Special Edition Created for Seneca College

Understanding Canadian Business

Seventh Edition

McGraw Hill Custom Publishing

MCGRAW-HILL RYERSON LIMITED

Understanding Canadian Business, Seventh Canadian Edition, by William Nickels, James McHugh, Susan McHugh, Rita Cossa, Bob Sproule. *ISBN 0-07-097027-0.*
Published by McGraw-Hill Ryerson, a subsidiary of the McGraw-Hill Companies, Inc., 1221 Avenue of the Americas, New York, NY, 10020. Copyright © 2008 by the McGraw-Hill Companies, Inc. All rights reserved.

Manager, Custom Learning Solutions: Jason Giles

ISBN-10: 0-07-105881-8
ISBN-13: 978-0-07-105881-0

Printed and bound in Canada.

Contents

APPENDIX A
Entrepreneur Readiness Questionnaire *176*

CHAPTER 7
Management and Leadership *178*

CHAPTER 8
Competing in Global Markets *206*

CHAPTER 11
Financial Management *298*

APPENDIX B
Risk Management *328*

CHAPTER 1

Managing Within the Dynamic Business Environment

LEARNING OBJECTIVES

AFTER YOU HAVE READ AND STUDIED THIS CHAPTER, YOU SHOULD BE ABLE TO:

LO ▶ 1 Describe the relationship of businesses' profit to risk assumption.

LO ▶ 2 Discuss the importance of stakeholders and non-profit organizations to business activities.

LO ▶ 3 Explain how entrepreneurship is critical to the wealth of an economy, and list the five factors of production that contribute to wealth.

LO ▶ 4 Review the six elements that make up the business environment and explain why the business environment is important to organizations.

LO ▶ 5 Understand how the service sector has replaced manufacturing as the principal provider of jobs, but why manufacturing remains vital for Canada.

Getting to Know Mike Lazaridis of Research In Motion Ltd.

Mike Lazaridis is known in the global wireless community as a visionary, innovator, and engineer of extraordinary talent. He traces his passion for his work to his hometown of Windsor, Ontario, where his love of science and fascination with electronics were nurtured in supportive family and school environments. Lazaridis studied electrical engineering at the University of Waterloo but dropped out two months before graduation. Using a small loan from his parents and a contract with General Motors, he founded Research In Motion Ltd. (RIM) in 1984.

RIM is a competitor in the ICT (information and communications technology—or technologies) sector. ICT is an umbrella term that includes any communication device or application encompassing radio, television, cellular phones, computer and network hardware and software, satellite systems and so on, as well as the various services and applications associated with them, such as videoconferencing and distance learning. The ICT sector contributed $57 billion to Canada's gross domestic product in 2007, accounting for 4.7 percent of Canadian output. Research and development (R&D) spending in the ICT sector has been steadily increasing over the years and is now at $6.0 billion, representing 38 percent of total Canadian private sector R&D expenditures. ICT sector employment is characterized by a highly educated workforce. The top three industries that employ the largest share of university-educated personnel are communications equipment, software and computer services, and computer equipment.

As RIM's President and Co-CEO, Lazaridis is responsible for product strategy, research and development, product development, and manufacturing. In fiscal 2009 (ended 28 February 2009), the company generated approximately US$11 billion in revenues. Today, RIM is a leading designer, manufacturer, and marketer of innovative wireless solutions for the worldwide mobile communications market. Through the development of integrated hardware, software, and services that support multiple wireless network standards, RIM provides platforms and solutions for seamless access to time-sensitive information. RIM technology also enables a broad array of third-party developers and manufacturers to enhance their products and services with wireless connectivity. RIM's portfolio of award-winning products, services, and embedded technologies are used by thousands of organizations around the world and include the BlackBerry wireless platform, the RIM BlackBerry Smartphone product line, software development tools, radio-modems, and software/hardware licensing agreements. The brand is becoming more global with products increasingly being introduced in new markets such as Vietnam, Malawi, and Egypt. Students and professionals alike have embraced the products. For example, do you know that a secure BlackBerry Smartphone was developed for U.S. President Barack Obama after he insisted on keeping a BlackBerry?

Lazaridis advocates for education and scientific research. He is a member of the Natural Sciences and Engineering Research Council of Canada (NSERC), the Ontario Research and Innovation Council, and a Governor of the Information Technology Association of Canada. He supports his community and country through generous philanthropic gifts made possible by his success in business. He has donated $100 million to the University of Waterloo to help establish the Institute for Quantum Computing. His gift of $150 million established the Perimeter Institute for Theoretical Physics. As a result of his leadership and tireless effort, more than $100 million has been generated in additional private and public sector funding for this world centre of excellence, based in Waterloo and affiliated with more than 30 Canadian universities.

In recognition of his contributions, Lazaridis has won many awards. Some examples include sharing Canada's most prestigious innovation prize, The Ernest C. Manning Principal Award. He was named an Officer to the Order of Canada in 2006, chosen as Canada's Outstanding CEO of the Year in 2006, listed on the *TIME* 100 List of Most Influential People in 2005, previously recognized as Canada's Nation Builder of the Year and was a recipient of Ontario's Entrepreneur of the Year award. He has been inducted into both the Canadian Business Hall of Fame and Canada's Telecommunications Hall of Fame.

The purpose of this text is to introduce you to the exciting and challenging world of business. Each chapter will begin with a story similar to this one. You will meet more successful entrepreneurs who have started a business. You will also learn about people who work for companies and have succeeded far beyond their original expectations. You will learn about all aspects of business: management, human resource management, marketing, accounting, finance, and more. You will also learn about businesses of all sizes. We begin by looking at some key terms and exploring the rapidly changing business environment so that you can prepare to meet tomorrow's challenges today.

Sources: "RIM's Executive Team – Mike Lazaridis," Research In Motion Ltd., 2009, http://www.rim.net/newsroom/ media/executive/index.shtml; "RIM 2008 Annual Report," Research in Motion Ltd., 2009, http://www.shareholder.com/visitors/DynamicDoc/document.cfm?DocumentID=2259&CompanyID=RIMM; "Canadian ICT Sector Profile," Industry Canada, 10 July 2008, http://www.ic.gc.ca/epic/site/ict-tic.nsf/en/h_it07229e.html; Brian Banks and Mark Evans, "Two Men and Their Baby," *Financial Post Business*, November 2006, 35; and "ICT Definition," SearchCIO-Midmarket.com, 14 January 2004, http://searchcio-midmarket.techtarget.com/sDefinition/0,,sid183_gci 928405,00.html#.

business
Any activity that seeks to provide goods and services to others while operating at a profit.

profit
The amount a business earns above and beyond what it spends for salaries and other expenses.

entrepreneur
A person who risks time and money to start and manage a business.

For an up-to-date list of the world's wealthiest citizens, visit www.forbes.com/billionaires/. Who is Canada's wealthiest person?

revenue
The total amount of money a business takes in during a given period by selling goods and services.

loss
When a business's expenses are more than its revenues.

BUSINESS AND ENTREPRENEURSHIP: REVENUES, PROFITS, AND LOSSES

Thousands of people have learned that one of the best ways to become a success in Canada, or almost anywhere else in the world, is to have a career in business. A **business** is any activity that seeks to provide goods and services to others while operating at a profit. **Profit** is the amount of money a business earns above and beyond what it spends for salaries and other expenses. Since not all businesses make a profit, starting a business can be risky. An **entrepreneur** is a person who risks time and money to start and manage a business.

Businesses provide people with the opportunity to become wealthy. *Forbes* magazine reports that in 2009 there were 790 billionaires around the world, of which 20 were of Canadian citizenship.[1] American business person and philanthropist Bill Gates, founder and Chairman of Microsoft Corporation, was said to be worth US$40 billion, making him the richest person in the world.[2] Maybe someday you will be a billionaire!

Businesses don't just make money for entrepreneurs. Businesses provide all of us with necessities such as food, clothing, housing, medical care, and transportation, as well as other goods and services that make our lives easier and better.

Matching Risk with Profit

Profit, remember, is the amount of money a business earns *above and beyond* what it pays out for salaries and other expenses. For example, if you were to start a business selling hot dogs in the summer, you would have to pay for the cart rental, for the hot dogs and other materials, and for someone to run the cart while you were away. After you paid your employee and yourself, paid for the food and materials you used, paid the rent on the cart, and paid your taxes, any money left over would be profit. Keep in mind that profit is over and above the money you pay yourself in salary. You could use any profit you make to rent or buy a second cart and hire other employees. After a few summers, you might have a dozen carts employing dozens of workers.

Revenue is the total amount of money a business takes in during a given period by selling goods and services. A **loss** occurs when a business's expenses are more than its revenues. If a business loses money over time, it will likely have to close, putting its employees out of work. In fact, approximately 125,000 businesses exit the marketplace

How well do you know yourself? Are you more excited at the prospect of starting your own small business or would you prefer to work for a large- or medium-sized business? The answer to this question may start with understanding your personal risk tolerance.

each year.[3] Some owners close down one business to start another one or to retire. Even though such closings are not failures, they are reported as exits by Industry Canada. Only a small proportion of firms that exit the marketplace end up filing for *bankruptcy*, which refers to the liquidation of the business debtor's assets and the end of the commercial entity's operations.[4] As discussed later in this textbook, most business failures are due to poor management or problems associated with cash flow.

Starting a business involves risk. **Risk** is the chance an entrepreneur takes of losing time and money on a business that may not prove profitable. Even among companies that do make a profit, not all make the same amount. Those companies that take the most risk may make the most profit. Decades ago, there was a lot of risk involved in, for example, producing automobiles to replace horse-drawn carriages. Today, we see investors betting on information highway pioneers such as Google as a way to prosper. Such is the nature of risk and reward in business.

As a potential business owner, you need to do research (e.g., talk to other business people and read business publications) to find the right balance between risk and profit for you. Different people have different tolerances for risk. To decide which is the best choice for you, you have to calculate the risks and the potential rewards of each decision. The more risks you take, the higher the rewards may be. In Chapter 6, you will learn more about the risks and rewards that come with starting a business.

risk
The chance an entrepreneur takes of losing time and money on a business that may not prove profitable.

Responding to the Various Business Stakeholders

Stakeholders are all of the people who stand to gain or lose by the policies and activities of a business. As noted in Figure 1.1, stakeholders include many different groups such as customers, employees, financial institutions (e.g., banks and credit unions), investors (e.g., stockholders), environmentalists, and government (e.g., federal, provincial, and municipal). All of these groups are affected by the products, policies, and practices of businesses, and their concerns need to be addressed. Don't forget that businesses can also influence government policies through the activities and efforts of their associations, lobbyists, and trade unions.

stakeholders
All the people who stand to gain or lose by the policies and activities of a business.

STAKEHOLDERS

FIGURE 1.1

A Business and Its Stakeholders
Often the needs of a firm's various stakeholders will conflict. For example, paying employees more may cut into stockholders' profits. Balancing such demands is a major role of business managers.

DEALING with CHANGE

Cirque du Soleil Tumbles to Success

With annual sales of more than US$700 million and nearly 10 million visitors a year, *Cirque du Soleil* is a Canadian (and international) success story. The company was formed in 1984 by a group of street performers that had a dream to create a Quebec circus and take it around the world. Since that time, it has become an international entertainment organization, growing to 18 shows in over 200 cities on five continents. Each show is a theatrical blend of circus arts and street performance, with spectacular costumes and fairyland sets. Due to its fast-paced growth and the complexity of staging shows around the world, *Cirque du Soleil* has outsourced its information technology needs in a $130-million, 10-year contract with Montreal-based CGI Group Inc. As part of this contract, CGI hired 84 of Cirque's employees that already were doing the job. CGI will help Cirque with everything from payroll to managing costume inventory to its Internet cafés that are set up when its shows travel.

Guy Laliberté is the founder, majority owner, and CEO of *Cirque du Soleil*. A former street performer himself, he guides the company that has a mission to invoke the imagination, provoke the senses, and evoke the emotions of people around the world. Creativity is the cornerstone of the organization's identity. Every concept and scenic element is created at the Studio, a training facility in Montreal. There, more than 1,000 employees work together to create new shows and costumes. Laliberté juggles the demands of creative and financial types and walks a tightrope among the almost 4,000 employees from over 40 different countries. With such diversity, you can see why the company's great strength is its ability to develop material that resonates with audiences worldwide.

Sources: Lori McLeod and Gordon Pitts, "From Quebec's Streets to Dubai," *The Globe and Mail*, 7 August 2008, B4; "Cirque du Soleil At a Glance," Cirque du Soleil, 26 July 2008 http://www.cirquedusoleil.com/cirquedusoleil/pdf/pressroom/en/cds_en_bref_en.pdf; Telios Demos, "Cirque du Balancing Act," *Fortune*, 12 June 2006, http://money.cnn.com/magazines/fortune/fortune_archive/2006/06/12/8379232/index.htm; and Shirly Won, "Cirque Faces New Balancing Act," *The Globe and Mail*, 7 April 2006, B3.

---

offshoring
Sourcing part of the purchased inputs outside of the country.

outsourcing
Assigning various functions, such as accounting, production, security, maintenance, and legal work to outside organizations.

The challenge of the twenty-first century will be for organizations to balance, as much as possible, the needs of all stakeholders. For example, the need for the business to make profits must be balanced against the needs of employees for sufficient income. The need to stay competitive may call for offshoring jobs to other countries, recognizing that this sound business strategy might do harm to the community because jobs would be lost.[5] **Offshoring** entails sourcing part of the purchased inputs outside of the country.[6] **Outsourcing** means contracting with other companies to do some or all of the functions of a firm, such as production or accounting.[7] One of the major themes of this text is managing change. There are special boxes called "Dealing with Change" throughout the text that discuss the rapidly changing business environment and the need to adjust to these changes. This first Dealing with Change box discusses how *Cirque du Soleil* is adapting to change.

You may be wondering, how are the terms outsourcing and offshoring that different? A Statistics Canada report highlights the distinction. As stated, "Outsourcing decisions affect the boundaries of the firm—what production takes place within the firm and what is purchased from outside the firm. Changes in offshoring may be, but are not necessarily, related to changes in outsourcing. They involve decisions both to purchase outside of the firm and to do so from abroad. Considerations to do the latter are at the heart of the study of international trade. Interest in outsourcing arises because it may foretell changes in industrial structure. Interest in offshoring arises because it may signify changes in international trading patterns."[8]

Companies have gone from outsourcing production jobs to offshoring research and development and design functions. Such decisions may prove disastrous to these firms doing the offshoring if the overseas companies use the information to produce their own competitive products.[9] In Canada, most of the offshoring that occurs is with the United States, though there has been some increase over the last decade with developing countries.[10] Canada is also an attractive offshoring location for U.S.-based firms, says Peter McAdam, president and CEO of Everest Group Canada:

> *Canada has essentially the same culture and many of the same companies have locations on both sides of the border. Education is similar and so is the concern for privacy and individual rights. You get all this plus polite, friendly, and helpful people at less cost.*

Companies are comfortable offshoring to Canada and callers/users are comfortable call-ing there. They find little difference between Canadians and American counterparts.[11]

This is especially true in the areas of software development related to business intelligence, industry-specific applications, business process outsourcing, and customer service-oriented call centres.

It is legal to outsource and offshore, but is that best for all stakeholders, including workers? Business leaders must make decisions based on all factors, including the need to make a profit. As you can see, pleasing all stakeholders is not easy and it calls for trade-offs that are not always pleasing to one or another stakeholder. Keep in mind that regard-less of temptations, company officials do have a responsibility to their stakeholders.

Such trade-offs are also apparent in the political arena. As will be discussed in Chapter 3, governments make policies that affect many stakeholders. However, budget limitations force governments to make difficult choices, and these decisions are often not popular. Consequently, after years of insufficient funding, any changes in the areas of the environ-ment, health care, and education generate a lot of attention. As you will learn, balancing the demands of stakeholders is not limited to for-profit businesses.

Using Business Principles in Non-Profit Organizations

Despite their efforts to satisfy all of their stakeholders, businesses cannot do everything that is needed to make a community all it can be. Non-profit organizations—such as schools, hospitals, and charities—also make a major contribution to the welfare of society. A **non-profit organization** is an organization whose goals do not include making a personal profit for its owners or organiz-ers.[12] Non-profit organizations often do strive for financial gains, but such gains are used to meet the stated social or educa-tional goals of the organization rather than personal profit.[13]

Social entrepreneurs are people who use business princi-ples to start and manage non-profit organizations and help countries with their social issues.[14] Canadian-born Jeff Skoll, eBay's first president, is one example. He left eBay to focus on philanthropic activities. The Skoll Foundation supports social entrepreneurs and innovative non-profit organizations around the world. The Spotlight on Small Business box fea-tures the Canadian Social Entrepreneurship Foundation. Would you consider becoming a social entrepreneur?

Your interests may lead you to work for a non-profit orga-nization. Millions of professionals, staffers, volunteers, and donors work for Canada's approximately 200,000 charities and non-profit organizations.[15] This doesn't mean, however, that you shouldn't study business. If you want to start or work in a non-profit organization, you'll need to learn business skills such as information management, leadership, market-ing, and financial management. Therefore, the knowledge and skills you acquire in this and other business courses will be useful for careers in any organization, including non-profits.

Starting any business, profit or non-profit, can be risky. Once an entrepreneur has started a business, there is usually a need for good managers and other workers to keep the business going. Not all entrepreneurs are skilled at being managers. We shall explore entrepreneurship right after the Progress Assessment.

non-profit organization
An organization whose goals do not include making a personal profit for its owners or organizers.

For more information about non-profit organizations, visit the Charity Village Web site at www.charityvillage.com. This site is dedicated to supporting Canada's charities and non-profit organizations as well as the stakeholders who support them.

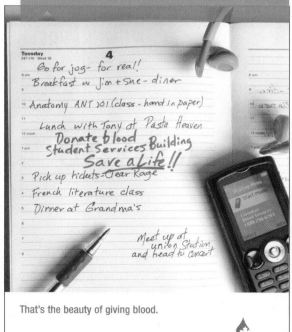

Non-profit organizations use for-profit business principles to achieve results. Canadian Blood Services is a national not-for-profit charitable organization whose mission is to manage the blood and blood products supply for Canadians. Did you know that approximately every minute of every day, someone in Canada needs blood? The good news is that one blood donation—in just one hour—can save up to three lives. This is a poster that has been used in schools across Canada with the purpose of encouraging people to donate blood.

SPOTLIGHT ON Small Business

Social Entrepreneurship

The Canadian Social Entrepreneurship Foundation (CSEF) site, sixty percent a virtual organization, was created in 2004 by Jason Carvalho to spur innovation and "bridge the gap" that was developing between the non-profit, business, and government sectors. Carvalho is an entrepreneur focused on creating sustainable value in a changing global economy. The motto of the CSEF is taken from a famous line which is as follows: "Some men and women see things as they are and say, 'Why?' I dream things that never were and say, 'Why not?'"

To begin to bridge this gap, the CSEF looks for social entrepreneurs who are under the age of 40 that want to develop and take a new service or product to market. Although social entrepreneurs share some characteristics and techniques with traditional business entrepreneurs—for example, an emphasis on innovation and the utilization of time-tested business theories and practices—their work and impact span the private, non-profit, and governmental sectors.

The CSEF provides access to funding, provincial/national/international networks, a wide variety of start-up resources, mentorship, and evaluation resources. It invests in Canadian social enterprises that focus on specific areas such as children and youth (e.g., employing at-risk youth), human rights, environment (e.g., clean technologies and energy efficiency), and economic development. Social economy enterprises are organizations that are run like businesses, producing goods and services, but which manage their operations on a not-for-profit basis. Instead, they direct any surpluses to the pursuit of social and community goals.

Can you see yourself as a social entrepreneur? You could become a small-business owner in Canada, but you could also use the business skills you learn in this course to be a social entrepreneur in Canada and other countries. Think of the possibilities.

Source: The Canadian Social Entrepreneurship Foundation. Copyright 2009, http://www.csef.ca. Used with permission.

Progress Assessment

- What is the difference between revenue and profit?
- What is risk, and how is it related to profit?
- What do the terms *stakeholders*, *offshoring*, and *outsourcing* mean?

ENTREPRENEURSHIP VERSUS WORKING FOR OTHERS

There are two ways to succeed in business. One is to rise up through the ranks of large companies such as Royal Bank of Canada or Manulife Financial. The advantage of working for others is that somebody else assumes the entrepreneurial risk and provides you with benefits such as paid vacation time and health insurance. Most people choose that option, which can lead to a happy and prosperous life.

The other, riskier path, is to start your own business and become an entrepreneur. When you consider Canada's wealthiest citizens, you will find that they arrived at their wealth as a result of this entrepreneurial spirit. Some well known billionaires and their companies include the Thomson family (Thomson-Reuters), Ted Rogers Jr. (Rogers Communications), Galen Weston (Loblaw Cos. Ltd.), and Paul Desmarais Sr. (Power Corp.).[16] Mike Lazaridis, the focus of this chapter's profile, also ranks in the top ten list of most affluent Canadians.[17] While you may hear about the success stories, keep in mind that many small businesses fail each year; thus, it takes a brave person to start a small business or to turn a business around. Furthermore, as an entrepreneur you don't receive any benefits such as paid vacation time and health insurance. You have to provide them for yourself!

Before you take on the challenge of entrepreneurship it makes sense to study the experiences of those who have succeeded to learn the process. Consider the example of Ron Joyce, who in 1963 purchased a Dairy Queen outlet. Two years later, he invested $10,000 to become a franchisee in the first Tim Hortons. (We will discuss franchising in Chapter 5.) By 1967, he became a full partner in the company with Tim Horton. In the early years, both partners worked on expanding the business. When Horton died in 1974, Joyce became the sole owner of the chain. In the following years, he continued to develop the business, spending hundreds of hours piloting his plane in search of new franchise opportunities and doing everything from training new store owners to baking donuts. When Joyce sold the chain to Wendy's for US$450 million in 1995, there were more than 1,000 Tim Hortons restaurants. Today, Tim Hortons is Canada's largest national chain in the coffee and fresh-baked goods segment, with 3,238 systemwide restaurants, including 2,930 in Canada and 527 in the United States.[18] What you can learn from successful entrepreneurs like Ron Joyce and Mike Lazaridis is that you need to find something that you love to do. Before he became an entrepreneur, Joyce was a police officer. He started to get experience in business with his Dairy Queen outlet, and from there went on to great success with his Tim Hortons restaurants. While there were many challenges along the way, he was willing to put in the long hours needed to be successful. In addition to the original coffee and donut offerings, he continuously added new products to the restaurants to meet his customers' needs.

Small businesses and entrepreneurs contribute enormously to the Canadian economy. While these terms have been briefly mentioned in this chapter, be aware that more time will be spent discussing their significance in Chapters 5 and 6. After all, without the initial ideas and risks taken by entrepreneurs, we would not have successful businesses today.

Charles Chang started Sequel Naturals Ltd. in his basement in 2001. Today the company, which manufactures premium natural health products and nutritional supplements (including the award-winning Vega brand of plant-based whole food products) is the eighth fastest-growing company in Canada with over 2,000 retailers carrying the company's products. Do you have a new product idea that could be turned into a successful business?

The Importance of Factors of Production to the Creation of Wealth

Have you ever wondered why some countries are relatively wealthy and others are poor? Economists have been studying the issue of wealth creation for many years. They began the process by studying potential sources of wealth to determine which are the most important. Over time, they came up with five factors that seemed to contribute to wealth, which they called **factors of production**. Figure 1.2 describes those five factors, which are:

1. Land (or natural resources)
2. Labour (workers)
3. Capital Goods (This includes machines, tools, buildings, or whatever else is used in the production of goods. It does not include money. Money is used to buy factors of production—it is not a factor itself.)
4. Entrepreneurship
5. Knowledge

factors of production
The resources used to create wealth: land, labour, capital goods, entrepreneurship, and knowledge.

Traditionally, business and economics textbooks have emphasized only four factors of production: land, labour, capital, and entrepreneurship. But management expert and business consultant Peter Drucker says that the most important factor of production in our economy is and always will be knowledge. The young workers in the high-tech industries are sometimes called *knowledge workers*. When high-tech businesses began

FIGURE | **1.2**

**The Five Factors
of Production**

LAND:	Land and other natural resources are used to make homes, cars, and other products.
LABOUR:	People have always been an important resource in producing goods and services, but many people are now being replaced by technology.
CAPITAL GOODS:	Capital includes machines, tools, buildings, and other means of manufacturing.
ENTREPRENEURSHIP:	All the resources in the world have little value unless entrepreneurs are willing to take the risk of starting businesses to use those resources.
KNOWLEDGE:	Information technology has revolutionized business, making it possible to quickly determine wants and needs and to respond with desired products.

to fail in the early 2000s, many knowledge workers had to find new jobs in other parts of the country, but their education and experience made this transition easier. Today, the environment is more competitive as new graduates are increasingly being sought by tech companies, such as Research In Motion Ltd. and Google Inc., looking to expand their operations domestically and internationally.[19]

Such results should motivate today's students to get as much education as possible to prepare themselves for knowledge-oriented jobs and to be prepared to change jobs as the economy demands.[20] Note that information is not the same as knowledge. There is usually too much information available and information management is critical.

If you were to analyze rich countries versus poor countries to see what causes the differences in the levels of wealth, you'd have to look at the factors of production in each country. Such analyses have revealed that some relatively poor countries often have plenty of land and natural resources. Russia and China, for example, both have vast areas of land with many resources, but they are not rich countries (yet). In contrast, Japan and Hong Kong are relatively rich countries but are poor in land and other natural resources. Therefore, land isn't the critical element for wealth creation.

Most poor countries have many labourers, so labour is not the primary source of wealth today. Labourers need to find work to make a contribution; that is, they need entrepreneurs to provide jobs for them. Furthermore, capital—machinery and tools—is now becoming available in world markets, so capital isn't the missing ingredient. Capital is not productive without entrepreneurs to put it to use.

What makes countries rich today is a combination of entrepreneurship and the effective use of knowledge. Together, lack of entrepreneurship and the absence of knowledge among workers, along with lack of freedom, contribute to keeping countries poor. The Reaching Beyond Our Borders box discusses the importance of freedom to economic development.

Entrepreneurship also makes some provinces and cities in Canada rich while others remain relatively poor. The business environment either encourages or discourages entrepreneurship. In the following section, we'll explore what makes up the business environment and how to build an environment that encourages growth and job creation.

Progress Assessment

- What are some of the advantages of working for others?
- What benefits do you lose by being an entrepreneur, and what do you gain?
- What are the five factors of production? Which factors are key to wealth?

Reaching Beyond Our Borders

Freedom Equals Prosperity

Recent studies have found that the freer a country is, the wealthier its citizens are. Freedom includes freedom from excess taxation, government regulations, and restrictions on trade. The average per capita gross domestic product (GDP)—the total value of all final goods and services produced in a country divided by the number of people in the country—for the freest countries greatly exceeds that in less-free countries. For example, Hong Kong is considered the freest country, and it has a per capita GDP of $39,062. Singapore, the second freest country, has a per capita GDP of $49,708. Canada's per capita GDP is $36,713. At the other end of the scale (less-free countries), you will find Libya with a per capita GDP of $11,622. Some countries make even less than that per capita: Haiti, for example, has a per capita GDP of $1,224 and Burundi's is just $333. As more countries become free (e.g., freedom from corruption), the standard of living around the world increases. And this is a good thing.

The 2009 Index of Economic Freedom covers 183 countries across 10 specific freedoms which include business freedom, trade freedom, fiscal freedom, government size, monetary freedom, investment freedom, financial freedom, property rights, freedom from corruption, and labour freedom. Canada's seventh place ranking was 0.3 percentage points higher than the year before, partly as a result of improved competitiveness in fiscal freedom accompanied by a reduced perception of corruption. Canada scores very high in seven of the 10 economic freedoms, especially business freedom, property rights, and freedom from corruption. The process for conducting a business is straightforward and encourages entrepreneurial activity. Overall, regulation is thorough but transparent. A strong rule of law ensures property rights, a low level of corruption, and transparent application of the commercial code. Canada trails the world average only in size and expense of government. Its elaborate social programs raise government spending. However, it has been able to establish sound fiscal management and federal budget surpluses in recent years, providing a competitive edge.

Numbers are always a good starting point when beginning to understand a situation. Keep in mind that the wealth of a country does not necessarily equate to health and happiness for all citizens, or even equity among citizens. Other sources, such as the Human Development Index or Genuine Progress Indicators, may shed more light on these issues.

Source: 2008 Index of Economic Freedom, Kim R. Holmes et al., eds., The Heritage Foundation and Dow Jones & Co., Inc., Washington, DC, 2008.

THE BUSINESS ENVIRONMENT

The **business environment** consists of the surrounding factors that either help or hinder the development of businesses. Figure 1.3, which summarizes some of the points discussed in this chapter, shows the six elements in the business environment:

business environment
The surrounding factors that either help or hinder the development of businesses.

1. The legal and regulatory environment
2. The economic environment
3. The technological environment
4. The competitive environment
5. The social environment
6. The global environment

Businesses grow and prosper in a healthy environment. The results are job growth and the wealth that makes it possible to have a high quality of life. The wrong environmental conditions, in contrast, lead to business failure, job losses, and a poor quality of life. In short, creating the right business environment is the foundation for social progress of all kinds, including good schools, clean air and water, good health care, and low rates of crime.

Companies should be aware of these elements and make it a practice to continuously assess the business environment for changes in trends. These trends could affect the organization's ability to achieve its objectives, steer clear of threats, or take advantage of new opportunities.

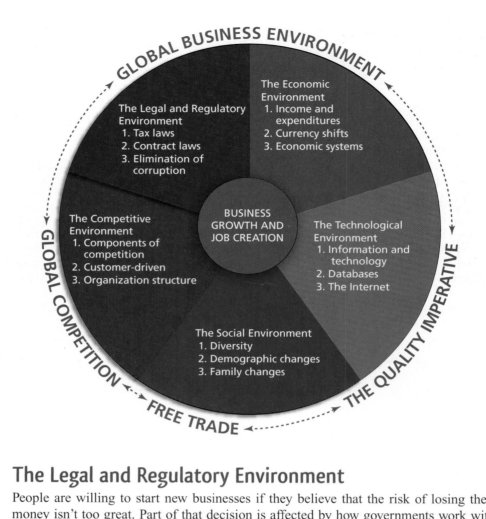

FIGURE | **1.3**

Today's Dynamic Business Environment

The Legal and Regulatory Environment

People are willing to start new businesses if they believe that the risk of losing their money isn't too great. Part of that decision is affected by how governments work with businesses. Governments can do a lot to lessen the risk of starting and running a business through the laws (also known as Acts) that are passed by its elected officials. The Constitution Act defines the powers that can be exercised by the different levels of government (i.e., federal and provincial). In Chapter 3, we will review some of the responsibilities of these different levels.

An important piece of legislation is the Competition Act. The purpose of the Competition Act is to:

> ... maintain and encourage competition in Canada in order to promote the efficiency and adaptability of the Canadian economy, in order to expand opportunities for Canadian participation in world markets while at the same time recognizing the role of foreign competition in Canada, in order to ensure that small- and medium-sized enterprises have an equitable opportunity to participate in the Canadian economy and in order to provide consumers with competitive prices and product choices.[21]

Other examples of laws include the Canada Small Business Financing Act, the Consumer Packaging and Labelling Act, and the Trade Unions Act. As you can imagine, these laws are relevant to many businesses.

Each legislation authorizes an agency (such as Industry Canada) to write regulations that interpret the law in more detail and indicate how it will be implemented and enforced. Consequently, **regulations** are rules or orders made by government to carry out the purposes set out in statutes.[22] These regulations exist to protect consumers as well as businesses. In Chapter 3, you will be introduced to some government departments that deal with businesses.

regulations
Rules or orders made by government to carry out the purposes set out in statutes.

Laws Affect Business

Businesses need to be aware of the laws that are in place (or may be passed) that will affect their business. For example, a government can keep taxes and regulations to a minimum, thereby encouraging entrepreneurship and increasing wealth. Entrepreneurs are looking for a high return on investment (ROI), including the investment of their time. If the government takes away much of what the business earns through high taxes, ROI may no longer be worth the risk. Provinces and territories that have high taxes and restrictive regulations tend to drive entrepreneurs out, while areas with low taxes and less restrictive regulations can attract entrepreneurs.

The government can also lessen the risks of entrepreneurship by passing laws that enable business people to write contracts that are enforceable in court.

There are many laws in Canada that are intended to minimize corruption, and businesses can flourish when these laws are followed. Nonetheless, corrupt and illegal activities at some companies do negatively affect the business community and the economy as a whole.[23] You hear about sports scandals (e.g., the taking of performance-enhancing drugs), church scandals, government scandals, and business scandals. In one high-profile case, a jury convicted media baron Conrad Black of obstructing justice and defrauding shareholders of his former newspaper company, Hollinger International Inc. As a result, he was sentenced to a 6½-year sentence. His three co-accused, namely John Boultbee, Peter Atkinson, and Mark Kipnis, were also convicted of mail fraud.[24]

Such scandals cross borders and organizations. (Think of the sub-prime mortgage scandal.) Ethics is so important to the success of businesses and the economy as a whole that we feature ethics boxes in each chapter and devote Chapter 4 to the subject. The Making Ethical Decisions box highlights the importance of individual ethical decision making.

The Economic Environment

The economic environment affects businesses as well as consumers. For our discussion, the focus will be on businesses. The economic environment looks at income, expenditures, and resources that affect the cost of running a business. Businesses review the results of major economic indicators such as consumer spending, employment levels, and productivity. This analysis will give them a sense of what is happening in the marketplace and what actions they may need to take. Since Chapter 2 is dedicated to how economic issues affect businesses, the discussion here will be very brief.

The movement of a country's currency relative to other currencies also pertains to this environment. Currency movements are especially critical for countries, such as Canada, that generate a great deal of business activity from exports. For instance, a lower Canadian dollar value relative to the U.S. dollar makes our exports cheaper and more attractive to the U.S. market, as consumers can buy more products with their higher-valued currency. The opposite is also true. For example in the late 2000s, the Ontario economy was negatively impacted as a result of the strong Canadian dollar, which surpassed parity with the U.S. dollar in the fall of 2007. The province lost tens of thousands of manufacturing jobs in just a few years as manufacturers shifted operations overseas. Some of the province's flagship employers, like General Motors, closed factories and trimmed production at others.[25]

Starting a business in some countries is much harder than in others. In India, for example, a person has to go through an extraordinary and time-consuming bureaucratic process to get permission to start a business—and with no certainty of success. Nonetheless, those businesses that do get started can become a major source of wealth and employment. This jewellery business is one example. Can you imagine the opportunities and wealth that might be created with just a little more freedom in this country of over one billion people?

Making Ethical Decisions

How Ethical Are You?

Despite the fact that the vast majority of business people are ethical, television, movies, and the print media all paint a dismal picture of ethics among business people, government officials, and citizens in general. It is easy to criticize the ethics of people whose names appear in the headlines. It is more difficult to see the moral and ethical misbehaviour of your own social group. Do you find some of the behaviours of your friends to be morally or ethically questionable? Some students have been known to tear out pages from books in the library or hide materials that are needed by classmates to complete an assignment. Other examples include cheating on tests and reusing work from someone else's assignment or from the Internet.

In the workplace, some employees call in sick when they are not sick. Rather than working, others have been seen completing their personal banking or visiting their Facebook account. One of the major trends in business today is that many companies are creating ethics codes to guide their employees' behaviour. We believe that this trend toward improving ethical behaviour is so important that we've made it a major theme of this book. Throughout the text you'll see boxes, like this one, called Making Ethical Decisions. The boxes contain short descriptions of situations that pose ethical dilemmas and ask what you would do to resolve them. The idea is for you to think about the moral and ethical dimensions of every decision you make.

Here is your ethical dilemma. You are doing a home project that requires paper, pens, and other materials available at work. You have noticed other employees taking home such materials, and are thinking about doing the same. What is the problem in this situation? What are your alternatives? What are the consequences of each alternative? Which alternative will you choose? Is your choice ethical?

One way for governments to actively promote entrepreneurship is to allow private ownership of businesses. In some countries, the government owns most businesses; thus, there's little incentive for people to work hard or create a profit. All around the world today, various countries in which the government formerly owned most businesses are selling those businesses to private individuals to create more wealth. In Chapter 2, we will discuss the different economic systems around the world.

You should soon realize, as we continue with our brief introduction to the other business environments, that the activities occurring in one environment have an impact on the others. In short, all of the environments are linked. For example, if a new government regulation decreases business taxes, then the impact will be seen in the economic environment when one considers expenditures. Therefore, as a business person you need to scan all of the environments to make good business decisions.

The Technological Environment

technology
Inventions or innovations from applied science or engineering research.

Technology refers to inventions or innovations from applied science or engineering research.[26] Technology can include (but is not limited to) everything from phones and copiers to computers, medical imaging devices, personal digital assistants, and the various software programs that make business processes' more effective, efficient, and productive. New technologies are dramatically changing business practices and the way businesses and customers buy and sell.[27]

Since prehistoric times, humans have felt the need to create tools that make their jobs easier. Few technological changes have had a more comprehensive and lasting impact on businesses than the emergence of information technology (IT), which includes computers, modems, cellular phones, and so on. We also discuss the Internet's impact on businesses throughout the text. In addition, we provide Internet exercises at the end of each chapter to give you some hands-on experience with various Internet sites.

Rogers Wireless is Canada's largest wireless provider. It provides wireless voice and data services to more than seven million customers. Are you a customer?

How Technology Benefits Workers and You

One of the advantages of working for others is that the company often provides the tools and technology to make your job more productive. **Productivity** is the amount of output you generate given the amount of input (e.g., hours worked). The more you can produce in any given period of time, the more money you are worth to companies. *Effectiveness* means producing the desired result. *Efficiency* means producing goods and services using the least amount of resources. Note that effectiveness is more important than efficiency. Companies look to technology to allow them to be more efficient, effective, and productive.

The Growth of Electronic Commerce (E-Commerce)

One of the more important changes of recent years is the growth of **e-commerce**, which encompasses the buying and selling of goods and services over the Internet.[28] There are two major types of e-commerce transactions: business-to-consumer (B2C) and business-to-business (B2B). As important as the Internet has been in the consumer market, it has become even more important in the B2B market, which consists of selling goods and services from one business to another. Such is the case for Richmond, British Columbia-based Talent Technology Corporation (considered one of Canada's fastest growing companies), whose largest clients, such as Oracle and SAP, pay up to $50,000 a year for its hosted recruitment software.[29] Traditional businesses have been learning how to deal with the competition from B2B and B2C firms. There are issues (e.g., security) surrounding such sites that companies need to consider and regularly monitor.

Do not confuse e-commerce with electronic business (e-business). Mostly done with Web technologies, the term **e-business** refers to any information system or application (e.g., business software) that empowers business processes.[30] While e-commerce is frequently mixed up with the term e-business, e-commerce only covers one aspect of e-business (i.e., the use of an electronic support for the commercial relationship between a company and individuals).[31]

productivity
The amount of output that is generated given the amount of input.

e-commerce
The buying and selling of goods and services over the Internet.

e-business
Any information system or application that empowers business processes.

According to the Survey of Electronic Commerce and Technology (SECT), the value of total online Canadian Internet sales in 2007 was $62.7 billion. For updated statistics on the digital economy, visit http://e-com.ic.gc.ca.

database
An electronic storage file in which information is kept; one use of databases is to store vast amounts of information about customers.

identity theft
Obtaining personal information about a person and using that information for illegal purposes.

Using Technology to Be Responsive to Customers

Another major theme of this text is that businesses succeed or fail largely because of the way they treat their customers. The businesses that are most responsive to customer wants and needs will succeed, and those that do not respond to customers will not be as successful. One way that traditional retailers can respond to the Internet revolution is to use technology to become much more responsive to customers. For example, businesses mark goods with Universal Product Codes (bar codes)—those series of lines and numbers that you see on most consumer packaged goods. Bar codes can be used to tell retailers what product you bought, in what size and colour, and at what price. A scanner at the checkout counter can read that information and put it into a database. A **database** is an electronic storage file in which information is kept. One use of databases is to store vast amounts of information about customers. For example, a retailer may ask for your name, address, and telephone number so it can put you on its mailing list. The information you give the retailer is added to the database. Using that information, the company can send you catalogues and other direct mail advertising that offers the kind of products you might want, as indicated by your past purchases. The use of databases enables stores to carry only the merchandise that the local population wants.

Alvin Amparo displays a selection of some of the paper shredders available at a Toronto office supply store. Whenever a TV show airs anything on identity theft, a flood of shoppers comes in to buy paper shredders, one of the best ways to guard against the crime, which is considered the fastest growing scam in North America. Once an identity thief has obtained your social insurance number, credit card number, address, and other such information, he or she can charge goods and services to your account. Do you know the limit you are liable for?

Unfortunately, gathering personal information about people has led to identity theft. **Identity theft** is the act of obtaining personal information about a person, such as social insurance number and/or credit card number, and using that information for illegal purposes, such as buying things with them. In response to consumer complaints, federal privacy laws have been created. The Personal Information Protection and Electronic Documents Act (PIPEDA) sets out ground rules for how private sector organizations may collect, use, or disclose personal information in the course of commercial activities.[32] If you think an organization covered by the Act is not living up to its responsibilities under the law, you have the right to lodge an official complaint.

To find out more about privacy legislation, visit the Office of the Privacy Commissioner of Canada's Web site at www.privcom.gc.ca.

Progress Assessment

- List the six elements of the business environment.
- What are four ways in which the government can foster entrepreneurship?
- How does technology benefit workers and customers?

The Competitive Environment

Competition among businesses has never been greater than it is today. Some companies have found a competitive edge by focusing on quality. The goal for many companies is zero defects—no mistakes in making the product.[33] However, simply making a high-quality product isn't enough to allow a company to stay competitive in world markets.

Components of Competition[34]

When developing their strategies, companies must consider the factors that drive competition: entry, bargaining power of buyers and suppliers, existing rivalries, and substitution possibilities. Scanning the competitive environment requires a look at all of these factors.

Entry   In considering the competition, a firm must assess the likelihood of new entrants. Additional producers increase industry capacity and tend to lower prices. *Barriers to entry* are business practices or conditions that make it difficult for new firms to enter the market. Barriers to entry can be in the form of capital requirements, product identity, distribution access, or switching costs. The higher the expense of the barrier, the more likely it will deter new entrants, and vice versa (e.g., barriers to exit).

Power of Buyers and Suppliers   Powerful buyers exist when they are few in number, there are low switching costs, or the product represents a significant share of the buyer's total costs. This last factor leads the buyer to exert significant pressure for price competition. A supplier gains power when the product is critical to the buyer and when it has built up switching costs.

Existing Competitors and Substitutes   Competitive pressure among existing firms depends on the rate of industry growth. In slow-growth settings, competition is more heated for any possible gains in market share. High fixed costs also create competitive pressures for firms to fill production capacity. (We will discuss production in Chapter 9.) For example, airlines offer discounts for making early reservations and charge penalties for changes or cancellations in an effort to fill seats, which represent a high fixed cost.

Competing by Exceeding Customer Expectations

Manufacturers and service organizations throughout the world have learned that today's customers are very demanding. Companies have to offer both high-quality products and outstanding service at competitive prices (value). Business is becoming customer-driven, not management-driven as in the past. This means that customers' wants and needs must come first.

Customer-driven organizations include Disney amusement parks (the parks are kept clean and appeal to all ages) and Moto Photo (it does its best to please customers with fast, friendly service). Such companies can successfully compete against Internet firms if they continue to offer better and friendlier service. Successful organizations must now listen more closely to customers to determine their wants and needs, then adjust the firm's products, policies, and practices to meet those demands.

Competing by Restructuring and Empowerment

To meet the needs of customers, firms must give their front-line workers (office clerks, front-desk people at hotels, salespeople, etc.) the responsibility, authority, freedom, training, and equipment they need to respond quickly to customer requests and to make other decisions essential to producing quality goods and providing good service. This is called **empowerment**, and we'll be talking about that process throughout this book. To implement a policy of empowerment, managers must train front-line people to make decisions within certain limits, without the need to consult managers.

empowerment
Giving front-line workers the responsibility, authority, and freedom to respond quickly to customer requests.

Empowering employees leads to developing entirely new organizational structures to meet the changing needs of customers and employees. As many companies have discovered, it sometimes takes years to restructure an organization so that managers are willing to give up some of their authority and employees are willing to assume more responsibility. We'll discuss such organizational changes and models in Chapter 9.

The Social Environment

demography
The statistical study of the human population with regard to its size, density, and other characteristics such as age, race, gender, and income.

Demography is the statistical study of the human population with regard to its size, density, and other characteristics such as age, race, gender, and income. In this book, we're particularly interested in the demographic trends that most affect businesses and career choices. The Canadian population is going through major changes that are dramatically affecting how people live, where they live, what they buy, and how they spend their time. Furthermore, tremendous population shifts are leading to new opportunities for some firms and to declining opportunities for others.

The Aging Population

The Canadian population has been aging for several decades. More people are living longer due to better medical knowledge and technology and better health habits, including proper nutrition, more exercise, and a reduction in the number of people who smoke. The portion of the population that is very young continues to decrease because of declining birth rates since the mid-1960s. Although the rate is low, the actual number of children being born is still large because of the baby-boom echo. The **baby-boom echo** (those born in the period from 1980 to 1995) represents the children of the large number of **baby boomers** (those born in the period from 1947 to 1966).[35] Most students are part of this echo generation.

baby-boom echo
A demographic group of Canadians that were born in the period from 1980 to 1995; the children of the baby boomers.

Figure 1.4 shows the population projections for Canada. You will notice that the 5 to 19 age group is declining, while the 65 years and over age group is increasing steadily. Based on these projections, it is expected that seniors will become more numerous than children sometime around 2015.

The projections use the 2005 population estimate as their base. The underlying assumption is that Canada will experience medium growth and recent migration trends. The median age of Canada's population will continue to rise as a direct result of the pronounced baby boom.

baby boomers
A demographic group of Canadians that were born in the period from 1947 to 1966.

What do such demographics mean for you and for businesses in the future? In his book *Boom Bust & Echo: Profiting from the Demographic Shift in the 21st Century*, economist and demographer David Foot writes that demographics play a pivotal role in the economic and social life of our country. According to Foot, demographics explain about two-thirds of everything—including which products will be in demand in five years.[36]

Think of the goods and services that the middle-aged and elderly will need—anything from travel and recreation to medicine, assisted-living facilities, and smaller apartments. Don't forget the impact of aging baby boomers; more grandparents with more money in their pockets will be buying more gifts for their grandchildren.

FIGURE | 1.4

Population Distribution by Age Group

Year	0–4	5–19	20–34	35–64	65 and Above
2006	5%	19%	21%	42%	13%
2011	5%	17%	21%	43%	14%
2016	5%	16%	20%	42%	16%
2021	5%	16%	19%	41%	19%
2026	5%	15%	18%	40%	21%
2031	5%	15%	17%	39%	23%

Source: Adapted from "Population Projections for Canada, Provinces and Territories 2005–2031," Cat. No. 91-520- XIE, December 2005.

Managing Diversity[37]

Canada has a strong multicultural population. Since the 1980s, it has welcomed 5.1 million immigrants. Between 2001 and 2006 alone, 1.4 million newcomers—or an annual average of 242,000 individuals—were admitted as permanent residents. Looking at Canada's overall population, 19.8 percent of the entire population (6,186,950) is made up of people who were born outside of Canada. The high level of annual admission of immigrants and the relatively slow rate of natural growth of the population explain why the proportion of the foreign-born in the Canadian population has been increasing since the 1990s. Companies have responded to this diverse customer base by hiring a more diversified workforce to serve them. For example, one of NAV CANADA's goals as an employer is to recruit and retain people who have not only talent and skill but a range of backgrounds and perspectives. Company officials believe that diversity in the workplace makes everyone a higher performer and it makes the company stronger by promoting new ideas and new ways of thinking. This generates creativity and adaptability, which are basic elements in at least two areas critical to NAV CANADA's future as a global leader: problem solving and innovation.[38]

The Family Portrait (Census 2006)[39]

Approximately 54 percent of all families in Canada are supported by two income earners. Factors that have contributed to the growth in two-income families include the high costs of housing and of maintaining a comfortable lifestyle, and more women wanting a career outside of the home. Families with a single parent, on the other hand, represented 15.9 percent of all census families, which was a slight increase from 2001 (15.7 percent). Companies have implemented a host of programs in response to such trends. For example, employee plans may include parental leave, flexible work schedules, and referral services for child care or elder care.

There were also several "firsts" recorded with the 2006 Census results. For example, there were more families comprised of couples without children (42.7 percent) than with children (41.4 percent). There were also more unmarried people aged 15 and over in Canada than legally married people. That is, just over one-half of Canada's population aged 15 and over was unmarried (i.e., never been legally married, were divorced, widowed, or separated). The proportion of young adults aged 20 to 29 who lived in the parental home continued to increase. In 2006, 43.5 percent of young adults lived at home, up substantially from 32.1 percent two decades earlier. Provincially, Newfoundland and Labrador (52.2 percent) and Ontario (51.5 percent) had the highest proportions of young adults in their twenties living in the parental home in 2006 while Alberta (31.7 percent) and Saskatchewan (31.8 percent) had the lowest proportions.

While this information is not exhaustive, it should give you an idea of some of the demographic trends that business people track as they develop their products and services. Can you think of some opportunities that are not currently being met as a result of some of these trends?

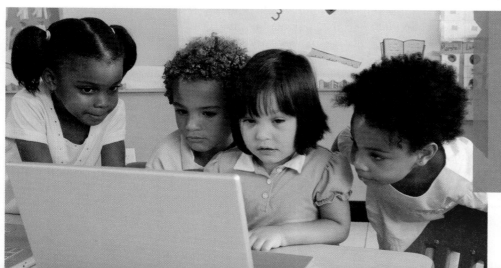

Kids & Company Ltd. is Canada's fastest growing company. Its business is providing backup and full-time child care to employees of dozens of corporate clients such as AGF, BP, and CIBC. The services are promoted as an employee benefit and an employee-retention tool.

Progress Assessment

- Describe the components of competition.
- What is empowerment?
- What social trends are evident in Canada?

The Global Environment

The global environment of business is so important that we show it as surrounding all other environmental influences (refer to Figure 1.3). Two important environmental changes in recent years have been the growth of international competition and the increase of free trade among nations. Two things that have led to more trade are the improvements in transportation and communication. These changes include more efficient distribution systems and communication advances such as the Internet. World trade (sometimes called *globalization*) has greatly improved living standards around the world. For example, the number of East Asian people living on less than $1 a day has declined from 56 percent to less than 16 percent.[40]

Better technology, machinery, tools, education, and training enable each worker to be more productive. It is the primary responsibility of businesses to focus on these areas to ensure success. Government support also contributes to domestic and global success. For example, the federal government has developed a science and technology (S&T) strategy, called *Mobilizing Science and Technology to Canada's Advantage*, that will foster a business environment by encouraging innovations that will provide solutions to environmental, health, and other important social challenges, while also improving the country's economic competitiveness. The government plans to do this by creating a policy environment that will encourage an entrepreneurial advantage, a knowledge advantage, and a people advantage.[41] Other government initiatives to support Canadian businesses will be discussed in Chapter 3.

Companies such as Bombardier Inc. (manufacturer of innovative transportation solutions, from commercial aircraft and business jets to rail transportation equipment, systems, and services) and CAE Inc. (provider of simulation and modelling technologies and integrated training solutions for the civil aviation industry and defence forces around the globe), as well as many smaller companies, are as good as or better than competing organizations anywhere in the world. But some businesses have gone beyond simply competing with organizations in other countries by learning to co-operate with international firms. Co-operation among businesses has the potential to create rapidly growing world markets that can generate prosperity beyond most people's expectations. The challenge is tremendous, but so is the will to achieve.

World trade has its benefits and costs. You'll read much more about the importance of global business in Chapter 8 and in the Reaching Beyond Our Borders boxes throughout the text.

There are an increasing number of terms that recognize today's preoccupation with how individual and business actions impact us nationally and internationally. Some examples include *carbon footprint* (defined as the impact of human activity measured in terms of the amount of carbon dioxide it causes to be emitted into the atmosphere), *food miles* (the distance travelled from the place where food is produced to the place where it is eaten, considered in terms of the environmental damage that transporting it entails), *green tax* (a tax imposed with the intention of discouraging activities that may damage the environment), and *eco-village* (a small-scale, environmentally friendly settlement designed for sustainable living).[42] In the Green Boxes throughout the text you will read about companies that recognize the importance in making changes as the planet's climate worsens. The first box highlights the activities of Global Footprint Network.

GreenBOX

Global Footprint Network, Advancing the Science of Sustainability

Global Footprint Network is non-profit organization established to enable a sustainable future where all people have the opportunity to live satisfying lives within the means of one planet. A focus is on advancing the scientific rigour and practical application of the Ecological Footprint, a resource accounting tool that measures how much nature we have, how much we use, and who uses what. Conceived in 1990 by Mathis Wackernagel and William Rees at the University of British Columbia, the Ecological Footprint is now in wide use by scientists, businesses, governments, agencies, individuals, and institutions working to monitor ecological resource use and advance sustainable development.

Global Footprint Network, through its numerous programs, aims to influence decision makers and create a critical mass of powerful institutions using the Footprint to put an end to ecological overshoot and get economies back into balance. The key to achieving this is to make the Ecological Footprint as prominent a metric as the gross domestic product. By 2015, through its flagship Ten-In-Ten campaign, Global Footprint Network aims to have at least ten key national governments managing their ecological wealth in the same way they manage their finances—by the numbers.

Since its inception in 2003, Global Footprint Network has made significant progress toward its goals. Over 90 organizations, spanning six continents, have become formal Global Footprint Network partners. Currently, six nations and numerous municipalities have adopted the Footprint to benchmark progress towards sustainability, make informed infrastructure and investment decisions, and identify solutions that will make a true difference to the ecological bottom line.

Source: Global Footprint Network, 22 June 2009, http://www.footprintnetwork.org.

THE EVOLUTION OF CANADIAN BUSINESS

Many managers and workers are losing their jobs in major manufacturing firms. Businesses in Canada have become so productive that, compared to the past, fewer workers are needed in industries that produce goods. **Goods** are tangible products such as computers, food, clothing, cars, and appliances. Due to the increasing impact of technology and global competition, shouldn't we be concerned about the prospect of high unemployment rates and low incomes? Where will the jobs be when you graduate? These important questions prompt us to look briefly at the manufacturing and service sectors.

goods
Tangible products such as computers, food, clothing, cars, and appliances.

Progress in the Agricultural and Manufacturing Industries

Canada has seen strong economic development since the nineteenth century. The agricultural industry led the way, providing food for Canadians and people in other parts of the world. Inventions such as the harvester and cotton gin did much to make farming successful, as did ongoing improvements to such equipment. The modern farming industry has become so efficient through the use of technology that the number of farms has dropped. Due to increased competition, many of the farms that existed even 50 years ago have been replaced by some huge farms, some merely large farms, and some small but highly specialized farms. The loss of farm workers over the past century is not a negative sign. It is instead an indication that Canadian agricultural workers are more productive.

Most farmers who lost their jobs went to work in factories. The manufacturing industry, much like agriculture, used technology to become more productive. The consequence, as in farming, was the elimination of many jobs. Again, the loss to society is minimal if the wealth created by increased productivity and efficiency creates new jobs elsewhere. This is exactly what has happened over the past 50 years. Many workers in the industrial sector found jobs in the service sector. Most of those who can't find work today are people who need retraining and education to become qualified for jobs that now exist.

Canada's Manufacturing Industry

The goods-producing sector includes the manufacturing, construction, utilities, agriculture, forestry, fishing, and mining industries. Of this sector, manufacturing employs a little over 7 percent of Canada's working population, as noted in Figure 1.5.

Tens of thousands of Canadian jobs were lost in the late 2000s. The rising Canadian dollar and increasing global competition were two of the reasons for these losses. Despite such losses, manufacturing still remains an important contributor to the Canadian economy. The Canadian Manufacturing Coalition highlights some of the reasons why this sector is important to Canada:

- Manufacturing directly accounts for 17 percent of the Canadian economy;
- Every $1 of manufacturing output in Canada generates $3.05 in total economic activity; and
- Manufacturing accounts for two-thirds of Canada's total exports of goods and services.[43]

While the manufacturing sector is much smaller today than it was 25 years ago, it is still clearly an integral part of our business economy. We will discuss the manufacturing sector and production in more detail in Chapter 9.

FIGURE 1.5

The Importance of the Goods-Producing and Services-Producing Sectors in Canada
Canada is a service economy, where the majority of jobs are generated in the services-producing sector. This excerpt from Statistics Canada's *Employment by Industry* for 2008 highlights the importance of manufacturing and agriculture (the two largest-employer industries in the goods-producing sector) to Canadians.

	Number of Employed (thousands)	Total Workforce (percent)
Total employed in Canada	17,125.8	100.0
Goods-producing sector	4,021.3	23.5
Agriculture	326.0	1.9
Manufacturing	1,970.3	7.2
Services-producing sector	13,104.5	76.5

Source: "Employment by Industry," Statistics Canada, CANSIM Table 282-0008. Retrieved from http://www40.statcan.ca/l01/cst01/econ40.htm?sdi=employment, (9 August 2008). Last modified 10 January 2008.

Agriculture is an important industry in Canada. The entire process of growing food and getting it to our tables is so smooth that it's easy to take for granted. But behind those well-stocked supermarkets is an army of farmers and distributors who supply our needs. Use of technology has led to increased productivity and made farmers more efficient, resulting in larger farms. This trend has meant less expensive food for us, but a continual reduction in the number of small, family-run farms. Is it still possible for small farms to be successful, and if so, how?

Progress in Service Industries

The service sector is distinct from the goods-producing sector. **Services** are intangible products (i.e., products that cannot be held in your hand) such as education, health care, insurance, recreation, and travel and tourism. In the past, the dominant industries in Canada produced goods such as steel, railroads, and machine tools. Over the last 30 years, the service sector in Canada and around the world has grown dramatically.

The shift in Canada's employment makeup began slowly early in the twentieth century, and has accelerated rapidly since the 1950s. Today, the leading firms are in services (such as legal, health, telecommunications, entertainment, financial services, etc.). As noted in Figure 1.5, the services-producing sector employs a little more than 76 percent of the working population.

There are several reasons why there has been growth in this sector. First, technological improvements have enabled businesses to reduce their payrolls while increasing their output. Since staffing has been downsized by many companies, business has become more complex and specialized companies have relied more heavily on outside services firms. Secondly, as large manufacturing companies seek to become more efficient, they contract out an increasing number of services, creating more opportunities for business people. Other service firms have risen or expanded rapidly to provide traditional services that used to be performed by women at home. Since many women have entered the workforce, there is increased demand for food preparation, child care, and household maintenance, to name just a few.

Your Future in Business

Despite the growth in the service sector, the service era now seems to be coming to a close as a new era is beginning. We're now in the midst of an information-based global revolution that will alter all sectors of the economy. It's exciting to think about the role you'll play in that revolution. You may be a leader; that is, you may be one of the people who will implement the changes and accept the challenges of world competition based on world quality standards. This book will introduce you to some of the concepts that will make such leadership possible.

Remember that most of the concepts and principles that make businesses more effective and efficient are also applicable to government agencies and non-profit organizations. This is an introductory business text, so we will focus on business. Business cannot prosper in the future without the co-operation of government and social leaders throughout the world.

services
Intangible products (i.e., products that can't be held in your hand) such as education, health care, insurance, recreation, and travel and tourism.

Visit http://jobfutures.ca to find out what the future's most promising jobs will be.

Progress Assessment

- What are two changes that have affected the global environment?
- Why is the manufacturing sector important to the economy?
- What is the major factor that caused people to move from farming to industry and from industry to the service sector?

SUMMARY

LO ▶ 1 Describe the relationship of businesses' profit-to-risk assumption.

1. A business is any activity that seeks to provide goods and services to others while operating at a profit.

What are the relationships between risk, profit, and loss?
Profit is money a business earns above and beyond the money it spends for salaries and other expenses. Business people make profits by taking risks. Risk is the chance an entrepreneur takes of losing time and money on a business that may not prove profitable. A loss occurs when a business's costs and expenses are more than its revenues.

LO ▶ 2 Discuss the importance of stakeholders and non-profit organizations to business activities.

2. Stakeholders include customers, employees, investors (e.g., stockholders), suppliers, dealers, people in the local community, environmentalists, and government.

Which stakeholders are most important to a business?
The goal of business leaders is to try to balance the needs of all stakeholders and still make a profit. Some businesses put the needs of stockholders above the other interests, but most businesses today seek a balance among the needs of the various stakeholders.

LO ▶ 3 Explain how entrepreneurship is critical to the wealth of an economy, and list the five factors of production that contribute to wealth.

3. Entrepreneurs are people who risk time and money to start and manage a business.

What importance does entrepreneurship hold in the list of the five factors of production?
Businesses use five factors of production: land (natural resources), labour (workers), capital goods (buildings and machinery), entrepreneurship, and knowledge. Of these, the most important are entrepreneurship and knowledge (managed information), because without them land, labour, and capital are not of much use.

LO ▶ 4 Review the six elements that make up the business environment and explain why the business environment is important to organizations.

4. The business environment consists of the surrounding factors that either help or hinder the development of businesses. The six elements are the legal and regulatory environment, the economic environment, the technological environment, the competitive environment, the social environment, and the global environment.

Explain why the business environment is important to organizations.
Scanning the business environment on a continual basis is important to organizations so that they can take advantage of trends. These trends could affect the organization's ability to achieve its objectives, steer clear of threats, or take advantage of new opportunities.

LO ▶ 5 Understand how the service sector has replaced manufacturing as the principal provider of jobs, but why manufacturing remains vital for Canada.

5. Canada has evolved from an economy based on manufacturing to one based on services.

Why is manufacturing still a vital industry for Canada?
While the services-producing sector employs a little more than 76 percent of the working population, the manufacturing industry employs a little over 7 percent of workers. Every $1 of manufacturing in Canada generates $3.05 in total economic activity. Directly, manufacturing accounts for 17 percent of economic activity, and two-thirds of Canada's exports of goods and services.

KEY TERMS

baby-boom echo 18

baby boomers 18

business 4

business environment 11

database 16

demography 18

e-business 15

e-commerce 15

empowerment 17

entrepreneur 4

factors of production 9

goods 21

identity theft 16

loss 4

non-profit organization 7

offshoring 6

outsourcing 6

productivity 15

profit 4

regulations 12

revenue 4

risk 5

services 23

stakeholders 5

technology 14

CRITICAL THINKING

Imagine that you are thinking of starting a restaurant in your community and answer the following questions.

1. You need to consider whether you will purchase using locally-grown produce versus foreign-grown produce. What are the advantages and disadvantages of using either, especially if the foreign-grown produce is cheaper or of better quality?

2. What are some of the things you could do to benefit your community other than provide jobs and generate tax revenue?

3. You are considering paying your employees the minimum wage. Do you think that you would attract better employees if your wages were higher?

4. How might you be affected by the six environmental factors outlined in this chapter? Which factor(s) might have the biggest impact on your business?

DEVELOPING WORKPLACE SKILLS

1. Make a list of non-profit organizations in your community that might offer you a chance to learn some of the skills you'll need in the job you hope to have when you graduate. How could you make time in your schedule to volunteer or work at one or more of those organizations? Write a letter to a non-profit organization to inquire about such opportunities.

2. Reading the news or surfing the Internet, find two examples of top executives who have disregarded their stakeholders. Present your findings to the class.

3. Imagine that you are a local business person who has to deal with the various issues involved with outsourcing.

You want to begin with the facts. How many jobs have been lost to outsourcing in your area, if any? Are there any foreign firms in your area that are creating jobs (insourcing)? You may want to use the Internet to find the data you need.

4. Form into teams of four or five and discuss the technological and e-commerce revolutions. How many students now shop for goods and services online? What have been their experiences? What other high-tech equipment (e.g., cellphones, personal digital assistants, etc.) do they use?

TAKING IT TO THE NET 1

Purpose

To gather data regarding trends in population and the social environment and to understand how this information affects Canadian businesses.

Exercise

To access this information, you will need to visit the Statistics Canada site at www.statcan.gc.ca.

1. Who is responsible for collecting the information found on this site? How is this information collected?

2. Statistics Canada conducts a census every five years. Why is the Census important? Who is included in the Census? Who will use this Census information? (To help answer these questions, click on Census on the bar on the left-hand side of the Statistics Canada home page.)

3. Return to the Statistics Canada home page. What is the population of Canada right now? How can businesses use this information?

TAKING IT TO THE NET 2

Purpose

To understand what influences tween spending.

Exercise

Tweens are Canadians aged 9 to 14. Visit YTV's Annual Tween Report site at www.corusmedia.com/ytv/research.asp.

1. What key topics are covered by the YTV Annual Tween Report?

2. How much money do tweens spend each year?

3. In what areas do tweens have a high level of influence?

4. What opportunities for product sales exist for businesses if they wish to target this group?

ANALYZING MANAGEMENT DECISIONS

Canada's Fastest-Growing Companies— PROFIT 100

Every year, *PROFIT* magazine publishes a list of Canada's 100 fastest-growing companies. The importance of many of the points we discussed in this chapter is evident in a recent issue, especially when one considers the breakdown among the types of companies. Services providers dominate the marketplace, which reinforces that Canada is a service economy. Here is a breakdown of the Top 100:

Focus	Number of Firms
Business services	42
Manufacturing	19
Software development	12
Consumer services	7
Construction	6
Natural resource production and services	6
Wholesale/distribution	5
Retail	3

While the companies were located across Canada, Ontario continued to support the largest share of these companies:

Ontario	42
Alberta	23
British Columbia	19
Quebec	12
Manitoba	2
Atlantic Canada	2

Clearly, great teams start with great people. Interesting statistics about the Top 100 company leaders include:

1. The age ranges from 27 to 67, with an average age of 43 years.

2. A substantial share (28 percent) are foreign-born.

3. An overwhelming 94 percent are male.

4. The average yearly compensation was $398,000.

What makes these companies leaders is that they grew rapidly, with a minimum explosive growth of 627 percent over the past five years. It does not matter whether they are high-tech or old-economy companies, manufacturing or service companies, they all were exceptional. A remarkable assortment of products and services are offered by these companies. Examples include child-care centres, IT staffing services, smoothies, air purifiers, custom clothing, and organic cranberries and blueberries. Seventy-five of the companies are exporters with 69 percent of sales ($7.9 billion) being thus generated. The top export markets are the United States, the United Kingdom, other Western European countries, Australia, the Pacific Rim (excluding China and Japan), Africa, the Middle East, and Eastern Europe (excluding Russia).

Source: Jim McElgunn, "Sights for Sore Eyes," *PROFIT*, June 2008, 38–58.

Discussion Questions

1. Which of these data support the information discussed in the chapter? Explain your answer.

2. Why do certain provinces or regions have so many (e.g., Ontario) or few (e.g., Atlantic Canada) companies?

3. Visit www.canadianbusiness.com/entrepreneur to see the latest information on the PROFIT 100 companies. How much has changed since these results were posted?

McGraw-Hill Connect™—Available 24/7 with instant feedback so you can study when you want, how you want, and where you want. Take advantage of the Study Plan—an innovative tool that helps you customize your learning experience. You can diagnose your knowledge with pre- and post-tests, identify the areas where you need help, search the entire learning package for content specific to the topic you're studying, and add these resources to your personalized study plan.

Visit www.mcgrawhillconnect.ca to register— take practice quizzes, search the e-book, and much more.

CHAPTER 2

How Economic Issues Affect Business

LEARNING OBJECTIVES

AFTER YOU HAVE READ AND STUDIED THIS CHAPTER, YOU SHOULD BE ABLE TO:

LO ▶ 1 Explain what capitalism is and how free markets work. As part of this discussion, define supply and demand and explain the relevance of the equilibrium point.

LO ▶ 2 Define socialism and its benefits and negative consequences.

LO ▶ 3 Understand communism and the challenges of such a system.

LO ▶ 4 Describe the mixed economy of Canada.

LO ▶ 5 Discuss the significance of key economic indicators and the business cycle.

Getting to Know Hernando de Soto: Economist for the Poor

A crowd of anxious fans pushes to get a glimpse of a celebrity visiting a poor community in Peru. Who is this person who has the town so excited? A rock singer, a famous athlete, a movie star? No. Would you believe he's an economist? Hernando de Soto, a noted economist, wrote one of Peru's bestselling books and the crowds were eager to hear his ideas about improving the country's economy—and thus their own lives.

Hernando de Soto was born in Peru. He went on to study in Canada, the United States, and Switzerland. Eventually he earned a graduate degree in international economics and law at the University of Geneva. He was successful enough to become managing director of Universal Engineering Corporation, a Swiss consulting firm. He made enough money to retire, but instead decided to devote his time to studying what makes some countries rich and others poor. He returned to Peru and studied the entrepreneurs there to see what held them back. What he learned was that the business owners were locked out of the formal, legal economy because there were no laws that provided property titles. That is, people could have houses, but no titles to them; farms, but no deeds to them; and businesses, but no statutes of incorporation. The lack of formal titling prevented owners from using their property as collateral, and thus prevented the capital embedded in these assets to be used for other purposes. This meant that entrepreneurs could not sell their property and use the money to invest. They also could not borrow money from banks to expand or improve their businesses. De Soto's book *The Other Path* outlined his findings.

De Soto found that another barrier to wealth in Peru and other less developed countries is government bureaucracy. It took de Soto and others 6.5 years and 207 administrative steps in 52 government offices to obtain legal authorization to build a house on state-owned land. It took 289 six-hour days and $1,231 (about 31 times the monthly minimum wage) in fees to legally open a garment workshop. In short, it is often very difficult and very expensive to become an entrepreneur in less developed countries.

De Soto estimates that the value of real estate held, but not owned, by the poor in less developed countries is at least $9.3 trillion. That's a lot of money that could be used to start or expand businesses, hire more people, and create wealth. De Soto's second book, *The Mystery of Capital*, goes into more detail about how property ownership leads to the creation of wealth.

De Soto is now the president of the Institute for Liberty and Democracy, a Lima, Peru–based think tank. He says that two-thirds of humanity is not in a position to participate in a modern market economy, and that is his biggest challenge. De Soto finds this to be true around the world and in countries such as Peru, Egypt, Russia, Africa, and the Philippines. He found, for example, that it takes 25 years of red tape to gain through legal means the kind of home in Manila that people now obtain through squatting. Roughly half of the world's people live in makeshift homes in squatter settlements and work in shadow economies. In many countries, more than 80 percent of all homes and businesses are unregistered. In the Philippines, the figure is 65 percent and in Tanzania, 90 percent. More than one-third of the developing world's GDP is generated in the underground economy, a figure that has increased steadily

over the past decade. He cites Switzerland and Japan as two countries that went from relative poverty to wealth by modifying their property laws.

As you can imagine, de Soto has his share of detractors. Articles have been written challenging his thinking, and his life has been threatened. But such challenges only help him bring the issue of poverty to the forefront and urge countries to change their laws to make prosperity a reality.

Many people don't realize the importance of the economic environment to the success of business. That is what this chapter is all about. You will learn to compare different economic systems to see the benefits and drawbacks of each. You will learn that the mixed economy is the system in Canada. By the end of the chapter, you should understand the direct effect that economic systems have on the wealth and happiness of communities throughout the world.

Sources: Madeleine Albright, "Giving The Poor Their Rights," *Time*, 5 July 2007, http://www.ild.org.pe/en/hernando-de-soto/blog/time/jul07; Hernando de Soto, *The Mystery of Capital: Why Capitalism Triumphs in the West and Fails Everywhere Else* (New York: Basic Books, 2003); Hernando de Soto, *The Other Path: The Invisible Revolution in the Third World* (New York: Harper and Row, 1989); "Hernando de Soto's Biography," www.Cato.org/special/friedman/desoto/; Jeremy Main, "How to Make Poor Countries Rich," *Fortune*, 16 January 1989; and N. Stephan Kinsella (ed.), book review, Journal of Libertarian Studies, Winter 2002; and www.nytimes.com/books/00/12/24/reviews/00124.24skidelt.html.

HOW ECONOMIC CONDITIONS AFFECT BUSINESS

If you want to understand the underlying situation and conditions in which Canadian businesses operate, it is essential that you (1) have some grasp of economics, (2) be aware of the impact of the global environment, and (3) understand the role of the federal and provincial governments in Canada.

The Canadian economy is an integral part of the world economy. Business firms use labour from other countries, export to and import from other countries, buy land in other countries for their facilities, and receive money from foreign investors. To understand events in the Canadian economy, therefore, one has to understand the world economy.

Why is South Korea comparatively wealthy and North Korea suffering economically, with many of its people starving? Why is China's annual gross domestic product per capita (PPP) of $6,757 much less than Switzerland's $35,633?[1] Such questions are part of the subject of economics. In this chapter, we explore the various economic systems of the world and how they either promote or hinder business growth, the creation of wealth, and a higher quality of life for all.

A major part of business success is due to an economic and social climate that allows businesses to operate freely. Foreign investors like Canada because we have a stable economic and political environment. Investing is risky enough without having to worry about unpredictable governments, massive corruption, and weak laws. Therefore, any change in our economic or political system can have a major influence on businesses.

What Is Economics?

economics

The study of how society chooses to employ resources to produce goods and services and distribute them for consumption among various competing groups and individuals.

Economics is the study of how society chooses to employ resources to produce goods and services and distribute them for consumption among various competing groups and individuals. Remember from Chapter 1 that these resources (land, labour, capital goods, entrepreneurship, and knowledge) are called *factors of production* .

Businesses may contribute to an economic system by inventing products that greatly increase available resources. For example, businesses may discover new energy sources, new ways of growing food, and new ways of creating needed goods and services.[2] Ballard Power Systems, a global leader in the design, development and manufacture of hydrogen fuel cells, is doing just this. Among other initiatives, Ballard is working with auto manufacturers to develop the next generation of efficient and clean engines for buses, automobiles, and trucks.[3]

Your buying behaviour falls under the study of macroeconomics. How does understanding spending patterns benefit a country's economy?

This is a close-up of a salmon farm in British Columbia. Environmental groups are concerned that some current mariculture practices create negative environmental impacts such as water pollution (e.g., due to chemicals used to control diseases), transfer of disease from caged species to wild populations, and the death of sea birds, turtles and marine mammals due to entanglement in nets.

There are two major branches of economics: **macroeconomics** looks at the operation of a nation's economy as a whole, and **microeconomics** looks at the behaviour of people and organizations in particular markets. For example, while macroeconomics looks at how many jobs exist in the whole economy, microeconomics examines how many people will be hired in a particular industry or a particular region of the country. Topics discussed in this chapter that are part of macroeconomics include gross domestic product, unemployment rate, and price indexes. Chapter topics that deal with microeconomic issues include pricing and supply and demand.

Some economists define economics as the allocation of "scarce" resources. They believe that resources are scarce and that they need to be carefully divided among people, usually by the government. There's no way to maintain peace and prosperity in the world by merely dividing the resources we have today among the existing nations. There aren't enough known resources available to do that. **Resource development** is the study of how to increase resources and to create the conditions that will make better use of those resources (e.g., recycling and oil conservation).[4] Outside of government, businesses may contribute to an economic system by inventing products that greatly increase available resources such as discovering new energy sources (e.g., hydrogen), new ways of growing food, and new ways of creating needed goods and services.[5] For example, people are starting to raise more fish in pens out in the ocean.[6] Such *mariculture* (the farming of aquatic plants and animals in land-based tanks and ponds or in sea cages) could lead to more food for everyone and more employment. The Green Box recognizes one company for its eco-winery philosophy.

Growth Economics and Adam Smith

Adam Smith was one of the first people to imagine a system for creating wealth and improving the lives of everyone. Rather than believing that fixed resources had to be divided among competing groups and individuals, Smith envisioned creating more resources so that everyone could become wealthier. The year was 1776. Adam Smith's book, *An Inquiry into the Nations and Causes of the Wealth of Nations* (simply called *The Wealth of Nations*), was later considered the foundation of the study and understanding of the newly developing capitalist industrial society.

macroeconomics
The part of economic study that looks at the operation of a nation's economy as a whole.

microeconomics
The part of economic study that looks at the behaviour of people and organizations in particular markets.

resource development
The study of how to increase resources and the creation of the conditions that will make better use of those resources (e.g., recycling).

GreenBOX

Stratus Winery Is LEEDing the Way

There are close to 500 wineries in Canada that provide jobs, preserve valuable agricultural land, and create tourist destinations. The sale of just one litre of Canadian wine provides over $4 in economic value to the Canadian economy. Wine sales in Canada are approaching $5 billion annually, and 40 percent of this total comes from Canadian brands. Canada's wine industry is characterized by new investments in world-class wineries, aggressive new plantings of vinifera varietals, diversified wine offerings, new technology, expanding exports, and greater recognition of the industry's ability to produce fine wines at competitive prices.

Stratus Vineyards, established in 2000, is one company that is achieving success with its eco-winery philosophy. Committed to responsible stewardship of the land, environmental sustainability is a core value of all involved in the design and operation of Stratus. Stratus is a sustainable, innovative winery located in Niagara-on-the-Lake. Its goal is to make limited quantities of premium wine with as minimal a carbon footprint as possible. The winery is the first building in Canada to achieve LEED® (Leadership in Energy and Environmental Design) certification from the Canada Green Building Council and it is the only winery worldwide to achieve this designation fully.

To qualify for LEED certification, the winery had to meet numerous criteria that reduced the negative impact on the environment both during construction and on a permanent, operational basis. Primary features include geothermal technology to heat and cool the building, the use of recycled materials in the construction and design, resource and energy-efficient electrical and plumbing systems, a toxin-free waste management program, herbicide-free vineyards, and a landscape plan that is organic and based on indigenous grasses and plants. For example, it estimated that 80 percent of the energy that is used is free. The company also uses a hybrid, gas-electric vehicle for winery deliveries.

Stratus is a strong example of the sustainable "triple bottom-line": plant, people, and profit. Its wines are critically acclaimed and have become benchmarks of quality within the Canadian wine industry.

Sources: Frederick G. Crane et al., *Marketing*, 7th Canadian ed. (Toronto: McGraw-Hill Ryerson Ltd., 2008), 5–6; Terri Meyer, "Case Studies in Canadian Sustainable Design: Stratus Winery," University of Waterloo, 27 June 2006, http://www.architecture.uwaterloo.ca/faculty_projects/terri/sustain_casestudies/stratus_gallery.html; and "Stratus Vineyards Becomes First Winery Worldwide to Achieve LEED Certification," CSRwire, 15 May 2005, http://www.csrwire.com/News/3943.html.

Adam Smith believed that freedom was vital to the survival of any economy, especially the freedom to own land or property and the freedom to keep profits from working the land or owning a business. He believed that people will work hard if they have incentives for doing so—that is, if they know that they will be rewarded.

He made the desire for improving one's condition in life the basis of his theory. According to Smith, as long as farmers, labourers, and business people (entrepreneurs) could see economic rewards for their efforts (i.e., receive enough money in the form of profits to support their families), they would work long hours and work hard. As a result of these efforts, the economy would prosper—with plenty of foods and all kinds of products available to everyone.

How Businesses Benefit the Community

Under Adam Smith's theory, business people don't necessarily deliberately set out to help others. They work primarily for their own prosperity and growth. Yet as people try to improve their own situation in life, Smith said, their efforts serve as an "invisible hand" that helps the economy grow and prosper through the production of needed goods, services, and ideas. Thus, the **invisible hand** turns self-directed gain into social and economic benefits for all.

invisible hand
A phrase coined by Adam Smith to describe the process that turns self-directed gain into social and economic benefits for all.

How is it that people working in their own self-interest produce goods, services, and wealth for others? The only way farmers in a given area can become wealthy is to sell some of their crops to others. To become even wealthier, farmers would have to hire workers to produce more food. As a consequence, people in that area would have plenty of food available and some would have jobs on the farms. So the farmers' self-centred efforts to become wealthy lead to jobs for some and food for almost all. Stop and think

Making Ethical Decisions

Helping After Natural Disasters

Natural disasters have highlighted the need to look beyond ourselves. The 2004 series of tsunamis that were triggered by the Indian Ocean earthquake, the flooding of New Orleans by Hurricane Katrina in 2005, and the 2008 Sichuan earthquake in Sichuan Province, China, are just some of the global events that you may recall. These disasters prompted worldwide efforts to help victims, with billions of dollars raised for disaster relief. While Canadian natural disasters do not generate such attention, examples have included wildfires in British Columbia (e.g., the 2003 wildfires in Okanagan Mountain Provincial Park) and floods in Manitoba (e.g., the 2009 Red River Flood).

Imagine you live in an area where the homes are medium priced. You have plenty of food to eat and spare rooms in your house. A deadly flood hits your neighbouring province. There has not been a national call for you to help out, but you know that the need is great and the ethical thing is for everyone to do his or her part. "We are all Canadians," the news media are saying, and you understand all that such a message means. You can send money to the Red Cross, the Salvation Army, or other charities; you can go to the endangered areas and try to help; or you can offer your home for protection and aid until things get better. What are the potential consequences of each action? What action are you most likely to take, if any? And why? What can ethical business people do to help?

Sources: Anna Mulrine, "To the Rescue," *U.S. News and World Report*, 12 September 2005, 20-26; "The Lost City," *Newsweek*, 12 September 2005, 40-52; various news reports on TV and radio, 2005; and "2004 Indian Ocean Earthquake," Wikipedia, 20 June 2006, http://en.wikipedia.org/wiki/2004_Indian_Ocean_earthquake.

about that process for a minute because it is critical to your understanding of economic growth in Canada and other countries in the world. The same principle applies to other products as well—everything from clothing to iPods.

Smith assumed that as people became wealthier, they would naturally reach out to help the less fortunate in the community.[7] This has not always happened, which is why government regulation in the public interest has always been required. Today, more business people are becoming concerned about social issues and their obligation to return to society some of what they've earned. Worldwide charitable donations in 2007 from Canadian banks totalled approximately $197.2 million, of which approximately $145.3 million remained within Canada.[8] Entrepreneur Bill Gates (the co-founder of Microsoft) and his wife Melinda set up the largest foundation in history, worth some $35.9 billion.[9] Among other initiatives, the Bill and Melinda Gates Foundation works to improve world health by providing vaccines (at least 700,000 lives in poor countries have been saved), training people in health matters, and more.[10] As we mentioned in Chapter 1, it is important for businesses to be ethical as well as generous. Unethical practices undermine the whole economic system; therefore, there needs to be more emphasis on ethics at all stages in business education. You can explore your own ethical position regarding responses to people in need by looking at the Making Ethical Decisions box.

Progress Assessment

- What is the difference between macroeconomics and microeconomics?
- What does Adam Smith's term *invisible hand* mean? How does the invisible hand create wealth for a country?

UNDERSTANDING FREE-MARKET CAPITALISM

Basing their ideas on free-market principles, such as those of Adam Smith, business people began to create more wealth than had ever been created before. They hired others to work on their farms and in their factories and nations began to prosper as a result. Business people soon became the wealthiest people in society. While there were great disparities between the wealthy and the poor, there was always the promise of opportunities to become wealthy.

A free market system is evident at a farmer's market. As a buyer, what can you do to ensure that you pay the best price for produce?

capitalism
An economic system in which all or most of the factors of production and distribution are privately owned and operated for profit.

The economic system that has led to wealth creation in much of the world is known as capitalism. **Capitalism** is an economic system in which all or most of the factors of production and distribution (e.g., land, factories, railroads, and stores) are privately owned (not owned by the government) and are operated for profit. In capitalist countries, business people decide what to produce, how much to pay workers, how much to charge for goods and services, where to sell these goods and services, and so on. Capitalism is the popular term used to describe free-market economies.

No country is purely capitalist, however. Often the government gets involved in issues such as determining minimum wages and subsidizing certain sectors, as the federal government does in Canada for the agriculture sector. Today, capitalism is the foundation for the economies of Canada, England, Australia, the United States, and most other developed nations. We will discuss Canada's mixed economy in some detail later in this book.

How Free Markets Work

The free market is one in which decisions about what to produce and in what quantities are made by the market—that is, by buyers and sellers negotiating prices for goods and services. Consumers (such as you and I) send signals to tell producers what to make, how many, in what colours, and so on. We do that by choosing to buy (or not to buy) certain goods and services. Note that just as no country is purely capitalist, no market is truly free. "Free" markets work not just from the interaction of buyers and sellers, but also from government signals (e.g., laws and regulations, taxes, warnings, advice, etc.).

How Prices Are Determined

In a free market, prices are not determined by sellers; they are determined by buyers and sellers negotiating in the marketplace. A seller may want to receive $50 for a T-shirt, but the quantity demanded at that price may be quite low. If the seller lowers the price,

With 75,000 hotel rooms and an estimated 300,000 visitors, some Vancouverites rented out their homes during the 2010 Vancouver Olympics. Would you pay $36,000 for a two-bedroom condo for one month?

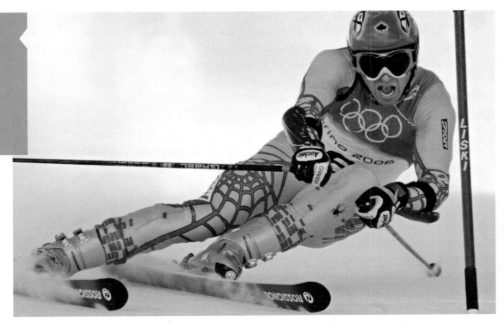

the quantity demanded is likely to increase. How is a price that is acceptable to both buyers and sellers determined? The answer is found in the microeconomic concepts of supply and demand.

The Economic Concept of Supply

Supply refers to the quantity of products that manufacturers or owners are willing to sell at different prices at a specific time. Generally speaking, the amount supplied will increase as the price increases because sellers can make more money with a higher price.

FIGURE | **2.1**

The Supply Curve at Various Prices
The supply curve rises from left to right. Think it through. The higher the price of T-shirts goes (the left margin), the more sellers will be willing to supply.

supply
The quantity of products that manufacturers or owners are willing to sell at different prices at a specific time.

Economists show this relationship between quantity supplied and price on a graph. Figure 2.1 shows a simple supply curve for T-shirts. The price of the T-shirts in dollars is shown vertically on the left of the graph. The quantity of T-shirts that sellers are willing to supply is shown horizontally at the bottom of the graph. The various points on the curve indicate how many T-shirts sellers would provide at different prices. For example, at a price of $5 a T-shirt, a vendor would provide only five T-shirts, but at $50 a T-shirt the vendor would supply 50 shirts. The supply curve indicates the relationship between the price and the quantity supplied. All things being equal, the higher the price, the more the vendor will be willing to supply. The Spotlight on Small Business box highlights how small businesses especially need to be aware of their capabilities when supplying customers.

The Economic Concept of Demand

Demand refers to the quantity of products that people are willing to buy at different prices at a specific time. Generally speaking, the quantity demanded will increase as the price decreases. Again, the relationship between price and quantity demanded can be shown in a graph. Figure 2.2 shows a simple demand curve for T-shirts. The various points on the graph indicate the quantity demanded at various prices. For example, at a price of $45, the quantity demanded is just five T-shirts, but if the price were $5, the quantity demanded would increase to 35 T-shirts. The line connecting the dots is called a demand curve. It shows the relationship between quantity demanded and price. The Dealing with Change box highlights some challenges when changes occur faster than a company is able to adapt.

demand
The quantity of products that people are willing to buy at different prices at a specific time.

The Equilibrium Point and the Market Price

It should be clear to you after reviewing Figures 2.1 and 2.2 that the key factor in determining the quantity supplied and the quantity demanded is *price*. Sellers prefer a high price, and buyers prefer a low price. If you were to lay one of the two graphs on top of the other, the supply curve and

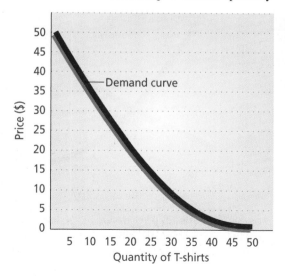

FIGURE | **2.2**

The Demand Curve at Various Prices
This is a simple demand curve showing the quantity of T-shirts demanded at different prices. The demand curve falls from left to right. It is easy to understand why. The lower the price of T-shirts, the higher the quantity demanded.

SPOTLIGHT ON Small Business

Pressing on with Kalikori

In 1950 in the region of Kalamata, Greece, Papou Vassily and his son Stavros Ligris planted an olive grove on land that had been passed down from generation to generation. Making olive oil became a family tradition as the olive oil was a central ingredient in many Greek dishes. Ligris passed the olive grove down to daughter, Effy, in 2003, and gave his blessing to the idea of marketing the olive oil in North America. Soon after, the Montreal-based company Kalikori was created.

All year long, the olive grove is nurtured. The olives are harvested in November, before all the olives are ripe. They are picked by hand, just as it's been done for hundreds of years. Then the olives are sent to the pressing machine, which washes and sorts the olives and extracts the oil. Within a year, Effy Ligris and partner Spyros Bourboulis imported their first batch of L'Olivier de Vassily Olive Oil. This is a single-variety, cold-pressed olive oil named after Ligris' grandfather.

Because of the early harvest, the amount of oil that is produced is small but of premium quality. The high quality is partly due to the rocky soil of the mountainous Kalamata region. The small green olives produced in the grove are the only ones used, as the overall product is not a blend. L'Olivier de Vassily was an instant success, so much so that the 4,000 units Kalikori imported sold out to specialty food shops within a few months, without any chance of restocking until the next year's harvest.

"Stocking too little or too much is a serious problem facing many startups," says Bakr Ibrahim, director of the Centre for Small Business and Entrepreneurial Studies at Concordia University. "But in the first year, they were only trying to test the market. Good entrepreneurs will test the market and use their gut feeling."

In 2007 the business partners knew that their business was in trouble when fire spread across Greece. While the olive grove that produced the olives for their cold-pressed olive oil wasn't torched, there were concerns about an insufficient harvest. To its credit, the company also imported red wine vinegar and handpicked sea salt. Ibrahim believes that this kind of diversification is the best way to combat impending olive oil supply problems. By increasing its vinegar production and choosing other complementary products, all of the company's products may not be affected by the same weather conditions.

Ligris believes there is a growing market for her rather expensive specialty product. "The small estate olive oils that are produced by the family are usually the real deal, the good stuff," she says. At $23 to $27 for a 375-millilitre bottle (compared with $6 to $9 for a bottle double that size of standard supermarket-variety oil), they are premium-priced to reflect the quality. Consumers seem to buy into Ligris' belief. Kalikori's sales more than doubled in the second year, and in the third year, sales were five times the first, at 20,000 units. In 2008, the company was seeking U.S. distributors to bring its products to the United States.

Sources: "L'Olivier de Vassily Olive Oil," Kalikori, 9 August 2008, http://kalikorioliveoil.com/en/about.html; and Regan Ray, "Slippery Business," *Canadian Business Magazine*, 24 September 2007, http://www.canadianbusiness.com/managing/strategy/article.jsp?content=20070918_19919_19919.

FIGURE 2.3

The Equilibrium Point
The place where quantity demanded and supplied meet is called the equilibrium point. When we put both the supply and demand curves on the same graph, we find that they intersect at a price where the quantity supplied and the quantity demanded are equal. In the long run, the market price will tend toward the equilibrium point.

market price
The price determined by supply and demand.

the demand curve would cross. At that crossing point, the quantity demanded and the quantity supplied are equal. Figure 2.3 illustrates that point. At a price of $15, the quantity of T-shirts demanded and the quantity supplied are equal (25 shirts). That crossing point is known as the *equilibrium point* or the *equilibrium price*. In the long run, that price would become the market price. **Market price**, then, is determined by supply and demand.

Supporters of a free market would argue that, because supply and demand interactions determine prices, there is no need for government involvement or government planning. If surpluses develop (i.e., if quantity supplied exceeds quantity demanded), a signal is sent to sellers to lower the price. If shortages develop (i.e., if quantity supplied is less than quantity demanded), a signal is sent to sellers to increase

DEALING with CHANGE

Adapting to Swings in Demand

Imagine that your local professional hockey team has not been winning many games in the last few years. We're sure that many of you can identify with that. Ticket prices are set and the season begins. Because of a few new people on the team, the team begins winning game after game and the demand for tickets goes up. The owners cannot raise the prices without creating great tumult among the fans, so the price remains stable. But an informal market (among fans) grows for tickets, often on the Internet. Prices for these tickets usually go up because interested purchasers may be willing to pay more than the ticket's face value. Revenue also goes up for the owners because they sell a lot more hot dogs and beverages.

But what happens if the team starts losing again? Demand for tickets falls. The owners begin losing money at the concession stand. What can the owners do to adjust? You can see how adapting to changes in demand are often difficult to do.

The same is true with auto sales. When gas prices go up dramatically, as they did in 2008, auto dealers find themselves with many large SUVs and light trucks in their inventories. This created opportunities as sales of subcompacts, compacts, and small sport utility vehicles jumped dramatically when consumers shifted sharply to more fuel-efficient models because of the gas-price shock. Toyota Canada Inc., for example, smashed a company record for July 2008 as sales shot up 18.3 percent. Business for the Corolla compact jumped 36 percent and sales for its hybrid Prius soared 137 percent. What other examples could you cite that show the lag between changes in supply and/or demand and the reaction by business people?

Sources: Tony Van Alphen, "Canadian Auto Sales Back in Gear," *The Toronto Star*, 2 August 2008, http://www.thestar.com/article/471543; and Victoria Murphy, "Seattle's Best Kept Secret," *Forbes*, 25 April 2005, 86–88.

---

the price. Eventually, supply will again equal demand if nothing interferes with market forces. Such price swings were evident when the oil supply was cut because of Hurricane Katrina. When supplies were low because of the hurricane, the price of gasoline went up (dramatically). When supplies were again plentiful, the price of gas fell.

In countries without a free market, there is no such mechanism to reveal to businesses (via price) what to produce and in what amounts, so there are often shortages (not enough products) or surpluses (too many products). In such countries, the government decides what to produce and in what quantity, but the government has no way of knowing what the proper quantities are. Furthermore, when the government interferes in otherwise free markets, such as when it subsidizes farm goods, surpluses and shortages may also develop.

Competition Within Free Markets

Economists generally agree that four different degrees of competition exist: (1) perfect competition, (2) monopolistic competition, (3) oligopoly, and (4) monopoly.

Perfect competition exists when there are many sellers in a market and no seller is large enough to dictate the price of a product. Under perfect competition, sellers produce products that appear to be identical. Agricultural products (e.g., apples, corn, potatoes) are often considered to be the closest examples of such products. You should know, however, that there are no true examples of perfect competition. Today, government price supports and drastic reductions in the number of farms make it hard to argue that even farming is an example of perfect competition.

Monopolistic competition exists when a large number of sellers produce products that are very similar but are perceived by buyers as different (e.g., hot dogs, candy, and T-shirts). Under monopolistic competition, product differentiation (the creation of real or perceived product differences) is a key to success. The fast-food industry, in which there are often promotional battles between hamburger restaurants, offers a good example of monopolistic competition.

An **oligopoly** occurs when a few sellers dominate a market. Oligopolies exist in industries that produce products in the areas of oil and gas, tobacco, automobiles, aluminum, and

perfect competition
The market situation in which there are many sellers in a market and no seller is large enough to dictate the price of a product.

monopolistic competition
The market situation in which a large number of sellers produce products that are very similar but that are perceived by buyers as different.

oligopoly
A form of competition in which just a few sellers dominate the market.

Although WestJet Airlines Ltd. operates within an oligopoly in Canada, it still has to listen to the needs of its customers and try to be innovative. Check-in choices include traditional counter, Web, mobile, self-service kiosks, and flow-through check-in.

aircraft. One reason some industries remain in the hands of a few sellers is that the initial investment required to enter the business is tremendous. In an oligopoly, prices for products from different companies tend to be close to the same. The reason for this is simple. Intense price competition would lower profits for all competitors, since a price cut on the part of one producer would most likely be matched by the others. As in monopolistic competition, product differentiation, rather than price, is usually the major factor in market success.

monopoly
A market in which there is only one seller for a product or service.

A **monopoly** occurs when there is only one seller for a good or service, and that one seller controls the total supply of a product and the price. Traditionally, monopolies were common in areas such as water, electricity, and telephone services that were considered essential to a community.[11] As a result of continuing deregulation, there are fewer examples in Canada of a monopoly. Figure 2.4 highlights where these forms of free-market competition fall when one considers the number of sellers (i.e., competitors) in the marketplace.

FIGURE **2.4**

Free-Market Competition

Benefits and Limitations of Free Markets

The free market—with its competition and incentives—was a major factor in creating the wealth that industrialized countries now enjoy. Free-market capitalism, more than any other economic system, provides opportunities for poor people to work their way out of poverty.

The free market allows open competition among companies. Businesses must provide customers with quality products at fair prices with good service. Otherwise, they will lose customers to those businesses that do provide good products, good prices, and good service.

Yet even as free-market capitalism has brought prosperity, it has brought inequality as well. Business owners and managers make more money and have more wealth than workers. There is much poverty, unemployment, and homelessness. People who are old, disabled, or sick may not be able to support themselves.

Smith assumed that as people became wealthier, they would naturally reach out and help the less fortunate in the community. As was discussed earlier, while this has not always happened, business people are becoming more concerned about social issues and their obligation to return to society some of what they've earned. For example, Warren Buffet, CEO of Berkshire Hathaway and ranked as one of the world's wealthiest people, has pledged to give away most of his money to the Bill and Melinda Gates Foundation.[12] In another example, Cirque du Soleil dedicates one percent of its revenues to social and cultural programs in the community.[13]

One of the dangers of free markets is that business people and others may let greed dictate how they act. Recent charges made against some big businesses indicate the scope of this danger. We hear more and more examples of business people deceiving the public about their products and others deceiving their shareholders about the value of their stock.[14] All of this was done to increase the executives' personal assets.

Clearly, some government rules and regulations are necessary to make sure that all of a business's stakeholders are protected and that people who are unable to work get the basic care they need. To overcome the limitations of capitalism, some countries have adopted an economic system called socialism. It, too, has its good and bad points. We explore the advantages and disadvantages of socialism after the Progress Assessment questions.

Progress Assessment

- How do business people know what to produce and in what quantity?
- How are prices determined?
- Describe the four degrees of competition.
- What are some of the limitations of free markets?

UNDERSTANDING SOCIALISM

Socialism is an economic system based on the premise that some, if not most, basic businesses—such as steel mills, coal mines, and utilities—should be owned by the government so that profits can be evenly distributed among the people.[14] Entrepreneurs often own and run the smaller businesses, but private businesses and individuals are taxed relatively steeply to pay for social programs.

Socialists acknowledge the major benefit of capitalism—wealth creation—but believe that wealth should be more evenly distributed than occurs in free-market capitalism. They believe that the government should be the agency that carries out the distribution. The major benefit of socialism is supposed to be social equality as income is taken from the wealthier people, in the form of taxes, and redistributed to the poorer members of the population through various government programs. Free education, health care, child care, and unemployment insurance are some of the benefits evident in socialist countries.

Socialism may create more equality than capitalism, but it takes away some of business people's incentives to work hard, as their profits will be heavily taxed. For example, tax rates in some nations once reached 85 percent. Socialism also results in fewer inventions and less innovation because those who come up with new ideas usually don't receive as much reward as they would in a capitalist system. Generally speaking, over the past decade or so, most socialist countries have simply not kept up with more capitalist countries in new inventions, job creation, or wealth creation.[15]

Communism may be considered an advanced version of socialism. We shall explore that system next.

socialism
An economic system based on the premise that some, if not most, basic businesses should be owned by the government so that profits can be evenly distributed among the people.

Socialism has been much more successful in some countries than in others. The photo on the left of Denmark's modern and clean transportation systems reflects the relative prosperity of that country. India (right photo) is not doing nearly as well, but it is experiencing economic growth as a result of a move away from agriculture toward more services and industrial firms. What other factors could account for this disparity in the economic success of these two socialist countries?

UNDERSTANDING COMMUNISM

The nineteenth-century German political philosopher Karl Marx saw the wealth created by capitalism, but he also noted the poor working and living conditions of labourers in his time. He decided that workers should take ownership of businesses and share in the wealth. In 1848, he wrote *The Communist Manifesto*, outlining the process, thus becoming the father of communism.

communism
An economic and political system in which the state (the government) makes all economic decisions and owns almost all of the major factors of production.

Communism is an economic and political system in which the state (the government) makes *almost all* economic decisions and owns almost all of the major factors of production. Communism affects personal choices more than socialism does. For example, some communist countries have not allowed their citizens to practise certain religions, change jobs, or move to the town of their choice.

One problem with communism is that the government has no way of knowing what to produce because prices don't reflect supply and demand as they do in free markets. As a result, shortages of many items may develop, including shortages of food and basic clothing. Another problem with communism is that it doesn't inspire business people to work hard, because the government takes most of their earnings. Therefore, although communists once held power in many nations around the world, communism is slowly disappearing as an economic form.

Most communist countries today are suffering economic depression, and some people (for example, in North Korea) are starving. Some parts of the former Soviet Union remain under communist concepts, but the movement there, until recently, was toward free markets. The trend toward free markets is also appearing in Vietnam and parts of China.[16]

THE TREND TOWARD MIXED ECONOMIES

The nations of the world have largely been divided between those that followed the concepts of capitalism and those that adopted the concepts of communism or socialism. Thus, to sum up the preceding discussion, the two major economic systems vying for dominance in the world today can be defined as follows:

1. **Free-market economies** exist when the market largely determines what goods and services are produced, who gets them, and how the economy grows. *Capitalism* is the popular term used to describe this economic system.

2. **Command economies** exist when the government largely decides what goods and services are produced, who gets them, and how the economy will grow. *Socialism* and *communism* are the popular terms used to describe variations of this economic system.

Experience has shown that neither of these systems has resulted in optimum economic conditions. Free-market mechanisms haven't been responsive enough to the needs of the poor, the old, or the disabled. Some people also believe that businesses in free-market economies have not done enough to protect the environment. Over time, voters in free-market countries, such as Canada, have therefore elected officials who have adopted social and environmental programs such as medicare, unemployment compensation, and various clean air and water acts.

Socialism and communism, for their part, haven't always created enough jobs or wealth to keep economies growing fast enough. As a consequence, communist governments are disappearing and socialist governments have been cutting back on social programs and lowering taxes for businesses and workers. The idea is to generate more business growth and thus generate more revenue.[17]

The trend, then, has been for so-called socialist countries (e.g., France) to move toward more capitalism. We say "so-called" because no country in the world is purely capitalist or purely socialist. All countries have some mix of the two systems. Thus, the long-term global trend is toward a blend of capitalism and socialism. This trend likely will increase with the opening of global markets as a result of the Internet.[18] The net effect of capitalist systems moving toward socialism and socialist systems moving toward capitalism is the emergence throughout the world of mixed economies.

Mixed economies exist where some allocation of resources is made by the market and some is made by the government. Most countries don't have a name for such a system. If the dominant way of allocating resources is by free-market mechanisms, then the leaders of such countries still call their system capitalism. If the dominant way of allocating resources is by the government, then the leaders call their system socialism. Figure 2.5 compares the various economic systems.

free-market economy
An economy in which the market largely determines what goods and services are produced, who gets them, and how the economy grows.

command economy
An economy in which the government largely decides what goods and services are produced, who gets them, and how the economy will grow.

mixed economies
Economic systems in which some allocation of resources is made by the market and some by the government.

Progress Assessment

- What led to the emergence of socialism?
- What are the benefits and drawbacks of socialism?
- What are the characteristics of a mixed economy?

	Capitalism	Socialism	Communism	Mixed Economy
Social and economic goals	Private ownership of land and business. Freedom and the pursuit of happiness. Free trade. Emphasis on freedom and the profit motive for economic growth.	Public ownership of major businesses. Some private ownership of smaller businesses and shops. Government control of education, health care, utilities, mining, transportation and media. Very high taxation. Emphasis on equality.	Public ownership of all businesses. Government-run education and health care. Emphasis on equality. Many limitations on freedom, including freedom to own businesses, change jobs, buy and sell homes, and assemble to protest government actions.	Private ownership of land and business with government regulation. Government control of some institutions (e.g., mail). High taxation for the common welfare. Empasis on a balance between freedom and equality.
Motivation of workers	Much incentive to work efficiently and hard, because profits are retained by owners. Workers are rewarded for high productivity.	Capitalist incentives exist in private businesses. Government control of wages in public institutions limits incentives.	Very little incentive to work hard or to produce quality products.	Incentives are similar to capitalism except in government-owned enterprises, which have few incentives.
Control over markets	Complete freedom of trade within and among nations. No government control of markets.	Some markets are controlled by the government and some are free. Trade restrictions among nations vary and include some free trade agreements.	Total government control over markets except for illegal transactions.	Some government control of trade within and among nations (trade protectionism).
Choices in the market	A wide variety of products is available. Almost no scarcity or oversupply exists for long because supply and demand control the market.	Variety in the marketplace varies considerably from country to country. Choice is directly related to government involvement in markets.	Very little choice among competing products.	Similar to capitalism, but scarcity and oversupply may be caused by government involvement in the market (e.g., subsidies for farms).

FIGURE   2.5

Comparisons of Key Economic Systems

CANADA'S MIXED ECONOMY

Like most other nations of the world, Canada has a mixed economy. The degree of government involvement in the economy today—in areas such as health care, education, and business regulation, just to name a few—is a matter of some debate. (In Chapter 3, we will discuss the role of government in more detail.) The government's perceived goal is to grow the economy while maintaining some measure of social equality. The goal is very hard to attain. Nonetheless, the basic principles of freedom and opportunity should lead to economic growth that is sustainable.

Several features have played a major role in Canada becoming an independent economic entity with high government involvement in the economy. First, we are one of the largest countries in the world geographically, but we have a small population (approximately 33.6 million in early 2009).[19] We have one of the lowest population densities in the world.

Most important, our neighbour to the south has ten times the population and an economy even greater than that proportion, speaks our language, is very aggressive economically, and is the most powerful country in the world. The United States exerts a very powerful influence on Canada as our largest trading partner. (We will discuss details in Chapter 8.)

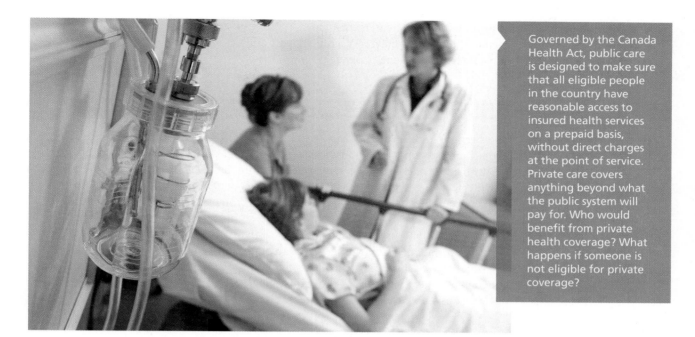

Governed by the Canada Health Act, public care is designed to make sure that all eligible people in the country have reasonable access to insured health services on a prepaid basis, without direct charges at the point of service. Private care covers anything beyond what the public system will pay for. Who would benefit from private health coverage? What happens if someone is not eligible for private coverage?

To control our destiny, Canadian governments have passed many laws and regulations to ensure that significant economic and cultural institutions, such as banks, insurance companies, and radio and TV stations, remain under Canadian control. (Even powerful countries like the United States and Japan have similar regulations.)

All of these factors led to the Canadian capitalist system taking on many characteristics of a mixed economy. Massive government support was necessary to build our first national rail line, the CPR, in the 1880s. When air transport was beginning in the 1930s no company wanted to risk investing heavily in such a large country with only 10 million people spread thinly across the land. So the government set up Air Canada (then called Trans Canada Airlines) to transport mail, people, and freight. There are many such examples of government action to protect the national interest.

In the 1980s, many countries, including Canada, began to reduce government involvement in, and regulation of, the economy. This trend toward deregulation was widespread. In Canada, airlines, banks, and the trucking industry have all seen a marked reduction in regulatory control.

This trend continues today as groups lobby the government to relax regulations to allow them to be more competitive. For example, to encourage competitiveness, the Competition Policy Review Panel recommends lowering barriers to foreign investment in a number of industries, including telecommunications and air transportation.[20] The Conference Board of Canada has released a report that warns that Canadian industries need to do a better job competing for global investment dollars, attracting foreign investors, and establishing new investments overseas.[21]

There are also many new players entering the Canadian marketplace that are competing with publicly funded (i.e., government-funded) institutions. One such industry is health care. Canada's health care spending in 2007 was expected to reach $160.1 billion, with public-sector spending representing $113.0 billion (70.6 percent) and private-sector spending (including privately insured and out-of-pocket expenses) representing the balance.[22] Private health care supporters continue to lobby for a greater presence in Canada. In the years to come, we can expect to see more examples of our mixed economy moving toward a more capitalist system, as the private sector will play a greater role in delivering some goods and services (e.g., health care) that have historically been managed by public institutions. Keep in mind that during tough economic times, voters demand more government involvement. Thus, it is a traditional and desirable role of government to increase expenditures (e.g., provide financial aid to industries, increase spending on infrastructure, etc.) to support and stabilize the economy. The question is how much involvement, debt, etc. is appropriate.

UNDERSTANDING CANADA'S ECONOMIC SYSTEM

The strength of the economy has a tremendous effect on business. When the economy is strong and growing, most businesses prosper and almost everyone benefits through plentiful jobs, reasonably good wages, and sufficient revenues for the government to provide needed goods and services. When the economy is weak, however, businesses are weakened, employment and wages fall, and government revenues decline as a result.

Because business and the economy are so closely linked, business literature is full of economic terms and concepts. It is virtually impossible to read business reports with much understanding unless you are familiar with the economic concepts and terms being used. One purpose of this chapter is to help you learn additional economic concepts, terms, and issues—the kinds that you will be seeing daily if you read the business press, as we encourage you to do.

Key Economic Indicators

Three major indicators of economic conditions are (1) the gross domestic product (GDP), (2) the unemployment rate, and (3) the price indexes. Another important statistic is the increase or decrease in productivity. When you read business literature, you'll see these terms used again and again. It will greatly increase your understanding if you learn the terms now.

Gross Domestic Product

gross domestic product (GDP)
The total value of goods and services produced in a country in a given year.

Gross domestic product (GDP) is the total value of final goods and services produced in a country in a given year. Either a domestic company or a foreign-owned company may produce the goods and services included in the GDP as long as the companies are located within the country's boundaries. For example, production values from Japanese automaker Toyota's factory in Cambridge, Ontario, would be included in the Canadian GDP. Likewise, revenue generated by the Ford Motor Company car factory in Mexico would be included in Mexico's GDP, even though Ford Motor Company is a U.S.-owned company.

If GDP growth slows or declines, there are often many negative effects on business. As noted in Figure 2.6, GDP growth has been slowing down in recent years. According to Statistics Canada, "2008 marked the first decline in exports since 2003 as trade of manufactured goods, particularly related to forestry and automotive products, were hard hit. Domestic demand grew at a slower pace than 2007, as growth of personal spending

Source: Economic Accounts Key Indicators, Canada, Statistics Canada, Provincial and Territorial Economic Accounts Review, Catalogue Number 13-016-X, www. statcan.gc.ca/pub/13-016-x/ 2009001/t/tab0101-eng.htm.

FIGURE 2.6

Canadian Real GDP, 2003–2008

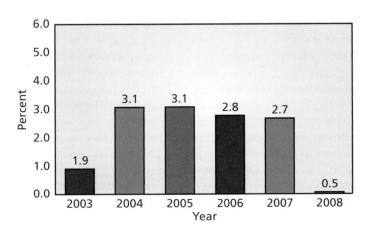

decelerated and housing construction slowed. Growth in services industries generally slowed."[23] An Economist Intelligence Unit report forecast that the real GDP would fall by 2.9 percent in 2009, driven by falls in real private consumption and investment. As well, it expected that weak global trade would cause a trade deficit in 2009.[24] Was this report accurate?

What can account for increases in GDP? A major influence on the growth of GDP is how productive the workforce is—that is, how much output workers create with a given amount of input. This is linked to the combination of creating jobs, working longer hours, or working smarter. Working smarter means being more productive through the use of better technology and processes and a more educated and efficient workforce. In the past, GDP growth has been affected by rising employment (to be discussed soon), low inflation, and low interest rates.[25]

The more you produce, the higher the GDP and vice versa. The economy benefits from a strong GDP. Money that is earned from producing goods and services goes to the employees that produce them in the form of wages. People who own the business generate a return on their investment, and government benefits from tax collection. A strong economy usually leads to a high standard of living for Canadians. The term **standard of living** refers to the amount of goods and services people can buy with the money they have. This includes homes, cars, trips, and the like.

Note that this is different from quality of life. **Quality of life** refers to the general well-being of a society in terms of political freedom, a clean natural environment, education, health care, safety, free time, and everything else that leads to satisfaction and joy. In your opinion, have too many people in Canada sacrificed their quality of life to have a higher standard of living by working more? Since productivity is central to a country's GDP, we will look at this next.

Productivity in Canada

Productivity is measured by dividing the total output of goods and services of a given period by the total hours of labour required to produce them. An increase in productivity means that a worker can produce more goods and services in the same period of time than before, usually through the use of machinery or other equipment.

Labour cost measures the same equation in dollars. The dollar value of outputs is divided by the dollar value of the work hours to arrive at the labour cost per unit. Anything that increases productivity or reduces labour costs makes a business, and a country, more competitive because prices can be lower. Productivity has gone up in recent years because computers and other technology have made the process of production faster and easier for many workers.[26] The higher productivity is, the lower costs are in producing products and the lower prices can be. Therefore, business people are eager to increase productivity. For example, the installation of self-serve registers in stores such as Home Depot and Zellers are attempts to decrease the number of cashiers and as a result, decrease labour costs. Do you prefer to deal with a cashier or check out your own purchases?

Starbucks, like all companies, is concerned about productivity. The faster an employee can make a venti-sized cold beverage, the more profits the store can make and the more productive the employee becomes. When someone discovered that it took two scoops of ice to make a venti-sized drink, a new scoop was invented to cut the production time by 14 seconds. A tall black drip coffee can be made in less than 20 seconds, while a venti Double Chocolate Chip Frappuccino Blended Crème takes closer to 90 seconds.[27] Which drink is more profitable for the store?

Since Canada is a service economy, productivity is an issue because firms are so labour-intensive. As a result of foreign competition, productivity in the manufacturing sector has been rising over the years. However, in the service sector, productivity is growing more slowly because there are fewer new technologies available to assist service workers (e.g., teachers, clerks, lawyers, and personal service providers such as barbers) than there are to assist factory workers. Computers, word processors, and other

standard of living
The amount of goods and services people can buy with the money they have.

quality of life
The general well-being of a society in terms of political freedom, a clean natural environment, education, health care, safety, free time, and everything else that leads to satisfaction and joy.

CANADIAN ECONOMY ONLINE, found at http://canadianeconomy.gc.ca, is a one-stop guide to the national economy that provides statistics, federal government facts, and more about economic concepts and events.

productivity
The total output of goods and services in a given period divided by the total hours of labour required to provide them.

REPORT CARD

	Economy	Innovation	Environment	Education and Skills	Health	Society
Australia	B	D	D	B	B	C
Austria	C	D	C	C	B	B
Belgium	B	C	C	B	n.a.	B
Canada	B	D	C	B	B	B
Denmark	B	C	C	C	D	A
Finland	B	C	A	A	B	B
France	D	C	B	C	B	B
Germany	D	B	C	B	B	B
Ireland	A	A	C	C	C	C
Italy	D	D	B	D	B	C
Japan	C	B	C	B	A	D
Netherlands	A	B	C	B	C	A
Norway	A	D	A	C	B	A
Sweden	A	B	A	B	B	A
Switzerland	A	A	A	B	A	B
U.K.	B	B	B	C	D	C
U.S.	B	A	D	C	D	D

Note: Data for the most recent year available used.
Source: Used with permission of the Conference Board of Canada.

According to the Conference Board of Canada, businesses need to work smarter to improve productivity. This includes producing higher-value-added products and services that are worth more in the marketplace. This report card summarizes country ratings in a variety of areas.

technological innovations have contributed to worker productivity. However, one problem is that an influx of machinery may add to the *quality* of the service provided but not to the *output per worker* (productivity).

For example, you've probably noticed that many computers have been installed on your campus. They add to the quality of education but don't necessarily boost professors' productivity. The same is true of some new equipment in hospitals, such as CAT scanners and PET scanners (more modern versions of the X-ray machine). They improve patient care but don't necessarily increase the number of patients that can be seen. In other words, today's productivity measures fail to capture the increase in quality caused by new technology.

Clearly Canada and other countries need to develop new measures of productivity for the service economy, measures that include quality as well as quantity of output. Productivity is extremely important to a country, as it is a measure of its economic prosperity. Canadian businesses are criticized for not spending enough on research and development, relative to other advanced countries. By not doing so, these businesses will fall behind in the fierce global competitive battle. We will discuss the importance of research and development in Chapter 9.

Of course, technological advances usually lead to people being replaced by machines, often contributing to unemployment. We will now examine this important issue.

The Unemployment Rate

unemployment rate
The percentage of the labour force that actively seeks work but is unable to find work at a given time.

The **unemployment rate** refers to the percentage of the labour force that actively seeks work but is unable to find work at a given time.[28] Figure 2.7 describes different types of employment and highlights Canada's unemployment rate over the past six years. The real rate is higher because Statistics Canada does not include people who have given up looking for jobs, those who are working at part-time or temporary jobs, those who stay in or return to school because they cannot find full-time work, and various other categories of

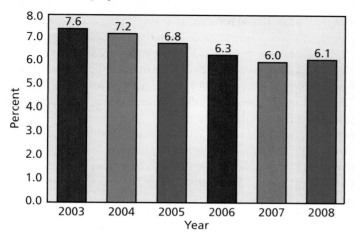

FIGURE | **2.7**

Canadian Unemployment Rate, 2003–2008

Source: "Labour Force Characteristics," Statistics Canada, 8 January 2009, http://www.40.statcan.ca/l01/cst01/econ10.htm.

The types of unemployment are:

- *Frictional unemployment* refers to those people who have quit work because they didn't like the job, the boss, or the working conditions and who haven't yet found a new job. It also refers to those people who are entering the labour force for the first time (e.g., new graduates) or are returning to the labour force after significant time away (e.g., parents who raised children). There will always be some frictional unemployment because it takes some time to find a first job or a new job.
- *Structural unemployment* refers to unemployment caused by the restructuring of firms or by a mismatch between the skills (or location) of job seekers and the requirements (or location) of available jobs (e.g., coal miners in an area where mines have been closed).
- *Cyclical unemployment* occurs because of a recession or a similar downturn in the business cycle (the ups and downs of business growth and decline over time). This type of unemployment is the most serious.
- *Seasonal unemployment* occurs where demand for labour varies over the year, as with the harvesting of crops.

people. The unemployment rate is a key indicator of the health of the economy and of society more generally. That is, when economic growth is strong, the unemployment rate tends to be low and a person who wants a job is likely to experience little trouble finding one. On the other hand, when the economy is stagnating or in recession, unemployment tends to be higher.[29]

People are unemployed in Canada for various reasons. Perhaps their employer goes out of business or their company cuts staff. Young persons enter the job market looking for their first job and other employees quit their jobs but have trouble finding new ones. Companies merge and jobs are consolidated or trimmed. Companies transfer their operations to another country, or a branch of a foreign company is closed down. Of course, in a period of economic recession, such as the early 1980s, the early 1990s, and the end of 2008, unemployment increases. When a job is lost, not only is it a loss to society and the economy, but the loss of income can also create hardship for individuals and families.

Armine Yalnizyan, Chief Economist for the Canadian Centre for Policy Alternatives, has written a report titled, *Exposed: Revealing Truths About Canada's Recession.* In this report, he shares that Canada took four years to restore the full-time jobs lost in the 1980s recession and seven years to restore the 1990s recession job losses. Recovery from the 2008 recession could take years. He cites that Canadians are more vulnerable to financial ruin than in any recession since the Great Depression for the following reasons: Canadians have the weakest unemployment insurance system since the 1940s; their personal savings rates are low and comparable to those of the 1930s; and household debt levels were at a record high even before the recession began. The report recommends improving benefits for the unemployed, given that six of out ten unemployed Canadians don't get jobless benefits today. In the last recession, only two out of ten unemployed had no income protection.[30]

One industry that has been particularly hard hit is the manufacturing industry where in 2008 alone, 84,800 jobs were lost.[31] Foreign demand continued to weaken due to the global downturn which, in part, continued to be impacted by the sub-prime mortgage situation and declining consumer confidence. As well, Canadian industries that were driven by discretionary consumer spending, such as motor vehicles and wood products (e.g., for residential construction), also saw a decrease in sales throughout much of 2008.[32] In Chapter 8, you will learn how countries are influenced by what is happening globally.

The Price Indexes

inflation
A general rise in the prices of goods and services over time.

The price indexes help measure the health of the economy by measuring the levels of inflation, disinflation, deflation, and stagflation. **Inflation** refers to a general rise in the prices of goods and services over time. Rapid inflation is scary. If the cost of goods and services goes up by just 7 percent a year, everything will double in cost in just ten years or so. Inflation increases the cost of doing business. When a company borrows money, interest costs are higher, employees demand increases to keep up with the rise in the cost of living, suppliers raise their prices, and as a result the company is forced to raise its prices. If other countries succeed in keeping their inflation rates down, then Canadian companies will become less competitive in the world market.

disinflation
A situation in which price increases are slowing (the inflation rate is declining).

Disinflation describes a condition where price increases are slowing (the inflation rate is declining). **Deflation** means that prices are actually declining.[33] It occurs when countries produce so many goods that people cannot afford to buy them all. That is, too few dollars are chasing too many goods. **Stagflation** occurs when the economy is slowing but prices are going up regardless.[34]

deflation
A situation in which prices are declining.

The **consumer price index (CPI)** is a monthly statistic that measures the pace of inflation or deflation. To calculate the Consumer Price Index, costs of a "basket" of about 600 goods and services for an average family—including housing, food, apparel, medical care, and education—are calculated to see if they are going up or down. For example, Canadian consumers paid, on average, 0.4 percent more in April 2009 than in April 2008 for the products included in the CPI basket.[35] According to Statistics Canada, some of the contributors to the increase were price increases for food and household operations and furnishings, which rose 7.1 percent and 2.8 percent respectively during the 12-month period. Price declines were reported for energy, natural gas prices, and transportation costs (which fell in the wake of year-over-year declines in prices for both gasoline and passenger vehicles).[36] The CPI is an important figure because it affects nearly all Canadians, either directly or indirectly. For example, government benefits (such as Old Age Security and Canada Pension Plan), rental agreements, some labour contracts, and interest rates are based on it.

stagflation
A situation in which the economy is slowing but prices are going up regardless.

consumer price index (CPI)
Monthly statistic that measures the pace of inflation or deflation.

Other indicators of the economy's condition include housing starts, retail sales, motor vehicle sales, consumer confidence, and changes in personal income. You can learn more about such indicators by reading business periodicals, contacting government agencies, listening to business broadcasts on radio and television, and exploring the Internet. In the Taking It to the Net exercise near the end of this chapter, you will learn that Statistics Canada (www.statcan.gc.ca) is an excellent source of economic information.

The Business Cycle

business cycles (economic cycles)
The periodic rises and falls that occur in economies over time.

Business cycles (also known as **economic cycles**) are the periodic rises and falls that occur in economies over time.[37] These fluctuations are often measured using the real gross domestic product.[38] Economists look at a number of types of cycles, from seasonal cycles that occur within a year to cycles that occur every 48 to 60 years. Economist Joseph Schumpeter identified the four phases of long-term business cycles as boom, recession, depression, recovery:

1. An economic boom is just what it sounds like—business is booming. Periods of economic boom bring jobs, growth, and economic prosperity. In Canada this was evidenced in the late 1990s and early 2000s.[39]

recession
Two or more consecutive quarters of decline in the GDP.

2. **Recession** is two or more consecutive quarters of decline in the GDP. In a recession, prices fall, people purchase fewer products, and businesses fail. A recession has many negative consequences for an economy: high unemployment, increased business failures, and an overall drop in living standards. The most recent recession was reported at the end of 2008 when the economy reflected two consecutive quarters of GDP decline. How long did this recession last?

3. A **depression** is a severe recession usually accompanied by deflation. Business cycles rarely go through a depression phase. In fact, while there were many business cycles during the twentieth century, there was only one severe depression (1929–1933).

4. A recovery occurs when the economy stabilizes and starts to grow. This eventually leads to an economic boom, starting the cycle all over again.

depression
A severe recession.

The goal of economists is to predict such ups and downs. That is very difficult to do. Business cycles are based on facts, but what those facts describe can be explained only by using theories. Therefore, one cannot say with certainty what will happen next. One can only theorize. But one thing is for sure: the economy will rise and fall.[40]

Since dramatic swings up and down in the economy cause all kinds of disruptions to businesses, the government tries to minimize such changes. The government uses fiscal policy and monetary policy to try to keep the economy from slowing too much or growing too rapidly. We will discuss both of these policies in Chapter 3.

Progress Assessment

- What factors have contributed to the decision to have a mixed economy in Canada?
- Name three economic indicators and describe how well Canada is doing using each one.
- What's the difference between a recession and a depression?

SUMMARY

1. Capitalism is an economic system in which all or most of the means of production and distribution (e.g., land, factories, railroads, and stores) are privately owned and operated for profit.

LO ▶ 1 Explain what capitalism is and how free markets work. As part of this discussion, define supply and demand and explain the relevance of the equilibrium point.

Who decides what to produce under capitalism?

In capitalist countries, business people decide what to produce; how much to pay workers; how much to charge for goods and services; whether to produce certain goods in their own countries, import those goods, or have them made in other countries; and so on.

How does the free market work?

The free market is one in which decisions about what to produce and in what quantities are made by the market—that is, by buyers and sellers negotiating prices for goods and services. Buyers' decisions in the marketplace tell sellers what to produce and in what quantity. When buyers demand more goods, the price goes up, signalling suppliers to produce more. The higher the price, the more goods and services suppliers are willing to produce. Price, then, is the mechanism that allows free markets to work.

What is supply and demand?

Supply refers to the quantity of products that manufacturers or owners are willing to sell at different prices at a specific time. Demand refers to the quantity of products that people are willing to buy at different prices at a specific time. The key factor in determining the quantity supplied and the quantity demanded is price.

What is the relevance of the equilibrium point?

The equilibrium point, also referred to as the equilibrium price, is the point where the quantity demanded is the same as the quantity supplied. In the long run, that price becomes the market price.

LO ▶ 2 Define socialism and its benefits and negative consequences.

2. Socialism is an economic system based on the premise that some businesses should be owned by the government.

What are the advantages and disadvantages of socialism?

Socialism creates more social equity. Compared to workers in capitalist countries, workers in socialist countries not only receive more education and health care benefits but also work fewer hours, have longer vacations, and receive more benefits in general, such as child care. The major disadvantage of socialism is that it lowers the profits of owners and managers, thus cutting the incentive to start a business or to work hard. Socialist economies tend to have a higher unemployment rate and a slower growth rate than capitalist economies.

LO ▶ 3 Understand communism and the challenges of such a system.

3. Under communism, the government owns almost all major production facilities and dictates what gets produced and by whom.

How else does communism differ from socialism?

Communism is more restrictive when it comes to personal freedoms, such as religious freedom. With communism, one can see shortages in items such as food and clothing, and business people may not work as hard as the government takes most of their earnings. While many countries practise socialism, only a few (e.g., North Korea) still practise communism.

LO ▶ 4 Describe the mixed economy of Canada.

4. A mixed economy is one that is part capitalist and part socialist. That is, some businesses are privately owned, but taxes tend to be high to distribute income more evenly among the population.

What countries have mixed economies?

Canada has a mixed economy, as do most other countries of the world.

What does it mean to have a mixed economy?

A mixed economy has most of the benefits of wealth creation that free markets bring plus the benefits of greater social equality and concern for the environment that socialism offers.

LO ▶ 5 Discuss the significance of key economic indicators and the business cycle.

5. Three major indicators of economic conditions are (1) the gross domestic product (GDP), (2) the unemployment rate, and (3) the price indexes.

What are the key terms used to describe the Canadian economic system?

Gross domestic product (GDP) is the total value of goods and services produced in a country in a given year. The unemployment rate represents the number of unemployed persons expressed as a percentage of the labour force. The Consumer Price Index (CPI) measures changes in the prices of about 600 goods and services that consumers buy. It is a monthly statistic that measures the pace of inflation (consumer prices going up) or deflation (consumer prices going down). Productivity is the total volume of goods and services one worker can produce in a given period. Productivity in Canada has increased over the years due to the use of computers and other technologies.

What are the four phases of business cycles?

In an economic boom, businesses do well. A recession occurs when two or more quarters show declines in the GDP, prices fall, people purchase fewer products, and businesses fail. A depression is a severe recession. Finally, recovery is when the economy stabilizes and starts to grow.

KEY TERMS

business cycles
(economic cycles) 48

capitalism 34

command economy 41

communism 40

consumer price index (CPI) 48

deflation 48

demand 35

depression 49

disinflation 48

economics 30

free-market economy 41

gross domestic product (GDP) 44

inflation 48

invisible hand 32

macroeconomics 31

market price 36

microeconomics 31

mixed economies 41

monopolistic competition 37

monopoly 38

oligopoly 37

perfect competition 37

productivity 45

quality of life 45

recession 48

resource development 31

socialism 39

stagflation 48

standard of living 45

supply 35

unemployment rate 46

CRITICAL THINKING

Many say that business people do not do enough for society. Some students choose to work for non-profit organizations instead of for-profit organizations because they want to help others. However, business people say that they do more to help others than non-profit groups because they provide jobs for people rather than giving them charity, which often precludes them from searching for work. Furthermore, they believe that businesses create all the wealth that non-profit groups distribute. Can you find some middle ground in this debate that would show that both business people and those who work for non-profit organizations contribute to society and need to work together more closely to help people? Could you use the concepts of Adam Smith to help illustrate your position?

DEVELOPING WORKPLACE SKILLS

1. Show your understanding of the principles of supply and demand by looking at the employment market today. Consider the high salaries that computer scientists are getting. Explain why some PhDs are being paid less than computer scientists who, in comparison, only have college diplomas or undergraduate degrees. Also consider the comparison in pay between graduates from a business program and those who have a skilled trade, such as electricians.

2. This exercise will help you understand socialism from different perspectives. Form three groups. Each group should adopt a different role in a socialist economy: one group will be the business owners, another group will be workers, and the third will be government leaders. Within your group, discuss and list the advantages and disadvantages to you of lowering taxes on businesses. Then have each group choose a representative to debate the tax issue with the representatives from the other groups.

3. Draw a line and mark one end "capitalism" and the other end "socialism." Mark where Canada is now on that line. Explain why you marked the spot you did. Students from other countries may want to do this exercise for their own countries and explain the differences to the class.

4. Break into small groups. In your group, discuss how the following changes have affected people's purchasing behaviour and attitudes toward Canada and its economy: the war in Iraq; new illnesses such as listeriosis; the growth of the Internet; and the numerous charges against big business behaving illegally and unethically. Have a group member prepare a short summary for the class.

TAKING IT TO THE NET 1

www.mcgrawhillconnect.ca

Purpose

To familiarize yourself with recent economic indicators that are important to business decision-makers.

Exercise

Statistics Canada (StatsCan) produces statistics that help Canadians better understand their country. If you want to find out about Canada's population, resources, economy, government, society, and culture, it is likely that StatsCan can help you. Go to the StatsCan Web site at www.statcan.gc.ca and answer the following questions as they pertain to Canada.

1. What is the latest CPI indicator? What percentage change was there from the previous year? What products reflected an increase in price since last year? What products reflected a decrease in price since last year? What products make up the eight most volatile components?

2. What is the latest unemployment rate indicator? How many new full-time jobs were created? How many part-time jobs were created? What sectors created these new jobs? What sectors laid off employees? What province saw the greatest increase in jobs? What province reflects the largest unemployment rate for this past quarter?

3. What is the latest GDP indicator? What percentage change was there from the previous month? What sectors contributed to an increase in production from the previous month? What is the dollar value of all products that were produced last month?

TAKING IT TO THE NET 2

www.mcgrawhillconnect.ca

Purpose

To become familiar with forecasting and analyzing tools.

Exercise

1. Analyses of the constantly changing economy are made regularly by various experts and government departments. See if you can find some forecasts for the Canadian economy, using the keywords "Canadian economic forecasts" to search Web sites such as those offered by the *Globe and Mail* (www.theglobeandmail.com), the *National Post* (www.nationalpost.com), and *Canadian Business* magazine (www.canadianbusiness.com).

2. Visit www.td.com/economics and review the Latest Releases. What are the latest economic forecasts? Is Canada's economic outlook positive? Explain.

ANALYZING MANAGEMENT DECISIONS

Canada's Non-Profit Sector

You may recall from Chapter 1 that non-profit organizations are those whose goals do not include making a personal profit for their owners or organizers. Often referred to interchangeably as "civil society," the "voluntary," "third," or "independent" sector, this group of organizations plays a critical role in society and is central to community engagement and to the building of social capital. This sector encompasses service delivery organizations in areas such as health, education, social services, community development, and housing, as well as those that serve "expressive" functions in arts and culture, religion, sports, recreation, civic advocacy, environmental protection, and through business, labour, and professional associations.

Non-Profit Organizations in 2004: Non-profit organizations continue to make a significant contribution to the economic and social well-being of Canada. In 2004, the value added, or gross domestic product, of the overall non-profit sector amounted to $83.4 billion, accounting for 6.9 percent of the total Canadian economy. This sector is over seven times larger than the motor vehicle manufacturing industry, and over three times larger than each of the agriculture and the accommodation and food services industry. It also exceeded the value of the entire retail trade industry. Economic activity is dominated by hospitals (42.7 percent), and universities and colleges (21.8 percent).

During this time, $135.5 billion was collected in income. A little over half (55.5 percent on average) was received by hospitals, universities and colleges. From this, 95 percent originated from only two sources: government transfers and sales of goods and services. For the other core non-profit organizations, the situation was quite different. Sales of goods and services were, by far, the most important source of revenue, accounting for 41.7 percent of the total. Government transfers were significant at 20.3 percent. In addition to these funds, core non-profit organizations derived more than one-third of their revenue from three additional sources: membership fees (17.2 percent), transfers from households (13.7 percent), and investment income (5.3 percent).

Volunteering in 2000 (Most Recent Data Available): Because the non-profit sector relies heavily on volunteers to undertake its activities, the value of volunteer work is based on the replacement cost approach. That is, it represents how much it would cost to replace volunteer effort if the same services were purchased on the paid labour market. The replacement cost value of work was approximately $14.0 billion, compared to $55.9 billion for paid labour. Put another way, volunteering continues to represent a considerably larger resource to the non-profit sector than monetary and in-kind donations from households. The replacement cost value of volunteering was estimated at $14.0 billion, which was more than double the $6.6 billion of donations received from households.

The use of volunteers relative to paid labour varies considerably by type of organization. The majority of volunteer work is concentrated in three fields of activity: culture and recreation, social services, and religion, with these three groups accounting for nearly three-quarters of the total in the core segment. Large service providers in health and education rely more heavily on paid labour, as do business and professional associations.

The value of volunteer work declined between 1997 and 2000, due to a drop in hours volunteered. While a million fewer Canadians offered volunteer services, those who did invested more hours on average, partially mitigating this decline. Non-profit and voluntary organizations appear to be experiencing difficulties fulfilling their missions or achieving their organizational objectives. Just over one-half report having problems planning for the future, recruiting the types of volunteers needed, and obtaining Board members.

Sources: "Satellite Account of Non-profit Institutions and Volunteering: 1997 to 2004," Statistics Canada, 10 July 2008, http://www.statcan.ca/english/freepub/13-015-XIE/13-015-XIE2007000.pdf; and Michael H. Hall et al., "The Canadian Nonprofit and Voluntary Sector in Comparative Perspective," The John Hopkins Institute for Policy Studies, 2005, http://nonprofitscan.imaginecanada.ca/files/en/misc/jhu_report_en.pdf.

Discussion Questions

1. If Canada followed a pure capitalist system, how would the non-profit sector be affected?

2. Do you agree with the standard measure of GDP for non-profit organizations (i.e., to include a replacement cost value of volunteer work)? Explain.

3. Why do you think these organizations are experiencing difficulties in recruiting volunteers? How could you be encouraged to volunteer?

CHAPTER 3
The Role of Government in Business

LEARNING OBJECTIVES

AFTER YOU HAVE READ AND STUDIED THIS CHAPTER, YOU SHOULD BE ABLE TO:

LO ▶ 1 Understand the six categories of government activities that can affect business.

LO ▶ 2 Trace the historical role of government in the Canadian economy and understand why Crown corporations were created.

LO ▶ 3 Discuss why understanding laws and regulations at all levels of government is critical to business success.

LO ▶ 4 Explain how taxation and financial policies affect the Canadian economy.

LO ▶ 5 Describe how government expenditures benefit consumers and businesses alike.

LO ▶ 6 Illustrate how purchasing policies and services assist Canadian businesses.

PROFILE

Getting to Know Melody Dover of Fresh Media Inc.

Melody Dover founded Fresh Media Inc. in 2003 after working as a professional graphic designer for more than ten years. Prior to opening this business, she broke her right wrist while working for a graphic designer, which prompted her to rethink her career. She decided to enrol in the Interactive Multimedia course at Holland College offered in partnership with Sheridan College. With her newly gained skills, she entered an Atlantic region animation and web design competition, Animediafest, where she took first prize. "People started contacting me to do work for them, and so in June of 2003 I registered the business," says Dover.

Fresh Media is a advertising and branding agency based in Charlottetown, Prince Edward Island (P.E.I.). A creative company with eight employees, it is focused on giving other businesses the best design solutions for their promotional and branding needs. Fresh Media started out with only three clients, but within a year business "just started to swell," says Dover. "Word of mouth was incredible." Now, Fresh Media's clients include a broad range of P.E.I. businesses as well as some off-Island, and sales have continued to increase steadily. As a successful entrepreneur, Dover speaks to students interested in becoming entrepreneurs. "I tell them you have to have passion, because that's what drives you to reach your goal," she says. "Being an entrepreneur is a lifestyle. Your business is a living, breathing creature that you have to take care of . . . When you're an entrepreneur, you have to be prepared for the unknown. You have to be really flexible and ready to accommodate whatever comes along, whether it's a challenge, a catastrophe, or something positive." Dover's company also contributes to the community. Fresh Media adopts one charitable organization each year and provides services free of charge to help promote it. "The community side of the business is really important to me," says Dover. "I believe everyone deserves quality material—even if they can't afford it."

There are many government agencies mandated to provide support for entrepreneurs, and we will discuss several of them in this chapter. One example is the Business Development Bank of Canada (BDC), a financial institution wholly owned by the Government of Canada. This Crown corporation plays a leadership role in delivering financial, investment, and consulting services to Canadian small business, with a particular focus on the technology and export sectors of the economy.

BDC also supports young entrepreneurs. Winner of the 2005 BDC Young Entrepreneur of the Year Award for Prince Edward Island, "Melody is an example of the best of Canada's young entrepreneurs," says BDC President and CEO Jean-René Halde. "The energy and commitment with which she runs her business have resulted in success for herself and generated opportunities for others. She has shown that creativity, passion, and dedication make for a powerful combination and drive the Canadian economy."

Sources: "The Fresh Family," Fresh Media Inc., 28 March 2009, www.fresh media.ca/fresh_family.php?MELODY%20DOVER; and "Melody Dover Takes Creative Leap into Business," Business Development Canada, 18 October 2005, http://www.bdc.ca/en/about/mediaroom/news_releases/2005/2005101805.htm.

GOVERNMENT AFFECTS BUSINESS

Government activities that affect business may be divided into six categories: Crown corporations, laws and regulations, taxation and financial policies, government expenditures, purchasing policies, and services. Because all of these activities are scattered among different levels of government and many departments, agencies, and corporations, it is not possible to present this information in such neatly divided categories. However, as you make your way through the rest of the chapter you will be able to see elements of these different aspects of government actions affecting business.

Since the focus of this chapter is on the role of government in business, there will be limited discussion on how business affects government. It should become obvious as you read that governments are trying to respond to business needs. This can be anything from creating laws that create a level playing field to providing services that support business initiatives. Reviewing Figure 3.1 will give you a sense of the scope of this relationship.

FIGURE **3.1**

Government Involvement with Business
Government activities that affect business can be divided into six categories.

1. **Crown Corporations.** There are hundreds of such companies, and they play an important role in the economy. Crown corporations sometimes compete with for-profit businesses.

2. **Laws and Regulations.** These cover a wide range, from taxation and consumer protection to environmental controls, working conditions, and labour–management relations.

3. **Taxation and Financial Policies.** All levels of government collect taxes—income taxes, the GST, sales taxes, and property taxes. Taxation is also fine-tuned by government to achieve certain goals or to give effect to certain policies. This is called fiscal policy.

4. **Government Expenditures.** Governments pay out billions of dollars to Canadians. When these recipients spend this money, businesses benefit. All levels of government provide a host of direct and indirect aid packages as incentives to achieve certain goals. These packages consist of tax reductions, grants, loans, and loan guarantees.

5. **Purchasing Policies.** Governments are very large purchasers of ordinary supplies, services, and materials to operate the country. Because the federal government is the single largest purchaser in Canada, its policies regarding where to purchase have a major effect on particular businesses and the economy.

6. **Services.** These include a vast array of direct and indirect activities, among them helping companies go international, bringing companies to Canada, training and retraining the workforce, and providing a comprehensive statistics service through Statistics Canada.

GOVERNMENT INVOLVEMENT IN THE ECONOMY

As noted in Chapter 2, the Canadian economic system is described as a mixed economy—that is, an economic system in which some allocation of resources is made by the market and some is made by the government. If you look at the Government of Canada section (and equivalent provincial government sections) in a city telephone directory, you will get some idea of the degree of government involvement in our economy today. Every country's government is involved in its economy, but the specific ways in which the governments participate vary a great deal. There are particular historical reasons why Canada developed into a nation in which governments play very important roles.

When Canada was formed as a country in 1867, the federal government was given the power to "regulate trade and commerce." When the western provinces later joined this Confederation, it became clear that it would take special efforts to build a unified Canada. The very small population was scattered across a huge country, and there was no railway to connect it. Trading patterns were in a north to south configuration because, like today, most people lived near the U.S. border.

The United States developed much faster and with a much larger population and a bigger economy—which provided products not available in the provinces, either because they were not made in Canada or because there was no transportation to distribute them.

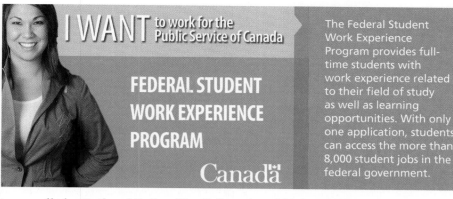

This led the Canadian governments, starting with our first prime minister, Sir John A. Macdonald, to develop what was called a **National Policy**. The Policy placed high tariffs on imports from the United States to protect Canadian manufacturing, which had higher costs. (Since that time, trade agreements such as the North American Free Trade Agreement, discussed in Chapter 8, the Canada-Peru Free Trade Agreement, and the Canada-European Free Trade Association have focused on eliminating such tariffs between countries. Note that in 2009, Canada was discussing the creation of a Canada–European Union Trade Agreement.) In addition, the government began to grapple with the difficult question of building a costly rail line to the west coast.

National Policy
Government directive that placed high tariffs on imports from the United States to protect Canadian manufacturing, which had higher costs.

These two issues set the tone for the continuing and substantial involvement of Canadian governments in developing and maintaining the Canadian economy. As you make your way through this chapter and see their complex activities, you should not be surprised to learn that the different levels of government are large employers in the country. The federal government and the provinces with the largest populations and levels of economic activity—namely, Ontario, Quebec, British Columbia, and Alberta—in particular have been excellent sources of employment for graduates in the past.

As you will see in this chapter, we also have an interventionist government that through its activities (e.g., monetary policy and expenditures) tries to create a stable economy for businesses. Before we go into more detail, let us briefly review how government affects business. You never know, one day you may have a job in one of these areas.

CROWN CORPORATIONS

In Canada, an important aspect of the role of government is expressed through **Crown corporations**, which are companies that are owned by the federal or provincial governments. Review Figure 3.2 for a brief list of the top Crown corporations in Canada. Crown corporations were set up for several reasons. They provided services that were not being provided by businesses, which is how Air Canada came into being in the 1930s. Crown corporations were created to bail out a major industry in trouble, which is how the Canadian National Railway was put together in 1919. Lastly, they provided some special services that could not otherwise be made available, as in the case of the Bank of Canada.

Crown corporation
A company that is owned by the federal or provincial government.

Each province also owns a variety of Crown corporations. Typically, a Crown corporation owns the province's electric power company. Some examples are New Brunswick's Power Corporation, Sask-Power, and Hydro-Québec. Alberta owns a bank called Alberta Treasury Branches (ATB), originally set up to help farmers in bad times. Two other examples in Alberta and Quebec are discussed next.

FIGURE 3.2

Canada's Largest Crown Corporations by Revenue

Rank	Company	2008 Revenue ($ Billions)
1	Hydro-Québec	12.7
2	Canada Mortgage and Housing Corporation	9.6
3	Canadian Wheat Board	8.4
4	Canada Post Corp.	7.5
5	Ontario Lottery and Gaming Corp.	6.2

Source: "Largest Crown Corporations," *Financial Post Business*, 2 June 2009, p. 82. Material reprinted with the express permission of The National Post Company.

The Financial Role of Two Special Provincial Crown Corporations

The Alberta Heritage Savings Trust Fund was established in the 1970s, when the Alberta economy was prospering as a result of the oil boom. The government set aside a part of its oil royalty revenue to start the fund. In 2008 the Fund's assets totalled $14.5 billion.[1] It must operate on a sound financial basis, but, as much as possible, it makes investment decisions that will benefit Alberta.

Quebec has the Caisse de dépôt et placement du Québec (which means Quebec Deposit and Investment Fund), a giant fund that was established to handle the funds collected by the Quebec Pension Plan. With $220.4 billion in total assets under management in 2008, it is one of the largest pools of funds in North America.[2] This plan was set up parallel to the Canada Pension Plan in 1966. The fund also handles other Quebec government funds, and it is a very powerful investment vehicle that is used to guide economic development in Quebec. Although it, too, must operate on a sound financial basis, it has a lot of scope to make decisions that will benefit the Quebec economy.

The Role for Government

Since the 1990s, federal and provincial governments have embarked upon a series of measures designed to reduce the role of government in the economy. Over the years, former large corporations like Teleglobe Canada, Air Canada, and Canadian National Railway (CNR) were sold. The national system of air traffic control, the management of airports, hundreds of ports and ferries, and other maritime installations were also sold.

privatization
The process of governments selling Crown corporations.

This disposal of government assets and companies signalled a minor revolution in Canadian history. The whole process of selling publicly-owned corporations is called **privatization**. As well, during this time, industries that had been regulated, such as airlines, oil and gas, and trucking, were partially or completely deregulated.

Similar activities were undertaken by provincial governments. Alberta privatized its liquor board. Ontario sold the toll-road Highway 407 and its share in a land-registry firm. Saskatchewan reduced its interest in giant uranium producer Cameco Corporation and the British Columbia provincial government sold BC Rail Ltd.

Municipal governments are also looking to privatize services such as water systems, garbage collection, and cleaning. Everywhere you look, government agencies, like for-profit organizations, are looking at ways to lower costs and improve efficiencies.

The federal government sold its remaining stake in Petro-Canada, an oil and gas company, in 2005. Here you see the Hanlan Robb gas plant near Edson, Alberta.

Progress Assessment

- What are the six categories of government involvement with business?
- What are Crown corporations? Why were they created?
- What does privatization refer to? Can you cite any examples?

LAWS AND REGULATIONS

In Chapter 1 you were introduced to the importance of the legal and regulatory environment. These laws and regulations are created by the politicians who, for the most part, have been elected by Canadians. Consequently, the political parties in power can greatly affect the business environment. This is also why it is important to be aware of the beliefs of the different parties. Some think the government should have more say in business, while others think that less government intervention is best.

The power to make laws is based on the British North America Act, 1867 (BNA Act). The BNA Act was passed by the British Parliament in 1867. It is the law that created the Canadian Confederation and it sets the legal ground rules for Canada. In 1982, the BNA Act became part of the new Constitution and was renamed the Constitution Act, 1867.

Laws are derived from four sources: the Constitution, precedents established by judges, provincial and federal statutes, and federal and provincial administrative agencies.[3] As a business person, you will be affected by current (and potential) laws and regulations.

Canada has a legislature in each province and territory to deal with local matters. The Parliament in Ottawa makes laws for all Canadians. The Constitution defines the powers that can be exercised by the federal and provincial governments. In the event of a conflict, federal powers prevail.

The Supreme Court of Canada has the final decision on constitutional questions and on important cases of civil and criminal law. It deals also with appeals from decisions of the provincial courts of appeal.

Federal Government Responsibilities

The federal government is responsible for issues that affect citizens across Canada. Its primary responsibility is to ensure and support the country's economic performance. Some other responsibilities that may have an impact on business operations include:

- trade regulations (interprovincial and international)
- incorporation of federal companies
- taxation (both direct and indirect)
- the banking and monetary system
- national defence
- unemployment
- immigration
- criminal law
- fisheries

In addition to the above-noted areas, the federal government also oversees such industries as aeronautics, shipping, railways, telecommunications, and atomic energy.[4]

As noted in Chapter 1, competition has never been greater than it is today, both internationally and domestically. For example, despite trade agreements, new government policies (e.g., the "Buy American" provisions of U.S. President Obama's massive economic stimulus package, which encourages priority for contracts with U.S. firms) can create barriers to trade.[5] The federal government lobbies other country governments to decrease such trade barriers in an attempt to create business opportunities for Canadian firms. This flip side to this is that these countries may request the same of Canada.

Domestically, the Competition Bureau listens to business and consumer complaints and, in some instances, launches investigations to ensure fair competition. You may recall that Industry Canada is the federal agency that administers a variety of laws affecting businesses and consumers. One of the most relevant pieces of legislation is the Competition Act, which aims to ensure that mergers of large corporations will not restrict

Canadian Agricultural Products Standards Act covers a wide range of farm products, such as meat, poultry, eggs, maple syrup, honey, and dairy products.

Consumer Packaging and Labelling Act applies to all products not specifically included in other acts.

Food and Drugs Act covers a whole range of regulations pertaining to quality, testing approval, packaging and labelling.

Hazardous Products Act covers all hazardous products.

Textile Labelling Act includes apparel sizing and many other special areas.

Weights and Measures Act applies to all equipment that measures quantities (scales, gas pumps, and so forth).

FIGURE | 3.3

Some Major Federal Consumer Protection Laws These laws all provide consumers with information and protection in various ways. There are also provincial consumer protection laws.

How Canadians Govern Themselves is a publication that describes Canada's Constitution, the judicial system, and government powers.

competition and that fair competition exists among businesses. (Some of the major consumer protection laws are shown in Figure 3.3.) The Act covers many laws, including discriminatory pricing, price fixing, misleading advertising, and the refusal to deal with certain companies. Let us look at some examples. The first considers price fixing and the second considers a concern (unproven at the time this chapter was being written) of unfair competition:

- In 2008, the Competition Bureau of Canada laid charges against 11 gas companies and 13 individuals associated with them for conspiring to fix prices in four Quebec municipalities. Three of the firms pleaded guilty on the spot. The other accused faced trial later that year—and, if found guilty, faced fines up to $10 million or five years in jail for individuals. Newly released court documents show that investigators who have been plowing through the wiretap evidence from the investigation have found references to pricing in half a dozen other towns, including Montreal. The Bureau says more charges might come of the continuing investigation, and that similar investigations are under way in other parts of the country.[6]

- The Competition Bureau of Canada is reviewing a proposed search engine partnership between Yahoo Inc. and Google Inc. amid concerns the deal will lead to rising costs for Canadian companies that advertise online. If the Bureau were to determine that the deal violates the Competition Act, it could force the companies to alter the terms of the partnership or squash it altogether. Google controls nearly 80 percent of the search market in Canada, while Yahoo controls less than 4 percent. Keyword prices on Yahoo could rise as much as 22 percent if the company decides to pursue a "profit maximization strategy," according to a recent report from search engine marketing firm SearchIgnite.[7]

Consider the clothes you wear. They are required to have a label showing the country of origin, size, type of fabric, and washing instructions. When you buy 25 litres of gasoline, you can feel confident that you have received a true measure because of the sticker on the equipment showing when it was last inspected. There are laws that give consumers the right to cancel contracts or return goods within a certain period of time. It is not possible to go through a day and not find an instance where laws have helped you in some way.

Marketing Boards

In Canada, we have a special system of **marketing boards** that control the supply or pricing of certain agricultural products. Consequently, they often control trade. This supply

marketing boards
Organizations that control the supply or pricing of certain agricultural products in Canada.

management is designed to give some stability to an important area of the economy that is normally very volatile. Farmers are subject to conditions that are rather unique and that have a great effect on their business and on our food supply. Weather and disease are major factors in the operation of farms and are beyond the control of the individual farmer. So are unstable prices and changes in supply resulting from uncoordinated decision making by millions of farmers around the world, or the exercise of market power by concentrated business organizations.

In the past farmers have experienced periods of severe drought, flooding, severe cold, and diseases that affected crops, livestock, and poultry. The situation regarding international markets and supply has a serious impact on Canada's grain farmers, since Canada exports much more wheat than it consumes domestically. This market fluctuates greatly depending on the supply in other major grain-exporting countries such as the United States, Argentina, and Australia. The market also depends on demand from major importers such as China and Russia, whose abilities to meet their own requirements are subject to wide variation. Often the Canadian government (like other governments) grants substantial loans with favourable conditions to enable these countries to pay for their imports of our wheat and other agricultural products.

Because we export billions of dollars of agricultural products annually, the ability to hold our own in international markets has a major impact on the state of the Canadian economy. When farmers are flourishing, they buy new equipment and consumer goods and their communities feel the effects of ample cash flow. So does the transportation industry. Conversely, when farmers are suffering, all of these sectors hurt as well.

To smooth out the effects of these unusual conditions on this sector of our economy, and to ensure a steady supply of food to consumers at reasonable prices, six government agencies have been set up to control wheat and barley, dairy products, and poultry. The Canadian Wheat Board operates in the three Prairie provinces. (Read the Reaching Beyond Our Borders box for more details.) The Canadian Dairy Commission controls the output and pricing of milk and other dairy products. The Canadian Egg Marketing Agency, Chicken Farmers of Canada, the Canadian Turkey Marketing Agency, and the Canadian Broiler Hatching Egg Marketing Agency consist of representatives from the provinces that produce these items.

All of these bodies, except the Canadian Wheat Board, control the amount of production for all of the products under their supervision by allocating quotas to each province that produces them. Provincial agencies administer these quotas and set prices for their province. Each agency controls products that are sold only in its province.

The Canadian system of marketing boards has been under attack by various organizations because it does not permit normal competitive conditions to operate in this field. This, they argue, distorts the whole industry and raises prices to Canadian consumers. Defenders of the system argue that other countries have different systems that have the same effect as our marketing boards but are just less visible. The European Union spends billions of dollars on subsidies for their farmers. The United States, which often complains about other countries' unreasonable trade barriers, has its own restrictions, such as on sugar imports.

In Chapter 8, we will refer to the World Trade Organization, whose main purpose is to reduce barriers to trade among countries. If the organization is successful, we may see a very different picture emerging worldwide over the next decade: limited protection for domestic markets, reduced tariffs and other restrictions, and the market having a much greater impact on prices and production. The effect on Canadian farmers and on the agricultural industry in general would be enormous, as everyone would be trying to cope with the necessary adjustments to such new conditions.

Provincial Government Responsibilities[8]

Each province has its own government, while the territories are still governed federally. Issues that affect provincial residents but do not necessarily affect all Canadians are

Reaching Beyond Our Borders

The Canadian Wheat Board

While some erroneously believe that the Canadian Wheat Board (CWB) provides and receives subsidies from the Government of Canada, in fact it is a farmer-controlled organization that markets wheat and barley grown by western Canadian producers. Based in Winnipeg, the CWB is one of the world's largest grain-trading companies, marketing 22 to 24 million tonnes of wheat and barley annually both domestically and to over 70 countries worldwide. Annual sales revenues average between US$3 to $4 billion. While farmers decide what to produce, the role of the CWB is to sell these grains for the best possible price. Sales revenues earned, less marketing costs, are passed back to farmers.

Western Canadian farmers control their marketing organization through the election of ten fellow farmers to the board of directors. The board also includes five directors that are appointed by the federal government. It is up to these 15 directors to oversee the management of the CWB. The CWB's value to farmers is based on three pillars:

- **Single-desk selling.** Instead of competing against one another for sales, these farmers sell as one through the CWB and can therefore command a higher return for their grain. Single-desk selling is the mainstay of the CWB. Without it, customers could choose to buy their products from several different competitors. Farmers would be left with an open market where customers could choose to deal with whoever gives them the lowest price, resulting in lower returns for all farmers.
- **Price pooling.** Price pooling means that all CWB sales during an entire crop year (August 1 to July 31) are deposited into pool accounts. This ensures that all farmers delivering the same grade of wheat or barley receive the same return at the end of the crop year, regardless of when their grain is sold during the year.

- **Government guarantee.** Farmers get a partial payment upon delivery of their grain, and the Government of Canada guarantees this payment. The government also guarantees the CWB's borrowings.

There is a perception that Canadian farmers are more subsidized than farmers in other countries. According to information gathered by the Organisation for Economic Co-operation and Development (OECD), Canadian farmers received 17 percent of their income from subsidies. American wheat producers received 49 percent of their income from subsidies, while European Union wheat farmers received 43 percent of their income from subsidies. The U.S. government has investigated or studied the CWB eight times in the past decade. Each time, the CWB has been found to be trading fairly and in full compliance with all of Canada's international trade obligations. The World Trade Organization negotiations on agriculture to try to reduce practices and policies that distort trade have been unsuccessful to date.

Increasingly, some farmers are calling for an end to this marketing monopoly. Prime Minister Stephen Harper promised to move toward dual marketing, eliminating the monopoly. Under this model, farmers could market their wheat without having to go through the CWB. Since this box was written, what changes have been imposed as a result of WTO negotiations (Doha round)? Has Parliament altered the role of the CWB?

Sources: "About Us," Canadian Wheat Board, 29 June 2009 and 7 September 2008, www.cwb.ca; "Canadian Wheat Board Gag Order Unconstitutional, Court Rules," CBC.ca, 20 June 2008, http://www.cbc.ca/canada/saskatchewan/story/2008/06/20/cwb-ruling.html; and "Strahl Must Defend Canadian Wheat Board and Supply Management," Liberal Party of Canada, 15 March 2006, www.liberal.ca/news_e.aspx? id=11502.

governed at the provincial level. Provincial governments are responsible for the following areas:

- regulation of provincial trade and commerce
- natural resources within their boundaries
- direct taxation for provincial purposes
- incorporation of provincial companies
- licensing for revenue purposes
- the administration of justice
- health and social services
- municipal affairs
- property law
- labour law
- education

DEALING with CHANGE

Free Trade Between Provinces

While interprovincial trade is a $300-billion industry in Canada, many Canadian companies and individuals face obstacles when trying to do business outside of their home province or territory. Some trade barriers exist because governments created them to protect their economies from outside competition. Governments also put policies in place to protect the environment, establish workforce standards, or achieve other regulatory purpose. Estimates on the costs of these interprovincial barriers in Canada are $14 billion per year. Interprovincial trade barriers are damaging to the economy and to Canadians' standard of living. These protectionist barriers discourage competition, distort market forces, and reduce efficiency.

The Agreement on Internal Trade (AIT) was signed in 1995 by the first ministers of Canada to allow freer trade between the provinces so that all may benefit. Its purpose is to foster improved interprovincial trade by addressing obstacles to the free movement of persons, goods, services, and investments within Canada. The objective is to reduce extra costs to Canadian businesses by making internal trade more efficient, increasing market access for Canadian companies, and facilitating work mobility for tradespeople and professionals. For example, the Certified General Accountants of New Brunswick successfully appealed to the Internal Trade Secretariat to have the government of Quebec stop restricting access to those that were recognized as qualified to practise accounting in that province.

In 2008, Canada's provincial premiers finally reached a deal to remove barriers that have made it difficult, and sometimes impossible, for workers from one province or territory to work in another. While it is not expected that the amendments will address all barriers, it is a step in the right direction. Amendments to the AIT will lead to full labour mobility for workers and professionals, except where protection of public health or safety justifies barriers. They will also provide for an effective dispute resolution mechanism, including monetary penalties for ignoring a trade panel ruling. Penalties will range from a maximum of $250,000 for the smallest provinces and territories to $5 million for Quebec and Ontario. The issue is especially important to British Columbia, where a shortage of 350,000 workers is forecast between now and 2015. Alberta Premier Ed Stelmach estimates that Alberta will create 400,000 jobs over the next decade. Labour mobility is seen as key to filling these jobs.

Sources: "Certified General Accountants Applaud Movement on Labour Mobility and Resolving Disputes," Certified General Accountants Association of Canada, 30 July 2008, www.cga-canada.org/en-ca/MediaCentre/CurrentMediaReleases/Pages/ca_mdr_2008-07-30.aspx; "Labour Mobility Deal Will Enhance Competitiveness; B.C.'s Campbell and Alberta's Stelmach Deserve Praise for Getting Other Premiers to Sign Up," *Vancouver Sun*, 22 July 2008, A10; "Improving Internal Trade: A Bold Approach," Certified General Accountants Association of Canada, 2008, www.cga-canada.org/en-ca/DiscussionPapers/ca_rep_internal_trade_position-paper2008.pdf; "Overview of the Agreement on Internal Trade, 2009" Internal Trade Secretariat, www.intrasec.mb.ca/index_en/ait.htm; and Paul Vieira, "Internal Barriers an Obstacle," *National Post*, 26 April 2006.

The participation of all provincial governments in federal–provincial, shared-cost arrangements for hospital insurance and medicare has helped ensure nationwide standards of service, despite some differences in their modes of financing and program coverage. While the federal government is responsible for health care, it is still up to the provinces to implement these policies, and their co-operation is critical for success. In contrast, the retention of a high degree of provincial autonomy in the provision of elementary and secondary school education and the accommodation of religious and linguistic preferences has resulted in a variation in school systems. Both government levels also fund programs for post-secondary education. Some changes that are being implemented by the federal and one provincial government with respect to student loans are examined below. The Dealing with Change box highlights provincial decisions that have an impact on the Canadian economy.

Education[9]

Both the federal and provincial governments run their own student loan programs. The federal government plans to phase out interest and other debt relief options for borrowers under the Canada Student Loans Program. Under the new program, known as the Repayment Assistance Plan (RAP), payments will be geared to income and no payments on federal loans will be required for those individuals with a gross annual income of $20,000 or less. Borrowers who are not eligible for RAP will be able to apply to extend their repayment period to reduce their monthly loan payments. This is especially good news for those that owe thousands of dollars in student loans. Statistics Canada reports that about 27 percent of 2005 graduates with bachelor's degrees still owed an average of $16,200 in government loans two years later, another 15 percent owed an average of $31,600 in government and other loans. Fully 43 percent of those owing more than $25,000 reported having difficulty paying their loans, although fewer than 11 percent were unemployed.

Provincially, the Newfoundland and Labrador government has made an effort to improve its post-secondary education policies. Changes to the student loan program include it being the first province to eliminate interest on student loans and extending a long-running freeze on tuition fees at Memorial University and other post-secondary institutions. "We're extremely excited about this," Daniel Smith, the provincial chair of the Canadian Federation of Students said after the program was revealed. This is going to ease the burden of student debt for students of Newfoundland and Labrador. Almost 50,000 people who currently fall under the student loan portfolio here in the province are going to be in a much better situation coming out of this."

Municipal Government Responsibilities[10]

Municipal governments—cities, towns, villages, counties, districts, and metropolitan regions—are set up by the provincial legislatures. Their authority is defined by the specific province in which they operate. There are roughly 4,000 municipal governments in Canada that provide a variety of services.

Municipalities also play a role in consumer protection. For example, they have regulations and laws regarding any establishment that serves food. Inspectors regularly examine the premises of all restaurants for cleanliness. Local newspapers often publish lists of restaurants fined for failing to maintain required standards. There are similar laws (called zoning laws) about noise, odours, signs, and other activities that may affect a neighbourhood. Certain zones are restricted to residences, and others permit only certain quiet businesses to operate.

Zoning requirements also limit the height of buildings and define how far they must be set back from the road. Most Canadian cities require that all high-rise buildings have a certain ratio of garage space so that cars have off-street parking spots. Parking problems in residential areas due to overflow of vehicles from adjacent businesses have led to parking being limited to residential permit holders on certain streets, so that stores and other places of business must offer commercial parking lots for their customers. And, of course, there are speed limits set by municipal or provincial authorities.

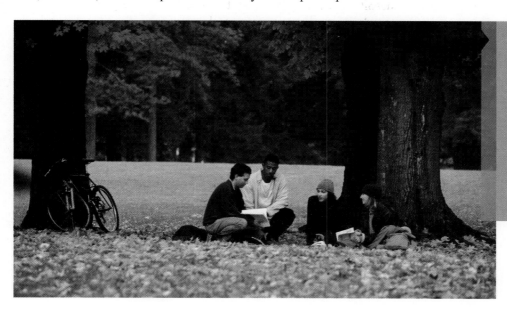

Municipalities provide services such as water supply, sewage and garbage disposal, roads, sidewalks, street lighting, building codes, parks, playgrounds, libraries, and so forth. Schools are generally looked after by school boards or commissions elected under provincial education Acts

All businesses usually must obtain a municipal licence to operate so the appropriate department can track them to ensure they are following regulations. Many municipalities also have a business tax and a charge for water consumption.

In summary, each level of government has its own roles and responsibilities. Sometimes there is overlap and in other instances, there is downloading of responsibilities. Such is the case with some municipal services. An understanding of these responsibilities will contribute to a better understanding of who is responsible for developing, implementing, and overseeing policies that are important to business.

TAXATION AND FINANCIAL POLICIES

Mention the word taxes and most people frown. That's because taxes affect almost every individual and business in the country. Taxes are how all levels of government redistribute wealth. The revenue that is collected allows governments to discharge their legal obligations. This revenue is used to pay for public services (e.g., fire, police, and libraries), pay down debt, and fund government operations and programs. Taxes have also been used as a method of encouraging or discouraging taxpayers. For example, if the government wishes to reduce the use of certain classes of products (e.g., cigarettes, alcohol, etc.), it passes what is referred to as a sin tax. It is hoped that the additional cost of the product from increased taxes discourages additional consumption.

In other situations, the government may encourage business to hire new employees or to purchase new equipment by offering a tax credit. A tax credit is an amount that can be deducted from a tax bill. Research In Motion (RIM) opened a technical support operations centre in Halifax that is expected to create 1,200 jobs over five years. As an incentive, the Nova Scotia government offered RIM $19 million in subsidies (some consider this a tax credit), including $14 million in payroll rebates and $5 million for training and recruitment.[11]

Taxes are levied from a variety of sources. Income (personal and business), sales, and property are the major bases of tax revenue. The federal government receives its largest share of taxes from personal income. Figure 3.4 illustrates the impact that taxation has on the price of gasoline.

FIGURE 3.4

What Goes Into the Price of Gasoline?
Gasoline prices are impacted by the cost of crude oil (approximately 50 percent of cost), taxes, and refining and marketing costs. They are also subject to market forces (e.g., supply of crude oil). This breakdown is based on gas costing $1.24 per litre, the average price in Canada in May 2008.

Factor	Cost per Litre
Crude Oil Barrel Cost	78¢
Taxes	32¢ – 33¢
Federal Excise Tax*	10¢
Provincial Tax	ranges from 6.2¢ in Yukon to 16.5¢ in Newfoundland and Labrador
Goods and Services Tax	5%
or Harmonized Sales Tax	13% in Newfoundland and Labrador, Nova Scotia, and New Brunswick
Provincial Sales Tax	in Quebec only
Municipal Taxes in Three Cities	1.5¢ in Montreal, 12.0¢ in Vancouver, and 3.5¢ in Victoria
Refining, Marketing Costs, and Margins	13¢

*The federal government raises $4 billion a year.

Source: Based on "What Goes into the Price of Gasoline?" CBC News, 14 May 2009, http://www.cbc.ca/consumer/story/2009/05/14/f-gas-prices-oil.html.

Stabilizing the Economy Through Fiscal Policy

Fiscal policy refers to the federal government's effort to keep the economy stable by increasing or decreasing taxes or government spending. The first half of fiscal policy involves taxation. Theoretically, high tax rates tend to slow the economy because they draw money away from the private sector and are remitted to the government. High tax rates may discourage small business ownership because they decrease the profits businesses can make, and this can make the effort less rewarding. It follows then that, theoretically, low tax rates would tend to give the economy a boost.[12] The government can use taxation to help move the economy in a desired direction. For example, taxes may be lowered to stimulate the economy when it is weak. Similarly, taxes may be raised when the economy is booming to cool it off and slow down inflation.

Federal and provincial governments constantly use the lever of fiscal policy to stimulate specific geographic and industrial areas. They offer special tax credits to companies that open plants in areas of chronically high unemployment, such as Cape Breton or Newfoundland and Labrador. All companies that invest in specific activities considered desirable by the government (such as the technology sector) receive a tax credit that reduces the income tax they have to pay. Unfortunately, many of these programs have been scaled back or eliminated due to budget constraints.

The second half of fiscal policy involves government spending. The government spends money in many areas including social programs, highways, the environment, and so on. If the government spends over and above the amount it gathers in taxes for a specific period of time (namely, a fiscal year), then it has a **deficit**.

One way to lessen annual deficits is to cut government spending. This is difficult to do. Every year, there is demand by the provinces (to be discussed later) and territories for increased transfer payments, the need for funds due to unexpected situations (such as the massive flooding in New Brunswick), more pressure from international bodies to increase peacekeeping support, and so on. Some people believe that spending by the government helps the economy grow. Others believe that the money the government spends comes out of the pockets of consumers and business people—especially when taxes have been increased—and that this slows growth. What do you think? Let us look at government actions that have been taken over the past decade.

The National Debt (Federal Debt)

For many years, the Canadian government spent more than it received in revenues, and it had to borrow heavily. However, it did not reduce spending when times were good to pay back these loans. In Canada, 25 years of annual deficits, starting in the mid-1970s, resulted in a huge (net) national debt of $588 billion by 1997.[13] The **national debt** (also known as the **federal debt**) is the accumulation of government surpluses and deficits over time. This debt was approximately $458 billion in 2008.[14]

After relentless pressure from business organizations and right-wing political groups, the Canadian government decided in 1996 that the only way out of that recession was to eliminate annual deficits and stop the debt from growing. This plan meant cutting expenses and cash outlays as much as possible, including reducing transfers to the provinces to pay for health care, education, and welfare. The government reduced employment insurance payments by raising eligibility standards, paying for shorter periods, and paying smaller amounts. The government also laid off thousands of people and reduced pension payments to wealthier senior citizens.

fiscal policy
The federal government's effort to keep the economy stable by increasing or decreasing taxes or government spending.

deficit
Occurs when a government spends over and above the amount it gathers in taxes for a specific period of time (namely, a fiscal year).

national debt (federal debt)
The accumulation of government surpluses and deficits over time.

Making Ethical Decisions

Tackling the Deficit

In the late 1990s the federal government was under strong pressure from the business community to reduce or wipe out the annual deficit in the annual budget. Business was convinced that these constant deficits and the resulting accumulated debt were dragging the Canadian economy down and making Canada uncompetitive with other major countries. To arrive at the surpluses that we have seen since, the federal government drastically cut its expenditures.

This resulted in significant reductions in funding to the provinces for health care, post-secondary education, and other important activities. Combined with other budget-cutting measures that have led to lower and fewer payments to the unemployed, the result has been an increase in poverty levels, especially among children and women.

These facts lead to some ethical questions. How could such severe budget cuts have been avoided? Does the business community bear some responsibility for the increase in poverty in Canada? In other words, was it ethical for business to allow our national debt to grow so large and not challenge the government's annual deficits much earlier? What do you think?

These reductions in spending contributed to Canada's slow recovery from the recession. Increased government borrowing and spending stimulates an economy, while cuts in spending have the opposite effect—they slow down the economy.

The drastic slashing of government spending in the 1990s was strongly opposed by left-wing political groups and many organizations such as churches, unions, welfare groups, food banks, and other community-centred groups because of the hardship these cuts inflicted on many people. Reduced employment insurance and welfare payments, a reduction in hospital funding, the closing of hospitals, and so on, affected many poor and sick people. Cuts to post-secondary education funding resulted in fewer instructors and more students per class, higher fees, increased costs for some services, and a reduction of other services. Food banks across Canada reported a jump in the number of people seeking food. When economic problems become severe, attempts to remedy them can be difficult and painful. Part of budget surpluses since that time were used to restore some of the funding cuts to health and education. The Making Ethical Decisions box highlights the results of the drastic cuts during this time.

Why is it important to control the debt? Financial security is critical to a country's investment in its people and businesses. A lower debt means that less money will need to go toward paying down the national debt and any outstanding interest. Reducing government spending on interest charges will allow the government to spend more money on social programs or to lower taxes. Lower taxes will stimulate the economy, as companies and individuals will have more disposable income.

With a lower debt, Canada could also be considered a more attractive country to invest in—a healthy and educated workforce is able to work and buy products. In addition, employers like well-funded social programs, as there is less risk that they will be asked to increase employee benefits. A lower debt load also means that in times of economic slowdown or when unexpected events occur (such as SARS) the government may have funds available to alleviate the ensuing pressures. Of course, if the debt is high, there is less money that can be dedicated to social programs and initiatives to assist businesses in becoming more competitive.

surplus
An excess of revenues over expenditures.

Reductions in the national debt have been the result of surpluses—a **surplus** is an excess of revenues over expenditures. As the debt comes down, the annual interest costs are also reduced. This reduction in the national debt has translated into a savings of billions of dollars each year on debt interest payments. In the mid-1990s, this number was as high as 37.6 cents of each revenue dollar.[14]

The Federal Budget

In late February of most years the federal finance minister releases a blueprint for how the government wants to set the country's annual economic agenda. This document, called the **federal budget**, is a comprehensive report that reveals government financial policies for the coming year. This political document shows how much revenue the government expects to collect, any changes in income and other taxes, and whether a deficit or a surplus is expected. The federal budget answers questions that affect businesses and Canadians, such as: How much money will go to pay down the debt? How much money will go to social programs such as health care? Will there be more money for research and development? and, Will taxes go up or down?

The budget is reviewed carefully by businesses, consumers, and other countries because the information it contains affects all of these stakeholders. It reflects revenues (from taxation) and expenditures (e.g., Canada Pension Plan payments) for the past year. In addition, the government will communicate program changes for the future, as well as forecasted growth projections. From this document, stakeholders can get an idea of what issues are important to the government.

Keep in mind that promises made by the federal government in a budget are not necessarily permanent. If a new political party is elected, it can reverse these decisions and announce its own initiatives. This is why the first budget after an election is critical. It clearly communicates to the population whether a new government will support its campaign promises. As well, it sends strong signals to businesses and international markets about the government's priorities.

Provincial governments also release their own budgets. A province's financial stability affects political decisions and, ultimately, the business environment within the province's boundaries.

federal budget
A comprehensive report that reveals government financial policies for the coming year.

The Reversal of a Trend: Federal Budget Deficits[16]

After over ten years of budget surpluses, Canada will experience a budget deficit in 2009–2010. Projected to be $50 billion, three factors that have contributed to the projected deficit include a falling world GDP, a continuing U.S. recession, and a drop in commodities prices. (You can see how an understanding of economics and global business is critical when reviewing the federal budget.) As a result of these economic conditions the federal government has been trying to stimulate the economy through initiatives such as increased spending (e.g., infrastructure) and lowering taxes. While the federal government has predicted that the budget will be balanced by 2013–2014, Toronto-Dominion Bank economists Derek Burleton and Don Drummond disagree. They predict that over the next five years, Ottawa will rack up $170 billion in new debt. Increased pressure will come from an aging population that will demand more health-care spending. The baby boom generation is the largest single group in Canada's population and its aging will drive up hospital bills and long-term care costs for taxpayers. "On average, somebody over the age of 65 costs double in terms of somebody under the 65," says Drummond. What are the implications for you, as a young adult, of this growing deficit? What social programs do you think may be cut in order to decrease expenditures?

Using Monetary Policy to Keep the Economy Growing

Have you ever wondered who lends the federal government money when it spends more than it collects in taxes? One source is the Bank of Canada, a Crown corporation. Its role is to "promote the economic and financial well-being of Canada." The day-to-day administration of monetary policy is the responsibility of the Bank of Canada, in co-operation and in consultation with the federal finance minister.

Monetary policy is the management of the money supply and interest rates. It is controlled by the Bank of Canada. When the economy is booming, the Bank of Canada tends to raise interest rates in an attempt to control inflation. This makes money more

monetary policy
The management of the money supply and interest rates.

expensive to borrow. Businesses thus borrow less, and the economy slows as business people spend less money on everything, including labour and machinery. The opposite is true when the Bank of Canada lowers interest rates. When this happens, businesses tend to borrow more, and the economy improves. Raising and lowering interest rates should therefore help control the business cycles.

The Bank of Canada also controls the money supply. A simple explanation of how this works is that the more money the Bank of Canada makes available to business people and others, the faster the economy grows. To slow the economy, the Bank of Canada lowers the money supply. If you are eager to learn more about the money supply, you can turn to Chapter 10 now. A recent example of the Canadian government stepping in to stimulate the economy is its reaction to the U.S. subprime crisis that impacted the global economy. Read about this in the next section.

In summary, the government makes two major efforts to control the economy: fiscal policy (taxes and spending) and monetary policy (control over interest rates and the money supply). The economic goal is to keep the economy growing so that more people can rise up the economic ladder and enjoy a satisfying quality of life.[17]

The Subprime Mortgage Crisis[18]

Subprime mortgages are loans targeted at people who couldn't qualify for regular mortgages because their credit records were not good enough or they did not have a credit history. Some mortgages were also interest-only loans and lower in cost as no principal was being paid down. Initially, these loans came with very low rates (thus, subprime). At the end of this term (e.g., two years), interest rates were much higher and people couldn't afford to make their payments. As housing prices started to fall, they often found they could not longer afford to sell the home either. The fallout has seen decreasing home sales and prices, and rising foreclosures. The resulting crisis contributed to approval of a US$700 billion bank bailout by the U.S. Congress in October 2008 to stabilize the financial sector and reinforce hundreds of financial institutions. The U.S. bailout was not sufficient for its intended purpose. In 2009, President Obama anticipated a new US$750 billion bank bailout. Bank bailouts soon followed in England, Germany, France, Italy, and Spain.

While Canadian financial institutions did not face the high default rates experienced in the United States, they were having trouble borrowing money because banks and other lenders in other countries were more cautious. This credit squeeze sent stock markets (read more about this in Chapter 11) crashing and there were worries of a global meltdown. The federal government announced in October 2008 that it would take over $25 billion worth of bank-held mortgages to ease the growing liquidity problems faced by the country's financial institutions. This would provide more money to financial institutions. To further stimulate the economy and encourage banks to continue lending money, the Bank of Canada continued to lower its lending rate, effectively hitting 0.25 percent, the lowest it can go using conventional monetary policy.

The government did not agree with critics who characterized this action as a bailout of an industry that generated record profits. "This is not a bailout; this is a market transaction that will cost the government nothing," said Prime Minister Harper. "We are not going in and buying bad assets. What we're doing is simply exchanging assets that we already hold the insurance on and the reason we're doing this is to get out in front. The issue here is not protecting the banks." He believes that the problem the country's financial institutions face is not solvency but the availability of credit. It is expected that this action will make loans and mortgages more available and more affordable for ordinary Canadians and businesses. One month later, another $50 billion allocation was announced. Do you agree that this is not a bailout? What would have been the implications for business people and consumers if more money had not been made available by financial institutions?

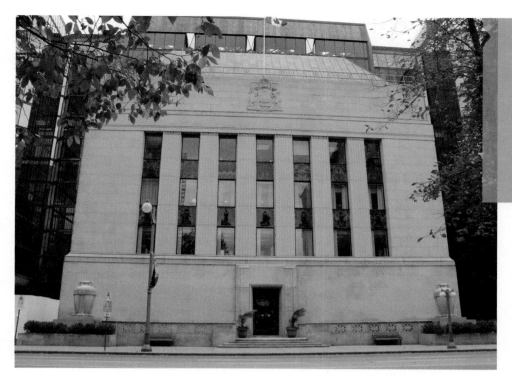

The Bank of Canada is Canada's central bank. It is not a commercial bank and it does not offer banking services to the public. Rather, it has the responsibilities for Canada's monetary policy, bank notes, financial system, funds management, and retail debt.

Progress Assessment

- How does the government manage the economy using fiscal policy?
- What is Canada's national debt? Has it been increasing or decreasing over the past six years?
- Explain the purpose of the federal budget.
- What does the term *monetary policy* mean? What organization is responsible for Canada's monetary policy?

GOVERNMENT EXPENDITURES

Governments in Canada help disburse tens of billions of dollars annually in old-age pensions, allowances to low-income families or individuals, employment insurance, welfare, workers' compensation, and various other payments to individuals. These transfers give Canadians more purchasing power and, therefore, the creation of a more viable market for businesses.

As people spend their money, large numbers of Canadian companies and their employees benefit as a result of this purchasing power. Increasing or lowering the rates or eligibility for these payments results in further fine-tuning of the economy. Again, government cutbacks have resulted in the reduction of such payments in recent years.

Governments also spend huge sums of money on education, health, roads, ports, waterways, airports, and various other services required by businesses and individuals. They also provide aid through direct and indirect government programs designed to help businesses. The Canadian Subsidy Directory lists more than 3,200 sources of financing and government programs for anyone searching for Canadian grants, loans, and government programs.[19] Governments also intervene on an ad hoc (special or unplanned) basis in important cases. Aid to Saskatchewan and Alberta farmers and Newfoundland and B.C. fishers when their industries faced severe hardships are examples.

A visit to Atlantic Canada Opportunities Agency (www.acoa.ca) will introduce you to projects that facilitate development in this region. See if you can find other Web sites for parallel agencies.

Financial Aid

All levels of government offer a variety of direct assistance programs to businesses, including grants, loans, loan guarantees, consulting advice, information, and other aids that are designed to achieve certain purposes. For example, the Northwest Territories government gave a $34-million loan to Discovery Air to refinance its existing debt. Said Finance Minister Michael Miltenberger, "We have to look at this, because this is a big outfit, has lots of northern content, hundreds and hundreds of jobs."[20] In another example, the Newfoundland government created a program worth up to $18 million to help crab workers affected by the late start to the fishery; the program focused on employment projects to help the approximately 8,500 workers.[21]

Some government aid is designed to help industries or companies that are deemed to be very important—at the cutting edge of technology, providing highly skilled jobs, and oriented toward exports. Bombardier, which makes the Learjet, plans to use $315 million in aid from the United Kingdom, $350 million from Canada, and further help from Quebec authorities, to create a new commercial jet to compete with the smaller offerings of Boeing and Airbus. The company said that plants in Belfast, Northern Ireland, Saint-Laurent and Mirabel in Quebec, and Kansas City, Missouri, will be involved in designing and constructing the new aircraft.[22]

Major companies often hint or announce outright that they are planning to close a plant that they claim is not efficient enough to be competitive. They often suggest that they will consolidate operations with other plants in Canada or the United States. These announcements naturally result in a flurry of efforts by all affected parties to prevent the closure. Unions, municipalities, and provincial and federal governments all work to save the jobs and economies of the area. Such examples are evident in a variety of businesses, including auto plants, pulp and paper mills, food processing plants, oil refineries, shipbuilding yards, meat-packing plants, and steel mills.

While in many cases the closures could not have been prevented, some have been saved by such concerted action. For example, in 2009 GM Canada received an auto bailout of $10.8 billion ($7.1 billion from the federal government and $3.5 billion from Ontario provincial government). What Canada gets is five GM plants in Ontario remaining

Ford Motor Company invested $1 billion to redevelop its Oakville, Ontario, plant as a state-of-the-art flexible manufacturing system. Project Centennial also received $200 million from the Ontario provincial government and from the Government of Canada. The Government of Canada's $100-million contribution is part of a larger commitment to the automotive industry that was supported with the creation of a $1-billion, five-year incentive fund for other automakers and manufacturers. What are the benefits of such government support?

open, while GM is shutting down many plants in the United States, and a guarantee that at least 16 percent of its North America assembly will be done in this country, including a new hybrid, as well as a promise of $2.2 billion in new investments over the next seven years. All this to save less than 5,000 jobs in the assembly plants. This works out to an investment of $1.4 million to save each job. However, in addition to saving these auto assembly jobs, auto parts suppliers can also continue to remain in Canada.[23]

Some of these rescue efforts end in costly failures. For example, in 2004 the P.E.I. government bought Polar Foods, as its bankruptcy put at risk tens of millions of dollars in government investments and brought into question where Island lobsters would be sold.[24] It was estimated that the government lost close to $27 million when it later sold the company. To assist the approximately 800 unemployed fish plant workers, the government set aside close to $1 million in an aid package. Was it worthwhile to spend such sums to provide hundreds of jobs in chronically depressed areas? Was it the best way to help the unemployed in areas of high unemployment? How do you decide what businesses or industries to help and which ones to ignore? These questions are constantly being asked in Canada.

Equalization of Transfer Payments[25]

Canada is a very large country with uneven resources, climate, and geography, which has led to uneven economic development. Ontario and Quebec, with large populations, proximity to the United States, an abundance of all kinds of natural resources, and excellent rail and water transport, were the earliest to develop industrially.

Nova Scotia and New Brunswick began to suffer when wooden ships gave way to metal ships in the last half of the nineteenth century and their lumber industries declined. The west was sparsely populated until well into the twentieth century. Alberta and British Columbia became strong industrially only in the last 30 years as oil, gas, coal, hydroelectric power, and forestry became significant competitive resources for them. Saskatchewan and Manitoba are essentially tied to the volatile agricultural industry. Newfoundland, which became part of Canada in 1949 and was far below the average Canadian living standard, has relied mainly on fisheries and pulp and paper. With the collapse of the cod fishery, Newfoundland and Labrador now looks to Hibernia and other offshore oil fields to become major factors in its economic growth in the twenty-first century. Nova Scotia is counting on the development of the huge gas fields off Sable Island. The three territories—Yukon, the Northwest Territories, and Nunavut—are very lightly populated and have difficult climates. The Northwest Territories is rich in diamonds and gas exploration.

Transfer payments are direct payments from governments to other governments or to individuals. Federal transfer payments to individuals include elderly benefits and employment insurance. Such payments provide social security and income support. **Equalization** is a federal government program for reducing fiscal disparities among provinces. These payments enable less prosperous provincial governments to provide their residents with public services that are roughly comparable to those in other provinces, at roughly comparable levels of taxation. While provinces are free to spend the funds on public services according to their own priorities, these payments are intended to fund medicare, post-secondary education, and smaller programs.

In 2009–2010, Ottawa distributed $14.2 billion in equalization payments to six provinces (P.E.I., Nova Scotia, New Brunswick, Quebec, Ontario, and Manitoba). Introduced in 1957, this system of payments (transfers) to poorer provinces is financed by wealthier ones, such as Alberta. While traditionally Ontario has been considered a "have" province, it received equalization payments for the first time due to a downturn in the manufacturing sector. This was also the first time Newfoundland and Labrador did not receive payments. According to Premier Williams, this can be attributed to Newfoundland and Labrador "operating on its own resources and its own monies because of oil revenues, corporate income taxes, commodity prices, and retail sales."

transfer payments
Direct payments from governments to other governments or to individuals.

equalization
A federal government program for reducing fiscal disparities among provinces.

The Taking It to the Net exercise near the end of this chapter will encourage you to become more familiar with the details of this program. Note that the Territorial Formula Financing program provides territorial governments with funding to support public services, in recognition of the higher cost of living in the north.

Progress Assessment

- Explain how governments in Canada spend tax dollars to help Canadians.
- Give two examples of how government has provided financial aid to businesses.
- What two groups benefit from equalization transfer payments?

PURCHASING POLICIES

Most governments are very large purchasers and consumers of goods and services; indeed, in Canada they are the largest buyers. The federal and provincial governments use this enormous purchasing power to favour Canadian companies. The provinces favour these companies in their own territories and have even set up trade barriers between provinces (as discussed earlier). When advanced technology items—civilian or military—must be obtained from foreign companies, our governments usually insist that a certain minimum portion be manufactured in Canada. This enables Canadian companies to acquire advanced technology know-how and to provide employment.

Contracts are awarded most often to help Canadian businesses even if they are sometimes more expensive than bids by non-Canadian companies. This is particularly true in the military acquisitions programs. Whatever can be produced or serviced in Canada—ships, electronics, trucks, artillery, ammunition—is acquired from Canadian companies. These federal and provincial policies are being modified as a result of the general movement to freer trade due to NAFTA. See the Spotlight on Small Business box for an example of a company that benefits from a government contract.

SPOTLIGHT ON Small Business

Ink Isle

Located in Charlottetown, Prince Edward Island (P.E.I.), Ink Isle is the only business of its kind in the province that remanufactures inkjet cartridges and resells other generic inkjet and toner cartridges. This is an environmentally-friendly alternative to throwing out unused inkjet and toner cartridges.

A proud Mi'kmaq member of the Abegweit First Nation, entrepreneur Jacob Jadis discovered his business idea during several exciting travel opportunities for Aboriginal youth across Canada, Australia, and the United States. During these trips he noticed several seemingly successful ink refilling kiosks located mostly in malls. This was a type of business that had not yet reached P.E.I., and with further research it became evident that he could create a better business by remanufacturing, instead of just refilling, ink cartridges. Jadis spent a year on business planning activities including researching the industry, writing a business plan, seeking start-up funding, receiving specialized

training in Colorado, searching for a storefront location and finally purchasing the equipment and products he needed to start Ink Isle. Not only is he fulfilling one of his lifetime goals of being an entrepreneur, but he is also enjoying it because the future is in his hands.

Since he started his business in 2005, Jadis has been receiving orders for toners from a large federal government agency on the Island. As you can infer, the different levels of government not only provide funding for small businesses, but they are also a good source of potential revenue generation. Jadis has also been recognized as the 2007 Prince Edward Island Best Business Award Winner, Winner of the 2006 Aboriginal Entrepreneur of the Year Award for Prince Edward Island, and second place for Atlantic Canada Youth Aboriginal Entrepreneur of the Year.

Source: © Thomas I. White.

SERVICES

The federal government has departments that provide services to businesses and consumers. We will look at two of these important departments: Industry Canada and Foreign Affairs and International Trade Canada. There are corresponding departments in many of the provinces, especially the four largest and most developed ones (British Columbia, Alberta, Ontario, and Quebec).

Industry Canada

For many years, the federal government has implemented a variety of programs to help small businesses get started. These programs are part of a larger one that involves setting up Canada Business service centres in every province and territory. These centres are operated jointly with provincial governments and certain local organizations. Industry Canada publishes brochures, booklets, and guides informing business people of the help available and how and where to get it. Industry Canada also participates in the production of publications to promote Canadian businesses internationally.

Other programs are designed to encourage businesses to establish themselves or expand in economically depressed areas of the country. These are populated regions that are industrially underdeveloped, have high unemployment, and have lower standards of living. The programs include help for the tourism industry and for Aboriginal residents of remote areas who want to establish businesses.

The National Research Council

The National Research Council (NRC) is a federal agency that began in 1916. It reports to Parliament through Industry Canada. The NRC plays a significant role in research that helps Canadian industry remain competitive and innovative. It has been mandated to provide substantial resources to help Canada become one of the world's top five R&D performers by 2010.[26]

This organization of some 4,000 scientists, researchers, and technicians represents Canada's principal science and technology agency. NRC also benefits from the efforts of guest workers, drawn from Canadian and foreign universities, companies, and public- and private-sector organizations. Located in every province, areas of research and industry support are aerospace, biotechnology, engineering and construction, fundamental sciences, information and communications technologies, and manufacturing.

NRC researchers are using thermographic cameras to design tools for physicians to rapidly identify tissue damage. Thermographic video cameras record infrared radiation, or heat, rather than visible light. This heat-imaging camera is thus able to identify differences in blood flow. Warmer areas have greater blood flow, and areas of tissue damage will register abnormally low levels of flow and thus heat. Here, a healthy subject's nose has less blood flow and is cooler (bluer) than her cheeks and the sides of her neck, which are warmer (redder).

Foreign Affairs and International Trade Canada

Because exports are particularly important to Canada's economic well-being, the government has a very large and elaborate system to assist companies in their exporting and foreign-investment activities. The federal government and most provincial and all large municipal governments have various ministries, departments, and agencies that provide a variety of such services. These include information, marketing, financial aid, insurance and guarantees, publications, and contracts. All major trading countries provide similar support to their exporters.

FIGURE **3.5**

FIGURE **3.5**

Some Government Sources Available to Assist Canadian Businesses

Government Source	Mission	Web Site
Business Development Bank of Canada (BDC)	BDC provides small- and medium-sized businesses with flexible financing, affordable consulting services, and venture capital. BDC has a particular focus on the emerging and exporting sectors of the economy.	www.bdc.ca
Export Development Canada (EDC)	EDC provides Canadian exporters with financing, insurance, and bonding services as well as foreign market expertise.	www.edc.ca
Industry Canada	The Department's mission is to foster a growing, competitive, knowledge-based Canadian economy. Program areas include developing industry and technology capability, fostering scientific research, and promoting investment and trade.	www.ic.gc.ca/ic_wp-pa.htm
National Research Council Canada (NRC)	NRC helps turn ideas and knowledge into new processes and products. Businesses work with partners from industry, government, and universities.	www.nrc-cnrc.gc.ca
Canada Business	Canada Business is a government information service for businesses and start-up entrepreneurs in Canada. It serves as a single point of access for federal and provincial/territorial government services, programs, and regulatory requirements for business.	www.canadabusiness.ca

See Figure 3.5 for a list of government sources that are available to assist Canadian businesses. All of them also provide some support for those that wish to succeed in global markets. We have discussed some of these organizations already in this textbook.

Progress Assessment

- Why do federal and provincial governments tend to favour Canadian companies when contracts are approved?
- How does the NRC contribute to technology advancement in Canada?
- List four organizations that aim to help exporters.

ROLE OF THE CANADIAN GOVERNMENT— SOME FINAL THOUGHTS

What should be clear is that government always has a critical role to play. Some people believe that the best way to protect the Canadian economy is for the federal government to reverse its current direction of privatization. Instead of withdrawing from active direction and participation in the economy, it should develop a long-term industrial policy of leadership and an active role in shaping the future of the economy. An **industrial policy** is a comprehensive, coordinated government plan to guide and revitalize the economy. An industrial policy requires close consultation with business and labour to develop a comprehensive program for long-term sustainable industrial development.

Others are opposed in principle to such government involvement. As mentioned earlier in this chapter, the 1980s witnessed the start of a movement toward deregulation, privatization, and less government involvement within Canada and other countries. Some believe that these were the right steps for the government to take, and that it should continue with these activities. One organization that supports less government involvement is the Fraser Institute. You will be asked to investigate some of its opinions

industrial policy
A comprehensive, coordinated government plan to guide and revitalize the economy.

in the Developing Workplace Skills section of this chapter. Interestingly enough, when events such as SARS or a recession appear, some groups that normally lobby for less government involvement in their industries suddenly believe that government should step in and provide financial assistance. While this is contrary to free-market principles, troubled times are usually followed by calls for more government involvement.

The Constitution Act outlines the powers of all levels of government. Each level of government is focused on creating a competitive environment for businesses of all sizes. As we move forward, the federal government will continue to focus on international trade initiatives to provide opportunities for Canadian businesses. This chapter has highlighted some of the resources that are available to businesses to assist them in their operations.

It is natural for disputes to arise as industries and countries attempt to act in their best interests. These disputes arise even between established trading partners such as Canada and the United States, as evidenced by the long-running lumber dispute. However, in most instances, trade agreements create opportunities. Did you know, for example, that 95 percent of Canada–U.S. trade due to NAFTA is problem-free?[27] While disputes will not be resolved overnight, they are being addressed in a global arena, and this is at least a step in the right direction. Since Canada is a large exporter of goods and services, it must also be aware how its policies on the environment may impact future trade. Read the Green Box for more information.

Green BOX

The Environment and the Economy

Governments have many policy options available to reduce greenhouse gas emissions. Some are more politically acceptable and easier to implement than others, and not all approaches are likely to be equally effective. Experience in addressing other environmental issues has shown that using a mix of policy measures is more likely to succeed and to spread the responsibility around fairly. It has been a challenge for governments in Canada to come up with effective policy options to address climate change, partly because all three levels of government (federal, provincial, and municipal) have a stake in this issue as well as responsibilities and opportunities. Not all policy options are suitable for all levels of government, so co-operation and collaboration will be important to make sure that effective measures are put in place without overlap and duplication.

The National Round Table on the Environment and the Economy has recommended that Canada immediately put in place a hard cap regime on emissions by 2015, with auctioning of carbon permits to businesses by 2020. To do otherwise would face dire environmental and economic consequences. Round table chairman Bob Page says the United States is moving quickly on capping emissions and will penalize Canadian exports if Canada does not follow suit. "It is the most serious protectionist challenge we've had to face. Now we're going to see in place of the softwood lumber issue, we're going to see the issue that cuts right across manufacturing in Ontario and Quebec, and natural resource products like the oil sands in Alberta and Saskatchewan ... those products will be subject to a carbon intensity surcharge at the American border" unless Canada meets new American standards." Alberta won't like it, but will likely agree, since the oil sands producers are likely concerned about being shut out of the United States and possibly world markets, said Page, a professor of sustainable development at the University of Calgary.

The Report says it is imperative that Canada move from the patchwork approach adopted by different provinces and for Ottawa to have a unified policy with identical standards across jurisdictions and industries. And it says it is critical that Canadian policy be compatible with that of its largest trading partners, particularly the United States. The cap-and-trade system is designed to put a price on pollution, but instead of taxing energy use by individuals directly, the cost is borne first by large emitters, who are expected to pass it on to consumers. Emissions permits can be traded on an open market between firms that need extra quota and those who have quota to sell.

While this system will involve a major transformation on the cost, the usage, and even the nature of energy in Canada, it is expected that the Canadian economy will continue to grow through the transformation period and that new industries will be created.

Sources: "Control Greenhouse Emissions or Face Trade Sanctions, Panel Tells Governments," The Canadian Press, 16 April 2009, www.cbc.ca/news/story/2009/04/16/tech-090416-cap-and-trade-greenhouse-gas.html; and "Government Policy Options," The Pembina Foundation, 2009, www.greenlearning.ca/climate/policy/canadian-policy-directions/2.

SUMMARY

LO ▶ 1 Understand the six categories of government activities that can affect business.

1. There are six categories of government involvement in Canada.

What are the government activities that affect business?

The six categories of government activities are Crown corporations, laws and regulations, taxation and financial policies, government expenditures, purchasing policies, and services. See Figure 3.1 for a brief description of each activity.

What is the relationship between Canada's economic system and government involvement?

As noted in Chapter 2, Canada has a mixed economy, which is an economic system in which some allocation of resources is made by the market and some by the government. As a result of the Constitution Act, the different levels of government (federal, provincial, and municipal) have responsibilities and jurisdiction over certain matters of the economy and population.

LO ▶ 2 Trace the historical role of government in the Canadian economy and understand why Crown corporations were created.

2. The Canadian government played a key role from the beginning of the country in 1867 in protecting young manufacturing industries and getting the railroad built to the west coast, helping to bind the country together.

Why did the government have to do what it did?

It had the legal power and responsibility to do so, as a result of the Constitution Act. The United States threatened to overwhelm our industry, which was not strong enough by itself to resist or to build the railway.

Why were Crown corporations necessary?

Companies were not willing or able to assume certain responsibilities or fill some needs in the marketplace. The CNR, Air Canada, Hydro-Québec, and Atomic Energy of Canada Ltd. are some important examples. (The CNR and Air Canada are no longer Crown corporations.)

What is the recent trend with Crown corporations?

In recent years, we have seen an increasing trend where governments (both federal and provincial) have been selling Crown corporations. This is called privatization. Some examples include the sale of remaining Petro-Canada shares and the sale of BC Rail Ltd.

LO ▶ 3 Discuss why understanding laws and regulations at all levels of government is critical to business success.

3. Businesses need to understand the laws and regulations that affect them. The Constitution Act defines the powers that can be exercised by the federal government and provincial governments. In the event of a conflict, federal powers prevail.

What are some federal government responsibilities?

The federal government's responsibilities include trade regulations, the incorporation of federal companies, national defence, immigration, and the fisheries.

What are some provincial government responsibilities?

Among other areas, provincial governments oversee natural resources within their boundaries, the administration of justice, municipal affairs, and education.

What are some municipal government responsibilities?

Municipal governments—cities, towns, villages, counties, districts, metropolitan regions—are set up by the provincial legislatures. Municipalities provide services such as water supply, sewage and garbage disposal, roads, sidewalks, street lighting, building codes, parks, playgrounds, libraries, and so forth. They play a role in consumer protection (e.g., inspectors examine restaurants) and the establishment of zoning requirements.

4. Each level of government collects taxes from companies. These taxes allow governments to discharge their legal obligations and to fund social programs.

What is fiscal policy?

Fiscal policy refers to the federal government's effort to keep the economy stable by increasing or decreasing taxes or government spending.

What is the national debt?

The national debt is the accumulation of past government surpluses and deficits. Since the late 1990s, the national debt has been decreasing. In 2008, it was approximately $458 billion.

How is monetary policy different from fiscal policy?

Controlled by the Bank of Canada, monetary policy is the management of the money supply and interest rates. When the economy is booming, the Bank of Canada tends to raise interest rates in an attempt to control inflation. Since money is more expensive to borrow, businesses borrow less, and the economy slows as business people spend less money on everything.

> **LO ▶ 4** Explain how taxation and financial policies affect the Canadian economy.

5. Government expenditures benefit consumers and businesses alike.

How do governments assist consumers with their tax dollars?

Governments disburse tens of millions of dollars annually in social program spending (e.g., old-age pensions, employment insurance, allowances to low-income families, etc.). These transfers give consumers more purchasing power.

How do businesses benefit from government expenditures?

All levels of government provide direct and indirect aid packages as incentives to achieve certain goals. These packages can consist of tax reduction, tariffs and quotas on imports, grants, loans, and loan guarantees.

> **LO ▶ 5** Describe how government expenditures benefit consumers and businesses alike.

6. Purchasing policies and services assist Canadian businesses.

Why is preferential treatment given to Canadian companies when they bid for a government contract?

Contracts are awarded most often to help Canadian businesses. This way, Canadians are employing and contributing to a strong economy.

What are two government departments that are particularly focused on assisting Canadian businesses?

Industry Canada and the Department of Foreign Affairs and International Trade assist businesses domestically and internationally.

> **LO ▶ 6** Illustrate how purchasing policies and services assist Canadian businesses

KEY TERMS

Crown corporation 57	industrial policy 76	National Policy 57
deficit 67	marketing boards 61	privatization 58
equalization 73	monetary policy 69	surplus 68
federal budget 69	national debt (federal debt) 67	transfer payments 73
fiscal policy 67		

CRITICAL THINKING

1. The issue of how much government should be involved in the economy has been the subject of much debate

in Canada. In the United States, ideology has played a major role in influencing Americans to believe that, in principle, government should "butt out." This thinking ignores the significant role that the U.S. government has played and continues to play in the country's economy. In Canada, we are less negative and perhaps more pragmatic: If it works, let's do it. But where do we go from here? Do we need less or more government involvement? Is it a question of the quality of that involvement? Could it be smarter rather than just less? How can the cost of government involvement decrease?

2. What are the implications of a minority federal government to the Canadian political scene? Explain. (A minority government exists when no one party has a majority of seats in a legislative assembly. To pass legislation and other measures, that government would need the support of at least some members of other parties in the assembly.[28])

3. If you represented the federal government, how would you respond to industries that have been seeking government action (e.g., bailout money or changes to policies) but to no avail? (For example, take the position of the forestry industry in Canada which in the past six years has lost about 130,000 jobs in Canada.[29]) Keep in mind that the other industries (e.g., auto) have received such support (i.e., bailout money).

DEVELOPING WORKPLACE SKILLS

1. Scan your local newspapers, the *Globe and Mail*, the *National Post*, or a Canadian magazine such as *Canadian Business* for references to government programs that help Canadian businesses or have assisted a specific company. Bring these articles to class and discuss.

2. Many U.S. states and foreign governments have developed strong marketing campaigns to attract Canadian businesses. They also offer many incentives (including financial ones) to lure businesses to move there. Should anything be done about this? Most provincial governments have similar programs to attract foreign companies to their jurisdictions. Check out your provincial government's Web site to see what it is doing in this regard. Bring your information to class to discuss this kind of government expenditure.

3. The Fraser Institute is a Canadian think tank that believes in a competitive marketplace, lower taxes, and less regulation. It supports a limited role for government in the marketplace. In a group of four, review some of its research. Some possibilities are economic freedom, government spending, privatization, and trade. Present your findings to the class. (Hint: You can find information at www.fraserinstitute.ca.)

4. Although unemployment remains high, especially among young people, business people complain that they cannot find trained employees to fill existing vacancies. Job candidates lack math and science backgrounds and their written English-language skills are weak. (In Quebec, there are similar complaints, but the language problems are with French.) Further, too many candidates are high school dropouts. What can be done about this serious problem? Should business or government be working on it? What exactly should they be doing? Discuss this in a group of three.

TAKING IT TO THE NET 1

www.mcgrawhillconnect.ca

Purpose
To become familiar with the financial budget and Canada's fiscal balance.

Exercise
Visit the Department of Finance Canada's Web site at www.fin.gc.ca. Click on Budget Info and answer the following questions.

1. What was the largest component of budgetary expenditures for last year's budget, as communicated in the most recent budget? How was this different from the previous year's budget?

2. What was the largest component of budgetary revenues for last year's budget, as communicated in the most recent budget? How was this different from the previous year's budget?

3. Common revenue sources for provincial (and federal) governments include personal income taxes, corporate income taxes, sales taxes (except in Alberta), and payroll taxes. List other provincial revenue sources.

4. Did Canada experience a deficit or a surplus last year?

TAKING IT TO THE NET 2

www.mcgrawhillconnect.ca

While still on the Department of Finance Canada's site, click on Transfer Payments to Provinces. Answer the following questions.

1. What is the estimated equalization entitlement for next year?

2. How are equalization payments calculated?

3. What provinces are scheduled to receive equalization payments?

ANALYZING MANAGEMENT DECISIONS

Gambling: A Cash Cow for Provincial Governments

Starting slowly in Quebec in the late 1960s, but catching on quickly across the country, lotteries, casinos, bingo, video-lottery terminals (VLTs), and other forms of gambling had become, by the end of the twentieth century, a major source of revenue for many provincial governments.

You can get some idea of how large the gambling business has become by looking at the revenues and profits for the Ontario and Quebec governments. For the year ended 31 March 2008, the Ontario Lottery and Gaming Corporation generated $3.7 billion in economic activity. Total revenue at Loto-Québec was a little over $3.8 billion. Over the years, both organizations have generated billions of dollars for their respective governments. Both operations also allot millions of dollars to help gamblers whose obsession with gambling has proven destructive to themselves or their families.

Sources: "2008 Annual Report," Loto-Québec, 2008, www.loto-quebec.com, http://www.loto-quebec.com/corporatif/pdf/2008_annual_report.pdf#page=1; and "OLG Gives Back," Ontario Lottery and Gaming Corporation, 2008, http://www.olg.ca/about/economic_benefits/index.jsp.

Discussion Questions

1. Some people and organizations argue that governments should not be in the gambling business, that encouraging gambling is a bad idea. Others argue that private enterprise should run that kind of business, and argue further that companies would generate more profit for governments. Governments reply that they want to prevent organized crime from controlling gambling, so they must own and run such operations. What do you think? Is it okay for governments to be in the gambling business?

2. Governments seem to believe that gambling is a great way to raise money because Canadians don't seem to mind creating revenue by having some fun, and a chance at big winnings, instead of just paying higher taxes. Besides, they argue, nobody is forced to gamble, so it's a kind of voluntary tax. How do you feel about that? Do you buy that argument? Explain.

3. Some churches and other institutions concerned with personal and family welfare point to the rising number of family and personal breakdowns caused by people becoming gambling addicts. Also, easy access to VLTs is very bad for young persons. Do you agree with either of these concerns? Why? What can be done to improve the situation?

4. Suppose that you agree with those who are totally opposed to governments encouraging gambling. Wouldn't taxes have to be raised to replace these revenues? Would you mind paying more taxes? Do you think your parents or family members would mind? Do you have any other suggestions?

CHAPTER 4

Ethics and Social Responsibility

LEARNING OBJECTIVES

AFTER YOU HAVE READ AND STUDIED THIS CHAPTER, YOU SHOULD BE ABLE TO:

LO ▶ 1 Explain why legality is only one step in behaving ethically.

LO ▶ 2 Describe management's role in setting ethical standards and distinguish between compliance-based and integrity-based ethics codes.

LO ▶ 3 List the six steps that can be considered when setting up a corporate ethics code.

LO ▶ 4 Define corporate social responsibility and examine corporate responsibility to various stakeholders.

LO ▶ 5 Discuss the responsibility that business has to customers, investors, employees, society, and the environment.

PROFILE

Getting to Know Mary Dawson, Canada's Conflict of Interest and Ethics Commissioner

In 2006, the Federal Accountability Act was implemented to help strengthen accountability and increase transparency and oversight in government operations. The Federal Accountability Act created the Conflict of Interest Act. As Canada's Conflict of Interest and Ethics Commissioner, Mary Dawson is responsible for administering the Conflict of Interest Act ("Act") and helping public office holders avoid conflicts of interest. The Act sets out clear conflict of interest and post-employment rules applicable to public office holders. Public office holders are ministers, parliamentary secretaries, full- and part-time ministerial staff and advisors, and Governor in Council and ministerial appointees (deputy ministers, heads of agencies and Crown corporations, members of federal boards and tribunals).

The main responsibilities of the Office in administering the Act are to advise public office holders on their obligations under the Act; to receive confidential reports of assets, liabilities, and activities of certain public office holders; to maintain confidential files of required disclosures; to maintain a public registry for publicly declarable information; and to conduct examinations into alleged contraventions of the Act. In her role, Dawson is also responsible for administering the Conflict of Interest Code for Members of the House of Commons.

Dawson holds a Bachelor of Arts (Philosophy) and a Bachelor of Civil Law from McGill University, a Bachelor of Laws from Dalhousie University and a post-graduate degree in Public Law from the University of Ottawa. She began her career in the public service in 1967 as a researcher with the Department of National Revenue. Joining the Department of Justice in 1968, she subsequently held positions of increasing scope and responsibility.

To highlight some of her roles, Dawson held the position of Associate Chief Legislative Counsel from 1980 to 1986 and was the Assistant Deputy Minister of the Public Law Sector of Justice from 1986 to 1995. She was personally involved in the drafting of numerous pieces of legislation, including key statutes such as the Constitution Act, 1982, as well as the Meech Lake Accord and the Charlottetown Accord. In 1987 she was appointed as Chairperson of the Statute Revision Commission, a legislative body responsible for revising and consolidating the public general statutes of Canada. In 1995, Dawson became Associate Deputy Minister with responsibility for the Constitutional Affairs and Canadian Unity Section and, as such, supported the Minister of Justice, the Minister of Intergovernmental Affairs and the Prime Minister, through the Clerk of the Privy Council, on all constitutional matters. Since her retirement from the Department of Justice, Dawson has acted as a consultant on a variety of projects, both in the public and the private sectors. She often speaks to university classes and other groups and participates from time to time on panels. In 2007, she was named a member of the Order of Canada.

This chapter introduces you to the importance of ethical behaviour. With the media saturated by stories of high-

profile business and government failures, why do we open this chapter on ethics with a profile of Mary Dawson and the Office of the Conflict of Interest and Ethics Commissioner? Because by attempting to improve oversight in government operations, the Office plays a key role in promoting good governance and accountability, the key to which is a high standard of ethical behaviour. The need for improved governance and better accountability to stakeholders has recently assumed increasing prominence in the private sector as well.

In this chapter, we explore the responsibility of businesses to all of their stakeholders: customers, investors, employees, and society. We also look at the responsibilities of individuals. After all, responsible business behaviour depends on the responsible behaviour of each individual in the organization.

Sources: "About the Office," Office of the Conflict of Interest and Ethics Commissioner, 31 July 2008, http://ciec-ccie.gc.ca/Default.aspx?pid=8&lang=en; "About the Commissioner," Office of the Conflict of Interest and Ethics Commissioner, 24 July 2008, http://ciec-ccie.gc.ca/Default.aspx?pid=3&lang=en; and "Prime Minister Welcomes New Conflict of Interest and Ethics Commissioner," Office of the Prime Minister, 9 July 2007, http://www.pm.gc.ca/eng/media.asp?category=1&id=1740.

ETHICS IS MORE THAN LEGALITY

It is not uncommon to hear of instances where business people are involved in unethical behaviour. Some examples of Canadian companies that have been caught in such scandals include Livent, CIBC World Markets, Nortel, and WestJet. After two years of denying accusations, WestJet Airlines Ltd. admitted to spying on Air Canada. In a news release, WestJet apologized for accessing a confidential Air Canada Web site designated for reservations: "This practice was undertaken with the knowledge and direction of the highest management levels of WestJet and was not halted until discovered by Air Canada. This conduct was both unethical and unacceptable and WestJet accepts full responsibility for such misconduct."[1] As part of the settlement, WestJet paid Air Canada's investigation and litigation costs of $5.5 million and it made a $10 million donation in the name of both airlines to children's charities across Canada.[2] The Canadian business environment has also been impacted by notable scandals in other countries such as Enron, Arthur Andersen, Tyco, and Parmalat, just to name a few.

It is not just for-profit business people that exhibit unethical behaviour. In the mid-2000s, Canadians were shocked to learn of the Auditor General's findings related to the advertising and sponsorship program run by the federal Public Works Department. It was disclosed that "senior government officials running the federal government's advertising and sponsorship contracts in Quebec, as well as five Crown corporations—the Royal Canadian Mounted Police (RCMP), Via Rail, Canada Post, the Business Development Bank of Canada, and the Old Port of Montreal—wasted money and showed disregard for rules, mishandling millions of dollars since 1995."[3] In 2007, the Atlantic Lottery Corporation announced it was turning over its files to police over concerns of retailers stealing winning tickets from customers.[4] This was soon followed by the British Columbia government's audit announcement of the province's lottery system following the Ombudsman report that found the lottery system was open to fraud.[5] In Figure 4.1, you will see a brief summary of some of the most-publicized corporate scandals in recent years.

Given the ethical lapses that are so prevalent today, what can be done to restore trust in the free-market system and leaders in general? First, those who have broken the law need to be punished accordingly. Arresting business leaders and sending them to jail may seem harsh, but it is a first step toward showing the public that it is time to get serious about legal and ethical behaviour in business. No one should be above the law: not religious people, not government people, and not business people. New laws making accounting records more transparent (easy to read and understand) and more laws making business people and others more accountable may help. But laws don't make people honest, reliable, or truthful. If laws alone were a big deterrent, there would be much less crime than exists today.

The danger in writing new laws to correct behaviour is that people may begin to think that any behaviour that is within the law is also acceptable. The measure of behaviour, then, becomes: "Is it legal?" A society gets in trouble when it considers ethics and legality to be the same. Ethics and legality are two very different things. Although following the law is an important first step, ethical behaviour requires more than that. Ethics reflects people's proper relations with one another: How should people treat others? What responsibility should they feel for others? Legality is more narrow. It refers to laws we have written to protect ourselves from fraud, theft, and violence. Many immoral and unethical acts fall well within our laws.[6]

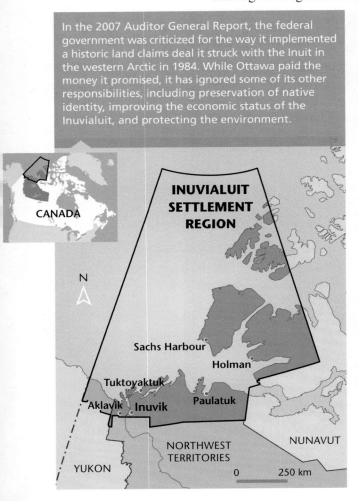

In the 2007 Auditor General Report, the federal government was criticized for the way it implemented a historic land claims deal it struck with the Inuit in the western Arctic in 1984. While Ottawa paid the money it promised, it has ignored some of its other responsibilities, including preservation of native identity, improving the economic status of the Inuvialuit, and protecting the environment.

CANADA

N

INUVIALUIT SETTLEMENT REGION

Sachs Harbour

Holman

Tuktoyaktuk

Aklavik   Inuvik   Paulatuk

NUNAVUT

NORTHWEST TERRITORIES

YUKON   0   250 km

Lottery Corporations: In March 2007, Ontario Ombudsman Andre Marin's Report blasted the Ontario Lottery and Gaming Corporation for not cracking down on retailers who collected tens of millions of dollars in jackpots between 1999 and 2006, some of them fraudulently. Police began probing allegations of fraudulent lottery prize claims by retailers after Marin accused the Corporation of "coddling" ticket sellers and playing "games" with customers who complained they had been cheated of their jackpots. In May 2007, the Atlantic Lottery Corporation announced it was turning over its files to police over similar concerns of retailers stealing winning tickets from customers. Also in May, the British Columbia government announced an audit of the province's lottery system following a negative report by the ombudsman that found it was open to fraud.

Research In Motion (RIM) Stock Option Scandal: An Ontario court approved a settlement between the company and the Ironworkers of Ontario Pension Fund over allegations RIM had backdated stock options to company executives. Under terms of the settlement, RIM's co-founders Jim Balsillie and Mike Lazaridis agreed to pay $2.5 million each (in addition to the $5 million the executives had each agreed to repay earlier). The company has also ceased giving stock options to directors, added more independent directors to the board and tightened up its executive compensation practices. Both the Ontario Securities Commission and the U.S. Securities and Exchange Commission announced they are looking at allegations of stock options backdating at the company.

Federal Government Sponsorship Scandal: The Auditor General's 2004 Report found that $100 million was paid to a variety of communications agencies in the form of fees and commissions, and said that the program was basically designed to generate commissions for these companies rather than to produce any benefit for Canadians. Implicated in this scandal were high-level officials. Charles Guité, a former senior bureaucrat, was sentenced to 42 months in prison for defrauding the federal government. Other scandal participants who received prison sentences, and whose advertising agencies benefited from these funds, include Jean Brault (30 months) and Paul Coffin (18 months). Gilles-André Gosselin, who headed Gosselin Communications, was charged in 2008 with nineteen criminal charges, including fraud.

Hollinger International Inc.: Conrad Black, who once headed the Hollinger International Inc. media empire, was convicted of obstruction of justice in 2007. In addition to three other former Hollinger executives, he was also found guilty of fraud for funneling US$6.1 million from the media company. Black was sentenced to 6½ years in federal prison and ordered to pay a small six-figure fine plus restitution of $6.1 million. Throughout the trial, Black has maintained his innocence. Before he was sentenced, he voiced his "deep regret" for the $1.2 billion in shareholder value lost to the company by the inept management of his successors. Three former Hollinger executives also received sentences: Jack Boultbee (27 months), Peter Atkinson (24 months), and Mark Kipnis (placed on probation with six months of house arrest). David Radler, one-time CEO of Hollinger International, pleaded guilty to mail fraud. He received a 29-month sentence and agreed to pay a US$250,000 fine.

Sources: Mark Steyn, "Conrad Black Trial," *Maclean's*, 24 December 2008, http://forums.macleans.ca/advansis/?mod=for&act=dis&eid=52&so=1&sb=1&ps=5; "Former Sponsorship Ad Exec Facing Criminal Charges," CBC News, 17 December 2008, http://www.cbc.ca/canada/story/2008/12/17/gosselin-charges.html; "Chicago Judges Reject Request to Reconsider Conrad Black's Appeal," CBC News, 21 August 2008, http://www.cbc.ca/money/story/2008/08/21/black.html; "Police Probe in Lottery Scandal not Over Yet," CBC News, 20 December 2007, http://www.cbc.ca/canada/toronto/story/2007/12/20/lottery-investigation.html; "Forgive and (Maybe) Forget," Canadian Business Online, 6 November 2007, http://www.canadianbusiness.com/columnists/john_gray/article.jsp?content=20071106_153800_5340; "Lotto 6/49 Bonus Rounds Coincided with Lottery Scandals," CBC News, 30 May 2007, http://www.cbc.ca/canada/toronto/story/2007/05/30/lotto649-bonus-rounds.html; "U.S. Judge Decides not to Revoke Black's Bond," CTV.ca, 26 June 2006, http://www.ctv.ca/servlet/ArticleNews/story/CTVNews/20060626/black_bond_060626/20060626/; Ross Marowits, "Guite Sentenced to 3 1/2 Years in Prison," Canoe Inc., 19 June 2006, http://CNRews.canoe.ca/CNREWS/Law/2006/03/29/1511103-cp.html; and "Federal Sponsorship Scandal," CBC News Online, 19 June 2006, http://www.cbc.ca/news/background/groupaction/.

FIGURE **4.1**

Brief Summary of Some Corporate Scandals

Ethical Standards Are Fundamental

ethics

Standards of moral behaviour; that is, behaviour that is accepted by society as right versus wrong.

We define **ethics** as the standards of moral behaviour; that is, behaviour that is accepted by society as right versus wrong. Many people today have few moral absolutes. Many decide situationally whether it's okay to steal, lie, or drink and drive. They seem to think that what is right is whatever works best for the individual, that each person has to work out for himself or herself the difference between right and wrong. That is the kind of thinking that has led to the recent scandals in government and business. This isn't the way it always was. However, in the past decade there has been a rising tide of criticism in Canada (and other countries) of various business practices that many Canadians consider unacceptable.

In a country like Canada, with so many diverse cultures, you might think it would be impossible to identify common standards of ethical behaviour. However, among sources from many different times and places—such as the Bible, Aristotle's *Ethics*, William Shakespeare's *King Lear*, the Quran, and the *Analects* of Confucius—you'll find the following basic moral values: integrity, respect for human life, self-control, honesty, courage, and self-sacrifice are right; cheating, cowardice, and cruelty are wrong. Furthermore, all of the world's major religions support a version of the Golden Rule: Do unto others as you would have them do unto you.[7]

Ethics Begins with Each of Us

It is easy to criticize business and political leaders for their moral and ethical shortcomings, but we must be careful in our criticism to note that ethics begins with each of us. Ethical behaviour should be exhibited in our daily lives, not just in a business environment.

The Fraser Institute's annual Generosity Index measures the propensity to give to charitable donations. Based on the 2008 Generosity Index, and as highlighted in Figure 4.2, the Institute found that 24.7 percent of Canadian tax filers donated to registered charities in 2006. The average annual donation was $1,470. Manitoba and Ontario rank as leaders in both the percentage of tax filers who donate and the percentage of income donated. Though the extent of charitable giving in almost every province from 1996 to 2006 has decreased, the percentage of aggregate personal income donated in Canada has increased.[8] What do you think accounts for this trend?

Young people learn from the behaviour of others. In a study conducted on one college campus, 80 percent of the students surveyed admitted to cheating. At the University of Maryland, a group of instructors conducted a "techno sting" by posting false answers to an accounting exam on a Web site. Twelve students used the false answers, including a few who admitted to getting the answers from the site during the exam itself by using their cellphones. To fight the problem of plagiarism, many instructors now use services such as Turnitin.com, which scans students' papers against over 64 million student papers in the Student Paper Database.[9] Have you seen students cheat on assignments or exams? How did this make you feel? Students use many reasons to rationalize such behaviour, such as "Everyone else is doing it" or "I ran out of time to prepare, but I will do all my own work next time." What do you think of these reasons?

Two studies found that there is a strong relationship between academic dishonesty among undergraduate students and dishonesty later when these same students were in the working world.[10] In response, many schools are adopting stricter

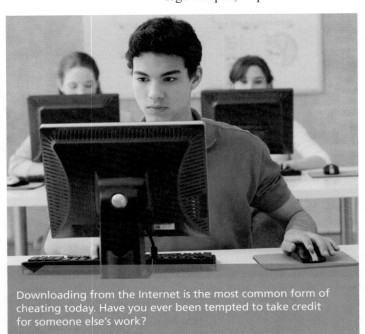

Downloading from the Internet is the most common form of cheating today. Have you ever been tempted to take credit for someone else's work?

FIGURE 4.2

The Fraser Institute's 2008 Generosity Index

Province	Percent of Returns with Charitable Donations (%)	Rank for Percent of Returns with Charitable Donations	Percent of Income Donated (%)	Rank for Percent of Income Donated	Average Charitable Donation ($)	Rank for Average Charitable Donation
British Columbia	23.4	7	0.84	5	1,713	4
Alberta	25.0	5	0.86	4	2,057	1
Saskatchewan	26.0	4	0.91	3	1,440	6
Manitoba	28.1	1	1.14	1	1,734	3
Ontario	26.7	2	0.92	2	1,746	2
Quebec	22.3	9	0.33	11	613	13
New Brunswick	22.9	8	0.76	6	1,291	7
Nova Scotia	23.9	6	0.73	8	1,263	8
Prince Edward Island	26.4	3	0.76	7	1,075	11
Newfoundland & Labrador	21.6	10	0.49	9	944	12
Yukon	20.7	11	0.38	10	1,174	10
Northwest Territories	17.3	12	0.29	12	1,213	9
Nunavut	10.8	13	0.25	13	1,549	5
Canada	**24.7**		**0.76**		**1,470**	

Sources: "Generosity in Canada and the United States: The 2008 Generosity Index," The Fraser Institute, December 2008, http://www.fraserinstitute.org/Commerce.Web/product_files/Generosity_Index_2008.pdf; Canada Revenue Agency, 2008a; and Statistics Canada, 2008a.

honour policies that provide serious consequences for cheating. Do you think that such policies make a difference to student behaviour?

It is always healthy when discussing moral and ethical issues to remember that ethical behaviour begins with you and me. We cannot expect society to become more moral and ethical unless we as individuals commit to becoming more moral and ethical ourselves.

The purpose of the Making Ethical Decisions boxes you see throughout the text is to demonstrate to you that it is important to keep ethics in mind whenever you are making a business decision. The choices are not always easy. Sometimes the obvious solution from an ethical point of view has drawbacks from a personal or professional point of view. For example, imagine that your supervisor at work has asked you to do something you feel is unethical. You have just taken out a mortgage on a new house to make room for your first baby, due in two months. Not carrying out your supervisor's request may get you fired. What would you do? Sometimes there is no desirable alternative. Such situations are called ethical dilemmas because you must choose between equally unsatisfactory alternatives. It can be very difficult to maintain a balance between ethics and other goals such as pleasing stakeholders or advancing in your career. It is helpful to ask yourself the following questions when facing an ethical dilemma:[11]

1. *Is it legal?* Am I violating any law or company policy? Whether you are thinking about having a drink and then driving home, gathering marketing intelligence, designing

a product, hiring or firing employees, planning on how to get rid of waste, or using a questionable nickname for an employee, it is necessary to think about the legal implications of what you do. This question is the most basic one in behaving ethically in business, but it is only the first.

2. *Is it balanced?* Am I acting fairly? Would I want to be treated this way? Will I win everything at the expense of another party? Win–lose situations often end up as lose–lose situations. There is nothing like a major loss to generate retaliation from the loser. You can see this in the stock market today. Many companies that were merely suspected of wrongdoing have seen their stock drop dramatically. Not every situation can be completely balanced, but it is important to the health of our relationships that we avoid major imbalances over time. An ethical business person has a win–win attitude. In other words, such a person tries to make decisions that benefit all parties involved.

3. *How will it make me feel about myself?* Would I feel proud if my family learned of my decision? My friends? Would I be able to discuss the proposed situation or action with my immediate supervisor? The company's clients? How would I feel if my decision were announced on the evening news? Will I have to hide my actions or keep them secret? Has someone warned me not to disclose my actions? Am I feeling unusually nervous? Decisions that go against our sense of right and wrong make us feel bad—they corrode our self-esteem. That is why an ethical business person does what is proper as well as what is profitable.

It is important to note that there are no easy solutions to ethical dilemmas. Individuals and companies that develop a strong ethics code and use the three ethics-check questions presented above have a better chance than most of behaving ethically. If you would like to know which style of recognizing and resolving ethical dilemmas you favour, fill out the ethical orientation questionnaire in Figure 4.3.

FIGURE | **4.3**

Ethical Orientation Questionnaire

Please answer the following questions.

1. Which is worse?
   A. Hurting someone's feelings by telling the truth.
   B. Telling a lie and protecting someone's feelings.

2. Which is the worse mistake?
   A. To make exceptions too freely.
   B. To apply rules too rigidly.

3. Which is it worse to be?
   A. Unmerciful.
   B. Unfair.

4. Which is worse?
   A. Stealing something valuable from someone for no good reason.
   B. Breaking a promise to a friend for no good reason.

5. Which is it better to be?
   A. Just and fair.
   B. Sympathetic and feeling.

6. Which is worse?
   A. Not helping someone in trouble.
   B. Being unfair to someone by playing favourites.

7. In making a decision you rely more on
   A. Hard facts.
   B. Personal feelings and intuition.

8. Your boss orders you to do something that will hurt someone. If you carry out the order, have you actually done anything wrong?
   A. Yes.
   B. No.

9. Which is more important in determining whether an action is right or wrong?
   A. Whether anyone actually gets hurt.
   B. Whether a rule, law, commandment, or moral principle is broken.

To score: The answers fall in one of two categories, J or C. Count your number of J and C answers using this key:
1. A = C, B = J; 2. A = J, B = C; 3. A = C, B = J; 4. A = J, B = C; 5. A = J, B = C; 6. A = C, B = J; 7. A = J, B = C; 8. A = C; B = J; 9. A = C, B = J

(continued)

What your score means: The higher your J score, the more you rely on an ethic of *justice*. The higher your C score, the more you prefer an ethic of *care*. Neither style is better than the other, but they are different. Because they appear so different they may seem opposed to one another, but they're actually complementary. In fact, your score probably shows you rely on each style to a greater or lesser degree. (Few people end up with a score of 9 to 0.) The more you can appreciate both approaches, the better you'll be able to resolve ethical dilemmas and to understand and communicate with people who prefer the other style.

An ethic of justice is based on principles such as justice, fairness, equality, or authority. People who prefer this style see ethical dilemmas as conflicts of rights that can be solved by the impartial application of some general principle. The advantage of this approach is that it looks at a problem logically and impartially. People with this style try to be objective and fair, hoping to make a decision according to some standard that's higher than any specific individual's interests. The disadvantage of this approach is that people who rely on it might lose sight of the immediate interests of particular individuals. They may unintentionally ride roughshod over the people around them in favour of some abstract ideal or policy.

An ethic of care is based on a sense of responsibility to reduce actual harm or suffering. People who prefer this style see moral dilemmas as conflicts of duties or responsibilities. They believe that solutions must be tailored to the special details of individual circumstances. They tend to feel constrained by policies that are supposed to be enforced without exception. The advantage of this approach is that it is responsive to immediate suffering and harm. The disadvantage is that, when carried to an extreme, this style can produce decisions that seem not simply subjective, but arbitrary.

To learn more about an ethic of justice, consult the writings of Lawrence Kohlberg. To learn more about an ethic of care, consult the research of Carol Gilligan.

Source: © Thomas I. White.

Progress Assessment

- What is ethics?
- How does ethics differ from legality?
- When faced with ethical dilemmas, what questions can you ask yourself that might help you make ethical decisions?

MANAGING BUSINESSES ETHICALLY AND RESPONSIBLY

It cannot be stressed enough that organizational ethics begin at the top. Ethics is caught more than it is taught. That is, people learn their standards and values from observing what others do, not from hearing what they say. This is as true in business as it is at home. The leadership and example of strong top managers can help instill corporate values in employees. The majority of CEOs surveyed recently attributed unethical employee conduct to the failure of the organization's leadership in establishing ethical standards and culture.[12]

Any trust and co-operation between workers and managers must be based on fairness, honesty, openness, and moral integrity. (This can be challenging as there is less mutual loyalty and trust given the increasing focus on profits at the expense of jobs.) The same can be said about relationships among businesses and among nations. A business should be managed ethically for many reasons: to maintain a good reputation; to keep existing customers; to attract new customers; to avoid lawsuits; to reduce employee turnover; to avoid government intervention (the passage of new laws and regulations controlling business activities); to please customers, employees, and society; and simply to do the right thing.

Some managers think that ethics is a personal matter—that individuals either have ethical principles or they don't. These managers feel that they are not responsible for an individual's misdeeds and that ethics has nothing to do with management. But a growing number of people think that ethics has everything to do with management. Individuals do not usually act alone; they need the implied, if not direct, co-operation of others to behave unethically in a corporation.

Setting Corporate Ethical Standards

Formal corporate ethics codes are popular these days. Eighty-nine percent of the organizations surveyed have written codes of ethics.[13] Figure 4.4 offers a sample from one company's code of ethics.

Although ethics codes vary greatly, they can be classified into two major categories: compliance-based and integrity-based. **Compliance-based ethics codes** emphasize preventing unlawful behaviour by increasing control and by penalizing wrongdoers. Whereas compliance-based ethics codes are based on avoiding legal punishment, **integrity-based ethics codes** define the organization's guiding values, create an environment that supports ethically sound behaviour, and stress a shared accountability among employees. See Figure 4.5 for a comparison of compliance-based and integrity-based ethics codes.

The following six-step process can help improve business ethics:

1. Top management must adopt and unconditionally support an explicit corporate code of conduct.

2. Employees must understand that expectations for ethical behaviour begin at the top and that senior management expects all employees to act accordingly.

3. Managers and others must be trained to consider the ethical implications of all business decisions.

4. An ethics office must be set up. Phone lines to the office should be established so that employees who don't necessarily want to be seen with an ethics officer can inquire about ethical matters anonymously. **Whistleblowers** (people who report illegal or unethical behaviour) must feel protected from retaliation as oftentimes this exposure can lead to great career and personal cost.

5. Outsiders such as suppliers, subcontractors, distributors, and customers must be told about the ethics program. Pressure to put aside ethical considerations often comes from the outside, and it helps employees to resist such pressure when everyone knows what the ethical standards are.

6. The ethics code must be enforced. It is important to back any ethics program with timely action if any rules are broken. This is the best way to communicate to all employees that the code is serious.[14]

This last step is perhaps the most critical. No matter how well intended a company's ethics code is, it is worthless if it is not enforced. Enron had a code of ethics. However, by ignoring this code, Enron's board and management sent employees the message that rules could be shelved when they were inconvenient.[15]

---

compliance-based ethics codes
Ethical standards that emphasize preventing unlawful behaviour by increasing control and by penalizing wrongdoers.

integrity-based ethics codes
Ethical standards that define the organization's guiding values, create an environment that supports ethically sound behaviour, and stress a shared accountability among employees.

whistleblowers
People who report illegal or unethical behaviour.

FIGURE | 4.4

Overview of Johnson & Johnson's Code of Ethics
Johnson & Johnson calls this code of ethics its Credo.

Written in 1943 by long-time Chairman General Robert Wood Johnson, the Johnson & Johnson Credo serves as a conscious plan that represents and encourages a unique set of values. Our Credo sums up the responsibilities we have to the four important groups we serve:

- Our customers—We have a responsibility to provide high-quality products they can trust, offered at a fair price.
- Our employees—We have a responsibility to treat them with respect and dignity, pay them fairly and help them develop and thrive personally and professionally.
- Our communities—We have a responsibility to be good corporate citizens, support good works, encourage better health and protect the environment.
- Our stockholders—We have a responsibility to provide a fair return on their investment.

The deliberate ordering of these groups—customers first, stockholders last—proclaims a bold business philosophy: If we meet our first three responsibilities, the fourth will take care of itself … To ensure our adherence to Credo values, we periodically ask every employee to evaluate the company's performance in living up to them. We believe that by monitoring our actions against the ethical framework of Our Credo, we will best ensure that we make responsible decisions as a company.

Features of Compliance-Based Ethics Codes		Features of Integrity-Based Ethics Codes	
Ideal:	Conform to outside standards (laws and regulations)	Ideal:	Conform to outside standards (laws and regulations) and chosen internal standards
Objective:	Avoid criminal misconduct	Objective:	Enable responsible employee conduct
Leaders:	Lawyers	Leaders:	Managers with aid of lawyers and others
Methods:	Education, reduced employee discretion, controls, and penalties	Methods:	Education, leadership, accountability, decision processes, controls, and penalties

FIGURE | 4.5

Strategies for Ethics Management
Both codes have a concern for the law and use penalties as enforcement. Integrity-based ethics codes move beyond legal compliance to create a "do-it-right" climate that emphasizes core values such as honesty, fair play, good service to customers, a commitment to diversity, and involvement in the community. These values are ethically desirable, but not necessarily legally mandatory.

An important factor in the success of enforcing an ethics code is the selection of the ethics officer. The most effective ethics officers set a positive tone, communicate effectively, and relate well with employees at every level of the company. They are equally comfortable serving as counsellors or as investigators. While many ethics officers have backgrounds in law, it is more important that they have strong communication skills than a background in specific rules, regulations, and risks. Effective ethics officers are people who can be trusted to maintain confidentiality, can conduct objective investigations and ensure that the process is fair, and can demonstrate to stakeholders that ethics is important in everything that the company does.

As more organizations are recognizing the importance of this role, associations are also providing support for those in these roles. One such example is the Ethics Practitioners' Association of Canada (EPAC). EPAC's mission is "to enable individuals to work successfully in the field of ethics in organizations by enhancing the quality and availability of ethics advice and services across Canada." This organization supports ethics officers, consultants, educators, students, and others who are interested in the field of ethics as applied to organizations of all kinds.

The Sarbanes-Oxley Act of 2002 (SOX)[16]

The major corporate and accounting scandals in the United Sates in the early 2000s (e.g., Enron, Tyco, Adelphia, and WorldCom) gave rise to the implementation of U.S. federal legislation known as the Sarbanes-Oxley Act (SOX). The legislation established stronger standards to prevent misconduct and improve corporate governance practices. SOX applies to all publicly-traded companies whose shares are listed on the stock exchanges under the jurisdiction of the U.S. Securities and Exchange Commission. The goal of SOX is to ensure the accuracy and reliability of published financial information, and therefore the main part of the legislation requirements deal with the proper administration routines, procedures, and control activities. In response to SOX, Canada also implemented similar corporate governance legislation.

As Vice President for Corporate Development at Enron, Sherron Watkins sensed that something was rotten with the company's financial reporting. She "blew the whistle" on her bosses, who hid billions of dollars of debt and operating losses from investors and employees. Watkins said she would have come forward sooner, but she was afraid of losing her job. SOX now also protects whistleblowers like Watkins from any company retaliation as it requires that all public corporations provide a system that allows employees to submit concerns regarding accounting and auditing issues both confidentially and anonymously. Obviously, the purpose is to motivate employees to

As the office manager, Linda Merk discovered that the president and business manager of Ironworkers Union Local 771 were double dipping on their travel expenses. She was fired when she went to the police after the union's international office ignored her concerns. In a precedent-setting decision, the Supreme Court of Canada ruled in her favour. Merk received a settlement and was reinstated to her position.

report any wrongdoing. For example, the legislation provides for reinstatement and back pay to people who were punished by their employers for passing information about frauds to authorities.

Whistleblowing Legislation in Canada[17]

Clearly, one might suggest that for the six steps mentioned earlier to work, there must first be protection in place for the whistleblower. Otherwise, how effective can such a process be? Bill C-11: The Public Servants Protection Disclosure Act is Canada's only national whistleblower legislation. Passed in 2005, Bill C-11 applies to almost the entire public sector. It provides for significant powers to investigate wrongdoing, it contains a clear legal prohibition of reprisal against those who make good-faith allegations of wrongdoing, and it proposes measures to protect the identity of persons making disclosures.

As noted in the chapter profile, the Federal Accountability Act was implemented to help strengthen accountability and increase transparency and oversight in government operations. Reforms include a five-year lobbying ban on former ministers, their aides, and senior public servants (i.e., to communicate in an attempt to influence), the elimination of corporate and union donations to political parties and candidates, and protection for whistleblowers. Critics condemn the Act as they believe that loopholes have actually weakened government accountability. For example, Democracy Watch (Canada's leading citizen group advocating democratic reform, government accountability, and corporate responsibility) points out that one year after the Act was passed, despite a staff of 21 and a budget of $6.5 million, the Public Service Integrity Commissioner did not report a single instance of wrongdoing or a single case of reprisal against a whistleblower in the entire federal public sector. Review the Dealing with Change box for more information on another organization, the Federal Accountability Initiative for Reform, that also believes that Canada needs stronger legislation.

Both of these Acts protect public sector workers but there is no provision to protect private-sector whistleblowers. In a KPMG survey on private corporations' policies on whistleblowers, almost two-thirds of respondents to the business ethics survey stated that they have a written policy requiring employees to report fraud or misconduct in the workplace. However, only 40 percent of respondents reported having formal systems designed to protect whistleblowers from retaliation. One-fifth of respondents lacked any type of protection system.

Petro-Canada communicates its Whistleblower Protection Policy on its Web site (www.petro-canada.ca). This policy includes the implementation of an anonymous 1-800 "whistleblowing line." A third-party service provider answers the telephone line and reports all calls to the appropriate members of Petro-Canada's executive or audit committee, depending on the nature of the call. Employees are informed that they will not be discharged, demoted, suspended, threatened, harassed, or in any other manner discriminated against in the terms and conditions of employment, or otherwise, because of any lawful act done by an employee in the provision of information to superiors, or to appropriate government agencies, regarding conduct that the employee reasonably believes violates the Petro-Canada Code of Business Conduct or any applicable governmental laws, rules, and regulations, or in assisting in an investigation of these types of violations.

Progress Assessment

- How are compliance-based ethics codes different from integrity-based ethics codes?
- What are the six steps to follow in establishing an effective ethics program in a business?
- What protection is being offered to whistleblowers in the public sector?

DEALING with CHANGE

Federal Accountability Initiative for Reform

Founded in 1998, the Federal Accountability Initiative for Reform (FAIR) promotes integrity and accountability within government by empowering employees to speak out without fear of reprisal when they encounter wrongdoing. Its aim is to support legislation and management practices that will provide effective protection for whistleblowers and hence occupational free speech in the workplace. A registered Canadian charity, it is Canada's only public interest organization dedicated to protecting employees who blow the whistle on government misconduct.

Many public service scandals have come to light in Canada over the past several years. A few notable examples are the tainted blood scandal (in which 60,000 Canadians were infected with hepatitis C, many of them fatally), the gun registry scandal (in which a program with a budget of $2 million spent $1 billion without authorization or reporting of the cost overrun to Parliament), and the sponsorship scandal (in which millions of dollars of public money were diverted illegally to government-favoured advertising agencies). While these cases received extensive media coverage, there was very little media coverage or public debate regarding what Canada could do to prevent such abuses in the future.

Since these cases, the federal government implemented several key pieces of legislation. One example is the Public Servants Disclosure Protection Act (PSDPA), which purports to protect Canadians who blow the whistle on federal government wrongdoing. A central part of the Federal Accountability Act, the PSDPA establishes a process for whistleblowers' allegations of wrongdoing to be investigated, and for whistleblowers to seek protection from reprisals. FAIR believes that the "ironclad" protection provided for whistleblowers by this legislation is misleading. For example, it believes that the legislation provides no assurance that any wrongdoing reported by the whistleblower will be corrected. On another point, it denies whistleblowers access to our normal system of public courts.

FAIR has developed five points for judging any whistleblower legislation. Meeting all these in full will ensure that the legislation can be made to work effectively. Failing to meet any of these will create loopholes that may render the entire system useless. In the opinion of FAIR, there is still much work to be done with whistleblower legislation in Canada today. The five points are as follows:

1. *Full Free Speech Rights*—Whistleblowers must be able to blow the whistle on wrongdoing anywhere, anytime, and to any audience unless release of the information is specifically prohibited by statute, in which case disclosure must still be permitted to law enforcement and/or to Parliament.

2. *Right to Disclose All Illegality and Misconduct*—Disclosure must extend to any illegality, gross waste, gross mismanagement, abuse of authority, substantial and specific danger to public health or safety, as well as the contravention of any workplace policy, regulation, rule, professional statement, directive, or code of conduct.

3. *No Harassment of Any Kind*—Any harassment must be banned.

4. *Forum for Adjudication, with Realistic Burden of Proof and Appropriate Remedies*—Whistleblowers must have access to an effective judicial process, which includes access to the courts. Whistleblowers also require realistic burdens of proof. The law must therefore provide a reverse onus whereby once the whistleblower has shown that the whistleblowing was a contributing factor in the action taken against them (i.e., a short time frame between the whistleblowing and the retaliation), the burden shifts to the employer to show by clear and convincing evidence that the employer had other legitimate reasons for taking the action. Finally, if the whistleblower prevails, the relief must be comprehensive to cover all direct, indirect, and future consequences of the reprisal. This may mean relocation, medical bills, and compensation in lieu of salary.

5. *Mandatory Corrective Action*—Employees remain silent for two key reasons: one, they have no faith that anything will change; and two, fear of reprisal. To promote true accountability, persons who engage in harassment against an employee must be held personally responsible. As well, ministers must be required to take remedial action on the wrongdoing.

Source: "Our Mission," Federal Accountability Initiative for Reform, 22 December 2008, http://fairwhistleblower.ca/. Used with permission.

CORPORATE SOCIAL RESPONSIBILITY

corporate social responsibility (CSR)
A business's concern for the welfare of society as a whole.

Just as you and I need to be good citizens, contributing what we can to society, corporations need to be good citizens as well. **Corporate social responsibility (CSR)**, also known as *corporate responsibility*, is the concern businesses have for the welfare of society. It is based on a company's concern for the welfare of all of its stakeholders, not just the owners. CSR goes well beyond merely being ethical. It is based on a commitment to such basic principles as integrity, fairness, and respect.[18]

There is discussion in this chapter about ethics and CSR. It is important to note that both of these are often judgement calls, depending on which side of the issue you are on. To clarify, one person's unethical behaviour can be considered another person's sound business decision. Also, do not underestimate the impact of cultural values. Differences from country to country also contribute to varying perspectives on the same issue. This can result in decision making that is not in line with one's personal values but is congruent with what is considered ethical in a country.

Not everyone thinks that CSR is a good thing. Some critics of CSR believe that a manager's sole role is to compete and win in the marketplace. Economist Milton Friedman made a classic statement when he said that the only social responsibility of business is to make money for stockholders. He thought that doing anything else was moving dangerously toward socialism.[19] CSR critics believe that managers who pursue CSR are doing so with other people's money—money they invested to make more money, not to improve society. They view spending money on CSR activities as stealing from their investors.

CSR defenders, on the other hand, believe that businesses owe their existence to the societies they serve. Businesses cannot succeed in societies that fail. They are given access to society's labour pool and its natural resources, things that every member of the society has a stake in. Even Adam Smith, the father of capitalism, believed that the self-interested pursuit of profit was wrong. He argued that benevolence was the highest virtue. CSR defenders acknowledge that businesses have deep obligations to investors, and that businesses should not attempt government-type social responsibility projects. However, they also argue that CSR makes more money for investors in the long run. They base their arguments on studies that have shown that companies with good ethical reputations attract and retain better employees, draw more customers, and enjoy greater employee loyalty. Very simply, CSR is simply good business because it is what society demands. What do you think?

corporate philanthropy
Dimension of social responsibility that includes charitable donations.

The social performance of a company has several dimensions:

Tim Horton Children's Foundation is a private organization that is supported by Tim Hortons. Every year, thousands of children from economically challenged homes participate in camps that are run by the Foundation.

- **Corporate philanthropy** includes charitable donations to non-profit groups of all kinds. Strategic philanthropy involves companies making long-term commitments to one cause, such as the Canadian Tire Foundation for Families. Since its launch in 1999, the Foundation has donated more than $30 million to charitable organizations that support families in local communities by helping to ensure that life's basic needs are met.[20] The Spotlight on Small Business box highlights how CanadaHelps.org provides a channel for those that wish to make charitable donations.

SPOTLIGHT ON Small Business

Giving Online Through E-philanthropy

The voluntary sector is dealing with the effects of two major changes: while government funding has diminished over the past several years, the definition of what role charities are expected to play in the lives of Canadians has expanded. With this increased burden charities need to make the most effective use possible of every dollar donated. Meanwhile, technology is changing at a rapid pace and the complexities around accepting online donations are many. Most charities quite simply have neither the resources nor the expertise to understand the complexity around e-commerce.

CanadaHelps.org believes that charities should focus on their core activities, such as protecting the environment, educating the population, or providing relief to the less fortunate. CanadaHelps is Canada's only donation portal that provides access to all of Canada's 80,000 charities, from larger organizations such as national cancer charities to smaller groups such as local animal shelters and soup kitchens. It provides information and ideas about how people can help their communities.

Three university students—Ryan Little, Matthew Choi, and Aaron Pereira—launched CanadaHelps.org in December 2000. They recognized the opportunity that e-commerce presented to the voluntary sector to increase efficiency. Together with a diverse group of volunteers and a committed board of advisers and directors and staff, the company has gained the support of individuals and organizations in the charitable and corporate sectors.

"Because of Canadians' increasingly hectic lifestyles, making charitable donations online has clicked in a big way," says Little. This service is available in both official languages to all Canadians, living domestically and abroad, who wish to make a donation to a Canadian charity. Making your donation is simple. You search/browse for the charity you wish to donate to, add it to your "Giving Basket" and then pay for the gift. One of the newest options is the CanadaHelps Give the Gift of Giving™ program. This gift card service allows donors to give a charitable donation to friends and family. Donors purchase a gift card in a certain amount, and the gift recipient chooses which charity receives the donation amount.

Once the donation has been paid, the donor receives an immediate, secure PDF tax receipt, issued by CanadaHelps via e-mail. CanadaHelps then disburses the funds (less a 3 percent transaction fee) to the designated charity.

Not only is donating online convenient and efficient for donors, but charities are benefiting as well. CanadaHelps provides a cost-effective alternative to setting up their own online donations facilities: there is no set-up fee or annual charge, and charities receive immediate notification when a donation is received. Charities are only charged when a donation is actually made, thereby ensuring that a charity does not pay for a service that is not being used. (Raising funds through the Internet is estimated to cost about 20 percent less than direct mail or telemarketing.) Today, CanadaHelps facilitates more than $10 million in donations to Canadian charities annually.

Sources: "How It Works," CanadaHelps.org, 21 December 2008, www.canadahelps.org; "Giving Just Got Easier," 3 November 2003, St. John's: Community Services Council Newfoundland and Labrador, http://www.envision.ca/templates/news.asp?ID=4718; and "Volunteers of the Year Awards 2001," Toronto: City of Toronto, http://www.city.toronto.on.ca/volunteer_awards/winners_2001.htm.

- **Corporate social initiatives** include enhanced forms of corporate philanthropy that are more directly related to the company's competencies. For example, as part of the 2004 Asian tsunami disaster relief, UPS and FedEx shipped emergency relief supplies for free from all over the world, Johnson & Johnson sent medical supplies, and other pharmaceutical companies sent antibiotics, nutritional supplements, and baby formula.[21]

- **Corporate responsibility** includes everything from hiring minority workers to making safe products, minimizing pollution, using energy wisely, and providing a safe work environment—that is, everything that has to do with acting responsibly within society and toward employees. We will discuss this in more detail later in the chapter.

- **Corporate policy** refers to the position a firm takes on social and political issues.

So much news coverage has been devoted to the problems caused by corporations that people tend to develop a negative view of the impact that companies have on society. If the news were more balanced, much more could be said about the positive contributions that businesses make. Few people know, for example, that Xerox has a program called Social Service Leave, which allows employees to take a leave of absence for up to a year to work for a non-profit organization. While on Social Service Leave, the Xerox employee

corporate social initiatives
Dimension of social responsibility that includes enhanced forms of corporate philanthropy that are more directly related to the company's competencies.

corporate responsibility
Dimension of social responsibility that includes everything from hiring minority workers to making safe products.

corporate policy
Dimension of social responsibility that refers to the position a firm takes on social and political issues.

receives full salary and benefits, including job security.[22] Microsoft Canada belongs to the I CAN Program. The I Volunteer element of this program permits employees to volunteer 40 hours during regular Microsoft work hours.[23]

Two-thirds of the MBA students surveyed by a group called Students for Responsible Business said they would take a lower salary to work for a socially responsible company. But when the same students were asked to define a socially responsible company, things got complicated. It appears that even those who want to be socially responsible can't agree on what it involves.

Corporate Responsibility in the Twenty-First Century

What should be the guiding philosophy for business in the twenty-first century? For most of the twentieth century, there was uncertainty regarding the position top managers should take, and this question is still being debated today. How a company answers this question depends on its fundamental belief of how stakeholders should be treated and its responsibility to society. There are two different views of corporate responsibility to stakeholders:

1. *The Strategic Approach.* The strategic approach requires that management's primary orientation be toward the economic interests of shareholders. The rationale is this: as owners, shareholders have the right to expect management to work in their best interests; that is, to optimize profits. Furthermore, Adam Smith's notion of the invisible hand suggests that the maximum social gain is realized when managers attend only to their shareholders' interests.

   Friedman and others argue that since (in their view), only people can have social responsibilities, corporations are only responsible to their shareholders and not to society as a whole. Although they accept that corporations should obey the laws of the countries within which they work, they assert that corporations have no other obligation to society.[24] For example, when John Akers was the CEO of IBM, he said that an IBM decision about whether to cease operations in a country would be a business decision: "We are not in business to conduct moral activity; we are not in business to conduct socially responsible action. We are in business to conduct business." The strategic approach encourages managers to consider an actions' effects on stakeholders other than owners, but asserts that others' interests are secondary. Often those interests are considered only when they would adversely affect profits if ignored.

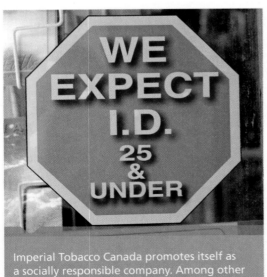

Imperial Tobacco Canada promotes itself as a socially responsible company. Among other programs, it supports Operation I.D., a youth smoking prevention program. Overall, what view of corporate responsibility to stakeholders do you believe this company supports?

2. *The Pluralist Approach.* This approach recognizes the special responsibility of management to optimize profits, but not at the expense of employees, suppliers, and members of the community. This approach recognizes the moral responsibilities of management that apply to all human beings. Managers don't have moral immunity when making managerial decisions. This view says that corporations can maintain their economic viability only when they fulfill their moral responsibilities to society as a whole. When shareholders' interests compete with those of the community, as they often do, managers must decide, using ethical and moral principles.

The guiding philosophy for the twenty-first century will be some version of the pluralist approach. Managerial decision making won't be easy, and new ethical guidelines may have to be drawn. But the process toward such guidelines has been started, and a new era of more responsible and responsive management is under way. Perhaps it would be easier to understand social responsibility if we looked at the concept through the eyes of the stakeholders to whom businesses are responsible: customers, investors, employees, society in general, and the environment.

Responsibility to Customers

One responsibility of business is to satisfy customers by offering them goods and services of real value. A recurring theme of this book is the importance of pleasing customers. This responsibility is not as easy to meet as it seems. Keep in mind that more than half of new businesses fail—perhaps because their owners failed to please their customers. One of the surest ways of failing to please customers is not being totally honest with them. For example, a consumer magazine reported that the Suzuki Samurai was likely to roll over if a driver swerved violently in an emergency. When Suzuki executives denied there was a problem, sales plummeted.

In contrast, Daimler-Benz suffered a similar problem during a test simulating a swerve around a wayward elk, when its A-class Baby Benz rolled over. The company quickly admitted a problem, came up with a solution, and committed the money necessary to put that solution into action. In addition, company representatives continued to answer questions in spite of aggressive press coverage. Daimler took out full-page ads that read: "We should like to thank our customers most warmly for their loyalty. You have given us the chance to remedy a mistake." Following the test flip, only 2 percent of the orders for the vehicle were cancelled. The solution cost the company $59 million in the first year and $118 million in the next. Analysts say those costs probably eliminated any profit on the vehicle. However, the quick resolution of the problem protected the company's reputation, thus allowing its other models to become such hits that Daimler's net earnings remained the same.[25]

The payoff for socially conscious behaviour could result in new business as customers switch from rival companies simply because they admire the company's social efforts—a powerful competitive edge. Consumer behaviour studies show that, all else being equal, a socially conscious company is likely to be viewed more favourably than less socially responsible companies. The important point to remember is that customers prefer to do business with companies they trust and who share their values. This means that they do not want to do business with companies they don't trust.

Responsibility to Investors[26]

Some people believe that before you can do good, you must do well (i.e., make a lot of money); others believe that by doing good, you can also do well. What we do know is that ethical behaviour is good for shareholder wealth. It doesn't subtract from the bottom line, but rather adds to it. On the other hand, unethical behaviour does cause financial damage. Those cheated by financial wrongdoing are the shareholders themselves. Unethical behaviour may seem to work for the short term, but it guarantees eventual failure. The following are two examples:

- In the early 2000s, accounting irregularities reported at Nortel Networks Corp., once the most-traded stock in Canada, damaged investor trust and subsequently the company's share value. Years later, the company was still being scrutinized amid rumours of bankruptcy when its share price was under $1. In early 2009, the company declared bankruptcy.

- Co-founders Garth Drabinsky and Myron Gottlieb, of the theatre company Livent Inc., were found guilty in 2009 of defrauding investors of about half a billion dollars. It was found that both deliberately misrepresented their company's finances before the company went public in the early 1990s. Both men pleaded not guilty to all charges, arguing that they were victims of collusion by a group of former employees who sought to frame them. The verdict came more than 10 years after police began probing what they called one of the biggest fraud cases in Canadian history. The convictions on two counts each of fraud and one of forgery carry respective maximum sentences of 10 and 14 years.[27]

Unfortunately, we continue to read of individual business people who abuse the trust that individual investors have placed in them. Some high-profile examples in recent years include Bernard Madoff and Earl Jones. Financier Bernard Madoff is serving a 150-year sentence after admitting he squandered tens of billions of dollars in investors' money. Madoff's crimes have left many investors impoverished and some charities decimated. At the time this chapter was written, an investigation was underway against financier Earl Jones. He was accused by between 100 and 150 investors of cheating them out of millions of dollars. Quebec's financial securities regulator has alleged the amount could be as high as $50 million. What was the resolution of these charges?

Many people believe that it makes financial as well as moral sense to invest in companies that are planning ahead to create a better environment. By choosing to put their money into companies whose goods and services benefit the community and the environment, investors can improve their own financial health while improving society's health. In the 2005 Canada's Most Respected Corporations survey, 89 percent of Canadian CEOs agreed with the statement that "companies that are more respected by the public enjoy a premium in their share price," while only 9 percent disagreed. The same survey also confirmed that 65 percent of CEO respondents agree with the statement that they are "finding a greater part of his/her job these days involves building respect for his/her company among the general public."

Insider Trading[28]

insider trading
An unethical activity in which insiders use private company information to further their own fortunes or those of their family and friends.

A few investors, known as inside traders, have chosen unethical means to improve their own financial health. **Insider trading** involves insiders using private company information to further their own fortunes, or those of their family and friends. For example, Andrew Rankin, a former executive with RBC Dominion Securities, was charged by the Ontario Securities Commission (OSC) with ten counts of tipping his friend, Daniel Duic. Investigators found that Rankin had alerted Duic to upcoming mergers and acquisitions before they were publicly known. The OSC alleges that, based on this information, Duic bought and sold investments in ten companies and saw his investment increase following the release of the merger and acquisition news. Duic agreed to pay just over $3 million in the form of a penalty, taxes, and lawyer's fees and to testify against Rankin. Under the Ontario Securities Act, Rankin was sentenced to six months in jail for Canada's first conviction for illegal stock tipping.

Responsibility to Employees

Businesses have several responsibilities to employees. First, they have a responsibility to create jobs if they want to grow. It's been said that the best social program in the world is a job. Once a company creates jobs, it has an obligation to ensure that hard work and talent are fairly rewarded. Employees need realistic hope of a better future, which comes only through a chance for upward mobility. People need to see that integrity, hard work, goodwill, ingenuity, and talent pay off. Studies have shown that the factor that most influences a company's effectiveness and financial performance is human resource management.

High-risk groups lined up for hours at public clinics when the H1N1 vaccine was released in October 2009, while many non-high-risk Canadians (e.g., some professional athletes and private-clinic members) received the vaccine courtesy of their employers. For weeks following the initial rollout, thousands of those on the priority list did not receive the vaccine due to the shortage. Were the actions of these employers ethical?

If a company treats employees with respect, they usually will respect the company as well. That respect can make a huge difference in a company's bottom line. In their book *Contented Cows Give Better Milk*, Bill Catlette and Richard Hadden compared "contented cow" companies with "common cow" companies. The companies with the contented employees outgrew their counterparts by four to one for more than ten years. The "contented cow" companies outearned the "common cow" companies by nearly $40 billion and generated 800,000 more jobs. The authors attribute this difference in performance to the commitment and caring that the companies demonstrate for their employees.[29]

When employees feel they've been treated unfairly, they often strike back. Getting even is one of the most powerful incentives for good people to do bad things. Not many disgruntled workers are desperate enough to resort to violence in the workplace, but a great number do relieve their frustrations in more subtle ways, such as blaming mistakes on others, not accepting responsibility for decision making, manipulating budgets and expenses, making commitments they intend to ignore, hoarding resources, doing the minimum needed to get by, making results look better than they are, or even stealing. The loss of employee commitment, confidence, and trust in the company and its management can be very costly indeed. Employee larceny costs Canadian businesses billions of dollars every year. According to the Association of Certified Fraud Examiners, fraud and theft cost employers an average of $9 a day per employee, with the average organization losing about five percent of its total annual revenue to thieves.[30] On average, most victimized firms lose around $159,000, up more than one-third since 2002.[31] Canadian retailers alone are relieved of approximately $8 million of merchandise every day, with employees outstealing the shoplifters.[32]

Responsibility to Society

One of business's responsibilities to society is to create new wealth, which is disbursed to employees, suppliers, shareholders, and other stakeholders. But if businesses don't create wealth, who will? Non-profit organizations play an important role in distributing the funds they receive from donors, governments, and even their own investments in billions of shares in publicly-held companies. As those stock prices increase, more funds are available to benefit society. However, for stock prices to increase, the publicly-held company must be successful. For companies to prosper, they need to provide customers with safe products. Businesses today, more than ever before, need to develop long-term profitable relationships with their customers. There is no question that repeat business is based on buying safe and value-laden goods and services, at reasonable prices.

Businesses are also partially responsible for promoting social justice. Business is perhaps the most crucial institution of civil society. For its own well-being, business depends on its employees being active in politics, law, churches and temples, arts, charities, and so on. Many companies believe that business has a role in building a community that goes well beyond giving back. To them, charity is not enough. Their social contributions include cleaning up the environment, building community toilets, providing computer lessons, caring for the elderly, and supporting children from low-income families.[33] Samsung, a Korean electronics conglomerate, emphasizes volunteer involvement. For example, a busload of Samsung employees and managers are transported each month to a city park, where they spread out to pick up garbage, pull weeds, and plant saplings. Managers even volunteer to help spruce up employee homes. Local employees feel such loyalty to the company that in the height of an unrest that destroyed many businesses in Indonesia, local employees and their neighbours pulled together to protect Samsung's refrigerator factory there and shielded foreign managers from violence. With the help of relatives in the countryside, the local employees set up a food supply network that helped protect their colleagues from skyrocketing prices for food staples such as rice and palm oil.

The focus of this book is on business; however, one should not forget that government decisions also affect business and society. The Walkerton, Ontario, E. coli tragedy that killed seven people and made half of the town's 5,000 residents ill from contaminated water is one such example. After hearing testimony from more than 100 witnesses over nine months, Justice O'Connor concluded that the catastrophe could have been prevented if brothers Stan and Frank Koebel, who ran Walkerton's water system, had properly chlorinated the water and if the Ontario government had heeded warnings that cuts to the provincial environment ministry were resulting in ineffective testing.[34] Clearly, the Koebel brothers were responsible for their individual decisions.

Responsibility to the Environment[35]

Businesses are often criticized for their role in destroying the environment. Such was the case when images of the slow death of 500 ducks on a toxic oil sands tailings pond in northern Alberta flashed around the world. This led to federal and provincial charges against Syncrude Canada Ltd., which was charged under the Alberta Environmental Enhancement and Protection Act and the federal Migratory Birds Convention Act. While Syncrude attempted to rescue some of the ducks that landed in the tailings pond, only a handful were taken out of the water for cleaning and none survived.

We are seeing more efforts being made to reverse years of neglect to the environment. For example, the Sydney Tar Ponds in Nova Scotia are North America's largest hazardous waste site. More than 80 years of discharges from the steel-producing coke ovens near the harbour have filled Muggah Creek with contaminated sediments. By 1983, Environment Canada had pinpointed the coke ovens as the major source of pollution in the Sydney area. Fishing was banned and the Sydney lobster fishery was closed. Statistics show significantly higher levels of cancers and other debilitating diseases than anywhere else in Canada. The disposal of the toxic waste has been slow. Two decades later, there have been several attempts and more than $100 million spent to clean up this toxic site. In May 2004, the governments of Canada and Nova Scotia committed $400 million to the cleanup. It is expected that this cleanup will take ten years.

This is not the only example of government getting involved with business. The Great Lakes—lakes Superior, Michigan, Huron, Erie, and Ontario—span more than 1,200 kilometres. The Great Lakes basin is home to more than one-quarter of Canada's population and more than one-tenth of the U.S. population. Some of the world's largest concentrations of industrial capacity are located in the Great Lakes region. In spite of their large size, the Great Lakes are sensitive to the effects of a wide range of pollutants, including runoff of soils and farm chemicals from agricultural lands, waste from cities, and discharges from industrial areas.

One hot spot is Sarnia's Chemical Valley. There have been hundreds of spills in the St. Clair River since 1986. Chemical Valley is home to dozens of chemical and petroleum companies. They account for about 40 percent of Canada's chemical production and 20 percent of the nation's refineries. Thousands of residents in the area are concerned about spills because they draw their drinking water from the river. Efforts since 1987 were supposed to have reduced the spills into the river to virtually zero. In the Sarnia area, Health Canada

The Ethical Funds Company selects investments based on financial as well as social and environmental criteria. The company does not invest in corporations that derive a significant portion of their income from military weapons, tobacco, or nuclear power. Would you invest in companies on the basis of their environmental, social, and governance performance?

statistics show that residents have a higher rate of illnesses than in the rest of Canada, ranging from cancer to birth defects. Despite these efforts and the fact that companies have been heavily fined, spills still occur. What do you think should be the next step to stop these spills? Is it realistic to expect zero spills? The Analyzing Management Decisions case near the end of this chapter discusses the implications of an oil spill in Alberta.

Some governments are taking more responsibility for improving the environment, as highlighted in the Green Box. Businesses are also taking more responsibility for helping to make their own environment a better place. Environmental efforts may increase the company's costs, but they also may allow the company to charge higher prices, to increase market share, or both. For example, Ciba Specialty Chemicals, a Swiss textile-dye manufacturer, developed dyes that require less salt than traditional dyes. Since used dye solutions must be treated before they are released into rivers or streams, having less salt and unfixed dye in the solution means lower water-treatment costs. Patents protect Ciba's low-salt dyes, so the company can charge more for its dyes than other companies can charge for theirs. Ciba's experience illustrates that, just as a new machine enhances labour productivity, lowering environmental costs can add value to a business.

Environmental practices are of interest to many stakeholders, including investors. Jantzi Research Inc. has developed the Canadian Social Investment Database™, which contains social and environmental profiles of approximately 300 Canadian companies and income trusts. Institutional investors that incorporate social and environmental criteria—such as corporate governance, environmental performance, ethical business practices, human rights issues, and tobacco and weapons-related production—into their investment decisions use this tool. According to Michael Jantzi, President, "Companies that look at social and environmental issues in a consistent, clear way do better than their counterparts."

Environmental quality is a public good; that is, everyone gets to enjoy it regardless of who pays for it. The challenge for companies is to find the right public good that will appeal to their target market. Many corporations are publishing reports that document their net social contribution. To do that, a company must measure its positive social contributions and subtract its negative social impacts. We will discuss that process next.

Social Auditing

It is nice to talk about having organizations become more socially responsible. It is also encouraging to see some efforts made toward creating safer products, cleaning up the environment, designing more honest advertising, and treating women and minorities fairly. But is there any way to measure whether organizations are making social responsibility an integral part of top management's decision making? The answer is yes, and the term that represents that measurement is *social auditing*.

A **social audit** is a systematic evaluation of an organization's progress toward implementing programs that are socially responsible and responsive. One of the major problems of conducting a social audit is establishing procedures for measuring a firm's activities and its effects on society. What should be measured? Many social audits consider such things as workplace issues, the environment, product safety, community relations, and respecting the rights of local people.[36] See Figure 4.6 for an outline of business activities that could be considered socially responsible.

A commitment to corporate social responsibility implies a commitment to some form of **triple-bottom line** ("**TBL**," "**3BL**," or "**People, Planet, Profit**") reporting.[37] TBL is used as a framework for measuring and reporting corporate performance against economic, social, and environmental parameters.[38] Such corporations focus on the economic value they add, but also on the environmental and social value they add and destroy.[39]

There is some question as to whether positive actions should be added (e.g., charitable donations and pollution control efforts) and negative effects subtracted (e.g., layoffs and overall pollution levels) to get a net social contribution. Or should only positive actions be recorded? In general, social responsibility is becoming one of the aspects of corporate success that business evaluates, measures, and develops.

social audit
A systematic evaluation of an organization's progress toward implementing programs that are socially responsible and responsive.

triple-bottom line (TBL, 3BL, or People, Planet, Profit)
A framework for measuring and reporting corporate performance against economic, social, and environmental parameters.

Green BOX

To Carbon Tax or Not?

The carbon tax, sometimes called a green tax, can refer to any number of measures designed to increase the cost of burning fossil fuels like oil, gas, and coal. In basic terms, it is a tax on greenhouse gas emissions levied with the aim of reducing pollution to combat climate change. Those emissions spewing from exhaust pipes or industrial smokestacks are made up primarily of carbon dioxide, which is produced when fossil fuels containing carbon—such as coal, natural gas, or diesel—are burned. "It's a really important tool for fighting climate change," says Clare Demerse, a senior policy analyst with the Pembina Institute. "It's a way to make sure pollution carries a cost."

A carbon tax would provide an incentive to stop the social harm and move to more positive alternatives. The idea is both to change behaviour (e.g., turn people and businesses away from "bad" fossil fuels and toward "good" clean alternatives) and to set aside a fund to help smooth the transition to a cleaner economy.

A carbon tax can be (1) an across-the-board levy on all fuels based on CO_2 (carbon dioxide) emissions, (2) applied to just the businesses that produce carbon emissions, leaving it up to them whether or not to pass costs along to consumers, or (3) directly levied on consumers. Another alternative is a "revenue-neutral carbon tax" in which any levies extracted from a particular sector (e.g., transportation) would be given back in some other form of subsidy or tax break, that would reward more fuel-efficient behaviour. The most common form of this has been the fairly modest tax breaks on small and hybrid cars.

The tax is described in terms of a dollar value per tonne of gas produced. This can then be translated into a cost on the fuel that emits the greenhouse gases (e.g., 10 cents a litre on gasoline). The Pembina Institute and the David Suzuki Foundation say that Canada needs a carbon tax of $30/tonne immediately, at least $50/tonne by 2015 and $75/tonne by 2020 for the country to do its part in cutting greenhouse gas pollution.

Opposition to carbon taxes includes suggestions that they are merely a cash grab to bolster government revenue and will just push jobs and business to cheaper jurisdictions. In Alberta, for example, where oil and gas production are such a strong segment of the economy, there is little support for any kind of across-the-board carbon tax. Depending on how the tax is introduced, and whether it is accompanied by tax cuts, financial assistance for people with lower incomes or other incentives to encourage consumers to make choices that reduce pollution, its costs may not be distributed evenly in the economy.

Quebec was the first province to introduce a carbon tax in 2007. The levy was just under one cent for a litre of gas, with funds to pay for energy-saving initiatives such as improvements to public transit. British Columbia followed in 2008, taxing carbon-based fuels such as gasoline, diesel, natural gas, and home heating fuel, at a rate of $10 per tonne of greenhouse gases generated. The carbon tax will reach $30 per tonne in 2012. This works out to an extra 2.4 cents a litre on gasoline, increasing to 7.24 cents per litre by 2012. The provincial government has said that all carbon tax revenue—about $1.8 billion over three years—will be returned to British Columbians through reductions to income and business taxes. To soften the impact of the carbon tax, the government gave a $100 climate action dividend to each British Columbian.

Compare these taxes to those imposed in Finland, where drivers pay a carbon surtax of about eight Canadian cents per litre. In Sweden, people pay almost 40 cents extra per litre in carbon taxes at the pumps. What do you think? Could governments, businesses, and consumers be doing more? Do you agree or disagree with a green tax?

Sources: "Just What Is a Carbon Tax?" CBC News, 29 September 2008, http://www.cbc.ca/news/canadavotes/story/2008/09/19/f-carbontaxprimer.html; "Carbon Taxes: Cash Grab or Climate Saviour?" CBC News, 19 June, 2008, http://www.cbc.ca/canada/story/2008/06/18/f-carbon-tax.html; and "B.C. Carbon Tax Kicks in on Canada Day," CBC News, 1 July 2008, http://www.cbc.ca/canada/british-columbia/story/2008/06/30/bc-carbon-tax-effective.html.

FIGURE **4.6**

Socially Responsible Business Activities

Community-related activities such as participating in local fundraising campaigns, donating employee time to various non-profit organizations (including local government), and participating in urban planning and development.
Employee-related activities such as establishing equal opportunity programs, offering flextime and other benefits, promoting job enrichment, ensuring job safety, and conducting employee development programs.
Political activities such as taking a position on nuclear safety, gun control, pollution control, consumer protection, and other social issues; and working more closely with local, provincial, and federal government officials.
Support for higher education, the arts, and other non-profit social agencies.
Consumer activities such as ensuring product safety, creating truthful advertising, handling complaints promptly, setting fair prices, and conducting extensive consumer education programs.

In addition to the social audits conducted by the companies themselves, there are four types of groups that serve as watchdogs regarding how well companies enforce their ethical and social responsibility policies:

1. *Socially conscious investors* who insist that a company extend its own high standards to all its suppliers. Social responsibility investing (SRI) is on the rise. Be aware that SRI is highly subjective. Different people have different values, so what's ethically appropriate for one is not for another.
2. *Environmentalists* who apply pressure by naming names of companies that don't abide by the environmentalists' standards.
3. *Union officials* who hunt down violations and force companies to comply to avoid negative publicity.
4. *Customers* who take their business elsewhere if a company demonstrates unethical or socially irresponsible practices.

What these groups look for constantly changes as the world view changes. One important thing to remember is that it isn't enough for a company to be right when it comes to ethics and social responsibility. It also has to *convince* its customers and society that it's right.

Sustainable Development[40]

Sustainable development means implementing a process that integrates environmental, economic, and social considerations into decision making. This reinforces the World Commission on Environment and Development's conclusion that development should be sustainable for the benefit of current and future generations. Such a focus has created opportunities for new ventures such as Revive. Corporations that wish to eliminate no-longer-needed facility assets (e.g., chairs, desks, etc.) can deal with Revive, which provides a cost-effective alternative to having these items removed. These items are then redistributed to needy non-profit organizations, schools, and health clinics then receive critically needed equipment and supplies, and planet Earth is given relief from the pressures of expanding population and waste.

In another example, Canada's two largest grocery chains, Loblaw Companies Limited and Sobeys, are gradually eliminating free plastic bags at their checkout counters. The plastic bags will be available only on request, and will cost five cents each. "It represents the next natural step forward as we continue to acknowledge and respond to Canadians' desire to support environmental initiatives," Loblaw executive chairman Galen Weston Jr. said. Most of the proceeds from the sale of Loblaw's bags will be used to cover the cost of its plastic bag reduction program. As well, "we'll take some of the money and invest it in lower food prices ... [and] in our sustainability projects and a couple of environmental charities," said Weston.

Other companies have also implemented similar actions. The Liquor Control Board of Ontario (LCBO) has ended its use of plastic shopping bags, offering shoppers paper bags instead. Furniture retailer IKEA Canada charges five cents for plastic bags, donating proceeds to Tree Canada to help plant trees throughout the country. Would you shop more at a retailer that supports such initiatives?

sustainable development
Implementing a process that integrates environmental, economic, and social considerations into decision making.

Progress Assessment

- What is corporate social responsibility, and how does it relate to each of a business's major stakeholders?
- How does the strategic approach differ from the pluralist approach?
- What is a social audit, and what kinds of activities does it monitor?

INTERNATIONAL ETHICS AND SOCIAL RESPONSIBILITY

Ethical problems and issues of social responsibility are not unique to Canada. Top business and government leaders in Japan were caught in a major "influence-peddling" (read bribery) scheme in Japan. Similar charges have been brought against top officials in South Korea, the People's Republic of China, Italy, Brazil, Pakistan, and Zaire. What is new about the moral and ethical standards by which government leaders are being judged? They are much stricter than in previous years. The Reaching Beyond Our Borders box highlights some areas that require improvement in reducing corruption.

Government leaders are not the only ones being held to higher standards. Many businesses are demanding socially responsible behaviour from their international suppliers by ensuring that suppliers do not violate domestic human rights and environmental standards. For example, Sears will not knowingly import products made by Chinese prison labour. The clothing manufacturer Phillips–Van Heusen said it would cancel orders from suppliers that violate its ethical, environmental, and human rights code. McDonald's denied rumours that one of its suppliers grazed cattle on cleared rain forest land, but wrote a ban on the practice anyway.

In contrast to companies that demand that their suppliers demonstrate socially responsible behaviour are those that have been criticized for exploiting workers in less developed countries. Nike, the world's largest athletic shoe company, has been accused by human rights and labour groups of treating its workers poorly while lavishing millions of dollars on star athletes to endorse its products. Nike is working to improve its reputation, in part by joining forces with Patagonia, Gap, and five other companies and six leading anti-sweatshop groups to create a single set of labour standards with a common factory-inspection system. The goal of the Joint Initiative on Corporate Accountability & Workers' Rights, as the project is called, is to replace the current multitude of approaches with something that is easier and cheaper to use, in the hope that more companies will adopt the standards as well.[41] Nike has established key targets to be met by 2011: eliminate excessive overtime in its contract factories; implement tailored human resource management systems and educational training for workers in its focus factories; implement Freedom of Association Educational Programs in 100 percent of its focus factories; and lead multi-brand collaboration on compliance issues in 30 percent of its supply chain.[42]

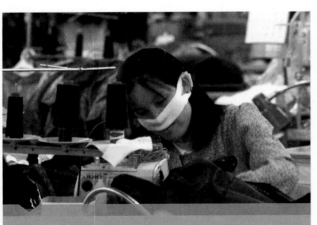

Ethical responsibility does not stop at North American borders. Many colleges and universities have adopted standards that prohibit their schools' names or logos from being displayed on apparel made in foreign sweatshops. Sweatshops are factories with very low pay and poor health and safety standards. Would you be willing to buy products from a manufacturer that produces its goods in substandard facilities in foreign nations?

The justness of requiring international suppliers to adhere to domestic ethical standards is not as clear-cut as you might think. For example, what could be considered a gift in one culture is considered a bribe in another.[43] Is it always ethical for companies to demand compliance with the standards of their own countries? What about countries in which child labour is an accepted part of the society and families depend on the children's salaries for survival? What about foreign companies doing business in Canada? Should these companies have to comply with Canadian ethical standards? What about multinational corporations? Since they span different societies, do they not have to conform to any one society's standards? None of these questions are easy to answer, but they give you some idea of the complexity of social responsibility issues in international markets. The Reaching Beyond Our Borders box highlights one external body that can assist countries in developing laws and regulations to fight corruption. The UN Global Compact (the focus of a Taking It To The Net exercise) is another organization that provides a practical framework for companies that are committed to sustainability and responsible business practices around the world.

Reaching Beyond Our Borders

An Assessment of Action on Anti-Corruption Commitments

Transparency International (TI) is the global civil society organization leading the fight against corruption. TI raises awareness of the damaging effects of corruption and works with partners in government, business, the private sector, and civil society to develop and implement effective measures to tackle corruption.

A recent report assessed commitments made by the Group of Eight (G8) since 2002 with respect to reducing corruption and found that overall, they had fallen short. While there has been significant enforcement of anti-bribery laws in France, Germany, and the United States, this has not been the case with Canada, Japan, and the United Kingdom. For example, for Canada there has been only one minor case against a company for a small payment allegedly made to a U.S. immigration official to gain access to the United States for business purposes.

Furthermore, Canada is the only Organisation for Economic Co-Operation and Development (OECD) country not to have adopted nationality jurisdiction in its legislation through the Corruption of Foreign Public Officials Act. Canadian courts apply "territorial" jurisdiction in almost all criminal matters and do not interpret it broadly. It has been recommended that the Government of Canada amend this Act to clarify that it applies extraterritorially to Canadian nationals. As it now stands, permitting nationals to pay foreign bribes as long as they do outside Canada creates an easy loophole that should be closed.

Experts have called on the Canadian government to do more to promote anti-bribery compliance programs among small- and medium-sized businesses and to make greater efforts within those agencies engaged in other countries and with foreign trade initiatives to report bribery allegations "up the line" and ultimately, to enforcement authorities.

In a positive development, following Canada's ratification of the United Nations Convention Against Corruption, the Royal Canadian Mounted Police established two International Anti-Corruption Teams that focus on the detection, investigation, and prevention of international corruption such as bribery, embezzlement, and money laundering.

Source: Reprinted from Transparency International, "2008 G8 Progress Report." Copyright 2009 Transparency International: The Global Coalition Against Corruption. Used with permission. For more information, visit www.transparency.org.

SUMMARY

1. Ethics goes beyond obeying laws. It also involves abiding by the moral standards accepted by society.

LO ▶ 1 Explain why legality is only one step in behaving ethically.

How is legality different from ethics?
Ethics reflects people's proper relation with one another. Legality is more limiting; it refers only to laws written to protect people from fraud, theft, and violence.

What influences our ethical decision making?
Ethical behaviour begins with you and me. We are influenced by our society and what it considers to be ethical, the behaviour of others (both socially and in a work setting), and by our own personal values and beliefs.

How can we tell if our business decisions are ethical?
There is no universally-accepted approach when answering this question. One suggestion is to ask yourself three questions: (1) Is it legal? (2) Is it balanced? and (3) How will it make me feel? Companies (and individuals) that develop strong ethics codes and use these three questions have a better chance than most of behaving ethically.

LO ▶ 2 Describe management's role in setting ethical standards and distinguish between compliance-based and integrity-based ethics codes.

2. Some managers think that ethics is an individual issue that has nothing to do with management, while others believe that ethics has everything to do with management.

What is management's role in setting ethical standards?

Managers often set formal ethical standards, but more important are the messages they send through their actions. Management's tolerance or intolerance of ethical misconduct influences employees more than written ethics codes do.

What's the difference between compliance-based and integrity-based ethics codes?

Whereas compliance-based ethics codes are concerned with avoiding legal punishment, integrity-based ethics codes define the organization's guiding values, create an environment that supports ethically sound behaviour, and stress a shared accountability among employees.

LO ▶ 3 List the six steps that can be considered when setting up a corporate ethics code.

3. Business ethics can be improved if companies follow a six-step process.

What are the six steps that can improve business ethics?

The six steps are as follows: (1) top management must adopt and support an explicit corporate code of conduct; (2) employees must understand that expectations for ethical behaviour begin at the top and that senior management expects all employees to act accordingly; (3) managers and others must be trained to consider the ethical implications of all business decisions; (4) an ethics office must be set up, and phone lines to the office should be established; (5) outsiders such as suppliers, subcontractors, distributors, and customers must be told about the ethics program; and (6) the ethics code must be enforced.

Which step is the most critical in this six-step process?

The last step is most critical because a company's ethics policy must be enforced to be taken seriously.

LO ▶ 4 Define corporate social responsibility and examine corporate responsibility to various stakeholders.

4. Corporate social responsibility goes beyond merely being ethical.

Define *corporate social responsibility*.

Corporate social responsibility is the concern businesses have toward stakeholders.

What are the dimensions of corporate social responsibility?

The social performance of a company has several dimensions. Corporate philanthropy includes charitable donations to non-profit groups. Corporate responsibility includes everything from hiring minority workers to making safe products. Corporate policy refers to the position a firm takes on social and political issues.

Discuss the two views of corporate responsibility to stakeholders.

The strategic approach requires that management's primary orientation be toward the economic interests of shareholders. This approach encourages managers to consider an actions' effects on stakeholders other than owners, but ultimately others' interests are secondary. Often these interests are considered only when they would adversely affect profits if ignored. The pluralist approach recognizes the special responsibility of management to optimize profits, but not at the expense of employees, suppliers, and members of the community. This approach recognizes the moral responsibilities of management that apply to all human beings. The guiding philosophy for the twenty-first century will be some version of the pluralist approach.

LO ▶ 5 Discuss the responsibility that business has to customers, investors, employees, society, and the environment

5. Business has a responsibility to many stakeholders.

What responsibility does business have to customers?

Business's responsibility to customers is to satisfy them with goods and services of real value.

What responsibility does business have to investors?

Business is responsible for making money for its investors. Implicit is that decisions are good not only for the economic bottom line but also for the social responsibility bottom line.

What responsibility does business have to employees?

Business has several responsibilities to employees: to create jobs, to maintain job security, and to see that hard work and talent are fairly rewarded. This should be accomplished within a safe work environment.

What responsibility does business have to society?

Business has several responsibilities to society: to create new wealth, to promote social justice, and to contribute to making its own environment a better place.

What responsibility does business have to the environment?

Business has the responsibility to minimize its negative impact on the environment.

How are a company's social responsibility efforts measured?

A corporate social audit measures an organization's progress toward social responsibility. Some people believe that the audit should sum the organization's positive actions and then subtract the negative effects of business to get its net social benefit.

KEY TERMS

compliance-based ethics codes 90

corporate philanthropy 94

corporate policy 95

corporate responsibility 95

corporate social initiatives 95

corporate social responsibility (CSR) 94

ethics 86

insider trading 98

integrity-based ethics codes 90

social audit 101

sustainable development 103

triple-bottom line (TBL, 3BL, or People, Planet, Profit) 101

whistleblowers 90

CRITICAL THINKING

1. Think of a situation you have been involved in that tested your ethical behaviour. For example, perhaps your best friend forgot about a term paper due the next day and asked you if he could copy and hand in a paper you wrote for another instructor last semester. What are your alternatives, and what are the consequences of each one? Would it have been easier to resolve the dilemma if you had asked yourself the three questions in the ethics check? Try answering them now and see if you would have made a different choice.

2. In Chapter 3 we discussed how the granting of subprime mortgages contributed to a crisis in the financial markets. Was it ethical for firms to provide mortgages to individuals that were unlikely to be able to afford them? How about for investors? How about for the homeowners?

3. Companies appear to act with corporate responsibility but the underlying motive seems to be to increase profits. Does this motive undermine the value of corporate responsibility or is it only the actions that are important? That is, do you think less of a company if you know it is being responsible only to increase its profits?

DEVELOPING WORKPLACE SKILLS

1. Newspapers and magazines are full of stories about individuals and businesses that are not socially responsible. What about those individuals and organizations that do take social responsibility seriously? We don't normally read or hear about them. Do a little investigative reporting of your own. Identify a public interest group in your community and identify its officers, objectives, sources and amount of financial support, and size and characteristics of membership. List some examples of its recent actions and/or accomplishments. Consider environmental groups, animal protection groups, political action committees, and so on. Call your local Chamber of Commerce, the Better Business Bureau, or local government agencies for help. Try using one of the Internet search engines to help you find more information.

2. You are the manager of a coffee house called the Morning Cup. One of your best employees wants to be promoted to a managerial position; however, the owner is grooming his son for the promotion your employee seeks. The owner's act of nepotism may hurt a valuable employee's chances for advancement, but complaining may hurt your own chances for promotion. What do you do?

3. You are a salesperson at a clothing store. You walk into the storage room to start ticketing some clothes that came in that morning and see a co-worker quickly take some pants from a box and put them into her knapsack. Your colleague does not see you enter the room. What do you do? Do you leave and not say anything to your employer? Do you say something to your colleague? Do you tell your employer about this incident? Is your responsibility to your organization, your colleague, or both? What might be the implications of your decision?

4. Contact a local corporation and ask for a copy of its written ethics code. Would you classify its code as compliance-based or integrity-based? Explain.

 ## TAKING IT TO THE NET 1

www.mcgrawhillconnect.ca

Purpose

To learn about a corporate social responsibility (CSR) resource available to support business decisions that will improve performance and contribute to a better world.

Exercise

Canadian Business for Social Responsibility (CBSR) is a non-profit, member-led organization that is committed to corporate social responsibility. Go to www.cbsr.ca and answer the following questions.

1. What is the CSBR approach?
2. Looking at the Resources tab, what are some of the recent CSR trends?
3. What is the focus of the next Summit? (Hint: Visit the Conferences & Events tab.) What are some of the workshop themes?

 ## TAKING IT TO THE NET 2

www.mcgrawhillconnect.ca

Purpose

To be aware of an external body that can help firms develop ethical codes of conduct.

Exercise

The UN Global Compact has the mandate to be both a policy platform and to provide a practical framework for companies that are committed to sustainability and responsible business practices. Visit the site (http://www.unglobalcompact.org/) and answer the following questions:

1. What are the two complementary objectives that the UN Global Compact aims to advance?
2. What are companies that voluntarily join the Global Compact expected to do?
3. Considering human rights, labour, the environment, and anti-corruption, what are the ten principles of the UN Global Compact?

ANALYZING MANAGEMENT DECISIONS

CNR Charged with Spill

Canadian National Railway (CNR) was charged by Alberta Environment with failing to take all reasonable measures to remedy and confine the spill from a train derailment into a northern Alberta lake in August 2005. In the incident, 43 cars derailed next to Wabamun Lake, west of Edmonton, spilling almost 800,000 litres of heavy fuel and a potentially cancer-causing wood preservative. The environmental offence is punishable by a maximum fine of $500,000.

Alberta Environment spokeswoman Kim Hunt said the charges were laid by Alberta Justice after a review. "It's the law in Alberta that the polluter pays," Hunt told the Canadian Press. After the spill, Alberta Environment issued an Environmental Protection Order to CNR. The company was ordered to clean up the spill, begin long-term environmental planning and monitoring of the area, and keep the public informed on its progress. Residents of Wabamun were told in June 2006 that they could use the lake again for swimming and boating, but not for washing dishes, cleaning vegetables, or bathing. At that time, CNR said in a statement that it was committed to the monitoring and testing of the lake, and announced that the cleanup was expected to be completed by the end of the month.

The spill initially left a slick on the surface of the lake and coated migrating waterfowl. While most of the oil has been removed, residents claim that balls of tar still occasionally wash up onshore. Wabamun Lake residents' committee chairman Doug Goss said that while CNR has already spent $75 million removing the mess, he hopes in future that the provincial government will clean up spills immediately and send the bill to the company responsible.

CNR offered nearly $7.5 million on a sliding scale to the area's 1,600 residents. The payments, which ranged from $1,500 to $27,000 for those closest to the spill, were in recognition of loss of property use as a result of the derailment. The Paul First Nation, whose reserve is on the western shore of the lake, also filed a multi-million-dollar lawsuit against CNR, Ottawa, and the province, alleging that the spill destroyed its traditional way of life. In September 2008, CNR reached a $10 million settlement with the band. "This money will play a major part in implementing the band's business development plan, which we are confident will result in a much stronger economic situation for our people," said Chief Daniel Paul. Earlier in 2008, three charges were laid by Environment Canada and Fisheries and Oceans Canada against CNR: one for allegedly depositing a substance harmful to migratory birds into a lake and the other two for alleged disruption of a fish habitat.

Sources: "Canadian National Railway to Pay $10M to Alta. Band in Derailment Along Lake," CANOE Inc., 12 September 2008, http://cnews.canoe.ca/CNEWS/Politics/2008/09/12/6751421-cp.html; "Oil Spill Nets CN Rail Three Charges from Feds," *Canadian Geographic*, 18 March 2008, http://www.canadiangeographic.ca/cea/archives/news_item.asp?articleid=493; Gordon Kent and Kelly Cryderman, "Wabamun Residents Unhappy with CN Charge," CanWest News Service, 6 June 2006, http://www.canada.com/topics/news/national/story.html?id=14a77881-cc1b-4ec0-90a7-fd86af5a9c7c&k=58041; and "CN Rail Charged in Oil Spill at Alta. Lake," The Canadian Press, 6 June 2006, http://sympaticomsn.ctv.ca/servlet/ArticleNews/story/CTVNews/20060605/cn_wabamun_060506.

Discussion Questions

1. What stakeholders were impacted by this incident?

2. Conduct some research into this story. As a result of this derailment, what changes were implemented by CNR and Environment Alberta?

3. Do you feel that the costs associated with this incident are excessive? Explain.

RUNNING CASE

Canadian Tire Financial Services: Adapting to the Business Environment

As the financial arm of Canadian Tire Corporation, Ltd. (Canadian Tire), Canadian Tire Financial Services (CTFS) primarily engages in financing and managing the Canadian Tire Options® MasterCard for more than five million card members. CTFS also markets related financial products and services to retail and petroleum customers including personal loans, insurance and warranty products, and emergency roadside assistance through the Canadian Tire Auto Club. A banking pilot is currently underway at Canadian Tire Bank offering high-interest savings accounts, guaranteed investment certificates, residential mortgages, and the One-and-Only™ account.

CTFS originated in 1961 as Midland Shoppers Credit Limited, a small financial services company offering third-party credit processing for local retailers. During the 1960s, the Canadian Tire Associate Stores became clients. In 1968, Midland became a subsidiary of Canadian Tire Corporation and was renamed Canadian Tire Acceptance Limited (CTAL). In the decades that followed, CTAL continued to provide credit processing. In 1995, it became the first non-deposit-taking financial institution worldwide to launch a MasterCard. In 2000, it expanded the Canadian Tire "Money" loyalty program by launching Canadian Tire "Money" On The Card. People could accumulate Canadian Tire "Money" On The Card by using their MasterCard anywhere in the world and redeem Canadian Tire "Money" On The Card in any Canadian Tire store on merchandise, auto parts, or auto labour.

Changes to the Bank Act in 2001 created opportunities for non-traditional banks to enter the Canadian industry. During this time, a project group was formed and consultants were hired to investigate the benefits of creating a bank. A major benefit would be that CTFS would need to comply with one set of federal rules and legislation rather than to the individual provincial and territorial government rules and legislation. As well, CTFS would be able to compete with what banks could offer. Third, a bank structure would change the terms and conditions of existing products. In 2002, CTAL's name was changed to Canadian Tire Financial Services to better reflect the company's stronger and broader position within the financial services industry. In 2003, CTFS established Canadian Tire Bank to enable greater marketing flexibility for its card operations, and to facilitate continued expansion into the high growth bank card market. Canadian Tire Bank is a federally chartered, federally regulated bank. Operating the credit card business under Canadian Tire Bank enables the company to offer customers credit card services consistently across the country.

As part of its 2007–2012 Strategic Plan, CTFS continues its focus on growth in the areas of insurance and warranty, the credit card portfolio, and its retail banking products. Approximately 46 percent of Canadian Tire's 2009 first quarter earnings were generated by CTFS's activities. Looking at 2009 alone, CTFS will be relaunching credit cards with PayPass® capability, testing new credit cards, and providing select investments in balance transfer offers.

Each year, corporate donations to the community exceed $1 million. CTFS believes that a portion of its earnings should be reinvested into the community from which they are derived. Overarching CTFS committees work to support different charities and worthy causes. For example, the Corporate Donations Committee sets aside an annual budget with a third allocated to sports (e.g., employee and youth teams), a third allocated to the arts (e.g., Niagara Symphony, local theatres, etc.), and a third allocated to the community (e.g., Welland Food Festival). Employees contribute to some of these causes as evidenced by the annual Employee Giving Campaign. In 2008, more than $286,000 was raised for local charities through this endeavour. More recently, and in partnership with Canadian Tire Jumpstart Charities, CTFS raised $300,000 in support of Goodwill's Stokes Community Village and the Niagara-area Canadian Tire Jumpstart Chapter.

Sources: "Canadian Tire Corporation Overview," Canadian Tire Corporation, Ltd., 9 June 2009, http://corp.canadiantire.ca/EN/Pages/default.aspx; Lara V. Strebul, Senior Communications Consultant Corporate Communications, Canadian Tire Financial Services, interview, 9 June 2009; Marco Marrone, President, Canadian Tire Financial Services, interviews, 13 August 2008 and 10 March 2006; and *Canadian Tire Financial Times*, Spring 2008 and Fall/Winter 2007.

Discussion Questions

1. List some stakeholders that must be considered when top executives at CTFS develop policies and strategies.

2. How does CTFS incorporate social responsibility in its business practices? How does the company benefit as a result of this community involvement?

3. Consider the elements in the business environment. What are some trends that must be analyzed as CTFS moves forward with its growth strategy?

CHAPTER 5

Forms of Business Ownership

LEARNING OBJECTIVES

AFTER YOU HAVE READ AND STUDIED THIS CHAPTER, YOU SHOULD BE ABLE TO:

LO ▶ 1 List the advantages and disadvantages of sole proprietorships.

LO ▶ 2 Describe the advantages and disadvantages of partnerships. Include the differences between general and limited partners.

LO ▶ 3 Discuss the advantages and disadvantages of corporations.

LO ▶ 4 Define and give examples of three types of corporate mergers, and explain the role of leveraged buyouts and taking a firm private.

LO ▶ 5 Outline the advantages and disadvantages of franchises, and discuss the challenges of global franchising.

LO ▶ 6 Describe the role of co-operatives in Canada.

Getting to Know Michelle Strum and David Eisnor, Co-Owners of Halifax Backpackers Hostel

Michelle Strum and David Eisnor have been friends for all of their lives. They have travelled extensively and lived for many months in various hostels around the world. With the number of travellers visiting Halifax growing, they felt that there would be a need for more budget accommodations in the city.

Their first business expense was a personal computer. On the day after they made this purchase, they registered their business name, Halifax Backpackers Hostel. The hostel provides budget accommodation for travellers who can share rooms or come together in common areas, such as the kitchen where they can prepare their own meals or the café that is run by another local entrepreneur. Guests also have access to the Internet and laundry facilities.

From the day they opened Halifax Backpackers Hostel in August 2001, Strum and Eisnor knew it was going to take off. "We were full from that day right into the middle of October," says Strum. "It was quite amazing." Since opening, they bought the building that houses the hostel, doubled the accommodation it provides, and continue to focus on efforts to help revitalize the neighbourhood.

Getting started required a lot of elbow grease and hard work by the partners, who quickly learned about doing renovations themselves and the challenges of financing the business. They received two $15,000 young entrepreneur loans, applied for a bunch of credit cards and did a lot of bartending to pay for drywall! "We've had to be creative," explains Eisnor. "For example, in the summertime, we share employees with the café owner to cut down on payroll costs."

Whether you dream of going into business for yourself, starting a business with a friend, or someday leading a major corporation, it's important to know that each form of business ownership has advantages and disadvantages. You will learn more about them in this chapter.

Sources: "History—Our Story," Halifax Backpackers Hostel, 13 September 2008, www.halifaxbackpackers.com; Bonnie Schiedel, "Spirit: A Hundred Grand," *Chatelaine*, November 2005, http://www.northstarwriting.ca/articles/article_100K.html; and "Co-owners David Eisnor and Michelle Strum Win BDC's Young Entrepreneur Award for Nova Scotia," Business Development Bank of Canada, 19 October 2004, http://www.bdc.ca/en/about/mediaroom/news_releases/2004/2004101903.htm.

STARTING A SMALL BUSINESS

Like Michelle Strum and David Eisnor, thousands of people start new businesses in Canada every year. Chances are, you have thought of owning your own business or know someone who has. One key to success in starting a new business is understanding how to get the resources you need. You may have to take on partners or find other ways of obtaining money. To stay in business, you may need help from someone with more expertise than you have in certain areas, or you may need to raise more money to expand. How you form your business can make a tremendous difference in your long-term success. You can form a business in one of several ways. The three major forms of business ownership are (1) sole proprietorships, (2) partnerships, and (3) corporations.

It can be easy to get started in your own business. You can begin a word-processing service out of your home, open a car repair centre, start a restaurant, develop a Web site, or go about meeting other unmet wants and needs in your community. A **sole proprietorship** is one person owning and operating a business, without forming a corporation.[1] (We will discuss corporations soon.) In a sole proprietorship, the business and the owner are a single entity. As noted in Figure 5.1, almost 24 percent of all registered businesses in Canada fall under this form of ownership.

Many people do not have the money, time, or desire to run a business on their own. They prefer to have someone else or a group of people get together to form the business. When two or more people legally agree to become co-owners of a business, the organization is called a **partnership**.

There are advantages to creating a business that is separate and distinct from the owners. A legal entity with authority to act and have liability separate from its owners is called a **corporation**. There are more than 1.5 million corporations in Canada, and they have the largest share of business revenue by far, as noted in Figure 5.1.

As you will learn in this chapter, each form of business ownership has advantages and disadvantages. It is important to understand these advantages and disadvantages before attempting to start a business. Keep in mind that just because a business starts in one form of ownership, it doesn't have to stay in that form. Many companies start out in one form, then add (or drop) a partner or two, and eventually may become corporations. The advantages and disadvantages that are highlighted in this chapter may give you an idea of why there may be a change in ownership form as the business grows.

Another thing that must be looked at before proceeding is the meaning of the term *liability*. **Liability** is often just another word for debt, but it also has a wider and important meaning, as you will see in the following pages. Liability for a business includes the responsibility to pay all normal debts and to pay:

1. Because of a court order
2. Because of a law

---

sole proprietorship
A business that is owned and operated by one person, without forming a corporation.

partnership
A legal form of business with two or more parties.

corporation
A legal entity with authority to act and have liability separate from its owners.

liability
For a business, it includes the responsibility to pay all normal debts and to pay because of a court order or law, for performance under a contract, or payment of damages to a person or property in an accident.

FIGURE 5.1

Business Distribution by Type, Number, and Revenue
The category of *partnerships/joint ventures* represents unincorporated businesses.

Business Type	Number of Businesses	Business (%)	Revenue (%)
Incorporations	1,576,866	69.1	88.9
Sole Proprietorships	544,858	23.9	2.9
Partnerships/Joint Ventures	100,860	4.4	5.4
Other/Unknown	51,646	2.3	0.9
Government	7,413	0.3	1.4
Trust and Special Funds	1,328	0.1	0.5
Total	**2,282,971**		**100.0**

Source: "Business Distribution by Type, Number, and Revenue," adapted from Statistics Canada, special tabulation, unpublished data (Business Register Database), June 2008.

3. For performance under a contract

4. For damages to a person or property

Let's begin our discussion by looking at the most basic form of ownership—the sole proprietorship.

SOLE PROPRIETORSHIPS

Advantages of Sole Proprietorships

Sole proprietorships are the easiest kind of businesses for you to explore in your quest for an interesting career. Every town has sole proprietors you can visit. Talk with some of these business people about the joys and frustrations of being on their own. Most will mention the benefits of being their own boss and setting their own hours. Other advantages they mention may include the following:

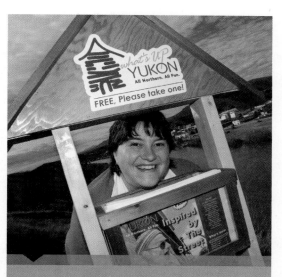

Tammy Beese started *What's Up Yukon*, a free weekly magazine that features 100 percent local content. Printed on newsprint, the magazine covers Yukon news about arts and culture, sports and recreation, and "all things fun and entertainment."

1. *Ease of starting and ending the business.* All you have to do to start a sole proprietorship is buy or lease the needed equipment (e.g., a saw, a word processor, a tractor, a lawn mower) and put up some announcements saying you are in business. It is just as easy to get out of business; you simply stop. There is no one to consult or to disagree with about such decisions. You may have to get a permit or licence from the local government, but often that is no problem.

2. *Being your own boss.* As noted earlier, this is one of the most common reasons cited for starting a sole proprietorship. Working for others simply does not have the same excitement as working for yourself—at least, that's the way sole proprietors feel. You may make mistakes, but they are your mistakes—and so are the many small victories encountered each day.

3. *Pride of ownership.* People who own and manage their own businesses are rightfully proud of their work. They deserve all the credit for taking the risks and providing needed products.

4. *Retention of company profit.* Other than the joy of being your own boss, there is nothing like the pleasure of knowing that you can earn as much as possible and not have to share that money with anyone else (except the government, in taxes).

5. *No special taxes.* All profits of a sole proprietorship are taxed as the personal income of the owner, and the owner pays the normal personal income tax on that money. Another tax advantage for sole proprietors is that they can claim any business losses against other earned income. These losses would decrease the personal taxes they would need to pay. Understanding tax planning is an important factor in choosing the appropriate form of business organization and often requires the advice of professional accountants.

6. *Less regulation.* While proprietorships are regulated by the provincial/territorial governments, and the proprietorship may have to be registered, overall they are less regulated than corporations.[2] As well, the administration of a proprietorship is less costly than that of a corporation.

Disadvantages of Sole Proprietorships

Not everyone is equipped to own and manage a business. Often it is difficult to save enough money to start a business and keep it going. The costs of inventory, supplies, insurance, advertising, rent, computers, utilities, and so on may be too much to cover alone. Other disadvantages of owning your own business are listed on the next page.

unlimited liability
The responsibility of business owners for all of the debts of the business.

1. *Unlimited liability—the risk of personal losses.* When you work for others, it is their problem if the business is not profitable. When you own your own business, you and the business are considered one. You have **unlimited liability**; that is, any debts or damages incurred by the business are your debts and you must pay them, even if it means selling your home, your car, or whatever else you own. This is a serious risk, and one that requires not only thought but also discussion with a lawyer, an insurance agent, an accountant, and others.

2. *Limited financial resources.* Funds available to the business are limited to the funds that the one (sole) owner can gather. Since there are serious limits to how much money one person can raise, partnerships and corporations have a greater probability of obtaining the needed financial backing to start a business and keep it going.

3. *Management difficulties.* All businesses need management; that is, someone must keep inventory records, accounting records, tax records, and so forth. Many people who are skilled at selling things or providing a service are not so skilled at keeping records. Sole proprietors often find it difficult to attract good, qualified employees to help run the business because they cannot compete with the salary and benefits offered by larger companies.

4. *Overwhelming time commitment.* Though sole proprietors may say they set their own hours, it's hard to own a business, manage it, train people, and have time for anything else in life. This is true of any business, but a sole proprietor has no one with whom to share the burden. The owner often must spend long hours working. The owner of a store, for example, may put in 12 hours a day, at least six days a week—almost twice the hours worked by a non-supervisory employee in a large company. Imagine how this time commitment affects the sole proprietor's family life. Tim DeMello, founder of the successful company Wall Street Games Inc., echoes countless other sole proprietors when he says, "It's not a job, it's not a career, it's a way of life."

5. *Few fringe benefits.* If you are your own boss, you lose the fringe benefits that often come from working for others. You have no paid health insurance, no paid disability insurance, no sick leave, and no vacation pay. These and other benefits may add up to approximately 30 percent of a worker's income.[3]

6. *Limited growth.* Expansion is often slow since a sole proprietorship relies on its owner for most of its creativity, business know-how, and funding.

7. *Limited lifespan.* If the sole proprietor dies, is incapacitated, or retires, the business no longer exists, unless it is sold or taken over by the sole proprietor's heirs. While the net business assets pass to the heirs, valuable leases and contracts may not.[4]

8. *Possibly pay higher taxes.* If the business's income exceeds $400,000, it will usually be paying higher taxes than if it was incorporated as a Canadian Controlled Private Corporation (CCPC).[5] That is, tax rates are more advantageous if the business is incorporated. We will expand on this point later on in the chapter under the corporations discussion.

Talk with a few local sole proprietors about the problems they have faced in being on their own. They are likely to have many interesting stories to tell about problems in getting loans from the bank, problems with theft, problems simply keeping up with the business, and so on. These problems are also reasons why many sole proprietors choose to find partners to share the load.

Progress Assessment

- What are the three forms of business ownership?
- Most people who start businesses in Canada are sole proprietors. What are the advantages and disadvantages of sole proprietorships?
- Why would unlimited liability be considered a major drawback of sole proprietorships?

PARTNERSHIPS

A partnership is a legal form of business with two or more parties. The business can be a partnership of individuals, corporations, trusts, other partnerships, or a combination of these.[6] Two types of partnerships are general partnerships and limited partnerships. A **general partnership** is a partnership in which all owners share in operating the business and in assuming liability for the business's debts. A **limited partnership** is a partnership with one or more general partners and one or more limited partners.

A **general partner** is an owner (partner) who has unlimited liability and is active in managing the firm. Every partnership must have at least one general partner. A **limited partner** is an owner who invests money in the business but does not have any management responsibility or liability for losses beyond the investment. **Limited liability** means that limited partners are not responsible for the debts of the business beyond the amount of their investment—their liability is limited to the amount they put into the company; therefore, their personal assets are not at risk.

Advantages of Partnerships

There are many advantages to having one or more partners in a business, as we will list for you next. Some professionals who enjoy the advantages of partnerships today are physicians, lawyers, dentists, and accountants. The advantages of a partnership include the following:

1. *More financial resources.* When two or more people pool their money and credit, it is easier to pay the rent, utilities, and other bills incurred by a business. A limited partnership is specially designed to help raise capital (money). As mentioned earlier, a limited partner invests money in the business but cannot legally have any management responsibility and has limited liability. Read the Reaching Beyond Our Borders box for how taking on a partner has allowed Inder Bedi to grow his business.

2. *Shared management and pooled/complementary skills and knowledge.* It is simply much easier to manage the day-to-day activities of a business with carefully chosen partners. Partners give each other free time from the business and provide different skills and perspectives. Some people find that the best partner is a spouse. That is why you see so many husband-and-wife teams managing restaurants, service shops, and other businesses.

3. *Longer survival.* One study that examined 2,000 businesses started since 1960 reported that partnerships were four times as likely to succeed as sole proprietorships. Being watched by a partner can help a business person become more disciplined.

4. *Shared risk.* A partnership shares the risk among the owners. This includes financial risk in starting the business and ongoing risks as the business grows.

5. *No special taxes.* As with sole proprietorships, all profits of partnerships are taxed as the personal income of the owners, and the owners pay the normal income tax on that money. Similarly, any business losses can be used to decrease earned income from other sources.

6. *Less regulation.* Like a sole proprietorship, a partnership is less regulated than a corporation.

Disadvantages of Partnerships

Any time two people must agree, there is the possibility of conflict and tension. Partnerships have caused splits among families, friends, and marriages. Let's explore the disadvantages of partnerships:

1. *Unlimited liability.* Each general partner is liable for the debts of the firm, no matter who was responsible for causing those debts. You are liable for your partners' mistakes as well as your own. Like sole proprietors, general partners can lose their homes, cars, and everything else they own if the business loses a lawsuit or goes bankrupt.

general partnership
A partnership in which all owners share in operating the business and in assuming liability for the business's debts.

limited partnership
A partnership with one or more general partners and one or more limited partners.

general partner
An owner (partner) who has unlimited liability and is active in managing the firm.

limited partner
An owner who invests money in the business but does not have any management responsibility or liability for losses beyond the investment.

limited liability
The responsibility of a business's owners for losses only up to the amount they invest; limited partners and shareholders have limited liability.

Reaching Beyond Our Borders

Bags That Travel

It started with a challenge to forgo animal products for thirty days. Today, matt & nat's line of vegan handbags and wallets for men and women is known to an ever-growing number of consumers across Canada, the United States, and Europe. Celebrity followers include Brad Pitt, Eva Mendes, and Natalie Portman. Founded eleven years ago by Inder Bedi, 35, the company has expanded to include 18 employees, an office in the United Kingdom, and revenues that have grown 1,000 percent from 2001 to 2007.

Bedi started matt & nat fresh out of university. "I dreamed of something that no one else in the market was doing: a lifestyle brand that embraces a philosophy of positivity and is environmentally conscious," he says. "Being a vegetarian, I wanted the line to be cruelty-free, using no animal products. But beyond that, I wanted the product to reflect a philosophy, which is why there is a positivity message stamped on all bags, something that has universal appeal."

When he began, Bedi lived with family until he saved enough money to fund the business start-up, while learning everything he could about design and the trade. "In the first years of the company, the line was produced locally in Montreal," says Bedi. "I got to the point where I wanted to bring the business to the next level. Seven years ago, I brought in a business partner and we took production to Asia. This allowed us to make the line more affordable, while maintaining our designer appeal. Due to the attention we give to design and details, we have managed to maintain the perception of a high-end line while taking it to mass market."

matt & nat has successfully distinguished itself in the crowded fashion accessories industry with three key factors: fashion-forward designs, a philosophy, and reasonable pricing. The company targets boutique businesses and has, over time, defined a recognizable matt & nat style that appeals to a wide range of people. "We keep our designs as practical as possible without compromising style. Our strategy is to carefully select who we sell to and be the most affordable line in high-end stores," says Bedi. matt & nat has garnered attention in the fashion media for its distinctive message tags and eco-conscious offerings. "We have specifically chosen not to advertise through traditional ways," adds Bedi. "We want the brand and the product to speak for themselves."

The company opened an office in London, England, three years ago and is developing its presence internationally with sales representatives throughout Canada, as well as in the United States, Germany, Poland, and Dubai. Distribution agreements are in the works with Japan, Korea, and Sweden. "Long-term, we would be looking to open our own showrooms as well as matt & nat concept stores throughout North America," says Bedi.

Sources: "About Us," matt & nat, 2008, http://www.mattandnat.ca/about_us; and "Inder Bedi Wins BDC's Young Entrepreneur Award for Québec," Business Development Bank of Canada, 16 October 2007, http://www.bdc.ca/en/about/mediaroom/news_releases/2007/2007101603.htm.

2. *Division of profits.* Sharing risk means sharing profits, and that can cause conflicts. There is no set system for dividing profits in a partnership, so profits are not always divided evenly. For example, two people form a partnership in which one puts in more money and the other puts in more hours working the business. Each may feel justified in asking for a bigger share of the profits. Imagine the resulting conflict.

3. *Disagreements among partners.* Disagreements over money are just one example of potential conflict in a partnership. If things are going badly, one partner may blame the other. Who has final authority over employees? Who hires and fires employees? Who works what hours? What if one partner wants to buy expensive equipment for the firm and the other partner disagrees? Potential conflicts are many. All too often, not enough effort is spent at the creation of the partnership delineating the nature of the relationship through a partnership agreement. Because of such problems, all the terms of the partnership should be spelled out in writing to protect all parties and to minimize misunderstandings.[7] Figure 5.2 gives you some ideas about what should be included in a partnership agreement. The Spotlight on Small Business offers some suggestions on what to consider when choosing the right partner.

4. *Difficult to terminate.* Once you have committed yourself to a partnership, it is not easy to get out of it (other than by death, which immediately terminates the partnership). Sure, you can end a partnership just by quitting. However, questions about who gets what and what happens next are often very difficult to solve when the partnership ends. Surprisingly, law firms often have faulty **partnership agreements** (legal documents that specify the rights and responsibilities of each partner) and find that breaking up is hard to do. How do you get rid of a partner you don't like? It is best to decide such questions up front in the partnership agreement. In the absence of an agreement, or if certain provisions are not addressed in the agreement, provincial or territorial laws will determine some or all of the terms of the partnership.[8]

5. *Possibly pay higher taxes.* Similar to a sole proprietorship, if the partnership is very profitable, it may be paying higher taxes than if it was incorporated as a Canadian Controlled Private Corporation (CCPC).[9]

The best way to learn about the advantages and disadvantages of partnerships is to interview several people who have experience with such agreements. They will give you insights and hints on how to avoid problems. The Making Ethical Decisions box leaves you with a dilemma to consider when it comes to making decisions in a partnership.

One common fear of owning your own business or having a partner is the fear of losing everything you own if the business loses a lot of money or someone sues the business. Many business people try to avoid this and the other disadvantages of sole proprietorships and partnerships by forming corporations. We discuss this basic form of business ownership in the next section.

partnership agreement
Legal document that specifies the rights and responsibilities of each partner

Progress Assessment

- What is the difference between a limited partner and a general partner?
- What are some of the advantages and disadvantages of partnerships?
- State four provisions usually included in a partnership agreement.

SPOTLIGHT ON Small Business

Choose Your Partner

Suppose you need money and want help running your business, and you decide to take on a partner. You know that partnerships are like marriages and that you won't really know the other person until after you live together. How do you choose the right partner? Before you plunge into a partnership, do three things:

1. Talk to people who have been in successful—and unsuccessful—partnerships. Find out what worked and what didn't. Ask them how conflicts were resolved and how decisions were made.

2. Interview your prospective partner very carefully. Do you share the same goals? What skills does the person have? Are they the same as yours, or do they complement your skills? What contacts, resources, or special attributes will the person bring to the business? Do you both feel the same about family members working for the business? Do you share the same vision of the company's future?

3. Evaluate your prospective partner as a decision maker. Ask yourself, "Is this someone with whom I could happily share authority for all major business decisions?"

As in a good marriage, the best way to avoid major conflicts is to begin with an honest communication of what each partner expects to give and get from the partnership.

Making Ethical Decisions

Outsourcing or Outsmarting?

Imagine that you and your partner own a construction company. You receive a bid from a subcontractor that you know is 20 percent too low. Such a loss to the subcontractor could put him out of business. Accepting the bid will certainly improve your chances of winning the contract for a big shopping centre project. Your partner wants to take the bid and let the subcontractor suffer the consequences of his bad estimate. What do you think you should do? What will be the consequences of your decision?

FIGURE | 5.2

Partnership Agreement Provisions

It's not hard to form a partnership, but it's wise for each prospective partner to get the counsel of a lawyer experienced with such agreements. Lawyers' services are usually expensive, so would-be partners should read all about partnerships and reach some basic agreements before calling a lawyer.

For your protection, be sure to put your partnership agreement in writing. The following provisions are usually included in a partnership agreement:

1. The name of the business. All provinces require the firm's name to be registered with the province if the firm's name is different from the name of any of the partners.
2. The names and addresses of all partners.
3. The purpose and nature of the business, the location of the principal offices, and any other locations where business will be conducted.
4. The date the partnership will start and how long it will last. Will it exist for a specific length of time, or will it stop when one of the partners dies or when the partners agree to discontinue?
5. The contributions made by each partner. Will some partners contribute money, while others provide real estate, personal property, expertise, or labour? When are the contributions due?
6. The management responsibilities. Will all partners have equal voices in management, or will there be senior and junior partners?
7. The duties of each partner.
8. The salaries and drawing accounts of each partner.
9. Provision for sharing of profits or losses.
10. Provision for accounting procedures. Who'll keep the accounts? What bookkeeping and accounting methods will be used? Where will the books be kept?
11. The requirements for taking in new partners.
12. Any special restrictions, rights, or duties of any partner.
13. Provision for a retiring partner.
14. Provision for the purchase of a deceased or retiring partner's share of the business.
15. Provision for how grievances will be handled.
16. Provision for how to dissolve the partnership and distribute the assets to the partners.

CORPORATIONS

Although the word *corporation* makes people think of big businesses such as the Bank of Montreal or Irving Oil, it is not necessary to be big to incorporate (start a corporation). Obviously, many corporations are big. However, incorporating may be beneficial for small businesses also.

A corporation is a federally or provincially chartered legal entity with authority to act and have liability separate from its owners. The corporation's owners (called stockholders/shareholders, as they hold stock/shares of ownership in the company) are not liable for the debts or any other problems of the corporation beyond the money they invest. Corporate stockholders do not have to worry about losing their houses, cars, and other personal property if the business cannot pay its bills—a very significant benefit. A corporation not only limits the liability of owners, but it also enables many people to share in the ownership (and profits) of a business without working there or having other commitments to it. We will discuss the rights of stockholders in Chapter 11.

In Canada, corporations are divided into two classes: public and private. A **public corporation** has the right to issue stock (ownership in the company through shares) to the public, which means its shares may be listed on a stock exchange. This offers the possibility of raising large amounts of capital, regardless of the size of the company. That is, public corporations can be small and large companies.

A **private corporation** is not allowed to issue stock to the public, so its shares are not listed on a stock exchange, and it is limited to 50 or fewer stockholders. This greatly reduces the costs of incorporating. Many small corporations are in the private category. This is the vehicle employed by individuals or partners who do not anticipate the need for substantial financing but want to take advantage of limited liability. Private corporations can be very large. Examples include Sun Life Assurance of Canada, Katz Group, and Honda Canada.

There are several advantages that Canadian-owned private corporations have over public corporations, especially from a taxation perspective. For example, a Canadian controlled private corporation (CCPC) pays a much lower rate of federal tax (small business rate) on the first $400,000 (in 2007) of active business income than would be paid by an unincorporated business, due to the small business deduction.[10] The combined federal and provincial small business tax rate varies from approximately 16 percent to 22 percent, depending on the province, and the threshold amount subject to the lower rate also varies between provinces.[11] With each federal and provincial budget, accountants study the impact of changes to corporate taxes. Such was the case when the 2006 federal budget reduced the general corporate tax rate from 21 percent to 19 percent, effective 1 January 2010.[12]

Another important advantage for the owner of a private corporation is that he or she can issue stock to a daughter, a son, or a spouse, making them co-owners of the company. This procedure is not available to a sole proprietor. It is a simple and useful way of recognizing the contribution of these or other family members, or employees, to the company. This procedure may also be a good way for the owner to prepare for retirement by gradually transferring ownership and responsibility to those who will be inheriting the business.

Keep in mind that with any kind of succession planning in private corporations, conflict may arise. In the mid-1990s, brothers Wallace and Harrison McCain of McCain Foods were bitterly divided over who should be picked to lead the company when they were gone. Wallace wanted his son Michael to take over, while Harrison preferred outside management. The fight ultimately wound up in a New Brunswick court, which sided with Harrison. Ousted from the company, Wallace ended up in Toronto, where he took over Maple Leaf Foods with sons Michael and Scott.[13] The Dealing with Change box discusses some of the challenges associated with taking over a family business.

public corporation
Corporation that has the right to issue shares to the public, so its shares may be listed on a stock exchange.

private corporation
Corporation that is not allowed to issue stock to the public, so its shares are not listed on stock exchanges; it is limited to 50 or fewer shareholders.

Chapman's Ice Cream is a private corporation. Started in 1973 by David and Penny Chapman, it is now Canada's largest independent ice cream manufacturer. Did you know that vanilla is the world's most popular ice cream flavour?

To find out the details on how one would set up a corporation, visit the Business Start-Up Assistant site at http://bsa.canadabusiness.ca.

There is a formal procedure for forming a corporation that involves applying to the appropriate federal or provincial agency. It is always recommended that company owners seek the services of a competent lawyer and accountant prior to proceeding with any incorporation. The procedure for large or public corporations is much more complex and expensive and definitely requires hiring a legal firm. These costs can easily run into the thousands of dollars.

Advantages of Corporations

Most people are prepared to risk some pre-determined amount when they invest in a business, but are not willing to risk everything to go into business. Yet, for businesses to grow and prosper and create economic opportunity, many people need to invest their money. One way to manage the risk is to create an artificial being, an entity that exists only in the eyes of the law—a corporation. A corporation has a separate legal identity from the owners—the stockholders—of the company. The corporation files its own tax returns. This entity is a technique for involving people in business without risking their other personal assets. Advantages include:

1. *Limited liability.* A major advantage of corporations is the limited liability of owners. Many corporations in Canada have the letters *Ltd.* after their name. This stands for "limited liability," probably the most significant advantage of corporations. Remember, limited liability means that the owners of a business are responsible for losses only up to the amount they invest. Corporations can also end their names with *Inc.* or *Corp.* to indicate their status.

   Be aware that you should not incorporate if it is your intention to use this ownership form as a way to avoid your debts. As a sole proprietorship or partnership, the debts the business incurs remain personal liabilities even after they are taken over by a corporation. Legally, it is the status existing at the time the debts were incurred that governs, not what happens subsequently.

2. *More money for investment.* To raise money, a corporation can sell ownership (stock) to anyone who is interested. This means that thousands of people can own part of major companies such as Rogers Communications Inc., TD Bank Financial Group, Manulife Financial Corp., EnCana Corp., Canadian National Railway Co., Loblaw Companies Ltd., and smaller companies as well. If a company sold 1 million shares for $50 each, it would have $50 million available to build plants, buy materials, hire people, manufacture products, and so on. Such a large amount of money would be difficult to raise any other way.

The TDL Group (owner of the Tim Hortons chain) was a private corporation owned by Wendy's International, Inc. In 2006, Wendy's sold 15 percent of the TDL Group to raise approximately $671 million. This money was used to repay debt owed by Wendy's. Today, Tim Hortons is considered the fourth largest publicly traded quick service restaurant chain in North America.

FIGURE 5.3

Canada's Largest Publicly Traded Corporations

Rank	Company	2008 Revenue ($ Billions)	Industry Group
1	Royal Bank of Canada	$37.6	Financial Services
2	Power Corp. of Canada	$37.1	Conglomerates
3	Manulife Financial	$33.0	Insurance
4	George Weston Ltd.	$32.1	Retail Services
5	EnCana Corp.	$31.2	Major Integrated Oil and Gas

Source: "Canada's 500 Largest Corporations 2009," *Financial Post Business Magazine*, 2 June 2009, 42. Material reprinted with the express permission of The National Post Company.

Corporations can also borrow money from individual investors by issuing bonds. Corporations may also find it easier to obtain loans from financial institutions, since lenders find it easier to place a value on the company when they can review how the shares are trading. Many small or individually owned corporations that do not trade actively may not have such opportunities, however. You can read about how corporations raise funds through the sale of stock and bonds in Chapter 11.

3. *Size.* That one word summarizes many of the advantages of some corporations. Because they have the ability to raise large amounts of money to work with, corporations can build modern factories or software development facilities with the latest equipment. They can also hire experts or specialists in all areas of operation. Furthermore, they can buy other corporations in other fields to diversify their risk. (What this means is that a corporation can be involved in many businesses at once so that if one is not doing well, the negative impact on the total corporation is lessened.) In short, a large corporation with numerous resources can take advantage of opportunities anywhere in the world.

When one considers size, different criteria can be used. This can include the number of employees, revenues, assets, and profits. Note that corporations do not have to be large to enjoy the benefits of incorporation. Professionals (such as physicians and lawyers) can incorporate, as will soon be highlighted in the discussion of professional corporations. Other individuals and partnerships can also incorporate. Figure 5.3 lists some of Canada's largest publicly traded corporations.

4. *Perpetual life.* Because corporations are separate from those who own them, the death of one or more owners does not terminate the corporation.

5. *Ease of ownership change.* It is easy to change the owners of a corporation. All that is necessary is to sell the stock to someone else.

6. *Ease of drawing talented employees.* Corporations can attract skilled employees by offering benefits such as a pension plan, dental plan, and stock options (the right to purchase shares of the corporation for a fixed price). To be competitive, sole proprietorships and partnerships may offer money or other benefits to compete with such plans.

7. *Separation of ownership from management.* Corporations are able to raise money from many different investors without getting them involved in management. A corporate hierarchy is shown in Figure 5.4.

The pyramid in Figure 5.4 shows that the owners/stockholders are separate from the managers and employees. The owners/stockholders elect a board of directors. The directors hire the officers of the corporation and oversee major policy issues. The owners/stockholders thus have some say in who runs the corporation, but they have no control over the daily operations.

How Owners Affect Management
Owners have an influence on how business is managed by electing a board of directors. The board hires the top managers (or fires them). It also sets the pay for top managers. Top managers then select other managers and employees with the help of the human resources department.

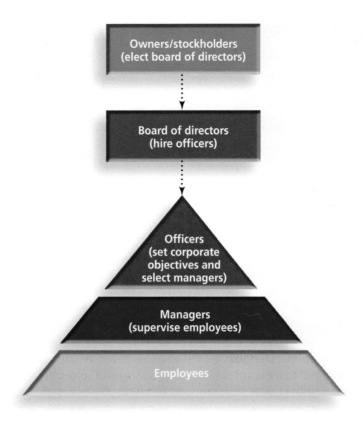

Disadvantages of Corporations

There are so many sole proprietorships and partnerships in Canada that clearly there must be some disadvantages to incorporating. Otherwise, more people would incorporate their businesses. The following are a few of the disadvantages:

1. *Extensive paperwork.* The paperwork filed to start a corporation is just the beginning. Tax laws demand that a corporation prove that all of its expenses and deductions are legitimate. Corporations must therefore process many forms. A sole proprietor or a partnership may keep rather broad accounting records; a corporation, in contrast, must keep detailed financial records, the minutes of meetings, and more.

2. *Double taxation.* Corporate income is taxed twice. First the corporation pays tax on income before it can distribute any to stockholders. Then the stockholders pay tax on the income (dividends) they receive from the corporation. While this is *double* taxation, it is not *excessive* taxation, as the tax system is designed to provide some offsetting credits such as the dividend tax credit for investors.

3. *Two tax returns.* If an individual incorporates, he or she must file both a corporate tax return and an individual tax return. Depending on the size of the corporation, a corporate return can be quite complex and require the assistance of an accountant.

4. *Size.* Size may be one advantage of corporations, but it can be a disadvantage as well. Large corporations sometimes become too inflexible and too tied down in red tape to respond quickly to market changes.

5. *Difficulty of termination.* Once a corporation is started, it's relatively difficult to end. Legal procedures are costly and more complex than for unincorporated companies.

6. *Possible conflict with stockholders and board of directors.* Some conflict may brew if the stockholders elect a board of directors that disagrees with the present management.

FIGURE 5.5

Comparison of Forms of Business Ownership

	Sole Proprietorship	Partnerships		Corporation	
		General Partnership	Limited* Partnership	Public Corporation	Private Corporation
Documents Needed to Start Business	None, may need permit or licence	Partnership agreement (oral or written)	Written agreement; must file certificate of limited partnership	Articles of incorporation, bylaws	Articles of incorporation, bylaws; must meet criteria
Ease of Termination	Easy to terminate: just pay debts and quit	May be hard to terminate, depending on the partnership agreement	Same as general partnership	Hard and expensive to terminate	Not difficult; pay off debts, sell off assets, withdraw cash, and pay taxes
Length of Life	Terminates on the death of owner, sale, or retirement	Terminates on the death or withdrawal of partner	Same as general partnership	Perpetual life	Perpetual life
Transfer of Ownership	Business can be sold to qualified buyer	Must have agreement of other partner(s)	Same as general partnership	Easy to change owners; just sell stock	Easy—just sell stock†
Financial Resources	Limited to owner's capital and loans	Limited to partners' capital and loans	Same as general partnership	More money to start and operate: sell stock and bonds; loans	Owners' capital and loans; no public stock issue allowed
Risk of Losses	Unlimited liability	Unlimited liability	Limited liability	Limited liability	Limited liability
Taxes	Taxed as personal income	Taxed as personal income	Same as general partnership	Corporate, double taxation	Same as public corporation
Management Responsibilities	Owner manages *all* areas of the business	Partners share management	Can't participate in management	Separate management from ownership	Owners usually manage all areas
Employee Benefits	Usually fewer benefits and lower wages	Often fewer benefits and lower wages; promising employee could become a partner	Same as general partnership	Usually better benefits and wages, advancement opportunities	Same as public corporation

* There must be at least one general partner who manages the partnership and has unlimited liability.
† Unless the agreement specifies otherwise.

Since the board of directors chooses the company's officers, entrepreneurs could find themselves forced out of the very company they founded. This is what happened to Rod Canion, one of the founders of Compaq Computer.

7. *Initial cost.* Incorporation may cost thousands of dollars and involve the services of expensive lawyers and accountants.

Many people are discouraged by the costs, paperwork, and special taxes that corporations must pay. However, many other business people believe that the challenges of incorporation outweigh the advantages. Figure 5.5 compares the three main types of organizations.

Other Types of Corporations

When reading about corporations, you will find that there are variations of private and public corporations.

Professional Corporations[14]

Not all corporations are large organizations with hundreds of employees or thousands of stockholders. Individuals can also incorporate. A *professional corporation* is a Canadian-controlled private corporation engaged in providing professional services. The member must be part of a profession that is governed by a professional body that allows its members to practise through a corporation, as opposed to a sole proprietorship or partnership. Each province has different laws and rules as to which professions have these governing bodies. Professions that can incorporate include accountants, architects, lawyers, physicians, dentists, and engineers. Normally, individuals who incorporate do not issue shares to those outside of their business or family; therefore, they do not share all of the same advantages and disadvantages of large public corporations (such as more money for investment and size). Limited liability is a benefit, depending on your professional service. For example, all legislation relating to physician practices in Canada specifically prohibits any limitation of personal liability. The major benefit of professional corporations is tax advantages: professional corporations can benefit from the Small Business Deduction (discussed earlier), income splitting with family members, and the capital gains exemption for qualifying small business corporation shares (if shares are later sold).

Non-Resident Corporations

A *non-resident corporation* conducts business in Canada but has its head office outside Canada. For example, most foreign airlines are non-resident corporations.

Non-Profit Corporations

A *non-profit corporation* is formed for charitable or socially beneficial purposes. As mentioned in Chapter 1, it is not run for profit. It has many features of business corporations, but it pays no income taxes and it does not issue shares. In short, it does not have owners or stockholders. In some towns, property is tax exempt if it belongs to a non-profit organization such as a religious institution, hospital, college, museum, YMCA, or athletic, artistic, or charitable organization.

Crown Corporations

Note that this chapter does not discuss another type of corporation that we reviewed in Chapter 3. You will recall that *Crown corporations* are companies that only the federal or a provincial government can set up.

Corporate Governance

corporate governance
The process and policies that determine how an organization interacts with its stakeholders, both internal and external.

Corporate governance refers to the process and policies that determine how an organization interacts with its stakeholders—both internal and external. Rules outline how the organization is to be managed by the board of directors and the officers. Corporate governance is necessary because of the evolution of public ownership. In public corporations, unlike sole proprietorships and partnerships, there is a separation between ownership and management.[15] As a result, the board of directors was created.

The pyramid in Figure 5.4 shows that the owners/stockholders elect a board of directors. These board members have the responsibility of representing the best interests of the stockholders. The board assumes many of the same responsibilities that would typically rest with the sole proprietors, partners, or owners of a private corporation. Board members are often chosen based on their business experience and level of expertise. They have responsibilities such as hiring the officers of the corporation and overseeing major policy

As a result of corporate scandals, board members are under increasing scrutiny to ensure that they are effectively fulfilling their roles and responsibilities to their stakeholders. Professional development programs for board and committee members have been created to address this need. Two such examples are the Directors College (www.thedirectorscollege.com) and the Institute of Corporate Directors (www.icd.ca).

issues. Be aware that those who serve on boards (both for-profit and non-profit) may be held personally liable for the misconduct of the organization. Having directors insurance is one way to try to limit this risk. Risk will be discussed in more detail in Appendix B.

The owners/stockholders thus have some say in who runs the corporation but they have no control over the daily operation. This is up to the officers and their management team. We will discuss the levels of management in Chapter 7.

In the past, many boards were made up of officers of the company. It was not uncommon to have the chief executive officer hold the chairman of the board position. In the wake of corporate scandals, companies and their boards of directors are being scrutinized. Is the board independent from officers? Does the company have a statement of corporate governance practices? To truly represent the stockholders, are directors elected every year? These are just some of the questions that are being addressed by boards across Canada.

The annual *Report on Business* Board Games ranking of Canadian companies' corporate governance practices assesses a variety of governance issues including board composition, compensation, shareholder rights, and disclosure practices.[16] A trend reveals that Canadian companies are giving shareholders a growing volume of information about their executive compensation and their boards of directors as shareholders have particularly demanded greater information to explain and justify growing executive pay packages.[17] Bill Mackenzie, director of special projects for the powerful Canadian Coalition for Good Governance, says the expanded disclosure is a reform particularly championed by shareholders: "If we paid a whole lot of money for this CEO, the idea is to be able to figure out if we got the value we paid for or not," he says. "The key is to tell us how you got there, so we can figure out if it makes sense over the long term."[18]

Business Regulations

Companies that wish to operate in Canada must follow federal and provincial business laws and regulations. Among other things, this applies to registration and to reporting and information.

Registration

Governments need to know what businesses are in operation to ensure that a wide range of laws and regulations are being followed. Guaranteeing that the names of businesses are not duplicated is important to avoid confusion. Additionally, governments have to be sure that taxes are being paid. To ensure these and other goals, every company must register its business. This is a simple, routine, and inexpensive procedure.

Companies wanting to incorporate must fill out articles of incorporation and file these with the appropriate provincial/territorial or federal authority. **Articles of incorporation** are a legal authorization from the federal or provincial/territorial government for a company to use the corporate format. The main advantage of being a federally incorporated company is that incorporation gives the company name added protection and guarantees its usage across Canada. Depending on the type of business you are considering, you may be required to incorporate federally.

Reporting and Information

Businesses receive many documents from governments during the course of a year. Some are just information about changes in employment insurance, the Canada or Quebec Pension Plan, or tax legislation as it affects them or their employees. Then there are various forms that all companies must complete so that governments can compile statistical reports that businesses, individuals, research organizations, and governments need to operate effectively. Statistics Canada maintains vast databases and creates useful reports from this information.

All public corporations must file annual reports containing basic data about themselves. An annual report should include the name of the officers, how many shares have been issued, and the head office location. Of course, every corporation must also file an annual tax return containing financial statements and pay the necessary taxes during the year.

> ## Progress Assessment
> - What are the major advantages and disadvantages of incorporating a business?
> - What is the role of owners (stockholders) in the corporate hierarchy?
> - If you buy stock in a corporation and someone is injured by one of the corporation's products, can you be sued? Why or why not?

CORPORATE EXPANSION: MERGERS AND ACQUISITIONS

The last decade saw considerable corporate expansion. It was not uncommon to read of a new merger or acquisition on a weekly basis. It seemed as though each deal was intended to top the one before it. Most of the new deals involved companies trying to expand within their own fields to save costs, enter new markets, position for international competition, or adapt to changing technologies or regulations. Those proved to be unattainable goals for many of the merged giants. Read the Dealing with Change box for some examples.

What's the difference between mergers and acquisitions? A **merger** is the result of two firms forming one company. It is similar to a marriage joining two individuals as one. An **acquisition** is one company's purchase of the property and obligations of another company. It is more like buying a house than entering a marriage.

There are three major types of corporate mergers: vertical, horizontal, and conglomerate. A **vertical merger** is the joining of two firms involved in different stages of related businesses. Think of a merger between a soft drink company and a company that produces artificial sweetener. Such a merger would ensure a constant supply of sweetener needed by the soft drink manufacturer. It could also help ensure quality control of the soft drink company's products. A **horizontal merger** joins two firms in the same industry and allows them to diversify or expand their products. An example of a hori-

---

articles of incorporation
A legal authorization from the federal or provincial/territorial government for a company to use the corporate format.

merger
The result of two firms forming one company.

acquisition
One company's purchase of the property and obligations of another company.

vertical merger
The joining of two companies involved in different stages of related businesses.

horizontal merger
The joining of two firms in the same industry.

DEALING with CHANGE

The Urge to Merge

Two-thirds of the merged giants of the late 1990s failed to meet their goals. The greatest merger mania in history unravelled before our eyes. These failing corporate giants lost trillions of dollars in market value. The once high-flying WorldCom filed for bankruptcy. The 2000 AOL/Time Warner marriage was so rocky that the company's stock lost two-thirds of its value in 2001. In 2009, AOL separated from Time Warner.

Why did CEOs have the urge to merge if so many land mines lay in the way? The booming markets in the mid-1990s convinced many CEOs that they needed to beef up to compete and to achieve the double-digit growth that Wall Street expected. The stock market's remarkable upward spiral gave dot-com entrepreneurs rising stock prices. They used that high-priced stock to buy other companies, which increased their earnings, which raised their stock prices higher, which allowed them to buy more and bigger businesses. Of course, if the CEOs got a big bonus for merger deals no matter what happened to the share price, they were even more eager to merge. Joseph Nacchio, CEO of Qwest Communications, received a $26 million "growth payment" when Qwest bought US West, and Solomon Trujillo of US West got $15 million for selling. (The deal was not as profitable for the company's shareholders. Qwest's value fell $20 to $30 billion in late 2000 when the merger was completed and continued to free-fall for the next two years. If you had bought 100 shares of the stock at its height in mid-2000, you'd have paid $8,500. If you still held the stock in 2005, the shares would have been worth a mere $400—that's a 95 percent loss.)

Some economists see merger waves in terms of games that CEOs play. When one company merges with another, its competitors ask themselves what their next move should be to get not the best outcome, but the least bad outcome. Since they fear being left behind, the first deal inspires others. For example, after Daimler bought Chrysler, Ford and GM each bought other carmakers. But which carmakers have remained the most profitable? BMW, Porsche, and Toyota—all of which stayed out of the mania.

Following Competition Bureau approval, Petro-Canada and Suncor Energy Inc. merged under the Suncor name. Both company CEOs have emphasized the benefits of being huge: The merged company will be "able to compete with global supermajors," it "will have a commanding presence as Canada's largest energy company and the fifth largest in North America," it will be "large enough to compete in the top tier of global energy companies," and the combination would make for a more efficient player in Canada's oil patch, which will insulate the new Canadian firm from potential foreign takeovers. Have these predictions come to fruition?

Change is constant, of course, so every merger wave is followed by a counterwave. More than a third of the largest international mergers completed in the preceding decade are now being "demerged." For example, luxury goods giant LVMH sold bits of the empire it accumulated in the 1990s. However, after avoiding big deals for more than three years, a new wave of mergers surged in early 2005 as corporations announced 48 deals of $1 billion or more, totalling $357 billion in just three months. Procter & Gamble paid $57 billion for Gillette. Will P&G's shares collapse as has happened with many of the mega mergers of the past? According to analysts, P&G must increase profits from Gillette's razor, batteries, and other businesses by 12 percent each year for the next five years to cover the costs of the merger. In the past five years, Gillette's profits have risen at only one-third that rate. So, meeting that goal may be a close shave.

Sources: "Merged Suncor, Petro-Canada Ready to Compete with 'Global Supermajors'," CBC News, 4 June 2009, http://www.cbc.ca/canada/calgary/story/2009/06/04/suncor-petrocanada-merger.html; "Time Warner Inc. Announces Plan to Separate AOL," Time Warner Inc., 28 May 2009, http://www.timewarner.com/corp/newsroom/pr/0,20812,1901397,00.html; Gregory Zuckerman and Ian Mcdonald, "Time to Slice the Mergers," *The Wall Street Journal*, 10 January 2006, C; Harry Berkowitz, "Time Warner Pays $2.4B to Settle Class-Action Suit," *Newsday*, 4 August 2005; Robert Barker, "P&G's $57 Billion Bargain," *BusinessWeek*, 25 July 2005; and Shawn Tully, "The Urge to Merge," *Fortune*, 21 February 2005.

zontal merger is the merger of a soft drink company and a mineral water company. The business can now supply a variety of drinking products. A **conglomerate merger** unites firms in completely unrelated industries. The primary purpose of a conglomerate merger is to diversify business operations and investments. The merger of a soft drink company and a snack food company would be an example of a conglomerate merger. Figure 5.6 illustrates the differences between the three types of mergers.

There are many benefits to a merger. One of them is that a merger may allow regional players to work together and compete more effectively. This is the case with the merger of salted snack food companies Old Dutch Foods Ltd. and Humpty Dumpty Snack Foods Inc. The combined entity will have $300 million in annual sales and about 25 percent of

conglomerate merger
The joining of firms in completely unrelated industries.

FIGURE 5.6

Types of Mergers

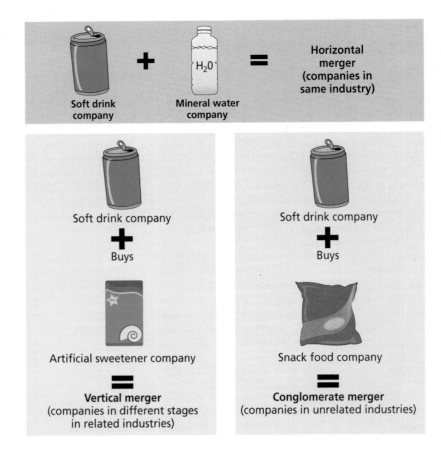

the Canadian market, says Steve Aanenson, president, CEO, and co-owner of Old Dutch Foods Inc.[19] It is estimated that the market leader, Frito-Lay (a division of PepsiCo. Inc.), has more than 60 percent of the Canadian market. The newly merged company will also have new clout when negotiating with national retailers and undertaking marketing and promotional activities, an important consideration given ongoing consolidation in the food retail and consumer products industries.[20]

Rather than merge or sell to another company, some corporations decide to maintain control, or in some cases regain control, of a firm internally. Years ago, the former owners of Cara Operations Limited, the largest operator of full-service restaurants in Canada, decided to take the firm private. Taking a firm private involves the efforts of a group of stockholders or management to obtain all of the firm's stock for themselves.[21] Cara's wholly owned businesses include Swiss Chalet, Harvey's, Second Cup, Kelsey's Neighbourhood Bar & Grill, Montana's Cookhouse, Milestone's Grill and Bar, Cara Air Terminal Restaurant Division, Cara Airport Services Division, and Summit Food Service Distributors Inc. Prior to going private in 2004, the company's annual system sales were in excess of $1.8 billion.[22]

Suppose the employees in an organization feel there is a good possibility they may lose their jobs. Or what if the managers believe that corporate performance could be enhanced if they owned the company? Do either of these groups have an opportunity to take ownership of the company? Yes—they might attempt a leveraged buyout. A **leveraged buyout (LBO)** is an attempt by employees, management, or a group of investors to purchase an organization primarily through borrowing. The funds borrowed are used to buy out the stockholders in the company. The employees, managers, or investors now become the owners of the firm. LBOs have ranged in size from millions to billions of dollars and have involved everything from small family businesses to giant corporations such as R.J.R. Nabisco and Toys "R" Us.[23]

leveraged buyout (LBO)
An attempt by employees, management, or a group of investors to purchase an organization primarily through borrowing.

FRANCHISING

Some people are not comfortable starting their own business from scratch. They would rather join a business with a proven track record through a franchise agreement. A **franchise agreement** is an arrangement whereby someone with a good idea for a business (the **franchisor**) sells the rights to use the business name and to sell a good or service (the **franchise**) to others (the **franchisee**) in a given territory. As you might suspect, both franchisors and franchisees have a stake in the success of the franchise.

A franchise can be formed as a sole proprietorship, partnership, or corporation. Business students often mistakenly identify franchising as an industry. It is important to stress a few things before we go any further. Franchising is a method of distributing a good or service, or both, to achieve a maximum market impact with a minimum investment. It is not a separate form of business ownership from those already discussed in Figure 5.5 and it does not replace a form of business. How the franchisee sets up the franchise business (i.e., sole proprietorship, partnership, or corporation) and operates it, however, is dependent on the advantages and disadvantages of each form of business ownership.

Often, what looks like a chain of stores—Canadian Tire, Quiznos Sub, Buck or Two—is usually a franchise operation with each unit owned by a different person or company. Sometimes one person or group may own and operate more than one franchise unit. Regardless of the form of business ownership (e.g., sole proprietorship), all units are part of a franchise operation. In the following pages you will see the advantages and disadvantages of this type of business operation, and you will learn what to consider before buying a franchise unit.

Canada has the second largest franchise industry in the world, led only by the United States.[24] As noted in Figure 5.7, franchises employ more than 1.5 million people and generate annual sales of more than $100 billion. Of the franchises that opened in Canada within the last five years, 86 percent are still under the same ownership and 97 percent are still in business.[25]

Canadian food franchises that you may be familiar with are Booster Juice, Mr. Sub, Crabby Joe's Tap & Grill, and Edo Japan. Keep in mind that there are also non-food

franchise agreement
An arrangement whereby someone with a good idea for a business sells the rights to use the business name and sell its goods and services in a given territory.

franchisor
A company that develops a product concept and sells others the rights to make and sell the products.

franchise
The right to use a specific business's name and sell its goods or services in a given territory.

franchisee
A person who buys a franchise.

SupperWorks is a meal preparation business that has been helping families and students save time while providing nutritious, cost-effective meals. Would you consider using this company's services?

FIGURE **5.7**

Franchising in Canada

Total franchise units	75,809
Annual sales	Over $100 billion
Rate of new franchises	One opens every 2 hours, 365 days a year
Employment	More than 1.5 million people
Average franchise fee	$25,000
Average franchisee investment	$166,600

Source: "Interesting Facts," CANAM Franchise Development Group, 2008, http://www.canamfranchise.com/interestingfacts.cfm. Used with permission.

franchises, such as Shoppers Drug Mart, Molly Maid, Oxford Learning, 1-800-GOT-JUNK?, Home Hardware, and Budget Brake & Muffler. Have you ever considered owning one of these?

A growing number of companies, including franchise systems, deliver goods and services that directly or indirectly protect the environment. The Green Box highlights some of these examples.

GreenBOX

Franchises Going Green

According to Barry Young, President and CEO of Lord & Partners Holdings, a franchisor specializing in environmentally friendly commercial cleaning agents, the Canadian environmental business sector represents $30 billion each year. The global sector generates $900 billion annually. Lord & Partners is a worldwide venture with more than 100 cleaning agents and solvents that are developed in two plants in Huntsville, Ontario, and the list is growing as increasingly stringent regulatory guidelines force industries to seek alternatives to hazardous chemicals.

Two years before regulations required it to do so, Maaco Systems Canada's owners of the company's 36 franchises started using water-based paints, as opposed to those containing solvents. They had to invest in new spray guns as well as oscillation equipment. The cost of converting ran anywhere from $6,000 to $75,000, depending on the age of the equipment. A volatile organic compound (VOC) is a class of chemicals that produces ground-level ozone, commonly known as smog. The company's reduction in VOCs emissions was equivalent to taking 1,000 cars off the road. "If our small chain of stores can do that," says Gary Dohring, President and CEO, "imagine the effect if the country's 6,500 body shops changed their ways."

Harvey's Restaurants, a division of Cara Operations, is overhauling its 280 stores across the country. Each of its locations will either be extensively renovated or rebuilt from scratch, says company President Rick McNabb. Over the next five years, Harvey's will build 100 stores and most will occupy about 2,200 square feet versus the typical 2,300 square feet of today. For starters, this smaller footprint will consume fewer building materials. New store features will include an added layer of insulation around the exterior of the building, cold cathode compact fluorescents (which are 90 percent more efficient than conventional incandescent lights), and awnings over the windows to reduce solar heat gain during the warm weather months.

Banks that provide franchising financing are also looking to become more environmental. TD Canada Trust became the first Canadian bank to pledge that it would become carbon neutral by 2010. While it can never eliminate emissions entirely, it can reduce consumption through better lighting practices, among other things, and by acquiring green energy. Through its Friends of the Environment Foundation, which was set up in 1990 to support community-based, eco-friendly initiatives, TD Canada Trust has funded over 16,000 green initiatives.

Sources: Roma Ihnatowycz, "Ecology Economics," *Franchise Canada Magazine*, July/August 2008, 22–24; and D'Arcy Jenish, "Going Green," *Franchise Canada Magazine*, July/August 2008, 34–39. Reprinted with permission from *Franchise Canada Magazine*, published by the Canadian Franchise Association.

Advantages of Franchises

Franchising has penetrated every aspect of Canadian and global business life by offering goods and services that are reliable, convenient, and competitively priced. The world-wide growth of franchising could not have been accomplished by accident. Franchising clearly has some advantages:

1. *Management and marketing assistance.* Compared with someone who starts a business from scratch, a franchisee (the person who buys a franchise) has a much greater chance of succeeding because he or she is selling an established product (e.g., Domino's pizza). As well, the franchisor provides assistance in all phases of the operation. This assistance can include help in choosing a location, setting up an accounting system, training staff, and marketing. It is like having your own store with full-time consultants available when you need them.

   Franchisors provide intensive management training, since they want the franchisees to succeed. For example, franchisor Boston Pizza International offers its franchisees eight weeks of training and support in its corporate training centre, one week of business management sessions, and ongoing training as needed.[26] McDonald's sends all new franchisees to Hamburger University. To be eligible as franchisees, applicants are also required to complete 1,600 hours of on-the-job training.

   Some franchisors are helping their franchisees succeed by helping with local marketing efforts rather than having franchisees depend solely on national advertising. Furthermore, franchisees have a network of fellow franchisees that face similar problems and can share their experiences. For example, The UPS Store provides its franchisees with a software program that helps them build data banks of customer names and addresses. The company also provides one-on-one phone support and quick e-mail access through its help desk. The help desk focuses on personalizing contact with the company's franchisees by immediately addressing their questions and concerns.

2. *Personal ownership.* A franchise operation is still your store, and you enjoy many of the incentives and profit of any sole proprietor. You are still your own boss, although you must follow more rules, regulations, and procedures than you would with your own privately owned store.

3. *Nationally recognized name.* It is one thing to open a gift shop or ice cream store. It is quite another to open a new Hallmark store or a Baskin-Robbins. With an established franchise, you get instant recognition and support from a product group with established customers around the world.

4. *Financial advice and assistance.* A major problem with small businesses is arranging financing and learning to keep good records. Franchisees get valuable assistance and periodic advice from people with expertise in these areas. In fact, some franchisors will even provide financing to potential franchisees they believe will be valuable partners of the franchise system.

5. *Lower failure rate.* Historically, the failure rate for franchises has been lower than that of other business ventures. Some experts say that independent businesses fail eight times more often than franchised businesses.[27] However, franchising has grown so rapidly that many weak franchises have entered the field, so you need to be careful and invest wisely.

Canadian Business Franchise is a bimonthly magazine that features articles on franchise advice from bankers, lawyers, and franchise specialists. Visit www.cgb.ca for advice and to view profiles on individual franchises.

Disadvantages of Franchises

It almost sounds like franchising is too good to be true. There are, however, some potential pitfalls. You must be sure to check out any such arrangement with present franchisees and possibly discuss the idea with a lawyer and an accountant. Disadvantages of franchises are listed on the next page.

Canadian Tire is Canada's most-shopped retailer. To own a franchise, candidates must be willing to make a personal and financial investment. A minimum of $125,000 of accessible capital is needed to become an associate dealer. In addition, successful dealer candidates will be charged a dealer training and development fee of $100,000 upon receiving their first store.

1. *Large start-up costs.* Most franchises will demand a fee just for the rights to the franchise. Fees for franchises can vary considerably. Start-up costs for a Kumon Math and Reading Centre include $1,000 for the franchise fee and a minimum investment ranging from $10,000 to $20,000.[28] But if you want to own a Keg Restaurant, you will need more money. The franchise fee is $50,000 and capital requirements range from $2.0 to $3.25 million.[29]

2. *Shared profit.* The franchisor often demands either a large share of the profits in addition to the start-up fees or a percentage commission based on sales rather than profit. This share demanded by the franchisor is generally referred to as a royalty. For example, if a franchisor demands a 10-percent royalty on a franchise's sales, 10 cents of every dollar collected at the franchise (before taxes and other expenses) must be paid to the franchisor.

3. *Management regulation.* Management "assistance" has a way of becoming managerial orders, directives, and limitations. Franchisees feeling burdened by the company's rules and regulations may lose the spirit and incentive of being their own boss with their own business. One of the biggest changes in franchising in recent years has been the banding together of franchisees to resolve their grievances with franchisors rather than each fighting their battles alone.

4. *Coattail effects.* What happens to your franchise if fellow franchisees fail? Quite possibly you could be forced out of business even if your particular franchise has been profitable. This is often referred to as a *coattail effect.* The actions of other franchisees clearly have an impact on your future growth and level of profitability. If customers have a negative experience at one franchise location, this may destroy the reputation of other franchisees. Franchisees must also look out for competition from fellow franchisees. For example, TCBY franchisees' love for frozen yogurt melted as the market became flooded with new TCBY stores. McDonald's franchisees complain that due to the McDonald's Corporation's relentless growth formula, some of the new stores have cannibalized (taken away) business at existing locations, squeezing franchisees' profits.

5. *Restrictions on selling.* Unlike owners of private businesses who can sell their companies to whomever they choose on their own terms, many franchisees face restrictions in the reselling of their franchises. To control the quality of their franchisees, franchisors often insist on approving the new owner, who must meet their standards.

6. *Fraudulent franchisors.* Contrary to common belief, most franchisors are not large systems like McDonald's or Subway. Most franchisors are honest, but there has been an increase in complaints about franchisors that deliver little or nothing of what they promised.[30]

If you are interested, Figure 5.8 provides some tips on evaluating a franchise.

Home-Based Franchises

Home-based businesses offer many obvious advantages, including relief from the stress of commuting, extra time for family activities, and low overhead expenses.

For example, when Henry and Paula Feldman decided to quit sales jobs that kept them on the road for weeks, they wanted to find a business to run at home together. The Feldmans started their home-based franchise, Money Mailer, Inc. (a direct mail advertiser), with nothing more than a table and a telephone. Five years later, they owned 15 territories, which they ran from an office full of state-of-the-art equipment. They grossed more than $600,000 during their fifth year. Henry says that the real value of being in a franchise is that the systems are in place: "You don't have to develop them yourself. Just be willing to work hard, listen, and learn. There's no greater magic than that."

FIGURE 5.8

FIGURE 5.8

Buying a Franchise

Since buying a franchise is a major investment, be sure to check out a company's financial strength before you get involved.

CHECKLIST FOR EVALUATING A FRANCHISE

The franchise

Did your lawyer approve the franchise contract you're considering after he or she studied it paragraph by paragraph?

Does the franchise give you an exclusive territory for the length of the franchise?

Under what circumstances can you terminate the franchise contract and at what cost to you?

If you sell your franchise, will you be compensated for your goodwill (the value of your business's reputation and other intangibles)?

If the franchisor sells the company, will your investment be protected?

The franchisor

How many years has the firm offering you a franchise been in operation?

Does it have a reputation for honesty and fair dealing among the local firms holding its franchise?

Has the franchisor shown you any certified figures indicating exact net profits of one or more going firms that you personally checked yourself with the franchisee? Ask for the company's disclosure statement.

Will the firm assist you with

    A management training program?
    An employee training program?
    A public relations program?
    Capital?
    Credit?
    Merchandising ideas?

Will the firm help you find a good location for your new business?

Has the franchisor investigated you carefully enough to assure itself that you can successfully operate one of its franchises at a profit both to itself and to you?

You, the franchisee

How much equity capital will you need to purchase the franchise and operate it until your income equals your expenses?

Does the franchisor offer financing for a portion of the franchising fees? On what terms?

Are you prepared to give up some independence of action to secure the advantages offered by the franchise? Do you have your family's support?

Does the industry appeal to you? Are you ready to spend much or all of the remainder of your business life with this franchisor, offering its good or service to the public?

Your market

Have you conducted any studies to determine whether the good or service that you propose to sell under the franchise has a market in your territory at the prices you'll have to charge?

Will the population in the territory given to you increase, remain static, or decrease over the next five years?

Will demand for the good or service you're considering be greater, about the same, or less five years from now than it is today?

What competition already exists in your territory for the good or service you contemplate selling?

Sources: U.S. Department of Commerce, *Franchise Opportunities Handbook*; and Rhonda Adams, "Franchising Is No Simple Endeavour," Gannett News Services, 14 March 2002.

But one of the disadvantages of owning a business based at home is the feeling of isolation. Compared to home-based entrepreneurs, home-based franchisees feel less isolated. Experienced franchisors share their knowledge of building a profitable enterprise with franchisees.

E-Commerce in Franchising

We've already talked about how e-commerce is revolutionizing the way we do business. Online business is not limited to those with technical knowledge and the desire to take on the challenge of starting their own business from scratch. Today, Internet users are able to obtain franchises to open online retail stores stocked with merchandise made in all parts of the world. Before you jump online and buy a web-based franchise, however, make certain that you check out the facts fully.

PropertyGuys.com is an example of a franchise that uses e-commerce as an important component of the service it offers. Formed in 1998 in Moncton, New Brunswick, PropertyGuys.com has built on the "For Sale by Owner (FSBO)" Internet concept. The

Holiday Inn's InterContinential Amstel hotel in Amsterdam has been celebrated as the Netherlands' most beautiful and luxurious hotel. Holiday Inn franchises try to complement the environment of the area they serve. This hotel is on the crossroads of Amsterdam's financial and exclusive shopping districts. What do you think would have been the reaction if Holiday Inn built the typical American-style hotel in this area?

service is a no-commission, low-cost alternative to pricey real estate commissions. PropertyGuys.com has been used to list homes, land, apartments, commercial buildings, and cottages. According to company literature, what differentiates this company from other FSBO sites is its personal touch. Company representatives will set up clients, install signage, take photos, and make themselves available during the process. Furthermore, the company does not rely solely on the Internet to display properties. Packages include a combination of print advertising, direct mail, electronic mail, seller's documentation, a "For Sale" sign, a Web site listing, and a phone answering service.

Some franchisees with existing brick-and-mortar stores are expanding their businesses online. Franchisees that started with a limited territory are now branching out globally. Other franchisors prohibit franchisee-sponsored Web sites. Conflicts between franchisors and franchisees can erupt if the franchisor then creates its own Web site. The franchisees may be concerned that the site will pull sales from their brick-and-mortar locations. Sometimes the franchisors send "reverse royalties" to outlet owners who feel that their sales were hurt by the franchisor's Internet sales, but that doesn't always bring about peace. Before buying a franchise, you would be wise to read the small print regarding online sales.

Franchising in International Markets[31]

What makes franchising successful in international markets is what makes it successful domestically: convenience and a predictable level of service. Because of proximity and language, the United States is by far the most popular target for Canadian-based franchises. Let us look at some examples.

In 1986, brothers Michael and Aaron Serruya, then aged 19 and 20, wanted to buy a franchise, but no one would take a chance on them. So, they started their own frozen yogurt shop, Yogen Früz. Today, Yogen Früz has grown to be a world leader in the frozen yogurt category, with over 1,100 locations operating in 20 countries around the world.

Montreal-based Couche-Tard Inc. is the largest convenience store operator in Canada with a network of over 2,000 stores in Canada as well as a considerable presence in the United States, with more than 3,000 additional stores. The stores are primarily operated under the Couche-Tard® and Mac's® trademarks in Canada and the Circle K® trademark in the United States. In addition to the North American Couche-Tard network, there are approximately 3,500 Circle K licensed stores located in seven other regions worldwide (Japan, Hong Kong, China, Indonesia, Guam, Macao, and Mexico).

Beavertails Pastry is another successful franchisor story. First introduced in Ottawa in 1978, there are now more than 130 locations in seven countries. One of the company's products is a hot pastry treat that resembles—you guessed it—a beaver tail. Expansion opportunities exist in amusement parks, sports venues, tourist destinations, and ski hills.

Not only is the United States an attractive market for our franchisors, but Canada is also an attractive market for American franchisors. Taco Del Mar, a Seattle-based quick-service restaurant chain specializing in Baja style "mondo burritos and rippin' tacos," has inked a deal with B.C.-based TDM Federal Holdings, Inc. to develop restaurants across Canada. The deal could produce 600 Taco Del Mar franchises in Canada by 2014.

CO-OPERATIVES[32]

Some people dislike the notion of having owners, managers, workers, and buyers as separate individuals with separate goals. They envision a world where people co-operate with one another more fully and share the wealth more evenly. These people have formed a different type of organization that reflects their social orientation. This is called a co-operative, or co-op. A **co-operative** is an organization owned by members and customers who pay an annual membership fee and share in any profits (if it is a profit-making organization). Often the members work in the organization for a certain number of hours per month as part of their duties.

Co-operatives in Canada represent a large and diverse heritage of Canadians working together to build better communities based upon co-operative principles. Collectively, there are over 10,000 co-operatives and credit unions, providing products and services to over 10 million Canadians. Co-operatives employ over 150,000 Canadians and they can be found in many sectors of the economy, including the finance, insurance, and service sectors. They are especially significant in rural and remote regions of the country, where they meet the economic needs of producers in agriculture, the fisheries, arts and crafts production, and manufacturing. Some co-ops are listed in Canada's top 500 companies and several financial co-operatives have been rated the best places to work in Canada.

Co-operatives differ from other businesses principles in several ways:

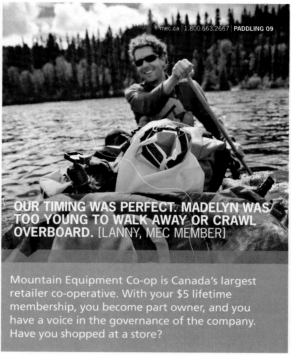

OUR TIMING WAS PERFECT. MADELYN WAS TOO YOUNG TO WALK AWAY OR CRAWL OVERBOARD. [LANNY, MEC MEMBER]

Mountain Equipment Co-op is Canada's largest retailer co-operative. With your $5 lifetime membership, you become part owner, and you have a voice in the governance of the company. Have you shopped at a store?

- *A different purpose.* The primary purpose of co-operatives is to meet the common needs of their members. Most investor-owned businesses have a primary purpose to maximize profit for their stockholders.

- *A different control structure.* Co-operatives use the one-member/one-vote system, not the one-vote-per-share system used by most businesses. This helps the co-operative serve the common need rather than the individual need.

- *A different allocation of profit.* Co-operatives share profits among their member-owners on the basis of how much they use the co-op, not on how many shares they hold. Profits tend to be invested in improving services for the members.

co-operative
An organization that is owned by members and customers, who pay an annual membership fee and share in any profits.

Because co-ops distribute their profits to members as a reduction in members' costs, these profits are not subject to income tax. From time to time, various business organizations assert that many co-ops are now more like large businesses and should be taxed. So far, this viewpoint does not appear to have extensive support.

WHICH FORM OF OWNERSHIP IS BEST FOR YOU?

As you can see, you may participate in the business world in a variety of ways. You can start your own sole proprietorship, partnership, and/or corporation. You can purchase a franchise and structure your business as a sole proprietorship, partnership, or corporation. Co-operatives are corporations that usually have a different motivation than traditional for-profit businesses. There are advantages and disadvantages to each. However, there are risks no matter which form you choose. Before you decide which form is best for you, you need to evaluate all of the alternatives carefully.

Progress Assessment

- What are some of the factors to consider before buying a franchise?
- What opportunities are available for starting a global franchise?
- What is a co-operative?

SUMMARY

LO ▶ 1 List the advantages and disadvantages of sole proprietorships.

1. The major forms of business ownership are sole proprietorships, partnerships, and corporations.

   What are the advantages and disadvantages of sole proprietorships?
   The advantages of sole proprietorships include ease of starting and ending the business, being your own boss, pride of ownership, retention of profits, no special taxes, and less regulation than for corporations. The disadvantages include unlimited liability, limited financial resources, difficulty in management, overwhelming time commitment, few fringe benefits, limited growth, limited lifespan, and the possibility of paying higher taxes depending on the level of income.

LO ▶ 2 Describe the advantages and disadvantages of partnerships. Include the differences between general and limited partners.

2. The three key elements of a general partnership are common ownership, shared profits and losses, and the right to participate in managing the operations of the business.

   What are the main differences between general and limited partners?
   General partners are owners (partners) who have unlimited liability and are active in managing the company. Limited partners are owners (partners) who have limited liability and are not active in the company.

   What are the advantages and disadvantages of partnerships?
   The advantages include more financial resources, shared management and pooled knowledge, longer survival, and less regulation than for corporations. The disadvantages include unlimited liability, division of profits, possible disagreements among partners, difficulty of termination, and the possibility of paying higher taxes depending on the level of income.

LO ▶ 3 Discuss the advantages and disadvantages of corporations.

3. A corporation is a legal entity with authority to act and have liability separate from its owners.

   What are the advantages and disadvantages of corporations?
   The advantages include more money for investment, limited liability, size, perpetual life, ease of ownership change, ease of drawing talented employees, and separation of ownership from management. The disadvantages include initial costs, paperwork, size, difficulty of termination, double taxation, and possible conflict with a board of directors.

   What is a professional corporation?
   A professional corporation is a Canadian-controlled private corporation engaged in providing professional services. The member must be part of a profession that is governed by a professional body that allows its members to practise through a corporation, as opposed to a sole proprietorship or partnership. Members may include physicians and lawyers.

LO ▶ 4 Define and give examples of three types of corporate mergers, and explain the role of leveraged buyouts and taking a firm private.

4. This decade has witnessed increased activity in the area of mergers.

   What is a merger?
   A merger is the result of two firms forming one company. The three major types of mergers are vertical mergers, horizontal mergers, and conglomerate mergers. A vertical merger is the joining of two companies involved in different stages of related businesses. A horizontal merger is the joining of two firms in the same industry. A conglomerate merger is the joining of firms in completely unrelated industries.

   What are leveraged buyouts, and what does it mean to take a company private?
   Leveraged buyouts are attempts by managers and employees to borrow money and purchase the company. Individuals who, together or alone, buy all of the stock for themselves are said to take the company private.

5. A person can participate in the entrepreneurial age by buying the rights to market a new product innovation in his or her area.

LO ▶ 5 Outline the advantages and disadvantages of franchises, and discuss the challenges of global franchising.

What are the benefits and drawbacks of being a franchisee?
The benefits include a nationally recognized name and reputation, a proven management system, promotional assistance, and pride of ownership. Drawbacks include high franchise fees, managerial regulation, shared profits, and transfer of adverse effects if other franchisees fail.

What is the major challenge to global franchises?
It may be difficult to transfer an idea or product that worked well in Canada to another culture. It is essential to adapt to the region.

6. Co-operatives have a different purpose, control structure, and allocation of profit than traditional for-profit businesses.

LO ▶ 6 Describe the role of co-operatives in Canada.

What is the role of a co-operative?
Co-operatives are organizations owned by members/customers. Some people form co-operatives to give members more economic power than they would have as individuals. Small businesses often form co-operatives to give them more purchasing, marketing, or product development strength.

What types of co-operatives are found in the economy?
Co-operatives can be found in many sectors of the economy, including the finance, insurance, agri-food and supply, wholesale and retail, housing, health, and service sectors.

KEY TERMS

acquisition 128
articles of incorporation 128
conglomerate merger 129
co-operative 137
corporate governance 126
corporation 114
franchise 131
franchise agreement 131
franchisee 131

franchisor 131
general partner 117
general partnership 117
horizontal merger 128
leveraged buyout (LBO) 130
liability 114
limited liability 117
limited partner 117
limited partnership 117

merger 128
partnership 114
partnership agreement 119
private corporation 121
public corporation 121
sole proprietorship 114
unlimited liability 116
vertical merger 128

CRITICAL THINKING

1. Have you ever dreamed of opening your own business? If so, what kind of business? Could you start such a business in your own home? How much would it cost to start? Could you begin the business part-time while you attended school? What satisfaction and profit could you get from owning your own business? What could you lose? (Be aware that you must be careful not to use a name for your business that has already been used or registered by someone else. You may face some local restrictions and license requirements if you operate from your residence such as number of parking spaces, size and type of vehicle and signage, noise by-laws, etc.)

2. Is it fair to say that franchisees have the true entrepreneurial spirit? Could you see yourself as a franchisee or franchisor? Which one? Do you have an idea that you think could eventually grow into a franchise? Explain.

DEVELOPING WORKPLACE SKILLS

1. Research businesses in your area and identify two companies that use the following forms of ownership: sole proprietorship, partnership, and corporation. Arrange interviews with managers from each form of ownership and get their impressions about their business. (If you are able to work with a team of fellow students, divide the interviews among team members.) Some questions that you might ask include: How much did it cost to start this business? How many hours do you work? What are some drawbacks that you have encountered with the way your business is set up (i.e., business form), if any? What are the specific benefits of this business? Share the results with your class.

2. Have you thought about starting your own business? What opportunities seem attractive? Think of a friend or friends whom you might want as a partner or partners in the business. List all of the financial resources and personal skills you will need to launch the business. Then make separate lists of the personal skills and the financial resources that you and your friend(s) might bring to your new venture. How much capital and what personal skills do you need but lack? Develop an action plan to obtain them.

3. Let's assume you want to open one of the following new businesses. What form of business ownership would you choose for each business? Why?
   a. Video game rental store
   b. Wedding planning service
   c. Software development firm
   d. Computer hardware manufacturing company
   e. Online bookstore

4. Find out how much it costs to incorporate a company in your province or territory. Then compare it to the cost of a federal incorporation. Is there a significant difference? Why might you choose not to incorporate federally?

TAKING IT TO THE NET 1

www.mcgrawhillconnect.ca

Purpose
To find information about co-operatives.

Exercise
There are several sources of information for Canadian co-operatives. The Canadian Co-operative Association (www.coopscanada.coop) is a national umbrella organization representing co-operatives and credit unions. The Co-operative Secretariat (www.agr.gc.ca/ rcs-src/coop/) was established in 1987 to help the federal government respond more effectively to the concerns and needs of co-operatives.

1. Visit each of these sites. What are some recent statistics about co-operatives in Canada?
2. Profile how co-operatives affect a sector of the economy.
3. Describe the history and relevance of co-operatives in your province.

TAKING IT TO THE NET 2

www.mcgrawhillconnect.ca

Purpose
To explore current franchising opportunities and to understand more about the challenges of starting a franchise.

Exercise
Go to BeTheBoss Canada (www.betheboss.ca).

1. On the home page, click on the Franchise Directory tab. Choose Browse by Company Name. Key in some franchise names that you recognize. Are you surprised by any of the information (e.g., start-up cost, level of franchisor support, etc.)? Click on Browse by Investment Level. Would you be interested in any of the franchises in the $0 to $10,000 range? How about in any of the other ranges such as the $200,001 to $500,000 range?

2. Visiting Sponsored Links (lower left-side of the home page), what sources can you review to get more information on franchising?

3. On the home page, click on the Resources tab (near the top of the page). Clicking on Introduction to Franchising, list the Ten Golden Rules (found under Franchising Basics). Review the Worksheets. If you were interested in franchising, would you consider completing them?

ANALYZING MANAGEMENT DECISIONS

Going Public

George Zegoyan and Amir Gupta face a difficult decision. Their private auto parts manufacturing company has been a great success—too quickly. They cannot keep up with the demand for their product. They must expand their facilities, but have not had time to accumulate sufficient working capital, nor do they want to acquire long-term debt to finance the expansion. Discussions with their accountants, lawyers, and stockbrokers have confronted them with the necessity of going public to raise the required capital.

Zegoyan and Gupta are concerned about maintaining control if they become a public company. They are also worried about loss of privacy because of the required reporting to various regulatory bodies and to their stockholders. Naturally, they are also pleased that the process will enable them to sell some of their shareholdings to the public and realize a fair profit from their past and expected future successes. They will be able to sell 40 percent of the shares for $500,000, which is ten times their total investment in the company. It will also allow them to raise substantial new capital to meet the needs of their current expansion program.

The proposed new structure will allow them to retain 60 percent of the outstanding voting shares, so they will keep control of the company. Nevertheless, they are somewhat uneasy about taking this step, because it will change the nature of the company and the informal method of operating they are used to. They are concerned about having "partners" in their operations and profits. They are wondering whether they should remain as they are and try to grow more slowly, even if it means giving up profitable orders.

Discussion Questions

1. Are Zegoyan and Gupta justified in their concerns? Why?

2. Do they have any other options besides going public? Is the franchise route a viable option? Explain?

3. Do you think they should try to limit their growth to a manageable size to avoid going public, even if it means forgoing profits now? Why?

4. Would you advise them to sell their business now if they can get a good price and then start a new operation? Explain.

CHAPTER 6

Entrepreneurship and Starting a Small Business

LEARNING OBJECTIVES

AFTER YOU HAVE READ AND STUDIED THIS CHAPTER, YOU SHOULD BE ABLE TO:

LO ▶ 1 Explain why people are willing to become entrepreneurs, and describe the attributes of successful entrepreneurs.

LO ▶ 2 Discuss the importance of small business to the Canadian economy.

LO ▶ 3 Summarize the major causes of small-business failure.

LO ▶ 4 List ways to learn about how small businesses operate.

LO ▶ 5 Analyze what it takes to start and run a small business.

LO ▶ 6 Outline the advantages and disadvantages that small businesses have in entering global markets.

PROFILE

Getting to Know Marlene Ross of Marlene Ross Design

Marlene Ross has changed the face of hockey around the world. She has designed and painted original pieces of "Mask Art" for Martin Brodeur, Roberto Luongo, J.S. Giguere, Marc-Andre Fleury, Grant Fuhr, and Ron Hextall, just to name a few. For over twenty years, she has been the premier artist for goalies in the NHL, international and Olympic competition, NCAA and CIS Leagues, major motion pictures, and for amateurs in minor hockey around the world.

Ross didn't have much to do with hockey when she was growing up in Merrickville, southwest of Ottawa. The self-taught painter began her career as a cartoonist and serious portrait artist. She soon developed a reputation for being able to paint on any medium. When she was 19, a goalie playing in an adult recreational league offered her $225 to paint his mask to look like the face of Batman's nemesis, the Joker. At a hockey tournament, the mask caught the eye of everyone who saw it—including Gerry Wright, of the Chicago hockey company Itech, which makes goalie helmets. For a while, Ross painted masks for Itech, and she was offered a contract. But she wanted to remain independent, so she turned the offer down. It has proved to be the right decision. Ross owns the rights to all of her designs and collects royalties from Pinnacle hockey trading cards, McDonald's restaurants, EA sports video games, and Corinthian mini masks.

There is an eight-week wait to have a mask custom painted, each of which takes about 25 to 30 hours to paint. Each goalie is provided with detailed preliminary drawings with custom design for approval. Ross might spend anywhere from 20 to 80 hours brainstorming one idea. She listens to people, helps them flesh out their ideas and then follows inspiration through to design the original custom mask. The artistic process is the same for all of her art, as amateur players and professionals receive the same quality work.

Stories about people like Marlene Ross who take risks are commonplace in this age of the entrepreneur. As you read about such risk-takers in this book, maybe you will become inspired to become an entrepreneur yourself!

Sources: "Behind the Mask," Marlene Ross Design, 2008, http://www.marlene rossdesign.com/aboutus.html; and Jody Kingsbury, "The Woman Behind the Mask," Capital Arts Online, 1 February 2006, http://www.carleton.ca/sjc/capitalarts/2006/s10.shtml.

ENTREPRENEURSHIP AND SMALL BUSINESS[1]

The 2.6 million people in Canada who are self-employed represent approximately 15 percent of all employed workers in the Canadian economy. Increasingly, young people are considering starting a small business when they graduate. Others, like Marlene Ross, start even earlier. "The perception is out there among young people that a job with an IBM for 30 years is not likely to happen," said Bruce Phillips, a senior fellow in regulatory studies at the National Federation of Independent Business Research Foundation. "Thus, working in or starting a small business has increased appeal…where there is a feeling that you control more of your own destiny."

Schools are responding to this trend by offering more courses on the subject of entrepreneurship. **Entrepreneurship** is accepting the challenge of starting and running a business. The word entrepreneur originates from the French word, *entreprendre*, which means "to undertake." In a business context, it means to start a business. You can imagine how the concept of entrepreneurship has a wide variety of meanings. On the one extreme, an entrepreneur is a person of very high aptitude who pioneers change, possessing characteristics found in only a very small fraction of the population. On the other extreme of definitions, anyone who wants to work for himself or herself is considered an entrepreneur. It is for this reason that we discuss both topics in this chapter.

While many people use the terms entrepreneurship and small business interchangeably, there are significant differences. Entrepreneurial ventures differ from small businesses in the following four ways:[2]

1. *Amount of Wealth Creation.* Rather than simply generating an income stream that replaces traditional employment, a successful entrepreneurial venture creates substantial wealth, typically in excess of several million dollars of profit.
2. *Speed of Wealth Creation.* While a successful small business can generate several million dollars of profit over a lifetime, entrepreneurial wealth creation often is rapid. For example, this may occur within five years.
3. *Risk.* The risk of an entrepreneurial venture must be high. Otherwise, with the incentive of sure profits, many people would pursue the idea of entrepreneurship, making business ventures impossibly competitive.
4. *Innovation.* Entrepreneurship often involves substantial innovation beyond what a small business might exhibit. This innovation gives the venture the competitive advantage that results in wealth creation. Innovation may be in new products, new production methods, new markets, and new forms of organizations.

From this list, you can quickly gather that entrepreneurship is not always small and small business is not always entrepreneurial.

While most businesses start small, it's the intent to stay small that separates them from entrepreneurship. Explore this chapter and think about the possibilities. That is, the possibility of entrepreneurship and the possibility of starting a small business in your future. Or, the possibility of working for an entrepreneur or an agency that supports entrepreneurship.

Well-Known Canadian Entrepreneurs[3]

Entrepreneurs have played a major role in developing the Canadian economy. Consider just a few of the many entrepreneurs who have created companies that are now household names in Canada:

- Jim Pattison acquired a Pontiac Buick dealership in Vancouver in 1961 and started Jim Pattison Lease. In 1965, he was awarded a license to operate Vancouver AM radio station CJOR. In subsequent years he continued acquisitions across the country until today the Jim Pattison Group is the third largest private company in Canada. Headquartered in Vancouver, British Columbia, it is comprised of over 410 locations

---

entrepreneurship
Accepting the challenge of starting and running a business.

worldwide focusing on the automotive, media, packaging, food sales and distribution, magazine distribution, entertainment, export, and financial industries.

- In 1922, two brothers, John W. and Alfred J. Billes, with a combined savings of $1,800, bought Hamilton Tire and Garage Ltd. Today, nine out of ten adult Canadians shop at Canadian Tire at least twice a year, and 40 percent of Canadians shop at Canadian Tire every week. Canadian Tire Corporation, Limited, is engaged in retail (which includes PartSource and Mark's Work Wearhouse), financial services, and petroleum.

- Ablan Leon began his career selling clothing from a suitcase door-to-door. When he had enough money, he bought a small building in Welland, Ontario, in 1909 and the A. Leon Company was established. When he died in 1942, operation of the family business became the responsibility of his children. Today, Leon's Furniture Limited is Canada's largest retailer of home furnishings.

In 1957, brothers Harrison and Wallace McCain began producing frozen french fries in Florenceville, New Brunswick. Today, privately-owned McCain Foods Limited is the world's largest french fry manufacturer. The company's products, which include green vegetables, desserts, pizzas, juices and beverages, oven meals, entrees, and appetizers, are sold in more than 125 countries.

- In 1969, Jean Coutu (founder of The Jean Coutu Group) and his associate at the time, Louis Michaud, opened a discount pharmacy in Montreal. They offered a large array of products, high-quality professional services, and longer store-opening hours. By 1973, there were five branches of the "Jean Coutu Discount Pharmacies" and a franchise system was established. Today, The Jean Coutu Group is a leading pharmacy franchisor in Canada with 353 stores in Quebec, Ontario, and New Brunswick. It also holds a significant interest in Rite Aid Corporation, an American national drugstore chain with more than 4,900 drugstores.

- In 1907, J. W. Sobey started a meat delivery business in Stellarton, Nova Scotia. With a horse-drawn meat cart, he purchased and collected livestock from local farmers for resale. The first modern Sobeys supermarket opened in 1947. Today, Sobeys Inc. is one of Canada's two national retail grocery and food distributors. Sobeys owns or franchises more than 1,300 corporate and franchised stores in all ten provinces under retail banners that include Sobeys, IGA, and Price Chopper.

- Kenneth Colin Irving opened Bouctouche, New Brunswick's first garage and service station in 1924. That same year, he opened a Ford dealership in Saint John and established Irving Oil. He was 25 years old. Today, Irving Oil is a regional energy processing, transporting, and marketing company. It sells a range of finished energy products including gasoline, diesel, home heating fuel, jet fuel, and complementary products.

These stories are all very much the same: one entrepreneur or a couple of entrepreneurs had a good idea and started a business. Each one now employs thousands of people and helps the country prosper.

WHY PEOPLE TAKE THE ENTREPRENEURIAL CHALLENGE

Taking the challenge of starting a business can be scary and thrilling at the same time. One entrepreneur described it as almost like bungee jumping. You might be scared, but if you watch six other people do it and they survive, you're then able to do it yourself. There are many triggers to why people become entrepreneurial and some reasons may include unexpected structural unemployment, a sudden inheritance that allows them to try something different, a change in health that forces a career path adjustment, a change in family responsibility that sparks a search to increase income, or even disliking a supervisor so much that being self-employed is an attractive option. Other reasons why people are willing to take the challenge of starting a business are described in more detail below:

- *New Idea, Process, or Product.* Some entrepreneurs are driven by a firm belief, perhaps even an obsession, that they can produce a better product, or a current product at a lower cost, than anybody else. Perhaps they have gotten hold of a new widget or have conceived of an improvement that they are convinced has a large potential market. That's how Travel CUTS (Canadian Universities Travel Service) started. In 1969, Canadian students established a national travel bureau to provide travel opportunities for students. Travel CUTS, co-owned and operated by the Canadian Federation of Students Society and the Canadian Student Horizons Group, is Canada's only national student travel bureau that provides unique student-oriented products in over 70 locations on or near Canadian university and college campuses.[4] The Spotlight on Small Business highlights another business that was started by a student while he was still in school.

- *Independence.* Many entrepreneurs simply do not enjoy working for someone else. They like doing things their own way without someone standing over them. This type of person gets a great deal of satisfaction out of what he or she achieves. Some corporate managers get tired of big-business life and quit their jobs to start their own small businesses. They bring with them their managerial expertise and their enthusiasm.

- *Challenge.* Closely related to the previous factors are the excitement and the challenge of doing something new or difficult. Many people thrive on overcoming challenges. These people welcome the opportunity to run their own business.

- *Family Pattern.* Some people grow up in an atmosphere in which family members have started their own businesses, perhaps going back several generations. The talk at the dinner table is often about business matters. This background may predispose young men or women to think along the same lines. Sometimes there is a family business, and the next generation grows up expecting to take its place there in due course.

    For example, the Anne of Green Gables Museum in Prince Edward Island is on a 110-acre property. The property includes the museum, an antique shop, a craft shop that sells Anne of Green Gables products, a tearoom, and a variety of activities for families. The Campbell home was built in 1872 by author L. M. Montgomery's uncle and aunt. Montgomery often visited this location, and it has become popular with tourists from around world. Campbells first settled on the property in 1776 and it is still in the Campbell family after two hundred years.[5]

- *Profit.* It's natural for people to benefit monetarily from their ideas and dedication and to be rewarded for the money they risk and their hard work when they run a business. Yet long after a business has produced substantial profits and amassed personal fortunes for its owners, many continue to enjoy the challenge of overcoming the endless problems that every business faces and the satisfaction of continued success.

Company's Coming, Canada's most popular name in cookbooks, began in the home of Jean Paré in Vermilion, Alberta. Since 1981, Paré has sold more than 28 million cookbooks. *Company's Coming* has turned into a family business. Grant Lovig, Jean's son and co-founder of *Company's Coming*, is the president. Jean's daughter, Gail, is responsible for marketing and distribution. Do you know of any other successful family businesses?

SPOTLIGHT ON Small Business

Riding the Tracks to Otter Valley Railroad at www.ovrtrains.com

Lorne James started Otter Valley Railroad with his father, Roger, while he was in the third year of his undergraduate Commerce program at the DeGroote School of Business at McMaster University. The name is derived from Otter Valley, an area in southern Ontario along Lake Erie, where generations of Jameses have lived. James's passion for trains started when his father gave him his first model train at the age of eight. Wanting to do something fun with his son, it was not long before a small train table led to a home layout. Over the years, father and son went to hobby shops and trade shows as they built their layout. Along the way, they met other modellers and joined some groups and associations.

There are several reasons why James started his business: "Over the years, I was getting tired of the poor service, lack of support, and the high prices that traditional local hobby stores were charging other hobby enthusiasts. After scanning the business environment, I realized that there was a market for a new player, and coupled with my father's support and the ease of starting a business, Otter Valley Railroad was created in May 2003."

To develop his business, James made connections with several manufacturers, wholesalers, and distributors to ensure the availability of products at competitive prices. He began to build his client base by promoting the company at local and regional trade shows. He, his father, and mother, Cheryl, became the face of Otter Valley Railroad. As they met other modellers, they stressed the company's products, services (e.g., layout consultation), convenience, and especially their great prices. Due to low overhead and high product turnover, they are able to offer prices 10 to 20 percent lower than traditional local hobby stores.

While the Jameses attend 12 to 15 trade shows in Ontario each year and a few out-of-province trade shows,

they feel that they have saturated the mid-West Ontario market. So, what are the future plans for Otter Valley Railroad? James wishes to become a leader in the Canadian market and have one of the biggest catalogues in the country. In the meantime, he is working toward becoming a Chartered Accountant. While studying for his School of Accountancy examination, he developed the marketing plan and Web site for the company's new e-commerce site. His strategy is to gain market share of the Canadian e-commerce market, eventually ship coast-to-coast, and offer unique custom runs. It will also allow him to serve U.S. customers with a goal to eventually ship anywhere in the world. In addition, new products and suppliers are being brought on board.

Another growth area is creating digital custom control sound. There are customers who wish to have sound-equipped locomotives that are customized to their locomotives and specific routes. This is an alternative to factory sound, which is purchased from a manufacturer. To create the custom sound, James researches the locomotive history on the Internet (versus going through old books) and collects sounds digitally from different sources (e.g., videos, the Internet, his recordings, and modellers around the world). Then, he modifies the sound based on locomotive matches. This "sound detailing" allows customers to have a realistic, trackside sound.

Is there a hobby that you have that can be turned into a business? Could you make the time to develop such as business while you are in school? What are some of the sacrifices and rewards that one would face if such a "track" was followed?

Sources: Lorne James, co-owner, Otter Valley Railroad, personal interviews, 3 August 2008 and 6 May 2006.

- *Immigrants.* Some immigrants who come to Canada lack education. This, combined with no Canadian job experience and weak language skills, makes it difficult for them to find employment. However, they often have the drive and desire to succeed, and if they can obtain the capital, they can start their own business. We see this in the many immigrants who run convenience stores (called dépanneurs in Quebec) as well as other types of businesses, such as importing and manufacturing. Other immigrants arrive with capital, skills, and strong entrepreneurial backgrounds. Vancouver, and British Columbia in general, have been major beneficiaries of such immigrants from Hong Kong.

What Does It Take to Be an Entrepreneur?

Would you succeed as an entrepreneur? You can learn about the managerial and leadership skills needed to run a firm. However, you may not have the personality to assume the risks, take the initiative, create the vision, and rally others to follow your lead. Those traits are harder to learn or acquire. The following page lists some important entrepreneurial attributes. Do you have them?[6]

- *Self-directed.* You should be a self-starter, with a lot of confidence in yourself. You do not hesitate to step into any situation. You should be comfortable and self-disciplined, even though you are your own boss. You will be responsible for your success or possible failure. The best lesson Rebecca MacDonald, Executive Chair and co-CEO of Energy Savings Income Fund, ever learned is "to believe in yourself, because business throws you curveballs on a minute-to-minute basis. If you start second-guessing yourself, your confidence can be shaken very quickly, and lack of confidence is going to create lack of performance."

- *Determined.* Closely related to self-direction is the drive you need to see you through all of the obstacles and difficulties you will encounter. You have to believe in your idea even when no one else does, and be able to replenish your own enthusiasm. In short, you have to keep going when others would give up. This often accompanies the high degree of self-confidence mentioned earlier.

- *Action-Oriented.* Great business ideas are not enough. The most important thing is a burning desire to realize, actualize, and build your dream.

- *Highly Energetic.* It's your own business and you must be emotionally, mentally, and physically able to work long and hard. For example, when starting Extreme Pita, brothers Mark and Alex Rechichi were so consumed with work that they often slept on cots in the shop's backroom after their evening shift. That way, the entrepreneurs could get a few hours of sleep before starting all over again the next morning.

- *Tolerant of Uncertainty.* Successful entrepreneurs take only calculated risks (if they can help it). On a day-to-day basis, you must make decisions that involve varying degrees of risk. Remember, entrepreneurship is not for anyone who is squeamish or bent on security.

- *Able to Learn Quickly.* Making errors is inevitable. Only those who do nothing make no mistakes. What is important is what you learn from them. Good entrepreneurs are quick to learn such lessons. They adapt and change direction as required instead of letting pride stand in the way of admitting a mistake.

While courage is not considered a skill, it is nevertheless an important element of an entrepreneur. Courage is required to challenge the status quo, to see an opportunity, and then most importantly, to try to do something about it. Entrepreneurs are doers. They don't just think and talk about an idea, they act on it! Also be aware that even if you possess many (or even all) of these attributes, there is no guarantee that you will be successful with every endeavour.

It is important to know that most entrepreneurs don't get the ideas for their goods and services from some flash of inspiration. Rather than a flash, the source of innovation is more like a flashlight. Imagine a search party, walking around in the dark, shining lights, looking around, asking questions, and looking some more. The late Sam Walton used such a flashlight approach. He visited his stores and those of competitors and took notes. He'd see a good idea on Monday, and by Tuesday every Walmart manager in the country knew about it. He expected his managers to use flashlighting too. Every time they travelled on business, they were expected to come back with at least one idea worth more than the cost of their trip. "That's how most creativity happens," says business author Dale Dauten. "Calling around, asking questions, saying 'What if?' 'till you get blisters on your tongue."

Keep in mind that necessity isn't always the mother of invention. Entrepreneurs don't always look for what customers need—they look for what they *don't* need as well. Aaron Lapin thought we didn't need the hassles of the touchy process of whipping heavy cream to top our pies. He made millions selling his invention: Reddi Wip. Although we'd rather reach for a can in the refrigerator than whip our own cream, Reddi Wip isn't a necessity. If you think you may have the entrepreneurial spirit in your blood, complete the Entrepreneur Readiness Questionnaire that appears in the appendix at the end of this chapter. There is also some advice for would-be entrepreneurs in Figure 6.1.

FIGURE | **6.1**

Advice for Potential Entrepreneurs

- Work for other people first and learn on their money.
- Research your market, but don't take too long to act.
- Start your business when you have a customer. Maybe try your venture as a sideline at first.
- Set specific objectives, but don't set your goals too high. Remember, there's no easy money.
- Plan your objectives within specific time frames.
- Surround yourself with people who are smarter than you—including an accountant and an outside board of directors who are interested in your well-being and who'll give you straight answers.
- Don't be afraid to fail. Former football coach Vince Lombardi summarized the entrepreneurial philosophy when he said, "We didn't lose any games this season, we just ran out of time twice." New entrepreneurs must be ready to run out of time a few times before they succeed.

Sources: Kathleen Lynn, "Entrepreneurs Get Tips on Weathering Recession," *Bergen County (New Jersey) Record*, 5 March 2002, I5; and Keith Lowe, "Setting Clear Goals," Entrepreneur.com, 5 August 2002.

Women Entrepreneurs[7]

A major phenomenon since the late 1970s is the large number of women who have gone into business for themselves. Throughout this book, you will see examples of such enterprises. Statistics Canada's *Labour Force Survey* reports that there were 877,000 self-employed women in Canada in 2006, accounting for about one-third of all self-employed persons. Between 1996 and 2006 (the most recent data available), the number of self-employed women grew by 18 percent, compared with 14 percent growth in male self-employment. It was estimated that 47 percent of small and medium-sized enterprises (SMEs) have some degree of female ownership: 16 percent of SMEs were majority-owned by women, 20 percent were owned in equal partnerships between male and female owners, and 11 percent have a minority female ownership. The term **SME** refers to all businesses with fewer than 500 employees. CIBC predicts that 1 million Canadian women will own a small business by 2010.

Women owners of SMEs tend to operate in the wholesale, retail, and professional services industry. One such example is Rachel Arseneau-Ferguson, president of Centre Transmed Center Inc. in Campbellton, New Brunswick. While teaching bilingual medical transcription at a local college, Arseneau-Ferguson started her business after her research revealed that there was no other company in Canada providing bilingual medical transcriptions. Transmed provides bilingual medical transcription and translation for large hospital corporations, private clinics, and doctors' offices throughout central and eastern Canada. Doctors dictate medical reports into a digital voice system to be transcribed for patient files. The company's software can link to any hospital and download voice files with medical reports. Doctors can also punch in codes and dictate reports directly into Transmed's system. "We can do work for anyone, anywhere in the world. It's just a matter of having a phone line," says Arseneau-Ferguson.

Studies have shown a variety of reasons for the significant emergence of female entrepreneurs:

- *Financial Need.* The previous decade saw the average real incomes of Canadian employees drop and unemployment fluctuate. This has forced many women to support the family budget by starting a business.

- *Lack of Promotion Opportunities.* Most positions in higher management are still dominated by men. In a recent survey conducted by Toronto-based Rosenzweig & Co., only 5 percent

small and medium-sized enterprises (SMEs)
Refers to all businesses with fewer than 500 employees.

Visit http://www. canadianbusiness.com/ rankings/w100/ for a list of Canada's top women entrepreneurs.

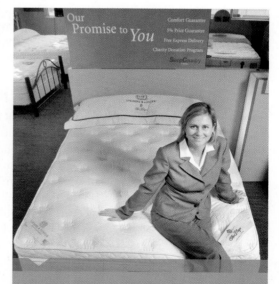

Christine Magee started Sleep Country Canada with partners Steve Gunn and Gord Lownds based on their dream to give customers what they want. Today, the company is the number one mattress specialist in Canada.

of the top 500 senior executives in Canada are women.[8] Although the situation is improving, the pace is extremely slow. Many women who are frustrated by this pace take the entrepreneurial route.

- *Women Returning to the Workforce.* Many women who return to the job market after raising a family find that their skills are outdated. They also encounter subtle age discrimination. These factors encourage many to try self-employment.

- *Family and Personal Responsibility.* The high rate of divorced women and single mothers in recent years has created a situation in which many women find themselves with children and little or no financial support. Some even refuse such support to be more independent. The development of affordable personal computers and other modern technology has made it possible for women to start home-based businesses.

- *Public Awareness of Women in Business.* As more publicity highlights the fact that growing numbers of women have started their own ventures, the idea catches on and gives others the confidence to try. Often two or more women will team up to form a partnership.

- *Part-Time Occupations.* Often women with some particular talent—for example, publicity, writing, designing, making clothes, cooking, organizing, or human relations—are encouraged to develop their hobby or skills on a part-time basis to see how far they can go with it. This focus has resulted in many notable success stories, some of which are reported in this book.

- *Higher Rate of Success for Women.* Women entrepreneurs seem to have a better success rate than men. Various factors may account for this. Women feel less pressured than men to achieve quick results. They are a little more cautious, so they make fewer mistakes. They also accept advice more readily than men, who may have a macho image of having to know it all. It will be interesting to follow this process to see if women continue to start ventures at the same rate and maintain their remarkable track record.

There are many resources available to help women entrepreneurs network and get general support. Some examples include Canadian Women's Business Network (www.cdnbizwomen.com), Women Entrepreneurs of Canada (www.wec.ca), and Canadian Association of Women Executives & Entrepreneurs (www.cawee.net). Financial institutions also offer small business products and services, which can be accessed on their sites. One example is www.rbcroyalbank.com/sme/women/.

Entrepreneurial Teams

entrepreneurial team
A group of experienced people from different areas of business who join together to form a managerial team with the skills needed to develop, make, and market a new product.

An **entrepreneurial team** is a group of experienced people from different areas of business who join together to form a managerial team with the skills needed to develop, make, and market a new product.[9] A team may be better than an individual entrepreneur because team members can combine creative skills with production and marketing skills right from the start. Having a team also can ensure more co-operation and coordination among functions.

When you think of Apple Computers, the name Steven Jobs may spring to mind. However, while Jobs was the company's charismatic folk hero and visionary, it was Steve Wozniack who invented the first PC model and Mike Markkula who offered the business expertise and access to venture capital.[10] The key to Apple's early success was that the company was built around this "smart team" of entrepreneurs. The team wanted to combine the discipline of a big company with an environment where people could feel they were participating in a successful venture. The trio of entrepreneurs recruited seasoned managers with similar desires. All of the managers worked as a team. Everyone worked together to conceive, develop, and market products.

Progress Assessment

- What are key differences between entrepreneurial ventures and small businesses?
- Why are people willing to become entrepreneurs?
- What are the advantages of entrepreneurial teams?

Micropreneurs and Home-Based Businesses

Not every person who starts a business has the goal of growing it into a mammoth corporation. Some are interested in simply enjoying a balanced lifestyle while doing the kind of work they want to do. The smallest of small businesses are called **micro-enterprises**, most often defined as having fewer than five employees.[11] While other entrepreneurs are committed to the quest for growth, **micropreneurs** (owners of micro-enterprises) know they can be happy even if their companies never appear on a list of top-ranked businesses.

Many micropreneurs are owners of home-based businesses. According to Industry Canada, approximately 55 percent of all employer businesses (597,432 in number) were micro-enterprises, with almost 43 percent of these businesses operating in the service sector.[12] Micropreneurs include writers, consultants, video producers, architects, book-keepers, and such. In fact, the development of this textbook involved many home-based business owners. The authors, the developmental editors, the copy editor, and even the text designer operate home-based businesses.

Many home-based businesses are owned by people who are trying to combine career and family.[13] Don't misunderstand and picture home-based workers as female child-care providers; men also run home-based businesses. In addition to helping business owners balance work and family, other reasons for the growth of home-based businesses include the following:[14]

- *Computer Technology.* Computer technology has levelled the competitive playing field, allowing home-based businesses to look and act as big as their corporate competitors. Broadband Internet connections, fax machines, and other technologies are so affordable that setting up a business takes a much smaller initial investment than it used to.

- *Corporate Downsizing.* Downsizing has made workers aware that there is no such thing as job security, leading some to venture out on their own. Meanwhile, the work of the downsized employees still needs to be done and corporations are outsourcing much of the work to smaller companies; that is, they are contracting with small companies to temporarily fill their needs.

- *Change in Social Attitudes.* Whereas home-based entrepreneurs used to be asked when they were going to get a "real" job, they are now likely to be asked instead for "how-to-do-it" advice.

Working at home has its challenges, of course. In setting up a home-based business, you could expect the following major challenges:[15]

- *Getting New Customers.* Getting the word out can be difficult because you don't have signs or a storefront, especially if the business does not have a Web presence.

micro-enterprise
A small business defined as having fewer than five employees.

micropreneurs
Small-business owners with fewer than five employees who are willing to accept the risk of starting and managing the type of business that remains small, lets them do the kind of work they want to do, and offers them a balanced lifestyle.

Chef Michael Smith, Canada's best-known chef, is host of several cooking shows on Food Network Canada and in 26 other countries. He is an award-winning cookbook author, newspaper columnist, restaurant chef, and home cook who works from his home. His third series, *Chef At Home*, features some of his home cooking.

FIGURE **6.2**

Some Home-Based Business Ideas

Starting your own business at home can be a viable business opportunity. It is important to note that some home-based businesses may be subject to the approval of local authorities (e.g., health, zoning, etc.).

Look for a business that meets these important criteria: (1) Pick a business that interests you, for which you have a talent or expertise, for which there is a need, and which you can afford to finance; (2) Do your market research; (3) Complete a business plan; (4) Check on and obtain all necessary licences, permits, and registrations; and (5) Advertise. The following are examples of ideas for home-based businesses.

1. Antique refinishing and repair
2. Music/dance lessons
3. Bed and breakfast
4. Accounting
5. Consulting

6. Research
7. Catering
8. Gift basket service
9. Trade (e.g., electrician)
10. Clothing design

Source: "Home-Based Business Ideas," Government of Canada, 2008, http://www.canadabusiness.ca.

- *Managing Time.* Of course, you save time by not commuting, but it takes self-discipline to use that time wisely.
- *Keeping Work and Family Tasks Separate.* Often it is difficult to separate work and family tasks. It's great to be able to throw a load of laundry in the washer in the middle of the workday if you need to, but you have to keep such distractions to a minimum. It is also difficult to leave your work at the office if the office is your home. Again, it takes self-discipline to keep work from trickling out of the home office and into the family room.
- *Abiding by City Ordinances.* Government ordinances restrict the types of businesses that are allowed in certain parts of the community and how much traffic a home-based business can attract to the neighbourhood.
- *Managing Risk.* Home-based entrepreneurs should review their homeowner's insurance policy, since not all policies cover business-related claims. Some even void the coverage if there is a business in the home.

Those who wish to get out of an office building and into a home office should focus on finding opportunity instead of accepting security, getting results instead of following routines, earning a profit instead of earning a paycheque, trying new ideas instead of avoiding mistakes, and creating a long-term vision instead of seeking a short-term pay-off. Figure 6.2 lists ten ideas for potentially successful home-based businesses. You can find a wealth of online information about starting a home-based business at http://sbin-focanada.about.com and www.entrepreneur.com.

Web-Based Businesses

The Internet has sprouted a world of small Web-based businesses that sell everything from staplers to refrigerator magnets to wedding dresses. These small businesses compete with other small businesses as well as large Web-based and bricks-and-mortar businesses. Take a moment and ponder the opportunities that have been created by eBay alone for entrepreneurs. This has been such a powerful channel for part-time and full-time entrepreneurs that a book has been developed, titled *eBay for Dummies,* to teach people how to successfully use this Web site (www.ebay.ca) to buy and sell products and services.

While 87 percent of firms used the Internet in 2007, only 41 percent reported having a Web site.[16] A Statistics Canada report highlights some of the recent trends. Internet sales, including not only retailers but all enterprises in the private and public sectors, grew to an estimated $62.7 billion in 2007, up 26 percent over the year before. The private sector constituted the largest part of that, with sales of $58.2 billion, which was a 25 percent increase over 2006. Nevertheless, Statistics Canada said "e-commerce still represents a relatively small fraction of total economic activity. In 2007, online sales of private-sector firms accounted for just under 2 percent of total operating revenue." In the private sector, business-to-business sales made up 62 percent of online sales, down from 68 percent in 2006. Statistics Canada's report also shows Canadian enterprises are more inclined to be consumers than creators of online commerce: 48 percent of private-sector firms were reported to be purchasers of goods and services online versus only 8 percent who were sellers.[17]

KEH Camera Brokers began as a hobby, grew into a mail-order business, and is now a flourishing Web-based business (www.keh.com). More than 57 percent of the store's sales are made online. Customers have found that the Web site is an efficient pipeline for buying and selling cameras. The far reach of the Web was a natural fit for the company. "The Web is a much better vehicle for our customers [compared with a mail-order catalogue]," store manager Pat Mulherin said. "They want to be able to see our inventory." When KEH's first Web page went active, it was an immediate success. "Within two months it was accounting for 35 percent of our business, then quickly went up." Prior to the Web, the small store produced mail-order catalogues listing used cameras for sale. Creating and mailing the catalogues was a slow process; by the time a customer saw a product and tried to order it, another customer could have already purchased it. The KEH Web site's listing of available cameras is updated every four hours. A used camera is listed for sale on the Web site a few hours after it enters KEH's inventory.

Don't get the idea that a Web-based business is always a fast road to success. It can sometimes be a shortcut to failure. Hundreds of high-flying dot-coms crashed after promising to revolutionize the way we shop.[18] That's the bad news. The good news is that you can learn from someone else's failure and spare yourself some pain. Startupfailures.com serves as a community for those who have tried and failed. To help future Web-based entrepreneurs understand online-business fundamentals and how to avoid the failed dot-coms' mistakes, visit www.businessplanarchive.org. There, you will see a database of dot-com business plans and marketing documents.

intrapreneurs
Creative people who work as entrepreneurs within corporations.

Entrepreneurship Within Firms

Entrepreneurship in a large organization is often reflected in the efforts and achievements of intrapreneurs. **Intrapreneurs** are creative people who work as entrepreneurs within corporations. The idea is to use a company's existing resources—human, financial, and physical—to launch new products and generate new profits.[19]

At 3M, which produces a wide array of products from adhesives (Scotch tape) to non-woven materials for industrial use, managers are expected to devote 15 percent of their time to thinking up new products or services.[20] You know those brightly coloured Post-it Notes that people use to write messages on just about everything? That product was developed by Art Fry, a 3M employee. He needed to mark the pages of a hymnal in a way that wouldn't damage or fall out of the book. He came up with the idea of the self-stick, repositionable paper. The 3M labs soon produced a sample, but distributors thought the product wasn't important and market surveys were inconclusive. Nonetheless, 3M kept sending samples to secretaries of top executives. Eventually, after launching a major sales and marketing program, the orders began pouring in, and Post-it Notes became a big winner. The company continues to update the product; making the notes from recycled paper is just one of many innovations. Post-it Notes have gone international as well—the notepads sent to Japan are long and narrow to accommodate vertical writing. Now you can even use Post-it Notes electronically—the software program Post-it Software Notes allows you to type messages onto brightly coloured notes and store them on memo boards, embed them in documents, or send them through e-mail.

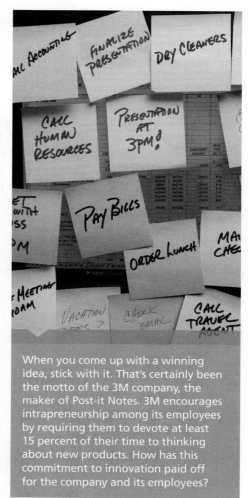

When you come up with a winning idea, stick with it. That's certainly been the motto of the 3M company, the maker of Post-it Notes. 3M encourages intrapreneurship among its employees by requiring them to devote at least 15 percent of their time to thinking about new products. How has this commitment to innovation paid off for the company and its employees?

ENCOURAGING ENTREPRENEURSHIP: WHAT GOVERNMENT CAN DO[21]

The different levels of government provide many services to help entrepreneurs and small businesses to succeed. Canada Business (http://canadabusiness.gc.ca) is a federal government information service for entrepreneurs that serves as a single point of access for federal and provincial/territorial government services, programs, and regulatory requirements for business. Canada Business's mandate is to serve as the primary source of up-to-date and accurate business-related information and to provide referrals on government programs, services, and regulations—without charge—in all regions of Canada. The mission of Canada Business is to improve the start-up, survival, and growth rates of small and medium-sized enterprises. This includes assisting with sound business planning, market research, and the use of strategic business information.

There are also specialized programs. For example, the Aboriginal Business Service Network (ABSN) provides Aboriginal entrepreneurs with information and resources to improve their access to capital and to establish or develop their business. ABSN is one element of the Aboriginal Business Development Initiative.

Industry Canada's Small Business Research and Policy Web site is designed to encourage small business researchers and policy analysts across Canada to share information. It includes an extensive database of research literature on small business and entrepreneurship, recent reports on small-business financing, small-business statistics, and lists of researchers and policy development offices across Canada. The *Small Business Quarterly* (*SBQ*) provides a quick and easy-to-read snapshot of the recent performance of Canada's small-business sector. (For additional government sources, review the Services section in Chapter 3.)

Entrepreneurs and new start-ups can also find assistance from incubators. Incubators were first developed to be centres that offered new businesses low-cost offices with basic business services such as accounting, legal advice, and secretarial help. Since then, the "networked" incubator has emerged with the creation of innovation centres. The networked incubator goes beyond the simple provision of office space and provides entrepreneurs and new companies with access to more services. According to the Canadian Association of Business Incubation (www.cabi.ca), **incubators** today provide hands-on management assistance, education, information, technical and vital business support services, networking resources, financial advice, as well as advice on where to go to seek financial assistance. In fact, the average survival rate of companies in Canada that go through business incubation has been shown to be higher than 80 percent after five years.

The goal of an incubator is not only to ensure that the small business survives the start-up period, but also to produce confident, successful graduates who will run a productive business in the future. One example of an incubator that has received worldwide recognition is the Quebec Biotechnology Innovation Centre (QBIC) in Laval. It provides start-ups in the health, environment, agri-food, and forestry sectors with lab space, scientific equipment, and mentoring services. Located in Laval's Biotech City, QBIC is just one organization that fosters entrepreneurship.

According to the National Incubation Association, there are over 1,400 business incubators in North America (including 120 in Canada) and about 5,000

incubators
Centres that provide hands-on management assistance, education, information, technical and vital business support services, networking resources, financial advice, as well as advice on where to go to seek financial assistance.

The National Research Council (NRC) supports Industrial Partnership Facilities (IPFs). Similar to incubators, each IPF has a focus on a different technology sector, depending on the specialization of its host institute. IPFs offer start-ups access to specialized laboratory space and equipment, regular interaction with researchers, and the opportunity to benefit from a range of NRC technology-transfer initiatives. The NRC Plant Biotechnology Institute in Saskatoon (viewed here) strengthens the region's agricultural biotechnology cluster.

worldwide. The government can also have a significant effect on entrepreneurship by offering investment tax credits that give tax breaks to businesses that make the kind of investments that create jobs. For example, the Biotechnology Development Centre is a tenant in Laval's Biotech City. This Centre is supported by the Canadian and Quebec governments in addition to the City of Laval. These government bodies encourage research and development by granting corporations and individuals tax incentives that foster scientific and technological development. One incentive includes a 30 percent refundable tax credit on capital or rental costs for eligible equipment (up to three years).

While the government provides a great deal of assistance, it is still primarily up to the entrepreneur to make a success of the new business.

Visit http://www.canadaone. com/magazine/loan_programs. html for a list of Canadian grant and loan programs for young entrepreneurs.

Progress Assessment

- How do micropreneurs differ from other entrepreneurs?
- What are some of the opportunities and risks of Web-based businesses?
- List some services for entrepreneurs provided by the federal government.

STARTING A SMALL BUSINESS

Let's suppose you have a great idea for a new business, you have the attributes of an entrepreneur, and you are ready to take the leap into business for yourself. How do you start a business? How much paperwork is involved? That is what the rest of this chapter is about. We will explore small businesses, their role in the economy, and small-business management. It may be easier to identify with a small neighbourhood business than with a giant global firm, yet the principles of management are similar. The management of charities, government agencies, churches, schools, and unions is much the same as the management of small and large businesses. So, as you learn about small-business management, you will make a giant step toward understanding management in general. All organizations demand capital, good ideas, planning, information management, budgets (and financial management in general), accounting, marketing, good employee relations, and good overall managerial know-how. We shall explore these areas as they relate to small businesses and then, later in the book, apply the concepts to large firms, even to global organizations.

Small Versus Big Business[22]

The Business Registrar of Statistics Canada maintains a count of business establishments. A **business establishment** must have at least one paid employee, have annual sales revenue of $30,000, or be incorporated and have filed a federal corporate income tax return at least once in the previous three years. While there are a little over 2.3 million business establishments in Canada, approximately 1.1 million of them are employer businesses. An **employer business** meets one of the business establishment criteria and usually maintains a payroll of at least one person, possibly the owner. The rest are classified as "indeterminate." Figure 6.3 breaks down the number of businesses by sector and number of employees.

It would be helpful to define what is meant by the term *small business*. Giant companies like Telus Corporation or Magna International may look at most companies as small. A **small business** is often defined as a business that is independently owned and operated, is not dominant in its field, and meets certain standards of size in terms of employees or annual revenues.

Many institutions define small business according to their own needs. For example, the Canadian Bankers Association classifies a loan authorization of less than $250,000 as small. Industry Canada often uses a definition based on the number of employees: goods-producing firms are considered small if they have fewer than 100 employees, while services-

business establishment
Has at least one paid employee, annual sales revenue of $30,000, or is incorporated and has filed a federal corporate income tax return at least once in the previous three years.

employer business
Meets one of the business establishment criteria and usually maintains a payroll of at least one person, possibly the owner.

small business
A business that is independently owned and operated, is not dominant in its field, and meets certain standards of size in terms of employees or annual revenues.

FIGURE | 6.3

Number of Business Establishments by Sector and Firm Size (Number of Employees)
A little over 95 percent of Canadian companies are considered small businesses.

	Percentage of Employer Businesses	No. of Business Establishments		
		Total	Goods-Producing Sector	Service-Producing Sector
Indeterminate[1]		**1,300,594**	**315,798**	**984,796**
Employer Businesses		**1,085,719**	**238,279**	**847,440**
Small businesses (1–49 employees)	95.2	1,033,803	225,266	808,447
Medium-sized businesses (50–499 employees)	4.5	48,976	12,444	36,622
Large businesses (500+ employees)	0.3	2,940	569	2,371
Total		**2,386,313**	**554,077**	**1,832,236**

Note 1: The "indeterminate" category consists of incorporated or unincorporated businesses that do not have a Canada Revenue Agency (CRA) payroll deductions account. The workforce of such businesses may consist of contract workers, family members, and/or owners.

Source: "Number of Business Establishments by sector and size (Number of Employees)," adapted from Statistics Canada, special tabulation, unpublished data, (Business Register Database), June 2008.

producing firms with 50 employees or less are considered small. Generally speaking, 50 employees is the upper limit most used when defining a small business based on the number of employees. Medium-sized businesses have 50 to 499 employees, while large businesses employ more than 500 people. In Figure 6.3, of the approximately 1.1 million employer businesses in Canada, 0.3 percent have more than 500 employees. Businesses employing fewer than 50 employees account for the vast majority (95.2 percent) of all employer businesses.

As you can see, small business is really a big part of the Canadian economy. How big a part? We'll explore that question next.

Importance of Small Businesses[23]

The small-business sector is a dynamic part of the Canadian economy. Nearly all small businesses are Canadian-owned and -managed. This is in contrast to large businesses, of which many are foreign-owned and -managed. Small business thus plays a major role in helping to maintain the Canadian identity and Canadian economic independence.

Small businesses also continue to be feeders for future large businesses. As they prosper and develop new goods and services, they are often bought out by large companies, which in turn become more competitive. Alternatively, after small businesses establish a good track record, some of them convert from private to public companies, enabling them to obtain significant financing and become larger companies.

Here are some quick facts about small businesses (defined by Industry Canada as firms that have fewer than 100 employees):

- On average, 130,000 new small businesses are created in Canada each year.
- Small businesses employ approximately 5 million individuals in Canada, or 48 percent of the total private labour force.
- Small businesses account for almost 98 percent of all employer businesses.

Key Small Business Statistics is a semi-annual publication that provides baseline data on the small-business sector in Canada. Visit the Web site (http://www.ic.gc.ca/eic/site/sbrp-rppe.nsf/eng/h_rd01252.html) to find up-to-date information.

- On average, small businesses that have fewer than 50 employees contributed about 26 percent to Canada's gross domestic product.
- Approximately 15 percent (2.6 million) of all employed workers in the Canadian economy were self-employed.

Since most of Canada's jobs are in small businesses, there is a very good chance that you will either work in a small business some day or start one. One-quarter of small businesses list "lack of qualified workers" as one of their biggest obstacles to growth. In addition to providing employment opportunities, small firms believe that they offer other advantages that larger companies do not. Owners of small companies report that their greatest advantages over big companies are their more personal customer service and their ability to respond quickly to opportunities.

Bigger is not always better. Picture a hole in the ground. If you fill it with big boulders, there are many empty spaces between them. However, if you fill it with sand, there is no space between the grains. That's how it is in business. Big businesses don't serve all the needs of the market. There is plenty of room for small companies to make a profit filling those niches.

Wide Diversification

Another significant aspect of small business is the wide diversification of its activities. If you look, you will find small businesses in many sectors:

1. *Service Businesses.* You are already familiar with the services provided by car mechanics, dry cleaners, travel agencies, lawn care firms, salons, and other services that cater to you and your family. In your career search, be sure to explore opportunities provided by hotels and motels, health clubs, amusement parks, income tax preparation organizations, employment agencies, accounting firms, rental firms of all kinds, management consulting, repair services (e.g., computers, DVD players), insurance agencies, real estate firms, stockbrokers, and so on. A growth area is in computer consulting and the knowledge-based industries.

2. *Retail Businesses.* You only have to go to a major shopping mall to see the possibilities in retailing. There are stores selling shoes, clothes, hats, skis, housewares, sporting goods, ice cream, groceries, and more. Much more. Watch the trends and you will see ideas such as fancy popcorn stores and cafés with Internet access areas.

3. *Construction Firms.* Drive through any big city and you will see huge cranes towering over major construction sites. Would you enjoy supervising such work? Visit some areas where construction firms are building bridges, roads, homes, schools, buildings, and dams. There is a feeling of power and creativity in such work that excites many observers. How about you? Talk to some of the workers and supervisors and learn about the risks and rewards of small construction firms.

4. *Wholesalers.* Have you ever visited a wholesale food warehouse, jewellery centre, or similar wholesale firm? If not, you are missing an important link in the small-business chain, one with much potential. Wholesale representatives often make more money, have more free time, travel more, and enjoy their work more than similar people in retailing.

5. *Manufacturing.* Of course, manufacturing is still an attractive career for tomorrow's graduates. Surveys show that manufacturers make the most money among small-business owners. There are careers for designers, machinists, mechanics, engineers, supervisors, safety inspectors, and a host of other occupations. Visit some small manufacturers in your area and inquire about such jobs to get some experience before starting your own manufacturing business. Today's high-tech world opens up many opportunities, if you are interested.

There are also thousands of small farmers who enjoy the rural life and the pace of farming. Small farms have been in great trouble for the last few years, but some that specialize in exotic or organic crops do quite well. Similarly, many small mining operations attract college and university students who have a sense of adventure. People who are not sure what career they would like to follow have a busy time ahead. They need to visit service firms, construction firms, farms, mines, retailers, wholesalers, and all other kinds of small and large businesses to see the diversity and excitement available in Canadian business.

Small-Business Success and Failure

You can't be naive about business practices, or you will go broke. There is some debate about how many new small businesses fail each year. There are many false signals about entries and exits. When small-business owners go out of business to start new and different businesses, they may be included in the "failure" category when obviously this is not the case. Similarly, when a business changes its form of ownership from partnership to corporation, it may be counted as a failure. Retirements of sole owners may also be in this category.

As mentioned in Chapter 1, thousands of businesses enter and exit the marketplace throughout the year. Statistics Canada reports that about 96 percent of small businesses that enter the marketplace survive for one full year, 85 percent survive for three years, and 70 percent survive for five years.[24] Figure 6.4 lists reasons for small-business failure. Managerial incompetence and inadequate financial planning are two of the biggest reasons for these failures.

Choosing the right type of business is critical. Many of the businesses with the lowest failure rates require advanced training to start—veterinary services, dental practices, medical practices, and so on. While training and degrees may buy security, they do not tend to produce much growth. If you want to be both independent and rich, you need to go after growth. Often high-growth businesses, such as technology firms, are not easy to start and are even more difficult to keep going.

In general, it seems that the easiest businesses to start are the ones that tend to have the least growth and the greatest failure rate (e.g., restaurants). The easiest businesses to keep alive are difficult ones to get started (e.g., manufacturing). And the ones that can

FIGURE | 6.4

Causes of Small-Business Failure

The following are some of the causes of small-business failure:
- Plunging in without first testing the waters on a small scale.
- Underpricing or overpricing goods or services.
- Underestimating how much time it will take to build a market.
- Starting with too little capital.
- Starting with too much capital and being careless in its use.
- Going into business with little or no experience and without first learning something about the industry or market.
- Borrowing money without planning just how and when to pay it back.
- Attempting to do too much business with too little capital.
- Not allowing for setbacks and unexpected expenses.
- Buying too much on credit.
- Extending credit too freely.
- Expanding credit too rapidly.
- Failing to keep complete, accurate records, so that the owners drift into trouble without realizing it.
- Carrying habits of personal extravagance into the business.
- Not understanding business cycles.
- Forgetting about taxes, insurance, and other costs of doing business.
- Mistaking the freedom of being in business for oneself for the liberty to work or not, according to whim.

FIGURE 6.5

Situations for Small-Business Success

The following factors increase the chances of small-business success:
- The customer requires a lot of personal attention, as in a beauty parlour.
- The product is not easily made by mass-production techniques (e.g., custom-tailored clothes or custom auto-body work).
- Sales are not large enough to appeal to a large firm (e.g., a novelty shop).
- A large business sells a franchise operation to local buyers. (Don't forget franchising as an excellent way to enter the world of small business.)
- The owner pays attention to new competitors.
- The business is in a growth industry (e.g., computer services or Web design).

make you rich are the ones that are both hard to start and hard to keep going. See Figure 6.5 to get an idea of the business situations that are most likely to lead to success.

When you decide to start your own business, you must think carefully about what kind of business you want. You are not likely to find everything you want in one business—easy entry, security, and reward. Choose those characteristics that matter the most to you; accept the absence of the others; plan, plan, plan; and then go for it!

LEARNING ABOUT SMALL-BUSINESS OPERATIONS

Hundreds of would-be entrepreneurs of all ages have asked the same question: How can I learn to run my own business? Many of these people had no idea what kind of business they wanted to start; they simply wanted to be in business for themselves. That seems to be a major trend among students today.

There are several ways to get into your first business venture:

1. Start your own company.
2. Buy an existing business.
3. Buy a franchise unit (see Chapter 5).
4. Inherit / takeover a family business.

Here are some hints for learning about small business.

Start Your Own Company

Your search for small-business knowledge might begin by investigating your local area schools for classes on the subject. There are entrepreneurship programs in post-secondary schools throughout Canada. One of the best things about such courses is that they bring together entrepreneurs from diverse backgrounds. (Many entrepreneurs have started businesses as students—see the Analyzing Management Decisions case near the end of the chapter for an example.) An excellent way to learn how to run a small business is to talk to others who have already done it. They will tell you that location is critical. They will caution you not to be undercapitalized; that is, not to start without enough money. They will warn you about the problems of finding and retaining good workers. And, most of all, they will tell you to keep good records and hire a good accountant and lawyer before you start. Free advice like this is invaluable.

Get Some Experience

There is no better way to learn small-business management than by becoming an apprentice or working for a successful entrepreneur. Many small-business owners got the idea for their businesses from their prior jobs. An industry standard is to have three years' experience in a comparable business.

MBAs Without Borders (MWB) was co-founded by Tal Dehtiar (seen here meeting with some Masai in Kenya) and Michael Brown. MWB gives MBAs experience by helping to promote enterprise in developing nations. According to Dehtiar, "The classroom and office are great environments for education, but MWB forces MBAs to not only think outside of the box, but out of this world."

Many new entrepreneurs come from corporate management. They are tired of the big-business life or are being laid off because of corporate downsizing. Such managers bring their managerial expertise and enthusiasm with them. Such was the case with Tom Heintzman and Greg Kiessling, co-founders of Bullfrog Power, the focus of this chapter's Green Box. Prior to starting the company, Heintzman had experience in the private and non-governmental organizations sectors as a consultant and more recently, as the director of corporate development for Zenon Environmental. Kiessling had 18 years of private sector experience leading high-growth, entrepreneurial organizations.

By running a small business part-time during your off hours or on weekends, you can experience the rewards of working for yourself while still enjoying a regular paycheque. This is what John Stanton, founder of the Running Room, did when he first started his company. He kept his full-time job as a vice-president in the grocery sector and he opened the Running Room in a house in Edmonton. At first, he only sold cotton T-shirts and running shoes. Four years later, he was confident that the company had growth potential. He quit his job and concentrated on building the Running Room chain. Today, there are more than 92 locations from coast to coast with expansion plans for Canada and the United States.

Green BOX

Are You Interested in Becoming Bullfrog-Powered?

Conventional electricity production is among the largest industrial sources of carbon dioxide, a primary greenhouse gas that is linked to climate change. Electricity production is also a major source of pollutants including nitric oxide, sulphur dioxide, mercury, and particulates that contribute to poor air quality and smog conditions.

Founded in 2005 by Tom Heintzman and Greg Kiessling, Bullfrog Power is a leading provider of 100 percent green electricity, with service available to Ontario and Alberta residents and businesses. Bullfrog Power provides customers with a convenient way to support locally generated renewable power as all of Bullfrog's power comes from clean, green sources like wind power and low-impact water power.

When customers switch to Bullfrog Power, they continue to draw their power from the province's grid in the same way that they always have. They don't need any special equipment or wiring and there is no change in the reliability of the service. Bullfrog Power injects green power onto the grid to match the amount of power a customer's home (or office building) uses. Customers receive estimates of their emission/waste reductions on their billing statements.

So while greening a building's electricity costs a little extra, customers have the comfort of knowing that their electricity dollars are supporting clean, renewable power instead of polluting and carbon-intensive sources like coal. To date, thousands of Canadian homeowners and hundreds of businesses have made the decision to become "bullfrogpowered." What's more, this support helps the company bring more new, renewable power online in Canada. For example, new wind turbines have already been commissioned in Canada as a direct result of support from Bullfrog Power customers.

Source: "About Bullfrog Power," Bullfrog Power, 22 September 2008, http://www.bullfrogpower.com/about/about.cfm.

Sabotaging Your Employer

Suppose you've worked for two years in a company and you see signs that the business is beginning to falter. You and a co-worker have ideas about how to make a company similar to your boss's succeed. Rather than share your ideas with your boss, you and your friend are considering quitting your jobs and starting your own company together. Should you approach other co-workers about working for your new venture? Will you try to lure your old boss's customers to your own business? What are your alternatives? What are the consequences of each alternative? What's the most ethical choice?

Learning a business while working for someone else may also save you money because you are less likely to make "rookie mistakes" when you start your own business. (See the Making Ethical Decisions box, though, for a scenario that raises a number of questions.)

Buy an Existing Business

Small-business management takes time, dedication, and determination. Owners work long hours and rarely take vacations. After many years, they may feel stuck in their business. They may think they can't get out because they have too much time and effort invested. Consequently, there are some small-business owners out there eager to get away, at least for a long vacation.

This is where you come in. Find a successful business person who owns a small business. Tell him or her that you are eager to learn the business and would like to serve an apprenticeship—that is, a training period. State that at the end of the training period (one year or so), you would like to help the owner or manager by becoming assistant manager. As assistant manager, you would free the owner to take off weekends and holidays, and to take a long vacation—a good deal for him or her. For another year or so, work very hard to learn all about the business—suppliers, inventory, bookkeeping, customers, promotion, and so on. At the end of two years, make the owner this offer: he or she can retire or work only part-time and you will take over the business. You can establish a profit-sharing plan for yourself plus a salary. Be generous with yourself; you will earn it if you manage the business. You can even ask for 40 percent or more of the profits.

The owner benefits by keeping ownership in the business and making 60 percent of what he or she earned before—without having to work. You benefit by making 40 percent of the profits of a successful firm. This is an excellent deal for an owner about to retire—he or she is able to keep the firm and a healthy profit flow. It is also a clever and successful way to share in the profits of a successful small business without any personal investment of money. If you think that this is not realistic, be aware that nearly half of Canada's small-business owners plan to retire before 2020—and 500,000 are set to leave the workforce by 2011.[25]

If profit-sharing doesn't appeal to the owner, you may want to buy the business outright. How do you determine a fair price for a business? Value is based on (1) what the business owns, (2) what it earns, and (3) what makes it unique. Naturally, your accountant will need to help you determine the business's value.

If your efforts to take over the business through either profit-sharing or buying fail, you can quit and start your own business fully trained.

Franchising

In Chapter 5, you were introduced to franchising. Many business people first get into business via franchising. Recall that franchising is a method of distributing a good or service, or both, to achieve a maximum market impact with a minimum investment. From

Reaching Beyond Our Borders

Canadian Franchisor Cleans Up

Molly Maid International Inc. set out to provide domestic cleaning services in Mississauga, Ontario, in 1979. The company is built on the fact that families are now busier than ever and need time-saving, convenient services to help manage their responsibilities at home. Since that time, Molly Maid has performed more than 6 million home cleanings across Canada and more than 12 million around the world. This year alone, the company is expecting to perform 2 million home cleanings.

Molly Maid's success should not be surprising when you scan the business environment. Much of the company's growth results from the increased participation of women in the workforce. While the majority of women between the ages of 18 and 65 now hold jobs outside the home, most are still responsible for the majority of the housework. Statistics reveal that working mothers spend as much as five hours each day on household chores—in addition to the almost eight hours spent working for employers.

Independent market research shows that Molly Maid is the most recognized brand in the cleaning industry. Eight of ten Canadians are familiar with the Molly Maid name and four of ten Canadians mention it first when

asked to name a cleaning service. Today, Molly Maid is the largest Canadian-based cleaning company in the world with over 500 franchises and global sales in excess of $200 million. It has a presence on three continents and can be found in seven countries including Canada, the United States, the United Kingdom, Portugal, and Japan.

Franchise owners have received numerous industry awards. For example, *Success* magazine ranked Molly Maid first in residential cleaning and fourth in the franchising industry overall in its annual Franchise Gold 200. *Income Opportunities* magazine ranked Molly Maid first in residential cleaning and second in the franchising industry overall. *Entrepreneur* magazine has ranked Molly Maid in the top 100 of their Franchise 500 for over six years.

Sources: "History," Molly Maid International Inc., 22 October 2008, http://www.mollymaid.ca/news/index.php; "The Real Dirt on Canadians and Their Homes," Canada NewsWire, 19 March 2007, http://proquest.umi.com; "Molly Maid Still Cleaning Up in Canada After 25 years," *Canadian Business Franchise*, March/April 2004, 80–81; and "Pioneer in Home Cleaning Business Continues to Meet the Needs of the Modern Family," Canada NewsWire, 13 April 2004, http://proquest.umi.com.

your investment perspective, you are not creating a product or service from scratch. Rather, you are benefiting from the experience of the franchisor. In addition to the two methods mentioned earlier, franchising is a way that you can start a business venture, especially if you are more comfortable doing so with an established product and process. When deciding which method is best for you in terms of getting into your first business venture—whether it be starting your own company from scratch, buying an existing business, or franchising—be sure to weigh the advantages and disadvantages of each option before proceeding. One example a successful franchise business is Molly Maid International Inc., a leader in the cleaning industry. The Reaching Beyond Our Borders introduces you to this company.

INHERIT OR TAKE OVER A FAMILY BUSINESS[26]

It is not uncommon for the dream of one to evolve into a family business. Some examples highlighted in this textbook include Company's Coming and Irving Oil. Husband and wife teams (such as Timothy Snelgrove and Teresa Snelgrove, founders of Timothy's World Coffee, and David and Penny Chapman, founders of Chapman's Ice Cream) are also quite common when you review the Canadian landscape of family businesses.

There are a number of factors that make family businesses unique. One is ownership. Public companies are typically owned by a large number of shareholders whose primary interest in ownership is generating the best return on investment. However, family businesses are often owned by a much smaller group whose ownership often has elements of personal identity, family legacy, and community responsibility entwined

DEALING with CHANGE

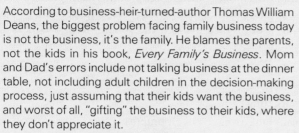

Some Unique Challenges of Family Businesses

According to business-heir-turned-author Thomas William Deans, the biggest problem facing family business today is not the business, it's the family. He blames the parents, not the kids in his book, *Every Family's Business*. Mom and Dad's errors include not talking business at the dinner table, not including adult children in the decision-making process, just assuming that their kids want the business, and worst of all, "gifting" the business to their kids, where they don't appreciate it.

Management problems in a family-owned business are somewhat different from similar problems in non-family businesses. When close relatives work together, emotions often interfere with business decisions. When you put up your own money and operate your own business, you prize your independence. "It's my business," you tell yourself. However, "It's our business" in a family company.

Conflicts sometimes abound because relatives look upon the business from different viewpoints. Those relatives who are silent partners, shareholders, and directors may only see dollar signs when judging capital expenditures, growth, and other major matters. Relatives who are engaged in daily operations judge major matters from the viewpoint of the production, sales, and personnel necessary to make the company successful. Obviously, these two viewpoints may conflict in many instances. This natural conflict can be aggravated by family members who have no talent for money or business.

While the majority of family business owners would like to see their business transferred to the next generation, it is estimated that 70 percent will not survive into the second generation and 90 percent will not survive into the third generation. With 90 percent of businesses being family businesses, and half of all business owners planning to retire over the next decade, Canada's economic health clearly hinges on creating more successful successions.

One factor that might contribute to a successful transfer is governance. The key to effective governance for a family business is recognizing when the family business is moving from one stage to another, such as from the controlling owner (i.e., the original entrepreneur) to a sibling partnership where siblings have an ownership interest and/or some family shareholders are not working in the business. By designing revisions to the governance structure that will meet the needs of the owners for the next stage, expectations and responsibilities are likely to be clearer, contributing to a more successful business venture.

Sources: "Problems in Managing a Family-Owned Business," *Canada Business*, 5 October 2005, http://www.canadabusiness.ca/servlet/Content Server?cid=1081945276597&pagename=CBSC_FE%2Fdisplay&lang= en&c=GuideFactSheet; "Governance for the Family Business," KPMG in Canada, 2008, http://www.kpmg.ca/en/services/enterprise/issuesGrowth Governance.html; "The Parent Trap," *PROFIT*, October 2008, 13; and Grant Walsh, Family Business Succession, KPMG Enterprise™, 2008, http://www.kpmg.ca/en/services/enterprise/documents/3468_Succession.pdf.

---

with its economic interests. This "emotional ownership" often results in family businesses having a longer-term view. Another factor that tends to separate successful family firms from their public counterparts is the concept of stewardship. Many family businesses have a clear understanding that the business is something to be preserved and grown for future generations. As Bill Ford, the chairman of Ford Motor Company once said, "I'm working for my children and grandchildren and feel I'm working for our employees' children and grandchildren as well."

As with any form of business, there are some challenges associated with a family business, as highlighted in the Dealing with Change box. Regardless of such challenges, inheriting or taking over a family business is another way that one can learn about small business.

Progress Assessment

- Why are small businesses important to Canada?
- What are causes of small-business failure?
- How can one get into a business venture?

MANAGING A SMALL BUSINESS

The number-one reason for small-business failure is poor management. Keep in mind, though, that the term *poor management* covers a number of faults. It could mean poor planning, poor record keeping, poor inventory control, poor promotion, or poor employee relations. Most likely it would include poor capitalization.[27] To help you succeed as a business owner, in the following sections we explore the functions of business in a small-business setting:

- planning your business
- financing your business
- knowing your customers (marketing)
- managing your employees (human resource development)
- keeping records (accounting).

Although all of the functions are important in both the start-up and management phases of the business, the first two functions—planning and financing—are the primary concerns when you start your business. The remaining functions are the heart of the actual operations once the business is started.

Begin with Planning

It is amazing how many people are eager to start a small business but have only a vague notion of what they want to do. Eventually, they come up with an idea for a business and begin discussing the idea with professors, friends, and other business people. It is at this stage that the entrepreneur needs a business plan. A **business plan** is a detailed written statement that describes the nature of the business, the target market, the advantages the business will have in relation to competition, and the resources and qualifications of the owner(s). A business plan forces potential owners of small businesses to be quite specific about the goods or services they intend to offer. They must analyze the competition, calculate how much money they need to start, and cover other details of operation. A business plan is also mandatory for talking with bankers or other investors. Put another way, a business plan is a tool that is used to transition the entrepreneur from having an idea to actually developing a strategic and operational framework for the business.

If you are looking for bank financing, here are some tips. First, pick a bank that serves businesses the size of yours, have a good accountant prepare a complete set of financial statements and a personal balance sheet, and make an appointment before going to the bank. Second, go to the bank with an accountant and all of the necessary financial information and demonstrate to the banker that you're a person of good character: civic minded and respected in business and community circles. Finally, ask for all the money you need, be specific, and be prepared to personally guarantee the loan.

Writing a Business Plan

A good business plan takes a long time to write, but you've got to convince your readers (e.g., prospective lenders and investors) in five minutes not to throw it away. While there is no such thing as a perfect business plan, prospective entrepreneurs do think out the smallest details. Jerrold Carrington of Inroads Capital Partners advises that one of the most important parts of the business plan is the executive summary. The summary has to catch the reader's interest. Bankers receive business plans every day. "You better grab me up front," says Carrington. Figure 6.6 gives you an outline of a comprehensive business plan.

Getting the completed business plan into the right hands is almost as important as getting the right information into the plan. Finding proper funding requires research. Next, we will discuss some of the many sources of money available to new business ventures. All of them call for a comprehensive business plan. The time and effort you invest before starting a business will pay off many times over. With small businesses, the big payoff is survival.

business plan
A detailed written statement that describes the nature of the business, the target market, the advantages the business will have in relation to competition, and the resources and qualifications of the owner(s).

FIGURE 6.6

Sample Outline of a Business Plan

LENGTH OF A COMPREHENSIVE BUSINESS PLAN

A good business plan is between 25 and 50 pages long and takes at least six months to write.

Cover letter

Only one thing is certain when you go hunting for money to start a business: You won't be the only hunter out there. You need to make potential funders want to read your business plan instead of the hundreds of others on their desks. Your cover letter should summarize the most attractive points of your project in as few words as possible. Be sure to address the letter to the potential investor by name. "To Whom It May Concern" or "Dear Sir" is not the best way to win an investor's support.

Section 1—Executive Summary

Begin with a two-page or three-page management summary of the proposed venture. Include a short description of the business, and discuss major goals and objectives.

Section 2—Company Background

Describe company operations to date (if any), potential legal considerations, and areas of risk and opportunity. Summarize the firm's financial condition, and include past and current balance sheets, income and cash-flow statements, and other relevant financial records. (You will learn about these financial statements in Chapter 16.) It is also wise to include a description of insurance coverage. Investors want to be assured that death or other mishaps do not pose major threats to the company.

Section 3—Management Team

Include an organization chart, job descriptions of listed positions, and detailed resumés of the current and proposed executives. A mediocre idea with a proven management team is funded more often than a great idea with an inexperienced team. Managers should have expertise in all disciplines necessary to start and run a business. If not, mention outside consultants who will serve in these roles and describe their qualifications.

Section 4—Financial Plan

Provide five-year projections for income, expenses, and funding sources. Don't assume the business will grow in a straight line. Adjust your planning to allow for funding at various stages of the company's growth. Explain the rationale and assumptions used to determine the estimates. Assumptions should be reasonable and based on industry/historical trends. Make sure all totals add up and are consistent throughout the plan. If necessary, hire a professional accountant or financial analyst to prepare these statements.

Stay clear of excessively ambitious sales projections; rather, offer best-case, expected, and worst-case scenarios. These not only reveal how sensitive the bottom line is to sales fluctuations but also serve as good management guides.

Section 5—Capital Required

Indicate the amount of capital needed to commence or continue operations, and describe how these funds are to be used. Make sure the totals are the same as the ones on the cash-flow statement. This area will receive a great deal of review from potential investors, so it must be clear and concise.

Section 6—Marketing Plan

Don't underestimate the competition. Review industry size, trends, and the target market segment. Discuss strengths and weaknesses of the good or service. The most important things investors want to know are what makes the product more desirable than what's already available and whether the product can be patented. Compare pricing to the competition's. Forecast sales in dollars and units. Outline sales, advertising, promotion, and public relations programs. Make sure the costs agree with those projected in the financial statements.

Section 7—Location Analysis

In retailing and certain other industries, the location of the business is one of the most important factors. Provide a comprehensive demographic analysis of consumers in the area of the proposed business as well as a traffic-pattern analysis and vehicular and pedestrian counts.

Section 8—Manufacturing Plan

Describe minimum plant size, machinery required, production capacity, inventory and inventory-control methods, quality control, plant personnel requirements, and so on. Estimates of product costs should be based on primary research.

Section 9—Appendix

Include all marketing research on the good or service (off-the-shelf reports, article reprints, etc.) and other information about the product concept or market size. Provide a bibliography of all the reference materials you consulted. This section should demonstrate that the proposed company won't be entering a declining industry or market segment.

FIGURE | 6.7

Sources of Financing for SMEs
Many companies use multiple sources of financing. Half of all SMEs rely on financial services firms to provide them with business debt financing. Beyond business credit, however, SMEs also make use of other sources of financing such as:

- supplier credit (51.9%)
- personal savings (56.9%)
- personal credit cards (50.0%)
- retained earnings (53.7%)
- business credit cards (48.4%)
- personal lines of credit (45.2%)
- leasing (30.4%)
- personal loans (33.2%)
- loans from friends and relatives (24.2%)
- government lending agencies (20.9%)
- angel investment (15.1%)

Source: "Where Does the Money Come From?" Canadian Bankers Association, 2008, www.cba.ca.

venture capitalists (VCs)
Individuals or companies that invest in new businesses in exchange for partial ownership of those businesses.

angel investors
Private individuals who invest their own money in potentially hot new companies before they go public.

Getting Money to Fund a Small Business

An entrepreneur has several potential sources of capital for a small business, as listed in Figure 6.7. Half of all SMEs rely on financial services firms to provide them with business financing. While banks provide 54 percent of this financing, credit unions and caisses populaires, finance companies, insurance companies, and venture capital/ investment funds also play a significant role in financing SMEs.[28]

Investors known as **venture capitalists (VCs)** may finance your project— for a price. Venture capitalists may ask for a hefty stake (as much as 60 percent) in your company in exchange for the cash to start your business. If the VC demands too large a stake, you could lose control of the business. This may have been the case with Chris & Larry's Clodhoppers. Chris Emery and Larry Finnson started Krave's in 1996. Their Clodhopper treats are bite-sized pieces of graham wafer and chocolate candy. By the mid-2000s, they had accepted venture capital financing and management advice when their sales kept growing but they were still broke. In October 2005, Finnson stepped down as president and he and Emery turned the running of the company over to a management company so they could focus on marketing. Five months later, the assets of the company were sold to Brookside Foods. Harold Heide, vice-president of investments at ENSIS Growth Fund, which owned about 45 percent of Krave's, said the deal made sense: "The time had simply come in ENSIS's investing cycle to sell its position in Krave's."[29]

According to *PROFIT*'s "Financing Guide," financing from VCs ranges from $500,000 to $20 million.[30] In 2008, the average amount invested per company was $3.6 million, with total venture capital investment in Canada reaching $1.3 billion.[31] If you are interested in finding out more, visit Canada's Venture Capital & Private Equity Association (www.cvca.ca), which represents Canada's venture capital and private equity industry.

An alternate source of funds, if you cannot get venture capital, is to consider finding an angel investor. **Angel investors** are private individuals who invest their own money in potentially hot new companies before they go public.[32] Angel investors usually target their support (generally $20,000 to $500,000) to pre-start-up and early-stage companies with high growth prospects.[33] If your proposed venture does require millions of dollars to start, experts recommend that you talk with at least five investment firms and their clients to find the right VCs.

There are many information sources for financing. You can visit government sites such as the Business Development Bank of Canada or Industry Canada's Financing Web site. The Industry Canada site provides information aimed at helping small- and medium-sized businesses, companies, and entrepreneurs in Canada find financing from public- and private-sector sources. You can also find a listing of federal and provincial government assistance programs, tax incentives for small businesses, and a listing of financial providers, including

Dragon's Den is a CBC production where aspiring entrepreneurs pitch their business concepts and products to a panel of Canadian business moguls. If you can convince them to lend you money, they will expect ownership in the business in exchange.

VCs. Examples of government grants and programs include the Scientific Research and Experimental Development program, the National Research Council's Industrial Research Assistance Program, and Ontario Centres of Excellence Investment Accelerator Fund.[34] Another useful source is www.canadianbusiness.com/entrepreneur/financing.

Obtaining money from banks, VCs, and government sources can be a challenge for most small businesses. (You will learn more about financing in Chapter 11.) Those who do survive the planning and financing of their new ventures are eager to get their businesses up and running. Your success in running a business depends on many factors. Three important factors for success are knowing your customers, managing your employees, and keeping efficient records. These topics will be discussed next.

Knowing Your Customers

One of the most important elements of small-business success is knowing the market. In business, a **market** consists of people with unsatisfied wants and needs who have both the resources and the willingness to buy. For example, we can confidently state that many of our students have the willingness to own a brand new car. However, few of them have the resources necessary to satisfy this want. Would they be considered a good market for a luxury car dealer to pursue?

Cervélo Cycles is the world's largest manufacturer of time trial and triathlon bikes. Cervélo founders and co-owners Phile White (left) and Gerard Vroomen (right) have launched their own Cervélo TestTeam. In 2008, the Tour de France was won aboard a Cervélo bike.

Once you have identified your market and its needs, you must set out to fill those needs. The way to meet your customers' needs is to offer top quality at a fair price with great service. Remember, it isn't enough to get customers—you have to keep them. Everything must be geared to bring the customers the satisfaction they deserve. Gérard Vroomen and Phil White founded Cervélo Cycles Inc. when they were engineering students and wished to market the new time-trial bikes they were developing. Today, the company produces road and triathlon racing bikes, and Cervélo is internationally recognized as one of the most innovative bike manufacturers. According to Vroomen, "Our basic philosophy is that we start by having very strong products. It's much easier to market a good product than a bad one."[35]

One of the greatest advantages that small businesses have over larger ones is the ability to know their customers better and to adapt quickly to their ever-changing needs. Now let's consider the importance of effectively managing the employees who help you serve your market.

market
People with unsatisfied wants and needs who have both the resources and the willingness to buy.

Managing Employees

As a business grows, it becomes impossible for an entrepreneur to oversee every detail, even if he or she is working 60 hours per week. This means that hiring, training, and motivating employees are critical.

It is not easy to find good, qualified help when you offer less money, fewer benefits (if any), and less room for advancement than larger firms do. That is one reason why employee relations is such an important part of small-business management. Employees of small companies are often more satisfied with their jobs than are their counterparts in big business. Why? Quite often they find their jobs more challenging, their ideas more accepted, and their bosses more respectful.

Often entrepreneurs reluctantly face the reality that to keep growing, they must delegate authority to others. Nagging questions such as "Who should be delegated authority?" and "How much control should they have?" create perplexing problems.

This can be a particularly touchy issue in small businesses with long-term employees, and in family businesses. As you might expect, entrepreneurs who have built their companies from scratch often feel compelled to promote employees who have been with them from the start—even when those employees aren't qualified to serve as managers. Common sense probably tells you this could be detrimental to the business.

The same can be true of family-run businesses that are expanding. Attitudes such as "You can't fire family" or "You must promote certain workers because they're family" can hinder growth. Entrepreneurs can best serve themselves and the business if they gradually recruit and groom employees for management positions. By doing this, entrepreneurs can enhance trust and the support of the manager among other employees and themselves.

When Heida Thurlow of Chantal Cookware suffered an extended illness, she let her employees handle the work she once had insisted on doing herself. The experience transformed her company from an entrepreneurial one into a managerial one. She says, "Over the long run that makes us stronger than we were."

Keeping Records

Small-business owners often say that the most important assistance they received in starting and managing the business involved accounting. A business person who sets up an effective accounting system early will save much grief later. Computers simplify record keeping and enable a small-business owner to follow the progress of the business (sales, expenses, profits) on a daily basis. An inexpensive computer system can also help owners with other record-keeping chores, such as inventory control, customer records, and payroll.

A good accountant is invaluable in setting up such systems and showing you how to keep the system operating smoothly. Many business failures are caused by poor accounting practices. A good accountant can help make decisions such as whether to buy or lease equipment and whether to own or rent the building. Help may also be provided for tax planning, financial forecasting, choosing sources of financing, and writing up requests for funds.[36]

Other small-business owners may tell you where to find an accountant experienced in small business. It pays to shop around for advice.

Looking for Help

Small-business owners have learned, sometimes the hard way, that they need outside consulting advice early in the process. This is especially true of legal, tax, and accounting advice but may also be true of marketing, finance, and other areas. Most small- and medium-sized firms cannot afford to hire such experts as employees, so they must turn to outside assistance. As a start, ask friends, other entrepreneurs, or family to recommend someone.

A necessary and invaluable aide is a competent, experienced lawyer—one who knows and understands small businesses. Partners have a way of forgetting agreements unless the contract is written by a lawyer and signed. Lawyers can help with a variety of matters, including leases, contracts, and protection against liabilities.

Marketing decisions should be made long before a product is produced or a store is opened. An inexpensive marketing research study may help you determine where to locate, whom to select as your target market, and what would be an effective strategy for reaching those people. Thus, a marketing consultant with small-business experience can be of great help to you.

Given the marketing power of the Internet, your business will benefit from a presence on the Internet, even if you do not sell products or services directly from the Web. This applies to both small and large companies. For example, while the Forzani Group Ltd. is the largest and only national sporting goods retailer in Canada, you can visit its site to view products but you cannot buy anything online.[37]

Two other invaluable experts are a commercial account officer and an insurance agent. The commercial account officer can help you design an acceptable business plan and give you valuable financial advice as well as lend you money when you need it. An insurance agent will explain the risks associated with a small business and how to cover them most efficiently with insurance and other means (e.g., safety devices, sprinkler systems).

Often, local schools have business professors who will advise small-business owners for a small fee or for free. Some universities have clubs or programs that provide consulting services by master of business administration (MBA) candidates for a nominal fee. Does your school provide such services?

It also is wise to seek the counsel of other small-business owners. Other sources of counsel include local chambers of commerce, the Better Business Bureau, national and local trade associations (such as the Canadian Federation of Independent Business), the business reference section of your library, and many small business-related sites on the Internet. Some have been noted in this chapter.

GOING INTERNATIONAL: SMALL-BUSINESS PROSPECTS

As we will note in Chapter 8, the world market is a much larger, much more lucrative market for small businesses than Canada is alone. In spite of that potential, most small businesses still do not think internationally, and only a small percentage of small businesses export.

Why are so many companies missing the boat to the huge global markets? Primarily because the voyage involves a few major hurdles: (1) financing is often difficult to find, (2) many would-be exporters don't know how to get started, (3) potential global business people do not understand the cultural differences of prospective markets, and (4) the bureaucratic paperwork can threaten to bury a small business. See the Reaching Beyond Our Borders box for a story about how one company has become a leader in its field.

Besides the fact that most of the world's market lies outside of Canada, there are other good reasons for going international. For instance, exporting products can absorb excess inventory, soften downturns in the domestic market, and extend product lives. It can also spice up dull routines.

Jen Kluger and Suzie Orol met while studying for their business degrees. They set out to build their company, Foxy Originals, with a vision: high-style fashion jewellery accessible to young women. Upon graduation, they focused full-time on their business. Their products are found in hundreds of stores across North America and they are quickly expanding beyond. What are some challenges they might have encountered in global markets?

Small businesses have several advantages over large businesses in international trade:

- overseas buyers enjoy dealing with individuals rather than with large corporate bureaucracies
- small companies usually can begin shipping much faster
- small companies provide a wide variety of suppliers
- small companies can provide more personal service and more undivided attention, because each overseas account is a major source of business.

The growth potential of small businesses overseas is phenomenal. This is why there are many organizations that offer assistance. Some of these have been cited in this chapter as well as in Chapter 3. Web-based business applications are helping small businesses cross boundaries like never before and, in some instances, levelling some of the advantages that large businesses traditionally have had.

Progress Assessment

- What are the five functions of business?
- There are nine sections in the business plan outline in this chapter. Can you describe at least five of those sections now?
- What are some of the advantages that small businesses have over large businesses in selling in global markets?

SUMMARY

LO ▶ 1 Explain why people are willing to become entrepreneurs, and describe the attributes of successful entrepreneurs.

1. There are many reasons why people are willing to take the risks of entrepreneurship.

What are significant differences between the entrepreneurial venture and the small business?
Entrepreneurial ventures differ from small businesses in four ways: amount of wealth creation, speed of wealth creation, risk, and innovation.

What are a few of the reasons people start their own businesses?
Reasons include profit, independence, opportunity, and challenge.

What are the attributes of successful entrepreneurs?
Successful entrepreneurs are self-directed, determined, action-oriented, highly energetic, tolerant of uncertainty, and able to learn quickly.

LO ▶ 2 Discuss the importance of small business to the Canadian economy.

2. Businesses employing fewer than 50 employees account for approximately 95 percent of all employer businesses.

What does the "small" in small business mean?
A small business is often defined as a business that is independently owned and operated, is not dominant in its field, and meets certain standards of size in terms of employees or annual revenues. Many institutions define small business according to their own needs.

Why are small businesses important to the Canadian economy?
Small business that have fewer than 100 employees contribute approximately 26 percent to Canada's gross domestic product. Perhaps more important to tomorrow's graduates, small businesses employ a large portion of the total private labour force.

3. Thousands of businesses enter and exit the marketplace throughout the year.

LO ▶ 3 Summarize the major causes of small-business failure.

How many small businesses fail each year?

Statistics Canada reports that 60 percent of micro-enterprises fail within their first four years, with a slightly lower percentage (58 percent) for businesses with five to ninety-nine employees.

Why do so many small businesses fail?

Many small businesses fail because of managerial incompetence and inadequate financial planning. See Figure 6.4 for a list of causes of small-business failure. Some of these causes include attempting to do too much business with too little capital, underestimating how much time it will take to build a market, and not allowing for setbacks and unexpected expenses.

What factors increase the chances for success?

Figure 6.5 outlines some situations for small-business success. This includes whether the product is not easily made by mass-production techniques, whether sales are not large enough to appeal to a large firm, and whether the owner pays attention to new competitors.

4. Most people have no idea how to go about starting a small business.

LO ▶ 4 List ways to learn about how small businesses operate.

What hints would you give someone who wants to learn about starting a small business?

An entrepreneur can improve the odds by learning from others. First, take courses and talk with some small-business owners. Second, get some experience working for others. Third, take over a successful firm. Finally, study the latest in small-business management techniques, including the use of computers for things such as payroll, inventory control, and mailing lists.

5. Writing a business plan is the first step in organizing a business.

LO ▶ 5 Analyze what it takes to start and run a small business.

What goes into a business plan?

See Figure 6.6 to see what goes into a business plan. A business plan includes a section on company background, the financial plan, and the location analysis.

What sources of funds should someone wanting to start a new business consider investigating?

A new entrepreneur has several sources of capital: personal savings, relatives, banks, finance companies, venture capital organizations, government agencies, angel investors, and more.

What are some of the special problems that small-business owners have in dealing with employees?

Small-business owners often have difficulty finding competent employees and grooming employees for management responsibilities.

Where can potential entrepreneurs find help in starting their businesses?

Help can be found from many sources: accountants, lawyers, marketing researchers, loan officers, insurance agents, the Business Development Bank of Canada, and even professors.

What online sources are available to assist entrepreneurs?

Entrepreneurs can start by visiting government sources, such as the Industry Canada Web site. Financial services providers, such as RBC Financial Group and CIBC, also have sites dedicated to small businesses.

LO ▶ 6 Outline the advantages and disadvantages that small businesses have in entering global markets.

6. The future growth of some small businesses is in foreign markets.

What are some advantages small businesses have over large businesses in global markets?

Foreign buyers enjoy dealing with individuals rather than large corporations because (1) small companies provide a wider variety of suppliers and can ship products more quickly and (2) small companies give more personal service.

Why don't more small businesses start trading internationally?

There are several reasons: (1) financing is often difficult to find, (2) many people don't know how to get started, (3) many do not understand the cultural differences in foreign markets, and (4) the bureaucratic red tape is often overwhelming.

KEY TERMS

angel investors 166

business establishment 155

business plan 164

employer business 155

entrepreneurial team 150

entrepreneurship 144

incubators 154

intrapreneurs 153

market 167

micro-enterprise 151

micropreneurs 151

small and medium-sized enterprises (SMEs) 149

small business 155

venture capitalists (VCs) 166

CRITICAL THINKING

1. There was mention in the chapter that small businesses continue to be feeders for future large businesses. As they prosper and develop new goods and services, they are often bought out by large companies. Is this good or bad? Should we do anything about it? If so, what?

2. Are there any similarities between the characteristics demanded of an entrepreneur and those of a professional athlete? Would an athlete be a good prospect for entrepreneurship? Why or why not? Could teamwork be important in an entrepreneurial effort?

3. Imagine yourself starting a small business. What kind of business would it be? How much competition is there? What could you do to make your business more attractive than those of competitors? Would you be willing to work 60 to 70 hours a week?

DEVELOPING WORKPLACE SKILLS

1. Find issues of *Canadian Business*, *Canadian Business Franchise*, and *PROFIT* magazines in the library, your local bookstore, or on the Internet. Read about the entrepreneurs who are heading today's dynamic new businesses. Write a profile about one entrepreneur.

2. Select a small business that looks attractive as a career possibility for you. Talk to at least one person who manages such a business. Ask how he or she started the business. Ask about financing, personnel problems (hiring, firing, training, scheduling), accounting problems, and other managerial matters. Prepare a summary of your findings, including whether the job was rewarding, interesting, and challenging—and why or why not.

3. Contact a government agency such as Export Development Canada or Business Development Bank of Canada. Write a brief summary of the services that they provide for small businesses. (Hint: Each organization has a Web site: www.edc.ca and www.bdc.ca.)

4. Contact a local bank and make an appointment to speak with a commercial accounts officer. Ask this person what a small business owner should consider if she or he is looking for financing. Discuss other sources of financing that might be available to an entrepreneur. Find out what resources this bank has available to assist small-business owners. Bring this information to class and share it with your peers.

5. There has been some discussion in this chapter about entrepreneurship and traits of entrepreneurs. In a group, highlight the differences between a business person and an entrepreneur.

TAKING IT TO THE NET 1

www.mcgrawhillconnect.ca

Purpose

To assess your potential to succeed as an entrepreneur.

Exercise

Go to www.bizmove.com/other/quiz.htm and take the interactive entrepreneurial quiz to find out if you have the qualities needed to be a successful entrepreneur.

TAKING IT TO THE NET 2

www.mcgrawhillconnect.ca

Purpose

To write a business plan.

Exercise

Sometimes one of the most difficult tasks in writing a business plan is knowing where to start. One source is *Canadian Business*'s Interactive Business Planner, which assists entrepreneurs in preparing a three-year business plan for their new or existing business.

Go to http://www.canadabusiness.ca/ibp/eng/intro.cfm. How will this tool assist an entrepreneur in preparing a business plan? What are the key features in this tool?

ANALYZING MANAGEMENT DECISIONS

Starting a Small Business While in School

Milun Tesovic, co-founder and owner of Metroleap Media Inc., was named the 2009 national CIBC Student Entrepreneur of the Year by Advancing Canadian Entrepreneurship Inc. (ACE). The company won over the judges because of the accomplishments Tesovic has achieved as a small-business owner while attending Simon Fraser University as a full-time student. Started in 2004, the company hosts a music lyric Web site (www.metrolyrics.com) that provides music lovers with the written lyrics of their favourite songs. In creating a market and revenue stream for the music industry, Metroleap Media Inc. was named the second-largest music Web site online (as of January 2009 by Hitwise), reaching 32 million visitors per month. It has been growing 8 percent month over month.

Tesovic competed at the national level against five other regional champions, to a panel of 30 top executives.

In addition to the national title, he received a $10,000 cash prize. "You always hear people say that the youth of today are the future," says Tesovic. "...this Student Entrepreneur Competition puts that saying into perspective. I am proud to be representing Canada at the Global Student Entrepreneur Awards so I can demonstrate the amazing accomplishments students can do alongside a full course load. For me, ACE's Student Entrepreneur Competition has been a great source of publicity and recognition. Most importantly, it has put me in touch with other young entrepreneurs from across Canada."

Sources: "Milun Tesovic Named 2009 National Student Entrepreneur Competition Champion," Advancing Canadian Entrepreneurship Inc., 7 May 2009, http://www.acecanada.ca/news/newsItem.cfm?cms_news_id=32105.07.2009; and "British Columbia Student Entrepreneur Provincial Champion Named," Advancing Canadian Entrepreneurship Inc., 24 February 2009, http://www.acecanada.ca/news/newsItem.cfm?cms_news_id=277.

Discussion Questions

1. What are the advantages and potential problems of starting a business while in school?

2. What kinds of entrepreneurs are operating around your school? Talk to them and learn from their experiences.

3. What opportunities exist for satisfying student needs at your school? Pick one idea, write a business plan, and discuss it in class (unless it is so good you don't want to share it; in that case, good luck).

RUNNING CASE

Canadian Tire Corporation, Ltd.: Then and Now

In 1913, there were only 23,700 cars in Canada, but by 1922, the number had jumped to 210,333 in Ontario alone. That year, with a combined savings of $1,800, two brothers, John W. Billes and Alfred J. Billes, bought Hamilton Tire and Garage Ltd. in Toronto's east end. The brothers stocked a small range of repair parts for the two most popular car makes, tires, batteries, and a homemade brand of antifreeze at a time when Toronto's 40,000 cars were being accepted as transportation. A big part of their early earnings came from renting out parking spaces in their heated garage—a necessity in those days if a car was to start on a cold morning.

In 1927, Canadian Tire Corporation, Limited, was officially incorporated. "We chose Canadian Tire," A.J. Billes later recalled, "because it sounded big." From across the country, people began writing to the store, looking for automotive parts that were hard to find in more isolated areas. In 1928, to serve this market, the brothers produced their first catalogue featuring tire values on one side, and a handy road map of Ontario on the back.

Today, Canadian Tire Corporation, Limited, is Canada's most-shopped general merchandise retailer. As a public corporation, it generated net earnings of approximately $374.2 billion in 2008. Reporting to the parent corporation are five interrelated businesses: Canadian Tire Retail (CTR), PartSource, Canadian Tire Petroleum (CTP), Canadian Tire Financial Services (CTFS), and Mark's Work Wearhouse.

CTR operates 475 stores from coast to coast through its network of entrepreneurial associate dealers. Together, these stores offer customers a unique mix of products and services through three specialty categories: automotive parts, accessories, and service; sports and leisure products; and home products. Its Web site, www.canadiantire.ca, offers Canadians the opportunity to shop online and is among the country's busiest e-commerce sites.

PartSource is an automotive parts specialty chain with 86 stores designed to meet the needs of major purchasers of automotive parts. This includes professional automotive installers and serious do-it-yourselfers.

CTP is one of the country's largest and most productive independent retailers of gasoline, operating 273 gas bars, 266 convenience stores and kiosks, and 74 car washes. Petroleum is an important component of the company's total offering, giving customers discounts on store merchandise as well as loyalty rewards with every purchase.

As the financial arm of Canadian Tire Corporation, Ltd. (Canadian Tire), Canadian Tire Financial Services (CTFS) primarily engages in financing and managing the Canadian Tire Options® MasterCard for more than five million card members. CTFS also markets related financial products and services to retail and petroleum customers including personal loans, insurance and warranty products, and emergency roadside assistance through the Canadian Tire Auto Club. A banking pilot is currently underway at Canadian Tire Bank offering high-interest savings accounts, guaranteed investment certificates, residential mortgages, and the One-and-Only™ account.

Mark's Work Wearhouse is one of the country's leading apparel retailers, operating 372 stores in Canada. Under the Clothes that Work™ marketing strategy, Mark's sells apparel and footwear in work, work-related, casual, and active-wear categories, as well as health-care and business-to-business apparel. Its Web site, www.marks.com, offers Canadians the opportunity to shop for Mark's products online.

Source: "Corporate Profile," Canadian Tire Corporation, Limited, 2009, http://corp.canadiantire.ca/EN/AboutUs/Pages/CorporateProfile.aspx.

Discussion Questions

1. Entrepreneurs have played a major role in developing the Canadian economy. Visit http://corp.canadiantire.ca/EN/BusinessOpportunities/RetailOwnership/Pages/FAQs.aspx to learn read some commonly-asked questions by those considering applying for a store. How much does it cost to invest in an CTR store? What qualifications are needed in a Dealer? (Note that this term is used in the place of franchisee.)

2. What are some advantages and disadvantages to becoming an Associate Dealer?

3. What are some advantages and disadvantages of being a wholly owned subsidiary, as is the case for Canadian Tire Financial Services?

McGraw-Hill Connect™—Available 24/7 with instant feedback so you can study when you want, how you want, and where you want. Take advantage of the Study Plan—an innovative tool that helps you customize your learning experience. You can diagnose your knowledge with pre- and post-tests, identify the areas where you need help, search the entire learning package for content specific to the topic you're studying, and add these resources to your personalized study plan.

Visit www.mcgrawhillconnect.ca to register— take practice quizzes, search the e-book, and much more.

Entrepreneur Readiness Questionnaire

Not everyone is cut out to be an entrepreneur. The fact is, though, that all kinds of people with all kinds of personalities have succeeded in starting small and large businesses. There are certain traits, however, that seem to separate those who'll be successful as entrepreneurs from those who may not be. The following questionnaire will help you determine in which category you fit. Take a couple of minutes to answer the questions and then score yourself at the end. Making a low score doesn't mean you won't succeed as an entrepreneur. It does indicate, however, that you may be happier working for someone else.

Each of the following items describes something that you may or may not feel represents your personality or other characteristics about you. Read each item and then circle the response (1, 2, 3, 4, or 5) that most nearly reflects the extent to which you agree or disagree that the item seems to fit you.

Scoring:

Give yourself one point for each 1 or 2 response you circled for questions 1, 2, 6, 8, 10, 11, 16, 17, 21, 22, 23.

Give yourself one point for each 4 or 5 response you circled for questions 3, 4, 5, 7, 9, 12, 13, 14, 15, 18, 19, 20, 24, 25.

Add your points to see how you rate in the following categories:

21–25   Your entrepreneurial potential looks great if you have a suitable opportunity to use it. What are you waiting for?

16–20   This is close to the high entrepreneurial range. You could be quite successful if your other talents and resources are right.

11–15   Your score is in the transitional range. With some serious work you can probably develop the outlook you need for running your own business.

6–10   Things look pretty doubtful for you as an entrepreneur. It would take considerable rearranging of your life philosophy and behaviour to make it.

0–5   Let's face it. Entrepreneurship isn't really for you. Still, learning what it's all about won't hurt anything.

Looking at my overall philosophy of life and typical behaviour, I would say that …	RESPONSE				
	Agree Completely (1)	Mostly Agree (2)	Partially Agree (3)	Mostly Disagree (4)	Disagree Completely (5)
1. I am generally optimistic.	1	2	3	4	5
2. I enjoy competing and doing things better than someone else.	1	2	3	4	5
3. When solving a problem, I try to arrive at the best solution first without worrying about other possibilities.	1	2	3	4	5
4. I enjoy associating with co-workers after working hours.	1	2	3	4	5
5. If betting on a horse race I would prefer to take a chance on a high-payoff "long shot."	1	2	3	4	5
6. I like setting my own goals and working hard to achieve them.	1	2	3	4	5
7. I am generally casual and easy-going with others.	1	2	3	4	5
8. I like to know what is going on and take action to find out.	1	2	3	4	5
9. I work best when someone else is guiding me along the way.	1	2	3	4	5
10. When I am right I can convince others.	1	2	3	4	5
11. I find that other people frequently waste my valuable time.	1	2	3	4	5
12. I enjoy watching football, baseball, and similar sports events.	1	2	3	4	5
13. I tend to communicate about myself very openly with other people.	1	2	3	4	5
14. I don't mind following orders from superiors who have legitimate authority.	1	2	3	4	5
15. I enjoy planning things more than actually carrying out the plans.	1	2	3	4	5
16. I don't think it's much fun to bet on a "sure thing."	1	2	3	4	5
17. If faced with failure, I would shift quickly to something else rather than sticking to my guns.	1	2	3	4	5
18. Part of being successful in business is reserving adequate time for family.	1	2	3	4	5
19. Once I have earned something, I feel that keeping it secure is important.	1	2	3	4	5
20. Making a lot of money is largely a matter of getting the right breaks.	1	2	3	4	5
21. Problem solving is usually more effective when a number of alternatives are considered.	1	2	3	4	5
22. I enjoy impressing others with the things I can do.	1	2	3	4	5
23. I enjoy playing games like tennis and handball with someone who is slightly better than I am.	1	2	3	4	5
24. Sometimes moral ethics must be bent a little in business dealings.	1	2	3	4	5
25. I think that good friends would make the best subordinates in an organization.	1	2	3	4	5

Source: Kenneth R. Van Voorhis, *Entrepreneurship and Small Business Management* (New York: Allyn & Bacon, 1980).

CHAPTER 7
Management and Leadership

LEARNING OBJECTIVES

AFTER YOU HAVE READ
AND STUDIED THIS CHAPTER,
YOU SHOULD BE ABLE TO:

LO ▶ 1 Explain how the changes that are occurring in the business environment are affecting the management function.

LO ▶ 2 Describe the four functions of management.

LO ▶ 3 Describe the different types of planning and the importance of decision making in choosing the best alternative.

LO ▶ 4 Describe the organizing function of management and the three categories of skills needed by managers.

LO ▶ 5 Explain the differences between leaders and managers, and describe the various leadership styles.

LO ▶ 6 Summarize the five steps of the control function of management.

PROFILE

Getting to Know Richard (Rick) George of Suncor Energy

Suncor pioneered the commercial development of the oil sands. Suncor is a major North American energy producer and marketer with a team of over 6,500 employees. Operating an upgrader near Fort McMurray, Alberta, Suncor extracts and upgrades oil sands into high-quality, refinery-ready crude oil products. They also explore for and develop natural gas and sell refined products in Ontario and Colorado. Suncor is also investing in clean renewable energy sources. They have a number of wind power projects in operation with a total capacity of over 150 megawatts of renewable energy. In addition, they operate ethanol production facilities developing ethanol from non-food sources such as wood residues.

Rick George is the President and Chief Executive Officer of Suncor. Rick was named Canada's "Outstanding CEO of the Year" after leading a remarkable business turnaround at Suncor, lifting the company from an underperformer to a leader in Canada's energy industry. Since Rick took the company public in 1992, Suncor's market capitalization has increased to more than $40 billion from less than $1 billion.

Rick received the Canadian Business Leader Award in 2000 and served as chairperson of the Canadian Council of Chief Executives from 2003 to 2006. He has been a member of the North American Competitiveness Council since 2006 and was appointed an Officer of the Order of Canada in December 2007. He was a member of the Calgary Committee to End Homelessness in 2007 and chair of the 2008 Governor General's Canadian Leadership Conference. Originally from Brush, Colorado, Rick spent 10 years with Sun Company both in the United States and the United Kingdom. During this time he held various positions in project planning, production evaluation, exploration and production, and in the international oil business.

Rick led Suncor's move to new technologies and processes that propelled the oil sands from the margins of viability to a major Canadian energy source. Investment in technology to improve productivity and reduce environmental impacts has remained central to Rick's business philosophy. Suncor is one of Canada's top 20 research and development spenders, and putting technology into action forms a substantial part of the company's planned capital spending.

Under his leadership, Suncor has also invested outside the oil and gas industry to adopt a "parallel path" approach to reaching sustainable energy objectives: developing hydrocarbon resources responsibly to meet current needs while supporting the long-term diversification of energy sources. He talks about his concern for the environment both from the standpoint of current tar sands extraction and investment in renewable energy in the CEO messages on the Suncor Web site, which you are encouraged to visit.

With the majority of Suncor's business operations in northern Alberta, Rick has also taken a lead role in working with Canada's Aboriginal communities and leadership to build opportunities for aboriginals to participate in the growing economy. Under Rick's leadership, Aboriginal participation in Suncor's oil sands workforce has grown from less than 3 per cent to nearly 10 percent by 2005. From 2001 to 2003, Rick was co-chair of the Taking Pulse Initiative of the national Aboriginal Achievement Foundation.

In this chapter, you will read about management and the changes occurring in this area. Like George, most managers today are flexible and open to new ideas. They see opportunity and act much faster than they did in the past. They tend to give their workers more responsibility and authority and act more like leaders (visionaries) and coaches than hands-on managers who tell people what to do and how to do it.

Source: Suncor, 22 August 2008, www.suncor.com; and The Governor General's Canadian Leadership Conference, 22 August 2008, www.leadershipcanada.ca.

MANAGERS' ROLES ARE EVOLVING

resources

A general term that incorporates human resources, natural resources, and financial resources.

Managers must practise the art of getting things done through organizational resources. **Resources** is a general term that incorporates human resources (e.g., employees), natural resources (e.g., raw materials), and financial resources (e.g., money). Resources include the factors of production, which were introduced in Chapter 1. Every business has scarce resources, and management is about deciding how to effectively use these scarce resources. It is for this reason that you will be introduced to the study of management and how the different functional areas of business (operations, human resources, and marketing are the first three covered in this book) must work together.

At one time, managers were called bosses, and their job consisted of telling people what to do and watching over them to be sure they did it. They were typically more proficient and knew more than the employees they supervised. Bosses tended to reprimand those who didn't do things correctly, and generally were impersonal. Many managers still behave that way. Perhaps you've witnessed such behaviour.

Today, management is becoming more progressive. Managers are educated to guide, train, support, motivate, and coach employees rather than tell them what to do.[1] When coaching, managers are trying to get the best out of their employees. Management is an assignment; coaching is a choice.[2]

Managers of high-tech firms realize that workers often know much more about technology than they do. Thus, most modern managers emphasize teamwork and co-operation rather than discipline and giving orders.[3] Managers in some high-tech firms and in progressive firms of all kinds tend to be friendly and generally treat employees as partners rather than unruly workers.

In the past, an employee would expect to work for the same company for many years, maybe even a lifetime. Similarly, companies would proudly acknowledge employees who achieved milestones in terms of duration of employment. Today, many companies don't hesitate to lay off employees, and employees don't hesitate to leave if their needs are not being met. Today's top leaders of Fortune 100 companies are younger, and more of them are female. They tend to move from one company to another as their careers unfold.[4] Traditional long-term contracts between management and employees—and the accompanying trust—are often no longer there. This increases the difficulty of the management task because managers must earn the trust of their employees, which includes rewarding them and finding other ways to encourage them to stay in the firm.

In general, management is studied more and more. Managers in the future are likely to be working in teams and assuming completely new roles in the firm. Further, they'll have to deal with a different set of issues in developing nations—see the Reaching Beyond Our Borders box.

What this means for you and other graduates of tomorrow is that successful management will demand a new kind of person: a skilled communicator and team player as well as a planner, coordinator, organizer, and supervisor. These trends will be addressed in the next few chapters to help you decide whether management is the kind of career you would like.

management

The process used to accomplish organizational goals through planning, organizing, leading, and controlling people and other organizational resources.

planning

A management function that includes anticipating trends and determining the best strategies and tactics to achieve organizational goals and objectives.

organizing

A management function that includes designing the structure of the organization and creating conditions and systems in which everyone and everything work together to achieve the organization's goals and objectives.

FUNCTIONS OF MANAGEMENT

Well-known management consultant Peter Drucker says that managers give direction to their organizations, provide leadership, and decide how to use organizational resources to accomplish goals.[5] Such descriptions give you some idea of what managers do. In addition to those tasks, managers today must deal with conflict resolution, create trust in an atmosphere where trust has been badly shaken, and help create balance between work lives and family lives.[6] Managers look at the big picture, and their decisions make a major difference in organizations.[7] The following definition of management provides the outline of this chapter: **Management** is the process used to accomplish organizational goals through planning, organizing, leading, and controlling people and other organizational resources.

Reaching Beyond Our Borders

We Need Managers Over Here

OK, so there are many opportunities for growing a business overseas. What is keeping Canadian companies from expanding rapidly in global markets? Jack Welch, former CEO of General Electric, says the problem is not a lack of engineers or scientists; the problem is a lack of professional managers. Top managers from many companies are complaining that they can't find people to run their operations. That includes managers in all areas, from human resource management to finance. That means lots of opportunity for today's college graduates. If they can broaden their perspective to think of global markets, the potential is awesome.

The challenges are pretty daunting, however. Here is what the *Sloan Management Review* said in 2008: "Village roads can be impassable, home cooking is still a way of life, product prices can be below the cost of production . . . and local products often have generations

of loyal customers." Flexibility is a key to conquering such challenges. For example, companies are using motorcycles to get through on those supposedly impassible roads. Developing products that appeal to local markets is another strategy. That may mean selling cigarettes one by one instead of in packs. It may mean selling crank-up radios that run without electricity. The challenges can be fun as well as daunting. Sure, you'll have to learn how to negotiate with the government. Sure, you'll face all the issues discussed in this chapter. But the payoff is a rewarding managerial position in a growing country. Often the rewards far outstrip the costs.

Sources: Jack Welch and Suzy Welch, "Red Flags for the Decade Ahead," *BusinessWeek*, 19 May 2008; and Satish Shankar, Charles Ormiston, Nicolas Bloch, Robert Schaus and Vijay Vishwanath, "How to Win in Emerging Markets," *Sloan Management Review*, Spring 2008.

(Figure 7.1 provides a comprehensive listing of all the critical tasks in this process.)

Planning includes anticipating trends and determining the best strategies and tactics to achieve organizational goals and objectives. One of those objectives is to please customers.[8] The trend today is to have *planning teams* to help monitor the environment, find business opportunities, and watch for challenges. Planning is a key management function because the other management functions depend heavily on having a good plan.

Organizing includes designing the structure of the organization and creating conditions and systems in which everyone and everything work together to achieve the organization's goals and objectives.[9] Many of today's organizations are being designed around the customer. The idea is to design the firm so that everyone is working to please the customer at a profit. Thus, organizations must remain flexible and adaptable because customer needs change, and organizations must either change along with them or risk losing their business. General Motors, for example, has lost much of its customer base to more fuel-efficient cars.[10] It hopes to win them back by offering hydrogen-powered vehicles that could save consumers much money in fuel.[11]

Many managers today are working in teams, and this means working *with* employees rather than simply directing them. These teams are likely to be ethnically diverse and include people of varied ages and backgrounds. Since managers will function primarily as trainers, coaches, and motivators of teams, it is expected that member of the team will do year-end evaluations of the manager and vice versa. How do you think most managers will react to having lower-level employees evaluate *their* effectiveness?

Leading means creating a vision for the organization and communicating, guiding, training, coaching, and motivating others to work effectively to achieve the organization's goals and objectives. Researchers have spent a considerable amount of time studying motivation, given the direct relationship between motivation and output. This subject is explored further in Chapter 11. The trend is to empower employees, giving them as much freedom as possible to become self-directed and self-motivated. This function was once known as *directing*; that is, telling employees exactly what to do. In many smaller firms, that is still the role of managers. In most large modern firms, however, managers no longer tell people exactly what to do because knowledge workers and others often know how to do their jobs better than the manager. Nonetheless, leadership is necessary to keep employees focused on the right tasks at the right time along with training, coaching, motivating, and the other leadership tasks.[12]

leading
Creating a vision for the organization and guiding, training, coaching, and motivating others to work effectively to achieve the organization's goals and objectives.

FIGURE **7.1**

What Managers Do
Some modern managers perform all of these tasks with the full co-operation and participation of workers. Empowering employees means allowing them to participate more fully in decision making.

Planning
- Setting organizational goals.
- Developing strategies to reach those goals.
- Determining resources needed.
- Setting precise standards.

Organizing
- Allocating resources, assigning tasks, and establishing procedures for accomplishing goals.
- Preparing a structure (organization chart) showing lines of authority and responsibility.
- Recruiting, selecting, training, and developing employees.
- Placing employees where they'll be most effective.

Leading
- Guiding and motivating employees to work effectively to accomplish organizational goals and objectives.
- Giving assignments.
- Explaining routines.
- Clarifying policies.
- Providing feedback on performance.

Controlling
- Measuring results against corporate objectives.
- Monitoring performance relative to standards.
- Rewarding outstanding performance.
- Taking corrective action when necessary.

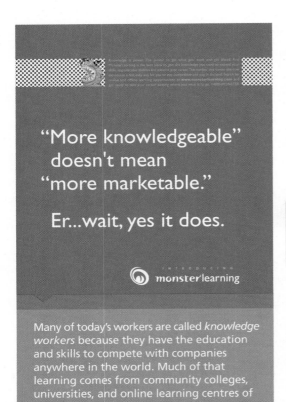

"More knowledgeable" doesn't mean "more marketable."

Er...wait, yes it does.

INTRODUCING
🌀 monster learning

Many of today's workers are called *knowledge workers* because they have the education and skills to compete with companies anywhere in the world. Much of that learning comes from community colleges, universities, and online learning centres of all kinds. What skills will make you more competitive in tomorrow's job market?

controlling
A management function that involves establishing clear standards to determine whether or not an organization is progressing toward its goals and objectives, rewarding people for doing a good job, and taking corrective action if they are not.

Controlling involves establishing clear standards to determine whether an organization is progressing toward its goals and objectives, rewarding people for doing a good job, and taking corrective action if they are not. Basically, it means measuring whether what actually occurs meets the organization's goals.

The four functions—planning, organizing, leading, and controlling—are the heart of management, so let's explore them in more detail. The process begins with planning; we'll look at that right after the Progress Assessment.

Progress Assessment

- What is the definition of management used in this chapter?
- What are the four functions of management?

PLANNING: CREATING A VISION BASED ON VALUES

Planning, the first managerial function, involves setting the organizational vision, values, goals, and objectives. Executives rate planning as the most valuable tool of their workbench. Part of the planning process involves the creation of a vision for the organization. A **vision** is more than a goal; it's an encompassing explanation of why the organization exists and where it's trying to head. A vision gives the organization a sense of purpose. **Values** are a set of fundamental beliefs that guide a business in the decisions they make. Values guide strategic planning through to day-to-day decisions by being mindful of how all stakeholders will be treated. Vision informs values, while values come alive through vision. Together, they unite workers in a common destiny. Managing an organization without first establishing a vision can be counterproductive. It's like motivating everyone in a rowboat to get really excited about going somewhere, but not telling them exactly where. As a result, the boat will just keep changing directions rather than speeding toward an agreed-on goal. Without a set of values, an organization has no basis for determining how their employees should interact with stakeholders. As a result, sustainable long-term relationships will be difficult.

Suncor's vision is "to become a sustainable energy company and so we manage our business to deliver superior shareholder returns, while providing social and economic benefits to our stakeholders and reducing the environmental impact of our operations and products." Notice the reference to corporate social responsibility, as discussed in Chapter 4, and to the environment, as seen in each chapter's Green Boxes. Their values include reference to safety, people and relationships, high performance, sustainability, and accountability.

A **mission statement** is an outline of the organization's fundamental purposes.[13] Mission statements are usually developed by top management, with some input from employees, depending on the size of the company. A meaningful mission statement should address:

- the organization's self-concept
- company philosophy and goals
- long-term survival
- customer needs
- social responsibility
- the nature of the company's product or service

Figure 7.2 contains Canadian Tire Financial Services' mission statement. How well does this mission statement address all of the issues listed above?

The mission statement becomes the foundation for setting specific goals and selecting and motivating employees. **Goals** are the broad, long-term accomplishments an organization wishes to attain. Goals need to be mutually agreed on by workers and management. Thus, goal setting is often a team process.

Objectives are specific, short-term statements detailing how to achieve the organization's goals. One of your goals for reading this chapter, for example, may be to learn basic concepts of management. An objective you could use to achieve this goal is to answer the chapter's Progress Assessment questions correctly. Objectives must be measurable. For example, you can measure your progress in answering questions by determining what percentage you answer correctly over time.

Planning is a continuous process. It's unlikely that a plan that worked yesterday would be successful in today's market. Most planning follows a pattern. The procedure you would follow in planning your life and career is basically the same as that used by businesses for their plans. Planning answers several fundamental questions for businesses:

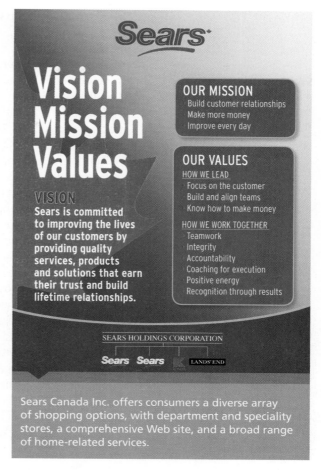

Sears Canada Inc. offers consumers a diverse array of shopping options, with department and speciality stores, a comprehensive Web site, and a broad range of home-related services.

vision
An encompassing explanation of why the organization exists and where it's trying to head.

values
A set of fundamental beliefs that guide a business in the decisions they make.

mission statement
An outline of the fundamental purposes of an organization.

goals
The broad, long-term accomplishments an organization wishes to attain.

objectives
Specific, short-term statements detailing how to achieve the organization's goals.

FIGURE 7.2

Canadian Tire Financial Services' Mission Statement

Canadian Tire's vision comes to life through our Team Values:
We are *learners* … who thrive in a challenging and fast-paced environment.
We are *committed* … to operate with honesty, integrity and respect.
We are *owners* … with a passion to continuously improve.
We are *driven* … to help customers achieve their goals.
We are *accountable* … to ourselves and each other.
We are *leaders* … who perform with heart.
The Canadian Tire Way is our foundation and inspiration that will continue to guide our future growth and success.

Source: Marco Marrone, president of Canadian Tire Financial Services.

SWOT analysis
A planning tool used to analyze an organization's strengths, weaknesses, opportunities, and threats.

1. What is the situation now? What trends are being observed in the business environment? What opportunities exist for meeting customers' needs? What products and customers are most profitable or will be most profitable? Why do people buy (or not buy) our products? Who are our major competitors? What threats are there to our business? These questions frame the **SWOT analysis**. This is an analysis of an organization's **S**trengths, **W**eaknesses, **O**pportunities, and **T**hreats—how can strengths be used and capitalized on, how can weaknesses be improved, how can opportunities be exploited, and how can threats be mitigated. Soliciting input from all key stakeholders, a company begins such a process with a general review of the business situation. Then it identifies its internal strengths and weaknesses, relative to its competitors. These strengths and weaknesses are for the most part within the control of the organization. They include elements that are referred to as PRIMO-F: people, resources, innovation and ideas, marketing, operations, and finance. Next, a business environment analysis (you were introduced to some elements, such as the legal environment, in Chapter 1) is conducted. Opportunities and threats in the marketplace are identified—and, while they cannot always be controlled or anticipated, they most definitely affect the organization. Opportunities and threats include concepts referred to as PESTLE: political, economic, social, technological, legal, and environmental. Given all of this information gathered in the SWOT analysis, a company can then create an action plan to address the business situation identified. Figure 7.3 lists some of the potential issues companies consider when conducting a SWOT analysis: Where do we want to go? How much growth do we want? What is our profit goal? What are our social objectives? What are our personal development objectives? A SWOT analysis is framed by the vision and when completed may result in the vision being revisited. The Dealing With Change box highlights how a large department store chain has used the results of such an analysis to plan a successful course of action.

2. How can we get there from here? This is the most important part of planning. It takes four forms: strategic, tactical, operational, and contingency. See Figure 7.4 for a visual of this. Notice the continuous connection between the four forms. Not only does this illustrate the relationship between them, but also that planning is a continuous process, which each of the forms being informed by another of the forms.

strategic planning
The process of determining the major goals of the organization and the policies and strategies for obtaining and using resources to achieve those goals.

Strategic planning outlines how the company will meet its objectives and goals. It provides the foundation for the policies, procedures, and strategies for obtaining and using resources to achieve those goals. In this definition, policies are broad guides to action,

FIGURE | 7.3

SWOT Analysis
This figure identifies potential strengths, weaknesses, opportunities, and threats that organizations may discover in a SWOT analysis.

Potential Internal Strengths
- an acknowledged market leader
- core competencies in key areas
- proven and respected management team

Potential Internal Weaknesses
- no clear strategic direction
- weak market image
- subpar profitability

Potential External Opportunities
- falling trade barriers in attractive foreign markets
- new government policies (e.g., incentives for R&D, lower taxes, industry deregulation)
- increases in market demand (due to changing buyer needs and tastes, growing incomes)

Potential External Threats
- recession and changing (negative) economic conditions
- introduction of substitute products (by competitors)
- costly regulatory requirements

DEALING with CHANGE

Hitting the Retail Bull's Eye

Target is certainly one of the success stories of the recent past in the U.S. retailing scene. It has the reputation that Sears, Kmart, and other large retailers once had. As the competition slows, Target management seems to be finding the right path to success. For one thing, Target managers have found a market niche for the company's online sales. Stores are good for buying items for yourself, but Web sites are often better for finding gifts for someone else. Therefore, management decided to go to the Web. Target.com aims its Web site at people who need to buy gifts. One fall, for example, Target sold thousands of Student Survival Kits to parents and other relatives of returning students. Some 22 percent of the site's sales come from bridal and baby registries. By responding quickly to such market opportunities, Target managers can keep the company in the vanguard. Target is also on Amazon.com's Web site. In short, Target seems to be on target when it comes to adapting to the Internet challenge. In this area, Target's success seems comparable to that of Walmart.

Target management has been less successful in competing with Walmart in the area of superstores. Target's superstores are less productive than its regular stores. Was it a mistake to go after Walmart's super-centres? Walmart has its own grocery warehouses, giving it a cost advantage. Target could create its own distribution centres to become more competitive, but that is dangerous ground. Such centres are costly. Adapting to change is never easy, but adapting to Walmart is truly daunting. Target has its own image and its own customer base. Sometimes change is good and sometimes it's not. By listening to its customer base and responding appropriately, Target's managers should be able to expand and increase profits. That may mean sticking to what Target knows best and not venturing into Walmart's strengths. Or, it may not. That's the future challenge for Target's managers.

Walmart has entered the Canadian market, first with smaller scale department stores and a number of Sam's Club Wholesale outlets. More recently, they are focusing their expansion on their SuperStore format, aggressively expanding their produce offerings including grocery products. Target continues to stay away from the Canadian marketplace. There has been no public talk in the past few years about them coming to Canada, even with the continuing problems at The Bay.

Sources: Jim Collins, "Bigger, Better, Faster," *Fast Company*, June 2003, 74–78; www.target.com, 2005; and Michael Barbaro, "Pinch Me—Is That a Wal-Mart?" *The Washington Post*, 7 August 2005, F1, F6.

---

and strategies determine the best way to use resources. At the strategic planning stage, the company decides which customers to serve, what goods or services to sell, and the geographic areas in which the firm will compete.[14] For example, GM is going through the painful process of deciding which products to keep and which to cut.[15] Poor decision making in the past has had disastrous consequences on this company.

In today's rapidly changing environment, strategic planning is becoming more difficult because changes are occurring so fast that plans—even those set for just months into the future—may soon be obsolete.[16] Therefore, some companies are making shorter-

FORMS OF PLANNING

STRATEGIC PLANNING
The setting of broad, long-range goals by top managers

TACTICAL PLANNING
The identification of specific, short-range objectives by lower managers

CONTINGENCY PLANNING
Backup plans in case primary plans fail

OPERATIONAL PLANNING
The setting of work standards and schedules

FIGURE 7.4

Planning Functions
Very few firms bother to make contingency plans. If something changes the market, such companies may be slow to respond. Most organization do strategic, tactical, and operational planning.

term plans that allow for quick responses to customer needs and requests.[17] The goal is to be flexible and responsive to the market.

tactical planning

The process of developing detailed, short-term statements about what is to be done, who is to do it, and how it is to be done.

Tactical planning is the process of developing detailed, short-term statements about what is to be done, who is to do it, and how it is to be done. Tactical planning is normally the responsibility of managers or teams of managers at *lower* levels of the organization, whereas strategic planning is the responsibility of the *top* managers of the firm (e.g., the president and vice-presidents of the organization). Tactical planning, for example, involves setting annual budgets and deciding on other details and activities necessary to meet the strategic objectives. If the strategic plan of a truck manufacturer, for example, is to sell more trucks in northern Canada, the tactical plan might be to fund more research of northern truck drivers' wants and needs, and to plan advertising to reach those customers.

operational planning

The process of setting work standards and schedules necessary to implement the company's tactical objectives.

Operational planning is the process of setting work standards and schedules necessary to implement the company's tactical objectives. Operational planning focuses on the specific responsibilities of supervisors, department managers, and individual employees. Operational plans can include operational budgets. You will read about budgets in more detail in Chapter 11. Or, The operational plan is the department manager's tool for daily and weekly operations. An operational plan could also include, say, the specific dates for certain truck parts to be completed and the quality specifications those parts must meet. You will read about operations management in more detail in Chapter 9.

contingency planning

The process of preparing alternative courses of action that may be used if the primary plans don't achieve the organization's objectives.

Contingency planning is the process of preparing alternative courses of action that may be used if the primary plans don't achieve the organization's objectives. The economic and competitive environments change so rapidly that it's wise to have alternative plans of action ready in anticipation of such changes. For example, if an organization doesn't meet its sales goals by a certain date, the contingency plan may call for more advertising or a cut in prices at that time. The global outbreak of SARS in 2003 forced many health agencies around the world to develop contingency plans to respond to this atypical pneumonia. The SARS experience (estimated to have cost the business community $50 billion) and mad cow disease ($7 billion and growing) have also forced companies in the private sector to develop contingency plans.[18]

Some believe that the H5N1 type of avian flu, which started in Korea in 2003 and has spread to other countries, or the H1N1 strain, sometimes referred to as swine flu, which gained prominence in 2009, is a pandemic-in-waiting. While no one knows conclusively when the next pandemic will occur, the World Health Organization warns that the global spread of a pandemic can't be stopped—but preparing properly will reduce its impact.[19] In response, the Public Health Agency of Canada, together with federal government departments and provincial and territorial governments, has taken many steps to protect Canadians from a possible influenza (flu) pandemic.[20] This includes maintaining the Canadian Pandemic Influenza Plan, which maps out how Canada will prepare for and respond to pandemic influenza. For example, the Plan has been revised in response to the 2009 H1N1 virus threat, and now includes an Annex that outlines a suggested planning framework for addressing the psychosocial implications of a pandemic influenza or any large-scale public health emergency.[21]

Some companies see opportunities where others see threats. Morneau Sobeco provides global benefits consulting, administration systems, and outsourcing services. It encourages companies to re-evaluate their thinking regarding contingency planning and the importance of anticipating health care–related emergencies (HREs). While there has been widespread media attention given to SARS, other diseases such as pneumonia and influenza (also known as the flu) lead to more deaths annually in Canada. Morneau Sobeco believes that most companies view contingency planning solely as a tool to prevent operational shutdowns. A company should be able to mitigate the potential damage and financial loss resulting from an unforeseen emergency or catastrophe. The benefits of developing an HRE contingency plan are numerous. However, the main goals of such

SPOTLIGHT ON Small Business

I'd Rather Be Blue

Some of the best-managed organizations can be found in the most unusual situations. Consider, for example, three entrepreneurs whose product involved shaving their heads, slathering themselves with blue paint, and drumming on homemade instruments such as PVC pipe. Enter the Blue Man Group. Today the original Blue Men—Matt Goldman, Phil Stanton, and Chris Wink—manage an organization of over 500 employees, 70 of whom appear nightly as Blue Men in 12 cities around the world. Their Megastar World Tour included a number of shows in central Canada featuring their unique music, comedy, and multimedia theatrics.

Like the founders of any other company, the Blue Man Group creators knew they had to tinker with their product if they wanted to expand and be successful. Planning and organization were critical. The partners locked themselves away for several days to write a detailed 132-page Blue Man operating manual. Writing the manual made the partners realize the vast market potential for their concept, but it also taught them the importance of managing the product's growth and everyday operations. They decided that company decisions would not be made on a majority vote but rather by consensus among the three of them. That policy continues today.

Sources: Liz Welch, "How We Did It: The Blue Man Group," *Inc.*, August 2008; and Blue Man Group, www.blueman.com, accessed 29 January 2009.

---

initiatives are ensuring business continuity, reducing risk to employees and their dependants, and maintaining productivity, as well as minimizing the possibility of litigation.[22]

Crisis planning is a part of contingency planning. **Crisis planning** involves reacting to sudden changes in the environment. At the 16th World Conference on Disaster Management, Peter Power, a veteran of the anti-terrorism branch of the London Metropolitan Police, stated that "nowhere near enough" Canadian companies are ready to deal with the fallout from an environmental, accidental, technological, or terrorist-driven catastrophe.[23] Crisis planning can be especially challenging to medium-sized and smaller companies due to fewer resources, said Carolee Birchall, vice-president and senior risk officer of technology and solutions at BMO Bank of Montreal.[24] In short, crisis planning is a critical component of contingency planning that requires understanding and acceptance throughout the whole organization, regardless of its size. You will read more about risk management in Appendix B.

Planning is a key management function because the other management functions depend on having good plans. Starting with a directional plan based on broad business objectives and performance targets over three to five years, companies can then focus their efforts through strategic planning. The idea is to stay flexible, listen to customers, and seize opportunities when they come, whether or not those opportunities were expected.[25] The opportunities, however, must fit into the company's overall goals and objectives or the company could lose its focus. Clearly, then, much of management and planning involves decision making.

Before we consider decision making, let us summarize some of the points in this chapter. A vision ("WHERE we are going..."), in combination with values (HOW we will treat our stakeholders...) ..."), and the mission statement ("Our purpose IS ..."), provides direction for the company. A company's objectives (WHAT we want to accomplish) are linked to its strategy (HOW we will accomplish the objectives). So, there is a progression from vision and values, to mission, to objectives, and to strategy. Once the strategy has been established, plans must be developed and implemented to ensure that objectives are met. There is never a strategy without there first being an objective. A SWOT analysis alone is almost useless unless you match it to the company's strategy and plan.

Clearly, then, much of management and planning requires decision making. The Spotlight on Small Business box illustrates how one unique small business handles planning and decision making.

crisis planning
Involves reacting to sudden changes in the environment.

The following YouTube video talks about car sharing in Kitchener-Waterloo: http://www.youtube.com/watch?v=43rEQzbk-c8.

GreenBOX

How About Car Sharing?

Car sharing is affordable for people who do not need a car every day. "When you want a glass of milk, do you buy a cow?" Cars are located in convenient locations, near bus lines. Members of a car share not-for-profit corporation do not pay for gas, repairs, or insurance; just a flat fee based on length of use (which could be as short as one hour) and a fixed cost per kilometre. Car sharing creates a culture of a more caring, respectful community, given that these are co-operative organizations. Car sharing has proven to reduce auto emissions by over 50 percent per member.

Considerable planning is required to initiate this business, which is so contrary to the norm for car ownership. It was in the early 1990s that car sharing started to take hold on a global basis, with the first North American location being in Quebec City. The concept needed to build a public profile. Local car shares operate as a co-operative, so funding continually needs to be planned for. Common sources of funding are government agencies and charitable foundations. In each of these applications, car sharing co-operatives need to demonstrate a thorough plan. The co-operative must start with the basics of a plan, including vision, values, and mission statements. Then it must produce operational plans showing how the not-for-profit entity is going to achieve financial stability. On an ongoing basis, contingency plans need to be in place to respond to the membership levels. Given the incremental increasing costs of car ownership and the concern for the environment, car sharing appears to be more than a passing phenomenon.

Source: Grand River Carshare and Hamilton Carshare, 20 October 2009, www.peoplescar.org.

DECISION MAKING: FINDING THE BEST ALTERNATIVE

decision making
Choosing among two or more alternatives.

All management functions involve some kind of decision making. **Decision making** is choosing among two or more alternatives. It sounds easier here than it is in practice. In fact, decision making is the heart of all management functions. The rational decision-making model is a series of steps that managers often follow to make logical, intelligent, and well-founded decisions.[26] These steps can be thought of as the seven Ds of decision making:

1. Define the situation.
2. Describe and collect needed information.
3. Develop alternatives.
4. Develop agreement among those involved.
5. Decide which alternative is best.
6. Do what is indicated (begin implementation).
7. Determine whether the decision was a good one and follow up.

Managers don't always go through this seven-step process. Sometimes decisions have to be made on the spot—with little information available. Managers must make good decisions in all such circumstances.

problem solving
The process of solving the everyday problems that occur. Problem solving is less formal than decision making and usually calls for quicker action.

Problem solving is the process of solving the everyday problems that occur. It is less formal than the decision-making process and usually calls for quicker action. Problem-solving teams are made up of two or more workers who are given an assignment to solve a specific problem (e.g., Why are customers not using our service policies?). Problem-solving techniques that companies use include **brainstorming** (i.e., coming up with as many solutions as possible in a short period of time with no censoring of ideas) and **PMI** (i.e., listing all the **P**luses for a solution in one column, all the **M**inuses in another, and the **I**nteresting in a third column). PMI is an tool developed by Edward de Bono as part of his work on lateral and creative thinking strategies. You can practise using the PMI system on almost all of your decisions. For example, should you stay home and study tonight? You would list all benefits of your choice (Pluses) in one column: better grades,

brainstorming
Coming up with as many solutions to a problem as possible in a short period of time with no censoring of ideas.

PMI
Listing all the pluses for a solution in one column, all the minuses in another, and the interesting in a third column.

improved self-esteem, more responsible, and so forth. In the other column, you would put the negatives (Minuses): boredom, less fun, etc. We hope that the pluses outweigh the minuses most of the time, and that you study often, but sometimes it is best to go out and have fun. In that case, the Interesting would be that having fun would not hurt your grades or job prospects.

Progress Assessment

- What's the difference between goals and objectives?
- What does a company analyze when it does a SWOT analysis?
- What's the difference between strategic, tactical, and operational planning?
- What are the seven Ds in decision making?

ORGANIZING: CREATING A UNIFIED SYSTEM

After managers have planned a course of action, they must organize the firm to accomplish their goals. Operationally, organizing means allocating resources (such as funds for various departments), assigning tasks, and establishing procedures for accomplishing the organizational objectives. When organizing, a manager develops a structure or framework that relates all workers, tasks, and resources to each other. That framework is called the organization structure.

Most organizations draw a chart showing these relationships. This tool is called an organization chart. An **organization chart** is a visual device that shows relationships among people and divides the organization's work; it shows who is accountable for the completion of specific work and who reports to whom. Figure 7.5 shows a simple one. Each rectangle indicates a position (and usually who holds this position) within the organization. The chart plots who reports to whom (as indicated by the lines) and who is responsible for each task.

organization chart
A visual device that shows relationships among people and divides the organization's work; it shows who is accountable for the completion of specific work and who reports to whom.

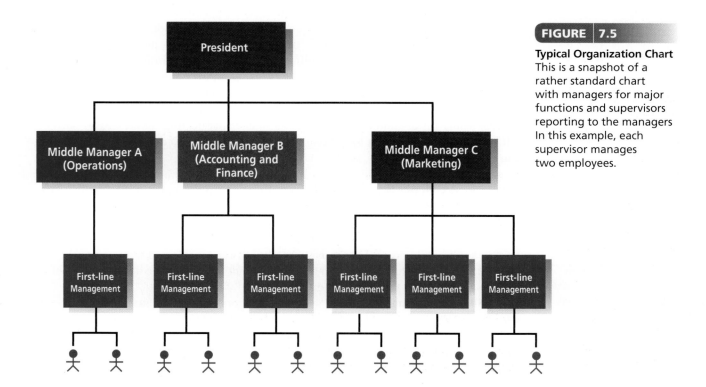

FIGURE | 7.5

Typical Organization Chart
This is a snapshot of a rather standard chart with managers for major functions and supervisors reporting to the managers In this example, each supervisor manages two employees.

FIGURE **7.6**

Levels of Management
This figure shows the three levels of management. In many firms, there are several levels of middle management. Recently, some firms have been eliminating middle-level managers because fewer are needed to oversee self-managed teams of employees.

top management
Highest level of management, consisting of the president and other key company executives, who develop strategic plans.

middle management
The level of management that includes general managers, division managers, and branch and plant managers, who are responsible for tactical planning and controlling.

For example, in Figure 7.5, Manager B is the accounting and finance manager, and this middle manager reports directly to the president. Reporting directly to the accounting and finance manager are two first-line supervisors; two employees report directly to each of these first-line supervisors. The corporate hierarchy illustrated on the organization chart includes top, middle, and first-line managers. The problems involved in developing an organization structure will be discussed later in the text. For now, it's important to know that the corporate hierarchy usually includes three levels of management (see Figure 7.6).

Top management (the highest level of management) consists of the president and other key company executives who develop strategic plans. Terms you're likely to see often are chief executive officer (CEO), chief operating officer (COO), chief financial officer (CFO), and chief information officer (CIO), or in some companies, chief knowledge officer (CKO). The CEO is often the president of the firm and is responsible for all top-level decisions in the firm. CEOs are responsible for introducing change into an organization. The COO is responsible for putting those changes into effect. His or her tasks include structuring work, controlling operations, and rewarding people to ensure that everyone strives to carry out the leader's vision. Many companies today are eliminating the COO function as a cost-cutting measure and are assigning that role to the CEO.[27] Often, the CFO participates in the decision to cut the COO position. The CFO is responsible for obtaining funds, planning budgets, collecting funds, and so on. The CIO or CKO is responsible for getting the right information to other managers so they can make correct decisions.

Loblaws has been making significant changes in their operations over the past few years. Faced with the growing presence of Walmart and general merchandising distribution problems, which resulted in significant losses for a few years, they are looking to Galen Weston Jr. to implement a series of strategic initiatives to restore their former glory. They are refocusing on their strong brands, including President's Choice, repricing some staple products to provide best-value-for-money, and improving efficiencies in their supply chain. Time will tell what impact these strategic decisions will have on Loblaws' place in the Canadian grocery world.[28]

Middle management includes general managers, division managers, and branch and plant managers (in your school, deans and department/area heads) who are responsible for tactical planning and controlling. Many firms have eliminated some middle managers through downsizing, and have given the remaining managers more employees to supervise.

Supervisory management includes those who are directly responsible for supervising workers and evaluating their daily performance; they're often known as first-line managers (or supervisors) because they're the first level above workers.[29]

Tasks and Skills at Different Levels of Management

Few people are trained to be good managers. Usually a person learns how to be a skilled accountant or sales representative or production-line worker, and then—because of his or her technical skills—is selected to be a manager. Once someone becomes a manager they spend more of their time in supporting those people they supervise, showing them how to do things, helping them, supervising them, and generally being very active in the operating task. Robert Katz developed a model to explain the types of skills and the mix of these skills through the various management levels.

The further up the managerial ladder a person moves, the less important his or her original job skills become. At the top of the ladder, the need is for people who are visionaries, planners, organizers, coordinators, communicators, morale builders, and motivators.[30] Figure 7.7 shows that a manager must have three categories of skills:

1. **Technical skills** involve the ability to perform tasks in a specific discipline (such as selling a product or developing software) or department (such as marketing or information systems).

2. **Human relations skills** involve communication and motivation; they enable managers to work through and with people. Such skills also include those associated with leadership, coaching, morale building, delegating, training and development, and help and supportiveness.

3. **Conceptual skills** involve the ability to picture the organization as a whole and the relationships among its various parts. Conceptual skills are needed in planning, organizing, controlling, systems development, problem analysis, decision making, coordinating, and delegating.

While it is not specifically stated, you can see how time management skills are a necessary component of each one of these categories of skills. Good managers must be able to effectively handle the daily points of contact that require their attention. This includes a lot of phone calls, interruptions, meetings, and numerous e-mails.

Looking at Figure 7.7, you'll notice that first-line managers need to be skilled in all three areas. However, most of their time is spent on technical and human relations tasks (assisting operating personnel, giving directions, etc.). First-line managers spend little time on conceptual tasks. Top managers, in contrast, need to use few technical skills. Instead, almost all of their time is devoted to human relations and conceptual tasks. A person who is competent at a low level of management may not be competent at higher levels, and vice versa. The skills needed are different at each level of management.

supervisory management
Managers who are directly responsible for supervising workers and evaluating their daily performance.

technical skills
Skills that involve the ability to perform tasks in a specific discipline or department.

human relations skills
Skills that involve communication and motivation; they enable managers to work through and with people.

conceptual skills
Skills that involve the ability to picture the organization as a whole and the relationships among its various parts.

FIGURE 7.7

Skills Needed at Various Levels of Management
All managers need human relation skills. At the top, managers need strong conceptual skills and rely less on technical skills. First-line managers need strong technical skills and rely less on conceptual skills. Middle managers need to have a balance between technical and conceptual skills.

Canadian Securities Registration Systems (CSRS) is a Canadian registry agent that offers registration and search services across Canada. A winner in Canada's 50 Best Managed Companies program, it attributes its successes to its vision, which is "to be a dynamic, innovative and responsive organization focused on building relationships with our clients and employees." Would you consider researching other companies that have been recognized with this award when looking for a job?

The Stakeholder-Oriented Organization

A dominating question of the past 20 years or so has been how to best organize a firm to respond to the needs of its stakeholders. Remember, stakeholders include customers, employees, suppliers, dealers, environmental groups, and the surrounding communities. The consensus seems to be that smaller organizations are more responsive than larger organizations. Therefore, many large firms are being restructured into smaller, more customer-focused units.

The point is that companies are no longer organizing to make it easy for managers to have control. Instead, they're organizing so that customers have the greatest influence. The change to a customer orientation is being aided by technology. For example, establishing a dialogue with customers on the Internet enables some firms to work closely with customers and respond quickly to their wants and needs. For instance, by allowing customers the option to book flights via the Web, WestJet Airlines not only generated cost savings (a cost of $2 for online booking compared with as much as $20 when a travel agent booked the flight), but customers could collect Air Miles and get a small discount off any round trip fare.[31]

There's no way an organization can provide high-quality goods and services to customers unless suppliers provide world-class parts and materials with which to work. Thus, managers have to establish close relationships with suppliers, including close Internet ties.[32] To make the entire system work, similar relationships have to be established with those organizations that sell directly to consumers—namely retailers. To continue to serve the travel agency market, as well as to acquire more of corporate Canada's business, WestJet increased the size and scope of its sales team.[33]

In the past, the goal of the organization function in the firm was to clearly specify who does what within the firm. Today, the organizational task is much more complex because firms are forming partnerships, joint ventures, and other arrangements that make it necessary to organize the whole system; that is, several firms working together, often across national boundaries.[34] One organization working alone is often not as effective as many organizations working together. Creating a unified system out of multiple organizations will be one of the greatest management challenges of the twenty-first century. This discussion will be re-visited in Chapter 9, when we look at operations management.

LEADING: PROVIDING CONTINUOUS VISION AND VALUES

In business literature there's a trend toward separating the notion of management from that of leadership. One person might be a good manager but not a good leader. Another might be a good leader without being a good manager. One difference between managers and leaders is that managers strive to produce order and stability, whereas leaders embrace and manage change. Leadership is creating a vision for others to follow, establishing corporate values and ethics, and transforming the way the organization does business to improve its effectiveness and efficiency. Good leaders motivate workers and create the environment for workers to motivate themselves.[35] *Management is the carrying out of the leadership's vision.*

Can we identify the characteristics of successful leaders? In looking at leaders in entrepreneurial situations, Murray Johannsen (a leading consultant on transformational leadership) identified nine characteristics: self-esteem, need to achieve, screening for opportunity, internal locus of control, goal orientation, optimism, courage, tolerance to ambiguity, and strong internal motivation. Leaders are motivated by intrinsic values: needs, desires, motive and will power: as opposed to extrinsic values: rewards and recognition.[36]

Transformational leadership has been another focus.[37] A famous quote from Robert Kennedy, when he was Attorney General of the United States, in 1961, illustrates this concept very well, " Some people see things the way they are and ask why, I see things as they could be and ask why not." Put another way, transformational leadership occurs where the leader takes a visionary position and inspires people to follow. Nine spheres of influence, at play when this type of leadership is at play, include authority, charisma, expertise, punishment, positive reinforcement, persuasion, coaching, relationship, and vision.

Now and in the future, all organizations will need leaders who can supply the vision as well as the moral and ethical foundation for growth. You don't have to be a manager to be a leader. All employees can lead. That is, any employee can contribute to producing order and stability and can motivate others to work well. All employees can also add to a company's ethical environment and report ethical lapses when they occur.

Companies can expect negative consequences if leaders do not behave in an ethical manner. For years, Clive Beddoe (former president and CEO of WestJet Airlines) had been recognized for his leadership. Under his management, WestJet had become Canada's second-largest airline. He won several awards, including Alberta's Most Respected Leader

Canada's Top 40 Under 40 honours Canadians who have reached a significant level of success before the age of 40. Winners have demonstrated excellence in areas such as vision and leadership, innovation, and community involvement. For a list of winners, visit www.top40awardcanada.org.

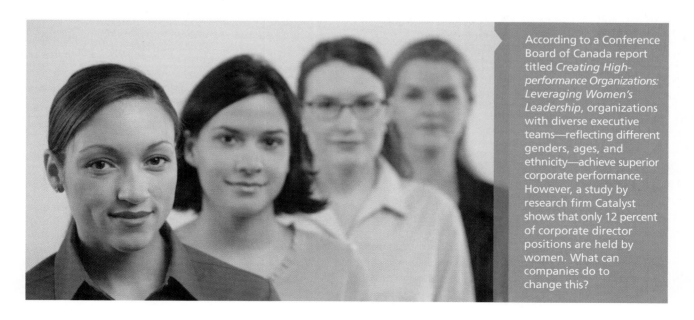

According to a Conference Board of Canada report titled *Creating High-performance Organizations: Leveraging Women's Leadership*, organizations with diverse executive teams—reflecting different genders, ages, and ethnicity—achieve superior corporate performance. However, a study by research firm Catalyst shows that only 12 percent of corporate director positions are held by women. What can companies do to change this?

Making Ethical Decisions

Are You Responsible for Your Boss's Success?

First-line managers assist in the decisions made by their department heads. The department heads retain full responsibility for the decisions—if a plan succeeds, it's their success; if a plan fails, it's their failure. Now picture this: As a first-line manager, you have new information that your department head hasn't seen yet. The findings in this report indicate that your manager's recent plans are sure to fail. If the plans do fail, the manager will probably be demoted and you're the most likely candidate to fill the vacancy. Will you give your department head the report? What will the consequences be of your decision?

(2004) and Top CEO in Canada (2003). In the Eleventh Annual Survey of Canada's Most Respected Corporations (2005), he was ranked third as the most respected leader in Canada. In 2006, WestJet admitted that the company was involved in corporate espionage against Air Canada (recall Chapter 4) and that it was "undertaken with the knowledge and direction of the highest management levels of WestJet." Some questioned whether Beddoe should be allowed to continue as CEO as the admission "raises a lot of questions about leadership and appropriateness of behaviour either in a complicit sense or supervisory sense that the board cannot ignore."[38] It remains to be seen, however, what the long-term impact will be on WestJet's corporate culture. "When the leader of a strong-culture organization admits wrongdoing—it's devastating," said Marc-David Seidel, a professor at the University of British Columbia's Sauder School of Business.[39] Do you agree? In 2007, the board of directors accepted Clive's resignation, and appointed him Chairperson of the Board. Since then, the company has performed very well.

Organizations will need workers and managers who share a vision and know how to get things done co-operatively. The workplace is changing from an environment in which a few dictate the rules to others to an environment in which all employees work together to accomplish common goals. Furthermore, managers must lead by doing, not just by saying. In summary, leaders must:

- *Communicate a vision and rally others around that vision.* In doing so, the leader should be openly sensitive to the concerns of followers, give them responsibility, and win their trust. They should ensure that employees get the message, through quality communication.

- *Establish corporate values.* These values (as discussed earlier in this chapter) include a concern for employees, for customers, for the environment, and for the quality of the company's products. When companies set their business goals today, they're defining the values of the company as well.

- *Promote corporate ethics.* Ethics include an unfailing demand for honesty and an insistence that everyone in the company is treated fairly. That's why we stress ethical decision making throughout this text. See the *Making Ethical Decisions* box for a scenario. Many business people are now making the news by giving away huge amounts to charity, thus setting a model of social concern for their employees and others.

- *Embrace transformational change.* A leader's most important job may be to transform the way the company does business so that it's more effective (does things better) and efficient (uses fewer resources to accomplish the same objectives).

Over the past ten years, there has been an increasing trend in compensation packages. These packages have been justified as necessary to attract and keep good leaders. McGill University's Henry Mintzberg has been vocal on his disagreement with the increasing

CEO compensation packages. In his view, many CEOs focus solely on the short-term increase in the share value of the company and their bonuses. "Find me a chief executive who refuses those bonuses, who takes the long-term view and says his team will share the spoils of their mandate in 10 years time, and I'll show you a leader," he said.[40] Do you agree that top executives should receive such lucrative packages in today's environment?

The Importance of Middle Managers to Leadership[41]

The Conference Board of Canada released a report on the changing role of middle managers, "Leading from the Middle: Managers Make the Difference." Researcher Carolyn Farquahar wrote, "A decade ago, senior managers viewed middle managers poorly— they thought middle managers blocked change and prevented the transfer of authority to front-line employees... A fundamental shift has occurred, and middle managers are now considered an essential link to making change throughout the organization and a training ground for executives of the future."

Carolyn Clark, vice-president of human resources for Fairmont Hotels & Resorts Inc., said that a growing body of research shows "people don't quit their companies, they quit their managers. Therefore, leadership quality is of critical importance at all levels of the company." Dofasco Inc. has also elevated the role of middle managers as key players "in repositioning the company for a new group of leaders." According to the Conference Board report, the greatest challenge facing Dofasco is its aging workforce. Most of the executive team will be gone in the next five to seven years, and over the next decade up to one-third of the workforce will turn over. Middle management will help ensure that Dofasco's unique culture is retained, even with the influx of a large number of new employees.

The Conference Board of Canada report notes that not all organizations recognize the importance of middle managers. However, there are more examples seen today than in the past. This is indeed positive news for those middle managers who survived the downsizing of the past five years and were left with heavy workloads. According to the report, opportunities for middle managers to do challenging and rewarding work are increasing. "In just a few years, middle managers have moved from traditional roles of planning, monitoring, and controlling, to assuming additional roles relating to strategy and process."

Leadership Styles

Nothing has challenged researchers in the area of management more than the search for the "best" leadership traits, behaviours, or styles. Thousands of studies have been undertaken of successful businesses to identify a common style. Intuitively, you would conclude about the same thing that researchers have found: leadership styles are hard to pin down. In fact, results of most studies on leadership have been neither statistically significant nor reliable. Some leaders are well groomed and tactful, while others are unkempt and abrasive—yet the latter may be just as effective as the former.

There's also no one style of leadership that works best in all situations. Even so, we can look at a few of the most commonly recognized leadership styles (see Figure 7.8) and see how they may be effective:

1. **Autocratic leadership** involves making managerial decisions without consulting others. Such a style is effective in emergencies and when absolute "followership" is needed— for example, when fighting fires. Autocratic leadership is also effective sometimes with new, relatively unskilled workers who need clear direction and guidance.

2. **Participative (democratic) leadership** consists of managers and employees working together to make decisions. Research has found that employee participation in decisions may not always increase effectiveness, but it usually increases job satisfaction. Many progressive organizations are highly successful at using a democratic style of leadership that values traits such as flexibility, good listening skills, and empathy.

The Conference Board of Canada's mission is to build leadership capacity for a better Canada by creating and sharing insights on economic trends, public policy, and organizational performance. Visit www.conferenceboard.ca to review some of its more recent findings.

autocratic leadership
Leadership style that involves making managerial decisions without consulting others.

participative (democratic) leadership
Leadership style that consists of managers and employees working together to make decisions.

FIGURE | 7.8

Various Leadership Styles

Boss-centred leadership ← ⋯⋯⋯⋯⋯⋯⋯⋯⋯⋯⋯⋯⋯⋯⋯⋯⋯ Subordinate-centred leadership

Use of authority by manager

Area of freedom for employee

| Manager makes decision and announces it | Manager "sells" decision | Manager presents ideas and invites questions | Manager presents tentative decision subject to change | Manager presents problem, gets suggestions, makes decision | Manager defines limits, asks group to make decision | Manager permits employee to function within limits defined by superior |

Autocratic   Participative/democratic   Free rein/laissez-faire

Source: Reprinted by permission of the *Harvard Business Review*. An exhibit from "How to Choose a Leadership Pattern" by Robert Tannenbaum and Warren Schmidt (May/June 1973). Copyright © 1973 by the President and Fellows of Harvard College, all rights reserved.

At meetings in such firms, employees discuss management issues and resolve those issues together in a democratic manner. That is, everyone has some opportunity to contribute to decisions. Many firms have placed meeting rooms throughout the company and allow all employees the right to request a meeting.

3. **Free-rein (laissez-faire) leadership** involves managers setting objectives and employees being relatively free to do whatever it takes to accomplish those objectives. In certain organizations, where managers deal with doctors, engineers, or other professionals, often the most successful leadership style is free rein. The traits needed by managers in such organizations include warmth, friendliness, and understanding. More and more firms are adopting this style of leadership with at least some of their employees.

free-rein (laissez-faire) leadership
Leadership style that involves managers setting objectives and employees being relatively free to do whatever it takes to accomplish those objectives.

Individual leaders rarely fit neatly into just one of these categories. Researchers illustrate leadership as a continuum with varying amounts of employee participation, ranging from purely boss-centred leadership to subordinate-centred leadership.

Which leadership style is best? Research tells us that successful leadership depends largely on what the goals and values of the firm are, who's being led, and in what situations. It also supports the notion that any leadership style, ranging from autocratic to free-rein, may be successful depending on the people and the situation. In fact, a manager may use a variety of leadership styles, depending on a given situation. A manager may be autocratic but friendly with a new trainee, democratic with an experienced employee who has many good ideas that can only be fostered by a flexible manager who's a good listener, and free-rein with a trusted, long-term supervisor who probably knows more about operations than the manager does.

There's no such thing as a leadership style that always works best. A truly successful leader has the ability to use the leadership style most appropriate to the situation and the employees involved. Figure 7.9 lists some rules of leadership.

FIGURE 7.9

The Rules of Leadership

The 12 Rules of Leadership	The 7 Don'ts of Leadership
1. *Set a good example.* Your subordinates will take their cue from you. If your work habits are good, theirs are likely to be too.	On the other hand, these items can cancel any constructive image you might try to establish.
2. *Give your people a set of objectives and a sense of direction.* Good people seldom like to work aimlessly from day to day. They want to know not only what they're doing but why.	1. *Trying to be liked rather than respected.* Don't accept favours from your subordinates. Don't do special favours in trying to be liked. Don't try for popular decisions. Don't be soft about discipline. Have a sense of humour. Don't give up.
3. *Keep your people informed of new developments of the company and how they'll affect them.* Let people know where they stand with you. Let your close assistants in on your plans at an early stage. Let people know as early as possible of any changes that will affect them. Let them know of changes that won't affect them but about which they may be worrying.	2. *Failing to ask subordinates for their advice and help.*
4. *Ask your people for advice.* Let them know that they have a say in your decisions whenever possible. Make them feel a problem is their problem too. Encourage individual thinking.	3. *Failing to develop a sense of responsibility in subordinates.* Allow freedom of expression. Give each person a chance to learn his or her superior's job. When you give responsibility, give authority too. Hold subordinates accountable for results.
5. *Let your people know that you support them.* There's no greater morale killer than a boss who resents a subordinate's ambition.	4. *Emphasizing rules rather than skill.*
6. *Don't give orders.* Suggest, direct, and request.	5. *Failing to keep criticism constructive.* When something goes wrong, do you tend to assume who's at fault? Do you do your best to get all the facts first? Do you control your temper? Do you praise before you criticize? Do you listen to the other side of the story?
7. *Emphasize skills, not rules.* Judge results, not methods. Give a person a job to do and let him or her do it. Let an employee improve his or her own job methods.	
8. *Give credit where credit is due.* Appreciation for a job well done is the most appreciated of fringe benefits.	6. *Not paying attention to employee gripes and complaints.* Make it easy for them to come to you. Get rid of red tape. Explain the grievance machinery. Help a person voice his or her complaint. Always grant a hearing. Practise patience. Ask a complainant what he or she wants to do. Don't render a hasty or biased judgment. Get all the facts. Let the complainant know what your decision is. Double-check your results. Be concerned.
9. *Praise in public.* This is where it will do the most good.	
10. *Criticize in private.*	
11. *Criticize constructively.* Concentrate on correction, not blame. Allow a person to retain his or her dignity. Suggest specific steps to prevent recurrence of the mistake. Forgive and encourage desired results.	7. *Failing to keep people informed.*
12. *Make it known that you welcome new ideas.* No idea is too small for a hearing or too wild for consideration. Make it easy for them to communicate their ideas to you. Follow through on their ideas.	

Sources: "To Become an Effective Executive: Develop Leadership and Other Skills," *Marketing News*, April 1984, 1; and Brian Biro, *Beyond Success* (New York: Berkley, 2001).

Managing Knowledge

There's an old saying that still holds true today: "Knowledge is power." Empowering employees means giving them knowledge—that is, getting them the information they need to do the best job they can. Finding the right information, keeping the information in a readily accessible place, and making the information known to everyone in the firm together constitutes **knowledge management**.[42] For example, Canadian Tire was the

knowledge management
Finding the right information, keeping the information in a readily accessible place, and making the information known to everyone in the firm.

first major Canadian retailer to use an Internet-based eLearning program. eLearning is an online training and education program that delivers product knowledge and skills training on everything from plumbing to paint mixing. The program is credited with improved customer and employee satisfaction levels. According to Janice Wismer, former vice-president of human resources, "People say the lessons have increased their confidence, that they're happier working here because the company is committing to their growth and development."[43] This is good news for store sales.

The first step to developing a knowledge management system is determining what knowledge is most important. Do you want to know more about your customers? Do you want to know more about competitors? What kind of information would make the company more effective or more efficient or more responsive to the marketplace? Once you have decided what you need to know, you set out to find answers to those questions.

Knowledge management tries to keep people from reinventing the wheel—that is, duplicating the work of gathering information—every time a decision needs to be made. A company really progresses when each person in the firm asks continually, "What do I still not know?" and "Whom should I be asking?" It's as important to know what's not working as what is working. Employees and managers now have e-mail, fax machines, intranets, and other means of keeping in touch with each other, with customers, and with other stakeholders. The key to success is learning how to process that information effectively and turn it into knowledge that everyone can use to improve processes and procedures. That is one way to enable workers to be more effective.

Progress Assessment

- What are some characteristics of leadership today that make leaders different from traditional managers?
- Explain the differences between autocratic and democratic leadership styles.
- What is the first step in developing a knowledge management system?

CONTROLLING: MAKING SURE IT WORKS

The control function involves measuring performance relative to the planned objectives and standards, rewarding people for work well done, and then taking corrective action when necessary. Thus, the control process (see Figure 7.10) is the heart of the management system because it provides the feedback that enables managers and workers to adjust to any deviations from plans and to changes in the environment that have affected performance. Controlling consists of five steps:

1. Establishing clear performance standards. This ties the planning function to the control function. Without clear standards, control is impossible.
2. Monitoring and recording actual performance (results).
3. Comparing results against plans and standards.
4. Communicating results and deviations to the employees involved.
5. Taking corrective action when needed and providing positive feedback for work well done.

FIGURE 7.10

The Control Process
The whole control process is based on clear standards. Without such standards, the other steps are difficult, if not impossible. With clear standards, performance measurement is relatively easy and the proper action can be taken.

This control process is ongoing throughout the year. Continuous monitoring ensures that if corrective action is required, there is enough time to implement changes. When corrective action is necessary, the decision-making process is a useful tool to apply (recall the seven Ds of decision making). Simply, managers are encouraged to review the situation and, based on collected information, develop alternatives with their staff and implement the best alternative. Or, in some circumstances, if significant changes have occurred, management can implement a contingency plan (as discussed earlier in the chapter). The focus is to meet the standards that were initially established during the planning stage or the standards that have since been modified. This process is also ongoing. It may take several attempts before standards are successfully met.

The control system's weakest link tends to be the setting of standards. To measure results against standards, the standards must be specific, attainable, and measurable. Vague goals and standards such as "better quality," "more efficiency," and "improved performance" aren't sufficient because they don't describe what you're trying to achieve. For example, let's say you're a runner and you want to improve your distance. When you started your improvement plan last year, you ran 2 kilometres a day. Now you run 2.1 kilometres a day. Did you meet your goal? You did increase your distance, but certainly not by very much. A more appropriate goal statement would be: To increase running distance from 2 kilometres a day to 4 kilometres a day by January 1. It's important to establish a time period for when specific goals are to be met. Here are examples of goals and standards that meet these criteria:

- Cut the number of finished-product rejects from 10 per 1,000 to 5 per 1,000 by March 31.

- Increase the number of times managers praise employees from 3 per week to 12 per week by the end of the quarter.

- Increase sales of product X from $10,000 per month to $12,000 per month by July 31.

One way to make control systems work is to establish clear procedures for monitoring performance. Accounting and finance are often the foundation for control systems because they provide the numbers management needs to evaluate progress. We shall explore both accounting and finance in detail later in the text.

A New Criterion for Measurement: Customer Satisfaction

external customers
Dealers, who buy products to sell to others, and ultimate customers (or end users), who buy products for their own personal use.

internal customers
Individuals and units within the firm that receive services from other individuals or units.

The criterion for measuring success in a customer-oriented firm is customer satisfaction. This includes satisfaction of both external and internal customers. **External customers** include dealers, who buy products to sell to others, and ultimate customers (also known as end users) such as you and me, who buy products for their own personal use. **Internal customers** are individuals and units within the firm that receive services from other individuals or units. For example, the field salespeople are the internal customers of the marketing research people who prepare research reports for them. One goal today is to go beyond simply satisfying customers to "delighting" them with unexpectedly good products.

Other criteria of organizational effectiveness may include the firm's contribution to society and its environmental responsibility in the area surrounding the business.[44] The traditional measures of success are usually financial; that is, success is defined in terms of profits or return on investment. Certainly these measures are still important, but they're not the whole purpose of the firm. The purpose of the firm today is to please employees, customers, and other stakeholders. Thus, measurements of success must take all of these groups into account. Firms have to ask questions such as: Do we have good relations with our employees, our suppliers, our dealers, our community leaders, the local media, our shareholders, and our bankers? What more could we do to please these groups? Are the corporate needs (such as making a profit) being met as well?

Let's pause now, review, and do some exercises. Management is doing, not just reading.

Progress Assessment

- What are the five steps in the control process?
- What's the difference between internal and external customers?

SUMMARY

1. Many managers are changing their approach to corporate management.

   What reasons can you give to account for these changes in management?
   Business people are being challenged to be more ethical and to make their accounting practices more visible to investors and the general public. Change is now happening faster than ever, and global competition is just a click away. Managing change is an important element of success, particularly in light of today's emphasis on speed in the global marketplace. National borders mean much less now than ever before, and co-operation and integration among companies have greatly increased. Within companies, knowledge workers are demanding managerial styles that allow for freedom, and the workforce is becoming increasingly diverse, educated, and self-directed.

   How are managers' roles changing?
   Managers are being educated to guide, train, support, and teach employees rather than tell them what to do.

   LO ▶ 1 Explain how the changes that are occurring in the business environment are affecting the management function.

2. Managers perform a variety of functions.

   What are the four primary functions of management?
   The four primary functions are (1) planning, (2) organizing, (3) leading, and (4) controlling.

   Describe each of the four functions.
   Planning includes anticipating trends and determining the best strategies and tactics to achieve organizational goals and objectives. Organizing includes designing the structure of the organization and creating conditions and systems in which everyone and everything works together to achieve the organization's goals and objectives. Leading involves creating a vision for the organization and guiding, training, coaching, and motivating others to work effectively to achieve the organization's goals and objectives. Controlling involves establishing clear standards to determine whether an organization is progressing toward its goals and objectives, rewarding people for doing a good job, and taking corrective action if they are not.

   LO ▶ 2 Describe the four functions of management.

3. The planning function involves the process of setting objectives to meet the organizational goals. Goals are broad, long-term achievements that organizations aim to accomplish.

   What are the four types of planning, and how are they related to the organization's goals and objectives?
   Strategic planning is broad, long-range planning that outlines the goals of the organization. Tactical planning is specific, short-term planning that lists organizational objectives. Operational planning is part of tactical planning and involves setting specific timetables and standards. Contingency planning involves developing an alternative set of plans in case the first set doesn't work out.

   What are the steps involved in decision making?
   Decision making is choosing among two or more alternatives and it is the heart of all management functions. The seven Ds of decision making are (1) define the situation, (2) describe and collect needed information, (3) develop alternatives, (4) develop agreement among those involved, (5) decide which alternative is best, (6) do what is indicated (begin implementation), and (7) determine whether the decision was a good one and follow up.

   LO ▶ 3 Describe the different types of planning and the importance of decision making in choosing the best alternative.

LO ▶ 4 Describe the organizing function of management and the three categories of skills needed by managers.

4. Organizing means allocating resources (such as funds for various departments), assigning tasks, and establishing procedures for accomplishing the organizational objectives.

What are the three levels of management in the corporate hierarchy?
The three levels of management are (1) top management (highest level consisting of the president and other key company executives who develop strategic plans); (2) middle management (general managers, division managers, and plant managers who are responsible for tactical planning and controlling); and (3) supervisory management (first-line managers/supervisors who evaluate workers' daily performance).

What skills do managers need?
Managers must have three categories of skills: (1) technical skills (ability to perform specific tasks such as selling products or developing software), (2) human relations skills (ability to communicate and motivate), and (3) conceptual skills (ability to see organizations as a whole and how all the parts fit together). Managers at different levels need different skills.

LO ▶ 5 Explain the differences between leaders and managers, and describe the various leadership styles.

5. Executives today must be more than just managers; they must be leaders as well.

What's the difference between a manager and a leader?
A manager plans, organizes, and controls functions within an organization. A leader has vision and inspires others to grasp that vision, establishes corporate values, emphasizes corporate ethics, and doesn't fear change.

Which leadership style is most effective?
Figure 7.8 shows a continuum of leadership styles ranging from boss-centred to subordinate-centred leadership. The most effective leadership style depends on the people being led and the situation.

LO ▶ 6 Summarize the five steps of the control function of management.

6. The control function of management involves measuring employee performance against objectives and standards, rewarding people for a job well done, and taking corrective action if necessary.

What are the five steps of the control function?
Controlling incorporates (1) setting clear standards, (2) monitoring and recording performance, (3) comparing performance with plans and standards, (4) communicating results and deviations to employees, and (5) providing positive feedback for a job well done and taking corrective action if necessary.

What qualities must standards possess to be used to measure performance results?
Standards must be specific, attainable, and measurable.

KEY TERMS

autocratic leadership 195
brainstorming 188
conceptual skills 191
contingency planning 186
controlling 182
crisis planning 187
decision making 188
external customers 200
free-rein (laissez-faire)
leadership 196
goals 183
human relations skills 191

internal customers 200
knowledge management 197
leading 181
management 180
middle management 190
mission statement 183
objectives 183
operational planning 186
organization chart 189
organizing 180
participative (democratic)
leadership 195

planning 180
PMI 188
problem solving 188
resources 180
strategic planning 184
supervisory management 191
SWOT analysis 184
tactical planning 186
technical skills 191
top management 190
values 183
vision 183

CRITICAL THINKING

1. Is the democratic management style most appropriate in all situations? Why or why not? Can you see a manager getting frustrated when he or she can't control others? Can someone who's trained to give orders (e.g., a military sergeant) be retrained to be a democratic manager? What problems may emerge? What kind of manager would you be? Do you have evidence to show that?

2. Sometimes when working in a team, one team member habitually overloads themselves with team requirements, while another deftly dodges everything the team asks them to do. What would you do in this situation? How would you frame the discussion? If you are aware of these traits, before assigning team work, how would you approach the assignment? How would you make team members responsible?

DEVELOPING WORKPLACE SKILLS

1. Allocate some time to do some career planning by doing a SWOT analysis of your present situation. What does the marketplace for your chosen career(s) look like today? What skills do you have that will make you a winner in that type of career? What weaknesses might you target to improve? What are the threats to that career choice? What are the opportunities? Prepare a two-minute presentation for the class.

2. Bring several decks of cards to class and have the class break up into teams of four or so members. Each team should then elect a leader. Each leader should be assigned a leadership style: autocratic, participative, or free-rein. Have each team try to build a house with a given design. The team that complete the task the most quickly wins. Each team member should then report his or her experience under that style of leadership.

3. Review Figure 7.8 and discuss managers you have known, worked for, or read about who have practised each style. Students from other countries may have interesting experiences to add. Which management style did you like best? Why? Which were most effective? Why?

4. Because of the illegal and unethical behaviour of a few managers, managers in general are under suspicion for being greedy and dishonest. Discuss the fairness of such charges, given the thousands of honest and ethical managers, and what could be done to improve the opinion of managers among the students in your class.

TAKING IT TO THE NET 1

www.mcgrawhillconnect.ca

Purpose

To discover some of Canada's leaders and find out what makes them great leaders.

Exercise

Many national awards are given out each year to recognize Canadian business leaders. Go on the Web and see if you can find some of these leaders. Two sites you may wish to visit are www.canadianbusiness.com/allstars and www.top40award-canada.org.

1. What are some common characteristics in these leaders?
2. Analyze the criteria used to choose these leaders. Are these measures reflective of the theory discussed in this chapter?
3. Referring back to your answer to the first question, what characteristics do you personally need to develop further and how do you plan on doing so?
4. Visit www.robmagazine.com and review the best-paid executives in Canada. Did you find some of Canada's top leaders on this list? Is salary reflective of a great leader? Explain.

TAKING IT TO THE NET 2

www.mcgrawhillconnect.ca

Purpose

To perform a simple SWOT analysis.

Exercise

Go to www.marketingteacher.com/ and then click on SWOT Analysis. Complete the SWOT analysis for the Highly Brill Leisure Center (click on Exercise).

1. What are the company's strengths, weaknesses, opportunities, and threats?
2. Analyze the company's weaknesses. How do you think the company's strengths might be used to overcome some of its weaknesses?
3. Analyze the opportunities and threats. What additional opportunities can you suggest? What additional threats can you identify?

ANALYZING MANAGEMENT DECISIONS

Leading in a Leaderless Company

In an issue of *Business Week* devoted to the future of business, writer John Byrne speculated about the future of leadership. He said that the twenty-first century would be unfriendly to leaders who try to run their companies by sheer force of will, and that success would come instead to companies that are "leaderless"—or companies whose leadership is so widely shared that they resemble ant colonies or beehives. In a world that is becoming more dependent on brainpower, having teams at the top will make more sense than having a single top manager. The Internet enables companies to act more like beehives because information can be shared horizontally rather than sent up to the top manager's office and then back down again. Decisions can be made instantly by the best people equipped to make them.

In the past, uniform thinking from the top could cripple an organization. Today, however, team leadership is ideally suited for the new reality of fast-changing markets. Urgent projects often require the coordinated contribution of many talented people working together. Such thinking does not happen at the top of the organization; it takes place down among the workers.

In the future, therefore, managers are more likely to be chosen for their team experience and their ability to delegate rather than make all key decisions themselves. Companies in the future, it is said, will be led by people who understand that in business, as in nature, no one person can be really in control.

Sources: John A. Byrne, "The Global Corporation Becomes a Leaderless Corporation," *Business Week*, 30 August 1999, 88–90; and Etienne C. Wenger and William M. Synder, "Communities of Practice: The Organizational Frontier," *Harvard Business Review*, January–February 2000, 139–145.

Discussion Questions

1. What would you look for on a resumé that would indicate that a candidate for work was a self-motivated team player? Are you that type? How do you know?

2. Given your experience with managers in the past, what problems do you see some managers having with letting employees decide for themselves the best way to do things and giving them the power to obtain needed equipment?

3. What would happen if all businesses in your area had their employees mix with customers to hear their comments and complaints? Would that be a good or bad thing? Why?

4. What are the various ways you can think of for companies to pay bonuses to team members? One way is to divide the money equally. What are other ways? Which would you prefer as a team member?

CHAPTER 8

Competing in Global Markets

LEARNING OBJECTIVES

AFTER YOU HAVE READ AND STUDIED THIS CHAPTER, YOU SHOULD BE ABLE TO:

LO ▶ 1 Discuss the growing importance of the global market and the roles of comparative advantage and absolute advantage in global trade.

LO ▶ 2 Explain the importance of importing and exporting and understand key terms used in global business.

LO ▶ 3 Illustrate the strategies used in reaching global markets and explain the role of multinational corporations in global markets.

LO ▶ 4 Evaluate the forces that affect trading in global markets.

LO ▶ 5 Debate the advantages and disadvantages of trade protectionism, define tariff and non-tariff barriers, and give examples of common markets.

LO ▶ 6 Discuss the changing landscape of the global market.

Getting to Know Lisa Olfman and Joy Rosen of Portfolio Entertainment Inc.

It all started in a spare bedroom with a borrowed typewriter, a $15,000 bank loan, and a determination to produce and export world-class television programs. Portfolio Entertainment Inc. was founded by co-presidents Lisa Olfman and Joy Rosen in 1991 after the production/distribution firm where they both worked stopped operating. Both partners had relevant experience in the industry. Rosen was formerly Head of Distribution and Marketing for Venture Entertainment Group. She also served in international sales and marketing positions at Sullivan Entertainment (where she was responsible for the worldwide sales of *Anne of Green Gables*). Olfman formerly served as the General Manager and Executive Producer for Venture Entertainment Group. Prior to her work at Venture she was the Supervising Producer for the Emmy Award–winning television series, *Lorne Greene's New Wilderness*. She launched her television career as an Associate Producer on a number of Canadian game shows, and created one of the first trivia-based game shows for CTV called *You Tell Us*.

The company is now one of Canada's leading independent producers and distributors of bold, award-winning television programs for kids, tweens, teens, and adults. Portfolio's newest projects include the preschool animated series *The Cat In The Hat Knows A Lot About That*, featuring Dr. Seuss's iconic "Cat" character; *Hood*, an animated adventure/comedy; and *Chinatown Cops*, a prime time animated comedy. Successful productions include Teletoon's hit series, *Carl*, which has been sold to Nickelodeon in Germany, Jetix in the Netherlands, and ABC in Australia; *Roboroach* for Teletoon, Animania in the United States, and Jetix internationally; *Stolen Miracle*, a Gemini Award–nominated movie of the week for Lifetime in the United States and CTV in Canada; and *Something from Nothing*, a film festival and perennial TV favourite. Offering an ambitious catalogue that consists of more than 2,000 episodes of programming, the company produces and exports over $20 million worth of programming each year. Its distribution arm, Portfolio International, sells to over 100 territories worldwide.

According to Olfman, the company's export success lies in its strong relationships. "We have developed a very strong network of contacts in every country we deal with," says Olfman. "And we don't wait for our phone to ring," adds Rosen. Instead, they're regularly in touch with foreign clients and contacts via telephone and e-mail, and maintain an up-to-date database to keep track of industry changes, such as personnel moves, industry trends, and new channel openings.

The company also advertises in trade magazines and takes booth space at each of the four major international trade shows each year. "That's our opportunity to sit down face-to-face with our clients and talk to them," says Rosen. "Our goal is also to meet new ones and increase our base of contacts. Without having those eyes and ears on the ground in other places, we'd be doing a lot of walking around in the dark."

Due to open markets and global trade, there are many opportunities for Canadian companies beyond our borders. This chapter will introduce some of the topics that explain the opportunities that exist in global markets and the challenges that business people such as Lisa Olfman and Joy Rosen face as they continue to look globally for growth and success.

Sources: Portfolio Entertainment Inc., 31 March 2009, http://www.portfolio entertainment.com/; and Susanne Baillie, "Secrets of an entertainment exporter," Canadian Business Online, 11 December 2003, http://www. canadianbusiness.com/entrepreneur/exporting/article.jsp?content=200312 11_131146_2932.

THE DYNAMIC GLOBAL MARKET

Have you ever dreamed of travelling to exotic cities such as Paris, Tokyo, Rio de Janeiro, or Cairo? In times past, the closest most Canadians ever got to working in such cities was in their dreams. Today, the situation has changed. It's hard to find a major Canadian company that does not cite global expansion as a link to its future growth.

If a career in global business has never crossed your mind, maybe a few facts will make the possibility of such a career interesting: Canada is a market of more than 33.6 million people, but there are almost 6.8 billion potential customers in the 195 countries that make up the global market.[1] (See Figure 8.1 for a map of the world and important statistics about the world's population.[2]) Perhaps more interesting is that a little less than 74 percent of the world's population lives in developing areas where technology, education, and per capita income still lag considerably behind those of developed (or industrialized) nations such as Canada.[3]

Canadian companies, both large and small, continuously look for opportunities to grow their businesses. For example, Scotiabank's acquisition of E*TRADE Canada from U.S.-based parent E*TRADE Financial Corporation "demonstrates our commitment to pursuing opportunities to grow our wealth management business and drive revenue growth," said Rick Waugh, President and CEO, Scotiabank. "This is consistent with our overall strategic focus on growing our wealth management business in Canada and around the world," he added.[4] Small-business Lija Style Inc. was started by Linda Hipp after she became frustrated with the unflattering golfwear available for women. The company employs 19 people and its products are sold in pro shops, resorts, and department stores. Today, exports (to be discussed soon) represent 80 percent of the company's sales.[5] Canadian companies also scan the marketplace to get ideas on what is working well elsewhere. The Green Box shares one example of how Paris's Velib program is influencing new programs being developed nationally.

Companies also continuously review their global operations to ensure that they are operating at a profit. One Canadian industry that has been particularly hard hit as a result of global trends is the auto industry. Factors such as the increasing price of gas and weakening demand for trucks and sport utility vehicles (SUVs) have forced companies to consider restructuring plans. As a result, thousands of Canadian jobs have been eliminated. Layoffs have occurred at General Motors Canada, Chrysler Canada, Ford Motor

FIGURE | 8.1

World Population By Continent

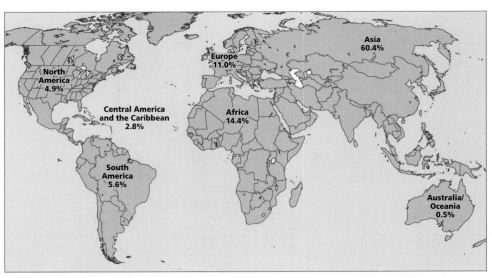

Source: Nations Online, "Current World Population, 2009," www.nationsonline.org/oneworld/world_population.htm.

Green BOX

Rent Your Wheels

The city of Toronto is rolling out a high-tech rent-a-bike program in 2009, similar to a successful one in Paris. Launched in Paris in 2006, Paris's Velib program already has more than 211,000 subscribers who have taken 31 million trips. The Paris program has about 20,000 bikes and 1,400 self-serve rental kiosks. For the equivalent of approximately $45 a year, cyclists can swipe their credit card at a kiosk, unlock a bike, ride it across town and drop it off at another kiosk. The first 30 minutes are free with fees starting at about $1.60 (1 euro) for each additional half hour. The bikes have a distinct appearance that makes them hard to steal, and a penalty is applied for lost or damaged bikes.

According to Councillor Adrian Heaps, head of Toronto's Cycling Committee, the city plans to emulate the best aspects of programs in other jurisdictions and would include automated stations with swipe-card access. A subscription would give users access to a bicycle that is a one-speed or three-speed, with a kind of mousetrap rack on the back where you can put books or a briefcase. At this stage of the planning, there are still some questions that need to be answered. What are the best locations for hubs? How many bicycles could work? Do we do it in the downtown core? Do we do it where there are subways and intermodal transportation hubs?

Such programs are gaining in popularity around the world with the rise of gas prices and environmental consciousness. Montreal and other U.S. cities (e.g., Denver, Minneapolis, and San Francisco) are kicking off similar programs, while Copenhagen, Lyon ,and Barcelona already have bike-sharing programs in place.

Source: Reprinted with permission—Torstar Syndication Services. Adapted from an article that originally appeared in the *Toronto Star* on 21 August 2008; and www.footprintnetwork.org/.

Company of Canada, and many parts suppliers, such as Polywheels Manufacturing and Progressive Moulded Products Ltd.[6] The global market is truly dynamic, and progressive companies continuously scan the business environment to ensure that they take advantage of the opportunities and minimize the impact of threats.

Canada is a large exporting nation. **Exporting** is selling goods and services to another country. **Importing** is buying goods and services from another country. Competition in exporting is very intense and Canadian companies face aggressive competition from exporters based in countries such as Germany, China, and Japan.

The purpose of this chapter is to familiarize you with the potential of global business, including its many challenges. The demand for students with training in global business is almost certain to grow as the number of businesses competing in global markets increases.[7] You might decide that a career in global business is your long-term goal. If you make that choice, prepare yourself to work hard and always be ready for new challenges.[8]

exporting
Selling goods and services to another country.

importing
Buying goods and services from another country.

Why Trade with Other Nations?

There are several reasons why countries trade with other countries. First, no country, not even a technologically advanced one, can produce all of the products that its people want and need. Second, even if a country did become self-sufficient, other nations would seek to trade with that country to meet the needs of their own people. Third, some nations have an abundance of natural resources and a lack of technological know-how (e.g., China and Russia), while other countries have sophisticated technology but few natural resources (e.g., Japan and Switzerland). Global trade enables a nation to produce what it is most capable of producing and to buy what it needs from others in a mutually beneficial exchange relationship. This happens through the process of free trade. **Free trade** is the movement of goods and services among nations without political or economic trade barriers. It is often a hotly debated concept. Figure 8.2 offers some of the pros and cons of free trade.

free trade
The movement of goods and services among nations without political or economic obstruction.

Pros	Cons
• The global market contains more than 6 billion potential customers for goods and services. • Productivity grows when countries produce goods and services in which they have a comparative advantage. • Global competition and less-costly imports keep prices down, so inflation does not curtail economic growth. • Free trade inspires innovation for new products and keeps firms competitively challenged. • Uninterrupted flow of capital gives countries access to foreign investments, which helps keep interest rates low.	• Domestic workers (particularly in manufacturing-based jobs) can lose their jobs due to increased imports or production shifts to low-wage global markets. • Workers may be forced to accept pay cuts from employers who can threaten to move their jobs to lower-cost global markets. • Moving operations overseas because of intense competitive pressure often means the loss of service jobs and white-collar jobs. • Domestic companies can lose their comparative advantage when competitors build advanced production operations in low-wage countries.

FIGURE | 8.2

The Pros and Cons of Free Trade

comparative advantage theory
Theory that states that a country should sell to other countries those products that it produces most effectively and efficiently, and buy from other countries those products that it cannot produce as effectively or efficiently.

absolute advantage
The advantage that exists when a country has the ability to produce a particular good or service using fewer resources (and therefore at a lower cost) than another country.

The Theories of Comparative and Absolute Advantage

Global trade is the exchange of goods and services across national borders. Exchanges between and among countries involve more than goods and services, however. Countries also exchange art, sports, cultural events, medical advances, space exploration, and labour. Comparative advantage theory, suggested in the early nineteenth century by English economist David Ricardo, was the guiding principle that supported this idea of free economic exchange.[9]

Comparative advantage theory states that a country should sell to other countries those products that it produces most effectively and efficiently, and buy from other countries those products it cannot produce as effectively or efficiently. Japan has shown this ability with cars and electronic items. Canada has such an advantage with certain forestry products, aluminum, and various minerals. In practice, it does not work so neatly. For various reasons, many countries decide to produce certain agricultural, industrial, or consumer products despite a lack of comparative advantage. To facilitate this plan, they restrict imports of competing products from countries that can produce them at lower costs. The net result is that the free movement of goods and services is restricted. We will return to the topic of trade protectionism later in the chapter.

A country has an **absolute advantage** if it has the ability to produce a particular good or service using fewer resources (and therefore at a lower cost) than another country.[10] Trade with other countries permits specialization, which allows resources to be used more productively.[11] For instance, Zambia has an absolute advantage over many countries in the production of copper due to its copper ore reserves.

Canada became a diamond producer in 1998 when the Ekati diamond mine opened about 300 kilometres northeast of Yellowknife. Here you see the Diavik Diamond Mine, located on a 20-square-kilometre island in the same area. Today Canada is the world's third largest diamond producer on a value basis, after Botswana and Russia.

GETTING INVOLVED IN GLOBAL TRADE

People interested in finding a job in global business often think of firms like Bombardier, IBM, and Sony, which have large multinational accounts. The real job potential, however, may be with small businesses. In Canada, small businesses account for 48 percent of the total private labour force and about 85 percent of exports.[12] With the help of government agencies, such as Foreign Affairs and International Trade Canada and Export Development Canada (EDC), many small businesses are becoming more involved in global markets.

Getting started globally is often a matter of observation, determination, and risk. What does that mean? First, it is important to observe and study global markets. Your library, the Internet, and your fellow classmates are good starting points for doing your research. Second, if you have the opportunity, travelling to different countries is a great way to observe foreign cultures and lifestyles and see if doing business globally appeals to you.

Importing Goods and Services

Imports for goods and services reached $529.4 billion in 2008, as noted in Figure 8.3. Services imports represented 16.3 percent of total imports, or almost one out of every six dollars of total imports. When considering merchandise trade, you will see that three categories (machinery and equipment, industrial goods and materials, and automotive products) represent almost 65 percent of imports. If imports keep increasing as they have, how might this affect our standard of living and quality of life?

Nickelback began as a cover band in Hanna, Alberta, and to date has sold millions of records worldwide. Other Canadian musicians who have exported their music and have global appeal include Avril Lavigne, Celine Dion, and Finger Eleven, just to name a few. Do you prefer to support Canadian talent?

Exporting Goods and Services

You may be surprised at what you can sell in other countries. The fact is, you can sell just about any good or service that is used in Canada to other countries—and often the competition is not nearly as intense for producers in global markets as it is at home. You can, for example, sell snowplows to the Saudi Arabians. Don't forget that services can be exported as well.

While Canada has a small population, it produces vast quantities of products, ranking high in terms of nations that export. Why is trade so important? Trade with other countries enhances the quality of life for Canadians and contributes to our country's economic well-being. Exports alone account for one in five Canadian jobs and generate 30 cents out of every dollar earned.[13]

Sales abroad by affiliates of Canadian companies are an important means by which Canadian companies engage in international business and are equivalent to almost 85 percent of the value of exports of goods and services.[14] Goods comprise the largest component of trade, being more than seven times as great as services on the export side (and about five times as great on the import side).[15] As highlighted in Figure 8.3, exports of goods and services were approximately $560.5 billion, which included service exports of approximately $70.5 billion. Industrial goods and materials, and machinery and equipment represented the two largest export categories for merchandise trade.

Spend some time reviewing Figure 8.3. By understanding these categories and their impact on our exports (as well as imports), you will realize why you hear so much about specific industries in the news. After all, such activities are vital to our economy. It's important for businesses to be aware of these great opportunities. But don't be misled: Selling in global markets is not by any means easy. Adapting goods and services to specific global markets is potentially profitable but can be very difficult. We shall discuss a number of forces that affect global trading later in this chapter.

Visit the Foreign Affairs and International Trade Canada site at http://www.international.gc.ca for updated statistics and information on Canada's state of trade.

FIGURE | **8.3**

Canada's Merchandise and Service Trade, 2008

CATEGORIES	EXPORTS $ Billions	EXPORTS %	IMPORTS $ Billions	IMPORTS %
MERCHANDISE TRADE **Industrial Goods and Materials** (incl. metals and metal ores, chemicals and plastics, other industrial goods and materials)	111.5	22.8	91.6	20.7
Machinery and Equipment (incl. industrial and agricultural machinery, aircraft and other transportation equipment, and other machinery and equipment)	93.0	19.0	122.6	27.7
Energy Products (incl. crude petroleum and other energy products such as natural gas and petroleum and coal products)	125.8	25.7	53.1	12.0
Automotive Products (incl. passenger autos and chassis, trucks and other motor vehicles, and motor vehicle parts)	61.1	12.5	72.0	16.3
Agricultural and Fishing Products (incl. wheat, fruits and vegetables, and other agricultural and fishing products such as live animals, feed, beverages, and tobacco)	40.9	8.3	28.5	6.4
Forestry Products (incl. lumber and sawmill products, wood pulp and other wood products, and newsprint and other paper products)	25.7	5.2	2.9	0.7
Other Consumer Goods (incl. apparel and footwear, and miscellaneous consumer goods such as watches, sporting goods and toys, television and radio sets)	18.2	3.7	57.5	13.0
Special Transactions Trade and Unallocated Adjustments	13.8	2.8	14.8	3.3
Merchandise Trade Total	**490.0**	**100.0**	**443.0**	**100.0**
SERVICE TRADE **Other Services** (incl. government services such as military activities and commercial services such as accounting, legal, and financial services)	41.8	59.3	39.8	42.7
Travel (incl. business travel and personal travel)	16.1	22.8	26.6	28.7
Transportation Services (incl. air transport services, water transport services, land and other transport services)	12.6	17.9	20.0	21.6
Service Trade Total	**70.5**	**100.0**	**86.4**	**100.0**
Merchandise and Service Trade Total	**560.5**		**529.4**	

Sources: "Canada's Merchandise and Service Trade, 2007," adapted from Statistics Canada Web site "Exports of Goods on a Balance-of-Payments Basis, by Product," Statistics Canada, 13 August 2008, http://www40.statcan.ca/l01/cst01/gblec04.htm; "Imports of Goods on a Balance-of-Payments Basis, by Product," Statistics Canada, 13 August 2008, http://www40.statcan.ca/l01/cst01/gblec05.htm; and "Canada's Balance of International Payments," Statistics Canada, 29 May 2008, http://www40.statcan.ca.libaccess.lib.mcmaster.ca/l01/cst01/econ01a.htm?sdi=services.

Measuring Global Trade

In measuring the effectiveness of global trade, nations carefully follow two key indicators: balance of trade and balance of payments. The **balance of trade** is a nation's ratio of exports to imports. A favourable balance of trade, or trade surplus, occurs when the value of the country's exports exceeds that of its imports. Overall, Canada has a favourable balance of trade. Since 1990, three of the seven major categories of goods—agricultural and fishing products, forestry, and energy products—have consistently posted trade surpluses and remain in surplus.[16] Two other categories—machinery and consumer goods—have always posted trade deficits.[17] An **unfavourable balance of trade**, or **trade deficit**, occurs when the value of the country's imports exceeds that of its exports. It is easy to understand why countries prefer to export more than they import. If I sell you $200 worth of goods and buy only $100 worth, I have an extra $100 available to buy other things. However, I'm in an unfavourable position if I buy $200 worth of goods from you and sell you only $100.

The **balance of payments** is the difference between money coming into a country (from exports) and money leaving the country (for imports) plus money flows coming into or leaving a country from other factors such as tourism, foreign aid, military expenditures, and foreign investment. The goal is always to have more money flowing into the country than flowing out of the country; in other words, a *favourable* balance of payments. Conversely, an *unfavourable* balance of payments is when more money is flowing out of a country than coming in.

balance of trade
A nation's ratio of exports to imports.

trade deficit (unfavourable balance of trade)
Occurs when the value of a country's imports exceeds that of its exports.

balance of payments
The difference between money coming into a country (from exports) and money leaving the country (for imports) plus money flows from other factors such as tourism, foreign aid, military expenditures, and foreign investment.

Trading in Global Markets: The Canadian Experience

At first glance, Canada's foreign trade statistics are impressive. As a country, we rank eleventh in the world as both exporter and importer in world merchandise trade.[18] While our abundant natural resources are a major area for exports, developing countries continue to give Canada stiff competition in these areas. When we look carefully at the numbers, we see that we are dependent on one country, the United States. Figure 8.4 shows that over 73 percent of our exports and a little under 69 percent of our imports are with the United States. No other modern industrialized country is so dependent on one country for trade and investments.

Trade in automotive products, for example, stems from agreements that have been signed between the two countries over the years, starting with the 1965 Automotive Products Trade Agreement (also known as the "Auto Pact") and reinforced by the North American Free Trade Agreement (NAFTA) in 1994. The Dealing with Change box highlights the importance of the auto sector to the Canadian economy. In recent years, Canada has been diversifying its trade away from the United States and focusing on other countries. Read the next section to learn about these priority markets.

FIGURE 8.4

Regional Shares of Canada's Trade in Goods and Services, 2007

	Exports %	Imports %
United States	73.5	68.8
European Union	9.9	10.7
Japan	2.2	2.6
Other OECD	4.4	5.1
Non-OECD	10.0	12.9

Source: Statistics Canada, CANSIM database, http://cansim2.statcan.ca/, Table 228-0003.

Canada's Priority Markets[19]

Technological advances in most fields, primarily in the area of transmission and storage of information, have shattered the archaic notions of how things ought to function, from production and trade to war and politics. The new ways of communicating, organizing, and working are inviting the most remote corners of the world to be actors on the global economic stage. These *emerging economies* are enjoying high growth rates, rapid increases in their living standards, and a rising global prominence. Tapping into these markets is crucial. For example, in thirty years a gain of just 0.1 percent in the Canadian share of the import markets of Brazil, Russia, India, and China (BRIC countries) would mean an export gain of $29 billion.

DEALING with CHANGE

Canada's Auto Sector

The automotive sector is a key player in Canada's economy. It is the single biggest contributor to Canada's manufacturing GDP at 12 percent nationally, and regionally it contributes over 20 percent in Ontario alone. One in seven Canadians is either directly or indirectly employed in the automotive industry. It supports hundreds of thousands of high-wage, high-skill manufacturing jobs across the country in 11 light-duty and 3 heavy-duty assembly plants, over 540 Original Equipment (OEM) parts manufacturers, thousands of dealerships (3,949) and many other directly related industries. It is estimated that every $1 billion in exports creates or maintains 11,000 jobs.

Canada's automotive manufacturers have made nearly $40 billion in direct investment in Canada since 1990. The positive impact on the Canadian economy is significant given the automotive sector's 3:1 economic multiplier. This means that for every dollar spent in the industry, three more are spent in the economy.

The sector has a huge export orientation, with roughly 85 percent of vehicle production and 60 percent of all parts production being exported. In fact, Canada is the ninth largest vehicle producer in the world. The Canadian vehicle assemblers are highly competitive, accounting for 3.7 percent of total world production of 68.6 million units and a global trade surplus in finished vehicles of more than $13.8 billion. This accounted for 31.4 percent of Canada's 2007 global trade surplus. Automotive exports totalled roughly $70 billion in 2007, with over $67 billion sent to the United States. This maintained the automotive sector as one of Canada's most significant export industries.

Despite all these positive points, Canada's assembly industry is shrinking due to globalization and environmental changes. Global automotive growth is shifting from the mature markets of North America and Western Europe to emerging markets. In the next five years, China will account for 39 percent of the growth in automobile sales, while India will account for 15 percent. North America will account for only 3 percent of the growth. Automobile assemblers are global in their reach, but they rationalize their production and investments on a regional basis. Over time, they will establish their plants where they sell the most vehicles.

At the time this box was written, the auto industry was undergoing a major transformation. In 2008, auto analysts had forecast that over the next several years, for every plant that opened in North America, another two were expected to close as a result of market shifts. (In emerging countries, in contrast, for every automotive plant that closes, another three are expected to open.) Other environmental trends that also contributed to the recent closure of plants included the rising Canadian dollar, rising fuel prices, and weakening U.S. demand for vehicles. Weakening demand in Canada has also been impacted by poor management decisions. That is, poor management decisions that have produced cars that do not meet the expectations of consumers.

Fast forward to 2009. Both the Canadian and U.S. governments spent billions of dollars bailing out both Chrysler LLC (it filed for bankruptcy protection in April) and General Motors Corporation (it filed for bankruptcy in June). In exchange for an 11.7 percent equity stake in General Motors (GM), the federal and Ontario provincial governments paid $10.5 billion. Equity stakes were also owned by the U.S. government (60 percent), the United Auto Workers (17.5 per cent), and unsecured bondholders (10 percent.) It is expected that once GM is up and running, the government can sell its stake in the company. It was feared that not approving the bailout loan would have forced the company out of Canada.

Do you agree with the government bailout? Why should taxpayers be paying for poor management decisions? As a condition of the bailout, union members were told to go back to the table several times to re-negotiate labour contract conditions to lower overall payroll costs. Was this fair given that there was already a contract in place that had been agreed upon by both management and labour? Why do you think the government did not mandate that management also be forced to take a pay cut? After all, poor management decisions also contributed greatly to the company's overall financial situation. What were the implications for Canada if the government did not get involved in these negotiations? Do you think the cost outweighs the benefits?

Sources: "GM Hoping for Speedy Sale and Exit from Chapter 11," Sympatico.msn. 2 June 2009, http://news.sympatico.msn.ctv.ca/abc/home/contentposting.aspx?isfa=1&feedname=CTV-TOPSTORIES_V3&showbyline=True&date=true&newsitemid=CTVNews%2f20090602%2fGM_sale_090602; "Canada, Ontario Commit $10.5B to Revamped GM," CBC News, 1 June 2009, http://www.cbc.ca/money/story/2009/06/01/harper-mcguinty-gm.html; "The Automotive Industry in Canada," Canadian Vehicles Manufacturers' Association, 2008, http://www.cvma.ca/eng/industry/industry.asp; "Strategic Automotive Policy," Canadian Vehicles Manufacturers' Association, 2008, http://www.cvma.ca/eng/issues/strategicauto.asp; "Role," Canadian Vehicles Manufacturers' Association, 2008, http://www.cvma.ca/eng/industry/role.asp; and "Notes for an Address by the Honourable Jim Prentice, PC, QC, MP, Minister of Industry," Industry Canada, 29 February 2008, http://www.ic.gc.ca/epic/site/ic1.nsf/en/01926e.html.

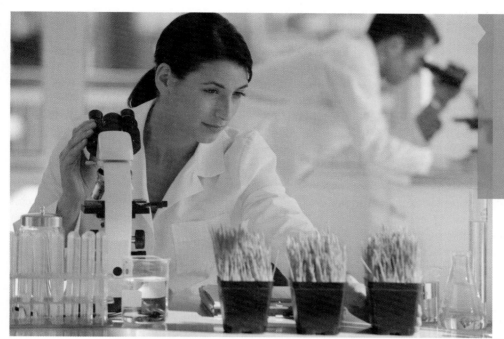

One objective of the federal government's Science and Technology program is to identify and incorporate world leading research into the development of innovative processes, goods, and services in Canada. What are some other benefits of such collaboration?

Based on extensive consultation with government, academic, and Canadian business and industry representatives, the federal government has identified 13 priority markets around the world where Canadian opportunities and interests have the greatest potential for growth. The priority markets are as follows: the Association of South East Asian Nations (Brunei Darussalam, Burma, Cambodia, Indonesia, Laos, Malaysia, Philippines, Singapore, Thailand, Vietnam), Australia and New Zealand, Brazil, China, Europe, Gulf Cooperation Council (Saudi Arabia, United Arab Emirates, Kuwait, Qatar, Bahrain and Oman), India, Japan, Korea, Latin America and the Caribbean, Mexico, Russia, and the United States. China and India are of particular interest as they are growing and emerging markets due to their size and economic transformation. A Conference Board of Canada report notes that by 2050, India will be the world's third-largest economy, with a GDP approaching US$30 trillion, behind only the United States and China, which will top the list. Steps already taken to encourage a stronger Canadian presence in the global marketplace include tax cuts, increased support for research and development, and critical investments in infrastructure at Canada–U.S. border crossings and Canada's Asia-Pacific Gateway. The federal government is investing $50 million a year to advance Canada's Global Commerce Strategy. Some specific initiatives include the International Science & Technology Partnerships Program and the Going Global Fund, which are programs that encourage research projects between Canada and China/India that have the potential for commercialization. Visit www.international.gc.ca/commerce/strategy-strategie/r.aspx to get an update on Canada's priority markets.

To learn about the recent global export forcecast, visit Export Development Canada's site at www.edc.ca.

Progress Assessment

- How do world population and market statistics support the expansion of Canadian businesses into global markets?

- What is comparative advantage? How does this differ from absolute advantage?

- How are a country's balance of trade and balance of payments determined?

STRATEGIES FOR REACHING GLOBAL MARKETS

Businesses use many different strategies to compete in global markets. The key strategies include exporting, licensing, franchising, contract manufacturing, creating international joint ventures and strategic alliances, and engaging in foreign direct investment. Each of these strategies provides opportunities for becoming involved in global markets, along with specific commitments and risks. Figure 8.5 places the strategies discussed on a continuum showing the amount of commitment, control, risk, and profit potential associated with each one. Take a few minutes to look over Figure 8.5 before you continue.

Exporting

The simplest way of going international is to export your goods and services (e.g., call centres, IT consultants, and cultural and performing artists). As you will see in the chapters on marketing, many decisions have to be made when a company markets a new product or goes into new markets with existing products. Often the first export sales occur as a result of unsolicited orders received. Regardless of how a company starts exporting, it must develop some goals and strategies for achieving those goals.

Canadian firms may be reluctant to go through the trouble of establishing foreign trading relationships. In such cases, specialists called export-trading companies (or export-management companies) are available to step in and negotiate and establish the trading relationships desired. An export-trading company not only matches buyers and sellers from different countries but also provides needed services (such as dealing with foreign customs offices, documentation requirements, even weights and measures) to ease the process of entering global markets. Export-trading companies also help exporters with a key and risky element of doing business globally: getting paid. If you are considering a career in global business, export-trading companies often provide internships or part-time opportunities for students. In Chapter 3 we illustrated how governments aid exporters.

Success in exporting often leads to licensing with a foreign company to produce the product locally to better serve the local market.

Licensing

A firm (the licensor) may decide to compete in a global market by **licensing** the right to manufacture its product or use its trademark to a foreign company (the licensee) for a fee (a royalty). A company with an interest in licensing generally needs to send company representatives to the foreign producer to help set up the production process. The licensor may also assist or work with a licensee in such areas as distribution, promotion, and consulting.

licensing
A global strategy in which a firm (the licensor) allows a foreign company (the licensee) to produce its product in exchange for a fee (a royalty).

FIGURE | 8.5

Strategies for Reaching Global Markets

| Exporting | Licensing | Franchising | Contract manufacturing | International joint ventures and strategic alliances | Foreign direct investment |

LEAST ◄————— Amount of commitment, control, risk, and profit potential —————► MOST

A licensing agreement can be beneficial to a firm in several different ways. Through licensing, an organization can gain additional revenues from a product that it normally would not have generated in its home market. In addition, foreign licensees must often purchase start-up supplies, component materials, and consulting services from the licensing firm. Such agreements have been very profitable for companies such as Disney, Coca-Cola,

The sun never sets on Mickey and the gang, which is making the Disney Company very happy. The firm has had great success licensing the famous mouse and his cast of characters in Europe and Asia. Here Mickey welcomes visitors to Tokyo Disneyland. What challenges does a company like Disney face in global markets?

and PepsiCo. These firms often enter foreign markets through licensing agreements that typically extend into long-term service contracts. For example, Oriental Land Company and the Hong Kong government have licensing agreements with Walt Disney Company. Oriental Land Company owns and operates Tokyo Disneyland and Tokyo Disney Sea Park under a licensing agreement; Disney also collects management and consulting fees.[20]

A final advantage of licensing worth noting is that licensors spend little or no money to produce and market their products. These costs come from the licensee's pocket. Therefore, licensees generally work very hard to see that the product they license succeeds in their market. However, licensors may also experience some problems. One major problem is that often a firm must grant licensing rights to its product for an extended period, maybe 20 years or longer. If a product experiences remarkable growth and success in the foreign market, the bulk of the revenues earned belong to the licensee. Perhaps even more threatening is that a licensing firm is actually selling its expertise in a product area. If a foreign licensee learns the company's technology or product secrets, it may break the agreement and begin to produce a similar product on its own. If legal remedies are not available, the licensing firm may lose its trade secrets, not to mention the agreed-on royalties.

Franchising

A variation of licensing is franchising. Franchising is an arrangement whereby someone with a good idea for a business sells the rights to use the business name and sell a product or service to others in a given territory. In Canada, there are thousands of franchise units—such as Canadian Tire, Molly Maid, Boston Pizza, and Japan Camera 1 Hour Photo—in many categories of business. Franchising is popular both domestically and internationally and was discussed in depth in Chapter 5.

Franchisors, however, have to be careful to adapt their good or service in the countries they serve. For example, KFC's first eleven Hong Kong outlets failed within two years. Apparently the chicken was too greasy, and eating with fingers was too messy for the fastidious people of Hong Kong. McDonald's made a similar mistake when entering the Netherlands market. It originally set up operations in the suburbs, as it does in North America, but soon learned that the Dutch mostly live in the cities. Pizza Hut originally approached the global market using a strategy of one-pie-fits-all. The company found out the hard way that Germans like small individual pizzas, not the large pies preferred in North America. Preferences in pizza toppings also differ globally. Japanese customers, for example, enjoy squid and sweet mayonnaise pizza.

Contract Manufacturing

Contract manufacturing involves a foreign company's production of private-label goods to which a domestic company then attaches its own brand name or trademark. The practice falls under the broad category of *outsourcing*, which we introduced in Chapter 1 and

contract manufacturing
A foreign country's production of private-label goods to which a domestic company then attaches its brand name or trademark; also called outsourcing.

will discuss in more depth in Chapter 9. For example, Dell Computer contracts with Quanta Computer of Taiwan to make notebook PCs, on which it then puts the Dell brand name, while Nike has almost 700 contract factories around the world that manufacture its footwear and apparel.[21]

Contract manufacturing enables a company to experiment in a new market without incurring heavy start-up costs such as a manufacturing plant. If the brand name becomes a success, the company has penetrated a new market with relatively low risk. A firm can also use contract manufacturing temporarily to meet an unexpected increase in orders and, of course, labour costs are often very low. One company, featured in *PROFIT* magazine's ranking of Canada's emerging growth companies, used contract manufacturing successfully. FouFou Dog is a dog apparel company whose collection includes canine track suits, hoodies, jewelled collars and leashes, as well as iChew and Fouberry chew toys. In 2004 and at the age of 24, Cheryl Ng, owner of a Maltese dog named Ernie, started the company because she liked how Paris Hilton dressed her dog. Today, the company exports 95 percent of its products. According to Ng, "All our stuff is made in Argentina. In China, quality control can be hit-and-miss or downright sloppy—you could have a disaster on your hands—but it's been consistently good from my suppliers." And she has other reasons for heading south instead of east: "My suppliers will make me a small quantity if I want to try something out. You can't get that from China anymore, and I don't want to be stuck with a colour or style nobody wants; besides, they let me check out the textiles before I buy and they always have good stuff." She also likes the shorter flights and the fact that she only has to cross two time zones.[22]

International Joint Ventures and Strategic Alliances

joint venture
A partnership in which two or more companies (often from different countries) join to undertake a major project or to form a new company.

A **joint venture** is basically a partnership in which two or more companies (often from different countries) join to undertake a major project or to form a new company. For example, to design a new biofuel engine British manufacturer Lotus has teamed up with Jaguar and Queen's University, who will help with every step of the development process.[23] Joint ventures can be mandated by governments, such as China where entry is difficult, as a condition of doing business in their country. It's often hard to gain entry into a country like China, but agreeing to a joint venture with a Chinese firm can help a company gain such entry. Such was the case for Volkswagen and General Motors, who have both had joint ventures with Shanghai Automotive Industrial Corporation to build cars in China.[24]

Joint ventures are developed for different business reasons as well. In the early 2000s, Campbell Soup Company formed a joint venture with Japan's Nakano Vinegar Company, called Campbell Nakano Inc., to expand its rather low share of the soup market in Japan. Nestlé and L'Oreal formed a joint venture to develop a line of inner-beauty products to improve the quality of a person's skin, hair, and nails.[25]

The benefits of international joint ventures are clear:

The Bank of Nova Scotia will pay US$15-million for 33 percent of a new mutual fund company in China that will be formed with the Bank of Beijing. The new joint venture, Bank of Beijing Scotiabank Asset Management Co. Ltd., will market mutual funds to retail and institutional customers through the Chinese bank's national branch network.

1. Shared technology and risk.

2. Shared marketing and management expertise.

3. Entry into markets where foreign companies are often not allowed unless goods are produced locally.

4. Shared knowledge of the local market, including local customs, government connections, access to local skilled labour and supplies, and awareness of domestic laws and regulations.

The drawbacks are not as obvious, but they are important. One partner can learn the other's technology and practices, then go off and use what has been learned. Also, over time, a shared technology may become obsolete or the joint venture may become too large to be as flexible as needed.

The global market is also fuelling the growth of strategic alliances. A **strategic alliance** is a long-term partnership between two or more companies established to help each company build competitive market advantages. Unlike joint ventures, however, they do not typically involve sharing costs, risks, management, or even profits. Such alliances can provide access to markets, capital, and technical expertise, causing executives and global consultants to predict that few companies in the future will succeed globally by going alone.[26] Plus, because of their flexibility, they can effectively link firms from different countries and firms of vastly different sizes.

Air Canada is expanding its access to overseas destinations by forming a strategic alliance with Continental Airlines Corp., clearing the way for the two airlines to work co-operatively on everything from ticketing to check-in to baggage transfer. Passengers benefit from coordinated frequent-flier rewards and access to each other's airport lounges around the world.[27] Continental, the fourth-largest airline in the United States, is a major player in the New York region with its hub at Newark, New Jersey, offering flights to Europe and Asia, while its Houston hub is a busy take-off point to Central and South America.[28] In another example, Consilient Technologies Corporation, a mobile software developer, and GroupM, a leading global media investment management operation, have created an alliance to enable both companies to cross promote their services and offerings to clients, end-users, and mobile operators throughout Asia Pacific.[29] GroupM will promote Consilient's Push™ e-mail advertising service as an advertising channel to their agencies in the region and Consilient will provide support and preferred access for GroupM's clients within their Push advertising service, which is commercially available through leading mobile operators in Asia Pacific.[30] For more information about Consilient Technologies, see the Spotlight on Small Business box.

strategic alliance
A long-term partnership between two or more companies established to help each company build competitive market advantages.

SPOTLIGHT ON Small Business

Newfoundland's Consilient Technologies Corporation

Founded in 2000, Consilient Technologies Corporation was formed by Trevor Adey (President and CEO) and Rod White (Senior Director). Consilient is a leading developer of wireless push e-mail for mobile devices and phones. Push e-mail means that e-mail travels directly to a customer's mobile phone or device—there's no need to pull the e-mail from a server or use desktop forwarding because e-mail is automatically pushed to the mobile phone or device.

The company's customer base comprises Global Fortune 500 companies, network operators, service providers, and government agencies. To meet the needs of its customers, Consilient has established strategic alliances with IT solution developers, network carriers, handheld device manufacturers (e.g., Research In Motion), system integrators, and application developers. Technology partners include industry leaders such as Oracle, Nokia, and Sun Microsystems.

People ask the St. John's entrepreneurs: Why would you build a software company in Newfoundland? Adey replies, "It's where I want to live. I don't have to rationalize it." Even so, he does: cheap office costs and, most of all, proximity to Memorial University. A Memorial University graduate himself, Adey believes that "what allows us to

build a company in St. John's like this is having a world-class university right here with students who want to stay in Newfoundland and Labrador, but don't think they can."

In recognition of its impact in the industry, Consilient was awarded the top Asian Mobile Innovation Award in 2007. "It is fitting that Consilient won the award, as our offering is the first of its kind that enables people to get free mobile services on their phones through brand advertising," said Adey. "Our approach and advanced mobile marketing platform has introduced a brand new business model for operators and advertisers. With this success under our belt, we will continue to partner with more mobile operators and market brands around the globe to bring free mobile applications, data, and advertising to the world's 2.5 billion mobile phone users."

Sources: "Consilient Wins Top Mobile Innovation Award in Asia," Consilient Technologies Corporation, 15 November 2007, http://www.consilient.com/media/press/top-mobile-innovation-award-winner.php; Simon Avery, "RIM's next rival may be an upstart from St. John's," *Report on Business*, 14 March 2006, http://global.factiva.com/aa/default.asp; Gordon Pitts, "Newfoundland Duo Battle Image Problem," *The Globe and Mail*, 25 November 2002, http://www.theglobeandmail.com; and Roy MacGregor, "And Not a Rubber Boot in Sight," *The Globe and Mail*, 18 October 2003, A11.

Foreign Direct Investment

Economists measure a nation's economic strength by comparing several factors. They calculate the amount of money a nation owes to foreign creditors and the value of what foreign creditors own in a particular country, referred to as foreign direct investment. **Foreign direct investment (FDI)** is buying permanent property and businesses in foreign nations. FDI provides benefits to Canadian firms through the transfer of knowledge, technology and skills, and increased trade related to investment, all of which contribute to productivity growth and competitiveness.[31] Some research in necessary before such an investment. For example, Simply Audiobooks Inc., an audiobook e-tailer, entered the U.S. market only after its test Web site attracted more U.S. than Canadian clients by 15 to 1. The company opened its first shipping facility in Buffalo, New York, about a month later, and today the U.S. market accounts for 90 percent of revenue. "When you're a startup, you can't afford a high risk/reward ratio," says CEO Sean Neville. "You can't think you're going to get 50 customers and only get one. This helped us narrow the deviation of what could be."[32]

Foreign direct investment is compared to how much money foreign creditors owe to a nation and the value of what a nation owns in other countries. Increasingly, economists and trade analysts have come to agree that a high amount of foreign direct investment in a nation is not necessarily a bad sign. In fact, the amount of foreign direct investment in a country means that other nations perceive that country as a strong economic leader. Figure 8.6 lists the countries with the largest direct foreign investment in Canada, as well as Canadian direct investment abroad.

As the size of a foreign market expands, many firms increase foreign direct investment and establish a foreign subsidiary. A **foreign subsidiary** is a company that is owned in a foreign country by another company (called the *parent company*). Such a subsidiary would operate much like a domestic firm, with production, distribution, promotion, pricing, and other business functions under the control of the foreign subsidiary's management.

The legal requirements of both the country where the parent firm is located (called the *home country*) and the foreign country where the subsidiary is located (called the *host country*) have to be observed. The primary advantage of a subsidiary is that the company maintains complete control over any technology or expertise it may possess. The major shortcoming of a subsidiary is that the parent company commits a large amount of funds and technology within foreign boundaries. Should relations with the host country falter, the firm's assets could be taken over by the foreign government. Such a takeover is called *expropriation*.

Canadian subsidiaries of American companies have played a major role in developing the Canadian economy. As noted in Figure 8.6, in 2008 U.S. companies alone invested more than $290 billion in Canada. There are, however, several disadvantages to foreign investment. One is that Canada has been criticized for having a "branch plant economy." This occurs when many subsidiaries are owned by foreign companies and profits are returned to the home country rather than reinvested in Canada. There are concerns that decisions made by the parent company are not primarily based on the needs of Canadians. For example, if a U.S. company decides to reduce its workforce or close a plant, it may more readily do that to a subsidiary than in its home country.

FIGURE | 8.6

Foreign Direct Investment in 2008

Canadian Direct Investment Abroad	2008 ($ Billions)
United States	310.7
United Kingdom	54.0
Barbados	45.0
Bermuda	22.3
Ireland	20.5
Cayman Islands	19.2
France	18.7
Hungary	10.8
Germany	10.5
Brazil	9.2
All other countries	116.5
Total	**637.4**
Foreign Direct Investment in Canada	
United States	293.6
United Kingdom	54.4
Netherlands	33.9
France	18.5
Switzerland	15.3
Japan	13.0
Brazil	11.9
Germany	9.4
Luxembourg	5.7
All other countries	49.1
Total	**504.9**

Source: "Foreign Direct Investment 2008," Statistics Canada, 8 April 2009, http://www.statcan.gc.ca/daily-quotidien/090408/dq090408a-eng.htm.

In the early 1990s, Michael Porter, the competition guru from Harvard University Business School, released a report titled *The Competitive Advantage of Nations* that was commissioned by the Canadian government. While this report is now more than 20 years old, some of his points still ring true today:

> *One of Canada's competitive problems is the high concentration of foreign-owned firms that perform little sophisticated production or R&D. It matters a lot where a multinational calls home, because a company's home base is where the best jobs exist, where core R&D is undertaken, and where strategic control rests... Home bases are important to an economy because they support high productivity and productivity growth.*

Regardless of these concerns, more countries are welcoming subsidiaries as a way to develop their economies.

Swiss-based Nestlé is an example of a major firm with many foreign subsidiaries. The consumer-products giant spent billions of dollars acquiring foreign companies such as Ralston Purina, Chef America (maker of Hot Pockets), Dreyer's Ice Cream, and Perrier in France. All told, Nestlé has approximately 283,000 employees in factories or operations in almost every country in the world.[33]

Nestlé is also an example of a multinational corporation. A **multinational corporation** is an organization that manufactures and markets products in many different countries; it has multinational stock ownership and multinational management. Multinational corporations are typically extremely large corporations, but not all large firms involved in global business are multinationals. For example, a business could literally be exporting everything it produces, deriving 100 percent of its sales and profits globally, and still not be considered a multinational corporation. Only firms that have *manufacturing capacity* or some other physical presence in different nations, such as Magna International Inc., can truly be called multinational.

Getting involved in global business requires selecting an entry strategy that best fits the goals of the business. The different strategies discussed reflect different levels of ownership, financial commitment, and risk that a company can assume. However, this is just the beginning. It's important to be aware of key market forces that affect a business's ability to trade in global markets. After the Progress Assessment, we will discuss these forces.

foreign direct investment (FDI)
The buying of permanent property and businesses in foreign nations.

foreign subsidiary
A company owned in a foreign country by the parent company.

multinational corporation
An organization that manufactures and markets products in many different countries and has multinational stock ownership and multinational management.

Bombardier Transportation won a contract to supply Bombardier Flexity Swift high-floor light rail vehicles to the Bursa Metropolitan Municipality, Turkey. The vehicles will be built at Bombardier's manufacturing facility in Bautzen, Germany. Bodies will come from the Siegen site, while the electrical equipment will be supplied by the Mannheim plant.

Progress Assessment

- What services are usually provided by an export-trading company?
- What are the advantages to a firm of using licensing as a method of entry in global markets? What are the disadvantages?
- What are the key differences between a joint venture and a strategic alliance?
- What is a multinational corporation?

FORCES AFFECTING TRADING IN GLOBAL MARKETS

Succeeding in any business takes work and effort due to the many challenges that exist in all markets. Unfortunately, the hurdles are higher and more complex in global markets than in domestic ones. This is particularly true when dealing with differences in sociocultural forces, economic forces, legal and regulatory forces, and technological forces. (Recall that these were introduced in Chapter 1.) Let's take a look at each of these global market forces to see how they challenge even the most established and experienced global businesses.

Sociocultural Forces

culture
The set of values, beliefs, rules, and institutions held by a specific group of people.

ethnocentricity
An attitude that one's own culture is superior to all others.

Canada is a multicultural country, yet understanding cultural diversity remains one of the true business challenges of the twenty-first century. The word **culture** refers to the set of values, beliefs, rules, and institutions held by a specific group of people.[34] Culture can also include social structures, religion, manners and customs, values and attitudes, language, and personal communication. An attitude that one's own culture is superior to all others is known as **ethnocentricity**. If you hope to get involved in global trade, it's critical to be aware of the cultural differences among nations.

Different nations have very different ways of conducting business. Canadian businesses that wish to compete globally must adapt to those ways. In North America, we like to do things quickly. We tend to call each other by our first names and try to get friendly even on the first encounter. In Japan, China, and other countries these actions would be considered surprising and even rude. Canadian negotiators will say no if they mean no, but Japanese negotiators usually say maybe when they mean no.

Religion is an important part of any society's culture and can have a significant impact on business operations. Consider the violent clashes between religious communities in India, Northern Ireland, and the Middle East—clashes that have wounded these areas' economies. Unfortunately, companies at times do not consider the religious implications of business decisions. Both McDonald's and Coca-Cola offended Muslims in Saudi Arabia by putting the Saudi Arabian flag on their packaging. The flag's design contains a passage from the Quran (Islam's sacred scripture), and Muslims feel that their holy writ should never be wadded up and thrown away.

Successful companies are those that can understand these differences and develop goods and services accordingly. The focus may be on a large global market or a smaller, yet profitable global market.

Understanding sociocultural differences can also be important when managing employees. In Latin American countries, workers believe that managers are placed in positions of authority to make decisions and be responsible for the well-being of their workers. Consider what happened to one North American manager in Peru who was unaware of this characteristic and believed that workers should participate in managerial functions. This manager was convinced that he could motivate his workers to higher levels of productivity by instituting a more democratic decision-making style than the one already in place. Soon workers began quitting their jobs in droves. When asked why, the workers said the new manager did not know his job and was asking the workers what to do. All stated that they wanted to find new jobs, since obviously this company was doomed due to incompetent managers.

The truth is that many companies still fail to think globally. A sound philosophy to adopt in global markets is: Never assume that what works in one country will work in another. Companies such as

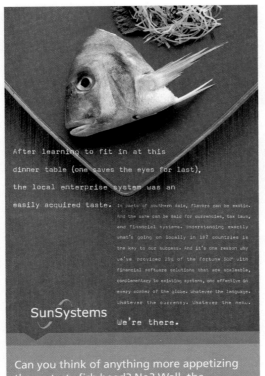

After learning to fit in at this dinner table (one saves the eyes for last), the local enterprise system was an easily acquired taste. In parts of southern Asia, flavors can be exotic. And the same can be said for currencies, tax laws, and financial systems. Understanding exactly what's going on locally in 187 countries is the key to our success. And it's one reason why we've provided 25% of the Fortune 500 with financial software solutions that are scaleable, complementary to existing systems, and effective in every corner of the globe. Whatever the language. Whatever the currency. Whatever the menu.

SunSystems

We're there.

Can you think of anything more appetizing than a tasty fish head? No? Well, the cheeseburgers and "finger-licking-good" chicken we devour in Canada often get similar reactions in other cultures. Understanding different sociocultural perspectives related to time, change, natural resources, and even food can be important in succeeding in global markets. How do you think companies can help employees being assigned to global markets adapt to the different cultures they will encounter and avoid culture shock?

PepsiCo attempted a Chinese translation of "Come Alive, You're in the Pepsi Generation" that read to Chinese customers as "Pepsi Brings Your Ancestors Back from the Dead."	
Coor's Brewing Company put its slogan "Turn It Loose" into Spanish and found it translated as "Suffer from Diarrhea."	
Perdue Chicken used the slogan "It Takes a Strong Man to Make a Chicken Tender," which was interpreted in Spanish as "It Takes an Aroused Man to Make a Chicken Affectionate."	
KFC's patented slogan "finger-lickin' good" was understood in Japanese as "Bite Your Fingers Off."	

FIGURE | 8.7

Oops, Did We Say That? A global marketing strategy can be very difficult to implement. Look at the problems these well-known companies encountered in global markets.

Roots, Nike, and Toyota have developed brand names with widespread global appeal and recognition. However, even these successful global marketers often face difficulties. To get an idea of the problems companies have faced with translations, take a look at Figure 8.7. "Think global, act local" is a valuable motto to follow.

Economic Forces

Economic differences can also make entering global markets more challenging. Surely it's hard for us to imagine buying chewing gum by the stick instead of by the package. Yet this buying behaviour is commonplace in economically depressed nations such as Haiti, because customers there have only enough money to buy small quantities. You might suspect that with more than 1 billion people, India would be a dream market for companies such as Hershey's, Skippy Peanut Butter, and Coca-Cola.[35] However, Indians annually consume an average of only three soft drinks per person, and the vast majority of people cannot afford chocolate or peanut butter due to their low per capita income level. So for these products, what seems like an unbelievable global opportunity is not viable due to economic conditions. Keep in mind that there may be opportunities for other goods and services. The challenge is to tailor products and strategies for local market conditions.

Global financial markets unfortunately do not have a worldwide currency. Mexicans shop with pesos, South Koreans with won, Japanese with yen, and Canadians with dollars. Globally, the U.S. dollar is considered the world's dominant and most stable form of currency. This doesn't mean, however, that the dollar always retains the same market value. In an international transaction today, one dollar may be exchanged for eight pesos; tomorrow, you may only get seven pesos for the same dollar. The **exchange rate** is the value of one nation's currency relative to the currencies of other countries.

Changes in a nation's exchange rates can have important implications in global markets. A *high value of the dollar* means that a dollar would be traded for more foreign currency than normal. The products of foreign producers would be cheaper because it takes fewer dollars to buy them, but the cost of Canadian-produced goods would become more expensive to foreign purchasers because of the dollar's high value. Conversely, a *low value of the dollar* means that a dollar is traded for less foreign currency than normal. Therefore, foreign goods become more expensive because it takes more dollars to buy them, but Canadian goods become cheaper to foreign buyers because it takes less foreign currency to buy Canadian goods.[36]

Global financial markets operate under a system called *floating exchange rates*, in which currencies "float" according to the supply and demand in the global market for the currency. This supply and demand is created by global currency traders, who develop a market for a nation's currency based on the perceived trade and investment potential of the country. Changes in currency values cause many problems globally. Consider a multinational corporation like Nestlé. Costs for labour, raw materials, and machinery can vary considerably as currency values shift, causing production to be juggled from one country to another.[37]

Currency valuation problems can be especially harsh on developing economies. At certain times a nation's government will intervene and adjust the value of its currency,

exchange rate
The value of one nation's currency relative to the currencies of other countries.

devaluation
Lowering the value of a nation's currency relative to other currencies.

countertrading
A complex form of bartering in which several countries may be involved, each trading goods for goods or services for services.

often to increase the export potential of its products. **Devaluation** is lowering the value of a nation's currency relative to other currencies. In other instances due to a nation's weak currency, the only possibility of trade in many developing nations is through one of its oldest forms: *bartering*, which is the exchange of merchandise for other merchandise or service for other service with no money involved.[38] **Countertrading** is a complex form of bartering in which several countries may be involved, each trading goods for goods or services for services. It has been estimated that countertrading accounts for more than 20 percent of all global exchanges, especially deals involving developing countries. For example, let's say that a developing country such as Jamaica wants to buy vehicles from Ford Motor Company in exchange for Jamaican bauxite. Ford, however, does not have a need for Jamaican bauxite but does have a need for computer monitors. In a countertrade agreement, Ford may trade vehicles to Jamaica, which then trades bauxite to another country—say, India—which then exchanges computer monitors with Ford. This countertrade is thus beneficial to all three parties. Trading products for products helps businesses avoid some of the financial problems and currency constraints that exist in global markets. Understanding economic conditions, currency fluctuations, and countertrade opportunities is vital to a company's success in global markets.

Legal and Regulatory Forces

In any economy, both the conduct and the direction of business are firmly tied to the legal and regulatory environment. In Canada, federal, provincial, and municipal laws and regulations heavily affect business practices. In global markets, no central system of law exists, so several groups of laws and regulations may apply. This makes the task of conducting global business extremely difficult as business people find myriad laws and regulations in global markets that are often inconsistent. Important legal questions related to antitrust rules, labour relations, patents, copyrights, trade practices, taxes, child labour, product liability, and other issues are written and interpreted differently country by country.[39]

Canadian businesses are required to follow Canadian laws and regulations in conducting business globally. For example, bribery is not considered legal in Canada. The problem is that this runs contrary to beliefs and practices in many countries where corporate or government bribery not only is acceptable, but also may be the only way to secure a lucrative contract.[40] Members of the Organisation for Economic Co-operation and Development (OECD) have been urged to lead a global effort to fight corruption and bribery in foreign markets. In Transparency International's annual Corruption Perceptions Index, Finland, Denmark, and New Zealand are perceived to be the world's least corrupt countries.[41] For the purposes of this Index, corruption is defined as the misuse of public power for private benefit. "Despite some gains, corruption remains an enormous drain on resources sorely needed for education, health and infrastructure," said Huguette Labelle, Chair of Transparency International. At the same time, deeply troubled states such as Afghanistan, Iraq, Myanmar, Somalia, and Sudan remain at the very bottom of the Index, with a strong correlation between corruption and poverty being evident. "Countries torn apart by conflict pay a huge toll in their capacity to govern. With public institutions crippled or non-existent, mercenary individuals help themselves to public resources and corruption thrives," said Labelle.[42]

It's important to remember that to be successful in global markets, it's often useful to contact local business people in the host countries and gain their co-operation and sponsorship. Such local contacts can help a company penetrate the market and deal with what can be imposing bureaucratic barriers. Local business people are also familiar with laws and regulations that could have an important impact on a foreign firm's business in their country.

Technological Forces

Certain technological forces can also have an important impact on a company's ability to conduct business in global markets. In fact, technological constraints may make it difficult given the nature of exportable products. For example, houses in most developing countries do not have electrical systems that match those of Canadian homes, in kind or in capacity. How would the differences in electricity available (110 versus 220 volts) affect a Canadian appliance manufacturer wishing to export?

Also, computer and Internet usage in many developing countries is rare or non-existent. You can see how this would make for a tough business environment in general and would make e-commerce difficult, especially as this is becoming a critical element of business. After the Progress Assessment, we will explore how trade protectionism affects global business.

Progress Assessment

- What are the major hurdles to successful global trade?
- What does *ethnocentricity* mean?
- Which cultural and social differences are most likely to affect global trade efforts? (Name at least two.)

TRADE PROTECTIONISM

As we discussed in the previous section, sociocultural, economic, legal and regulatory, and technological forces are all challenges to trading globally. What is often a much greater barrier to global trade, however, is trade protectionism. **Trade protectionism** is the use of government regulations to limit the import of goods and services. Supporters of trade protectionism believe that it allows domestic producers to survive and grow, producing more jobs. Those against trade protectionism argue that it not only impedes global trade, but that it also adds millions of dollars to the price of products, costing consumers billions of dollars.

Countries often use protectionist measures to guard against practices such as dumping. **Dumping** is the practice of selling products in a foreign country at lower prices than those charged in the producing country. Companies sometimes use this tactic to dispose of surplus products in foreign markets or to gain a foothold in a new market by offering products for lower prices than domestic competitors do. Dumping benefits foreign firms, as it generates more sales by intentionally charging lower prices. Dumping also benefits purchasers, as they can buy products at a lower price. However, domestic producers do not benefit. Dumping usually leads to a lower share of the market if they do not lower their prices. Lower prices may damage the domestic industry by leading to less revenues and potential job losses. It can take time to prove accusations of dumping, however. There's also evidence that some governments offer financial incentives to certain industries to sell goods in global markets for less than they sell them at home. To understand how trade protectionism affects global business, let's briefly review some global economic history.

Business, economics, and politics have always been closely linked. What we now call economics was once referred to as *political* economy, indicating the close ties between politics (government) and economics. In the seventeenth and eighteenth centuries, business people and governments advocated an economic principle called *mercantilism*. The overriding idea of mercantilism was for a nation to sell more goods to other nations than it bought from them; that is, to have a favourable balance of trade.[43] According to the mercantilists, this resulted in a flow of money to the country that sold the most globally. This philosophy led governments to implement **tariffs**, which are basically taxes on imports, thus making imported goods more expensive to buy.

trade protectionism
The use of government regulations to limit the import of goods and services.

dumping
Selling products in a foreign country at lower prices than those charged in the producing country.

tariff
A tax imposed on imports.

Generally, there are two different kinds of tariffs: protective and revenue. *Protective tariffs* (import taxes) are designed to raise the retail price of imported products so that domestic products will be more competitively priced. These tariffs are meant to save jobs for domestic workers and to keep industries (especially *infant industries*, which consist of new companies in the early stages of growth) from closing down entirely because of foreign competition. Such tariffs are usually met with resistance. After the Canada Border Service Agency ruled that grain was being subsidized in the United States and then sold in Canada below its true cost, the federal government imposed a duty of US$1.65 a bushel on U.S. corn imports.[44] In another instance, Canada, the United States, and the European Union successfully lodged a complaint to the World Trade Organization (to be discussed soon) arguing that China was imposing a 40 percent tariff on auto parts when it had promised not to treat parts as whole cars.[45] If it had been upheld, such a tariff would have forced manufacturers to source 40 percent of an auto's parts by value in China to avoid the tax on cars as the Chinese government considered auto parts as a complete vehicle if they accounted for 60 percent or more of the value of a final vehicle.[46]

Revenue tariffs are designed to raise money for the government. They are commonly used by developing countries to help infant industries compete in global markets.

An **import quota** limits the number of products in certain categories that a nation can import. Canada has import quotas on a number of products including textiles and clothing, agricultural products, steel products, and weapons and munitions.[47] Overall, the goal is to protect companies to preserve jobs. An **embargo** is a complete ban on the import or export of a certain product or the stopping of all trade with a particular country. Political disagreements have caused many countries to establish embargoes, such as Canada's embargo against the Burmese regime, reflecting its condemnation of the Burmese regime's complete disregard for human rights and ongoing repression of the democratic movement.[48]

Non-tariff barriers are not as specific or formal as tariffs, import quotas, and embargoes but can be as detrimental.[49] It's common for nations to set restrictive standards that detail exactly how a product must be sold in a country. For example, Denmark requires companies to sell butter in cubes, not tubs. For many years Japan argued it had some of the lowest tariffs in the world and welcomed foreign exports, yet business found it difficult to establish trade relationships with the Japanese. A Japanese tradition called *keiretsu* (pronounced "care-yet-sue") built "corporate families" (such as Mitsui and Mitsubishi)

import quota

A limit on the number of products in certain categories that a nation can import.

embargo

A complete ban on the import or export of a certain product or the stopping of all trade with a particular country.

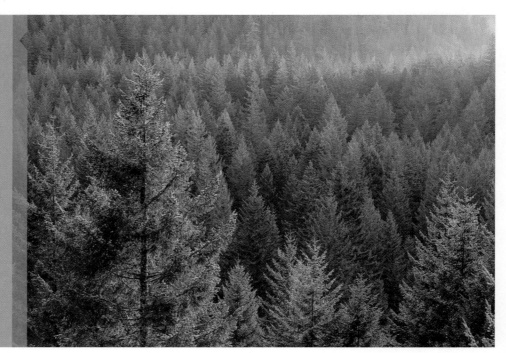

Canada's long dispute with the United States over softwood lumber cost the economy billions of dollars and thousands of jobs. In 2002, the United States imposed duties of 27 percent on Canadian softwood lumber, arguing that Canada unfairly subsidized producers of spruce, pine, and fir lumber. While international trade tribunals sided with Canada, it was not until July 2006 that an agreement between both countries was signed. The United States agreed to return over $4.5 billion in duties it had collected and remove tariffs on lumber.

that forged semi-permanent ties with suppliers, customers, and distributors with full support of the government.[50] The Japanese believed that corporate alliances would provide economic payoffs by nurturing long-term strategic thinking and mutually beneficial co-operation.

Other non-tariff barriers include safety, health, and labelling standards. The United States has stopped some Canadian goods from entering because it said that the information on the labels was too small. The discovery of mad cow disease resulted in a temporary import ban of Canadian beef by the United States, Japan, South Korea, Australia, and other countries.[51]

It would be easy for would-be exporters to view the trade barriers discussed above as good reasons to avoid global trade. Still, wherever you stand on the tariff issue, it's obvious that overcoming trade constraints creates business opportunities. Next, we'll look at organizations and agreements that attempt to eliminate trade barriers among nations.

The GATT and the WTO

In 1948, government leaders from 23 nations throughout the world formed the **General Agreement on Tariffs and Trade (GATT)**, which established an international forum for negotiating mutual reductions in trade restrictions. In short, the countries agreed to negotiate to create monetary and trade agreements that might facilitate the exchange of goods, services, ideas, and cultural programs. In 1986, the Uruguay Round of the GATT was convened to specifically deal with the renegotiation of trade agreements. After eight years of meetings, 124 nations at the Uruguay Round voted to modify the GATT. Under the agreement, tariffs were lowered an average of 38 percent worldwide, and new trade rules were expanded to areas such as agriculture, services, and the protection of patents.

The Uruguay Round also established the **World Trade Organization (WTO)** to assume the task of mediating future trade disputes. The WTO, headquartered in Geneva, Switzerland, is an independent entity now composed of 153 member nations, and its purpose is to oversee cross-border trade issues and global business practices among those nations.[52] It's the world's first attempt at establishing a global mediation centre. Trade issues are expected to be resolved within 12 to 15 months instead of languishing for years, as was the case in the past.

It would be a mistake to assume that the WTO has solved all problems in global trade. Legal and regulatory problems (discussed earlier) often impede trade expansion. Also, a wide divide exists between developed (e.g., Canada) and developing, or least-developed nations, which comprise over three quarters of the WTO membership.[53] "Few would contest the benefits that globalization and trade have brought in terms of greater prosperity for hundreds of millions, as well as greater stability among nations. But many individuals in different societies across the world have shared little or not all in the benefits. The challenges facing governments in managing globalization are formidable, and success in spreading prosperity more widely requires a strong common purpose" says WTO Director-General Pascal Lamy.[54] WTO challenges will likely persist throughout the current decade.

General Agreement on Tariffs and Trade (GATT)
A 1948 agreement that established an international forum for negotiating mutual reductions in trade restrictions.

World Trade Organization (WTO)
The international organization that replaced the General Agreement on Tariffs and Trade, and was assigned the duty to mediate trade disputes among nations.

The WTO has been trying since 2001 to secure a deal on the rules governing trade. But there have been continual disagreements between Western nations and emerging economic powers, such as India and China, over manufacturing and agricultural import rules.

The IMF and the World Bank

The **International Monetary Fund (IMF)** was created in 1944. The IMF is an international bank supported by its members that usually makes short-term loans to countries experiencing problems with their balance of trade. The IMF's basic objectives are to promote exchange stability, maintain orderly exchange arrangements, avoid competitive currency depreciation, establish a multilateral system of payments, eliminate exchange

International Monetary Fund (IMF)
An international bank that makes short-term loans to countries experiencing problems with their balance of trade.

restrictions, and create standby reserves. The IMF makes long-term loans at low interest rates to the world's most destitute nations to help them strengthen their economies. The function of the IMF is very similar to that of the World Bank.

The **World Bank** (also known as the **International Bank for Reconstruction and Development**), an autonomous United Nations agency, is concerned with developing infrastructure (e.g., roads, schools, hospitals, power plants) in less-developed countries. The World Bank borrows from more prosperous countries and lends at favourable rates to less-developed countries. In recent years, the IMF and the World Bank have forgiven some loans to highly indebted countries, such as Mozambique. To qualify for the program, numerous macroeconomic policies (such as inflation and poverty reduction) have to be implemented. These new requirements allow the lending organizations to continue to fulfill their objectives.

Some countries believe that their economies will be strengthened if they establish formal trade agreements with other countries. Some of these agreements, involving forming producers' cartels and common markets, are discussed next.

Producers' Cartels

Producers' cartels are organizations of commodity-producing countries. They are formed to stabilize or increase prices, optimizing overall profits in the long run. The most obvious example today is Organization of the Petroleum Exporting Countries (OPEC). Similar attempts have been made to manage prices for copper, iron ore, bauxite, bananas, tungsten, rubber, and other important commodities. These cartels are all contradictions to unrestricted free trade and letting the market set prices.

Common Markets

An issue not resolved by the GATT or the WTO is whether common markets create regional alliances at the expense of global expansion. A **common market** (also called a **trading bloc**) is a regional group of countries that have a common external tariff, no internal tariffs, and the coordination of laws to facilitate exchange among member countries. Two examples are the North American Free Trade Agreement and the European Union (EU). Let's look briefly at both.

The North American Free Trade Agreement (NAFTA)

A widely debated issue of the early 1990s was the ratification of the **North American Free Trade Agreement (NAFTA)**, which created a free-trade area among Canada, the United States, and Mexico. On 1 January 1993 NAFTA came into effect, replacing the previous Free Trade Agreement between Canada and the United States. The objectives of NAFTA were to (1) eliminate trade barriers and facilitate cross-border movement of goods and services among the three countries; (2) promote conditions of fair competition in this free-trade area; (3) increase investment opportunities in the territories of the three nations; (4) provide effective protection and enforcement of intellectual property rights (patents, copyrights, etc.) in each nation's territory; (5) establish a framework for further regional trade co-operation; and (6) improve working conditions in North America.

NAFTA was driven by the desire of Mexico to have greater access to the U.S. market. Improved access would spur growth, provide more employment for Mexicans, and raise the low standard of living in Mexico. The U.S. government was hoping to create jobs in Mexico and stop the flow of illegal immigrants that were entering its border. Canada was really a minor player in this deal; the Canadian government was concerned that it would be left out or penalized indirectly unless it joined the bloc. Canadians do have something to gain by having freer access to the growing Mexican market, but the country is still a minor customer for Canada.

Today, the three NAFTA countries have a combined population of over 445 million and a gross domestic product of more than $15.7 trillion.[55] The agreement permits all three

World Bank (International Bank for Reconstruction and Development)
An autonomous United Nations agency that borrows money from the more prosperous countries and lends it to less-developed countries to develop their infrastructure.

producers' cartels
Organizations of commodity-producing countries that are formed to stabilize or increase prices to optimize overall profits in the long run.

common market (trading bloc)
A regional group of countries that have a common external tariff, no internal tariffs, and a coordination of laws to facilitate exchange; also called a trading bloc.

North American Free Trade Agreement (NAFTA)
Agreement that created a free-trade area among Canada, the United States, and Mexico.

countries to reduce trade barriers with one another while maintaining independent trade agreements with other countries.

There is continuing concern by some groups (e.g., unions) in Canada and the United States that NAFTA has contributed to employment losses and that economic benefits were not realized. Some Canadian business people remain opposed because they did not like many of the details in NAFTA. In addition, Mexico has a poor policy on environmental problems, bad working conditions, and a poor record on human rights and political freedom. The country has repeatedly been condemned by many organizations in North America and abroad for serious flaws on all these counts. Others believe that NAFTA will force Mexico to gradually improve these conditions. This has been happening, but at a very slow pace.

Officially, almost all trade in the NAFTA region now flows tariff-free. But several major areas of dispute have yet to be resolved including trucking, immigration, the environment, and agricultural tariffs.

The European Union (EU)

The EU began in the late 1950s as an alliance of six trading partners (then known as the Common Market and later the European Economic Community). Today the EU is a group of 27 member nations, located primarily in Europe, with a population of almost 500 million citizens and an estimated 30 percent share of the world's nominal gross domestic product (US$18.4 trillion in 2008).[56] Today, the EU is the world's biggest trading power and member nations see this economic integration as the major way to compete for global business, particularly with the United States, China, and Japan.[57]

The path to European unification was not easy, but a significant step was taken in 1999, when the EU officially launched its joint currency, the euro. The formal EU transition to the euro occurred three years later, when 12 of the 15 member nations at that time agreed to a single monetary unit. (EU members Great Britain, Sweden, and Denmark elected not to convert to the euro at that time.) EU businesses saved billions each year with the entry of the euro, as currency conversions that were required prior to the euro were eliminated. Globally, the euro is certainly a worthy challenger to the U.S. dollar's dominance in global markets due to the economic strength and size of the EU.

A Canada-European Union Trade Agreement was being negotiated in 2009. A study estimated that Europe would gain $18.5 billion a year and Canada about $13 billion by cutting restrictions on services trade, removing tariffs, and reducing non-tariff barriers.[58] Was this agreement successfully negotiated and implemented?

The issues surrounding common markets and free-trade areas will extend far into the twenty-first century. Many fear that poor and developing countries that don't fit in the plans of the trading blocs will suffer. After the Progress Assessment, we'll look at the future of global trade.

To learn more about the countries that belong to the EU, visit http://europa.eu/abc/european_countries/index_en.htm.

Progress Assessment

- What are the advantages and disadvantages of trade protectionism?
- What is the difference between protective tariffs and revenue tariffs?
- What is the primary purpose of the WTO?
- State four objectives of NAFTA.
- What is the primary objective of a common market like the EU?

GLOBALIZATION AND YOUR FUTURE

Global trade opportunities grow more interesting, yet challenging, each day. New and expanding markets present great potential for trade and development. Changes in technology, especially through the Internet, have changed the landscape of business. Internet usage and advances in e-commerce enable companies worldwide to bypass historical distribution channels to reach a large market that is only a mouse click away. Take New England Potter Company, for example. Using the Internet, the company was able to speed up the flow of information between buyers and its manufacturing partners in Europe, South America, and Asia. The company became the world's largest vendor in the garden pottery industry.

The lure of more than 6 billion customers is hard to pass up, especially since the Internet makes the global market instantly accessible. With more than 600 million people worldwide now plugged into the Net, the global market is where opportunities exist.[59] However, nowhere on this planet is the lure to global markets keener than in the world's most populous country, China. With more than 1.2 billion people, China is an economy in high gear since shifting its philosophy from central planning to free markets.

Not long ago, foreign direct investment in China was considered risky and not worth the effort, but today this is not the case. Many view China as the fulfillment of a free trader's dream, where global investment and entrepreneurship are leading the nation to wealth and economic interdependence with the rest of the world. However, concerns remain about China's one-party political system, human rights policies, and growing trade imbalance.[60] Product piracy and counterfeiting are also significant problems. China's underground economy is still actively counterfeiting everything from Calloway golf clubs to Kiwi shoe polish to Louis Vuitton bags.[61] However, since its admission to the WTO in 2001, China has been more receptive to dealing with piracy and counterfeiting. Still, few expect problems to disappear anytime soon. Economists have warned that profits will take a long time to materialize for most companies doing business in China. Nonetheless, in a relatively short period of time, China has become an economic phenomenon. With its openness to trade and investment, educated workforce, and stable infrastructure, China is expected to be a key driver of the world economy.

While China clearly attracts most of the attention in Asia, it's important not to forget the rest of the continent. For example, India's 1.1 billion population (600 million of whom are under 25 years of age) and Russia's 150 million potential customers represent opportunities too good to pass up. Both nations are emerging markets that present business opportunities. India has seen huge growth in information technology, pharmaceuticals, and biotechnology.[62] Still, it remains a nation with extreme poverty and difficult trade laws. Russia is an industrialized nation with large reserves of oil, gas, and gold.[63] Unfortunately, political, currency, and social problems still persist in Russia. The developing nations of Asia, including Indonesia, Thailand, Singapore, the Philippines, Korea, Malaysia, and Vietnam also offer great potential for businesses—and possibly for you.

As you learned in Chapter 1, outsourcing means contracting with other companies to do some of all of the functions of a firm, rather than providing them within the company. In Canada, companies have outsourced payroll functions, accounting, and some manufacturing operations for many years. However, the shift in outsourcing manufacturing and services from domestic businesses to primarily low-wage markets outside of Canada is getting more attention. This shift is referred to as offshoring. The Making Ethical Decisions box offers an example of this practice.

Making Ethical Decisions

How Much Information Is Necessary?

Imagine that you're having a problem with your computer. Not able to fix the problem yourself, you take out the operator's manual and dial customer service. Your call is answered by a service technician who identifies himself as Jeff. You explain to Jeff the problem you are having and wait for his reply. Unfortunately, Jeff cannot solve your problem and transfers your call to his colleague Jennifer. Jennifer analyzes the situation and promptly provides a suggestion that fixes your computer. Impressed, you ask Jennifer for her direct line so you can call her if you have additional questions. She says she is unable to give you her direct number, according to company policy. Upset, you call customer relations and inquire why a service technician cannot give her direct number to a customer. The company representative says, in a rather disgusted tone, "Because the service centre is overseas. You were talking to people trained to identify themselves as Jeff and Jennifer." Should a company let customers know if its service facilities are being outsourced? Should service people be required to give their real names when dealing with customers? What are the consequences of each alternative?

To remain competitive, Canada must stay aware of the global challenge and focus on innovation and entrepreneurship. It's increasingly important for Canadian workers to get the proper education and training needed to stay ahead in the future.[64] The key thing to remember as you progress through this text is that globalization is for real, and competition promises to intensify. The Reaching Beyond Our Borders box highlights how Canada shapes up as a global competitor.

Whether you aspire to be an entrepreneur, a manager, or some other type of business leader, it's becoming increasingly important to think globally in planning your career. As this chapter points out, global markets offer many opportunities, yet they are laced with significant challenges and complexities. By studying foreign languages, learning about foreign cultures, and taking business courses (including a course in global business), you can develop a global perspective on your future.[65] But remember, the potential of global markets does not belong only to large, multinational corporations. Small- and medium-sized businesses are often better prepared to take the leap into global markets and react quickly to opportunities than are large firms saddled with bureaucracies. Also don't forget the global potential of franchising, which we examined in more detail in Chapter 5.

Progress Assessment

- What are the economic risks of doing business in countries like China?
- What might be some important factors that will have an impact on global trading?
- What can you do in the next few years to ready yourself for a career in global business?

Reaching Beyond Our Borders

How Does Canada Shape Up as an International Competitor?

How does Canada rank when compared to other industrialized countries? Canadian businesses have been criticized for not being more productive, because pro ductivity leads to competitiveness. However, productivity is just one important component. Assessing international competitiveness is complex and open to varying opinions.

There are several indexes that attempt to measure competitiveness, and different criteria and weightings are used by the agencies that produce them. You will notice the importance of economic conditions and the role of government when evaluating a country's attractiveness. The prestigious World Economic Forum (WEF) produces the annual Global Competitiveness Report. According to the WEF, one of its indexes—the Growth Competitiveness Index—is based on estimates of each country's ability to grow over the next five to ten years. Thus, economic conditions and institutions (e.g., government and financial markets) are reviewed. Canada's high tax rates, tax regulation, and inefficient government bureaucracy are cited as the most problematic factors for doing business in this country.

The International Institute for Management Development (IMD) produces the World Competitiveness Yearbook, which ranks the ability of a nation to provide an environment that sustains the competitiveness of enterprises. The ranking considers four criteria: economic performance, government efficiency, business efficiency, and infrastructure. While Canada ranks well on government policies conducive to competitiveness, IMD analysts suggest Canada would rank higher if it had a more enterprising business community.

YEAR	WEF'S GROWTH COMPETITIVENESS INDEX	IMD'S OVERALL COUNTRY RANKING
2009	10	8
2008	13	8
2007	12	10
2006	14	5
2005	15	3

It is clear that there is no one conclusive authority that is able to answer the question of how productive, and therefore how competitive, Canada is. These rankings, however, should give you an idea of how the business environment can change quickly and how challenging it is to be consistently competitive.

Sources: "The World Competitiveness Scoreboard 2009," IMD International, 20 May 2009, http://www.imd.ch/research/publications/wcy/upload/scoreboard.pdf; "The Global Competitiveness Report 2008–2009," World Economic Forum, 8 October 2008, http://www3.weforum.org/en/initiatives/gcp/Global%20Competitiveness%20Report/index.htm; and "David Crane, "Innovation: Management Gap Means Canada Is Falling Behind," *The Montreal Gazette*, 22 May 2008, B5.

SUMMARY

LO ▶ 1   **Discuss the growing importance of the global market and the roles of comparative advantage and absolute advantage in global trade.**

1. Canada has a population of more than 33 million people. The world market for trade is huge. Some 99 percent of the people in the world live outside Canada. Major Canadian companies routinely cite expansion to global markets as a route to future growth.

Why should nations trade with other nations?

Nations should trade globally as (1) no country is self-sufficient, (2) other countries need products that prosperous countries produce, and (3) natural resources and technological skills are not distributed evenly around the world.

What is the theory of comparative advantage?

The theory of comparative advantage contends that a country should make and then sell those products it produces most efficiently but buy those it cannot produce as efficiently.

What is absolute advantage?

Absolute advantage means that a country has the ability to produce a particular good or service using fewer resources (and therefore at a lower cost) than another country. For example, Zambia has an absolute advantage over many countries in the production of copper due to its copper ore reserves.

2. Anyone can get involved in world trade through importing and exporting. Business people do not have to work for big multinational corporations.

LO ▶ 2 Explain the importance of importing and exporting and understand key terms used in global business.

What kinds of products can be imported and exported?

Just about any kind of product can be imported and exported. Companies can sometimes find surprising ways to succeed in either activity. Selling in global markets is not necessarily easy, though.

What terms are important in understanding world trade?

Exporting is selling goods and services to other countries. Importing is buying goods and services from other countries. The balance of trade is the relationship of exports to imports. The balance of payments is the balance of trade plus other money flows such as tourism and foreign aid. Dumping is selling products for less in a foreign country than in your own country. Trade protectionism is the use of government regulations to limit the importation of products.

3. A company can participate in world trade in a number of ways.

LO ▶ 3 Illustrate the strategies used in reaching global markets and explain the role of multinational corporations in global markets.

What are some ways in which a company can get involved in global business?

Ways of entering world trade include exporting, licensing (which includes franchising), contract manufacturing, joint ventures and strategic alliances, and direct foreign investment.

How do multinational corporations differ from other companies that participate in global business?

Unlike other companies that are involved in exporting or importing, multinational corporations also have manufacturing facilities or some other type of physical presence in different nations.

4. Many forces affect foreign trade.

LO ▶ 4 Evaluate the forces that affect trading in global markets.

What are some of the forces that can discourage participation in global business?

Potential stumbling blocks to global trade include sociocultural forces (e.g., religion), economic forces (e.g., disposable income), legal and regulatory forces (e.g., law on bribery), and technological forces (e.g., Internet usage).

5. Political differences are often the most difficult hurdles to international trade.

LO ▶ 5 Debate the advantages and disadvantages of trade protectionism, define tariff and nontariff barriers, and give examples of common markets.

What is trade protectionism?

Trade protectionism is the use of government regulations to limit the import of goods and services. Advocates believe that it allows domestic producers to survive and grow, producing more jobs. The key tools of protectionism are tariffs, import quotas, and embargoes.

What are tariff and non-tariff barriers?

Tariffs are taxes on foreign products. There are two kinds of tariffs: (1) protective tariffs, which are used to raise the price of foreign products, and (2) revenue tariffs, which are used to raise money for the government. Non-tariff barriers include safety, health, and labelling standards.

What are some examples of trade organizations that try to eliminate trade barriers and facilitate trade among nations?

The World Trade Organization (WTO) replaced the General Agreement on Tariffs and Trade (GATT). The purpose of the WTO is to mediate trade disputes among nations. The International Monetary Fund (IMF) is an international bank that makes short-term loans to countries experiencing problems with their balance of trade. The World Bank is a United Nations agency that borrows money from the more prosperous countries and lends it to less-developed countries to develop their infrastructures.

What is a common market? State some examples.

A common market is a regional group of countries that have a common external tariff, no internal tariff, and a coordination of laws to facilitate exchange. The idea behind a common market is the elimination of trade barriers that existed prior to the creation of this bloc. Examples include the North American Free Trade Agreement (NAFTA) and the European Union (EU).

LO ▶ 6 Discuss the changing landscape of the global market.

6. The landscape of global business is changing.

What countries offer opportunities for Canadian businesses?

Expanding markets such as China, India, and Russia present great potential for trade and development.

What is outsourcing and how have companies used this business strategy?

Outsourcing is the purchase of goods and services from outside a firm rather than providing them inside the company. It has been a large part of business for many years. Today, more businesses are outsourcing manufacturing and services offshore.

KEY TERMS

absolute advantage 210

balance of payments 213

balance of trade 213

common market (trading bloc) 228

comparative advantage theory 210

contract manufacturing 217

countertrading 224

culture 222

devaluation 224

dumping 225

embargo 226

ethnocentricity 222

exchange rate 223

exporting 209

foreign direct investment (FDI) 221

foreign subsidiary 221

free trade 209

General Agreement on Tariffs and Trade (GATT) 227

import quota 226

importing 209

International Monetary Fund (IMF) 227

joint venture 218

licensing 216

multinational corporation 221

North American Free Trade Agreement (NAFTA) 228

producers' cartels 228

strategic alliance 219

tariff 225

trade deficit (unfavourable balance of trade) 213

trade protectionism 225

World Bank (International Bank for Reconstruction and Development) 228

World Trade Organization (WTO) 227

CRITICAL THINKING

1. You have read that global financial markets operate under a system called floating exchange rates. China is an exception as its exchange rate does not float. Research how this policy impacts the country's balance of trade. What is the reaction of other countries to this decision?

2. Countries like Canada that have a high standard of living are referred to as industrialized nations. Countries with a low standard of living and quality of life are called developing countries (terms formerly used were *underdeveloped* or *less-developed countries*). What prevents developing nations from fully industrializing? Consider economic indicators and political decisions as a starting point.

3. Two different types of tariffs—revenue and protective—are used by government to protect a country's trade. How would you justify the use of either a revenue or a protective tariff in today's global market?

DEVELOPING WORKPLACE SKILLS

1. Call, e-mail, or visit a business involved with importing foreign goods (perhaps a wine or specialty foods importer). Check with the owner or manager about the problems and joys of global trade and compile a list of advantages and disadvantages. Compare notes with your classmates about what they found in their research.

2. Prepare a short list of the advantages and disadvantages of trade protectionism. Share your ideas with others in the class and debate the following statement: Canada should increase trade protection to save Canadian jobs and companies.

3. The economies of Ontario and British Columbia depend heavily on exports. Ontario relies primarily on trade to the United States and Europe, while British Columbia relies heavily on trade with Asia. In a group of four, research these statements. Develop on Excel two graphs that break down the exporting countries that trade with each of these provinces. Present your findings to the class.

4. In a group of four, list the top ten Canadian-based multinationals. When researching, create a table that will include the following pieces of information: the company names, the year each was created, the number of global employees, the industry or industries in which they operate, annual revenues, and number of countries in which they have offices. Present your findings to the class.

 TAKING IT TO THE NET 1

www.mcgrawhillconnect.ca

Purpose

To discover the role the federal government plays in helping Canadian businesses compete successfully in international trade.

Exercise

Visit Foreign Affairs and International Trade Canada (www.international.gc.ca/). Answer the following questions:

1. What is the mandate for this federal department?

2. What are some of the services available for doing business abroad?

3. What are some of the most recent trade negotiations and agreements?

TAKING IT TO THE NET 2

www.mcgrawhillconnect.ca

Purpose

To identify those nations with high export potential and those with low export potential (except for basic goods such as food).

Exercise

Imagine that your company is ready to expand its products to foreign countries. Which countries are most likely to buy your products? The potential to export to a specific country is based on a number of factors, including the size of its population and the strength of its GDP.

1. From the population data given on the United Nations Population Information Network Web site (www.un.org/popin), prepare a list of the 20 countries with the largest populations.

2. Go to the InfoNation section of the UN's Cyber School Bus Web site (www.un.org/Pubs/CyberSchoolBus) and find the GDP per person for each of the nations on your population list. Rate each of the nations on your list for its export potential. Using the GDP per capita and the population size, place each of those nations into the following categories:

a. High export potential (those nations whose population is one of the ten largest and whose GDP per capita is greater than $20,000).

b. Medium-high export potential (those nations whose population is ranked 11 to 21 and whose GDP per capita is greater than $20,000).

c. Medium export potential (those nations whose population is one of the ten largest and whose GDP per capita is between $3,000 and $20,000).

d. Low export potential (those nations whose population is ranked 11 to 21 and whose GDP per capita is less than $3,000).

ANALYZING MANAGEMENT DECISIONS

The Challenge of Offshoring

The truth is that Canadian companies such as Bombardier and Celestica have outsourced manufacturing offshore for years. Fundamentally, as lower-level manufacturing became more simplified, Canadian companies shifted focus from assembling products to design and architecture. Today, economists agree that we are moving into the "second wave" of offshoring that involves sizable numbers of skilled, well-educated middle-income workers in service-sector jobs such as accounting, law, financial and risk management, health care, and information technology that were thought to be safe from foreign market competition. This shift is potentially more disruptive to the Canadian job market than was the first, which primarily involved manufacturing jobs. To take a look at the pros and cons of offshoring, review the following table.

PROS	CONS
1. Less strategic tasks can be outsourced globally so companies can focus on where they can excel and grow.	1. Jobs are lost permanently and wages fall due to low-cost competition offshore.
2. Outsource work allows companies to create efficiencies that in fact let them hire more workers.	2. Offshoring may reduce product quality, which can cause permanent damage to a company's reputation.
3. Consumers benefit from lower prices generated by effective use of global resources and developing nations grow, thus fuelling global economic growth.	3. Communication within the company, with its suppliers, and with its customers becomes much more difficult.

China and India are oftentimes named as country providers of offshoring. Currently, China is primarily involved with manufacturing at the low end of the technology scale, and India focuses on call centres, telemarketing, data entry, billing, and low-end software development. However, China is intent on developing advanced manufacturing technology and India has a deep pool of scientists, software engineers, chemists, accountants, lawyers, and physicians. The technology talent in these nations also keeps growing: China graduates 250,000 engineers each year and India about 150,000.

When you consider the impact of offshoring on Canada, research supports that more than two-thirds of imported services are from the United States, not China and India. A Statistics Canada paper calculates a number of correlations and finds that services offshoring doesn't seem to affect productivity or employment. It does seem to reduce wages in the service sector, though not in the goods-producing sector. Finally, on an industry-by-industry basis, rising offshoring of services seems to be associated with rising value-added. In the financial sector, for instance, low value-added activities such as general accounting are outsourced while high value-added activities such as strategizing are kept in-house and in-country.

Sources: William Watson, "Myth-Busting Offshoring," *National Post*, 30 May 2008, http://network.nationalpost.com/np/blogs/fpcomment/archive/2008/5/30/myth-busting-offshoring.aspx; Pete Engardio, "The Future of Outsourcing," *BusinessWeek*, 30 January 2006, 50–58; and Richard Ernsberger, "The Big Squeeze: A 'Second Wave' of Offshoring Could Threaten Middle-Income, White-Collar and Skilled Blue-Collar Jobs," *Newsweek International*, 30 May 2005.

Discussion Questions

1. Why are more Canadian companies investigating offshoring as a possible business strategy?

2. Do you think that offshoring is detrimental to the Canadian economy? Explain.

3. In your opinion, what are some business activities that should not be offshored? Explain.

McGraw-Hill Connect™—Available 24/7 with instant feedback so you can study when you want, how you want, and where you want. Take advantage of the Study Plan—an innovative tool that helps you customize your learning experience. You can diagnose your knowledge with pre- and post-tests, identify the areas where you need help, search the entire learning package for content specific to the topic you're studying, and add these resources to your personalized study plan.

Visit www.mcgrawhillconnect.ca to register— take practice quizzes, search the e-book, and much more.

CHAPTER 9

Producing World-Class Goods and Services

LEARNING OBJECTIVES

AFTER YOU HAVE READ AND STUDIED THIS CHAPTER, YOU SHOULD BE ABLE TO:

LO ▶ 1 Define operations management and explain what types of firms use it.

LO ▶ 2 Describe the operations management planning issues involved in both the manufacturing and the service sectors, including facility location, facility layout, and quality control.

LO ▶ 3 Discuss the problem of measuring productivity in the service sector, and tell how technology is leading to productivity gains in service companies.

LO ▶ 4 Explain how manufacturing processes can be used in the manufacturing sector.

LO ▶ 5 Describe seven manufacturing techniques that have improved the productivity of companies.

PROFILE

Getting to Know Pierre Beaudoin of Bombardier Inc.

After many ups and downs, in September 2009, Bombardier employed 60,000 people in 29 countries, had a market value of $1 billion, and is the world's No. 1 passenger train maker and No. 3 civil aircraft manufacturer. The company designs and manufactures a portfolio of rail vehicles and aviation products. Their competition includes Embraer, a state-owned aircraft manufactured from Brazil.

If you know anything about Bombardier, the one person who's name would come up is Laurent Beaudoin. He was the President and CEO for 35 years, the son-in-law of its founder, Joseph-Armand Bombardier. Laurent oversaw the development of this goliath—by Canadian standards—manufacturing company. So, who is Pierre Beaudoin, the 47-year-old who studied business administration and industrial relations at McGill and became President and CEO in June of 2008? Back in 1985, while Pierre was working for a sporting goods company, his father, Laurent, asked him to help develop the Sea-Doo. Pierre started as test driver for the first few prototypes of the Sea-Doo, and for the next 16 years he worked in various capacities for Bombardier Recreational Products. In 2001, he was appointed President of Bombardier Aerospace, and then in 2004 he was appointed Executive Vice President of Bombardier Inc.

In his short tenure as President of the parent company, Pierre has had to lead the company through both some very bad and good times. With the collapse of the global economy in the second half of 2008 and into 2009, which lead to a significant slowdown. However, Bombardier remained profitable in this difficult time and also committed to invest for the long term in research and development programs such as the *CSeries* commercial aircraft, the *Learjet 85* business jet, and the very high speed train, to prepare for the next economic cycle.

Pierre has supported a Code of Ethics and Business Conduct that addresses employee ethical conduct and business practices and relationships with external stakeholders. He has publicly supported the development of sustainable transportation systems including more fuel-efficient aircraft that have targeted a 20 percent reduction of carbon dioxide emissions, and rail products to increase energy efficiency by up to 50 percent (these commitments were included in their first Corporate Social Responsibility report, which was released in December 2008). Bombardier is an official supporter of the Vancouver 2010 Olympic and Paralympic Games, with total annual donations of $10 million. Pierre is a twenty-first-century leader of a truly world-class, Canadian-based manufacturer.

Sources: Joe Castaldo, "Laurent Beaudoin Interview, Déjà vu," *Canadian Business Magazine*, 7 August 2008; "Bombardier Signs Airline for Five Q400 NextGen Airliners," *Market Wire*, 3 August 2009; "Bombardier Signs 225 Million USD Contracts to Supply, Operate and Maintain an Automated People Mover System in Phoenix, USA," CCNMatthews, 14 July 2009; and www.bombardier.com.

CANADA TODAY

Canada is a large industrial country with many major industries. We are one of the largest producers of forest products in the world, with plants in nearly all provinces turning out a vast array of wood, furniture, and paper products. There are giant aluminum mills in Quebec and British Columbia, automotive-related manufacturing plants in Ontario and Quebec, and aircraft plants in Ontario, Quebec, and Manitoba. Oil, natural gas, and coal are produced in Alberta, Saskatchewan, Newfoundland and Labrador, Nova Scotia, and British Columbia, and are processed there or in other provinces; a vast array of metals and minerals come from all parts of Canada. These are only some of the thousands of components, products, and natural resources produced or processed in Canada.

Canada is facing some serious challenges to its ability to remain a modern, competitive industrial country. Today's business climate is characterized by constant and restless change and dislocation, as ever-newer technologies and increasing global competition force companies to respond quickly to these challenges. Many factors account for our difficulties in the world's competitive race. Among them are inadequate improvement in productivity and unrelenting competition from the United States, Japan, Germany, and more recently from India, China, and other Southeast Asian countries; inadequate education and retraining programs for our workforce; our "branch plant economy," whereby many subsidiaries are owned by foreign parent companies and profits are mostly returned to these foreign-based companies rather then invested in Canada; and not enough money spent on research and development. Where once a Canadian dollar was worth US$0.65, values closer to parity are forcing Canadian manufactures to improve productivity to remain competitive. Figure 9.1 lists these and other challenges.

Despite these challenges, Canada still ranks fairly well in world competitiveness, as discussed in Analyzing Management Decisions in Chapter 8. However, one cannot expect this to continue, as other countries are becoming stronger and more competitive. In response, the federal government's innovation strategy will, among other areas, focus on research and development as a way to improve our competitiveness. Let us look at research and development next.

FIGURE	**9.1**

Management Issues Survey
The Canadian Manufacturers & Exporters asked manufacturers to identify current and future challenges that will fundamentally change the nature of their business over the next five to ten years. For more information on each of these issues, visit http://cme-mec.ca/pdf/cme08.pdf.

Source: Courtesy Canadian Manufacturers & Exporters, http://cme-mec.ca/pdf/cme08.pdf, "Most Pressing Challenges," p. 11.

FUTURE BUSINESS CHALLENGES

- STRONGER CANADIAN DOLLAR
- INCREASING COMPETITION FROM CHINA
- CHANGING PATTERN OF CUSTOMER DEMAND
- HIGHER BUSINESS COSTS
- AVAILABILITY OF SKILLED PERSONNEL
- BRINGING NEW PRODUCTS ONTO MARKET
- INCREASING COMPETITION FROM OTHER COUNTRIES
- PROCESS INNOVATION
- HIGHER TAX & REGULATORY COSTS
- TECHNOLOGICAL CHANGE
- OVERCAPACITY
- MANAGING GROWTH
- ACCESS TO FOREIGN MARKETS
- AVAILABILITY & COST OF ENERGY
- COMPETITION FOR INVESTMENT & PRODUCT MANDATES

PERCENT OF MANUFACTURERS

Research and Development

According to the *Canadian Oxford Dictionary*, **research and development (R&D)** is defined as work directed toward the innovation, introduction, and improvement of products and processes. When evaluating why some companies are more competitive than others, the terms *technology* and *innovation* often come up. What do these terms mean?

The Centre for Canadian Studies at Mount Allison University, in co-operation with the Canadian Heritage Canadian Studies Programme, produces the *About Canada* series. Innovation in Canada is the focus of one of these documents.

> *Technology is know-how, knowing how to make and use the tools for the job. It's the combination of technology with markets that creates innovation and gives a competitive edge. An innovation is a new product or process that can be purchased. Put another way, an idea may lead to an invention, but it cannot be called an innovation until it is commercialized. When technological know-how is developed, sold, distributed, and used, then it becomes an innovation.*[1]

In the Survey of Innovation conducted by Statistics Canada, respondents indicated that the three most important objectives of innovation are to improve product quality, to increase production capacity, and to extend product range. Since that time, the Science, Innovation, and Electronic Information Division (SIEID) of Statistics Canada has piloted more surveys that focus on the importance of innovation. SIEID believes that innovation and the adoption and dissemination of innovative technologies and processes are vital to economic growth and development. It continues to elaborate by stating that, through innovation, new products are introduced in the market, new production processes are developed and introduced, and organizational changes are made. Through the adoption of newer, more advanced technologies and practices, industries can increase their production capabilities, improve their productivity, and expand their lines of new goods and services.[2]

Private industry, Canadian universities, hospitals, and government laboratories were expected to expend $29 billion on R&D in 2007.[3] The federal government alone—considered the principal source of R&D funds in Canada—spent an estimated $9.5 billion in 2007/2008 on science and technology.[4] Figure 9.2 outlines Canada's top ten corporate R&D spenders. Corporate spending on R&D continued to decline in 2006.[5] As you may note, four of the top 10 spenders were organizations that are part of the communications/telecommunications equipment and aerospace industries. Without the expenditures of Nortel, the decline in spending would have been even worse. A review of the corporate R&D spenders reflected that more companies spent more than $100 million while the largest spenders historically spent less. Such expenditures clearly show that relatively smaller companies understand that R&D is a critical component in ensuring their growth and competitiveness both domestically and internationally.

Based on its research, what does RE$EARCH Infosource Inc. forecast? "...in the 5 years (2002–2006) have seen an increase in corporate mergers...Brand name Canadian companies have disappeared, and this surely does not bode well for R&D investment, as their new owners inevitably rationalize company-wide R&D spending. For another, economic growth is being driven by the oil & gas and mineral and metals section, industries that have traditionally low levels of R&D spending. And manufacturing —which is typically a hotbed of R&D investment—has been hit hard by the fall of the U.S. dollar, squeezing profit margins and leaving fewer funds available for R&D, precisely at a time when more investment in innovation is needed."[6]

research and development (R&D)
Work directed toward the innovation, introduction, and improvement of products and processes.

FIGURE	9.2

Canada's Top Corporate R&D Spenders 2008

Rank			R&D Expenditures			Revenue	Research Intensity	
2007	2006	Company	FY2007 $000	FY2006 $000	% Change 2006–2007	FY2007 $000	R&D as % of Revenue**	Industry
1	1	Nortel Networks Corporation*	$1,851,880	$2,199,020	−15.8	$11,766,910	15.7	Comm/telecom equipment
2	2	Bell Canada	$1,260,000	$1,459,000	−13.6	$17,822,000	7.1	Telecommunications services
3	3	Magna International Inc.*	$725,490	$652,108	11.3	$28,016,812	2.6	Automotive
4	4	Pratt & Whitney Canada Corp.(fs)	$444,000	$481,000	−7.7	$3,300,000	13.5	Aerospace
5	6	IBM Canada Ltd.(fs)	$377,000	$360,000	4.7	nd		Software and computer services
6	8	Atomic Energy of Canada Limited	$288,982	$246,144	17.4	$554,113	52.2	Energy/oil and gas
7	11	Research in Motion*	$253,839	$178,767	42	$3,264,278	7.8	Comm/telecom equipment
8	10	Alcatel-Lucent(fs)	$236,000	$187,167	26.1	nd		Comm/telecom equipment
9		Sanofi-aventis Group++(fs)	$207,156	$216,987	−4.5	$660,769	31.4	Pharmaceuticals/ biotechnology
10	12	Apotex Inc.	$181,818	$178,757	1.7	$1,021,900	17.8	Pharmaceuticals/ biotechnology

NOTES:

We have attempted, wherever possible, to provide gross R&D expenditures before deduction of investment tax credits or government grants. FY2006 R&D expenditure figures may have been adjusted, as more accurate information became available.

Canadian-owned company results include worldwide R&D expenditures; foreign subsidiaries (fs) include R&D expenditures for Canadian operations only.

We have attempted, wherever possible, to provide revenue figures net of interest and investment income.

* = Converted to CDN$ at average 2007 = $1.0748, 2006 = $1.1341 (Bank of Canada)

++ = Includes sanofi-aventis Canada Inc. and Sanofi Pasteur Limited

** = $1 million or more of revenue

fs = Foreign subsidiary (includes R&D expenditures for Canadian operations only)

nd = Not disclosed

Source: RE$EARCH Infosource Inc., www.researchinfosource.com.

CANADA'S EVOLVING MANUFACTURING AND SERVICES BASE

Over the previous two decades, foreign manufacturers captured huge chunks of the North American market for basic products such as steel, cement, machinery, and farm equipment using the latest in production techniques. That competition forced companies to greatly alter their production techniques and managerial styles. Many firms are now as good as or better than competitors anywhere in the world. What have Canadian manufacturers done to regain a competitive edge? They've emphasized the following:

- focusing on customers
- maintaining close relationships with suppliers and other companies to satisfy customer needs
- practising continuous improvement
- focusing on quality
- saving on costs through site selection
- relying on the Internet to unite companies
- adopting production techniques such as enterprise resource planning, computer-integrated manufacturing, flexible manufacturing, and lean manufacturing

As you may recall from Figure 1.5 in Chapter 1, the manufacturing sector employs slightly over 7 percent of Canada's working population. Manufacturing not only is important in employing Canadians, but is also critical to our economy, as manufacturers perform 75 percent of private-sector R&D. They have also been increasing their use of advanced production technologies at an average annual rate of more than 20 percent over the last several years.[7]

As we progress through this chapter, you'll see that operations management has become a challenging and vital element of Canadian business. The growth of Canada's manufacturing base will likely remain a major business issue in the near future. There will be debates about the merits of moving production facilities to foreign countries. Serious questions will be raised about replacing workers with robots and other machinery. Major political decisions will be made regarding protection of Canadian manufacturers through quotas and other restrictions on free trade. Concerns about the impact of manufacturing on our environment will result in the development of new technologies as discussed in the Green Box. Regardless of how these issues are decided, however, there will be many opportunities along the way.

The service sector will also continue to get attention as it continues to become a larger part of the overall economy. Service productivity is a real issue, as is the blending of service and manufacturing through the Internet. Since many of tomorrow's graduates will likely find jobs in the service sector, it is important to understand the latest operations management concepts for this sector.

Each year companies discover new ways of automating that eliminate the need for human labour. This photo shows an automated apparatus known as a Flipper. It can pour a dozen pancakes and flip them when needed on one griddle while, at the same time, flipping burgers on another grill. Are any restaurants in your area already using equipment like this?

From Production to Operations Management

Production is the creation of goods and services using the factors of production: land, labour, capital, entrepreneurship, and knowledge. Production has historically been associated with manufacturing, but the nature of business has changed significantly in the last

production
The creation of finished goods and services using the factors of production: land, labour, capital, entrepreneurship, and knowledge.

GreenBOX

Carbon Capture and Storage

One of Canada's primary resources is its fossil fuels. Abundant supplies of oil, natural gas, and coal make this country one of the world's most attractive energy centres for continuing investment and development. However, with this economic opportunity comes a challenge, to mitigate greenhouse gas (GHG) emissions and their impact on climate change. More and more evidence is being gathered by the scientific community that global emissions growth could bring rapid climate change. The challenge is to reduce GHG emissions while continuing economic progress.

Carbon dioxide capture and storage (CCS) is one way to address the carbon challenge. With CCS, carbon dioxide emissions from large industrial facilities are separated from the plant's process or exhaust system, compressed, and injected deep underground.

CCS can be built as an add-on to existing fossil energy infra-structure or incorporated into new and future facilities. The main components of this operation are: capture, transportation, and storage. Once the carbon dioxide is captured at a plant, it needs to be transported to a location with the appropriate geological formation. These stable sedimentary rock formations, that securely held vast oil and gas reserves, can now be used to hold carbon dioxide, which will be injected into these formations.

Both the federal and a number of provincial governments are financially supporting the development of CCS and bringing forward legislation to reduce GHG emissions or the carbon footprint.

Carbon dioxide is also being used for enhanced oil recovery by companies including Encana. Since 2000, Encana has been injecting existing oil reserves with carbon dioxide to extract more resource.

Source: The Canadian CO_2 Capture and Storage Technology Network, Natural Resources Canada, www.CO_2network.gc.ca; and Racel Pulfer, "Burying King Coal," *Canadian Business*, 28 April 2008, 21–22.

---

20 years or so. The service sector, including Internet services, has grown dramatically, and the manufacturing sector has not grown much at all. As discussed in Chapter 1, Canada is a service economy—that is, one dominated by the service sector. This can be a benefit to future graduates because many of the top-paying jobs are in legal services, medical services, entertainment, broadcasting, and business services such as accounting, finance, and management consulting.

production management
The term used to describe all of the activities that managers do to help their firms create goods.

Production management has been the term used to describe all of the activities that managers do to help their firms create goods. To reflect the change in importance from manufacturing to services, the term *production* often has been replaced by *operations* to reflect both goods and services production. **Operations management**, then, is a specialized area in management that converts or transforms resources (including human resources) into goods and services. It includes inventory management, quality control, production scheduling, follow-up services, and more. In an automobile plant, operations management transforms raw materials, human resources, parts, supplies, paints, tools, and other resources into automobiles. It does this through the processes of fabrication and assembly. In a school, operations management takes inputs—such as information, professors, supplies, buildings, offices, and computer systems—and creates services that transform students into educated people. It does this through a process called education.

operations management
A specialized area in management that converts or transforms resources (including human resources) into goods and services.

Some organizations—such as factories, farms, and mines—produce mostly goods. Others—such as hospitals, schools, and government agencies—produce mostly services. Still others produce a combination of goods and services. For example, an automobile manufacturer not only makes cars but also provides services such as repairs, financing, and insurance. And at Harvey's you get goods such as hamburgers and fries, but you also get services such as order taking, order filling, and cleanup.

As this chapter's profile mentions, Bombardier is a Canadian-based, world-class manufacturing organization, which also earns substantial revenue from their service businesses. Bombardier Aerospace also is involved in fractional ownership, aircraft charter and management, aircraft maintenance, and pilot training.

Manufacturers Turn to a Customer Orientation and Services for Profit

Many manufacturers have spent an enormous amount of money on productivity and quality initiatives. Companies that have prospered and grown—General Electric and Dell, to name just a couple—have taken a similar road to success. They've expanded operations management out of the factory and moved it closer to the customer, providing services such as custom manufacturing, fast delivery, credit, installation, and repair.[8]

Another example of the growing importance of services is in the area of corporate computing. The average company spends only one-fifth of its annual personal computer budget on purchasing hardware. The rest (80 percent) goes to technical support, administration, and other maintenance activities. Because of this, IBM has shifted from its dependence on selling computer hardware to becoming a major supplier of computer services, software, and technology components.[9] Its purchase of Pricewaterhouse-Coopers' tech consulting affiliate was intended to increase its presence in the service sector. General Electric is doing the same; it generates more than $5 billion a year in worldwide revenues from Internet transactions.[10]

Companies such as Celestica and Ford have outsourced much of their production processes and are focusing more on building customer relationships and brand images.[11] As you can see, operations management has become much more focused on services, because by redirecting corporate thinking towards satisfying customer needs better than the competition, they retain their customers.

Progress Assessment

- What are some challenges that Canada is facing in its ability to remain a competitive country?
- How is innovation related to research and development?
- Explain the difference between production management and operations management.

OPERATIONS MANAGEMENT PLANNING

Operations management planning involves many of the same issues in both the service and manufacturing sectors. These issues include facility location, facility layout, and quality control. The resources used may be different, but the management issues are similar.

Facility Location

Companies today are making strategic decisions when establishing, operating, and closing facilities. **Facility location** is the process of selecting a geographic location for a company's operations. In keeping with the need to focus on customers, one strategy in facility location is to find a site that makes it easy for consumers to access the company's service and to maintain a dialogue about their needs. For example, Hewlett-Packard (Canada) Company opened a new computer manufacturing facility in Toronto in a bid to speed new machines to Canadian business customers as fast as archrival Dell Incorporated. In doing so, HP became the only major computer vendor active in Canada to actually assemble machines here.[12] Flower shops and banks are putting facilities in supermarkets so that their products are more accessible than they are in freestanding facilities. You can find a Second Cup inside some Home Depot stores and there are Tim Hortons outlets in some gas stations. Customers can buy gas and their meals, all in one location. Of course, the ultimate in convenience is never having to leave home to get services. That's why there is so much interest in Internet banking, Internet car shopping, Internet education, and so on. For brick-and-mortar businesses (e.g., retail stores) to beat such competition, they have to choose good locations and offer outstanding service to those who do come. Study the location of service-sector businesses—such as hotels, banks, athletic clubs, and supermarkets—and you will see that the most successful ones are conveniently located.

Facility Location for Manufacturers

A major issue of the recent past has been the shift of manufacturing organizations from one city or province to another in Canada, or to other foreign sites. In 2005, Gildan, a Canadian company and one of the world's largest manufacturers of T-shirts, closed two plants in Canada, transferring production to North Carolina.[13] Such shifts sometimes result in pockets of unemployment in some geographic areas and lead to tremendous economic growth in others that benefit from these shifts. The Making Ethical Decisions box considers some of the issues surrounding such moves.

Why would companies spend millions of dollars to move their facilities from one location to another? Issues that influence site selection include labour costs; availability of resources, such as labour; access to transportation that can reduce time to market; proximity to suppliers; proximity to customers; low crime rates; quality of life for employees; a lower cost of living; and the ability to train or retrain the local workforce.

One of the most common reasons for a business move is the availability of inexpensive labour or the right kind of skilled labour. Even though labour cost is becoming a smaller percentage of total cost in some highly automated industries, the low cost of labour remains a key reason that many producers move their plants. For example, low-cost labour is one reason why some firms are moving to Malaysia, Mexico, and other countries with low wage rates. Some of these firms have been charged with providing substandard working conditions and/or exploiting children in the countries where they have set up factories. Others, such as Grupo Moraira (Grupo M), a real estate construction and sales company in the Dominican Republic, are being used as role models for global manufacturing. Grupo M provides its employees with higher pay relative to local businesses, transportation to and from work, daycare centres, discounted food, and health clinics. Its operations are so efficient that it can compete in world markets and provide world-class services to its employees.

Inexpensive resources are another major reason for moving production facilities. Companies usually need water, electricity, wood, coal, and other basic resources. By moving

Making Ethical Decisions

Financial Support or Not?

In early 2009, both General Motors and Chrysler approached the federal and Ontario governments, along with their unions, looking for financial support and major concessions. Both companies indicated that without this support, they would be forced to close their Canadian operations. They claimed they were unable to compete with the lower wage costs of non-North American owned facilities. Closure of their operations would result in tens of thousands of job losses between their plants and their suppliers' operations. They sought billions of dollars from the governments to cover losses and update their production facilities while labour leaders had to agree to re-negotiate labour contracts significantly reducing labour costs. Do you think the governments and unions should have agreed to the demands of General Motors and Chrysler? What could have been the consequences if they didn't? What would you have chosen to do?

to areas where natural resources are inexpensive and plentiful, firms can significantly lower costs—not only the cost of buying such resources but also the cost of shipping finished products. Often the most important resource is people, so companies tend to cluster where smart and talented people are. Witness the Ottawa area, also known as Silicon Valley North.

Reducing time to market is another decision-making factor. As manufacturers attempt to compete globally, they need sites that allow products to move through the system quickly, at the lowest costs, so that they can be delivered rapidly to customers.[14] Access to various modes of transportation (such as highways, rail lines, airports, water, and the like) is thus critical. Information technology (IT) is also important to quicken response time, so many firms are seeking countries with the most advanced information systems.

Another way to work closely with suppliers to satisfy your customers' needs is to locate your production facilities near supplier facilities. That cuts the cost of distribution and makes communication easier.[15]

Many businesses are building factories in foreign countries to get closer to their international customers. That's a major reason why the U.S. automaker General Motors builds cars in Windsor, Ontario, and Japanese automaker Toyota builds cars in Cambridge, Ontario. Japanese-based automaker Honda opened an engine factory plant in Alliston, Ontario, in 2008, close to its two assembly plants. Honda Canada president Hiroshi Kobayashi told a news conference that this site selection "supports Honda's global strategic manufacturing focus of bringing manufacturing and sales operations to the local market."[16] When firms select foreign sites, they consider whether they are near airports, waterways, and highways so that raw materials and finished goods can be moved quickly and easily.

Businesses also study the quality of life for workers and managers. Quality-of-life questions include these: Are there good schools nearby? Is the weather nice? Is the crime rate low? Does the local community welcome new businesses? Do the chief executive and other key managers want to live there? Sometimes a region with a high quality of life is also an expensive one, which complicates the decision. In short, facility location has become a critical issue in operations management. The Dealing with Change box looks at how a major natural disaster can affect manufacturing and service organizations within the region and beyond. Nothing challenges firms more.

Outsourcing

The previous chapter noted that many companies now try to divide their production between core competencies, work they do best in-house, and outsourcing, letting outside companies service them by doing what they are experts at. The result sought is the best-quality products at the lowest possible costs.

Outsourcing goods and services has become a hot practice in North America. Software development, call-centre jobs, and back-office jobs have been moving to developing

With average labour costs about one-fortieth of those in Canada, China is now a leading manufacturer of not only textiles and consumer products, but also increasingly sophisticated electronic equipment, software, and other technologies. It is competing increasingly on the basis of high-end value-added products, as well as costs, using some of the world's best technologies and drawing from a pool of highly skilled talent.

countries for some time. The range of jobs now shifting to these countries includes accounting, financial analysis, medicine, architecture, aircraft maintenance, law, film production, and banking activities.[17] One estimate puts the current value of outsourced goods and services around the world at a whopping US$6 trillion a year.[18] Macadamian, an Ottawa-based software firm, estimates that by 2009, 90 percent of companies will outsource their software R&D, while only a quarter outsourced it in 2004.[19] Keep in mind that while outsourcing may look good on paper financially, if a company does not do its homework, outsourcing can become a problem due to language and cultural differences, differences in expectations, etc. A Canadian organization, the Centre for Outsourcing Research and Education (CORE), has been formed to provide organizations with the knowledge and skills to manage outsourcing activities.[20] CORE has released a report on new trends affecting companies outsourcing activities. More than just a cost-saving tool, outsourcing is being used as a strategic tool for focusing scarce human capital on core business activities.

One outsourcing model that is working involves the software company mentioned above, Macadamian Technologies Inc. Using software engineers in eastern Europe and India, Macadamian uses a distributed model with completely transparent communication. Using wikis, every small iteration on a project is reviewed by the rest of the team members, who then post comments. A project manager gets the final say. Everyone shares their work resulting in clients getting more flexibility and quicker turnaround.

Keep in mind that Canadian companies are also benefiting from other countries' outsourcing. For example, Procter & Gamble's bar soap for North America is now manufactured by Newmarket-based Trillium Health Care Products. This contract makes Trillium—already the leader in making private-label soap for retailers—the second- or third-largest bar soap maker on the continent.[21] Canada is one of the top IT outsourcing destinations in the world, especially for the United States. Reasons noted for why U.S. companies will outsource to Canada include: availability of highly skilled IT professionals, stable workforce without high attrition rates, similar culture and language, familiarity with American business processes, same time zones allowing for real time communication, and an excellent communication system between the two countries.[22]

There can be instances, however, when jobs do not need to be lost to foreign locations. When the Bank of Montreal (BMO) outsourced its human resources processing services to California-based Exult Inc., it negotiated an unusual condition: Take our business, take our people. As part of this $75-million-a-year contract for the next ten years, more than 100 former BMO employees now work for Exult in the same office

DEALING with CHANGE

Responding to a Major Disaster

Hurricane Katrina has been called "the largest natural disaster in American history." So what do you do if you have your corporate headquarters in New Orleans, where almost the whole city was flooded, and your only factory is in Long Beach, Mississippi, where the devastation was enormous? If you are Thomas Oreck, you plan to resume manufacturing in just two weeks. Here was the situation: The vacuum cleaner factory in Long Beach had no phone service, no electricity, and no water. Roads in and out of town were blocked. Hundreds of employees had lost their homes, and hundreds more were missing. The list of things needed to restart was long: diesel fuel, generators, food, water, and housing. One team of workers went looking for generators while another team searched for mobile homes.

Arrangements were made with United Parcel Service to distribute the vacuum cleaners and bring in food and water. The grounds around the manufacturing facility became a campus of sorts, with housing, health clinics, and offices. Web sites were established so that workers could contact each other and family members. The company was operating again as soon as it possibly could.

Businesses responded to the disaster in many ways. Getting old factories started again was a major contribution because it renewed old jobs and created some

hope. Hurricane Katrina closed 126 Walmart facilities, but all but 14 were operating again within a couple of weeks. Hundreds of businesses did what they could to help, and they responded quickly. Springs Industries of Fort Mill, South Carolina, sent sheets, blankets, and comforters. Anheuser Busch sent 2.5 million cans of drinking water *per week*! Bristol-Myers Squibb sent many cartons of baby formula. Eli Lilly sent 40,000 vials of insulin. Kellogg sent seven truckloads of crackers and cookies. Pfizer sent $2 million and a lot of medicine. The other pharmaceutical companies were equally or more generous. Amgen, for example, sent $2.5 million and offered to match any contributions made by employees. The list goes on and on.

Change management means more than adjusting to day-to-day challenges. It also means adjusting to catastrophic disasters, and reacting quickly. That is true for both manufacturing firms such as Oreck and service firms such as Walmart.

Sources: Jeffrey H. Birnbaum, "Stepping Up," *The Washington Post*, 4 September 2005, F1, F4; Jonathan Eig, "Manufacturer Finds More Than Vacuums At Stake in Recovery," *The Wall Street Journal*, 9 September 2005, B1, B5; Susan Morse, "A Tide of Giving," *The Washington Post*, 13 September 2005, F3.

---

tower. Exult sees this as an excellent opportunity to expand its business in Canada, and these new employees have a mandate to bring in more Canadian clients.[23] Unfortunately, examples such as this are not the norm.

Canada's Auto Industry[24]   The auto industry is critical to Canada's manufacturing economy. According to the Canadian Vehicle Manufacturers' Association, the auto sector is Canada's biggest contributor to manufacturing Gross Domestic Product (GDP) and its largest manufacturing employer, employing one out of every seven Canadians. The industry supports jobs across Canada in 13 assembly plants, more than 540 parts manufacturers, 3,900 dealerships, and many other related industries.

It is no wonder that this industry is Canada's largest, both domestically and in exports (recall the value of these exports from Chapter 8). As well, it should be of no surprise that this industry has also faced increased competition from international players. In recent years, faced with relatively high labour and pension costs, plants have closed, eliminating thousands of jobs. Other than Toyota in Cambridge and Woodstock, and Honda in Alliston (all these locations are in Ontario), plant expansion projects have gone south of the border.

To potential investors, Canada offers cost advantages due to our public medicare program and, until a few years ago, a low currency. However, southern U.S. states such as

The Canadian Auto Workers (CAW) has a Manufacturing Matters Campaign. Over 25,000 jobs have been lost in the last three to five years, due, in part, to incentives and cheaper wages offered in other countries. What other factors may influence companies to relocate?

A video called *The Toyota Production System* provides a very informative presentation of how this company has positioned itself as a leading global manufacturing entity. Go to www.toyota.ca, click on the "Company Info" tab, then "Toyota Motor Manufacturing Canada," then "How We Build" to find the video.

Alabama, Georgia, and Mississippi are luring billions of dollars' worth of auto industry assembly plants with more attractive incentives, including land and training. These incentives are also starting to be offered to parts makers. To respond to the decreasing trend in new auto investments, a joint industry–government council was established. A major goal of the Canadian Automotive Partnership Council (CAPC) is to improve the future of the assembly industry. The Council has acknowledged tax cuts and provincial government support for investment in environmental research as important to the survival of this industry in Canada. Time will tell if such initiatives will improve the industry's health.

Taking Operations Management to the Internet

Many of today's rapidly growing companies do very little production themselves. Instead, they outsource engineering, design, manufacturing, and other tasks to other companies that specialize in those functions. Furthermore, companies are creating whole new relationships with suppliers over the Internet, so that operations management is becoming an inter-firm process in which companies work together to design, produce, and ship products to customers. Coordination among companies today can be as close as coordination among departments in a single firm was in the past.

Many of the major manufacturing companies (e.g., Microsoft) are developing new Internet-focused strategies that will enable them and others to compete more effectively in the future.[25] These changes are having a dramatic effect on operations managers as they adjust from a one-firm system to an inter-firm environment, and from a relatively stable environment to one that is constantly changing and evolving. This linking of firms is called *supply chain management*. We will briefly introduce you to this concept later in the chapter.

Facility Location in the Future

Developments in information technology (computers, modems, email, voice mail, teleconferencing, etc.) are giving firms and employees more flexibility than ever before in choosing locations while staying in the competitive mainstream. Telecommuting (working from home via computer and modem) is a major trend in business.[26] Companies that no longer need to locate near sources of labour will be able to move to areas where land is less expensive and the quality of life may be nicer.

One big incentive to locate or relocate in a particular city or province is the tax situation and degree of government support. Those with lower taxes, such as Alberta, may be more attractive to companies. Some provinces and local governments have higher taxes than others, yet many engage in fierce competition by giving tax reductions and other support, such as zoning changes and financial aid, so that businesses will locate there. The Reaching Beyond Our Borders box explores how one company has handled the complex role of handling production facilities all over the world.

Facility Layout

facility layout
The physical arrangement of resources (including people) in the production process.

Facility layout is the physical arrangement of resources (including people) in the production process. The idea is to have offices, machines, storage areas, and other items in the best possible position to enable workers to produce goods and provide services for customers. Facility layout depends greatly on the processes that are to be performed. For services, the layout is usually designed to help the consumer find and buy things. More and more, that means helping consumers find and buy things on the Internet. Some stores have added kiosks that enable customers to search for goods on the Internet and then place orders in the store. The store also handles returns and other customer-contact functions. In short, services are becoming more and more customer oriented in how they design their stores and their Internet services. Some service-oriented organizations, such as hospitals, use layouts that improve the efficiency of the production process, just as manufacturers do. For manufacturing plants, facilities layout has become critical because the possible cost savings are enormous.

Reaching Beyond Our Borders

Lockheed Martin Goes Global

Can you imagine how hard it would be to manage the construction of a combat jet airplane? Now try to imagine how hard it would be if the plane was being built by 80 different suppliers in 187 different locations. Furthermore, while the plane is being constructed, the U.S. Air Force, Navy, and Marines; the British Ministry of Defence; and eight other U.S. allies will be watching the progress, making comments, and changing the plans if necessary. What kind of person could pull all of that together?

The man responsible for this huge project is Dain Hancock of Lockheed Martin. One of his successes at Lockheed was to consolidate three operating units into a single company. Now he has the responsibility, with the help of others, of uniting some 80 companies into a single production unit. To do that, Lockheed and its partner companies will be using a system of 90 Web software tools to share designs, track the exchange of documents, and keep an eye on progress. The Internet enables people from different companies with incompatible computer systems to meet on Web sites and speak a common language. They will be able to talk via their computers while looking at shared documents. They can also use electronic white boards on which two or more people can draw pictures or charts, in real time, as others watch and comment.

Hancock and other managers are taking operations management beyond the control of one plant to the control of multiple plants in multiple locations, often in multiple countries. The Internet has changed business in many ways, but none other may be as dramatic as this.

Many companies are moving from an *assembly line layout*, in which workers do only a few tasks at a time, to a *modular layout*, in which *teams* of workers combine to produce more complex units of the final product.[27] For example, there may have been a dozen or more workstations on an assembly line to complete an automobile engine in the past, but all of that work may be done in one module today. A *process layout* is one in which similar equipment and functions are grouped together. The order in which the product visits a function depends on the design of the item. This allows for flexibility. When working on a major project, such as a bridge or an airplane, companies use a *fixed-position layout* that allows workers to congregate around the product to be completed. Figure 9.3 illustrates typical layout designs.

Quality Control

Quality is consistently producing what the customer wants while reducing errors before and after delivery to the customer. Before, quality control was often done by a quality control department at the end of the production line. Products were completed *and then tested*. This resulted in several problems:

1. There was a need to inspect other people's work. This required extra people and resources.

2. If an error was found, someone would have to correct the mistake or scrap the product. This, of course, was costly.

3. If the customer found the mistake, he or she might be dissatisfied and might even buy from someone else thereafter.

Such problems led to the realization that quality is not an outcome; it is a never-ending process of continually improving what a company produces. Therefore, quality control should be part of the operations management planning process rather than simply an end-of-the-line inspection.

Companies have turned to the use of modern quality control standards, such as six sigma. **Six sigma quality** (just 3.4 defects per million opportunities) detects potential problems

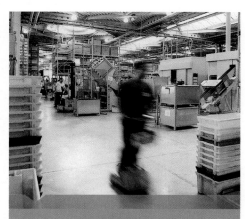

The Igus manufacturing plant in Cologne, Germany, can shrink or expand in a flash. Its flexible design keeps it competitive in a fast-changing market. Because the layout of the plant changes so often, some employees use scooters in order to more efficiently provide needed skills, supplies, and services to multiple workstations. A fast-changing plant needs a fast-moving employee base to achieve maximum productivity.

quality
Consistently producing what the customer wants while reducing errors before and after delivery to the customer.

six sigma quality
A quality measure that allows only 3.4 defects per million events.

FIGURE 9.3

Typical Layout Designs

A. ASSEMBLY-LINE LAYOUT
Used for repetitive tasks.

B. PROCESS LAYOUT
Frequently used in operations that serve different customers' different needs.

statistical quality control (SQC)
The process that some managers use to continually monitor all phases of the production process to ensure that quality is being built into the product from the beginning.

C. MODULAR LAYOUT
Can accommodate changes in design or customer demand.

statistical process control (SPC)
The process of taking statistical samples of product components at each stage of the production process and plotting those results on a graph. Any variances from quality standards are recognized and can be corrected if beyond the set standards.

D. FIXED POSITION LAYOUT
A major feature of planning is scheduling work operations.

What happens when you combine the zeal of technical innovators with the six sigma discipline of a large company like General Electric? You get a medical breakthrough. Janet Burki and her 280-person operations team developed the world's fastest CT scanner. It works ten times faster than other systems and produces clear 3-D images of the beating heart. Can you see how efforts to build in quality lead to better (and faster) products?

to prevent their occurrence. The Spotlight on Small Business box explores how small businesses can apply six sigma to their operations.

Statistical quality control (SQC) is the process that some managers use to continually monitor all phases of the production process to ensure that quality is being built into the product from the beginning. **Statistical process control (SPC)** is the process of taking statistical samples of product components at each stage of the production process and plotting those results on a graph. Any variances from quality standards are recognized and can be corrected if beyond the set standards. Ensuring that products meet standards all along the production process eliminates or minimizes the need for having a quality control inspection at the end. Any mistakes would have been caught much earlier in the process. SQC and SPC thus save companies much time and many dollars. Some companies call such an approach to quality control the Deming cycle (after W. Edwards Deming, the father of the movement toward quality).[28] The cycle steps are: Plan, Do, Check, Act (PDCA). Again, the idea is to find potential errors *before* they happen. Deming's approach, including implementing standards, was used for many years before the International Organization for Standardization (ISO), which we will talk about shortly, came into being.

The customer is ultimately the one who determines what the standard for quality should be. Businesses are getting serious about providing top customer service, and many are already doing it. Service organizations

SPOTLIGHT ON Small Business

Meeting the Six Sigma Standard

Six sigma is a quality measure that allows only 3.4 defects per million opportunities. It is one thing for Motorola or General Electric (GE) to reach for such standards, but what about a small company like Dolan Industries? Dolan is a 41-person manufacturer of fasteners. It spent a few years trying to meet ISO 9000 standards, which are comparable to six sigma.

Once the company was able to achieve six sigma quality itself, it turned to its suppliers and demanded six sigma quality from them as well. Dolan had to do that because its customers were demanding that level of quality. Companies such as Honeywell, Motorola, and Nortel Networks Corp. are all seeking six sigma quality. In his first conference call, Mike Zafirovski, president and CEO of Nortel, announced his intention to introduce the six sigma program in an attempt to improve performance via decreased costs and improved quality and process. Other benefits include increases in product performance and, more important, happy customers—and profit growth.

Here is how six sigma works: If you can make it to the level of one sigma, two out of three products will meet specifications. If you can reach the two sigma level, then more than 95 percent of products will qualify. But when you meet six sigma quality, as we've said, you have only 3.4 defects in a million opportunities (which means that 99.99966 percent of your products will qualify). The bottom line is that small businesses are being held to a higher standard, one that approaches perfection. Service organizations are also adopting six sigma standards.

So, how can a small business learn about such processes quickly? The answer is to use TRIZ. TRIZ is a Russian acronym for Theory of Inventive Problem Solving. The ideas are these: (1) Somebody, someplace, has already solved your problem or one similar to it. Creativity means finding that solution and adapting it to the current problem, and (2) Do not accept compromises; eliminate them. For example, farmers learned how to process manure to remove the water from studying the orange juice industry (that's how it makes concentrated orange juice). The pharmaceutical industry learned to manage foam in the production process by studying the beer industry. You get the idea. Today, searching for answers on the Internet is critical to a company's success. You might look at some of the sources below for examples.

Sources: Ellen Domb, "Enhance Six Sigma Creativity with TRIZ," *Quality Digest*, February 2004; Ellen Domb, "Think TRIZ for Creative Problem Solving," *Quality Digest*, August 2005, 35–40; www.TRIZ-journal.com, 2005; and Andrew Wahl, "Nortel's New Game Plan: Canada Telecom," *Canadian Business*, March 27–April 9, 2006, http://www.canadianbusiness.com/technology/companies/article.jsp;jsessionid=JGFKAOIDBBDD?content=20060327_75509_75509.

OVERALL BUSINESS PERFORMANCE

LEADERSHIP   PLANNING   CUSTOMER FOCUS

PEOPLE FOCUS   PROCESS MANAGEMENT   SUPPLIER/PARTNER FOCUS

PRINCIPLES FOR EXCELLENCE

The National Quality Institute is working to help companies understand and apply a focus on excellence through the adoption of the Canadian Framework for Business Excellence. This approach will help companies reduce rework, waste, and costs while improving productivity and competitiveness. Do you see how this framework incorporates principles discussed in this textbook?

are finding it difficult to provide outstanding service every time because the process is so labour intensive. Physical goods (e.g., a gold ring) can be designed and manufactured to near perfection. However, it is hard to reach such perfection when designing and providing a service experience such as a dance on a cruise ship or a cab drive through Vancouver.

Quality Award: The Canada Awards for Excellence[29]

The National Quality Institute (NQI), an independent, Canadian, not-for-profit organization, is the leading authority in Canada on workplace excellence based on quality systems and healthy workplace criteria. The Canada Awards for Excellence (CAE) are presented annually to private, public, and not-for-profit organizations that have displayed outstanding performance in the areas of quality and healthy workplace. The award has honoured hundreds of Canadian organizations, including the British Columbia Transplant Society, Delta Hotels, Statistics Canada, and the College of Physicians & Surgeons of Nova Scotia. Recent recipients include 3M Canada Company, Vincent Massey School, the City of Kamloops, and Manulife Financial. Other CAE awards include Healthy Workplace, Customer Service, and Health Care. For more information, visit www.nqi.ca.

ISO 9000 and ISO 14000 Standards

The International Organization for Standardization (ISO) is a worldwide federation of national standards bodies from more than 140 countries that set the global measures for the quality of individual products. ISO is a non-governmental organization established in 1947 to promote the development of world standards to facilitate the international exchange of goods and services. (ISO is not an acronym. It comes from the Greek word *isos*, meaning oneness.) **ISO 9000** is the common name given to quality management and assurance standards. The latest standards are called ISO 9004:2000.[30] The standards require that a company must determine what customer needs are, including regulatory and legal requirements. The company must also make communication arrangements to handle issues such as complaints. Other standards involve process control, product testing, storage, and delivery. Improving quality is an investment that can pay off in better customer relations and higher sales.[31]

It is important to know that ISO did not start as a quality certification, the way many people think. In the beginning, it simply meant that your process was under control. In short, it looked to see that companies were consistently producing the same products each time. There is a difference between consistency (flawed products every time) and quality (products free from defects). Today, ISO has developed over 17,000 international standards and 1,100 new standards are published every year.[32]

What makes ISO 9000 so important is that the European Union (EU) is demanding that companies that want to do business with the EU be certified by ISO standards. Some major Canadian companies are also demanding that suppliers meet these standards. There are several accreditation agencies in Europe and in North America whose function is to certify that a company meets the standards for all phases of its operations, from product development through production and testing to installation. SNC-Lavalin Group Inc. (www.snclavalin.com), one of the leading groups of engineering and construction companies in the world, has met such standards. It provides engineering, procurement, construction, project management, and project financing services to a variety of industry sectors in more than 120 countries. The Quality Policy at SNC-Lavalin is to "achieve client satisfaction through the careful management of our work processes, with due attention to value creation through scope, schedule, cost control, and with emphasis on safety and the environment." To best serve its various stakeholders, the company has implemented

ISO 9000

The common name given to quality management and assurance standards.

Lange Con Custom Homes Inc. has been building custom homes since 1983. It first obtained ISO 9001 certification in 2000, which it continues to maintain. Its processes are regularly reviewed to ensure high standards of quality, which supports its leadership position in the export of manufactured housing.

Client Satisfaction and Continual Improvement Programs in every division, business unit, geographic office, and subsidiary. These programs are based on the applicable requirements of ISO 9001 International Standard for Quality Management Systems.[33]

ISO 14000 is a collection of the best practices for managing an organization's impact on the environment. It does not prescribe a performance level. ISO 14000 is an environmental management system (EMS). The requirements for certification include having an environmental policy, having specific improvement targets, conducting audits of environmental programs, and maintaining top management review of the processes. Certification in both ISO 9000 and ISO 14000 would show that a firm has a world-class management system in both quality and environmental standards. In the past, firms assigned employees separately to meet both standards. Today, ISO 9000 and ISO 14000 standards have been blended so that an organization can work on both at once. ISO is now working on ISO 26000 standards, which are designed to give guidance on social responsibility.[34]

ISO 14000
A collection of the best practices for managing an organization's impact on the environment.

Supply Chain Management

Before we discuss this next topic, it is important to introduce some terms. **Logistics** involves those activities that focus on getting the right amount of the right products or services to the right place at the right time at the lowest possible cost. A **supply chain** is a sequence of firms that perform activities required to create and deliver a good or service to consumers or industrial users. Some companies have been successful in attracting more customers due to their supply chain management efficiencies. **Supply chain management** is the integration and organization of information and logistics activities *across* firms in a supply chain for the purpose of creating and delivering goods and services that provide value to customers.

Facilities included in supply chain management include: factories, processing centres, warehouses, distribution centres, and retail outlets. Functions and activities included are: forecasting, purchasing, inventory management, information management, quality assurance, scheduling, production, delivery, and customer service. Today, the major factors contributing to the importance of supply chain management include the need for improvement to remain competitive, the increase in outsourcing, shorter product life cycles and increased customization, increase in globalization, the growth of technology and e-commerce, the increase in complexity through just-in-time inventory (which will be talked about later in the chapter), and the need for better management of inventories. When implementing supply chain management, firms are trying to improve quality, reduce costs, increase flexibility and speed, improve customer service while reducing the number of suppliers used. Two examples are as follows:

logistics
Those activities that focus on getting the right amount of the right products or services to the right place at the right time at the lowest possible cost.

supply chain
The sequence of firms that perform activities required to create and deliver a good or service to consumers or industrial users.

supply chain management
The integration and organization of information and logistics activities *across* firms in a supply chain for the purpose of creating and delivering goods and services that provide value to customers.

- Canadian National Railway (CN) purchased supply chain management planning software from i2 Technologies to manage its intermodal business. CN has 10,000 freight cars and 7,000 containers that it owns, along with equipment belonging to shippers and other railways. While implementing this software is still a work in progress, CN expects to increase the level of speed and reliability of hauling containers and truck trailers from ports and major cities across North America.[35]

- Only Canada's Armed Forces surpasses the Cirque du Soleil in terms of the level of supply chain and logistics planning required to deploy large amounts of equipment, supplies, and people all over the world. According to Guy Migneron, director of international headquarters operations for Cirque du Soleil, "We use computers for a lot of what we do." The planning and logistics work for each performance begins 12 to 18 months before the first act enters the tent.[36]

Purolator Courier provides a video about Purolator's global supply services called "Connected to the World," concerning emerging worldwide manufacturing sectors and supply chain management. Go to http://purolator.com and click on "Purolator Global Supply Chain Services," then select "Connected to the World" from the list of available videos.

OPERATIONS MANAGEMENT IN THE SERVICE SECTOR

Operations management in the service industry is all about creating a good experience for those who use the service. For example, in a Four Seasons hotel, operations management includes restaurants that offer the finest in service, elevators that run smoothly, and a front desk that processes people quickly. It may include placing fresh-cut flowers in the lobbies and dishes of fruit in every room. More important, it may mean spending thousands of dollars to provide training in quality management for every new employee.

Operations management in luxury hotels is changing with today's new executives. As customers in hotels, executives are likely to want in-room Internet access and a help centre with toll-free telephone service. Also, when an executive has to give a speech or presentation, he or she needs video equipment and a host of computer hardware and other aids. Foreign visitors would like multilingual customer-support services. Hotel shops need to carry more than souvenirs, newspapers, and some drugstore and food items to serve today's high-tech travellers. The shops may also carry laptop computer supplies, electrical adapters, and the like. Operations management is responsible for locating and providing such amenities to make customers happy. In short, delighting customers by anticipating their needs has become the quality standard for luxury hotels, as it has for most other service businesses. But knowing customer needs and satisfying them are two different things. That's why operations management is so important: It is the implementation phase of management.

Information Mapping Canada helps leading organizations focus on improving performance through better written communication. Clients including Xerox Canada have increased productivity through better management of customer complaints. What types of measures could you implement to track how good a job was being done in managing customer complaints?

Measuring Quality in the Service Sector

There's strong evidence that productivity in the service sector is rising, but productivity measures don't capture improvements in quality. In an example from health care, positron emission tomography (PET) scans are much better than X-rays, but the quality difference is not reported in productivity figures. The traditional way to measure productivity involves tracking inputs (worker hours) compared to outputs (dollars). Notice that there is no measure for quality improvement. When new information systems are developed to measure the quality improvement of goods and services—including the speed of their delivery and customer satisfaction—productivity in the service sector will go up dramatically.

Using computers is one way in which the service sector is improving productivity, but not the only one. Think about labour-intensive businesses such as hospitals and fast-food restaurants, where automation plays a big role in controlling costs and improving service. Today, at Burger King, for example, customers fill their own drink cups from pop machines, which allows workers to concentrate on preparing the food. And because the people working at the drive-up window now wear headsets instead of using stationary mikes, they are no longer glued to one spot and can do four or five tasks while taking an order.

Most of us have been exposed to similar productivity gains in banking. For example, people in most cities no longer have to wait in long lines for tellers to help them deposit and withdraw money. Instead, they use automated teller machines (ATMs), which usually involve little or no waiting and are available 24 hours a day.

Another service that was once very slow was grocery store checkout. The system of marking goods with universal product codes (UPC) enables computerized checkout and allows cashiers to be much more productive than before. Now, many stores have set up automated systems that enable customers to go through the checkout process on their own. Some grocery chains, such as Longo's, are implementing Internet services that allow customers to place orders online and receive home delivery. The potential for productivity gains in this area are enormous.

In short, operations management has led to tremendous productivity increases in the service sector but still has a long way to go. Also, service workers are losing jobs to machines just as manufacturing workers did. The secret to obtaining and holding a good job is to acquire appropriate education and training. Such education and training must go on for a lifetime to keep up with the rapid changes that are happening in all areas of business. That message cannot be repeated too frequently.

International SOS is the world's leading provider of medical assistance, international health care, security services, and outsourced customer care. Customers include individuals, companies, and government agencies. As one of its many services, International SOS provides full support service to companies requiring 24/7 on-call and online services. This includes medical assistance and evacuation (as noted in this picture). Do you see how critical it is for service providers to respond in a timely manner?

Services Go Interactive

The service industry has always taken advantage of new technology to increase customer satisfaction. Jet travel enabled Purolator to deliver goods overnight. Cable TV led to pay-per-view services. And now interactive computer networks are revolutionizing services. Interactive services are already available from banks, stockbrokers, travel agents, and information providers of all kinds. More individuals may soon be able to participate directly in community and national decision making via telephone, cable, and computer networks.

eBay, an online auction and shopping Web site, is a huge phenomena. Revenues are between $5 and $10 billion. People and businesses buy and sell products and services worldwide. Regardless of what is being sold, however, the success of service organizations in the future will depend greatly on establishing a dialogue with consumers so that the operations managers can help their organizations adapt to consumer demands faster and more efficiently. Such information systems have been developed and should prove highly useful.

Progress Assessment

- Can you name and define three functions that are common to operations management in both the service and the manufacturing sectors?
- What are the major criteria for facility location?
- What is involved in implementing each of the following: six sigma, SQC, SPC, ISO 9000, and ISO 14000?

OPERATIONS MANAGEMENT IN THE MANUFACTURING SECTOR

Common sense and some experience have already taught you much of what you need to know about production processes. You know what it takes to write a term paper or prepare a dinner. You need money to buy the materials, you need a place to work, and you need

The Production Process
The production process consists of taking the factors of production (land, etc.) and using those inputs to produce goods, services, and ideas. Planning, routing, scheduling, and the other activities are the means to accomplish the objective—output.

form utility
The value added by the creation of finished goods and services.

to be organized to get the task done. The same is true of the production process in industry. It uses basic inputs to produce outputs (see Figure 9.4). Production adds value, or utility, to materials or processes. **Form utility** is the value added by the creation of finished goods and services, such as the value added by taking silicon and making computer chips or putting services together to create a vacation package. Form utility can exist at the retail level as well. For example, a butcher can produce a specific cut of beef from a whole cow or a baker can make a specific type of cake out of basic ingredients.

To be competitive, manufacturers must keep the costs of inputs down. That is, the costs of workers, machinery, and so on must be kept as low as possible. Similarly, the amount of output must be relatively high. The question today is: How does a producer keep costs low and still increase output? This question will dominate thinking in the manufacturing and service sectors for years to come. In the next few sections, we explore production processes and the latest technology being used to cut costs.

Production Processes

There are several different processes that manufacturers use to produce goods. Andrew S. Grove, chairman of computer chip manufacturer Intel, uses a great analogy to explain production:

> *To understand the principles of production, imagine that you're a chef and that your task is to serve a breakfast consisting of a three-minute soft-boiled egg, buttered toast, and coffee. Your job is to prepare and deliver the three items simultaneously, each of them fresh and hot.*

Grove goes on to say that the task here encompasses the three basic requirements of production: (1) to build and deliver products in response to the demands of the customer at a scheduled delivery time, (2) to provide an acceptable quality level, and (3) to provide everything at the lowest possible cost.

process manufacturing
That part of the production process that physically or chemically changes materials.

assembly process
That part of the production process that puts together components.

continuous process
A production process in which long production runs turn out finished goods over time.

intermittent process
A production process in which the production run is short and the machines are changed frequently to make different products.

Using the breakfast example, it's easy to understand two manufacturing terms: *process* and *assembly*. **Process manufacturing** physically or chemically changes materials. For example, boiling physically changes the egg. (Similarly, process manufacturing turns sand into glass or computer chips.) The **assembly process** puts together components (eggs, toast, and coffee) to make a product (breakfast). Cars are made through an assembly process that puts together the frame, engine, and other parts.

In addition, production processes are either continuous or intermittent. A **continuous process** is one in which long production runs (lots of eggs) turn out finished goods over time. As the chef in our diner, you could have a conveyor belt that lowers eggs into boiling water for three minutes and then lifts them out on a continuous basis. A three-minute egg would be available whenever you wanted one. (A chemical plant, for example, is run on a continuous process.)

It usually makes more sense when responding to specific customer orders to use an **intermittent process**. This is an operation where the production run is short (one or two eggs) and the machines are changed frequently to make different products (such as the oven in a bakery where you could make different types of bread). Manufacturers of custom-designed furniture would use an intermittent process.

As an example of a company that uses both long and short production runs, for the first time in nine years, Kodiak boots are being produced in Canada:

"At the end of the day, we're going to service customers a lot better through this core Canadian production," says Kevin Huckle, president of Kodiak Group Holdings Inc., which plans to do a third of its production in Canada. Domestic production offers quick, efficient service for Canadian retailers, who may require only small numbers of boots, but need them in a hurry. With Asian production, he has to contract for long production runs—more than 1,200 pairs—and has to carry a lot of inventory. With domestic manufacturing, the plant keeps enough materials around for relatively short runs. Because of automation and location, it can turn around Canadian production orders in 21 days, compared with 90 days for orders in Asia.[37]

Today, many new manufacturers use intermittent processes. Computers, robots, and flexible manufacturing processes allow firms to turn out custom-made goods almost as fast as mass-produced goods were once turned out.[38] We'll discuss how they do that in more detail in the next few sections as we explore advanced production techniques and the latest technology being used to cut costs.

Progress Assessment

- What are three basic requirements of production?
- Define and differentiate the following: process manufacturing, assembly process, continuous process, and intermittent process.

MODERN PRODUCTION TECHNIQUES

The ultimate goal of manufacturing and process management is to provide high-quality goods and services instantaneously in response to customer demand. As we have stressed throughout this book, traditional organizations were simply not designed to be so responsive to the customer. Rather, they were designed to make goods efficiently (inexpensively). The whole idea of mass production was to make a large number of a limited variety of products at very low cost.

Over the years, low cost often came at the expense of quality and flexibility. Furthermore, suppliers didn't always deliver when they said they would, so manufacturers had to carry large inventories of raw materials and components. Such inefficiencies made companies less competitive than foreign competitors that were using more advanced production techniques.

As a result of global competition, companies have had to make a wide variety of high-quality, custom-designed products at very low cost. Clearly, something had to change on the production floor to make that possible. Seven major developments have radically changed the production process: (1) materials requirement planning, (2) just-in-time inventory control, (3) purchasing, (4) flexible manufacturing, (5) lean manufacturing, (6) mass customization, and (7) computer-aided design and manufacturing.

Materials Requirement Planning (MRP)

Economic order quantity (also known as the Wilson EOQ Model, or simply the EOQ Model) is a model that defines the optimal quantity to order to minimize total variable costs required to order and hold inventory.[39] The theory gained wide acceptance in the early 1980s due to the benefits that such a model would generate. However, a major drawback was that businesses did not always understand the trade-off between ordering costs and holding costs. Another drawback was that the theory assumed that shortages or stockouts did not occur and it was difficult to guarantee this when demand was not always known (another assumption of the theory). Since this time, businesses and technology have become more sophisticated in the area of planning.

economic order quantity
A model that defines the optimal quantity to order to minimize total variable costs required to order and hold inventory.

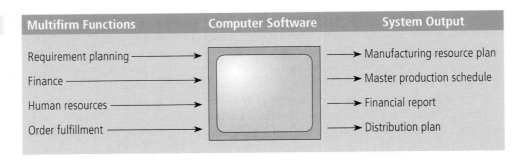

FIGURE | 9.5

Enterprise Resource Planning

Multifirm Functions	Computer Software	System Output
Requirement planning		Manufacturing resource plan
Finance		Master production schedule
Human resources		Financial report
Order fulfillment		Distribution plan

materials requirement planning (MRP)

A computer-based production management system that uses sales forecasts to make sure that needed parts and materials are available at the right time and place.

enterprise resource planning (ERP)

A computer application that enables multiple firms to manage all of their operations (finance, requirements planning, human resources, and order fulfillment) on the basis of a single, integrated set of corporate data.

Materials requirement planning (MRP) is a computer-based operations management system that uses sales forecasts to ensure that needed parts and materials are available at the right time and place *in a specific company*. In our diner, for example, we could feed the sales forecast into the computer, which would specify how many eggs and how much coffee to order and then print out the proper scheduling and routing sequence. The same can be done with the seats and other parts of an automobile. In the next section, you will read how just-in-time inventory control has a similar objective.

The newest version of MRP is **enterprise resource planning (ERP)**. ERP is a computer application that enables *multiple* firms to manage all of their operations (finance, requirements planning, human resources, and order fulfillment) on the basis of a single, integrated set of corporate data (see Figure 9.5). The result is shorter time between orders and payment, less staff to do ordering and order processing, reduced inventories, and better customer service for all firms involved. By entering customer and sales information in an ERP system, a manufacturer can generate the next period's demand forecast, which in turn generates orders for raw materials, production scheduling, and financial projections.

ERP software enables the monitoring of quality and customer satisfaction as it is happening. ERP systems are going global now that the Internet is powerful enough to handle the data flows. At the plant level, dynamic performance monitoring enables plant operators to monitor the use of power, chemicals, and other resources and to make needed adjustments. In short, flows to, through, and from plants have become automated.

Some firms are providing a service called sequential delivery. These firms are suppliers that provide components in an order sequenced to their customers' production process. For example, Ford's seat supplier loads seats onto a truck such that, when off-loaded, the seats are in perfect sequence for the type of vehicle coming down the assembly line.

While ERP can be an effective tool, it also can have its problems. The Royal Canadian Mint was having difficulties extracting and manipulating data. Departments were operated independently, and because it took so long to produce reports for analysis, employees did not trust the reliability of the information once it was in their hands. "Anyone who has used an ERP system knows that reporting can be problematic," says Azfar Ali Khan, director of operations and systems at the Mint's sales and marketing departments. "They're wonderful transactional engines, but getting the richness of the data in front of the people in a context they can understand is particularly challenging."[40]

Information technology (IT) has had a major influence on the entire production process, from purchasing to final delivery. Many IT advances have been add-ons to ERP. To solve its difficulties, the Mint turned to Cognos (www.cognos.com) for its enterprise solution. Cognos's Analytic Applications solution made it possible for users to access data right to the day, as well as to create new reporting opportunities. The Mint's self-service, web-enabled, enterprise-wide solution has allowed it to act quickly and thereby improve customer service. According to Ali

One of the biggest providers of Enterprise Resources Planning (ERP) software is SAS. Their business analytics software supports customers making better decisions faster through spending less time looking for data.

Khan, "Buying a prepackaged solution and customizing it to our own unique business requirements has saved us a lot of time and a lot of money."[41]

Just-in-Time Inventory Control

One major cost of production is holding parts, motors, and other items in storage for later use. Storage not only subjects such items to obsolescence, pilferage, and damage but also requires construction and maintenance of costly warehouses. To cut such costs, many companies have implemented a concept called **just-in-time (JIT) inventory control**. JIT systems keep a minimum of inventory on the premises and parts, supplies, and other needs are delivered just in time to go on the assembly line. To work effectively, however, the process requires excellent coordination with carefully selected suppliers. Sometimes the supplier builds new facilities close to the main producer to minimize distribution time.

JIT runs into problems when suppliers are farther away. Shipments may be delayed due to poor weather, worker strikes, and events such as the power outage in Ontario in August 2003. With more than $1.9 billion in goods and more than 300,000 people moving across the Canada–U.S. border each day, the efficient flow of products and people is vital to Canada's economy.[42] Any delays require that companies adjust their JIT schedules. Today, the longer delays at borders due to increased traffic and security measures have forced companies to do just that. Other limitations are that JIT works best with standard products, demand needs to be high and stable to justify the cost and savings, and suppliers need to be extremely reliable.

Here's how it works: A manufacturer sets a production schedule (using ERP) to determine what parts and supplies will be needed. Suppliers are connected electronically, so they know immediately what will be needed and when. The suppliers must then deliver the goods *just in time* to go on the assembly line. Naturally, this calls for more effort (and more costs) on the suppliers' part. The manufacturer maintains efficiency by linking electronically to the suppliers so that the suppliers become more like departments in the firm than separate businesses.

JIT systems ensure that the right materials are at the right place at the right time at the cheapest cost to meet both customer and production needs. That's a key step in modern production innovation. Part of that process is rethinking the purchasing process. We shall explore that issue next.

Huge warehouses such as the one depicted in the photo would become a thing of the past if all companies implemented just-in-time (JIT) inventory control. What are the advantages and disadvantages of having large amounts of inventory available?

just-in-time (JIT) inventory control
A production process in which a minimum of inventory is kept on the premises and parts, supplies, and other needs are delivered just in time to go on the assembly line.

Purchasing

Purchasing is the functional area in a firm that searches for quality material resources, finds the best suppliers, and negotiates the best price for quality goods and services. In the past, manufacturers tended to deal with many different suppliers with the idea that, if one supplier or another couldn't deliver, materials would be available from someone else. Today, however, manufacturers are relying more heavily on one or two suppliers because the firms share so much information that they don't want to have too many suppliers knowing their business. The Hudson's Bay Company shifted to single merchandise buyers for a growing number of departments at its Bay, Zellers, and Home Outfitters chains. This move was designed to help improve product selection and save money through less duplication and larger purchase orders.[43] The relationship between suppliers and manufacturers is thus much closer than ever before.[44]

The Internet has transformed the purchasing function in recent years. For example, a business looking for supplies can contact an Internet-based purchasing service and

purchasing
The functional area in a firm that searches for quality material resources, finds the best suppliers, and negotiates the best price for goods and services.

find the best supplies at the best price. Similarly, a company wishing to sell supplies can use the Internet to find all companies looking for such supplies. The cost of purchasing items has thus been reduced tremendously.

Flexible Manufacturing

flexible manufacturing
Designing machines to do multiple tasks so that they can produce a variety of products.

Flexible manufacturing involves designing machines to do multiple tasks so that they can produce a variety of products. Flexible manufacturing (also known as flex) not only leads to improved productivity, but it may also result in cost savings. Frank Gourneau, plant manager at Ford Motor Company of Canada Ltd., calls the $1-billion Oakville complex "a game changer" and a "jewel" with all the latest advances in auto technology. The first phase of the plant started production in 2006. According to Gourneau, "Undergoing major model changes in traditional plants means weeks of downtime and millions spent on new tooling and equipment. Once a flexible body shop is installed, downtime is reduced dramatically and the equipment changes consist mainly of repro-gramming robots. The point is to be able to cease assembly of one model on a Friday and start a new one on a Monday, instead of six, eight or 10 weeks later."[45] Gourneau esti-mates productivity will improve at least 20 percent in the new plant and the company expects to achieve $2 billion in production cost savings alone during the next decade.[46]

Allen-Bradley (part of Rockwell Automation), a maker of industrial automation controls, uses flexible manufacturing to build motor starters. Orders come in daily, and within 24 hours the company's 26 machines and robots manufacture, test, and package the starters—which are untouched by human hands. Allen-Bradley's machines are so flexible that a special order, even a single item, can be included in the assembly without slowing down the process. Did you notice that these products were made without any labour? One way to compete with cheap labour is to have as few workers as possible.

Lean Manufacturing

lean manufacturing
The production of goods using less of everything compared to mass production.

Lean manufacturing is the production of goods using less of everything compared to mass production: less human effort, less manufacturing space, less investment in tools, and less engineering time to develop a new product. A company becomes lean by continuously increasing its capacity to produce high-quality goods while decreas-ing its need for resources.[47] That's called "increasing productivity." You can see how technological improvements are largely responsible for the increase in productivity and efficiency of Canadian plants. That makes labour more productive and makes it possible to pay higher rates.

General Motors (GM) uses lean manufacturing. To make the Saturn automobile, for example, GM abandoned its assembly-line production process. The fundamental pur-pose of restructuring was to dramatically cut the number of worker hours needed to build a car. GM made numerous changes, the most dramatic of which was to switch to modular construction. GM suppliers pre-assemble most of the auto parts into a few large com-ponents called modules. Workers are no longer positioned along kilometres of assembly line. Instead, they're grouped at various workstations, where they put the modules together. Rather than do a few set tasks, workers perform a whole cluster of tasks. Trolleys carry the partly completed car from station to station. Compared to the assembly line, modular assembly takes up less space and calls for fewer workers—both of which are money-saving factors.

robot
A computer-controlled machine capable of performing many tasks requiring the use of materials and tools.

Finally, GM greatly expanded its use of robots in the manufacturing process. A **robot** is a computer-controlled machine capable of performing many tasks requiring the use of materials and tools. Robots, for example, spray-paint cars and do welding. Robots usually are fast, efficient, and accurate. Robots and other machines perform routine, repetitive jobs quickly, efficiently, and accurately. This provides opportunities for workers to be more creative.

Mass Customization

To *customize* means to make a unique good or provide a specific service to an individual. Although it once may have seemed impossible, **mass customization**, which means tailoring products to meet the needs of a large number of individual customers, is now practised widely. The National Bicycle Industrial Company in Japan, for example, makes 18 bicycle models in more than 2 million combinations, with each combination designed to fit the needs of a specific customer. The customer chooses the model, size, colour, and design. The retailer takes various measurements from the buyer and faxes the data to the factory, where robots handle the bulk of the assembly. Thus, flexible manufacturing (discussed earlier) is one of the factors that makes mass customization possible. Given the exact needs of a customer, flexible machines can produce a customized good as quickly as mass-produced goods were once made.

More and more manufacturers are learning to customize their products. For example, some General Nutrition Center (GNC) stores feature machines that enable shoppers to custom-design their own vitamins, shampoo, and lotions. Other companies produce custom-made books with a child's name inserted in key places, and custom-made greeting cards have appeared on the market. The Custom Foot stores use infrared scanners to precisely measure each foot so that shoes can be crafted to fit perfectly. Adidas can make each shoe fit perfectly for each customer.[48] InterActive Custom Clothes offers a wide variety of options in custom-made jeans, including four different rivet colours. You can even buy custom-made M&Ms.[49]

Mass customization can be used in the service sector as well. Health clubs offer unique fitness programs for individuals, travel agencies provide vacation packages that vary according to individual choices, and some schools allow students to design their own majors. Actually, it is much easier to custom-design service programs than it is to custom-make goods, because there is no fixed tangible good that has to be adapted. Each customer can specify what he or she wants, within the limits of the service organization—limits that seem to be ever widening.

mass customization
Tailoring products to meet the needs of individual customers.

computer-aided manufacturing (CAM)
The use of computers in the manufacturing of products.

computer-aided design (CAD)
The use of computers in the design of products.

Computer-Aided Design and Manufacturing

The one development in the recent past that appears to have changed production techniques and strategies more than any other has been the integration of computers into the design and manufacturing of products. The first thing computers did was help in the design of products; this is called **computer-aided design (CAD)**. The latest CAD systems allow designers to work in three dimensions. The next step was to involve computers directly in the production process; this is called **computer-aided manufacturing (CAM)**.

CAD/CAM (the use of both computer-aided design and computer-aided manufacturing) made it possible to custom-design products to meet the needs of small markets with very little increase in cost. A manufacturer programs the computer to make a simple design change, and that change can be incorporated directly into the production line. For example, CAD and CAM are used in the clothing industry. A computer program establishes a pattern and cuts the cloth automatically. Today, a person's dimensions can be programmed into the machines to create custom-cut clothing at little additional cost. In food service, CAM is used to make cookies in fresh-baked cookie shops. On-site, small-scale, semi-automated, sensor-controlled baking makes consistent quality easy to achieve.

CAD has doubled productivity in many firms. However, it's one thing to design a product and quite another to set the specifications

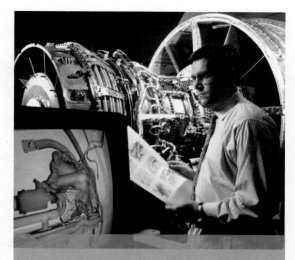

This photo shows computer-aided design (CAD) in operation. When linked with computer-aided manufacturing (CAM), these software systems can greatly improve the design and production process. What advantages might this technology offer to smaller manufacturing companies? What types of industries would benefit most from CAD/CAM?

computer-integrated manufacturing (CIM)
The uniting of computer-aided design with computer-aided manufacturing.

to make a machine do the work. The problem in the past was that CAD machines couldn't talk to CAM machines directly. Today, however, software programs unite CAD with CAM: the result is **computer-integrated manufacturing (CIM)**. The software is expensive, but it cuts as much as 80 percent of the time needed to program machines to make parts. The printing company JohnsByrne uses CIM in its Niles, Illinois, plant. The company noticed a decreased cost in overhead, reduced outlay of resources, and fewer errors. You can consult the *International Journal of Computer-Integrated Manufacturing* for other examples.

Progress Assessment

- What is the difference between materials resource planning (MRP) and enterprise resource planning (ERP)?
- What is just-in-time inventory control?
- How does flexible manufacturing differ from lean manufacturing?
- What are CAD, CAM, and CIM?

PREPARING FOR THE FUTURE

Canada is a major industrial country, but competition is growing stronger each year. This means that there are tremendous opportunities for careers in operations management as companies fight to stay competitive.

Today, relatively few graduates have majored in production and operations management, inventory management, and other areas involving manufacturing and operations management in the service sector. That means more opportunities for those students who can see the future trends and have the skills (e.g., high-level math) to own or work in tomorrow's highly automated, efficient factories, mines, service facilities, and other production locations. Students will need to keep a broad mind and seek information from a variety of sources to help them anticipate and plan for changes in the future.

SUMMARY

LO ▶1 Define operations management and explain what types of firms use it.

1. Operations management is a specialized area in management that converts or transforms resources (including human resources) into goods and services.

   What kinds of firms use operations managers?
   Firms in both the manufacturing and the service sectors use operations managers.

LO ▶2 Describe the operations management planning issues involved in both the manufacturing and the service sectors, including facility location, facility layout, and quality control.

2. Functions involved in both the manufacturing and the service sectors include facility location, facility layout, and quality control.

   What is facility location and how does it differ from facility layout?
   Facility location is the process of selecting a geographic location for a company's operations. Facility layout is the physical arrangement of resources (including people) to produce goods and services effectively and efficiently.

   Why is facility location so important, and what criteria are used to evaluate different sites?
   The very survival of manufacturing depends on its ability to remain competitive, and that means either making inputs less costly (reducing costs of labour and land)

or increasing outputs from present inputs (increasing productivity). Labour costs and land costs are two major criteria for selecting the right sites. Other criteria include whether (1) resources are plentiful and inexpensive, (2) skilled workers are available or are trainable, (3) taxes are low and the local government offers support, (4) energy and water are available, (5) transportation costs are low, and (6) the quality of life and quality of education are high.

What are the latest quality control concepts?

Six sigma quality (just 3.4 defects per million products) detects potential problems before they occur. Statistical quality control (SQC) is the process that some managers use to continually monitor all processes in production to ensure that quality is being built into the product from the beginning. Statistical process control (SPC) is the process of taking statistical samples of product components at each stage of the production process and plotting those results on a graph. Any variances from quality standards are recognized and can be corrected.

What quality standards do firms use in Canada?

International standards that Canadian firms strive to meet include ISO 9004:2000 (ISO 9000) and ISO 14000. The first is a European standard for quality and the second is a collection of the best practices for managing an organization's impact on the environment.

3. There's strong evidence that productivity in the service sector is rising, but this is difficult to measure.

LO ▶ 3 Discuss the problem of measuring productivity in the service sector, and tell how technology is leading to productivity gains in service companies.

Why is productivity so hard to measure?

The traditional way to measure productivity involves tracking inputs (worker hours) compared to outputs (dollars). Quality improvements are not weighed. New information systems must be developed to measure the quality of goods and services, the speed of their delivery, and customer satisfaction.

How is technology creating productivity gains in service organizations?

Computers have been a great help to service employees, allowing them to perform their tasks faster and more accurately. ATMs make banking faster and easier; automated checkout machines enable grocery clerks (and customers) to process items more quickly. In short, operations management has led to tremendous productivity increases in the service sector but still has a long way to go.

4. There are several different processes that manufacturers use to produce goods.

LO ▶ 4 Explain how manufacturing processes can be used in the manufacturing sector.

What is process manufacturing, and how does it differ from assembly processes?

Process manufacturing physically or chemically changes materials. Assembly processes put together components.

Are there other production processes?

Production processes are either continuous or intermittent. A continuous process is one in which long production runs turn out finished goods over time. An intermittent process is an operation where the production run is short and the machines are changed frequently to produce different products.

5. Companies are using seven production techniques to become more profitable: (1) materials requirement planning, (2) just-in-time inventory control, (3) purchasing, (4) flexible manufacturing, (5) lean manufacturing, (6) mass customization, and (7) computer-aided design and manufacturing.

LO ▶ 5 Describe seven manufacturing techniques that have improved the productivity of companies.

What relationship does enterprise resource planning (ERP) have with the production process?

ERP is a computer application that enables multiple firms to manage all of their operations (finance, requirements planning, human resources, and order fulfillment) on the basis of a single, integrated set of corporate data. The result is shorter time between orders and payment, less staff to do ordering and order processing, reduced inventories, and better customer service for all firms involved. It is an advanced form of materials requirement planning.

What is just-in-time (JIT) inventory control?

JIT involves having suppliers deliver parts and materials just in time to go on the assembly line so they don't have to be stored in warehouses.

How have purchasing agreements changed?

Purchasing agreements now involve fewer suppliers who supply quality goods and services at better prices in return for getting the business. Many new Internet companies have emerged to help both buyers and sellers complete the exchange process more efficiently.

What is flexible manufacturing?

Flexible manufacturing involves designing machines to produce a variety of products.

What is lean manufacturing?

Lean manufacturing is the production of goods using less of everything compared to mass production: less human effort, less manufacturing space, less investment in tools, and less engineering time to develop a new product.

What is mass customization?

Mass customization means making custom-designed goods and services for a large number of individual customers. Flexible manufacturing makes mass customization possible. Given the exact needs of a customer, flexible machines can produce a customized good as fast as mass-produced goods were once made.

How do CAD/CAM systems work?

Design changes made in computer-aided design (CAD) are instantly incorporated into the computer-aided manufacturing (CAM) process. The linking of the two systems—CAD and CAM—is called computer-integrated manufacturing (CIM).

KEY TERMS

assembly process 258

computer-aided design (CAD) 263

computer-aided manufacturing (CAM) 263

computer-integrated manufacturing (CIM) 264

continuous process 258

economic order quantity 259

enterprise resource planning (ERP) 260

facility layout 250

facility location 246

flexible manufacturing 262

form utility 258

intermittent process 258

ISO 9000 254

ISO 14000 255

just-in-time (JIT) inventory control 261

lean manufacturing 262

logistics 255

mass customization 263

materials requirement planning (MRP) 260

operations management 244

process manufacturing 258

production 243

production management 244

purchasing 261

quality 251

research and development (R&D) 241

robot 262

six sigma quality 251

statistical process control (SPC) 252

statistical quality control (SQC) 252

supply chain 255

supply chain management 255

CRITICAL THINKING

1. People on the manufacturing floor are being replaced by robots and other machines. On the one hand, that is one way in which companies compete with cheap labour from other countries. No labour at all is less expensive than cheap labour. On the other hand, automation eliminates many jobs. Are you concerned that automation may increase unemployment or under-employment in Canada and around the world? Why?

2. Computer-integrated manufacturing (CIM) has revolutionized the production process. Now everything from cookies to cars can be designed and manufactured much more cheaply than before. Furthermore, customized changes can be made with very little increase in cost. What will such changes mean for the clothing industry, the shoe industry, and other fashion related industries? What will they mean for other consumer and industrial goods industries? How will you benefit as a consumer?

3. One way to create new jobs in Canada is to have more innovation. Much innovation comes from new graduates from engineering and the sciences. What could Canada do to motivate more students to major in those areas?

DEVELOPING WORKPLACE SKILLS

1. Choosing the right location for a manufacturing plant or a service organization is often critical to its success. Form small groups and have each group member pick one manufacturing plant or one service organization in town and list at least three reasons why its location helps or hinders its success. If its location is not ideal, where would be a better one?

2. In teams of four or five, discuss the need for better operations management at clothing stores. Have the team develop a three-page report listing (1) problems that team members have encountered when clothes shopping, and (2) suggestions for improving operations so such problems won't occur in the future.

3. Discuss some of the advantages and disadvantages of producing goods overseas using inexpensive labour. Summarize the moral and ethical issues of this practice.

4. Think of any retail outlet (e.g., bookstore or food outlet) or service centre (e.g., library, copy centre) at your school and redesign the layout (make a pencil drawing placing people and materials) so that the facility could more effectively serve its customers and so that the workers would be more effective and efficient.

TAKING IT TO THE NET 1

www.mcgrawhillconnect.ca

Purpose
To illustrate production processes.

Exercise
Take a virtual tour of the Hershey Foods Corporation's chocolate factory by going to www.hersheys.com/discover/tour_video.asp.

1. Does Hershey use process manufacturing or the assembly process? Is the production of Hershey's chocolate an example of an intermittent or continuous production process? Justify your answers.

2. What location factors might go into the selection of a manufacturing site for Hershey's chocolate?

TAKING IT TO THE NET 2

Purpose

To understand the extent and importance of research and development (R&D) spending in Canada.

Exercise

RE$EARCH Infosource Inc. publishes an in-depth report on Canadian R&D trends. The top 100 R&D spending firms can be found by visiting www.researchinfosource. com/top100.shtml.

1. How has this ranking changed from last year's ranking?

2. What are the top ten R&D-intensive firms?

3. What is the future expectation for R&D spending in Canada?

ANALYZING MANAGEMENT DECISIONS

Why Big Companies Fail to Innovate

Matthew Kiernan, based in Unionville, Ontario, is a management consultant whose views command attention. He has a PhD degree in strategic management from the University of London and was a senior partner with an international consulting firm, KPMG Peat Marwick. Subsequently, he founded his own firm, Innovest Group International, with a staff operating out of Geneva, London, and Toronto. He was also a director of the Business Council for Sustainable Development based in Geneva.

His book *Get Innovative or Get Dead* took aim at big corporations for their poor record on innovation. Any five-year-old could tell you that companies must innovate to survive, he said, so what's the problem? According to Kiernan, it's one thing to understand something in your head but quite another thing to really feel it in your gut. This is further complicated by the difficulty of getting a big company to shift gears, to turn its culture around so that innovation becomes the norm rather than the special effort.

Kiernan called for a company to develop a style and atmosphere that favours individual risk-taking, the intra-preneurial approach discussed in Chapter 6. That means

that if a team tries something that doesn't work, you don't shoot it down. Encouraging innovation, which inevitably involves taking risks with the unknown, means accepting the fact that it may take two or three attempts before something useful is developed. Recently, Matthew has applied this principle to sustainable development, including the topic of carbon finance.

The 3M company is often used as a great example of a company that encourages creativity. Its policy dictates that 30 percent of annual sales come from products less than four years old. However, 3M wasn't always that progressive. When the now legendary Post-it Notes were first developed by an employee, he had a hard time getting the company to see the potential in his idea. This ultimately triggered a major change in the company's policy. Kiernan pointed out that most companies give lip service to the necessity of innovation but do not act in a credible way as far as their employees are concerned. If you mean business, you must take that "bright guy out of the basement, [the one] everybody knows is a genius, but whose last two enterprise efforts came to grief, and visibly promote him."

Discussion Questions

1. Do large companies find it difficult to innovate because they resist change? Is it because they are big or because they are afraid of the unknown? Why is that?

2. Do smaller companies do better at innovation because they are not so risk-averse? Is that because most of

them are private companies and not accountable to outside stakeholders?

3. If you were a vice-president in charge of operations management at a big corporation, how would you encourage innovation?

RUNNING CASE

Requisite Organization at Canadian Tire Financial Services (CTFS)

Requisite organization is a term created by Dr. Elliott Jaques. It is a scientific approach to the effective management of work systems. The word *requisite* is defined as "required by nature." The ideas in a requisite organization flow from the nature of things—the nature of tasks, work, and human behaviour. These systems include structure, leadership processes, and human resources.

The *structure*, which considers the total number of layers (or strata) in an organization, should be based on the complexity of the work to be performed. Work and accountability cascade downward in successive layers, and a system of organizational strata is formed. These strata comprise a series of levels in the organization with specified work to be done in each stratum. Jaques states that effective leadership in large corporations requires only seven layers (strata), including the CEO. Business units inside corporations, such as Canadian Tire Financial Services (formerly known as Canadian Tire Acceptance Limited), generally need five strata. At CTFS, the five levels are president, vice-presidents, associate vice-presidents, managers, and individual contributors.

A requisite structure, or any structure, in itself will not guarantee the success of an organization in meeting its business strategy. This is why the second major component of a requisite organization is to ensure that *competent individuals are performing work at each organizational level*. Once an assessment is made of the complexity of work to be performed, staffing of the role requires an individual who can manage the complexity.

The third key component of a requisite organization is that it sets a context for *human resource practices and procedures* that are fully integrated and supportive of the business strategy. A few of the key practices and procedures include assigning accountabilities and authority for decisions at the correct level and, as part of job design/job evaluation, determining the level of work for a role.

Jaques demonstrated in a wide variety of organizations that organizational effectiveness and efficiency (through gains in productivity and morale) could be increased by 20 to 50 percent by designing organizational structure and choosing people in ways consistent with those principles. Canadian companies that have implemented, in varying degrees, requisite practices include Essar Steel Algoma, Ontario Hydro, Sunoco, Health Canada, and the Public Service Commission. CTFS has been following this approach for almost over 20 years. Periodically, the structure is revisited to ensure that it is still efficient and effective.

Sources: Rich Morgan, "An Overview of Requisite Organization," Canadian Tire Acceptance Limited, December 1995; Marco Marrone, President, Canadian Tire Financial Service, in-person interview, 10 March 2006; Sharon Patterson, Vice-President Human Resources, Canadian Tire Financial Services, in-person interview, 5 April 2006; Requisite Organization International Institute, http://www.requisite.org/main.html, 6 November 2006; and Ken Shepard, "The Rigour of Requisite Organization," Queen's University iRC, http://irc.queensu.ca/articles/the-rigour-of-requisite-organization.

Discussion Questions

1. If a company wishes to implement a requisite organization structure, how would this process apply to each of the four management functions?

2. From your understanding of a requisite organization, what is the optimal span of control?

3. What role and accountabilities might a manager have within a requisite organization?

CHAPTER 10

The Financial Services Industry in Canada

PROFILE

Getting to Know Marco Marrone, President of Canadian Tire Financial Services Limited

Marco Marrone is the president of Canadian Tire Financial Services (CTFS), a wholly owned subsidiary of Canadian Tire Corporation, Ltd. As the financial arm of Canadian Tire, CTFS is primarily engaged in financing and managing the Canadian Tire Options® MasterCard to more than 4 million card members. CTFS also offers personal loans, markets a variety of insurance and warranty products to more than 6 million customers, and offers emergency roadside assistance through the Canadian Tire Auto Club.

CTFS originated in 1961 as Midland Shoppers Credit Limited, a small financial services company offering third-party credit processing for local retailers. During the 1960s, the Canadian Tire Associate Stores became clients. In 1968, Midland became a subsidiary of Canadian Tire Corporation and was renamed Canadian Tire Acceptance Limited (CTAL). In the decades that followed, CTAL continued to provide credit processing. In 1995, it became the first non–deposit-taking financial institution worldwide to launch a MasterCard. In 2000, it expanded the Canadian Tire "Money" loyalty program by launching Canadian Tire "Money" on the card. Card members could accumulate Canadian Tire Money by using their MasterCard anywhere in the world and then redeem it in any Canadian Tire store for merchandise, auto parts, or auto labour. In 2002, CTAL's name was changed to Canadian Tire Financial Services Limited to better reflect the company's stronger and broader position within the financial services industry. In 2003, CTFS established Canadian Tire Bank to enable greater marketing flexibility for its card operations and to facilitate continued expansion into the high-growth bank card market. Operating the credit card business under Canadian Tire Bank enables the company to offer customers credit card services consistently across the country.

Marrone is an example of a business person who has excelled and adapted to opportunities within the financial services business sector. During the 20 years at CTFS that preceded his current role, he held key management positions in finance, credit risk management, information technology, marketing, and operations. He was instrumental in many of the organization's most significant strategies. These include his role as vice-president of customer development with responsibility for the conversion of the company's retail card portfolio to Options® MasterCard, and the creation of Canadian Tire Bank, which he has led as chief operating officer (COO). As COO, he has had strategic and operational responsibility for the development of the credit card and personal loan businesses.

Marrone's ongoing education has contributed to his professional growth. Since becoming a certified management accountant, he has completed his MBA at McMaster University and the Leadership Development Program at the International Institute for Management Development in Switzerland. He is also a graduate of the McMaster University College for Corporate Directors. He is an officer of Canadian Tire, a member of the Canadian Tire Bank board of directors, a member of the MasterCard Advisory Board, and he serves in the community as the chair of the Niagara Health Systems Foundation board.

Today, CTFS is the second-largest MasterCard franchise in Canada, including the Options® MasterCard, the Gas Advantage MasterCard, and Commercial Link. The credit card portfolio has grown through adding new cards and features, including: Pay Pass, exclusive offers, product protector, credit protector, identity watch, line of credit, and road side assistance. While approximately 32 percent of Canadian Tire's overall earnings are generated through this division's activities, this contribution is expected to increase as new opportunities are explored. Under Marrone's leadership, initiatives will surely be in line with the company's purpose: "We build lifetime customer relationships by providing financial services which add trust and value to the Canadian Tire Brand." There are plans to expand CTFS's financial services products and services. Some of the products being piloted in select markets, include high-interest savings accounts, mortgages, and guaranteed investment certificates.

Sources: Marco Marrone, President, Canadian Tire Financial Services, interview, 10 March 2006; Rita Trichur, "Canadian Tire's Q2 Profit Rises 12% to $103.3 Million, Firm Raises Guidance," Canadian Press NewsWire, July 2008; and "2008 Investor Fact Sheet," Canadian Tire Corporation Ltd., http://investorrelations.canadiantire.ca.

THE FINANCIAL SERVICES INDUSTRY IN CANADA

In Chapter 11 we will talk about the role financial institutions play in supporting the financial needs of businessses. Now we focus our attention on all the product offered by the actual institutions: money, banking, investing, insurance, financing, and financial planning. Every day across the country, consumers, businesses, and governments depend on the products provided by financial institutions. In addition, the ever-changing environment in the financial services industry is supported by a number of new features provided by the Financial Consumer Agency of Canada, including:

- Model credit card application form
- Cost of banking guide
- Ten tips you need to know before signing any contract.[1]

According to this same agency, the financial services sector plays an important role in the Canadian economy, as it:

- Employs more than 600,000 Canadians
- Provides a yearly payroll of more than $35 billion
- Represents 6 percent of Canada's GDP, exceeded only by the manufacturing sector
- Yields more than $13 billion in tax revenue to all levels of government
- Is widely recognized as one of the safest and healthiest in the world[2]

Until the middle of the 1980s, the financial services industry in Canada was termed a "four-pillar system." These four pillars were banks, trust companies, insurance companies, and securities dealers. Regulation was designed to foster competition within each pillar, but not among them. When the government permitted commercial banks to acquire securities firms in 1987, this segregation of functions began to erode.

Since that time, changes in regulations have eliminated many of the old barriers that prohibited financial institutions from competing in each other's business. Today, it is increasingly difficult to distinguish firms by type of function, as this industry has become highly competitive. For example, a life insurance company can now own a bank, and vice versa. As a result of Bill C-8 (in force since October 2001), important changes were made to federal financial institutions legislation and how the financial services industry is regulated. Among other changes, ownership and organization rules for banks were loosened. Consequently, we see non-traditional financial services providers—such as Canadian Tire Financial Services (mentioned in the chapter-opening profile)—taking advantage of changes in the regulatory environment to offer new products and build on their customer base.

Participants in the Financial Services Industry

credit unions
Non-profit, member-owned financial co-operatives that offer a full variety of banking services to their members.

Canada's financial services industry consists of traditional banks (also called commercial banks), credit unions, caisses populaires, and trust companies. **Credit unions** are non-profit, member-owned financial co-operatives that offer a full variety of banking services to their members. Caisses populaires, a form of credit unions, are located predominantly in Quebec. A **trust company** is a financial institution that conducts activities like a bank. However, because of its fiduciary role, a trust company can administer estates, pension plans, and agency contracts, which banks cannot do. As a result of changes in legislation, we have seen instances of banks acquiring trust companies, such as Scotiabank's acquisition of Montreal Trust and National Trust.

trust company
A financial institution that can administer estates, pension plans, and agency contracts, in addition to other activities conducted by banks.

There are also a variety of other institutions that traditionally have been called non-banks. **Non-banks** are financial organizations that accept no deposits but offer many services provided by regular banks. Examples include pension funds, insurance companies, commercial finance companies, consumer finance companies, and brokerage houses. We will discuss brokerage houses soon.

non-banks
Financial organizations that accept no deposits but offer many services provided by regular banks.

Pension funds are amounts of money put aside by corporations, non-profit organizations, or unions to cover part of the financial needs of their members when they retire. Contributions to pension funds are made either by employees, by employers, or by both employees and employers.

Life insurance companies provide financial protection for policyholders, who periodically pay premiums. In addition, insurers invest the funds they receive from policyholders in a variety of vehicles, including corporate and government bonds. More insurance companies have begun to provide long-term financing for real estate development projects.

Commercial and consumer finance companies offer short-term loans to businesses or individuals who either cannot meet the credit requirements of regular banks or have exceeded their credit limit and need more funds. Typically, these finance companies' interest rates are higher than those of regular banks. The primary customers of these companies are new businesses and individuals with no credit history. One should be careful when borrowing from such institutions, because the interest rates can be quite high. Corporate financial systems established at major corporations such as General Electric, Sears, General Motors, and American Express offer considerable financial services to customers.

In the past, they were often called non-banks because they did not accept deposits but offered many of the services provided by regular banks. As competition among these organizations and banks has increased, the dividing line between banks and non-banks has become less and less apparent. Today, many of these non-banks offer select banking products, including taking deposits, making loans, and issuing credit cards.[3] Review Figure 10.1 to get an idea of the range of suppliers of financial services in Canada.

Since all of these financial institutions have one thing in common—money—we will discuss the importance of money to the economy. This will be followed by an introduction to three main players in the overall financial services industry: the banking industry, the securities industry, and the mutual fund industry. But first, let us briefly review how this industry is regulated.

FIGURE 10.1
The Canadian Financial Services Industry
• 70 domestic and foreign-owned banks
• 35 trust companies
• 70 life insurance companies
• 1,000 credit unions and caisses populaires
• 200 finance companies
Also, there are over 100 bank account packages and 96% of Canadians have an account with a financial institution.

Source: Courtesy of Canadian Bankers Association.

pension funds
Amounts of money put aside by corporations, non-profit organizations, or unions to cover part of the financial needs of their members when they retire.

How the Financial Services Industry Is Regulated[4]

Because of its important role in the economy, the financial industry is one of the most regulated sectors in the country. Regulation is designed to ensure the integrity, safety, and soundness of financial institutions and markets. Legislative, self-regulatory, and other initiatives help minimize crises and company failures. In addition, they protect investors, depositors, and policyholders. These detailed and varied compliance requirements take a considerable amount of time and money for companies in this industry to complete.

In Canada, there is no single body that regulates the entire industry. It's a responsibility shared among different organizations and levels of government. To start with, financial institutions may be regulated at either the federal or the provincial level, or jointly. For example, banks are federally regulated. Securities dealers, credit unions, and caisses populaires are provincially regulated. Insurance, trust and loan companies, and co-operative credit associations may be federally and/or provincially regulated, depending on the jurisdiction under which the company is incorporated or registered.

For institutions under federal responsibility, the Department of Finance is charged with overseeing their overall powers—in other words, what they can and cannot do. The Department of Finance relies on three federal agencies to supervise the ongoing operations of these institutions and their compliance with legislation:

- The Office of the Superintendent of Financial Institutions (www.osfi-bsif.gc.ca) monitors the day-to-day operations of institutions with respect to their financial soundness.

- Overseeing the deposit insurance system is the Canada Deposit Insurance Corporation (www.cdic.ca), which protects deposits that Canadians have in their federal financial institutions. CDIC will be discussed below.

- The Financial Consumer Agency of Canada (www.fcac-acfc.gc.ca) monitors financial institutions to ensure that they comply with federal consumer protection measures, which range from disclosure requirements to complaint-handling procedures.

For institutions under provincial jurisdiction, the province(s) in which a company is incorporated or registered is (are) responsible for regulating the company's overall powers. As at the federal level, provinces are supported by agencies and organizations that supervise the ongoing operations of these institutions.

The Canada Deposit Insurance Corporation[5]

The Canada Deposit Insurance Corporation (CDIC) is a federal Crown corporation that was created in 1967 to provide deposit insurance and contribute to the stability of Canada's financial system. CDIC insures eligible deposits at member institutions (e.g., banks and trust companies) against these institutions' failure or collapse. CDIC guarantees deposits up to $100,000 (principal and interest) in each member institution. It is funded primarily by premiums paid by banks and trust companies that belong to this program.

Keep in mind that CDIC does not cover all types of deposits. For example, foreign currency accounts, term deposits with a maturity of greater than five years, and investments in mortgages, stocks, and mutual funds are not covered.

To date, CDIC has provided protection to depositors in 43 member institution failures. As of April 2008, CDIC had insured some $477 billion in deposits.

Progress Assessment

- What components of the financial services industry were known as the four pillars?
- Describe some changes to the industry as a result of Bill C-8.
- Contrast credit unions and caisses populaires, and list some non-bank competitors.
- Describe the responsibilities of three federal agencies that oversee financial institutions.
- What deposits are not secured by CDIC?

WHY MONEY IS IMPORTANT

The Canadian economy depends heavily on money: its availability and its value relative to other currencies. Economic growth and the creation of jobs depend on money. Money is so important to the economy that many institutions have evolved to manage money and to make it available to you when you need it. Today, you can easily get cash from an automated teller machine (ATM) almost anywhere in the world, but in many places cash isn't the only means of payment you can use. Most organizations will accept a cheque, credit card, debit card, or smart card for purchases.[6] Behind the scenes of this free flow of money is a complex system of banking that makes it possible for you to do all of these things.

The complexity of the banking system has increased as the electronic flow of money from country to country has become as free as that from province to territory. Each day, more than $1.5 trillion is exchanged in the world's currency markets. Therefore, what happens to any major country's economy has an effect on the Canadian economy and vice versa. Looking back on the fall of 2008, the global inter-connnectivity of banking systems resulted in a widespread liquidity crisis which lead to major government interventions. Clearly, there's more to money and its role in the economies of the world than meets the eye. There's no way to understand the Canadian economy without understanding global money exchanges and the various institutions involved in the creation and management of money.

What Is Money?

Money is anything that people generally accept as payment for goods and services. In the past, objects as diverse as salt, feathers, stones, rare shells, tea, and horses have been used as money. In fact, until the 1880s, cowrie shells were one of the world's most abundant currencies. **Barter** is the trading of goods and services for other goods and services directly; though barter may sound like something from the past, many people have discovered the benefits of bartering online. Others still barter goods and services the old-fashioned way—face to face. For example, in Siberia, two eggs have been used to buy one admission to a movie, and employees of Ukraine's Chernobyl nuclear plant have been paid in sausages and milk. Some of the trade in Russia over recent years has been done in barter.

> **money**
> Anything that people generally accept as payment for goods and services.

> **barter**
> The trading of goods and services for other goods and services directly.

The problem is that eggs and milk are difficult to carry around. People need some object that's portable, divisible, durable, and stable so that they can trade goods and services without carrying the actual goods around with them. One answer to that problem over the years was to create coins made of silver or gold. Coins met all of the standards of a useful form of money:

- *Portability*. Coins are a lot easier to take to market than are pigs or other heavy products.

- *Divisibility*. Different-sized coins could be made to represent different values. Because silver is now too expensive, today's coins are made of other metals, but the accepted values remain.

- *Stability*. When everybody agrees on the value of coins, the value of money is relatively stable.

- *Durability*. Coins last for thousands of years, even when they've sunk to the bottom of the ocean, as you've seen when divers find old Roman coins in sunken ships.

- *Uniqueness*. It's hard to counterfeit, or copy, elaborately designed and minted coins. But with the latest colour copiers, people are able to duplicate the look of paper money relatively easily. Thus, the government has had to go to extra lengths to ensure that real dollars are readily identifiable. That's why some denominations have raised print or raised ink, watermarks, and fine-line patterns.[7]

When coins and paper money become units of value, they simplify exchanges. Most countries have their own coins and paper money, and they're all equally portable, divisible, and durable. However, they're not always equally stable. For example, the value of money in Russia is so uncertain and so unstable that other countries won't accept Russian money (rubles) in international trade.

Electronic cash (e-cash) is the latest form of money.[8] In addition to being able to make online bill payments using software programs such as Quicken or Microsoft Money, you can e-mail e-cash to anyone using Web sites such as PayPal.com (owned by eBay). Recipients get an e-mail message telling them that they have several choices for how they can receive the money: automatic deposit (the money will be sent to their bank), e-dollars for spending online, or a traditional cheque in the mail.

Some of the security features on the $5 note include a holographic stripe, watermark, see-through number, and windowed security thread. Additional features include raised ink, iridescent maple leaves, the hidden number 5, fine-line patterns printing, fluorescence, and a tactile feature. Do you check your notes for security features?

What Is the Money Supply?

money supply
The amount of money the Bank of Canada makes available for people to buy goods and services.

The **money supply** is the amount of money the Bank of Canada (introduced in Chapter 3) makes available for people to buy goods and services. The money supply can be measured in a number of different ways. Some of these different measures, called monetary aggregates, are described in Figure 10.2.

M1 represents money that can be accessed quickly and easily. M2, M2+, and M2++ are even broader measures of the money supply. Before we consider how the Bank of Canada controls the money supply, let us first consider why the money supply needs to be controlled and its impact on the global exchange of money.

Why Does the Money Supply Need to Be Controlled?

Imagine what would happen if governments or non-governmental organizations were to generate twice as much money as exists now. There would be twice as much money available, but there would be the same amount of goods and services. What would happen to prices in that case? Think about the answer for a minute. (Hint: Remember the laws of supply and demand from Chapter 2.) The answer is that prices would go up because more people would try to buy goods and services with their money and would bid up the price to get what they wanted. This is called inflation. That is why some people define inflation as "too much money chasing too few goods."

Now think about the opposite: What would happen if the Bank of Canada took some of the money out of the economy? What would happen to prices? Prices would go down because there would be an oversupply of goods and services compared to the money available to buy them; this is called deflation.[9] If too much money is taken out of the economy, a recession might occur. That is, people would lose jobs and the economy would stop growing.

Now we come to a second question about the money supply: Why does the money supply need to be controlled? The money supply needs to be controlled because doing so allows us to manage the prices of goods and services somewhat. And controlling the money supply affects employment and economic growth or decline.

The Global Exchange of Money

A falling dollar value means that the amount of goods and services you can buy with a dollar decreases.[10] A rising dollar value means that the amount of goods and services you can buy with a dollar goes up.

What makes the dollar weak (falling dollar value) or strong (rising dollar value) is the position of the Canadian economy relative to other economies. When the economy

FIGURE | 10.2

Measures of Money— Canada's Money Supply

Measures of Money (Monetary Aggregates)	Definition of the Monetary Aggregates
M1	The currency (bank notes and coins) in circulation plus personal chequing accounts and current accounts at banks.
M2	Includes personal savings accounts and other chequing accounts, term deposits, and non-personal deposits requiring notice before withdrawal, in addition to M1.
M2+	Includes all deposits at non-bank deposit-taking institutions, money-market mutual funds, and individual annuities at life insurance companies, in addition to M2.
M2++	Includes all types of mutual funds and Canada Savings Bonds, in addition to M2+.

Source: Bank of Canada, "Canada's Money Supply," January 2000, www.bankofcanada.ca/en/backgrounders/bg-m2.htm.

is strong, the demand for dollars is high, and the value of the dollar rises. As commodity prices rose from 2007 through 2008, the value of the Canadian dollar rose dramatically. After years of the exchange rate of a Canadian dollar being below par compared to a U.S. dollar, the exchange rate rose above parity. When the economy is perceived as weakening, however, the demand for dollars declines, and the value of the dollar falls. The value of the dollar thus depends on a strong economy. Clearly, control over the money supply is important. In the following section, we'll discuss briefly how the money supply is controlled.

Control of the Money Supply[11]

You already know that money plays a huge role in the world economies. Therefore, it's important to have an organization that controls the money supply to try to keep the economy from growing too fast or too slow. Theoretically, with proper monetary policy you can keep the economy growing without causing inflation. As mentioned in Chapter 3, the organization in charge of monetary policy is the Bank of Canada.

The Bank of Canada monitors the money supply. Indicators such as M1 provide useful information about changes that are occurring in the economy. The availability of money and credit must expand over time, and the Bank of Canada is responsible for ensuring that the rate at which more money is introduced into the economy is consistent with long-term stable growth.

The bank's economic research indicates that the growth of M1 provides useful information on the future level of production in the economy. The growth of the broader monetary aggregates is a good leading indicator of the rate of inflation.

The objective of the Bank of Canada's monetary policy is to support a level of spending by Canadians that is consistent with the Bank's goal of price stability. This is defined as keeping inflation within the inflation-control target range (of 1 to 3 percent). By influencing the rate at which the supply of money and credit is growing, total spending on goods and services in the economy can be stabilized.

The Bank of Canada manages the rate of money growth indirectly through the influence it exercises over short-term interest rates. When these rates change, they carry other interest rates—such as those paid by consumers for loans from commercial banks—along with them. When interest rates rise, consumers and businesses are apt to hold less money, to borrow less, and to pay back existing loans. The result is a slowing in the growth of M1 and the other broader monetary aggregates.[12]

The Bank of Canada has an influence on very short-term interest rates through changes in its target for the overnight rate. The target for the overnight rate is the main tool used by the Bank of Canada to conduct monetary policy. It tells major financial institutions the average interest rate the Bank of Canada wants to see in the marketplace where they lend each other money for one day, or "overnight." When the Bank changes the target for the overnight rate, this change usually affects other interest rates charged by commercial banks. The **prime rate** is the interest rate that banks charge their most creditworthy customers.

When the Bank changes the target for the overnight rate, this sends a clear signal about the direction in which it wants short-term interest rates to go. These changes usually lead to moves in the prime rate at commercial banks. The prime rate serves as a benchmark for many of their loans. These changes can also indirectly affect mortgage rates, and the interest paid to consumers on bank accounts, term deposits, and other savings.

When interest rates go down, people and businesses are encouraged to borrow and spend more, boosting the economy. But if the economy grows too fast, it can lead to inflation. The Bank may then raise interest rates to slow down borrowing and spending, putting a brake on inflation.

In choosing a target for the overnight rate, the Bank of Canada picks a level that it feels will keep future inflation low, stable, and predictable. Keeping inflation low and stable helps provide a good climate for sustainable economic growth, investment, and job creation.[13]

prime rate
The interest rate that banks charge their most creditworthy customers.

THE BANKING INDUSTRY

Following legislative changes in 1992, banks were allowed to own insurance, trust, and securities subsidiaries. Today, most of Canada's large banks have subsidiaries in these areas. As major players in Canada's financial industry, the banks serve millions of customers. They include individuals, small- and medium-sized businesses, large corporations, governments, institutional investors, and non-profit organizations. The major banks offer a full range of banking, investment, and financial services. They have extensive nationwide distribution networks and also are active in the United States, Latin America, the Caribbean, Asia, and other parts of the world. Close to half of their earnings are generated outside of Canada.

Figure 10.3 outlines Canada's six largest banks. Strong players in the Canadian economy, Canada's banks are were extremely profitable until the fall of 2008. These financial results have garnered criticism by some who believe that the banks are taking advantage of customers by charging high service charges. The reality is that bank revenues are increasingly being generated from international activities. As well, banks distribute a good portion of their net income to their shareholders. Most Canadians own bank shares, whether they know it or not; bank shares form a large part of many major mutual funds (to be discussed later in this chapter) and pension funds.[14] In 2007, Canada's banks distributed $8.7 billion of dividends to their shareholders, which represented 44 percent of the banks' net earnings.[15]

Some of the major banks have been trying to merge for several years. They believe that if they were permitted to merge, they would be able to take advantage of economies of scale and be more efficient. They argue that they are not big players globally (see Figure 10.4), and that they are increasingly being forced to look outside Canada for more opportunities due to the laws and regulations that control their domestic activities. Shareholders continue to demand good returns, and the banks are under more pressure to continue to

FIGURE	10.3

Canada's Six Largest Banks

Bank Name	Total Assets	Total Loans	Net Income for Fiscal Year Ended October 31, 2008
	($ millions)		
RBC Financial Group	723,859	334,236	4,555
Scotiabank	507,625	304,888	3,140
TD Bank Financial Group	563,214	262,049	3,833
BMO Financial Group	416,050	205,678	1,978
CIBC	353,930	207,072	(2,060)
National Bank of Canada	129,332	59,608	776
Total 6 Banks	2,694,010	1,373,529	12,222

Source: Courtesy of Canadian Bankers Association.

Reaching Beyond Our Borders

The Banking Crisis Goes Global

The banking crisis has become a global phenomenon, even in countries that appeared to be doing well, such as China. Even though the Chinese government could force banks to make loans, it is reluctant to do so now that capitalism seems to be working. Because banks began holding on to their money, some 67,000 small businesses in China went into bankruptcy in the first half of 2008.

Even some larger state-owned businesses felt the effects of the crisis. Pakistan recently went to China to borrow funds but could not get them and turned to the International Monetary Fund (IMF) for help. Several Eastern and Central European countries and former Soviet republics are also in trouble. The IMF has agreed to lend Ukraine over $16 billion and Hungary over $15 billion.

Turkey could need as much as $90 billion. Other countries are in similar straits. Even oil-rich Bahrain is suffering from the crisis.

Should the IMF and World Bank continue to give funds to countries suffering financial crises? Where do those funds come from? Should the United States and Canada, along with other G8 countries, continue to help provide money for such loans as it has pledged to do?

Sources: "Back in Business," *The Wall Street Journal*, 30 October 2008; David Stringer, "Struggling Nations Depleting IMF's Bailout," *Washington Times*, 29 October 2008; Ariana Eunjung Cha and Maureen Fan, "China Unveils $586 Billion Stimulus Plan," *The Washington Post*, 10 November 2008; and Chip Cummins, "Bahrain Credit Outlook Is Downgraded," *The Wall Street Journal*, 7 January 2009.

---

deliver, year after year. This is an issue that will not go away in the years to come. However, all the aggressive growth over the past few years has been stalled by the banking crisis that started at the end of 2008. The Reaching Beyond Our Borders box talks about the global nature of this banking crisis.

Commercial Banks

A **commercial bank** is a profit-seeking organization that receives deposits from individuals and corporations in the form of chequing and savings accounts and then uses some of these funds to make loans. Commercial banks have two types of customers: depositors and borrowers (those who take out loans). A commercial bank is equally responsible to both types of customers. Commercial banks try to make a profit by efficiently using the funds that depositors give them. In essence, a commercial bank uses customer deposits as inputs (on which it pays interest) and invests that money in interest-bearing loans to other customers (mostly businesses). Commercial banks make a profit if the revenue generated by loans exceeds the interest paid to depositors plus all other operating expenses.

| **FIGURE** | **10.4** |

Worldwide Bank Rankings, 2008

Rank	Bank	Assets (Cad$ Billions)
1	Royal Bank of Scotland	4,287
33	Royal Bank of Canada	883
47	Toronto-Dominion Bank	384
48	Scotiabank	614
53	Bank of Montreal	504
60	CIBC	428
116	National Bank of Canada	160
125	Desjardins Group	152

Source: Courtesy of Canadian Bankers Association.

Some Services Provided by Banks

Individuals and corporations that deposit money in a *chequing account* have the privilege of writing personal cheques to pay for almost any purchase or transaction. Typically, banks impose a service charge for cheque-writing privileges or demand a minimum deposit. Banks might also charge a small handling fee for each cheque written. For business depositors, the amount of the service charge depends on the average daily balance in the chequing account, the number of cheques written, and the firm's credit rating and credit history.

In addition to chequing accounts, commercial banks offer a variety of savings account options. As for the chequing accounts, each individual needs to evaluate the different features of each account as they differ from institution to institution.

A *term deposit* (also known as a guaranteed investment certificate or a certificate of deposit) is a savings account that earns interest to be delivered at the end of the specified

commercial bank
A profit-seeking organization that receives deposits from individuals and corporations in the form of chequing and savings accounts and then uses some of these funds to make loans.

Making Ethical Decisions

To Tell the Teller or Not?

You have been banking at the same bank for some time, but the tellers at the bank keep changing, so it is difficult to establish a relationship with any one teller. You do not like using the automated teller machine because the bank has decided to charge for each transaction. Therefore, you are working with a teller and withdrawing $300 for some expenses you expect to incur. The teller counts out your money and says: "Okay, here's your $300." Before you leave the bank, you count the money once more. You notice that the teller has given you $350 by mistake. You return to the teller and say, "I think you have made a mistake in giving me this money." She replies indignantly, "I don't think so. I counted the money in front of you."

You are upset by her quick denial of a mistake and her attitude. You have to decide whether to give her back the overpayment of $50. What are your alternatives? What would you do? Is that the ethical thing to do?

The Canadian Bankers Association has a series of free publications on a variety of financial topics. Some examples are Getting Started in Small Business, Small Business Financing, Getting Value for Your Service Fees, Investing Your Dollars, Managing Money, and Planning for Retirement. For more details, visit www.cba.ca.

period. The depositor agrees not to withdraw any of the funds in the account until the end of the specified term (e.g., one year). The longer the term deposit is to be held by the bank, the higher the interest rate for the depositor.

Banks also offer a variety of other products. Some examples of credit products for creditworthy customers include credit cards, lines of credit, loans, mortgages, and overdraft protection on chequing accounts. Additional products are access to automated teller machines (ATMs), life insurance coverage on credit products, brokerage services, financial counselling, telephone and Internet bill payment options, safe-deposit boxes, registered retirement accounts, and traveller's cheques. Visit a local bank branch to find out the details for all of these types of products. It is up to each individual to compare the different features on each type of account or service as they vary from institution to institution. Features and rates are competitive. The Making Ethical Decisions box highlights a human error that can easily be made.

ATMs give customers the convenience of 24-hour banking at a variety of outlets such as supermarkets, department stores, and drugstores, in addition to the bank's regular branches. Depositors can—almost anywhere in the world—transfer funds, make deposits, and get cash at their own discretion with the use of a computer-coded personalized plastic access card. Beyond all that, today's ATMs are doing even more. New ATMs can dispense maps and directions, phone cards, and postage stamps. They can sell tickets to movies, concerts, sporting events, and so on. They can even show movie trailers, news tickers, and video ads. Some can take orders for flowers and DVDs, and download music and games.[16] The convenience store chain 7-Eleven is testing machines that cash cheques and send wire transfers.[17] What will be next?

Services to Borrowers

In addition to other financial services firms and government agencies (such as the Business Development Bank of Canada), banks offer a variety of services to individuals and corporations in need of a loan. Generally, loans are given on the basis of the recipient's

SPOTLIGHT ON Small Business

How the Banking Crisis Affected Small Business

One of the consequences of the banking crisis of 2008–2009 was that it became more difficult to get a loan from a bank, especially if you ran a small business. It used to be that small businesses could get an "air-ball loan," that is, a loan based more on the borrower's personal relationship with the banker than on his or her assets. Today, however, banks are more reluctant to give out loans. Sometimes the bank will demand that the borrower make a "substantial" deposit—up to half the loan amount—to get a loan. Some banks have even cut lending to new customers to conserve available funds for existing customers. While the scope of the crisis has not been quite as severe in Canada compared to the United States, small business has found it more and more difficult to borrow from banks. Because borrowing from a bank has become so difficult, you might have to look to alternative sources of funds. For example, if you are buying equipment, you might ask the vendor for financing.

In Canada, banks have wanted to reduce their risk, so they have been advocating for more government guarantees for small business loans. There has also been talk about the governments providing a pool of funds to offset the decrease in loans being made by the banks, and the drying up of other credit options for small business.

Some small businesses use credit cards to get started, but the fees can be extremely high if the bills are not paid promptly. Many small-business owners turn to friends and family for loans, but that too can be dicey if the business does not do well. What other sources of funds are available? Angel investors are wealthy individuals who use their own money to fund start-up companies at the early stages of their development. They usually seek out high-growth companies in fields like technology and biotech that might issue stock or get profitably bought out in a few years. Local companies like restaurants, roofers, and deck cleaners usually cannot get a hearing, much less a loan. In short, banks and nonbanks are often reluctant to loan money to small businesses. Small business has to be far more diligent in searching out sources of funding as they try to expand their operations.

Sources: Norm Brodsky, "What the Financial Crisis Means to You," *Inc.*, November 2008; Binyamin Appelbaum and David Cho, "Small Banks, Tight Credit," *The Washington Post*, 27 August 2008; C. J. Prince, "Something to Bank On," *Entrepreneur*, August 2008; and Bob Seiwert, "Borrowing Trouble," *Black Enterprise*, January 2009.

creditworthiness. Banks want to manage their funds effectively and are supposed to screen loan applicants carefully to ensure that the loan plus interest will be paid back on time. Small businesses often search out banks that cater to their needs. The Spotlight on Small Business box discusses the new relationship between small businesses and banks after the 2008–2009 banking crisis.

Managing Your Personal Finances

A major reason for studying business is that it prepares you for finding and keeping a good job. You already know that one of the secrets to finding a well-paying job is to have a good education. With your earnings, you can take vacations, raise a family, make investments, buy the products you want, and give generously to others.

Money management, however, is not easy. You have to earn the money in the first place. Then you have to learn how to save money, spend money wisely, and insure yourself against any financial and health risks. While these topics are important from a personal perspective, they are outside the scope of this chapter. However, given their importance, you can visit the Online Learning Centre for an introduction to managing your personal finances. Starting with the six steps of learning to control your assets, we discuss ways to build a financial asset base, explain how to buy the appropriate insurance, and outline a strategy for retiring with enough money to last a lifetime.

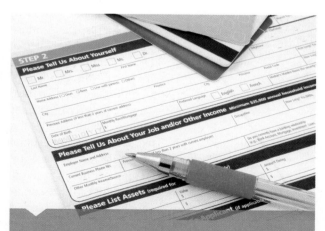

Many consumers, especially first-time credit card owners, are unable to properly manage their money and often end up with severely damaged credit ratings—or worse, in bankruptcy. That's why it may be a good idea for you to pass up the free T-shirt or other offer made by credit card companies.

DEALING with CHANGE

The Internet—Its Support for the Financial Meltdown and Rebirth

Facilitated by the use of the Internet, the breadth of financial flows on a global basis was mind boggling through the mid part of the first decade of 2000. In addition, the nature of the financial arrangements was so sophisticated that even seasoned financial experts were unable or unwilling to spend the time to properly ascertain the financial risks. This "house of cards" came crashing down in the latter part of 2008 with the global banking system meltdown. The United States and other economically powerful nations had an unprecedented string of bankruptcies happen in rapid succession. Both major and small financial institutions closed their doors. Governments were forced to inject billions and billions of dollars into their financial systems to head off a global recession that everyone felt would have been unprecedented in its scope and severity.

While the United States, in particular, and other countries to a lesser extent, has taken many months to try to deal with their problems, Canada has escaped the blood bath relatively unscathed. Our banking system has become the envy of the world due to its unwillingness to assume the same level of risk undertaken elsewhere. For example, in the United States, mortgages were given for home purchases to borrowers whose credit worthiness was questionable.

Given their relatively strong position, Canadian banks are looking for opportunities to expand globally by making sound investments at rock bottom prices. Many highly qualified investment bankers have been hired away from struggling firms in the United States and elsewhere. These individuals have supported expansion planning by all five major Canadian banks into countries that are viewed as having the greatest growth potential in the rebounding economy. Acquisitions or the opening of offices have been completed or are planned for China, India, Brazil, and Russia.

Sources: Daniel Fairlamb and Stanley Reed, "Uber Bank," *BusinessWeek*, 20 March 2000, 52–53; "The Global Giants," *The Wall Street Journal*, 14 October 2002, R10, R11; Stephanie Miles, "What's a Check?" *The Wall Street Journal*, 21 October 2002, R5; and Erik Portanger and Paul Beckett, "Banks Vie for Europe's Consumers," *The Wall Street Journal*, 24 February 2003, C1, C5.

Electronic Banking on the Internet

Not only have banking, insurance, and brokerage services been combined by financial service companies, but they are also available online. All of Canada's top banks allow customers to have access to their accounts online, and all have bill-paying capacity. Thus, you are now able to do all of your financial transactions from home, using your telephone or your computer. That includes banking transactions such as transferring funds from one account to another (e.g., savings to chequing), paying your bills, and finding out how much is in your various accounts.[18] In some instances, you can apply for a loan online and get a response almost immediately. The company can check your financial records and give you a reply while you wait. Buying and selling stocks and bonds is equally easy. The Dealing with Change box discusses how the Internet contributed to the financial crisis that started in late 2008.

Internet banks (such as ING) have been created that offer branchless banking. Such banks can offer high interest rates and low fees because they do not have the costs of physical overhead that traditional banks have. While many consumers are pleased with the savings and convenience, not all are entirely happy with the service they receive from Internet banks. Why are they dissatisfied? First, they are nervous about security. People fear putting their financial information into cyberspace, where others may see it. Despite all of the assurances of privacy, people are still concerned. Furthermore, some people want to be able to talk to a knowledgeable person when they have banking problems. They miss the service, the one-on-one help, and the security of local banks.

Because of these issues, the future seems to be with organizations like TD Bank Financial Group and BMO Financial Group, which are traditional banks that offer both online services and brick-and-mortar facilities.[19] Combined online and brick-and-mortar banks not only offer online services of all kinds but also have automated teller machines (ATMs), places to go to deposit and get funds, and real people to talk to in person.

Progress Assessment

- Why are banks interested in merging?
- List some services provided by commercial banks.
- What are some benefits of electronic banking to users?

THE INSURANCE INDUSTRY

Over the past few years, we seem to continually hear stories of natural disasters causing damages totalling in the billions of dollars. Where does the money come from to pay for these damages? How can we seem to deal with these huge costs so relatively easily? Insurance has served a vital role in dealing with the repairs and rebuilding.

The general insurance industry in Canada provides insurance protection for most homes, motor vehicles, and commercial enterprises throughout Canada.[20] Most general insurance is provided by private insurance companies, which are subject to either provincial or federal regulations. Auto insurance is provided through a combination of private and government-owned auto insurers. The latter exist in British Columbia, Saskatchewan, and Manitoba. Another major category of general insurance is liability or business interruption insurance. Liability insurance provides protection in the event that the insured causes bodily injury or property damage to others for which the insured is liable. In 2007, insurance sales totalled more than $38 billion, while insurance companies controlled assets of more than $116 billion.[21]

The idea of insurance is to share risk with others. Instead of having to set aside significant cash reserves to deal with possible losses that may arise, an ongoing, relatively small insurance premium allows those insured to have piece of mind that, in the event of a major catastrophe, their losses will be covered. Insurance companies collect insurance premiums from literally thousands of clients, using them to pay for the cost of the relatively few catastrophes that will inevitably occur.

Ever wonder why we typically have to pay insurance premiums at the start of an insurance period? Often, in a given year, the amount of claims paid out, in combination with the cost of running the insurance business, exceeds the premiums collected (we will get back to this anomaly shortly). The insurance industry is able to cover this shortfall with the interest it earns on the premiums it collects—it collects premiums before it has to pay out claims. Claims include theft, liability, natural disasters including hail and wind, water damage, and fire.

In most businesses, the selling price is set once all costs are determined. In the insurance industry, the exact opposite happens. Insurance premiums (the selling price) are set before the actual claims are paid out (the most significant cost). In setting premiums for the upcoming renewal period, an insurance company estimates the number and cost of current and future claims and the amount of investment income it will earn.

In recent years, skyrocketing claims costs have greatly increased the premiums for auto insurance, and in some instances even the availability of insurance. Costs for all forms of insurance have also increased significantly due to insurance crime, which results when individuals inflate the cost of a claim for a stolen item or when highly organized rings bilk insurers out of millions of dollars. In addition, liability claims, as awarded by courts, have increased dramatically.

From a consumer standpoint, we need to budget for premiums for at least auto and property insurance. From an employment standpoint, the insurance industry offers many opportunities.

THE CANADIAN SECURITIES INDUSTRY[22]

A **securities dealer** (also known as an investment dealer or brokerage house) is a firm that trades securities for its clients and offers investment services. Such firms also assist companies in raising all forms of capital for new and expanding businesses. As a result, this industry allows investors to trade in open capital markets. In 2003, there were 207 firms that employed more than 37,000 people. Since 1987, when federally regulated financial institutions were permitted to own securities firms, most of Canada's large, full-service securities firms have been bank-owned. Some examples are noted in Figure 10.5.

More Canadians are turning to the securities industry to ensure their financial security. The past decade has seen extraordinary growth in the number of individuals participating in Canadian capital markets. Roughly half of all working Canadians are directly and indirectly invested in the equities market. In the ten years prior to 2003, investors' holdings of shares have more than doubled to more than $660 billion. Ten years ago, 20 percent of the average investor's financial assets (bank accounts, registered retirement savings plans, pension, insurance, etc.) were stocks. Today, this ratio has grown to 27 percent. Not only are individuals choosing to invest more and more in the equities market, but so are companies and government agencies. Insurance companies will invest all of the excess of premiums they collect at the beginning of a policy year, over operating and claim costs. Pension plans, including the Canada Pension Plan, are investing a greater portion of their reserves. In all cases, investors want to increase their returns, but with increased risks.

Recently, increases in maximum foreign holdings of registered retirement savings plans have been granted in recognition of how proportionately small, on a global basis, the Canadian securities market is. The Canadian securities market is less than 3 percent of total world markets.

Securities Regulations[23]

As mentioned earlier in the textbook, one of the reasons why private corporations become public corporations is to raise capital to expand their existing operations. In recent times, companies such as Tim Hortons Inc., Sleep Country Canada, and the Brick became publicly traded companies following the successful completion of their first IPO.

Companies seeking public financing must issue a prospectus. A **prospectus** is a condensed version of economic and financial information that a company must make available to investors before they purchase the security. The prospectus must be approved by the securities commission in the province where the public funding is being sought. The **securities commission** is a government agency that administers provincial securities legislation.[24] For example, the mandate of the Ontario Securities Commission is to "protect investors from unfair improper and fraudulent practices, foster fair and efficient

FIGURE	10.5

Canada's Bank-Owned
Securities Firms

Firm	Majority owner
BMO Nesbitt Burns	Bank of Montreal
CIBC World Markets	Canadian Imperial Bank of Commerce
National Bank Financial	National Bank
RBC Dominion Securities	Royal Bank of Canada
Scotia Capital	The Bank of Nova Scotia
TD Securities	The Toronto-Dominion Bank

Source: Department of Finance Canada, "Canada's Securities Industry," January 2005, http://www.fin.gc.ca/toc/2005/cansec05_-eng.asp.

capital markets and maintain public and investor confidence in the integrity of those markets." Recently, stock promoter Stevens Demers was found guilty of multiple counts of securities violations.[25]

Canada's ten provinces and three territories are responsible for the securities regulations within their respective borders. The Canadian Securities Administrators (CSA) is a forum for these securities regulators to coordinate and harmonize regulation of the Canadian capital markets. The CSA brings provincial and territorial securities regulators together. The focus of these meetings is to share ideas, work at designing policies and regulations that are consistent across the country, and ensure the smooth operation of Canada's securities industry. By collaborating on rules, regulations, and other programs, the CSA helps avoid duplication of work and streamlines the regulatory process for companies seeking to raise investment capital and others working in the investment industry. However perceptions exist in capital markets that the level of enforcement of regulations varies from one jurisdiction to another.

Canada's regulatory framework has been reviewed over the past number of years. Successive Ministers of Finance have continued to encourage a solution that would address the problems of a costly, cumbersome regulatory framework. A steering committee made up of ministers from six provinces agreed in the summer of 2003 to try to fix Canada's patchwork regulatory system. In 2004, this steering committee recommended a national securities regulator. Quebec, Alberta, and British Columbia were opposed to giving up their control over securities regulations. Today, a national body has yet to be created to oversee all securities activities.

THE FUNCTION OF SECURITIES MARKETS

stock exchange
An organization whose members can buy and sell (exchange) securities for companies and investors.

A **stock exchange** is an organization whose members can buy and sell (exchange) securities for companies and investors. A security is a transferable certificate of ownership of an investment product such as a stock or bond.[26] The Toronto Stock Exchange and the Montreal Exchange are just two examples of securities markets in Canada. These institutions serve two major functions: First, they assist businesses in finding long-term funding to finance capital needs, such as beginning operations, expanding their businesses, or buying major goods and services. Second, they provide private investors with a place to buy and sell securities (investments), such as stocks, bonds, and mutual funds (to be discussed later in this chapter) that can help them build their financial future.

Securities markets are divided into primary and secondary markets. Primary markets handle the sale of new securities. This is an important point to understand. Corporations make money on the sale of their securities only once—when they are first sold on the primary market through an IPO.[27] After that, the secondary market handles the trading of securities between investors, with the proceeds of a sale going to the investor selling the stock, not to the corporation whose stocks are sold. For example, if you, the owner of Very Vegetarian, offer 2 million shares of stock in your company at $15 a share, you would raise $30 million at this initial offering. However, if Shareholder Jones sells 100 shares of her Very Vegetarian stock to Investor Smith, Very Vegetarian collects nothing from this transaction. Smith bought the stock from Jones, not from Very Vegetarian. However, it's possible for companies like Very Vegetarian to offer additional shares to raise additional capital.

The Toronto Stock Exchange and the TSX Venture Exchange are not the only fish in the stock exchange sea. Exchanges like the London Exchange (pictured here) are located throughout the world, even in former communist-bloc countries like Poland and Hungary. If you think a foreign company is destined to be the next Magna or Bombardier, call a broker and get in on the opportunity.

The importance of long-term funding to businesses cannot be overemphasized. Unfortunately, many new companies start without sufficient capital, and many established firms fail to do adequate long-term financial planning. If given a choice, businesses normally prefer to meet long-term financial needs by using retained earnings or by borrowing from a lending institution (bank, pension fund, insurance company). However, if such types of long-term funding are not available, a company may be able to raise funds by issuing corporate bonds (debt) or selling stock (ownership). As we will discuss in Chapter 11, the issuing of corporate bonds is a form of debt financing and selling stock in the corporation is a form of equity financing. These forms of debt financing or equity financing are not available to all companies, especially small businesses. However, many firms use such financing options to meet long-term financial needs.

Progress Assessment

- Describe the Canadian securities industry. Why are more Canadians turning to this industry?
- What is the role of the Canadian Securities Administrators?
- What is the primary purpose of a stock exchange? Can you name a stock exchange in Canada?

HOW TO INVEST IN SECURITIES

stockbroker

A registered representative who works as a market intermediary to buy and sell securities for clients.

Investing in bonds, stocks, or other securities is not very difficult. First, you decide what bond or stock you want to buy or that you have to sell. After that, it's necessary to use a registered representative authorized to trade stocks and bonds who can call a member of the stock exchange to execute your order. A **stockbroker** is a registered representative who works as a market intermediary to buy and sell securities for clients. Stockbrokers place an order with a stock exchange member, who goes to the place at the exchange where the bond or stock is traded and negotiates a price. After the transaction is completed, the trade is reported to your broker, who notifies you to confirm your purchase. Large brokerage firms like RBC Capital Markets and BMO Nesbitt Burns maintain automated order systems that allow their brokers to enter your order the instant you make it. Seconds later, the order can be confirmed.

A broker can be a valuable source of information about what stocks or bonds would best meet your financial objectives. It's important, however, that you learn about and follow stocks and bonds on your own, because investment analysts' advice may not always meet your specific expectations and needs.[28]

Investing Online

Investors can also use online trading services to buy and sell stocks and bonds in place of using traditional brokerage services.[29] BMO Investorline (www.bmoinvestorline.com), TD Waterhouse (www.tdwaterhouse.ca), and iTrade Canada (https://www.scotiaitrade.com) are a few of the leading providers of web-based stock trading services. The commissions charged by these trading services are far less than those of regular stockbrokers. Trades that used to cost hundreds of dollars with full-service brokerage firms may cost as low as $5 each on the Web.

Today, customers interested in online trading services are primarily investors willing to do their own research and make their own investment decisions without the assistance of a broker. The leading online services, however, do provide important market information such as company financial data, price histories of a stock, and consensus analysts' reports.

Whether you decide to trade stocks and bonds using an online broker or decide to invest through a traditional stockbroker, it is important to remember that investing means committing (and risking) your money with the expectation of making a profit.[30] As the market downturn in the fall of 2008 highlighted, investing is certainly a risky business. Therefore, the first step in any investment program is to analyze such factors as desired income, cash requirements, growth prospects, level of risk, and hedging against inflation. You are never too young or too old to get involved in investments, so let's look at some alternatives and questions you should consider before investing.

Choosing the Right Investment Strategy

As you might suspect, investment objectives change over the course of a person's life. Key investment decisions often centre on personal objectives such as growth and income. For example, a young person can afford more high-risk investment options (such as stocks) than a person nearing retirement. Often young investors are looking for significant growth in the value of their investments over time. Therefore, if stocks go into a tailspin and decrease in value, the younger person has time to wait for stocks to rise again. An older person, perhaps on a fixed income, doesn't have the luxury of waiting, and might be prone to invest in bonds that offer a steady return as a protection against inflation.

Inherent in any investment strategy is the risk/return trade-off. That's why it's important for investors to consider five key criteria when selecting investment options:

1. *Investment risk*—the chance that an investment will be worth less at some future time than it's worth now.

2. *Yield*—the expected rate of return on an investment, such as interest or dividends, usually over a period of one year.

3. *Duration*—the length of time your money is committed to an investment.

4. *Liquidity*—how quickly you can get back your invested funds if you want them or need them.

5. *Tax consequences*—how the investment will affect your tax situation.

Setting investment objectives such as growth or income should clearly set the tone for your investment strategy. Bonds, stocks, and mutual funds all offer opportunities for investors to enhance their financial future. We will look first at the potential of bonds as an investment, then move on to stocks and mutual funds.

INVESTING IN BONDS

For investors who desire low risk and guaranteed income, government bonds are a secure investment because these bonds have the financial backing and full faith and credit of the government. In recent history no government bond issue in Canada has been defaulted on. Corporate bonds are a bit more risky and challenging. However, bond interest is fully taxable in the hands of the bond holder, while dividend income qualifies for tax credits.

One question often bothers first-time corporate bond investors: If I purchase a corporate bond, do I have to hold it until the maturity date? The answer is no, you do not have to hold a bond until maturity. Bonds are bought and sold daily on major securities exchanges. However, if you decide to sell your bond to another investor before its maturity date, you are not guaranteed to get the face value of the bond (usually $1,000). For example, if your bond does not have features that make it attractive to other investors, you may be forced to sell your bond at a discount; that is, a price less than the bond's face value. But if your bond is highly valued by other investors, you may be able to sell it at a premium; that is, a price above its face value. Remember that with most bonds the interest rate is fixed throughout the term of the bond. Therefore, after the bond is first issued, more often than not, there is a difference between the bond interest rate and the market interest rate. Therefore, bond prices generally fluctuate inversely with current market interest rates. As market interest rates go up, bond prices fall, given that the bond interest rate remains constant, and vice versa. Thus, like all investments, bonds have a degree of risk.

Investors will invest in a bond that is considered risky only if the potential return to them is high enough. It's important to remember that investors have many investment options besides bonds. One such option is to buy stock.

INVESTING IN STOCKS

Buying stock makes the investor an owner of the firm. Stocks provide investors with an opportunity to participate in the success of emerging or expanding companies if the share price rises. In fact, since 1925, the average annual return on stocks has been about 12 percent, the highest return of any popular investment. This return is made up both of increases in the share price and of dividends that may be paid. For a discussion of dividends, refer to Chapter 11. As owners, however, stockholders can also lose money if a company does not do well or if the overall stock market is declining. The market fall of 2008 was proof of that. Again, it's up to investors to choose the investment that best fits their overall investment objectives.

According to investment analysts, the market price (and growth potential) of a common share depends heavily on the overall performance of the corporation in meeting its business objectives. If a company reaches its stated objectives, there are great opportunities for capital gains. **Capital gains** are the positive difference between the price at which you bought a stock and what you sell it for. For example, a $1,000 investment made in Microsoft when its stock was first offered to the public would be worth more than $1 million today. Stocks can be subject to a high degree of risk, however. While the late 1990s and early 2000s witnessed significant drops in the stock market, from 2004 to 2008 the Canadian stock market rose significantly as a result of the worldwide escalating demand for all types of natural resources. However, a financial crisis in the fall of 2008 drove markets down by close to 50 percent.

capital gains

The positive difference between the purchase price of a stock and its sale price.

Stock investors are often called bulls or bears depending on their perceptions of the market. *Bulls* are investors who believe that stock prices are going to rise, so they buy stock in anticipation of the increase. When overall stock prices are rising, the market is called a bull market. *Bears* are investors who expect stock prices to decline. Bears sell their stocks in anticipation of falling prices. When the prices of stocks decline steadily, the market is called a bear market.[31]

As we discussed previously, setting investment objectives such as growth, income, inflation protection, or cash can set the tone for your investment strategy. Investors may select several different investment opportunities in stock depending on their strategy. Growth stocks, for example, are stocks of corporations (often technology, biotechnology, or Internet-related firms) whose earnings are expected to grow at a rate faster than other stocks in the market. While often considered very risky, such stocks offer investors the potential for high returns. Another option is income stocks. These are stocks that offer investors a rather high dividend yield on their investment. Public utilities are often considered good income stocks that will generally keep pace with inflation.

The stock of high-quality companies such as Petro-Canada and Canadian National (CN) are referred to as *blue-chip stocks*. These stocks pay regular dividends and generally experience consistent growth in the company's stock price. Investors can even invest in a type of stock called a penny stock. *Penny stocks* are

Crystal Hanlan started with Home Depot as a cashier several years ago. She began buying shares in the company as part of an employee ownership plan and is now worth over a million dollars. There are over a million other employees who got to be millionaires the same way. Are you getting the idea that it is a good idea to participate in such ownership programs and to put the maximum you can into such accounts?

stocks that sell for less than $2 (some analysts say less than $5).[32] Such stocks frequently represent ownership in firms, such as mining or oil exploration companies, that compete in high-risk industries. Suffice it to say, penny stocks are considered very risky investments.

Investors who buy stock have more options for placing an order than investors buying and selling bonds. Stock investors, for example, can place a market order, which tells a broker to buy or to sell a stock immediately at the best price available. This type of order can be processed quickly, and the trade price can be given to the investor almost instantaneously. A limit order tells the broker to buy or to sell a particular stock at a specific price, if that price becomes available. Let's say, for example, that a stock is selling for $40 a share; you believe that the price will go up eventually but that it might drop a little before it goes higher. You could place a limit order at $36. The broker will buy the stock for you at $36 if the stock drops to that price. If the stock never falls to $36, the broker will not purchase it. See Figure 10.6 for a summary of some transactions. Which investments generated a capital gain (excluding any commissions) of more than $0.50 per share based on the closing price from the previous day?

Stock Indexes

Stock indexes measure the trend of different stock exchanges. Every country with a stock exchange has such indexes. In Canada, there are several thousand companies listed, and the prices of their shares fluctuate constantly. Some may be rising over a certain period and others may be falling. Various indexes have been developed to give interested parties useful information about significant trends. More and more indexes are being continually developed. Another use of an index is as an investment vehicle. Investors who do not have the time or expertise to actively manage their investments are choosing to be passive investors by investing in index funds.

In Canada, the largest index is the S&P/TSX Composite Index. There is no requirement for the index to hold a certain number of companies. The number of stocks that make up the index will vary over time and will be included in the index if they qualify (based on size and liquidity) after quarterly reviews.[33]

Staying abreast of what is happening in the market will help you decide what investments seem most appropriate to your needs and objectives. However, it's important to remember two key investment realities: (1) your personal financial objectives will change over time, and (2) markets can be volatile.

Buying on Margin

Buying on margin means you purchase securities by borrowing some of the cost from your broker, who holds them as collateral security until you pay the balance due. In effect, the broker lends you the money and charges you interest. Provincial regulatory agencies, such as the Ontario Securities Commission, control all aspects of this industry, including what minimum percentage of the purchase price must be paid in cash. For example, if the current rate is 50 percent for shares and 10 percent for bonds, you would have to invest a minimum of $4 to buy an $8 share (plus commissions to the broker), and $97 for a bond selling for $970.

Buying on margin is risky. If the stock or bond drops in price, you will get a margin call from your broker. This means that you will have to make a payment to your broker to maintain the margin of collateral protection that the broker is obligated to observe. In this case, the loan cannot exceed 50 percent of the stock value, or 90 percent of the bond value.

buying on margin
Purchasing securities by borrowing some of the cost from the broker.

Stock Splits

As the price of a stock rises, the number of potential owners falls. Companies and brokers usually don't like to see this happen. If such a situation is happening to a given company, they may declare a **stock split**; that is, they issue two or more shares for every share of stock that's currently outstanding. For example, if Very Vegetarian stock were selling for

stock split
An action by a company that gives shareholders two or more shares of stock for each one they own.

FIGURE 10.6

Daily Stock Transactions
This is a small segment of the list of stocks traded on the Toronto Stock Exchange, as reported on 27 October 2006, in *The Globe and Mail*.

Here is an explanation of what the column headings mean:

A & B: highest and lowest price in the last year

C: abbreviated name of the company

D: the symbol used to identify the company for trading purposes

E: annual dividend per share

F, G, & H: highest, lowest, and closing price for that day

I: change in closing price from the previous day

J: number of shares traded that day in hundreds (e.g., first line is 5,500 shares)

K: *yield* refers to the estimated percent income your investment would yield if you bought at closing price and kept the stock for a year. It is the ratio of annual dividend to closing price. There is no yield for those companies that show no dividend paid.

L: *P/E ratio* refers to ratio of closing price to estimated earnings per share (which is not shown but is known). Where no ratio is shown it means either that the company is not making any profits or that no estimate of earnings is available.

A	B	C	D	E	F	G	H	I	J	K	L
									vol.		p/e
365-day											
high	low	stock	sym	div	high	low	close	chg	(100s)	yield	ratio
1.80	0.75	Lab Intl	LAB		0.85	0.75	0.80		2731		
4.50	3.55	Lab Researc	LRI		4.30	4.05	4.10	−0.20	144		
10.95	3.75	♣ Labopharm	DDS		5.55	5.40	5.50		2482		
2.65	1.21	Lake Shore	LSG		1.45	1.38	1.43	+0.06	2840		
29.50	16.21	Laperriere	GLV.A		25.30	24.50	24.80	+0.30	419		14.4
8.50	4.06	Laramide	LAM		7.75	7.25	7.37	−0.16	3711		
36.72	28.01	Laurentn Bk	LB	1.16	29.15	28.97	29.10	+0.10	268	4.0	12.0
27.05	25.24	Lauren	LB.PR.B	1.50	26.30	26.04	26.20	+0.09	103	5.7	
27.85	24.70	Laurenti	LB.PR.E	1.312	26.68	26.60	26.60	+0.05	12	4.9	
59.40	36.00	Le Chatea	CTU.A	1.00	43.10	43.00	43.00	−0.45	82	2.3	12.4
158.00	92.85	Legg Masn	LMI	.944	101.00	99.38	101.00	+3.36	32	0.09	22.1
46.50	35.00	Leons Furnit	LNF	1.00	46.25	45.75	45.75	+0.25	39	2.2	15.8
14.72	14.00	Life & B	LBS	1.20	14.72	14.50	14.51	−0.07	747	8.3	
10.68	10.35	Life & B	LBS.PR.A		10.63	10.56	10.57	+0.01	1140		
16.74	10.81	Linamar	LNR	0.24	13.40	13.05	13.18	+0.14	220	1.8	8.9
7.76	3.15	Linear Gold	LRR		5.35	5.00	5.00	−0.25	225		
9.46	4.62	LionOre	LIM		9.46	9.11	9.26	+0.11	36528		
7.45	2.80	Liquidatin	LQW		6.60	6.45	6.60	+0.05	89		17.8
68.22	45.22	Loblaw Cos	L	0.84	46.38	46.00	46.30	+0.15	4133	1.8	17.5
0.49	.215	Lorus	LOR		0.24	0.23	0.23	−0.01	3498		
1.54	0.21	Lumina Res	LUR		1.45	1.38	1.43	+0.02	1030		
43.92	11.75	Lundin Min	LUN		41.22	40.19	41.00	+1.55	1703		17.2
0.38	0.03	Luxell Tech	LUX		.055	0.05	0.05	−0.01	427		
8.65	6.22	♣ MCM	MUH.A	1.20	7.53	7.52	7.52		60	16.0	5.0
16.05	15.14	♣ MCM	MUH.PR.A	.866	15.30	15.30	15.30		6	5.7	
23.20	18.25	MDS Inc	MDS	0.13	19.70	19.27	19.33	−0.15	1738	0.7	64.4
42.48	34.90	MI Dev	MIM.A	.674	42.25	41.57	41.79	−0.21	159	1.6	60.6
3.50	1.90	MKS	MKX	0.09	2.77	2.65	2.70	+0.05	183	3.3	13.5
52.49	33.00	MacDonld	MDA		42.29	41.19	41.61	−0.74	1844	—	21.6
3.34	2.11	Magellan	MAL		2.76	2.68	2.68	−0.10	233		
92.10	75.88	Magna Intl	MG.A	1.71	86.52	84.34	85.86	+0.73	1853	2.0	12.5
8.00	2.05	Mahalo Enr	CBM		3.15	2.85	2.85	−0.07	809		47.5
11.50	4.85	Mainstreet	MEQ		11.25	11.00	11.12	−0.13	48		
30.16	15.73	♣ Major Dril	MDI		23.25	21.60	22.59	+0.48	763		12.0
50.24	36.61	Manitob Tl	MBT	2.60	46.05	45.76	45.90	−0.09	2853	5.7	30.2
37.55	29.70	Manulife Fi	MFC	0.70	36.89	36.48	36.62	−0.01	38050	1.9	16.3
27.74	25.60	Manuli	MFC.PR.A	1.025	26.84	26.83	26.83		92	3.8	
25.80	24.25	Manuli	MFC.PR.B	1.162	25.26	25.14	25.26	−0.02	102	4.6	
25.05	23.77	Manuli	MFC.PR.C	1.125	24.98	24.76	24.81	+0.06	179	4.5	
17.15	11.00	Maple Leaf	MFI	0.16	12.58	12.00	12.40	−0.10	3067	1.3	45.9
42.00	16.85	March Netwo	MN		26.84	25.48	26.00	+0.85	746		9.5
9.99	7.18	Marsulex	MLX		8.65	8.65	8.65	+0.15	6		66.5
9.90	4.82	Martinrea	MRE		9.40	9.10	9.40	+0.20	1226		17.4
7.90	4.01	Maxin Pow	MXG		4.59	4.45	4.58	+0.08	1052		22.9
2.37	0.91	Medicure	MPH		1.70	1.51	1.57	−0.06	2448		
29.75	20.25	Mega Brands	MB		25.39	24.81	24.85	−0.05	738		13.6
5.625	1.255	Mega Urani	MGA		4.90	4.65	4.90	+0.28	8347		
22.25	9.80	Melcor Dev	MRD	0.30	20.61	20.25	20.61	+0.56	206	1.5	12.8
3.15	0.82	Mercator Min	ML		2.70	2.64	2.69	+0.06	668		40.1
42.30	21.44	MeridinGl	MNG		28.19	27.27	27.45	−0.13	5476		

$100 a share, you could declare a two-for-one stock split. Investors who owned one share of Very Vegetarian would now own two shares; each share, however, would now be worth only $50 (half the value before the split). As you can see, there is no change in the firm's ownership structure and no change in the investment's value after the stock split.[34] Investors, however, generally approve of stock splits because often the demand for the stock at $50 per share may be greater than the demand at $100 per share. Thus, the $50 stock price may go up in the near future.

Progress Assessment

- What is the key advantage to online investing? What do investors need to remember if they decide to do their investing online?
- What is a stock split? Why do companies sometimes split their stock?
- What is meant by buying on margin?

INVESTING IN MUTUAL FUNDS

A **mutual fund** is a fund that buys a variety of securities and then sells units of ownership in the fund to the public. A mutual fund company is similar to an investment company that pools investors' money and then buys stocks or bonds in many companies in accordance with the specific purpose of the fund. Mutual fund managers are experts who pick what they consider to be the best securities.

mutual fund
A fund that buys stocks and bonds and then sells units of ownership in the fund to the public.

Investors can buy shares of the mutual funds and thus take part in the ownership of many different companies that they may not have been able to afford to invest in individually or may not have had the time to thoroughly analyze. Thus, for a fee, mutual funds provide professional investment management and help investors diversify. So for the investor, they consider the trade-off between the fees paid for mutual fund management against the return earned by the mutual fund. The return over and above an index is expected to exceed all the fees paid.

Funds available range in purpose from very conservative funds that invest only in government securities or secure corporate bonds to others that specialize in emerging high-tech firms, Internet companies, foreign companies, precious metals, and other investments with greater risk. A number of mutual funds invest only in indexes (refer to the earlier discussion on stock indexes). Some mutual funds even invest exclusively in socially responsible companies. See the Green Box for a discussion of socially responsible investing.

In Canada, mutual fund companies fall under the jurisdiction of the provincial securities commissions. Some examples of companies that manage mutual fund assets include Investors Group, AIM Funds Management, Mackenzie Financial, and TD Asset Management. According to the Investment Funds Institute of Canada, total assets under administration were just less than $600 billion at the end of October 2008.[35]

With mutual funds, investors benefit from diversification. **Diversification** involves buying several different investment alternatives to spread the risk of investing. Consequently, a mutual fund investor is not 100 percent invested in only one company. So, if one company's shares decrease, hopefully there will be increases in the value of other companies' shares. This is also applicable if a mutual fund holds bonds.

diversification
Buying several different investment alternatives to spread the risk of investing.

One key advantage of mutual funds is that you can buy some funds directly and save any fees or commissions. The Internet has made access in and out of mutual funds easier than ever. A true no-load fund is one that charges no commission to investors to either buy or sell its shares. A load fund would charge a commission to investors to buy shares in the fund or would charge a commission when investors sell shares in the fund.

GreenBOX

Socially Responsible Investing

Also known as sustainable investing, Social Responsible Investing (SRI) is an investment strategy that seeks to achieve both financial return and social good. One of the focuses for SRI is environmental stewardship, including sustainability. Specifically, investment should be channeled away from companies that are perceived to negatively impact climate change.

On a global basis, by 2003, 200 SRI mutual funds existed, with assets over $160 billion. The proportion of mutual funds focused on SRI continues to grow exponentially. Shareholder activism has played an important role in either implementing a screening process that will exclude mutual funds from owning shares in certain companies, or divesting themselves of investment in other companies—with the latter being companies causing ethical objections. Government-controlled pension funds face growing pressure to undertake SRI.

A Canadian organization, Social Investment Organization, is mandated to promote the practice of SRI. They do this by taking a leadership role in supporting social and environmental criteria for investing decisions, raising public awareness of SRI, raising the case for environmental/social analysis with other investment organizations, and providing a forum for SRI. This organization sponsors a biennial conference, a list-serve (with data on the performance of SRI funds), a listing of financial advisors knowledgeable about SRI, a Web site and media relations activities. For more information, see their Web site at www.socialinvestment.ca.

Source: "Socially-Responsible Investing," http://en.wikipedia.org/wiki/Socially_responsible_investing.

Sprott Asset Management, with assets under management of nearly $4.4 billion, was founded by Eric Sprott. Recognized as a very good stock picker, he was recognized as the Fund Manager of the Year in 2007. A public offering of stock in his company made Eric Canada's newest billionaire in 2008.

It's important to check the costs involved in a mutual fund, such as fees and charges imposed in the managing of a fund, because these can differ significantly. It's also important to check the long-term performance record of the fund's management.[36] Some funds, called open-end funds, will accept the investments of any interested investors. Closed-end funds offer a specific number of shares for investment; once a closed-end fund reaches its target number, no new investors can buy into the fund.

Most financial advisers put mutual funds high on the list of recommended investments for small or beginning investors. Figure 10.7 evaluates bonds, stocks, and mutual funds according to risk, income, and possible investment growth (capital gain).

We hope you have enjoyed the discussion of investing in this chapter. It's critical for you to know that there's no such thing as easy money or a sure thing. Investing is a challenging and interesting field that's always changing.

Progress Assessment

- What is a mutual fund and what is the role of mutual fund managers?
- How do mutual funds benefit small investors?
- Describe the degree of risk, expected income, and possible growth one can expect with mutual funds.

FIGURE | **10.7**

Comparing Investments

Investment	Degree of risk	Expected income	Possible growth (capital gain)
Bonds	Low	Secure	Little
Preferred shares	Medium	Steady	Little
Common shares	High	Variable	Good
Mutual funds	Medium	Variable	Good

SUMMARY

1. Figure 10.1 briefly lists the variety of financial organizations that comprise this industry.

   Why is this industry important to Canada?

   The financial services industry employs more than 1 million Canadians, directly or indirectly. Its activities represent 5 percent of Canada's GDP. On a yearly basis, more than $9 billion in tax revenue to all levels of government is generated. Nearly $50 billion of services are exported annually. Because of its important role in the economy, the financial industry is one of the most regulated sectors in the country. Regulation is designed to ensure the integrity, safety, and soundness of financial institutions and markets.

   LO ▶ 1 Describe the importance of the financial services industry in Canada.

2. Money is anything that people generally accept as payment for goods and services.

   How is the value of money determined?

   The value of money depends on the money supply; that is, how much money is available to buy goods and services. Too much money in circulation causes inflation. Too little money causes deflation, recession, and unemployment.

   LO ▶ 2 Explain what money is and how its value is determined.

3. As major players in Canada's financial industry, banks serve millions of customers.

   Who benefits from the services offered by banks?

   Bank customers include individuals, small- and medium-sized businesses, large corporations, governments, institutional investors, and non-profit organizations. The major banks offer a full range of banking, investment, and financial services.

   LO ▶ 3 Discuss the role that banks play in providing services.

4. Insurance is big business and a key component of the financial services industry.

   What is the role of insurance as part of the financial services industry?

   Everyone who drives a vehicle is required to have auto insurance. All businesses typically carry a mix of insurance coverage from property, to liability, to crime, to business interruption insurance.

   LO ▶ 4 Discuss the nature and impact of insurance.

5. The risk/return trade-off is inherent in any investment strategy.

   What are the key criteria when selecting investment options?

   Five key criteria are investment risk (the chance that an investment will be worth less at some future time than it's worth now); yield (the expected rate of return on an investment over a period of time); duration (the length of time your investment is committed to an investment); liquidity (how quickly you can get your money back if you need it); and tax consequences (how the investment will affect your tax situation).

   LO ▶ 5 List the five key criteria when selecting investment options.

LO ▶ 6 Explain the opportunities in mutual funds as investments and the benefits of diversifying investments.

6. Diversification means buying several different types of investments (e.g., government bonds, preferred shares, common shares, etc.) with different degrees of risk. The purpose is to reduce the overall risk an investor would assume by investing in just one type of security.

How can mutual funds help individuals diversify their investments?
A mutual fund is a fund that buys a variety of securities and then sells units of ownership in the fund to the public. Individuals who buy shares in a mutual fund are able to invest in many different companies they could not afford to invest in otherwise.

KEY TERMS

barter 275

buying on margin 289

capital gains 288

commercial bank 279

credit unions 272

diversification 291

money 275

money supply 276

mutual fund 291

non-banks 272

pension funds 273

prime rate 277

prospectus 284

securities commission 284

securities dealer 284

stockbroker 286

stock exchange 285

stock split 289

trust company 272

CRITICAL THINKING

1. In the past few years, we have seen significant swings in the exchange rate of the Canadian dollar. The value of the Canadian dollar rose from as low as $.62 to over $1.00 and then back down to under $.80 (relative to the U.S. dollar). What have been some of the major contributors to the swings? What have been the impacts on the Canadian economy with both the rising and then the falling of the Canadian dollar's exchange rate?

2. The financial services marketplace is growing, changing, and becoming more competitive. Bill C-8 allowed more players into the marketplace. Despite increased competition, Canada's banks believe that they are still restricted in the business decisions they can make to achieve the size and scale they need to compete in the international marketplace. Do you agree with the claim that banks make that they are denied the opportunity to pursue legitimate strategies for growth, including insurance retailing and mergers? Do you believe that banks should be allowed to merge? (Note that at the time of this writing, no mergers had been approved.) Do you believe that consumers and businesses will suffer if bank mergers are permitted? Explain your position.

DEVELOPING WORKPLACE SKILLS

1. In a small group, discuss the following: What services do you use from banks? Does anyone use Internet banking? What seem to be the pros and cons of online banking? Use this opportunity to compare the rates and services of various local banks. compare the services at each (interest rates given on accounts, the services available, and the loan rates). If anyone uses an online service, see how those rates compare. If no one uses a credit union or online bank, discuss the reasons.

2. Poll the class to see who uses banks and who uses a credit union or caisse populaire. Have class members

3. Break up into small groups and discuss when and where you use cheques versus credit cards and cash.

Do you often write cheques for small amounts? Would you stop doing that if you calculated how much it costs to process such cheques? Discuss your findings with others in the class.

4. Write a one-page paper on the role of the World Bank and the International Monetary Fund in providing loans to countries. Is it important for Canadian citizens to lend money to people in other countries through such organizations? Why or why not? Be prepared to debate the value of these organizations in class.

TAKING IT TO THE NET 1

www.mcgrawhillconnect.ca

Purpose

To learn about how financial institutions combat money laundering, terrorist financing, and threats to the security of Canada.

Exercise

Visit the Financial Transactions and Reports Analysis Centre of Canada (www.fintrac.gc.ca) and answer the following questions.

1. Who is obligated to report suspicious transactions?

2. What types of transactions would qualify as suspicious?

3. What is it about terrorist financing that is more "legitimate" than money laundering?

TAKING IT TO THE NET 2

www.mcgrawhillconnect.ca

Purpose

To learn about services that are available to help consumers make educated financial decisions.

Exercise

Visit "For Consumers" at the Financial Consumer Agency of Canada (www.fcac-acfc.gc.ca/eng/consumers/default.asp) and answer the following questions.

1. What information must you receive when you open a bank account?

2. What do you do if you find unauthorized transactions on your credit card account?

3. What are some suggestions for protecting yourself against debit card fraud?

4. What information must a financial institution provide on a monthly basis, if you have a line of credit?

5. If you have a complaint or problem with a federally regulated financial institution, what are the steps that you need to follow?

ANALYZING MANAGEMENT DECISIONS

Becoming Financially Secure

Mike and Priscilla Thomas are a married couple with two incomes and no children. Their cars are both paid for. They've saved enough money to buy a new house without selling their old one. (Real estate is typically a sound investment.) They're renting out their townhouse for added income. They hope to buy more rental property to use as an income producer so that they can both retire at age 50!

Priscilla runs a company called Cost Reduction Services and Associates. It advises small firms on ways to cut overhead expenses. The couple also owned a window-washing business when they were in university. Priscilla loves being in business for herself because, she says, "When you own your own business, you can work hard and you get paid for your hard work." Mike is a pharmaceutical salesperson.

How did the Thomases get the money to start their own businesses and buy a couple of homes? They committed themselves from the beginning of their marriage to live on Mike's income and to save Priscilla's income. Furthermore, they decided to live frugally. The goal of early retirement was their incentive. They "lived like university kids" for five years, clipping coupons and saving every cent they could. They don't often go out to eat, and they rent movies for their VCR instead of going to the movie theatre.

Mike puts the maximum amount into his company's pension plan. It's invested in a very aggressive growth fund: half Canadian stocks and half international stocks. Now that the couple is financially secure, they're planning to have children.

Source: *Marketplace*, July 31, 2002.

Discussion Questions

1. When considering investment risk, where would you rank real estate relative to stocks, bonds, and mutual funds?

2. How can a financial services firm help a person develop a budget in order to achieve one's goals?

3. Do you agree with how Mike has allocated his pension plan contributions? Explain.

4. Can you see why money management is one of the keys to both entrepreneurship and personal financial security?

RUNNING CASE

Risk Management at Canadian Tire Financial Services

In 1995, Canadian Tire Financial Services (CTFS) became the first non-bank to receive a MasterCard® licence. While the company had experience with its retail card business (the card could be used in Canadian Tire stores only), the ultimate goal was to convert retail card users to the company's new Options® MasterCard®. Both cards are loyalty cards that encourage retail spending at Canadian Tire stores. The advantage of the Options® MasterCard® is huge growth potential, as the market now includes worldwide purchases (MasterCard is accepted at more than 24 million shops and services worldwide) rather than simply purchases in Canadian Tire stores. Thus, Options® MasterCard® holders generate more loyalty benefits through the increased use of this card. Before this could happen, a model had to be established to understand how the company could mitigate its risk.

The initial launch of the credit card was followed by the introduction of the Gas Advantage MasterCard in selected regions in 2006, followed by a full national roll-out in 2008. This credit card allows cardholders to earn discounts on gas purchases at all Canadian Tire Petroleum locations. The Gas Advantage MasterCard is a key initiative supporting interrelated businesses within Canadian Tire Corporation. Also in 2008, there was a re-issue of the entire Options MasterCard base incorporating new PayPass technology.

After changes to the Bank Act in 2001, CTFS launched Canadian Tire Bank in 2003. New controls had to be established to ensure compliance with regulatory require-

ments. Canadian Tire Bank had to ensure its documentation and reporting met the requirements of federal organizations (such as the Office of the Superintendent of Financial Institutions and the Financial Consumer Agency of Canada) and incorporate privacy legislation controls and anti–money laundering checks. In 2007 the Canadian Tire One and Only Account was launched. This product combines a customer's mortgage, chequing and savings accounts, loans, and credit card balances in one account.

Because of the Enron scandal and the increasing focus on ethics, organizational risk management has become even more critical within organizations. This became key as CTFS reviewed its operations under the new structure, which included Canadian Tire Bank. Risk had to be assessed across the organization. As a result, a team was created that was responsible for identifying, quantifying, and consolidating risk across the organization. This coordinated effort resulted in a disciplined approach to risk management. For example, when considering the credit risk function, policies and procedures were developed to ensure that the amount of credit risk-taking (that is, how much was loaned to a customer based on his or her creditworthiness or ability to repay) was within defined limits and subject to appropriate procedural controls. Such controls are critical for organizations to mitigate risk. To further manage their risk, in late 2007 Canadian Tire Bank began selling GICs through brokers as an alternative funding source to the securitization of credit card receivables, at reasonable and cost-effective interest rates, to fund operations.

This focus on risk management has resulted in an increasing level of complexity and rigour. Complex accounting and finance knowledge is required for employees to understand the increasing number of rules (e.g., SOX-like Canadian financial certification requirements) and how they are to be implemented, applied, and followed within the organization. The CEO and the CFO are now required to personally certify the accuracy of CTFS's financial statements, the design and effectiveness of disclosure controls and procedures, and the internal controls over financial reporting.

Sources: Dean McCann, Vice-President Finance, Canadian Tire Financial Services, interview, 13 April 2006; Gregory Craig, Vice-President Finance and Chief Financial Officer, Canadian Tire Bank, interview, 10 December 2008; and www.ctfs.com, 31 December 2008.

Discussion Questions

1. What are some of the operational needs that face CTFS? How would this differ for smaller organizations?

2. Conduct some research on the Internet. What are some additional products and services that have been introduced by CTFS, through Canadian Tire Bank, since this textbook was published?

3. Visit www.ctfs.com/Products/CreditCards/Options MasterCard/. What are the loyalty benefits of using the Options® MasterCard®? What is the purpose of the Pay Pass feature? What other features of this credit card help with personal security?

CHAPTER 11

Financial Management

LEARNING OBJECTIVES

AFTER YOU HAVE READ AND STUDIED THIS CHAPTER, YOU SHOULD BE ABLE TO:

LO ▶ 1   Describe the importance of finance and financial management to an organization, and explain the responsibilities of financial managers.

LO ▶ 2   Outline the financial planning process, and explain the three key budgets in the financial plan.

LO ▶ 3   Explain the major reasons why firms need funds, and identify various types of financing that can be used to obtain these funds.

LO ▶ 4   Identify and describe different sources of short-term financing.

LO ▶ 5   Identify and describe different sources of long-term financing.

PROFILE

Getting to Know Cynthia Devine, CFO of Tim Hortons

Very few brands enjoy the emotional ties and customer loyalty that Tim Hortons has earned. The company has spent the past 42 years building one of the most unique and successful brands in the highly competitive quick-service restaurant industry. On 24 March 2006, after ten very successful years as part of the Wendy's International organization, Tim Hortons completed an initial public offering (IPO) on the New York and Toronto stock exchanges. The offering of 33 million shares—or 17 percent of the company—raised net proceeds of $843 million and gave investors the opportunity to own part of this household name. On 29 September 2006, the remaining 83 percent of the company was divided out to Wendy's shareholders, launching Tim Hortons as a stand-alone public company. In September 2009, a merger and reorganization were approved by an overwhelming majority of the shareholders which resulted in Tim Hortons once again becoming a Canadian public company.

Cynthia Devine is the chief financial officer of Tim Hortons, where she is responsible for financial reporting, business planning and analysis, tax, and information technology. She has built an extensive 20-year financial career with some of the most established consumer product brands in Canada.

Devine began her career at Ernst & Young, where she obtained her chartered accountant designation. She then spent almost ten years in a variety of finance-related positions with Pepsi Canada. Her involvement in many initiatives at Pepsi helped her become chief financial officer of Pepsi-Cola Canada Ltd. During her term at Pepsi, Devine was heavily involved on the Canadian side with the spinoff of both the restaurant division and the bottling operations. This experience proved invaluable for her role at Tim Hortons during the IPO and ultimate spinoff. Prior to joining Tim Hortons, Devine held a senior financial position at Maple Leaf Foods, where she was very involved in all aspects of the business within the consumer products division. During her time at Maple Leaf, Devine was part of the team that completed the acquisition of Schneiders. This experience helped expand her knowledge of mergers and acquisition activity.

In late 2003, Devine joined Tim Hortons as chief financial officer and guided the company through its IPO and the building of a financial organization to become a stand-alone public company and support the ongoing needs of the business. Despite a busy workload, Devine enjoys spending time with her husband and two children.

In May 1964, Tim Horton, a National Hockey League All-Star defenceman, opened his first coffee and dough-nut shop on Ottawa Street in Hamilton, Ontario. In 1967, Ron Joyce, then the operator of three Tim Hortons restaurants, became partners with Tim Horton, and together they opened 37 new restaurants over the next seven years. In the early 1990s, Tim Hortons and Wendy's entered into a partnership to develop real estate and combination restaurants containing both brands under the same roof.

Tim Hortons has always had a focus on top-quality, always-fresh product, value, exceptional service, and community leadership. This has allowed the chain to grow into the largest quick-service restaurant chain in Canada, specializing in always-fresh coffee, baked goods, and homestyle lunches. By January 2009, there were more than 3,400 stores across Canada, and more than 500 locations in key markets in the United States. Tim Hortons has a diversified base of revenue and operating income generated from franchisee royalties and fees, rental income, warehouse sales, and company-operated stores. In fiscal 2008, it had total revenues of $2 billion, operating income of $444 million, and net income of $284 million.

Tim Hortons' commitment to maintaining a close relationship with franchisees and the communities in which it operates has helped generate immense customer loyalty and build Tim Hortons into one of the most widely recognized consumer brands in Canada. Tim Hortons was recognized as the best managed brand in Canada, according to annual surveys published by *Canadian Business* magazine in 2004 and 2005. It was also named one of Canada's most admired corporate cultures in 2005 by *Canadian Business*.

Risk, complexity, and uncertainty clearly define the role of financial management, especially in fast-growing companies such as Tim Hortons. Add to these challenges fluctuations in interest and exchange rates, expectations of investors and lenders, budgeting, and managing funds, and the job of the financial manager takes on even more intensity. In this chapter, you'll explore the role of finance in business, and learn about the tools that financial managers use to seek financial stability and future growth.

Source: Cynthia Devine, interview; Tim Hortons Web site, www.timhortons.com; Sharon Patterson, Vice President Human Resources, interview, 5 April 2006; and www.ctfs.com, 6 November 2006.

THE ROLE OF FINANCE AND FINANCIAL MANAGERS

finance
The function in a business that acquires funds for the firm and manages those funds within the firm.

The central goal of this chapter is to answer two major questions: "What is finance?" and "What do financial managers do?" **Finance** is the function in a business that acquires funds for the firm and manages those funds within the firm. Finance activities include preparing budgets; doing cash flow analysis; and planning for the expenditure of funds on such assets as plant, equipment, and machinery. **Financial management** is the job of managing a firm's resources so it can meet its goals and objectives. Without a carefully calculated financial plan, the firm has little chance for survival, regardless of its product or marketing effectiveness.

financial management
The job of managing a firm's resources so it can meet its goals and objectives.

An accountant could be compared to a skilled laboratory technician who takes blood samples and other measures of a person's health and writes the findings on a health report (in business, the equivalent of a set of financial statements).[1] A financial manager of a business is the doctor who interprets the report and makes recommendations to the patient regarding changes that will improve the patient's health. In short, **financial managers** examine the financial data prepared by accountants and make recommendations to top executives regarding strategies for improving the health (financial strength) of the firm. Refer to the Dealing with Change box for a description of how financial managers are doing major restorative work on a troubled Canadian organization.

financial managers
Managers who make recommendations to top executives regarding strategies for improving the financial strength of a firm.

It should be clear that financial managers can make sound financial decisions only if they understand accounting information. Similarly, a good accountant needs to understand finance. It's fair to say that accounting and finance go together like peanut butter and jelly. In large and medium-sized organizations, both the accounting and the finance functions are generally under the control of a chief financial office or a vice-president of finance.

Figure 11.1 highlights a financial manager's tasks. As you can see, a key responsibility is to obtain money and then control the use of that money effectively. Financial managers are responsible for seeing that the company pays its bills. Finance functions such as buying merchandise on credit (accounts payable) and collecting payment from customers (accounts receivable) are responsibilities of financial managers. Therefore, financial managers are responsible for paying the company's bills at the appropriate time and for collecting overdue accounts receivable to make sure that the company does not lose too much money to bad debts (people or firms that don't pay their bills). While these functions are critical to all types of businesses, they are particularly critical to small- and medium-sized businesses, which typically have smaller cash or credit cushions than large corporations. The role of advising top management on financial matters has become even more

FIGURE | **11.1**

What Financial Managers Do

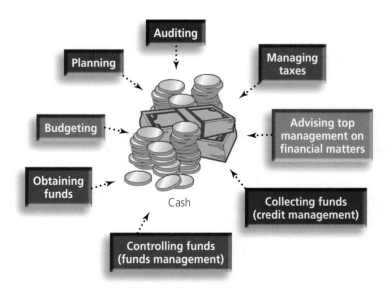

- Auditing
- Planning
- Managing taxes
- Budgeting
- Advising top management on financial matters
- Obtaining funds
- Cash
- Collecting funds (credit management)
- Controlling funds (funds management)

DEALING with CHANGE

Financial Restructuring for Canwest Global Communications

Canwest Global Communications and a number of affiliated companies have just applied for creditor protection under the Company's Creditors Arrangement Act (CCAA). This is a court-approved arrangement in which a major restructuring plan is submitted to and then hopefully approved by the shareholders and creditors.

In most cases, creditor protection is sought to provide a company with the time to develop a recapitalization plan. However, in this particular situation, Canwest entered creditor protection with what is called a prepackaged recapitalization plan, which has the support of its major debt holders and was backed up by up to $100 million in debtor in possession (DIP) financing to carry the businesses through the restructuring process.

This plan was developed in concert with the major debt holders to minimize business disruption and preserve the value of the business operations. It provides the time and the stability for Canwest to implement a controlled and orderly and consensual financial restructuring while continuing all its day-to-day operations. Because it is consensual the company is able to immediately begin to restructure its balance sheet, enabling it to emerge more quickly, providing a renewed financial outlook for the business units and putting them on a stronger, more stable footing for the future.

Creditor protection is normally approved by the Court based on the perception that the fundamental business of a company is viable. In the case of Canwest, the business operations of Global Television Network, three smaller specialty television channels, were generating operating profits even with recessionary level revenues. The National Post, originally part of the filing, has since been transitioned over into the Canwest publishing group (Canwest Limited Partnership) which is not part of this filing.

Over the past few years, Canwest undertook a massive expansion plan including the purchase of its publishing group from Conrad Black, a stable of 17 industry leading specialty channels from Alliance Atlantis, and radio operations in the United Kingdom and Turkey. They wanted to establish themselves as a global media heavyweight, and indeed are the largest media company in Canada. They choose to finance this growth with debt, and at the time of their filling, owed over $3.8 billion. The severe economic downturn over the past year resulted in an unprecedented decline in advertising revenue, which resulted in Canwest being unable to service their large debt.

During this time of restructuring, their financial managers have and will undertake to improve the operations of the companies through a combination of selling off non-core assets, closing unprofitable operations, and reducing operating expenses. The current net value of these companies is virtually zero and the restructuring plan calls for the conversion of a substantial portion of the debt into new equity. Operating under the CCAA will provide stability for the company while the financial managers complete all the complicated negotiations with the current shareholders and debtors.

Time will tell if all the efforts put into this restructuring will result in the emergence of Canwest as a far trimmer, healthier business organization.

You can access an audio presentation from the C.E.O., Leonard Asper, on the financial restructuring plans at www.canwestmediaworks.com/about/restructuring.asp.

Source: "About Us: Business and Financial Restructuring," CanWest Global Communications Web site, www.canwestmediaworks.com/about/restructuring.asp. Used with permission of CanWest Global Communications Corp.

---

important in recent years as risk has increased. Appendix B, immediately following this chapter, is devoted to the subject of Financial Risk.

As you may remember from Chapter 6, financing a small business is a difficult but essential function if a firm expects to survive those important first five years. The following are three of the most common ways for a firm to fail financially: (1) undercapitalization (lacking funds to start and run the business), (2) poor control over cash flow, and (3) inadequate expense control. Firms in a growth mode can often find themselves with large increases in their working capital as accounts receivable and inventory grow. Therefore, the need for careful financial management goes well beyond the first five years and remains a challenge that a business, large or small, must face throughout its existence.

The Importance of Understanding Finance

You can see the issues involved with all three of the items listed above when you consider the financial problems encountered by a small organization called Parsley Patch. Two friends, Elizabeth Bertani and Pat Sherwood, started the company on what can best be described as a shoestring budget. It began when Bertani prepared salt-free seasonings for her husband, who was on a no-salt diet. Her friend Sherwood thought the seasonings were good enough to sell. Bertani agreed, and Parsley Patch Inc. was born.

The business began with an investment of $5,000, which was rapidly eaten up for a logo and a label design. Bertani and Sherwood quickly learned the importance of capital in getting a business going. Eventually, the two women personally invested more than $100,000 to keep the business from experiencing severe undercapitalization.

The partners believed that gourmet shops would be an ideal distribution point for their product. Everything started well, and hundreds of gourmet shops adopted the product line. But when sales failed to meet expectations, the women decided that the health-food market offered more potential than gourmet shops, because salt-free seasonings were a natural for people with restricted diets. The choice was a good one. Sales soared and approached $30,000 a month. Still, the company earned no profits.

Bertani and Sherwood were not trained in monitoring cash flow or in controlling expenses. In fact, they had been told not to worry about costs, and they hadn't. They eventually hired a chartered accountant (CA) and an experienced financial manager, who taught them how to compute the costs of the various blends they produced and how to control their expenses. The financial specialists also offered insight into how to control cash coming in and out of the company (cash flow). Soon Parsley Patch earned a comfortable margin on operations that ran close to $1 million a year. Luckily, the owners were able to turn things around before it was too late.

If Bertani and Sherwood had understood finance before starting their business, they may have been able to avoid the problems they encountered. The key word here is *understood.* You do not have to pursue finance as a career to understand finance, which is important to anyone who wants to start a small business, invest in stocks and bonds (to be discussed later in this chapter), or plan a retirement fund.

Also, it's vital that financial managers in any business stay abreast of changes or opportunities in finance and prepare to adjust to them. For example, tax payments represent an outflow of cash from the business. Therefore, financial managers have become increasingly involved in tax management, and must keep abreast of changes in tax law. Financial managers also carefully analyze the tax implications of various managerial decisions in an attempt to minimize the taxes paid by the business.[2] It's critical that businesses of all sizes concern themselves with managing taxes.

Another responsibility of the firm's finance department, internal audit, checks on the journals, ledgers, and financial statements prepared by the accounting department. Another purpose of an internal audit is to safeguard assets, including cash. In short, finance and accounting are two areas everyone involved in business needs to study. Let's look more closely at what financial management is all about. We begin by looking at financial planning.

FINANCIAL PLANNING

Financial planning is a key responsibility of the financial manager in a business. Planning has been a recurring theme of this book. We've stressed planning's importance as a managerial function and offered insights into planning your career. Financial planning involves analyzing short-term and long-term money flows to and from the firm. The overall objective of financial planning is to optimize the firm's profitability and make the best use of its money.[3] The quality of a financial plan improves based on lived experiences. A start-up company's plan is of necessity, hopeful expectation, that can become more precise with experience and a track record.

Financial planning involves three steps: (1) forecasting both short-term and long-term financial needs, (2) developing budgets to meet those needs, and (3) establishing financial control to see how well the company is doing what it set out to do (see Figure 11.2). Let's look at each step and the role these steps play in improving the financial health of an organization.

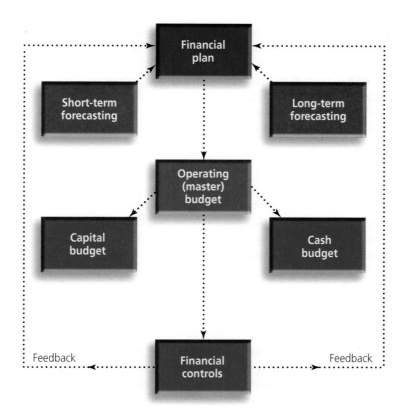

FIGURE | **11.2**

Financial Planning
Note the close link between
financial planning and
budgeting.

Forecasting Financial Needs

Forecasting is an important part of any firm's financial plan. A **short-term forecast** predicts revenues, costs, and expenses for a period of one year or less. This forecast is the foundation for most other financial plans, so its accuracy is critical. Part of the short-term forecast may be in the form of a **cash flow forecast**, which predicts the cash inflows and outflows in future periods, usually months or quarters. The inflows and outflows of cash recorded in the cash flow forecast are based on expected sales revenues and on various costs and expenses incurred and when the cash will be collected and costs will need to be paid.[4] The company's sales forecast estimates the firm's projected sales for a particular period. A business often uses its past financial statements as the starting point for projecting expected sales and various costs and expenses.[5]

A **long-term forecast** predicts revenues, costs, and expenses for a period longer than one year, and sometimes as far as five or ten years into the future. This forecast plays a crucial part in the company's long-term strategic plan, which asks questions such as these: What business are we in? Should we be in it five years from now? How much money should we invest in technology and new plant and equipment over the next decade? Will there be cash available to meet long-term obligations? Today, innovations in software assist financial managers in dealing with these long-term forecasting questions.

The long-term financial forecast gives top management, as well as operations managers, some sense of the income or profit potential possible with different strategic plans. Additionally, long-term projections assist financial managers with the preparation of company budgets.

Working with the Budget Process

The budgeting process depends on the accuracy of the firm's financial statements. Put simply, a budget is a financial plan.[6] Specifically, a **budget** sets forth management's expectations for revenues and, on the basis of those expectations, allocates the use of specific resources throughout the firm. The key financial statements—the balance sheet, income statement, and the cash flow statement—form the basis for the budgeting process. Often,

short-term forecast
Forecast that predicts revenues, costs, and expenses for a period of one year or less.

cash flow forecast
Forecast that predicts the cash inflows and outflows in future periods, usually months or quarters.

long-term forecast
Forecast that predicts revenues, costs, and expenses for a period longer than one year, and sometimes as far as five or ten years into the future.

budget
A financial plan that sets forth management's expectations, and, on the basis of those expectations, allocates the use of specific resources throughout the firm.

businesses use cost and revenue information, derived from past financial statements, as the starting point for forecasting company budgets.[7] The firm's budgets are compiled from short-term and long-term financial forecasts that need to be as accurate as possible. Since budgeting is clearly tied to forecasting, financial managers must take forecasting responsibilities seriously. A budget becomes the primary guide for the firm's financial operations and financial needs.

There are usually several types of budgets established in a firm's financial plan:

- An operating (master) budget
- A capital budget
- A cash budget

operating (master) budget
The budget that ties together all of a firm's other budgets; it is the projection of dollar allocations to various costs and expenses needed to run or operate the business, given projected revenues.

capital budget
A budget that highlights a firm's spending plans for major asset purchases that often require large sums of money.

cash budget
A budget that estimates a firm's projected cash inflows and outflows that the firm can use to plan for any cash shortages or surpluses during a given period.

The **operating (master) budget** ties together all of the firm's other budgets and summarizes the business's proposed financial activities. It can be defined more formally as the projection of dollar allocations to various costs and expenses needed to run or operate a business, given projected revenues.[8] How much the firm will spend on supplies, travel, rent, advertising, research, salaries, and so forth is determined in the operating (master) budget. The operating (master) budget is generally the most detailed (firms will prepare this budget for each of their divisions/departments) and most used budget that a firm prepares (see the following discussion on financial controls). Most firms will prepare an operating budget on a monthly basis for the next 12 months. Typically, those responsible for the activities reflected within the operating budget(s) will be involved in its preparation. Ultimately the firm's board of directors is responsible for approving all budgets. Often the entire budget process can take months and involve a significant amount of time.

A **capital budget** highlights a firm's spending plans for major asset purchases that often require large sums of money. The capital budget primarily concerns itself with the purchase of such assets as property, buildings, and equipment.

A **cash budget** estimates a firm's projected cash inflows and outflows that the firm can use to plan for any cash shortages or surpluses during a given period (e.g., monthly, quarterly). Cash budgets are important guidelines that assist managers in anticipating borrowing, debt repayment, operating expenses, and short-term investments.[9] A sample cash budget for our continuing example company, Very Vegetarian, is provided in Figure 11.3.

When first looking at the collection of sales, typically they occur over more than the month of sale. Sales, especially made in the latter part of a given month, will not be collected until the following month. The monthly cash collections in Figure 11.3 are based on collecting 20% of the current months sales and 80% of the prior month's sales. When forecasting the cash budget, not only do you want to identify the projected increase or decrease in cash for the month, but you also want to ensure that you maintain a minimum cash balance (a safety level). For planning purposes, you need to know when your projected cash balance may fall below the minimum, so that you can change how you will manage either your cash collections or your cash payments.

For example, when putting together the monthly cash budget in Figure 11.3, if the original payments schedule had projected salaries of $15,000, then February's cash budget would have ended up with total cash of $3,000. As such, after subtracting the minimum cash balance the excess cash would have had a balance of $−3,000. This amount would not be acceptable and therefore changes would have to be made to some of the assumptions. The other option would be to arrange for short-term financing to cover an expected shortfall.

Special processing equipment turns an average potato into the chips and fries we consume. The firm's capital budget is the financial tool that controls business spending for expensive assets such as this processing equipment. Such major assets are referred to as capital assets or property, plant, and equipment. What items are in your school's capital budget?

VERY VEGETARIAN Monthly Cash Budget			
	January	**February**	**March**
Sales forecast	$50,000	$45,000	$40,000
Collections			
Cash sales (20%)		$9,000	$8,000
Credit sales (80% of past month)		$40,000	$36,000
Monthly cash collection		$49,000	$44,000
Payments schedule			
Supplies and material		$11,000	$10,000
Salaries		12,000	12,000
Direct labour		9,000	9,000
Taxes		3,000	3,000
Other expenses		7,000	6,000
Monthly cash payments		$42,000	$40,000
Cash budget			
Cash flow		$7,000	$5,000
Beginning cash		−1,000	6,000
Total cash		$6,000	$11,000
Less minimum cash balance		−6,000	−6,000
Excess cash to market securities		$0	$5,000
Loans needed for minimum balance		0	0

FIGURE 11.3

A Sample Cash Budget for Very Vegetarian

Conversely, you should manage cash surpluses by planning for short-term investments (as illustrated in March in Figure 11.3) given the time value of money (which we will discuss later in this chapter). Regardless of how comfortable you are with your planning, investing your excess cash with fraudulent financiers like Bernie Madoff can have a devastating impact on your ability to carry on your business.

Clearly, financial planning plays an important role in the operations of the firm. This planning often determines what long-term investments are made, when specific funds will be needed, and how the funds will be generated. Once a company has forecast its short-term and long-term financial needs and established budgets to show how funds will be allocated, the final step in financial planning is to establish financial controls. We will discuss this topic in a moment. But first, the Spotlight on Small Business box challenges you to check your personal financial planning skill by developing a monthly budget for "You, Incorporated."

Establishing Financial Controls

Financial control is a process in which a firm periodically compares its actual revenues, costs, and expenses with its budget. Most companies hold at least monthly financial reviews as a way to ensure financial control. Such control procedures help managers identify variances to the financial plan and allow them to take corrective action if necessary. Financial controls also provide feedback to help reveal which accounts, which departments, and which people are varying from the financial plans. Finance managers can judge if such variances may or may not be justified, allowing them to make some financial adjustments to the plan when needed. The Making Ethical Decisions box details a situation a manager can face related to financial control. After the Progess Assessment, we will explore specific reasons why firms need to have funds readily available.

financial control
A process in which a firm periodically compares its actual revenues, costs, and expenses with its projected ones.

SPOTLIGHT ON Small Business

You, Incorporated, Monthly Budget

Let's develop a monthly budget for You, Inc. Be honest and think of everything that needs to be included for an accurate monthly budget for You! Much like a small business, when putting the monthly budget together, remember that the norm is to overestimate income and underestimate expenses. Often you need to revisit the budget a number of times before finalizing the numbers as you try to balance the income with the expenses to hopefully eliminate cash deficits.

	Expected	Actual	Difference
Monthly income:			
Wages (net pay after taxes)	_____	_____	_____
Savings account withdrawal	_____	_____	_____
Family support	_____	_____	_____
Other sources	_____	_____	_____
Total monthly income	_____	_____	_____
Monthly expenses:			
Fixed expenses			
Rent or mortgage	_____	_____	_____
Car payment	_____	_____	_____
Life insurance	_____	_____	_____
Tuition or fees	_____	_____	_____
Other fixed expenses	_____	_____	_____
Subtotal of fixed expenses	_____	_____	_____
Variable expenses			
Food	_____	_____	_____
Clothing	_____	_____	_____
Entertainment	_____	_____	_____
Transportation	_____	_____	_____
Phone	_____	_____	_____
Utilities	_____	_____	_____
Publications	_____	_____	_____
Internet connection	_____	_____	_____
Cable television	_____	_____	_____
Other expenses	_____	_____	_____
Subtotal of variable expenses	_____	_____	_____
Total expenses	_____	_____	_____
Total income − Total expenses = **Cash on hand/(Cash deficit)**	_____	_____	_____

Making Ethical Decisions

Playing It Safe

Suppose that you are the chairperson of the business administration department at a local community college. Like many other colleges, your campus has been affected financially by cuts in federal and provincial support and increasing expenses. As the end of the college's fiscal year approaches, you review your departmental budget and note that some unused travel funds, which you lobbied very hard to get for this year, are still available for faculty and staff development. The faculty and staff have not seemed interested in using the travel money for development purposes throughout the year, even though it has been readily available. You fear that if the funds are not spent this year, there's a good chance the college's chief financial officer will recommend cutting your travel budget for next year. That means if faculty and staff wish to travel for staff development next year and the needed funds are not available, you will have to limit the number of people who get to use the travel funds.

You consider telling faculty and staff that this money is available for about any type of travel or staff development they desire on a first-come, first-served basis, with no extensive justification needed concerning the educational benefit the college would receive from the travel requested. It's almost certain your superior will not contest any request you make for travel funds, and you can certainly be a hero in the eyes of your faculty and staff. However, you could also simply return the unused funds to the dean's office for disbursement to the college's general fund and risk what may happen next year. What will you do? What could result from your decision?

Progress Assessment

- Name three finance functions important to the firm's overall operations and performance.
- What are the three primary financial problems that cause firms to fail?
- In what ways do short-term and long-term financial forecasts differ?
- What is the organization's purpose in preparing budgets? Can you identify three different types of budgets?

THE NEED FOR FUNDS

In business, the need for funds never seems to cease. That's why sound financial management is essential to all businesses. Like our personal financial needs, those of a business change over time. For example, as a small business grows, its financial requirements shift considerably. (Remember the example of Parsley Patch.) The same is true with large corporations such as Barrick Gold Corporation, Irving Oil, and McCain Foods. As they venture into new product areas or markets, their capital needs increase, causing a need for funds for different reasons. In virtually all organizations, there are certain needs for which funds must be available. Key areas include:

- Managing day-to-day needs of the business
- Controlling credit operations
- Acquiring needed inventory
- Making capital expenditures

Let's look at the financial needs that affect both the smallest and the largest of businesses.

Managing Day-to-Day Needs of the Business

If workers expect to be paid on Friday, they don't want to have to wait until Monday for their paycheques. If tax payments are due on the fifteenth of the month, the government expects the money on time. If the payment on a business loan is due on the thirtieth, the

GreenBOX

Environmental Credits, Cap and Trade

In the late 1990s global leaders met in Kyoto, Japan, to address growing concern about the state of our environment. One of the initiatives coming out of these meeting was the Kyoto Protocol (an international agreement linked to the United Nations Framework Convention on Climate Change). The Protocol was a mechanism that would hopefully reduce global levels of greenhouse emissions (GHG). Starting in 2005, one of the ways countries could meet their respective targets was through the trading of carbon credits.

Carbon credits are meant to reduce greenhouse gas emissions and fight climate change through the use of carbon offsets. One popular form in Canada for carbon offsets involves tree planting. In the past few years, environmentalists and green-minded civilians have been jumping on board the carbon credit bandwagon, calculating their personal emissions and purchasing credits to neutralize the pollution they contribute to the atmosphere by the simple act of driving to work or running the dishwasher.

Carbon credits correspond to a determined tradable quantity of greenhouse gas (GHG) emissions. They are normally quoted in metric tonnes of carbon dioxide equivalent, and are used to offset emissions from the combustion of fossil fuels in any process that uses energy that emits GHGs, whether in industry, transportation, or the household.

In August of 2008, the province of British Columbia was the first Canadian jurisdiction to pass legislation dealing with climate change. They passed the Western Climate Initiative, which requires B.C. businesses to begin reducing their GHG emissions to 33 percent below their 2005 levels. If these greenhouse gases can't be reduced, companies will be required to offset their pollution via a new form of environmental currency, the carbon credit.

The city of Maple Ridge, British Columbia, and Shell Canada have had an agreement in place whereby a third party is planting trees in Maple Ridge, at no cost to the city, and selling the carbon credits to Shell Canada, who is then applying them to their Fort MacMurray operations. Companies (such as Planetair, a not-for-profit service offered by the Uniséfra International Centre) have been created to help individuals, corporations, and institutions reduce their climate footprint by raising awareness of how day-to-day activities impact global climate and supporting initiatives like the trading of carbon credits.

In 2007 the trading of carbon credits globally amounted to $30 billion. Many organizations now have to provide funds specifically for the purchase of these credits.

There's no shortage of carbon-neutral suppliers to choose from, but prices can vary. While some companies charge as little as US$5.50 per metric tonne of carbon dioxide, the price can go as high as US$13.00 per tonne.

Sources: Planetair Home Page, http://planetair.ca; and "Kyoto Protocol," United Nations Framework Convention on Climate Change, http://unfccc.int/kyoto_protocol/items/2830.php.

Collecting accounts receivable form some customers can be time-consuming and costly. Accepting credit cards like Visa, MasterCard, or American Express simplifies transactions, guarantees payment, and provides convenience for both customers and businesses at minimal cost. For what sort of purchases do you regularly use a credit card?

lender doesn't mean the first of the next month. Refer to the Green Box for a discussion of funding needs associated with an environmental issue. As you can see, funds have to be available to meet all operational costs of the business.

The challenge of sound financial management is to see that funds are available to meet these daily cash needs. Money has what is called a *time value*. In other words, if someone offered to give you $200 today or $200 one year from today, you would benefit by taking the $200 today. Why? It's very simple. You could invest the $200 you receive today, start collecting interest, and over a year's time your money would grow. The same thing is true in business; the interest gained on the firm's investments is important in maximizing the profit the company will gain. That's why financial managers encourage keeping a firm's cash expenditures to a minimum.[10] By doing this, the firm can free up funds for investment in interest-bearing accounts. It's also not unusual for finance managers to suggest that a company pay its bills as late as possible (unless a cash discount is available) but try to collect what's owed to it as fast as possible. This way, they maximize the investment potential of the firm's funds. Efficient cash management is particularly important to small firms in conducting their daily operations because their access to capital is generally much more limited than that of larger businesses.[11]

Controlling Credit Operations

Financial managers know that making credit available helps keep current customers happy and attracts new customers. In today's highly competitive business environment, many businesses would have trouble surviving without making credit available to customers.

The major problem with selling on credit is that a large percentage of a non-retailer's business assets could be tied up in its credit accounts (accounts receivable). At the same time the firm needs to pay the costs incurred for the making or provision of goods or services already sold to customers, who bought on credit. Financial managers in such firms must develop efficient collection procedures. For example, businesses often provide cash or quantity discounts to buyers who pay their accounts by a certain time. Also, finance managers carefully scrutinize old and new credit customers to see if they have a favourable history of meeting their credit obligations on time.[12] In essence, the firm's credit policy reflects its financial position and its desire to expand into new markets.

One way to decrease the time, and therefore expense, involved in collecting accounts receivable is to accept bank credit cards such as MasterCard or Visa.[13] This is convenient for both the customer and the business. The banks that issue such credit cards have already established the customer's creditworthiness, and have the expertise to manage credit. Businesses must pay a fee to accept credit cards, but the fees are generally not excessive compared to the benefits the cards provide. Accepting credit cards will enhance sales and a business no longer incurs the cost of running a credit department.

Acquiring Inventory

As we noted earlier in the text, effective marketing implies a clear customer orientation. This focus on the customer means that high-quality service and availability of goods are vital if a business expects to prosper in today's markets.[14] Therefore, to satisfy customers, businesses must maintain inventories that often involve a sizable expenditure of funds. Although it's true that firms expect to recapture their investment in inventory through sales to customers, a carefully constructed inventory policy assists in managing the firm's available funds and maximizing profitability. For example, Take-a-Dip, a neighbourhood ice cream parlour, ties up more funds in inventory (ice cream) in the summer than in the winter. It's obvious why. Demand for ice cream goes up in the summer.

Innovations such as just-in-time inventory (discussed in Chapter 9) help reduce the amount of funds a firm must tie up in inventory. Also, by carefully evaluating its inventory turnover ratio, a firm can better control its outflow of cash for inventory. It's important for a business of any size to understand that a poorly managed inventory system can seriously affect cash flow and drain its finances dry.

Making Capital Expenditures

Capital expenditures are major investments in either tangible long-term assets such as land, buildings, and equipment, or intangible assets such as patents, trademarks, and copyrights. In many organizations, the purchase of major assets—such as land for future expansion, manufacturing plants to increase production capabilities, research to develop new-product ideas, and equipment to maintain or exceed current levels of output—is essential. As you can imagine, these expenditures often require a huge portion of the organization's funds.

Expansion into new markets can cost large sums of money with no guarantee that the expansion will be commercially successful. Therefore, it's critical that companies weigh

capital expenditures
Major investments in either tangible long-term assets such as land, buildings, and equipment, or intangible assets such as patents, trademarks, and copyrights.

all possible options before committing what may be a large portion of their available resources.[15] Long-term financing could be used, as this type of expenditure should benefit a business for many years to come. For this reason, financial managers and analysts evaluate the appropriateness of such purchases or expenditures. Consider the situation in which a firm needs to expand its production capabilities due to increases in customer demand. One option is to buy land and build a new plant. Another option would be to purchase an existing plant or consider renting. Can you think of financial and accounting considerations that would come into play in this decision?

Obviously, the need for funds raises several questions in any firm: How does the firm obtain funds to finance operations and other business necessities? Will specific funds be needed by the firm in the long term or short term? How much will it cost to obtain these needed funds? Will these funds come from internal or external sources? Let's address these questions next.

Alternative Sources of Funds

debt financing
Funds raised through various forms of borrowing that must be repaid.

equity financing
Funds raised from operations within the firm or through the sale of ownership in the firm.

short-term financing
Borrowed funds that are needed for one year or less.

long-term financing
Borrowed funds that are needed for a period longer than one year.

Earlier in the chapter, you learned that finance is the function in a business that is responsible for acquiring and managing funds within the firm. Determining the amount of money needed and finding out the most appropriate sources from which to obtain these funds are fundamental steps in sound financial management. A firm can seek to raise needed capital through borrowing money (debt), selling ownership (equity), or earning profits (retained earnings). **Debt financing** refers to funds raised through various forms of borrowing that must be repaid. **Equity financing** is money raised from within the firm (from operations) or through the sale of ownership in the firm (e.g., the sale of stock). Firms can borrow funds either short-term or long-term. **Short-term financing** refers to funds needed for one year or less. In contrast, **long-term financing** refers to funds needed for a period longer than one year (usually two to ten years). Figure 11.4 summarizes the sources that can be used to acquire these needed short-term and long-term funds.

We'll explore the different sources of short-term and long-term financing fully in the next sections. For now it's important to know that businesses can use different methods of raising money. Before we go on, however, pause to check your understanding of what you just read by completing the Progress Assessment.

FIGURE | **11.4**

Sources of Short-Term and Long-Term Financing

Short-Term Financing	Long-Term Financing
Trade credit	**A. Debt Financing**
Promissory notes	Lending institutions (e.g., loan)
Family and friends	Selling bonds
Financial institutions (e.g., line of credit)	**B. Equity Financing**
Short-term loans	Retained earnings
Factoring	Venture capital
Commercial paper	Selling stock

Progress Assessment

- Money is said to have a time value. What does that mean?
- Why are accounts receivable a financial concern to the firm?
- What is the primary reason that an organization spends a good deal of its available funds on inventory and capital expenditures?
- What is the difference between debt financing and equity financing?

OBTAINING SHORT-TERM FINANCING

The bulk of a finance manager's job does not involve obtaining long-term funds. In fact, in small businesses, long-term financing is often out of the question. Instead, the day-to-day operation of the firm calls for the careful management of short-term financial needs. Firms need to borrow short-term funds to purchase additional inventory or to meet bills that come due. Also, as we do in our personal lives, a business sometimes needs to obtain short-term funds when the firm's cash reserves are low. This is particularly true, again, of small businesses.

Most small businesses are primarily concerned with just staying afloat until they are able to build capital and creditworthiness. Until a small business gets to that point, normally a lender will require some form of security for a loan. The security would typically be in the form of collateral (to be discussed later), or a personal guarantee. Firms can obtain short-term financing in several different ways. Let's look at the major forms of short-term financing and what's meant by secured and unsecured financing with regard to different ways of obtaining needed funds.

Trade Credit

The most widely used source of short-term funding, trade credit (an account payable), is the least expensive and most convenient form of short-term financing. **Trade credit** is the practice of buying goods or services now and paying for them later. For example, when a firm buys merchandise, it receives an invoice (a bill) much like the one you receive when you buy something with a credit card. As you will see, however, the terms that businesses receive are often different.

It is common for business invoices to contain items such as *2/10, net 30*. This means that the buyer can take a 2 percent discount if the invoice is paid within 10 days. The total bill is due (net) in 30 days if the purchaser does not take advantage of the discount. Finance managers need to pay close attention to such discounts because they create opportunities to reduce the firm's costs. Think about it for a moment: If the discount offered to the customer is 2/10, net 30, the customer will pay 2 percent more by using trade credit for an extra 20 days to pay the invoice.

Uninformed business people feel that 2 percent is insignificant, so they pay their bills after the discount period. By doing that, however, such firms lose a tremendous opportunity to save money—and it's much more than 2 percent! In the course of a year, 2 percent for 20 days adds up to a 36 percent interest rate (because there are eighteen 20-day periods in the year). If the firm is capable of paying within ten days, it is needlessly (and significantly) increasing its cost of financing by not doing so.

Some suppliers hesitate to give trade credit to organizations with a poor credit rating, no credit history, or a history of slow payment. In such cases, the supplier may insist that the customer sign a promissory note as a condition for obtaining credit. A **promissory note** is a written contract with a promise to pay a supplier a specific sum of money at a definite time. Promissory notes can be sold by the supplier to a bank at a discount (the amount of the note less a fee for the bank's services in collecting the amount due).

trade credit
The practice of buying goods and services now and paying for them later.

promissory note
A written contract with a promise to pay.

Family and Friends

Many small firms obtain short-term funds by borrowing money from family and friends. Because such funds are needed for periods of less than a year, friends or relatives are sometimes willing to help and the normal steps to obtain this type of funding are minimal. Such loans can create problems, however, if the firm does not understand cash flow.[16] As we discussed earlier, the firm may suddenly find itself having several bills coming due at the same time with no sources of funds to pay them. It is better, therefore, not to borrow from friends or relatives; instead, go to a commercial bank that fully understands the business's risk and can help analyze your firm's future financial needs.

Entrepreneurs appear to be listening to this advice. According to the National Federation of Independent Business, entrepreneurs today are relying less on family and friends as a source of borrowed funds than they have in the past. If an entrepreneur does, however, decide to ask family or friends for financial assistance, it's important that both parties (1) agree on specific loan terms, (2) put the agreement in writing, and (3) arrange for repayment in the same way they would for a bank loan. Such actions help keep family relationships and friendships intact.[17]

Commercial Banks and Other Financial Institutions

Banks are highly sensitive to risk and are often reluctant to lend money to small, relatively new, businesses. Nonetheless, a promising and well-organized venture may be able to get a bank loan. If a business is able to get such a loan, a small- or medium-sized business should have the person in charge of the finance function keep in close touch with the bank. It's also wise to see a banker periodically (as often as once a month) and send the banker all of the firm's financial statements and other required information so that the bank continues to supply funds when needed.

If you try to imagine the different types of business people who go to banks for a loan, you'll get a better idea of the role of financial management. Picture, for example, a farmer going to the bank to borrow funds for seed, fertilizer, supplies, and other needs. The farmer may buy these items in the spring and pay for them after the fall harvest. Now picture a local toy store buying merchandise for holiday-season sales. The store may borrow the money for such purchases in the summer and pay it back after the holidays. Restaurants may borrow funds at the beginning of the month and pay by the end of the month. It's evident that how much a business borrows and for how long often depends on the kind of business it is and how quickly the merchandise purchased with a bank loan can be resold or used to generate funds.

You can also imagine how important it is for specialists in a company's finance and accounting departments to do a cash flow forecast. Unfortunately, small-business owners generally lack the luxury of such specialists and must monitor cash flow themselves or look for outside help. By anticipating times when many bills will come due, a business can begin early to seek funds or sell other assets to prepare for a possible financial crunch. Often unplanned for events will happen and so it's important for a business person to keep friendly and close relations with his or her banker.[18] An experienced banker may spot cash flow problems early or be more willing to lend money in a crisis if a business person has established a strong, friendly relationship built on openness, trust, and sound management practices. It's important to remember that your banker

'Tis the season to shop. Ever wonder how retailers get the money to buy all of the items available during the holiday season? Department stores and other large retailers make extensive use of commercial banks and other lenders to borrow the money needed to buy merchandise to stock their shelves.

wants you to succeed almost as much as you do, so that the banker can earn interest as part of the repayment of loans. Bankers can be an invaluable support to any business, but especially to small, growing businesses.

Different Forms of Short-Term Loans

Banks and other financial institutions offer different types of loans to customers. A **secured loan** is a loan that's backed by something valuable, such as property. The item of value is called collateral. If the borrower fails to pay the loan, the lender may take possession of the collateral. For example, an automobile loan is a secured loan. If the borrower fails to pay the loan, the lender will repossess (take back) the car. Collateral takes some of the risk out of lending money.

Accounts receivable are assets that are often used by businesses as collateral for a loan; the process is called *pledging*. Some percentage of the value of accounts receivables pledged (usually about 75 percent) is advanced to the borrowing firm. As customers pay off their accounts, the funds received are forwarded to the lender in repayment of the funds that were advanced.[19] Inventory such as raw materials (e.g., coal, steel) can also be used as collateral or security for a business loan. Other assets that can be used as collateral include buildings, machinery, and company-owned stocks and bonds (to be discussed next).

The most difficult kind of loan to get from a bank or other financial institution is an unsecured loan. An **unsecured loan** doesn't require a borrower to offer the lending institution any collateral to obtain the loan. In other words, the loan is not backed by any assets. Normally, a lender will give unsecured loans only to highly regarded customers (e.g., long-standing customers or customers considered financially stable), who are seen as less risky.

If a business develops a good relationship with a bank, the bank may open a line of credit for the firm. A **line of credit** is a given amount of unsecured funds a bank will lend to a business. In other words, a line of credit is not guaranteed to a business. The primary purpose of a line of credit is to speed the borrowing process so that a firm does not have to go through the process of applying for a new loan every time it needs funds. The funds are generally available as long as the credit rating is satisfactory. As businesses mature and become more financially secure, the amount of credit often is increased, much like the credit limit on your credit card. Some firms will even apply for a **revolving credit agreement**, which is a line of credit that's guaranteed. However, banks usually charge a fee for guaranteeing such an agreement. Both lines of credit and revolving credit agreements are particularly good sources of funds for unexpected cash needs.

If a business is unable to secure a short-term loan from a bank, a financial manager may obtain short-term funds from **commercial finance companies**. These non-deposit-type organizations (often called non-banks) make short-term loans to borrowers who offer tangible assets (e.g., property, plant, and equipment) as collateral. Since commercial finance companies accept higher degrees of risk than commercial banks, they usually charge higher interest rates than banks. Commercial finance companies often make loans to individuals and businesses (e.g., General Electric loaned money to Air Canada as the airline restructured its business) that cannot get funds elsewhere.

Factoring Accounts Receivable

One relatively expensive source of short-term funds for a firm is **factoring**, which is the process of selling accounts receivable for cash. Factoring dates as far back as 4,000 years, during the days of ancient Babylon. Today, the Internet can help businesses find factors quickly so that they can solicit bids on a firm's accounts receivable promptly.[20] Here's how it works: Let's say that a firm sells many of its products on credit to consumers and other businesses, creating a number of accounts receivable. Some of the buyers may be slow to pay their bills, causing the firm to have a large amount of money due to it. A factor is a market intermediary (usually a financial institution such as a commercial bank or commercial finance company) that agrees to buy the accounts receivable from the firm,

secured loan
A loan backed by something valuable, such as property.

unsecured loan
A loan that's not backed by any specific assets.

line of credit
A given amount of unsecured funds a bank will lend to a business.

revolving credit agreement
A line of credit that is guaranteed by the bank.

commercial finance companies
Organizations that make short-term loans to borrowers who offer tangible assets as collateral.

factoring
The process of selling accounts receivable for cash.

at a discount, for cash. The discount rate charged depends on the age of the accounts receivable, the nature of the business, and the condition of the economy. The factor then collects and keeps the money that was owed the firm when it collects the accounts receivable.

Even though factoring can be an expensive way of raising cash, it is popular among small businesses. Factoring is very common in the clothing and furniture business, and is popular in financing a growing number of global trade ventures. What's important for you to note is that factoring is not a loan; factoring is the sale of an asset (accounts receivable). And while it's true that discount rates charged by factors are usually higher than loan rates charged by banks or commercial finance companies, remember that many small businesses cannot qualify for a loan. A company can reduce the cost of factoring if it agrees to reimburse the factor for slow-paying accounts, and it can reduce them even further if it assumes the risk of those people who don't pay at all.

Commercial Paper

commercial paper
Unsecured promissory notes of $100,000 and up that mature (come due) in 365 days or less.

Sometimes a large corporation needs funds for just a few months and wants to get lower rates of interest than those charged by banks. One strategy is to sell commercial paper. **Commercial paper** consists of unsecured promissory notes, in amounts of $100,000 and up, that mature (come due) in 365 days (366 days in a leap year) or less. Commercial paper states a fixed amount of money that the business agrees to repay to the lender (investor) on a specific date. The interest rate for commercial paper is stated in the agreement.

Still, because it is unsecured, only financially stable firms (mainly large corporations with excellent credit reputations) are able to sell commercial paper.[21] For these companies, it's a way to get short-term funds quickly and for less than the interest charged by commercial banks. Since most commercial paper matures in 30 to 90 days, it's also an investment opportunity for buyers who can afford to put up cash for short periods to earn some interest on their money at rates higher than they could earn by leaving surplus funds in their bank account. However, in late 2008 and into 2009, the ability for any large credit worthy corporation to sell commercial paper was significantly curtailed by the world-wide credit crunch.

Credit Cards

Letitia Mulzac seemed to have things going her way as she planned to open an imported gift and furniture shop. She had a great location and reliable business contacts lined up in India, Indonesia, and Morocco. Unfortunately, she didn't have enough money in her savings to start the business.[22] She did, however, have a Small Business Visa card with a high credit limit. Letitia was able to use her credit card to pay for the stock to start her business. Credit cards provide a readily available line of credit to a business that can save time and the likely embarrassment of being rejected for a bank loan. Of course, in contrast to the convenience that credit cards offer, they are extremely risky and costly. For example, interest rates can be exorbitant. There are also considerable penalties users must pay if they fail to make their payments on time. Credit cards are an expensive way to borrow money and are probably best used as a last resort. The recent credit problems were do in part to the excessive use of credit cards and the resulting inability of borrowers to make even the minimum monthly payments.

Progress Assessment

- What does the term "2/10, net 30" mean?
- What's the difference between trade credit and a line of credit at a bank?
- What's the difference between a secured loan and an unsecured loan?
- What is factoring? What are some of the considerations involved in establishing a discount rate in factoring?

OBTAINING LONG-TERM FINANCING

Forecasting helps the firm to develop a financial plan. This plan specifies the amount of funding the firm will need over longer time periods and the most appropriate sources for obtaining those funds. In setting long-term financing objectives, financial managers generally ask three major questions:

1. What are the organization's long-term goals and objectives?

2. What are the financial requirements needed to achieve these long-term goals and objectives?

3. What sources of long-term capital are available, and which will best fit our needs?

In business, long-term capital is used to buy capital assets such as plant and equipment, to develop new products, and to finance expansion of the organization. In major corporations, decisions involving long-term financing normally involve the board of directors and top management, as well as finance and accounting managers. Take pharmaceutical giant Pfizer, for example. Pfizer spends more than $8 billion a year researching and developing new products.[23] The actual development of a new innovative medicine can sometimes take ten years and cost close to $1 billion in company funds before the product is ever introduced in the market. It's easy to see why long-term financing decisions involve high-level managers at Pfizer. In small- and medium-sized businesses, it's also obvious that the owners are always actively involved in analyzing long-term financing opportunities that affect their company.

As we noted earlier in the chapter, long-term funding comes from two major types of financing: debt financing and equity financing. Let's look at these two important sources of long-term financing next. But first check out the Reaching Beyond Our Borders box to learn why a source of long-term funding is raising eyebrows in the financial community.

Reaching Beyond Our Borders

Sharing the Wealth?

When a nation's government has a budget surplus, it usually has many ways to invest the extra cash back into the country. But sometimes the surplus is too great to distribute immediately, so the country puts the money away in a sovereign wealth fund (SWF), where it can hold the excess assets for future investment.

For years, oil rich nations like United Arab Emirates (UAE) and Kuwait have been blessed with enormous budgetary surpluses, causing their SWFs to swell with capital. Kuwait's SWF boasts an impressive value of $200 billion, while UAE's fund Abu Dhabi Investment Authority (ADIA) is valued at an unbelievable $875 billion. With so much capital at their fingertips, these countries have started to run out of investment opportunities within their own borders, sending them on a search for foreign businesses to support, and their biggest target is the United States.

Though SWFs provide both distressed companies and those looking for significant investment capital with much-needed funds, the presence of foreign governments in the domestic business world concerns some who think SWFs will try to use their financial footholds to influence or even dictate government policy; some concerns have

also been expressed about the business acumen possessed by the managers of these funds. Despite such concerns, investment continues, and the United States and Canada remain an ideal investment target for foreign governments flush with funds.

For example, in 2007, a Chinese SWF invested billions of dollars in Morgan Stanley, a giant in the investment community. Similarly, ADIA dropped $7.5 billion in Citigroup, the largest bank in the United States, and bought out high-end retailer Barneys New York for $875 million. Resource-rich Canada has also attracted the interest of these funds. In 2009, a Chinese SWF invested $1.5 billion in Teck Resources. The huge funding requirements for the oil sands have also attracted a significant amount of interest.

Sources: Geoff Colvin, "America for Sale," *Fortune*, 18 February 2008; Emily Thornton and Stanley Reed, "A Power Player Emerges in the Gulf," *BusinessWeek*, 23 June 2008; Daniel Gross, "Exec Desperately Seeks SWF," *Newsweek*, 7 January 2008; and Bob Davis, "U.S. Pushes Sovereign Funds to Open to Outside Scrutiny," *The Wall Street Journal*, 26 February 2008.

Debt Financing

Debt financing involves borrowing money that the company has a legal obligation to repay. Firms can borrow funds by either getting a loan from a lending institution or issuing bonds.

Debt Financing by Borrowing Money from Lending Institutions

Firms that establish and develop rapport with a bank, insurance company, pension fund, commercial finance company, or other financial institution often are able to secure a long-term loan. Long-term loans are usually repaid within 3 to 7 years but may extend to 15 or 20 years. For such loans, a business must sign what is called a term-loan agreement. A **term-loan agreement** is a promissory note that requires the borrower to repay the loan in specified instalments (e.g., monthly or yearly). A major advantage of a business using this type of financing is that the interest paid on the long-term debt is tax deductible.

Sometimes the debt financing may result from selling an asset already owned to a financing company and then leasing the asset back. Ferries and railway rolling stock are two examples of assets that could be sold and leased back. The firm selling this type of asset immediately receives some cash and their future lease will be provided from the revenue earned from these assets.

Because they involve larger amounts of funding, long-term loans are often more complex than short-term loans. Also, since the repayment period could be quite long, lenders are not assured that their capital will be repaid in full. Therefore, most long-term loans require collateral, which may be in the form of real estate, machinery, equipment, stock, or other items of value. Lenders will also often require certain restrictions on a firm's operations to force it to act responsibly in its business practices. The interest rate for long-term loans is based on the adequacy of collateral, the firm's credit rating, and the general level of market interest rates. The greater the risk a lender takes in making a loan, the higher the rate of interest a lender requires. This principle is known as the **risk/return trade-off**.

Debt Financing by Issuing Bonds

If an organization is unable to obtain its long-term financing needs by getting a loan from a lending institution, it may try to issue bonds. A **bond** is a long-term debt obligation of a corporation or government. A company that issues a bond has a legal obligation to make regular interest payments to investors and to repay the entire bond principal amount at a prescribed time, called the maturity date.

Bonds can be issued by large organizations including different levels of government, government agencies, corporations, and foreign governments and corporations. Maybe your community is building a new stadium or cultural centre that requires selling municipal bonds. Potential investors (individuals and institutions) measure the risk involved in purchasing a bond against the return (interest) the bond promises to pay and the company's ability to repay the bond when promised. **Institutional investors** are large organizations—such as pension funds, mutual funds, insurance companies, and banks—that invest their own funds or the funds of others.

Interest is paid to the holder of the bond until the principal amount is repaid. Thus, in this context, **interest** is the payment the issuer of the bond makes to the bondholders for use of the borrowed money.

Like long-term loans, the interest rate paid on a bond varies according to factors such as the general level of market rates, the reputation of the company issuing the bond, and the going interest rate for government bonds or bonds of similar companies. Once an interest rate is set for a corporate bond issue (except in the case of what's called a floating-rate bond), it cannot be changed.

Bonds of all types are evaluated (rated) in terms of their risk to investors by independent rating firms such as Dominion Bond Rating Service (www.dbrs.com) and Standard & Poor's (www2.standardandpoors.com). Bond ratings can range from high quality to

term-loan agreement
A promissory note that requires the borrower to repay the loan in specified instalments.

risk/return trade-off
The principle that the greater the risk a lender takes in making a loan, the higher the interest rate required.

bond
A corporate certificate indicating that a person has lent money to a firm.

institutional investors
Large organizations—such as pension funds, mutual funds, insurance companies, and banks—that invest their own funds or the funds of others.

interest
The payment the issuer of the bond makes to the bondholders for use of the borrowed money.

bonds considered junk (which we discuss later in this chapter). Naturally, the higher the risk associated with the bond issue, the higher the interest rate the organization must offer investors. Investors should not assume high levels of risk if they don't feel that the potential return is worth it.

Bonds are issued with a denomination, which is the amount of debt represented by one bond. (Bonds are almost always issued in multiples of $1,000.) The principal is the face value of a bond. The issuing company is legally bound to repay the bond principal to the bondholder in full on the **maturity date**. For example, if Very Vegetarian issues a $1,000 bond with an interest rate of 5 percent and a maturity date of 2025, the company is agreeing to pay a bondholder a total of $50 in interest each year until a specified date in 2025, when the full $1,000 must be repaid. Though bond interest is quoted for an entire year, it is usually paid in two instalments (semi-annually). Maturity dates for bonds can vary. For example, firms such as Disney and Coca-Cola have issued bonds with 50-year maturity dates.

maturity date
The exact date the issuer of a bond must pay the principal to the bondholder.

Advantages and Disadvantages of Issuing Bonds
Bonds offer several long-term financing advantages to an organization. The decision to issue bonds is often based on advantages such as the following:

- Bondholders are creditors, not owners, of the firm and seldom have a vote on corporate matters; thus, management maintains control over the firm's operations.
- Interest paid on bonds is tax deductible to the firm issuing the bond.
- When bonds are repaid the debt obligation is eliminated.
- Bonds can be repaid before the maturity date if they contain a call provision. Some may also be converted to common shares (which is discussed later in this chapter).

But bonds also have their drawbacks:

- Bonds increase debt (long-term liabilities, an additional risk) and may adversely affect the market's perception of the firm.
- Paying interest on bonds is a legal obligation. If interest is not paid, bondholders can take legal action to force payment.
- The face value (denomination) of bonds must be repaid on the maturity date. Without careful planning, this repayment can cause cash flow problems when the bonds come due.

Different Classes of Bonds
Corporations can issue two different classes of corporate bonds. The first class is unsecured bonds, which are not backed by any collateral (such as equipment). These bonds are usually referred to as **debenture bonds**. Generally, only well-respected firms with excellent credit ratings can issue debenture bonds, since the only security the bondholder has is the reputation and credit history of the company.

The second class of bonds is *secured bonds*, which are backed by some tangible asset (collateral) that is pledged to the bondholder if bond interest isn't paid or the principal isn't paid back when promised. For example, a mortgage bond is a bond secured by company assets such as land and buildings. In issuing bonds, a company can choose to include different features in the various bond issues. Let's look at some possible special bond features.

debenture bonds
Bonds that are unsecured (i.e., not backed by any collateral such as equipment).

Special Bond Features
By now you should understand that bonds are issued with an interest rate, are unsecured or secured by some type of collateral, and must be repaid at their maturity date. This repayment requirement often leads companies to establish a reserve account called a **sinking fund**, whose primary purpose is to ensure that enough money will be available to repay bondholders on the bond's maturity date. Firms issuing sinking-fund bonds periodically retire (set aside) some part of the bond principal prior to maturity so that enough capital will be accumulated by the maturity date to pay off

sinking fund
A reserve account in which the issuer of a bond periodically retires some part of the bond principal prior to maturity so that enough capital will be accumulated by the maturity date to pay off the bond.

the bond. Sinking funds can be attractive to issuing firms and potential investors for several reasons:

- They provide for an orderly retirement (repayment) of a bond issue
- They reduce the risk the bond will not be repaid
- The market price of the bond is supported because the risk of the firm not repaying the principal on the maturity date is reduced

Another special feature that can be included in a bond issue is a call provision. A *callable bond* permits the bond issuer to pay off the bond's principal (i.e., call the bond) prior to its maturity date. Call provisions must be included when a bond is issued, and bondholders should be aware of whether a bond is callable. Callable bonds give companies some discretion in their long-term forecasting. For example, suppose that Very Vegetarian issued $50 million in 20-year bonds in 2010 with an interest rate of 10 percent. The yearly interest expense would be $5 million ($50 million times 10 percent). If market conditions change in 2014, and bonds issued of the same quality are only paying 7 percent, Very Vegetarian would be paying 3 percent, or $1.5 million ($50 million times 3 percent), in excess interest yearly. Obviously, Very Vegetarian could benefit if it could call in (pay off) the old bonds and issue new bonds at the lower interest rate. If a company calls a bond before maturity, investors in the bond are often paid a price above the bond's face value.

Another feature sometimes included in bonds is convertibility. A *convertible bond* is a bond that can be converted into common shares in the issuing company.[24] This feature is often an incentive for an investor to buy a bond. Why, you may ask, would bond investors want to convert their investment to shares? That's easy. If the value of the firm's common shares grows sizably over time, bondholders can compare the value of continued bond interest with the possible sizable profit they could gain by converting to a specified number of common shares. When we discuss common shares in the next section, this advantage will become more evident to you.

Progress Assessment

- What are the major forms of debt financing available to a firm?
- What role do bond rating services play in the bond market?
- What does it mean when a firm states that it is issuing a 9 percent debenture bond due in 2025?
- What are advantages and disadvantages of bonds?
- Why do companies like callable bonds? Why might investors dislike them?
- Why are convertible bonds attractive to investors?

Equity Financing

Rather than obtaining a long-term loan from a lending institution, or selling bonds to investors, a firm may look for long-term funding from equity financing. Equity financing comes from the owners of the firm. Therefore, equity financing involves selling ownership in the firm in the form of stock, or using earnings that have been retained by the company to reinvest in the business (retained earnings). A business can also seek equity financing by selling ownership in the firm to venture capitalists. Figure 11.5 compares debt and equity financing options.

Equity Financing by Selling Stock

There usually comes a time when a firm needs additional funds. One way to obtain such funds is to sell stock to private investors. **Stocks** represent ownership in a company. Both common and preferred shares (to be discussed soon) form the company's capital stock, also known as equity capital.[25]

stocks
Shares of ownership in a company.

	TYPE OF FINANCING	
	Debt	**Equity**
Management influence	There's usually none unless special conditions have been agreed on.	Common shareholders have voting rights.
Repayment	Debt has a maturity date. Principal must be repaid.	Stock has no maturity date. The company is never required to repay equity.
Yearly obligations	Payment of interest is a contractual obligation.	The firm isn't usually legally liable to pay dividends.
Tax issues	Interest is tax deductible.	Dividends are paid from after-tax income and aren't deductible.

FIGURE 11.5

Differences Between Debt and Equity Financing

The purchasers of stock become owners in the organization. The number of shares of stock that will be available for purchase is generally decided by the organization's board of directors. The first time a corporation offers to sell new stock to the general public is called an **initial public offering (IPO)**.

initial public offering (IPO)
The first public offering of a corporation's stock.

Equity Financing from Retained Earnings

Have you ever heard a business person say that he or she reinvests the firm's profits right back into the business? The profits the company keeps and reinvests in the firm are called retained earnings. Retained earnings often are a major source of long-term funds, especially for small businesses, which have fewer financing alternatives, such as selling bonds or stock, than large businesses do. However, large corporations also depend on retained earnings for needed long-term funding. In fact, retained earnings are usually the most favoured source of meeting long-term capital needs, since a company that uses them saves interest payments, dividends (payments for investing in stock), and any possible underwriting fees for issuing bonds or stock. Also, if a firm uses retained earnings, there is no new ownership created in the firm, as occurs with selling stock.

Unfortunately, many organizations do not have sufficient retained earnings on hand to finance extensive capital improvements or business expansion. If you think about it for a moment, it makes sense. What if you wanted to buy an expensive personal asset such as a new car? The ideal way to purchase the car would be to go to your personal savings account and take out the necessary cash. No hassle! No interest! Unfortunately, few people have such large amounts of cash available. Most businesses are no different. Even though they would like to finance long-term needs from retained earnings, few have enough to accomplish this.

Equity Financing from Venture Capital

The hardest time for a business to raise money is when it is just starting or moving into early stages of expansion. A start-up business typically has few assets and no market track record, so the chances of borrowing significant amounts of money from a bank are slim. Recall from Chapter 6 that venture capitalists are a potential source of funds. **Venture capital** is money that is invested in new or emerging companies that are perceived as having great profit potential. Venture capital firms are a possible source of start-up capital for new companies or companies moving into expanding stages of business.

venture capital
Money that is invested in new or emerging companies that are perceived as having great profit potential.

An entrepreneur or finance manager must remember that venture capitalists invest in a company in return for part ownership of the business. Venture capitalists concede that they expect higher-than-average returns and competent management performance for their investment. Therefore, venture capital firms are careful when choosing a firm to invest in.

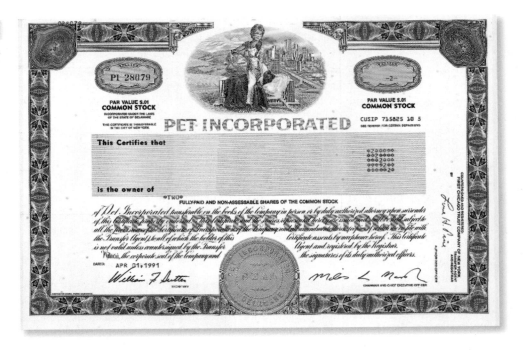

stock certificate
Evidence of stock ownership
that specifies the name of
the company, the number of
shares it represents, and the
type of stock being issued.

dividends
Part of a firm's profits that may
be distributed to shareholders
as either cash payments or
additional shares of stock.

A **stock certificate** is evidence of stock ownership that specifies the name of the company, the number of shares it represents, and the type of stock being issued (see Figure 11.6). Today, stock certificates are generally held electronically for the owners of the stock. Certificates sometimes indicate a stock's *par value*, which is a dollar amount assigned to each share of stock by the corporation's charter. Since par values do not reflect the market value of the stock, most companies issue "no-par" stock. **Dividends** are part of a firm's profits that may be distributed to shareholders as either cash payments or additional shares of stock. Dividends are declared by a corporation's board of directors and are generally paid quarterly. Although it's a legal obligation for companies that issue bonds to pay interest, companies that issue stock are not usually required to pay dividends.[26]

Advantages and Disadvantages of Issuing Stock

The following are some advantages to the firm of issuing stock:

- As owners of the business, shareholders never have to be repaid.
- There's usually no legal obligation to pay dividends to shareholders; therefore, income (retained earnings) can be reinvested in the firm for future financing needs.
- Selling stock has no risk since issuing stock creates no debt. (A corporation may also buy back its stock to improve its balance sheet and make the company appear stronger financially.)

Disadvantages of issuing stock include the following:

- As owners, shareholders (usually only common shareholders) have the right to vote for the company's board of directors. Typically one vote is granted for each share of stock. Hence, the direction and control of the firm can be altered by the sale of additional shares of stock.
- Dividends are paid out of profit after taxes and thus are not tax deductible.[27]
- Management's decisions can be affected by the need to keep stockholders happy.

Companies can issue two classes of shares: common and preferred. Let's see how these two forms of equity financing differ.

Issuing Common Shares **Common shares** are the most basic form of ownership in a firm. In fact, if a company issues only one type of stock, it must be common. Holders of common stock have the right (1) to vote for company board directors and important issues affecting the company, and (2) to share in the firm's profits through dividends, if approved by the firm's board of directors. Having voting rights in a corporation allows common shareholders to influence corporate policy since the elected board chooses the firm's top management and makes major policy decisions. Common shareholders also have what is called a pre-emptive right, which is the first right to purchase any new common shares the firm decides to issue. This right allows common shareholders to maintain a proportional share of ownership in the company.

Issuing Preferred Shares Owners of **preferred shares** enjoy a preference (hence the term *preferred*) in the payment of dividends; they also have a prior claim on company assets if the firm is forced out of business and its assets are sold. Normally, however, preferred shares do not include voting rights in the firm. Preferred shares are frequently referred to as a hybrid investment because they have characteristics of both bonds and stocks. To illustrate this, consider the treatment of preferred share dividends.

Preferred share dividends differ from common share dividends in several ways. Preferred shares are generally issued with a par value that becomes the base for the dividend the firm is willing to pay. For example, if a preferred share's par value is $100 a share and its dividend rate is 4 percent, the firm is committing to a $4 dividend for each share of preferred stock the investor owns (4 percent of $100 = $4). An owner of 100 shares of this preferred stock is promised a fixed yearly dividend of $400. In addition, the preferred shareholder is also assured that this dividend must be paid in full before any common share dividends can be distributed.[28]

Preferred shares are therefore quite similar to bonds; both have a face (or par) value and both have a fixed rate of return. Also, like bonds, rating services rate preferred shares according to risk. So how do bonds and preferred shares differ? Remember that companies are legally bound to pay bond interest and to repay the face value (denomination) of the bond on its maturity date. In contrast, even though preferred share dividends are generally fixed, they do not legally have to be paid; also shares (preferred or common) never have to be repurchased. Though both bonds and stock can increase in market value, the price of stock generally increases at a higher percentage than bonds. Of course, the market value of both could also go down. Figure 11.7 compares features of bonds and stock.

common shares
The most basic form of ownership in a firm; it confers voting rights and the right to share in the firm's profits through dividends, if offered by the firm's board of directors.

preferred shares
Stock that gives its owners preference in the payment of dividends and an earlier claim on assets than common shareholders if the company is forced out of business and its assets are sold.

	Bonds	Common Share	Preferred Share
Interest or Dividends			
Must be paid	Yes	No	Depends
Pays a fixed rate	Yes	No	Usually
Deductible from payor's income tax	Yes	No	No
Canadian payee is taxed at reduced rate		(if payor company is Canadian)	
	No	Yes	Yes
Stock or bond			
Has voting rights	No	Yes	Not normally
May be traded on the stock exchange	Yes	Yes	Yes
Can be held indefinitely	No	Yes	Depends
Is convertible to common shares	Maybe	No	Maybe

FIGURE | 11.7

Comparison of Bonds and Stock of Public Companies The different features help both the issuer and the investor decide which vehicle is right for each of them at a particular time.

Special Features of Preferred Shares   Preferred shares can have special features that do not apply to common shares. For example, like bonds, preferred shares can be callable. This means that preferred shareholders could be required to sell back their shares to the corporation. Preferred shares can also be convertible to common shares. Another important feature of preferred shares is that they can often be cumulative. That is, if one or more dividends are not paid when promised, the missed dividends will be accumulated and paid later to a cumulative preferred shareholder. This means that all dividends, including any back dividends, must be paid in full before any common share dividends can be distributed. Figure 11.8 lists some optional features of preferred shares.

FIGURE	11.8

Optional Features Available with Preferred Shares
Each feature holds some attraction for the potential investor.

Preferred Share Feature	Description
Convertible	The shares may be exchanged after a stated number of years for common shares at a preset rate, at the option of the shareholder.
Cumulative	If the dividend is not paid in full in any year, the balance is carried forward (accumulates). The cumulative unpaid balance must be paid before any dividends are paid to common shareholders.
Callable	The company that issued the shares has the right after a stated number of years to call them back by repaying the shareholders their original investment.*
Redeemable	After a stated number of years, the investor may return the stock and ask for repayment of his or her investment.*

*If the shares are also cumulative, all dividend arrears must be paid as well.

Progress Assessment

- What are the major forms of equity financing available to a firm?
- Name at least two advantages and two disadvantages of issuing stock as a form of equity financing.
- What are the major differences between common shares and preferred shares?
- In what ways are preferred shares similar to bonds? How are they different?

SUMMARY

1. Finance comprises those functions in a business responsible for acquiring funds for the firm, managing funds within the firm (e.g., preparing budgets and doing cash flow analysis), and planning for the expenditure of funds on various assets.

   What are the most common ways in which firms fail financially?
   The most common financial problems are (1) undercapitalization, (2) poor control over cash flow, and (3) inadequate expense control.

   What do financial managers do?
   Financial managers plan, budget, control funds, obtain funds, collect funds, audit, manage taxes, and advise top management on financial matters.

   LO ▶ 1 Describe the importance of finance and financial management to an organization, and explain the responsibilities of financial managers.

2. Financial planning involves forecasting short-term and long-term needs, budgeting, and establishing financial controls.

   What are the three budgets of finance?
   The operating (master) budget summarizes the information in the other two budgets; it projects dollar allocations to various costs and expenses given various revenues. The capital budget is the spending plan for expensive assets, such as property, plant, and equipment. The cash budget is the projected cash inflows and outflows for a period and the balance at the end of a given period.

   LO ▶ 2 Outline the financial planning process, and explain the three key budgets in the financial plan.

3. During the course of a business's life, its financial needs shift considerably.

   What are the major financial needs for firms?
   Businesses have financial needs in four major areas: (1) managing day-to-day needs of the business, (2) controlling credit operations, (3) acquiring needed inventory, and (4) making capital expenditures.

   What's the difference between short-term and long-term financing?
   Short-term financing refers to funds that will be repaid in less than one year, whereas long-term financing refers to funds that will be repaid over a specific time period of more than one year.

   What's the difference between debt financing and equity financing?
   Debt financing refers to funds raised by borrowing (going into debt), whereas equity financing is raised from within the firm (through retained earnings) or by selling ownership in the company to venture capitalists or by issuing shares to other investors.

   LO ▶ 3 Explain the major reasons why firms need operating funds, and identify various types of financing that can be used to obtain these funds.

4. Sources of short-term financing include trade credit, promissory notes, family and friends, commercial banks and other financial institutions, factoring, and commercial paper.

   Why should businesses use trade credit?
   Trade credit is the least expensive and most convenient form of short-term financing. Businesses can buy goods today and pay for them sometime in the future.

   What's a line of credit?
   It is an agreement by a bank to lend up to a specified amount of money to the business at any time, as long as certain conditions are met. A revolving credit agreement is a line of credit that guarantees a loan will be available—for a fee.

   What's the difference between a secured loan and an unsecured loan?
   An unsecured loan has no collateral backing it. Secured loans have collateral pledged as security such as accounts receivable, inventory, or other property of value.

   LO ▶ 4 Identify and describe different sources of short-term financing.

Is factoring a form of secured loan?
No, factoring means selling accounts receivable at a discounted rate to a factor (an intermediary that pays cash for those accounts).

What's commercial paper?
Commercial paper is a corporation's unsecured promissory note maturing in 365 days or less.

LO ▶ 5 Identify and describe different sources of long-term financing.

5. One of the important functions of a finance manager is to obtain long-term financing.

What are the major sources of long-term financing?
Debt financing involves the sale of bonds and long-term loans from banks and other financial institutions. Equity financing is obtained through the sale of company stock, from the firm's retained earnings, or from venture capital firms.

What are the two major forms of long-term financing?
Debt financing comes from two sources: selling bonds and borrowing from individuals, banks, and other financial institutions. Bonds can be secured by some form of collateral or can be unsecured. The same is true of loans.

KEY TERMS

bond 316
budget 303
capital budget 304
capital expenditures 309
cash budget 304
cash flow forecast 303
commercial finance companies 313
commercial paper 314
common shares 321
debenture bonds 317
debt financing 310
dividends 320
equity financing 310

factoring 313
finance 300
financial control 305
financial management 300
financial managers 300
initial public offering (IPO) 319
institutional investors 316
interest 316
line of credit 313
long-term financing 310
long-term forecast 303
maturity date 317
operating (master) budget 304
preferred shares 321

promissory note 311
revolving credit agreement 313
risk/return trade-off 316
secured loan 313
short-term financing 310
short-term forecast 303
sinking fund 317
stock certificate 320
stocks 318
term-loan agreement 316
trade credit 311
unsecured loan 313
venture capital 319

CRITICAL THINKING

1. Budgets are designed to keep decision-makers informed of progress compared to company plans. An important theme of this book is the need for managers to be flexible so that they can adapt quickly to rapidly changing conditions. This often means modifying previous plans. Do you see any conflict between budgets and such flexibility? How do managers stay within the confines of budgets when they must shift gears to accommodate a rapidly changing world?

Which forecasts are more affected by these problems, short-term or long-term? Why?

2. Considering the disadvantages and advantages of different forms of raising funds, which method would you adopt if you had to make that decision in your company? How would your decision be affected in a high-interest year? If your company was doing well, what would you do for short-term financing? For long-term financing? How would you justify your choices?

DEVELOPING WORKPLACE SKILLS

1. Visit a local bank lending officer. Ask what the current interest rate is and what rate small businesses pay for short-term and long-term loans. Ask for blank forms that borrowers use to apply for loans. Share these forms with your class, and explain the types of information they ask for.

2. Use information from Standard & Poor's and Dominion Bond Rating Service to find their evaluation of the bonds of three large Canadian companies. Ask the librarian what similar references are available. Report what you find to the class.

3. Many businesses try to raise funds through initial public offerings (IPOs). Access your library and use the services of Proquest, or visit securities dealers' Web sites such as www.bmonesbittburns.com and www.tdwaterhouse.ca. Find two IPOs that have been offered during the past six months. Track the performance of each IPO from its introduction to its present price.

4. Analyze the risks and opportunities of investing today in bonds and stock. Assume that your great-aunt Hildi just left you $10,000. Since you and your parents have already saved enough money to cover your education bills, you decide to invest the money so that you can start your own business after you graduate. How will you invest your money? Why? Name specific investments.

TAKING IT TO THE NET 1

www.mcgrawhillconnect.ca

Purpose

To research the current lending practices between banks and small businesses.

Exercises

1. Check out the Web site of the Canadian Bankers Association (www.cba.ca) to see if you can find information on the trend of lending to small businesses. What was the rate of refusal of loans to small businesses during the last few years? Is the refusal rate rising, declining, or unchanged?

2. Look through the Web site of the Business Development Bank of Canada (BDC) at www.bdc.ca to see how helpful it is. If you were starting a small business, would the information lead you to apply for a loan with the BDC? Is there anything you were looking for that you could not find? Is there much information for those wanting to start an Internet-based company?

TAKING IT TO THE NET 2

www.mcgrawhillconnect.ca

Purpose

To learn how small-business owners can obtain support for financing from the federal government.

Exercise

The Canada Small Business Financing Program (www.ic.gc.ca/eic/site/csbfp-pfpec.nsf/eng/home) seeks to increase the availability of loans and capital leases for establishing, expanding, modernizing, and improving small businesses. Visit the site and answer the following questions.

1. How does this financing program work?

2. Which financial institutions participate in the program?

3. What are the restrictions on which type of businesses can participate in the program?

4. What type of purchase is eligible for financing, what percentage of the purchase can be financed, and what is the maximum amount that can be financed?

ANALYZING MANAGEMENT DECISIONS

Making Dreams Come True

Carlos Galendez had big dreams but very little money. He had worked more than ten years washing dishes and then as a cook for two major restaurants. Finally, his dream to save enough money to start his own Mexican restaurant came true. Galendez opened his restaurant, Casa de Carlos, with a guaranteed loan. His old family recipes and appealing Hispanic decor helped the business gain immediate success. He repaid his small-business loan within 14 months and immediately opened a second location, and then a third. Casa de Carlos became one of the largest Mexican restaurant chains in the area.

Galendez decided that the company needed to go public to help finance expansion. He believed that continued growth was beneficial to the company, and that offering ownership was the way to bring in loyal investors. Nevertheless, he wanted to make certain that his family maintained a controlling interest in the firm's stock. Therefore, in its initial public offering (IPO), Casa de Carlos offered to sell only 40 percent of the company's available shares to investors. The Galendez family kept control of the remaining 60 percent.

As the public's craving for Mexican food grew, so did the fortunes of Casa de Carlos, Inc. By early 2007, the company enjoyed the enviable position of being light on debt and heavy on cash. But the firm's debt position changed dramatically when it bought out Captain Ahab's Seafood Restaurants and, two years later, expanded into full-service wholesale distribution of seafood products with the purchase of Ancient Mariner Wholesalers.

The firm's debt increased, but the price of its stock was up and all of its business operations were booming. Then tragedy struck the firm when Carlos Galendez died suddenly from a heart attack. His oldest child, Maria, was selected to take control as chief executive officer. Maria Galendez had learned the business from her father, who had taught her to keep an eye out for opportunities that seemed fiscally responsible. Even so, the fortunes of the firm began to shift. Two major competitors were taking market share from Casa de Carlos, and the seafood venture began to flounder (pun intended). Also, consumer shifts in eating habits and the slight recession in 2008 encouraged consumers to spend less, causing the company some severe cash flow problems. It was up to Maria Galendez as CEO to decide how to get the funds the firm needed for improvements and other expenses. Unfortunately, several local banks wouldn't expand the firm's credit line, so she considered the possibility of a bond or stock offering to raise capital for the business. Her decision could be crucial to the future of the firm.

Discussion Questions

1. What advantages do bonds offer a company such as Casa de Carlos? What disadvantages do bonds impose?

2. What would be the advantages and disadvantages of the company's offering new stock to investors?

3. Are any other options available to Maria Galendez?

4. What choice would you make and why?

APPENDIX B
Risk Management

UNDERSTANDING BUSINESS RISKS

The management of risk is a major issue for businesses throughout the country.[1] Almost every day you hear about a hurricane, earthquake, flood, fire, airplane crash, riot, or car accident that destroyed property or injured someone. An accident that involves a major personality may be front-page news for weeks. Such reports are so much a part of the news that we tend to accept these events as part of everyday life. But events involving loss mean a great deal to the business people involved. They must pay to restore the property and compensate those who are injured.

After two wars (Afghanistan and Iraq), corporate and government scandals, several major hurricanes and tornadoes, and the threat of terrorists and a pandemic flu, it is no surprise that risk management is getting more attention.[2] The risks of serious information security failures are manifold. Computer hackers and computer viruses have become a real threat, and identity theft has become commonplace.[3]

In addition to the newsmaking stories, thousands of other incidents involve business people in lawsuits. Lawsuits in recent years have covered everything from job-related accidents to product liability. In some provinces, insurance is not available or is too expensive for high-risk businesses. New legislation has been passed in some areas to lessen some of these risks so that companies can obtain insurance coverage again at a reasonable price.[4]

The outbreak of listeriosis in the late summer of 2008 claimed many lives. The financial impact on Maple Leaf Foods both in terms of lost sales and lawsuits was significant. Real financial risk relates to the variability of costs and revenues resulting in the inability to cover off all obligations. The future cannot be predicted but the financial risk that arises from uncertainty can be managed. Business needs to identify, measure, and appreciate the consequences of financial risk, and then take action to transfer or mitigate it. Financial risk management and risk taking are two sides of the same coin. Risk management is the process of understanding, costing, and efficiently managing unexpected levels of variability in the financial outcomes for a business. Risk management is about firms actively selecting the type and level of risk that is appropriate for them to assume. What current resources are sacrificed for future uncertain returns? Problems can arise when risk factors suddenly begin to act together.[5] Risk management is all about minimizing the losses from unexpected events.

How Rapid Change Affects Risk Management

Changes are occurring so fast in the business world that it is difficult to keep up with the new risks involved. For example, who in the organization can evaluate the risks of buying or selling products over the Internet or what the price of a barrel of oil will be six months from now? As companies reach global markets over the Internet, who in the company watches for fluctuations in the world's currencies and how they may affect profits? Will global warming affect weather conditions? How will climate change affect farms and cattle raising? What would happen to the economy if there were a series of terrorist attacks on the country? What would happen if a flu pandemic were to occur?[6] As you can see, risk management is getting more complex and more critical for all businesses. Those who do business in other countries face increasing risk from social unrest—think of the ongoing strife in the Middle East, Africa, and other third world countries.

The last 10 years have seen significant growth in new institutions that are in the business of taking and managing risks (hedge funds). Credit derivatives have been used to redistribute part or all of a company's credit-risk exposures, which if properly dispersed should minimize the shocks to the overall economic system. This thinking was turned on its head in the Fall of 2008. Derivative markets have made it easier to take on large amounts of risks, but as we saw in 2008, a "lemming" mentality can take over after a crisis gets underway, which increases market volatility. These problems might also be due to regulators who have colluded with the financial community to incorrectly value risky assets when the stakes are very high. Let's explore how companies go about managing risk. We'll begin by going over a few key terms.

MANAGING RISK

The term **risk** refers to the chance of loss, the degree of probability of loss, and the amount of possible loss. There are two different kinds of risk:

- **Speculative risk** involves a chance of either profit or loss. It includes the chance a firm takes to make extra money by buying new machinery, acquiring more inventory, and making other decisions in which the probability of loss may be relatively low and the amount of loss is known.[7] An entrepreneur takes speculative risk on the chance of making a profit.[8] In business, building a new plant is a speculative risk because it may result in a loss or a profit.[9]

- **Pure risk** is the threat of loss with no chance for profit. Pure risk involves the threat of fire, accident, or loss. If such events occur, a company loses money; but if the events do not occur, the company gains nothing.[10]

The risk that is of most concern to businesspeople is pure risk. Pure risk threatens the very existence of some firms. Once such risks are identified, firms have several options:

1. Reduce the risk
2. Avoid the risk
3. Self-insure against the risk
4. Buy insurance against the risk

We'll discuss the option of buying insurance in detail later. In the next sections, we will discuss each of the other alternatives for managing risk. These steps should be taken to lower the need for outside insurance.

Reducing Risk

A firm can reduce risk through internal controls and by establishing loss-prevention programs such as fire drills, health education, safety inspections, equipment maintenance, accident prevention programs, and so on. Many retail stores, for example, use mirrors, video

risk
The chance of loss, the degree of probability of loss, and the amount of possible loss.

speculative risk
A chance of either profit or loss.

pure risk
The threat of loss with no chance for profit.

cameras, and other devices to prevent shoplifting. Water sprinklers and smoke detectors are used to minimize fire loss. In industry, most machines have safety devices to protect workers' fingers, eyes, and so on.

Product recalls can also reduce risk. A classic example is the highly publicized decision by Johnson & Johnson Company to pull its Tylenol pills off the shelves across the country when sabotaged capsules killed several people. As mentioned already, the Listeriosis outbreak resulted in Maple Leaf Foods recalling all its production from their Toronto facility.[11]

Employees as well as managers can reduce risk. For example, truck drivers can wear seat belts to minimize injuries from accidents, operators of loud machinery can wear earplugs to reduce the chance of hearing loss, and those who lift heavy objects can wear back braces. The beginning of an effective risk management strategy is a good loss-prevention program. However, high insurance rates have forced some people to go beyond merely preventing risks to the point of avoiding risks, and in extreme cases by going out of business.

Avoiding Risk

Many risks cannot be avoided. There is always the chance of fire, theft, accident, or injury. But some companies are avoiding risk by not accepting hazardous jobs and by outsourcing shipping and other functions.[12] The threat of lawsuits has driven away some drug companies from manufacturing vaccines, and some consulting engineers refuse to work on hazardous sites. Some companies are losing outside members of their boards of directors for lack of liability coverage protecting them from legal action against the firms they represent.

Self-Insuring

self-insurance
The practice of setting aside money to cover routine claims and buying only "catastrophe" policies to cover big losses.

Many companies, municipalities, and other not-for-profit organizations have turned to self-insurance because they either can't find or can't afford conventional property/casualty policies. Such firms set aside money to cover routine claims and buy only "catastrophe" insurance policies to cover big losses. **Self-insurance**, then, lowers the cost of insurance by allowing companies to take out insurance only for larger losses.

Self-insurance is most appropriate when a firm has several widely distributed facilities or where many similar organizations, like universities, self-insure as a group. The risk from fire, theft, or other catastrophe is then more manageable. Firms with huge facilities, in which a major fire or earthquake could destroy the entire operation, usually turn to insurance companies to cover the risk.

Buying Insurance to Cover Risk

Although well-designed, consistently enforced risk-prevention programs reduce the probability of claims, accidents do happen. Insurance is the armour individuals, businesses, and non-profit organizations use to protect themselves from various financial risks. For this protection, such organizations spend about 10 percent of gross domestic product (GDP) on insurance premiums. Some insurance protection is provided by governments (see Figure B.1), but most risks must be covered by individuals and businesses on their own.[13] We will continue our discussion of insurance by identifying the types of risks that are uninsurable, followed by those that are insurable.

What Risks Are Uninsurable?

uninsurable risk
A risk that no insurance company will cover.

Not all risks are insurable, even risks that once were covered by insurance. An **uninsurable risk** is one that no insurance company will cover. Examples of things that you cannot insure include market risks (e.g., losses that occur because of price changes, style changes, or new products that make your product obsolete); political risks (e.g., losses from war or government restrictions on trade); some personal risks (such as loss of a job); and some risks of operation (e.g., strikes or inefficient machinery).

Type of Insurance	What It Does
Canadian Public Health Care	Provides all Canadians with free basic health care, free doctor visits, free hospital ward care, free surgery, and free drugs and medicine while in hospital.
Employment Insurance	Provides financial benefits, job counselling, and placement services for unemployed workers.
Old Age Security /Canada Pension Plan	Provides retirement benefits and life insurance.
Canada Mortgage Housing Corporation (CMHC)	Provides mortgage insurance to lenders to protect against default by home buyers.
Canada Deposit Insurance Corporation	Provides re-imbursement of up to $100,000 for funds held in banks, trusts, and loan companies that fail.
Provincial Auto Insurance (Manitoba, Saskatchewan, British Columbia)	Provides all citizens in these provinces with standard automobile insurance including collision, liability, and accident benefits.

FIGURE | **B.1**

Public Insurance
Provincial or federal government agencies that provide insurance protection.

What Risks Are Insurable?

An **insurable risk** is one that the typical insurance company will cover. Generally, insurance companies use the following guidelines when evaluating whether or not a risk is insurable:

1. The policyholder must have an **insurable interest**, which means that the policyholder is the one at risk to suffer a loss. You cannot, for example, buy fire insurance on your neighbour's house and collect if it burns down.
2. The loss should be measurable.
3. The chance of loss should be measurable.
4. The loss should be accidental.
5. The risk should be dispersed; that is, spread among different geographical areas so that a flood or other natural disaster in one area would not bankrupt the insurance company.
6. The insurance company can set standards for accepting the risk.

insurable risk
A risk that the typical insurance company will cover.

insurable interest
The possibility of the policy-holder to suffer a loss.

UNDERSTANDING INSURANCE POLICIES

An **insurance policy** is a written contract between the insured (an individual or organization) and an insurance company that promises to pay for all or part of a loss. A **premium** is the fee charged by the insurance company or, in other words, the cost of the insurance policy.

Like all other private businesses, an insurance company is designed to make a profit. Insurance companies therefore gather data to determine the extent of various risks. What makes the acceptance of risk possible for insurance companies is the law of large numbers.

The **law of large numbers** states that if a large number of people or organizations are exposed to the same risk, a predictable number of losses will occur during a given period of time. Once the insurance company predicts the number of losses likely to occur, it can determine the appropriate premiums for each policy it issues. The premium is supposed to be high enough to cover expected losses and yet earn a profit for the firm and its stockholders. Today, many insurance companies are charging high premiums not for past risks but for the anticipated costs associated with the increasing number of court cases and high damage awards.

Insurance companies can also earn revenue from investing the premiums they collect. Premiums are usually collected at the beginning of a policy period. Until policy claims need to be paid out, premiums can be placed in very secure interest paying investments.

insurance policy
A written contract between the insured and an insurance company that promises to pay for all or part of a loss.

premium
The fee charged by an insurance company for an insurance policy.

law of large numbers
Principle that if a large number of people are exposed to the same risk, a predictable number of losses will occur during a given period of time.

Rule of Indemnity

The **rule of indemnity** says that an insured person or organization cannot collect more than the actual loss from an insurable risk. One cannot gain from risk management; one can only minimize losses. One cannot, for example, buy two insurance policies and collect from both for the same loss. If a company or person carried two policies, the two insurance companies would calculate the loss and divide the reimbursement between them.

Types of Insurance Companies

There are two major types of insurance companies. A **stock insurance company** is owned by stockholders, just like any other investor-owned company. A **mutual insurance company** is owned by its policyholders. A mutual insurance company, unlike a stock company, does not earn profits for its owners. It is a non-profit organization, and any excess funds (over losses, expenses, and growth costs) go to the policyholders in the form of dividends or premium reductions.

INSURANCE COVERAGE FOR VARIOUS KINDS OF RISK

As we have discussed, risk management consists of reducing risk, avoiding risk, self-insuring, and buying insurance. There are many types of insurance that cover various losses: property and liability insurance, health insurance, and life insurance. Property losses result from fires, accidents, theft, or other perils. Liability losses result from property damage or injuries suffered by others for which the policyholder is held responsible. Let's begin our exploration of insurance by looking at health insurance.

Health Insurance

Canada provides universal health care for every citizen. The description of the coverage provided is found in Figure B.1. Above and beyond this insurance, individuals can be covered by benefit plans usually provided through their employer or a group the individual is affiliated with. Coverage typically includes dental, extended health care, survivors' benefits, worldwide travel benefits, income continuance, and pensions.

Dental coverage can vary from basic preventative care through to major procedures (e.g., dentures). Extended health care can cover prescription drugs, a number of paramedical services (e.g., massage), vision care, and upgraded hospital accommodation, normally up to a semi-private room. Worldwide travel benefits cover expenses that are the result of an accident or unexpected illness incurred while on business or vacation in a foreign country. Eligible expenses may include hospital accommodation and private duty nursing. Survivor benefits can include a death benefit (lump sum payment) for a spouse and dependent children, as well as a pension. Income continuance provides for both short- and long-term disability. Pensions will provide monthly income for a retired employee.

Over the past few years, the cost of benefit plans have increased significantly. As a result, coverage limits have been reduced, and a greater share of the cost has become the responsibility of the insured.

Disability Insurance

Disability insurance replaces part of your income (50 to 70 percent) if you become disabled and thus unable to work. There usually is a period during which you must be disabled (e.g., 60 days) before you can begin collecting. Many employers provide this type of insurance (as described above), but some do not. In either case, insurance experts recommend that you get disability insurance because the chances of becoming disabled by a disease or accident when young are much higher than the chance of dying. The premiums for such insurance vary according to age, occupation, and income.

Workplace Safety and Insurance

Provincial Workplace Safety and Insurance Boards guarantee payment of wages, medical care, and rehabilitation services (e.g., retraining) for employees who are injured on the job. Employers in all provinces and territories are required to provide this insurance. This insurance also provides benefits to the survivors of workers who die as a result of work-related injuries. The cost of insurance varies in relation to the company's safety record, its payroll, and the types of hazards faced by workers. For example, it costs more to insure a steelworker than an accountant.

Liability Insurance

Professional liability insurance covers people who are found liable for professional negligence. For example, if a lawyer gives advice carelessly and the client loses money, the client may then sue the lawyer for an amount equal to that lost which the insurance would cover. Professional liability insurance is also known as malpractice insurance. While you may think of doctors and dentists when you hear that term, the fact is that many professionals, including accountants, are buying professional liability insurance because of large lawsuits their colleagues have faced.

Product liability insurance covers liability arising out of products sold. If a person is injured by, say, a ladder or some other household good, he or she may sue the manufacturer for damages. Insurance usually covers such losses.

Personal liability insurance covers liability of any individual through a negligent act either at work or at home.

Premises liability insurance would cover claims resulting from an accident occurring either at a place of work or personal residence.

OTHER BUSINESS INSURANCE

This introductory course cannot discuss in detail all the insurance coverage that businesses may buy. Naturally, businesses must protect themselves against property damage, and they must buy car and truck insurance and more. Figure B.2 will give you some idea of the types of insurance available. Many businesses were happy that they had business interruption insurance after a major ice storm in Quebec and the 2003 blackout in Ontario.

The point to be made in this appendix is that risk management is critical in all firms. That includes the risk of investing funds and the risk of opening your own business (speculative risk). Remember from Chapter 1, though, that risk is often matched by opportunity and profits. Taking on risk is one way for an entrepreneur to prosper. Regardless of how careful we are, however, we all face the prospect of death, even entrepreneurs. To ensure that those left behind will be able to continue the business, entrepreneurs often buy life insurance that will pay partners and others what they will need to keep the business going.

Key Employee Insurance

A significant risk for businesses relates to the loss of a key employee. The best kind of insurance to cover executives in the firm is term insurance, but dozens of new policies with interesting features now exist.

Insurance Coverage for Home-Based Businesses

Homeowner's policies usually don't have adequate protection for a home-based business. For example, they may have a limit of $2,500 for business equipment. For more coverage, you may need to add an *endorsement* (sometimes called a rider) to your homeowners insurance. For about $25 a year, you can increase the coverage to $10,000.

Types of Insurance	What It Does
Property and Liability	
Fire	Covers losses to buildings and their contents from fire.
Automobile	Covers property damage, bodily injury, collision, fire, theft, vandalism, and other related vehicle losses.
Homeowners	Covers the home, other structures on the premises, home contents, expenses if forced from the home because of an insured peril, third-party liability, and medical payments to others.
Computer coverage	Covers loss of equipment from fire, theft, sometimes spills, power surges, and accidents.
Professional liability	Covers court-awarded losses stemming from mistakes made or bad advice given in a professional context.
Business interruption	Provides compensation for loss due to fire, theft, or similar disasters that close a business. Covers lost income, continuing expenses, and utility expenses.
Nonperformance loss protection	Protects from failure of a contractor, supplier, or other person to fulfill an obligation.
Criminal loss protection	Protects from loss due to theft, burglary, or robbery.
Commercial credit insurance	Protects manufacturers and wholesalers from credit losses due to insolvency or default.
Public liability insurance	Provides protection for businesses and individuals against losses resulting from personal injuries or damage to the property of others for which the insured is responsible.
Extended product liability insurance	Covers potentially toxic substances in products; environmental liability; and, for corporations, director and officer liability.
Fidelity bond	Protects businesses from employee dishonesty.
Surety bond	Covers losses resulting from a second party's failure to fulfill a contract.
Title insurance	Protects buyers from losses resulting from errors in title to property.
Health Insurance	
Extended health care	Pays a percentage of prescription drug costs, dental care, vision care, and paramedical services.
Disability income insurance	Pays income while the insured is disabled as a result of accident or illness.
Life Insurance	
Group life insurance	Covers all the employees of a firm or members of a group.
Owner or key executive insurance	Enables businesses of sole proprietors or partnerships to pay bills and continue operating, saving employee jobs if the owner or a key executive dies. Enables corporations to hire and train or relocate another manager with no loss to the firm.
Retirement and pension plans	Provides employees with supplemental retirement and pension plans.
Credit life insurance	Pays the amount due on outstanding credit (e.g., loan, line of credit, etc.) if the debtor dies.

If clients visit your office or if you receive deliveries regularly, you may need home-office insurance. It costs around $150 a year, but it protects you from slip-and-fall lawsuits and other risks associated with visitors. For more elaborate businesses, such as custom cabinetry shops and other types of manufacturing or inventory-keeping businesses, a business-owner policy may be needed which costs $300 a year or more. Unless you are an expert on insurance, you will need to consult an insurance agent about the best insurance for your home-business needs.

The Risk of Damaging the Environment

The risk of environmental harm reaches international proportions in issues such as global warming. The 1986 explosion at the Chernobyl nuclear power plant in what was then the Soviet Union caused much concern throughout the world. Due to high safety standards, Ontario nuclear power plants are closely watched for safety violations. Yet since coal-fired power plants are said to cause acid rain (and global warming), and other inexpensive fuel sources haven't been fully developed, nuclear power plants are still considered by some to be a necessity. However nuclear power plants also pose environment concerns.

Many people feel there is a need for a more careful evaluation of environmental risks than currently is done. How much risk is there in global warming? We don't know all the details yet, but the risks may be substantial.[14] Therefore, many companies are going out of their way to protect the environment.[15]

Clearly, risk management now goes far beyond the protection of individuals, businesses, and non-profit organizations from known risks. It means the evaluation of worldwide risks such as global warming.[16] It also means prioritizing these risks so that international funds can be spent where they can do the most good. No insurance company can protect humanity from such risks. These risks are the concern of businesses and governments throughout the world, with the assistance of the international scientific community.[17] They should also be your concern as you study risk management in all its dimensions.

SUMMARY

1. Risk management is becoming a critical part of management in most firms.

   What changes have made risk management more important?
   Global warming, terrorist threats, natural disasters, war, and an unstable economy have all contributed to additional risk and the need for more risk management.

   LO ▶ 1 Discuss the environmental changes that have made risk management more important.

2. There are several ways of handling risk.

   What are the four major ways of managing risk?
   The major ways of avoiding risk are: (1) reduce risk, (2) avoid risk, (3) self-insure, and (4) buy insurance.

   LO ▶ 2 Explain the four ways of managing risk.

3. Some risks are insurable and others are not.

   What's the difference between insurable and uninsurable risk?
   Uninsurable risk is risk that no insurance company will cover. Examples of things that you cannot insure include market risks, political risks, some personal risks (such as loss of a job); and some risks of operation (e.g., strikes or inefficient machinery). An insurable risk is one that the typical insurance company will cover. Generally, insurance companies use the following guidelines when evaluating whether or not a risk is insurable: (1) the policyholder must have an insurable interest, (2) the loss should be measurable, (3) the chance of loss should be measurable, (4) the loss should be accidental, (5) the risk should be dispersed, and (6) the insurance company can set standards for accepting risks.

   LO ▶ 3 Distinguish between insurable and uninsurable risk.

LO ▶ 4 Explain the rule of indemnity.

4. There are some things one should know about insurance company rules.

What is the rule of indemnity?

The rule of indemnity says that an insured person or organization cannot collect more than the actual loss from an insurable risk.

What are the two kinds of insurance companies?

A stock insurance company is owned by stockholders, just like any other investor-owned company. A mutual insurance company is owned by its policyholders.

LO ▶ 5 Discuss the various types of insurance that businesses may buy.

5. There are insurance policies to cover all different kinds of risk.

What kind of policy covers health risks?

Individuals can obtain benefit plans that cover dental care, extended health care, survivors' benefits, income continuance, and pensions. These coverages are over and above the universal health care system that operates in Canada. The cost of benefit plans has increased significantly in recent years. To manage these costs, coverage limits have been reduced and deductibles have been raised.

LO ▶ 6 Explain why businesses must carry workers' compensation insurance.

6. Businesses must explore many kinds of insurance.

What kinds of insurance do most businesses have?

Workers' compensation insurance guarantees payment of wages, medical care, and rehabilitation services (e.g., retraining) for employees who are injured on the job. Employers in all provinces and territories are required to provide this insurance. Professional liability insurance covers people who are found liable for professional negligence. Product liability insurance provides coverage against liability arising out of products sold. If a person is injured by a ladder or some other household good, he or she may sue the manufacturer for damages. Personal and premises liability insurance provides coverage for individuals based on their negligent acts or an accident occurring. Most businesses also have some kind of life insurance for the executives. If you conduct business from home, you should also have some form of home-office insurance to cover certain risks.

LO ▶ 7 Tell others why businesses cannot manage environmental damage on their own.

7. There is much discussion in the news about whether or not businesses are ruining the environment.

What are businesses doing to cover the risks of harming the environment?

Many businesses are doing what they can to minimize damage to the environment. Such risks, however, are often beyond what businesses can manage. They are the concern of governments around the world.

KEY TERMS

insurable interest 331
insurable risk 331
insurance policy 331
law of large numbers 331
mutual insurance company 332

premium 331
pure risk 329
risk 329
rule of indemnity 332

self-insurance 330
speculative risk 329
stock insurance company 332
uninsurable risk 330

CRITICAL THINKING

1. Are you self-insuring your apartment (or where you live) and your assets? What have you done to reduce the risk? Have you done anything to avoid risk? How much would it cost to buy insurance for your dwelling and the contents?

2. What risks do you take that cannot be covered by insurance?

3. What actions have you taken to avoid risk?

4. What can you do to lower the risk of natural disasters such as floods, hurricanes, and tornadoes?

DEVELOPING WORKPLACE SKILLS

1. Write a one-page paper about ways you could reduce risk in your life (e.g., drive more slowly). Form into small groups and share what you have written. Then discuss everything that you and your classmates might do to reduce the risk of loss or harm.

2. You cannot insure yourself against speculative risk. However, you can minimize the risks you take when investing. Compare and contrast the risks of investing in stocks versus bonds for the long term. Be prepared to discuss your results in class.

3. Much of risk management is observing the behaviour of others and then acting to reduce risky behaviour. What kind of risky behaviour have you observed among college students? What is being done, if anything, to inform them of such risks and to minimize them?

What has been the response? What can you learn from such observation? Discuss the merits of having a risk manager for education facilities.

4. Form into small groups and discuss liability insurance, automobile insurance, renter's insurance, life insurance, and disability insurance. Develop a list of questions to discuss openly in class so that everyone is more informed about these issues.

5. Write a short (two-page) essay on the perceived risks of a terrorist attack, a natural disaster, or a major health disaster such as bird flu. Which risk do you perceive as most likely? Most dangerous? Discuss what you could do to warn others of such risks and motivate them to do something about them.

TAKING IT TO THE NET

www.mcgrawhillconnect.ca

Purpose

To learn about insurance for your dwelling and property, and to examine the issue of liability.

Exercise

Go to Insurance-Canada at www.insurance-canada.ca. Explore the site and then answer the following questions:

1. What is homeowner's insurance?

2. What is in a standard policy?

3. What different types of homeowner's policies are there?

4. What is renter's insurance?

Endnotes

Chapter 1

1. Luisa Kroll, Matthew Miller, and Tatiana Serafin, "The World's Billionaires," Forbes.com, 11 March 2009, http://www.forbes.com/2009/03/11/worlds-richest-people-billionaires-2009-billionaires_land.html.
2. "#1 William Gates III," Forbes.com, 11 March 2009, http://www.forbes.com/lists/2009/10/billionaires-2009-richest-people_William-Gates-III_BH69.html.
3. "Key Small Business Statistics," Industry Canada, July 2008, http://www.ic.gc.ca/epic/site/sbrp-rppe.nsf/vwapj/KSBS_July2008_Eng.pdf/$FILE/KSBS_July2008_Eng.pdf.
4. Small Business Quarterly, "Business Insolvencies," Industry Canada, May 2008, http://www.ic.gc.ca/epic/site/sbrp-rppe.nsf/vwapj/SBQ_May2008_Eng.pdf/$FILE/SBQ_May2008_Eng.pdf.
5. Pete Engardio, "The Future of Outsourcing," *BusinessWeek*, 30 January 2006, 50–58.
6. John R. Baldwin and Wulong Gu, "Outsourcing and Offshoring in Canada," Statistics Canada, May 2008, http://www.statcan.ca/english/research/11F0027MIE/11F0027MIE2008055.pdf.
7. Erin White, "Smaller Companies Join the Outsourcing Trend," *The Wall Street Journal*, 8 May 2006, B3.
8. Baldwin and Gu, "Outsourcing and Offshoring in Canada."
9. Pete Engardio and Bruce Einhorn, "Outsourcing Innovation," *BusinessWeek*, 21 March 2005, 84–94.
10. Ibid.
11. Gary N. Bowen, "Nearshore? Farshore? Which Shore for CRM?" Everest Group, March 2005, http://www.outsourcing-journal.com/mar2005-canada.html.
12. William Foster and Jeffrey Bradach, "Should Nonprofits Seek Profits?" *Harvard Business Review*, February 2005, 92–100.
13. Steve Case, "Purpose and Profit Go Together," *The Wall Street Journal*, 10 May 2005, B2.
14. Amanda Bower, "Meet the Hard-Nosed Do-Gooders," *Time Inside Business*, January 2006, A24.
15. "Welcome to CharityVillage.com," Charity Village, 15 August 2008, http://www.charityvillage.com/.
16. John Gray et al., "It's A Rich Life," *Canadian Business*, Winter 2007/2008, 22.
17. Ibid.
18. "Corporate Profile," Tim Hortons, 24 July 2009, http://www.timhortons.com/en/about/profile.html.
19. Grant Robertson, "Boom Has Tech Grads Mulling Their Options," *The Globe and Mail*, 14 March 2006, B1.
20. Brook Manville and Josiah Ober, "Beyond Empowerment," *Harvard Business Review*, January 2003, 48–53.
21. "Competition Act C-34," Department of Justice Canada, 11 August 2008, http://laws.justice.gc.ca/en/showdoc/cs/C-34//20080816/en?command=home&caller=SI&search_type=all&shorttitle=competition%20act&day=16&month=8&year=2008&search_domain=cs&showall=L&statuteyear=all&lengthannual=50&length=50.
22. "Definitions: Understanding Legal Words," Manitoba Courts, 23 October 2006, http://www.manitobacourts.mb.ca/index.html.
23. "CEO Justice," *The Wall Street Journal*, 16 March 2005, A24.
24. "Conrad Black Complains Appeal Judges Don't Understand Case," CBC News, 10 June 2008, http://www.cbc.ca/world/story/2008/06/10/conrad-black-email.html; "Conrad Black's Lawyers File Appeal of his Conviction, CBC News, 14 March 2008, http://www.cbc.ca/world/story/2008/03/14/blackappeal.html.
25. "'Sense of Urgency,' as Premiers Meet with Central Banker," CBC News, 18 July 2008, http://www.cbc.ca/canada/saskatchewan/story/2008/07/18/premiers-economy.html.
26. Frederick G. Crane et al., *Marketing*, 7th Canadian ed., (Toronto: McGraw-Hill Ryerson Ltd., 2008), 81.
27. Ibid.
28. Paul Sloan, "Retail Without the Risk," *Business 2.0*, March 2006, 118.
29. "Talent Technology Corp.," PROFIT 100—Canada's Fastest Growing Companies, 2008 http://list.canadianbusiness.com/rankings/profit100/2008/DisplayProfile.aspx?profile=17.
30. "E-BUSINESS," Webster's Online Dictionary, 2009, http://www.websters-online-dictionary.org/definition/e-business.
31. "Introduction to e-Business," Kioskea.net, 16 October 2008, http://en.kioskea.net/contents/entreprise/e-business.php3.
32. Department of Justice Canada, "Competition Act C-34."
33. Mike Richman, "The Quest for Zero Defects," *Quality Digest*, April 2005, 40–43.
34. Crane et al., *Marketing*, 84–85.
35. David Foot with Daniel Stoffman, *Boom Bust & Echo 2000* (Toronto: Macfarlane Walter & Ross, 1998), 24–31.
36. "Boom, Bust & Echo, Profiting from the Demographic Shift in the 21st Century," Footwork Consulting Inc., 2008, http://www.footwork.com/21c.asp.
37. "Immigration Trends in Canada," Statistics Canada, 11 September 2007, http://www12.statcan.ca/english/census06/reference/Imm_trends_Canada.cfm; "Immigration in Canada: A Portrait of the Foreign-Born Population, 2006 Census: Highlights," Statistics Canada, 30 November 2007, http://www12.statcan.ca/english/census06/analysis/immcit/highlights.cfm.
38. "About Us—Careers," NAV CANADA, 2008, http://www.navcanada.ca/NavCanada.asp?Language=en&Content=ContentDefinitionFiles\AboutUs\Careers\ValuingDiversity\default.xml.
39. "Family Portrait: Continuity and Change in Canadian Families and Households in 2006: Highlights," Statistics Canada, 5 September 2007, http://www12.statcan.ca/english/census06/analysis/famhouse/highlights.cfm.
40. "Will Globalization Survive?" *Washington Times*, 10 April 2005, B2.
41. "Mobilizing Science and Technology to Canada's Advantage," Government of Canada, May 2007, http://www.ic.gc.ca/epic/site/ic1.nsf/vwapj/S&Tstrategy.pdf/$file/S&Tstrategy.pdf.
42. Associated Press, "Wardrobe Malfunction Joins the Credit Crunch," *Toronto Star*, 16 August 2008, http://www.thestar.com/article/478662.
43. "Manufacturing Our Future," Canadian Manufacturing Coalition, [2007?], http://www.cme-mec.ca/pdf/CMECoalitionFINAL.pdf.

Chapter 2

1. "Index of Economic Freedom, China," The Heritage Foundation, 2008, http://www.heritage.org/research/features/index/country.cfm?id=China; "Index of Economic Freedom, Switzerland," The Heritage Foundation, 2008, http://www.heritage.org/research/features/index/country.cfm?id=Switzerland.
2. Justin Gillis, "Old Laws, New Fish," *Washington Post*, 15 January 2003, E1.
3. "Transportation," Burnaby: Ballard Power Systems, 2004, http://www.ballard.com/tC.asp?pgid_44.
4. Anne Underwood, "Designing the Future," *Newsweek*, 16 May 2005, 40–45.
5. Kristin Ohlson, "Burst of Energy," *Entrepreneur*, February 2006, 46–47.
6. "Net Is Cast for Fish Farms," *Washington Times*, 4 April 2005, A8.
7. "Quirky Causes," *Forbes*, 28 March 2005, 172.
8. "Charitable Donations," Canadian Bankers Association, 2007, http://www.cba.ca/en/content/stats/DB%20283%20Eng%20(New)%202007.pdf.
9. "Foundation Fact Sheet," Bill & Melinda Gates Foundation, 30 June 2008, http://www.gatesfoundation.org/MediaCenter/FactSheet/; Amanda Ripley and Amanda Bower, "From Riches to Rags," *Time*, December–January 2006, 72–88.
10. Marilyn Chase, "Gates to Donate Extra $250 Million for Health Grants," *The Wall Street Journal*, 17 May 2005, D7.
11. Frederick G. Crane et al. *Marketing*, 7th Canadian ed. (Toronto: McGraw-Hill Ryerson Limited, 2008), 84.
12. "Bill Gates No Longer Tops World's-Richest List," *The Chronicle of Philanthropy*, 6 March 2008, http://philanthropy.com/news/philanthropytoday/4105/bill-gates-no-longer-tops-worlds-richest-list.

13. "About Us, History of Our Citizenship Action," Cirque du Soleil, 2008, http://www.cirquedusoleil.com/CirqueDuSoleil/en/cirquecitoyen/about/history.htm.

14. Richard Rahn, "Weapons of Mass Disinformation," *Washington Times*, 21 March 2005, A15.

15. Brian M. Carney, "Europe Hasn't Outgrown 'That '70s Show,'" *The Wall Street Journal*, 9 May 2005, A23.

16. Mark Henricks, "The New China?" *Entrepreneur*, February 2006, 17–18; Dexter Roberts, "How Rising Wages Are Changing the Game in China," *BusinessWeek*, 27 March 2006, 32–35.

17. Laura D'Andrea Tyson, "How Europe Is Revving Its Engine," *BusinessWeek*, 21 February 2005, 24.

18. Eric J. Savitz, "Look Who's Storming the Net," *Smart Money*, June 2005, 40–48.

19. "Latest Indicators, Population Estimate (January 2009)," Statistics Canada, 26 March 2009, http://www.statcan.gc.ca/start-debut-eng.html.

20. Matthew Coutts, "Complacency Hurts Nation: Think-Tank; Quality of Life Declining, Report Warns," *National Post*, 30 June 2008, A4.

21. Ibid.

22. "Health Care Spending to Reach $160 Billion This Year," Canadian Institute for Health Information, 13 November 2007, http://secure.cihi.ca/cihiweb/dispPage.jsp?cw_page=media_13nov2007_e.

23. "Provincial and Territorial Economic Accounts Review," Statistics Canada, 27 April 2009, http://www.statcan.gc.ca/pub/13-016-x/13-016-x2009001-eng.pdf.

24. "Country Report, Canada," The Economist Intelligence Unit, May 2009, http://portal.eiu.com.

25. "Country Profile 2005," The Economist Intelligence Unit, 1 September 2005, http://portal.eiu.com.

26. Richard S. Dunham, "The Struggle to Sell the Economy's Sizzle," *BusinessWeek*, 23 January 2006, 43.

27. Steven Gray, "Coffee on the Double," *The Wall Street Journal*, 12 April 2005, B1.

28. "Economic Concepts—Unemployment Rate," Government of Canada, 4 May 2007, http://canadianeconomy.gc.ca/english/economy/unemployment2.html.

29. Ibid.

30. Armine Yalnizyan, "Recession packs biggest wallop since 1930s: Study," Canadian Centre for Policy Alternatives, 28 April 2009.

31. Government of Canada, "Economic Concepts—Unemployment Rate."

32. "Study: The year in review in manufacturing," Statistics Canada, 29 April 2009, http://www.statcan.gc.ca/daily-quotidien/090429/dq090429b-eng.htm; "Study: The year in review in manufacturing," Statistics Canada, 29 April 2008, http://www.statcan.ca/Daily/English/080429/d080429a.htm.

33. David Pilling, "Japan Still in Grip of Deflation as Prices Fall," *Financial Times*, 27 April 2005, 7.

34. E. S. Browning, "Stagflation Fear Puts a Chill into Blue Chips," *The Wall Street Journal*, 29 April 2005, C1 and C4.

35. "Latest Release from the Consumer Price Index," Statistics Canada, 20 May 2009, http://www.statcan.gc.ca/subjects-sujets/cpi-ipc/cpi-ipc-eng.htm.

36. Ibid.

37. Victor Zarnowitz and Dara Lee, "Can U.S. Business Cycles Still Be Dated by Monthly Coincident Indicators Alone?" *Business Cycle Indicator*, March 2005, 3–4.

38. "Business Cycle," Wikimedia Foundation Inc., 18 August 2008, http://en.wikipedia.org/wiki/Business_cycle.

39. "Economic Concepts Business Cycle," Government of Canada, 4 May 2007, http://www.canadianeconomy.gc.ca/english/economy/business_cycle.html.

40. Lakshman Achuthan, "How Anyone Can Forecast Booms and Busts," *Bottom Line Personal*, 1 June 2005, 3–4.

Chapter 3

1. "Alberta Heritage Savings Trust Fund 2008–09 Third Quarter Update, February 26, 2009," Government of Alberta, 6 April 2009, http://www.finance.alberta.ca/business/ahstf/index.html.

2. "Assets Under Management," Caisse de Dépôt et Placement du Québec, 2009, http://www.lacaisse.com/en/chiffres/chiffres/Pages/faits-saillants.aspx.

3. "Sources of Canadian Law," Department of Justice Canada, 24 April 2003, http://canada.justice.gc.ca/en/dept/pub/just/CSJ_page7.html.

4. Eugene A. Forsey, *How Canadians Govern Themselves*, 6th ed., Government of Canada, 2005, http://www.parl.gc.ca/information/library/idb/forsey/index-e.asp.

5. Campbell Clark and Rheal Seguin, "Ottawa Pushes for New Chapter in Free Trade with U.S.," *The Globe and Mail*, 4 June 2009, A1.

6. "Price-Fixing Is Bad, No Matter Who Does It," *The Montreal Gazette*, 23 July 2008, A18.

7. Matt Hartley, "Competition Watchdog reviewing Google's Yahoo deal," *The Globe and Mail*, 28 August 2008, B2.

8. Forsey, *How Canadians Govern Themselves*.

9. James Daw, "High Interest, Bad Job Market Make Repaying Loans That Much Harder," *Toronto Star*, 30 May 2009, http://www.thestar.com/article/642879; "Elimination of Loan Interest Delights Students," CBC News, 27 March 2009, http://www.cbc.ca/canada/newfoundland-labrador/story/2009/03/27/student-loan-budget.html.

10. Forsey, *How Canadians Govern Themselves*.

11. "Research in Motion Opens Technical Support Centre in Halifax," Canadian Press, 21 April 2006, http://finance.sympatico.msn.ca/content/investing/other/P40361.asp.

12. Alan Reynolds, "Improvements . . . and Horror Replays," *Washington Times*, 12 January 2003, B8.

13. "The Federal Debt," Statistics Canada, 26 August 2004, http://142.206.72.67/03/03a/03a_055d_e.htm.

14. "Federal Debt," Government of Canada, 2 June 2009, http://canadianeconomy.gc.ca/english/economy/#top.

15. Presentation by the Honourable John Manley, P.C., M.P. to the House of Commons Standing Committee on Finance, Department of Finance Canada, 3 November 2003, http://www.fin.gc.ca/ec2003/speeche.html; Sandra Cordon, "Strong Growth Forecast," *Montreal Gazette*, 20 May 1999, A1; "Sheltered from the Global Storm," *ScotiaPlus*, Spring/Summer 1999, 5.

16. "Budget Deficit in 2009–10, Flaherty Confirms," CBC News, 17 December 2008, http://www.cbc.ca/canada/story/2008/12/17/finance-meeting.html; "Top TD Economist Sees Lingering Canadian Deficits," Reuters, 2 June 2009, http://finance.sympatico.msn.ca/investing/news/breakingnews/article.aspx?cp-documentid=20169426.

17. Richard S. Dunham, "The Struggle to Sell the Economy's Sizzle," *BusinessWeek*, 23 January 2006, 43.

18. "Glossary: Vocabulary for a Financial Crisis," CBC News, 24 March 2009, http://www.cbc.ca/money/story/2008/10/24/f-econoglossary.html; "Canada's Banks: Admired Worldwide for their Management—and Cash," CBC News, 3 March 2009, http://www.cbc.ca/money/story/2009/03/03/f-canada-banks.html; "$25B Credit Backstop for Banks 'Not a Bailout': Harper," CBC News, 10 October 2008, http://www.cbc.ca/canada/story/2008/10/10/flaherty-banks.html; Michel Chossudovsky, "Canada's 75 Billion Dollar Bank Bailout," Global Research, 25 January 2009, http://www.globalresearch.ca/index.php?context=va&aid=12007; Stefan Theil, "Europe's Bank Bailout: Is It Enough?" *Newsweek*, 13 October 2008, http://blog.newsweek.com/blogs/ov/archive/2008/10/13/europe-bank-bailout-is-it-enough.aspx; Kimberly Amadeo, "Understanding the Subprime Mortgage Crisis," About.com, 2008, http://useconomy.about.com/od/economicindicators/tp/Subprime-Mortgage-Primer.htm; Joel Schlesinger, "Why the Bank of Canada Is Doing What It's Doing," *Winnipeg Free Press*, 31 May 2009, http://www.winnipegfreepress.com/business/making-the-money-move-46566862.html?viewAllComments=y.

19. "Canadian Subsidy Directory," Canadian Publications, 2008, http://www.mgpublishing.net/grants-and-loans.htm#CSD.

20. "'Tolerable Risk' in Giving $34M Bailout Loan to Discovery Air: Miltenberger," CBC News, 3 February 2009, http://www.cbc.ca/canada/north/story/2009/02/03/discovery-loan.html.

21. "Nfld. Announces $18-million Aid for Crab Workers," Canadian Press Newswire, 28 June 2005, http://proquest.umi.com/pqdweb.

22. "U.S. Takes Dim View of Government Aid to Bombardier," CBC.ca, 11 August 2008, http://www.cbc.ca/money/story/2008/08/11/bombardier-aid.html.

23. L. Ian MacDonald, "Harper Had No Choice," *The Gazette*, 3 June 2009, http://www.montrealgazette.com/Business/Harper+choice/1657861/story.html.

24. "Ocean Choice Buys Polar Foods," PEI.CBC.CA 24 March 2004. Retrieved from http://pei.cbc.ca/regional/servlet/View?filename_pe_oceanbuys20040324.

25. "Equalization Program," Department of Finance Canada, 22 July 2008, http://www.fin.gc.ca/FEDPROV/eqpe.html; "A New Framework for Equalization and Territorial Formula Financing," Department of Finance Canada, 27 March 2006, http://www.

fin.gc.ca/toce/2004/eq_tff-e.html; "Equalization Payments," Department of Finance Canada, 11 May 2009, http://www.fin.gc.ca/fedprov/eqp-eng.asp; Kate Yule, "Ontario Receives First Equalization Payment," CFRA.com, 14 April 2009, http://www.cfra.com/?cat=3&nid=64463; "Have-not Is No More: N.L. Off Equalization," 3 November 2008, CBC News, http://www.cbc.ca/canada/newfoundland-labrador/story/2008/11/03/have-not.html.

26. "Just the Facts," National Research Council Canada, 10 September 2007, http://www.nrc-cnrc.gc.ca/aboutUs/facts_e.html.

27. "Trade and Investment at 10," Foreign Affairs and International Trade Canada, 10 July 2007, http://www.dfait-maeci.gc.ca/canada-magazine/issue24/06-title-en.asp.

28. Glossary of Key Terms: Minority Government," British Columbia Referendum Office, 2009, http://www.gov.bc.ca/referendum_info/first_past_the_post_bc_stv/glossary.html.

29. "Thousands of Forestry Workers Protest in Ottawa," CBC News, 2 June 2009, http://www.cbc.ca/canada/ottawa/story/2009/06/02/forestry-demonstration-ottawa002.html.

Chapter 4

1. Brent Jang, "WestJet Admits Spying," globeandmail.com, 29 May 2006, http://www.theglobeandmail.com/servlet/story/RTGAM.20060529.waircanada0529/BNStory/Business.

2. Ibid.

3. Auditor General's Report 2004, CBC News, 11 February 2004, http://www.cbc.ca/news/background/auditorgeneral/report2004.html.

4. "Lotto 6/49 Bonus Rounds Coincided with Lottery Scandals," CBC News, 30 May 2007, http://www.cbc.ca/canada/toronto/story/2007/05/30/lotto649-bonus-rounds.html.

5. Ibid.

6. Pallavi Guniganti, "Ethics' Place in Education," *University Wire*, 16 April 2002.

7. Kenneth Blanchard and Norman Vincent Peale, *The Power of Ethical Management* (New York: William Morrow, 1996); Shoshana Zuboff, "A Starter Kit for Business Ethics," *Fast Company*, 1 January 2005.

8. "Generosity in Canada and the United States: The 2008 Generosity Index," The Fraser Institute, December 2008, http://www.fraserinstitute.org/Commerce.Web/product_files/Generosity_Index_2008.pdf.

9. Product Specialist, iParadigms, LLC, E-mail interview, 27 October 2008, reqtii@turnitin.com; Jennifer Smith Richards, "OSU Sniffing Out Cheaters: Penalties Being Stiffened, More Cases Being Pursued in University Crackdown," *Columbus Dispatch*, 17 January 2006; Alicia Shepherd, "Psst . . . What's the Answer?" *People Weekly*, 24 January 2005; Camille Breland, "U. Mississippi Business School Warns Prospective Cheaters," *University Wire*, 21 January 2005.

10. David F. Martin, "Plagiarism and Technology: A Tool for Coping with Plagiarism," *Journal of Business Education*, 1 January 2005.

11. Blanchard and Peale, *The Power of Ethical Management*.

12. "Small Business Owners Doing Little to Promote Ethics," *Ascribe Newswire*, 25 June 2002.

13. Booz Allen Hamilton, "New Study Finds Link Between Financial Success and Focus on Corporate Values," *Business Wire*, 3 February 2005.

14. Craig Savoye, "Workers Say Honesty Is Best Company Policy," *Christian Science Monitor*, 15 June 2000, 3; Andrea Kay, "Tread Carefully Before Becoming a Whistleblower," *Gannett News Service*, 21 February 2002.

15. Alison Maitland, "How Ethics Codes Can Be Made to Work," *Financial Times*, 7 March 2005, 9.

16. Stephen Spector, "SOX and SOX North, Part 3 The Impact of SOX," Professional Development Network, https://www.cga-pdnet.org/Non_VerifiableProducts/ArticlePublication/SOX_E/SOX_part_3.pdf; "What is SOX?" Metso Corporation, 10 March 2006, http://www.metso.com/corporation/home_eng.nsf/FR?ReadForm&ATL=/corporation/articles_eng.nsf/WebWID/WTB-050704-2256F-A1200; Curtis Verschoor, "Is This the Age of Whistleblowers?" *Strategic Finance*, 1 February 2005; Guillermo Contreras, "San Antonio Whistleblower Doubly Rewarded in Exposing HealthSouth Fraud," *San Antonio Express News*, 14 January 2005; Paul K. Mcmasters, "Inside the First Amendment: Blowing the Whistle Can Also Blow a Career," *Gannett News Service*, 16 January 2006.

17. Larry Brown, "The Case for Whistleblowing Legislation in Canada," 3 November 2003, Nepean: National Union of Public and General Employees, http://www.nupge.ca/news_2003/

n06no03a.htm; "Whistleblowing and Bill C-11," Public Service Commission of Canada, 11 January 2006, http://www.psc-cfp.gc.ca/speech/2005/whistleblowing_e.htm; "Submission to the Standing Committee on Government Operations and Estimates," Public Service Integrity Office, 30 November 2004, http://www.psio-bifp.gc.ca/media/speech-discours/2004-11-30/part-2_e.php?printversion=1; "Reporting Abuses, Whistleblower Protection Policy," Petro-Canada, 21 March 2006, http://www.petro-canada.ca/eng/investor/9334.htm; Michele Brill-Edwards, Brian McAdam and David Hutton, "Whistleblower Legislation Might Have Prevented Listeriosis Outbreak, Say Activists," *The Hill Times*, 6 October 2008, http://fairwhistleblower.ca/news/articles/2008-10-06_Whistleblower_legislation_might_have_prevented_listeriosis_outbreak.html; "1 Year Later, Tory-Touted Accountability Act Scores 'D' Grade: Watchdog," CBC News, 12 December 2007, http://www.cbc.ca/canada/story/2007/12/12/accountabiliy-report.html; "Federal Accountability Act Becomes Law," Treasury Board of Canada Secretariat, 12 December 2006, http://www.tbs-sct.gc.ca/media/nr-cp/2006/1212-eng.asp; "The Lobbying Act and You," Government of Canada, 7 August 2007, http://www.faa-lfi.gc.ca/index-eng.asp.

18. John S. McClenahen, "Defining Social Responsibility," *Industry Week*, 1 March 2005.

19. Milton Friedman, "The Social Responsibility of Business is to Increase its Profits," *The New York Times Magazine*, 13 September 1970, http://www.colorado.edu/studentgroups/libertarians/issues/friedman-soc-resp-business.html.

20. "Canadian Tire Jumpstart®," The Canadian Tire Foundation for Families, 2009, http://www.canadiantire.ca/jumpstart/about.html.

21. William Damon, "Saints and Sinners in Business," *Security Management*, 1 January 2005.

22. "Trading Places," M2 Presswire, 31 January 2005.

23. "Empower Employees to be active in their communities" [n.d.], Redmond: Microsoft Corporation, http://www.microsoft.com/canada/ican/communityfocus/employees.mspx.

24. "Corporate Social Responsibility," Wikimedia Foundation, Inc., 5 June 2009, http://en.wikipedia.org/wiki/Corporate_social_responsibility.

25. Anita Lienhart, "She Drove, He Drove Mercedes C320," Gannett News Service, 9 January 2001; Menke-Gluckert, "Baby Benz Faces the Moose," *Europe*, 2 February 1998, 40–44; Earle Eldridge, "Luxury Sales Up: 'Move Up' Market Strong," *Edmonton Sun*, 21 June 2002, DR16.

26. "Nortel May Lose NYSE Listing," CBC News, 11 December 2008, http://www.cbc.ca/mobile/text/story_news-technology.html?/ept/html/story/2008/12/11/nortellisting.html; "Trustee Sues Madoff's Wife for $45M," CBS News, 29 July 2009, http://www.cbsnews.com/stories/2009/07/29/business/main5196249.shtml?source=related_story&tag=related; Sidhartha Banerjee, "Disgraced Financier Lived Lavishly," The Canadian Press, 30 July 2009, http://www.thestar.com/news/canada/article/673888; Robert Kuttner, "Dishonest Capitalism Won't Go Unpunished," *BusinessWeek*, 23 May 2005, 32; RBC Financial Group Voted Most Respected Corporation," KPMG LLP, 30 January 2006, http://www.mostrespected.ca/en/mrpr01.html.

27. Steven Skurka, "Black vs. Drabinsky: Two Trials, Two Very Different Systems," *National Post*, 4 June 2009, http://network.nationalpost.com/np/blogs/fullcomment/archive/2009/06/04/steven-skurka-on-black-vs-drabinsky-two-trials-two-very-different-systems.aspx; "Livent Sentencing Hearing Postponed," The Canadian Press, 3 June 2009, http://www.thestar.com/article/644834; Joe Schneider, "Livent Founders Convicted of C$500 Million Fraud (Update3)," Bloomber.com, 25 March 2009, http://www.bloomberg.com/apps/news?pid=20601082&sid=aBkY_Qtnf9y8&refer=canada.

28. "Former RBC Dominion Securities Exec Faces Insider Trading Charges," CBC News, 5 February 2004, http://www.cbc.ca/stories/2004/02/04/rankin040204; Nancy Carr, "Daniel Duic to Pay $1.9M, Stop Trading in Ont., Testify at Rankin Trial: OSC," Canoe Money, 3 March 2004, http://money.canoe.ca/News/Other/2004/03/03/369029-cp.html; Tara Perkins, "Andrew Rankin Gets 6 Months in Canada's 1st Stock-Tipping Conviction," CBC News, 10 April 2005, http://www.cbc.ca/cp/business/051027/b1027100.html.

29. "Background Checks—Know Who You Are Hiring," Hiring Smart, http://www.hiringsmart.ca/bc_stats.jsp.

30. Vicki O'Brien, "Hands in Your Pocket," BC Business Online, 1 August 2007, http://www.bcbusinessonline.ca/bcb/top-stories/2007/08/01/hands-your-pockets.

31. Ibid.

32. Ibid.
33. Jared Gilbert, "Alcoa Does Its Bit for the World—and Its Own Image—with Earthwatch Projects," *Workforce Management*, 1 March 2005; Katherine Mangu-Ward, "The Age of Corporate Environmentalism: Surprise—Big Business Has Learned That It's Pretty Easy Being Green," *Reason*, 1 February 2006.
34. Colin Perkel, "Harris Apologizes for Government's Role in Tragedy," 18 January 2002, Canoe C-Health, http://www.canoe.ca/EcoliTragedy/020118_report-cp.html.
35. Jim MacDonald, "Syncrude Charged After 500 Ducks Perished on Oilsands Pond," The Canadian Press, 9 February 2009, http://www.thestar.com/article/584719; "Tar Ponds in Sydney, Nova Scotia," PageWise Inc., 2002, http://tntn.essortment.com/tarpondssydney_rhxq.htm; "Sydney Nova Scotia Tar Ponds Move Closer to Cleanup" Ellicott, http://www.dredge.com/casestudies/enviro8.htm; "Our Site Overview," Province of Nova Scotia: Sydney Tar Ponds Agency, 2004, http://www.gov.ns.ca/stpa; "The Great Lakes Atlas," The United States Environmental Protection Agency, 2003, www.epa.gov/glnpo/atlas; Pat Currie, "All's Not Well in This Valley," *Lake Ontario Waterkeeper*, 3 April 2004, http://www.waterkeeper.ca/lok; Chris Sebastian, "Canada Getting Tough on Spills," *Times Herald*, 12 May 2004, http://www. thetimesherald.com/stories/20040512/localnews/403633.html; "Home," Jantzi Research, 2005, http://www.jantziresearch.com; "About Imagine—Who We Are," Imagine Canada, 2008, http://www.imagine.ca/content/about_imagine/who_we_are.asp?section=about.
36. Elizabeth Laurienzo, "Calvert Social Index Quarterly Adjustments," PR Newswire, 17 March 2005; "Corporate Social Concerns: Are They Good Citizenship, or a Rip-Off for Investors?" *The Wall Street Journal*, 6 December 2005.
37. "Triple Bottom Line," Wikipedia, 13 December 2008, http://en.wikipedia.org/wiki/Triple_bottom_line.
38. "What Is the Triple Bottom Line?" SustainAbility Ltd., http://www.sustainability.com/downloads_public/news/TBL.pdf.
39. Ibid.
40. "Defining Sustainability," Sustainability Reporting Program, 2000, http://www.sustreport.org/background/definitions.html; "Introducing Revive," Green Solutions North American, Inc., 2009, http://revive-d.com/revive_overview.cfm; "Loblaws, Sobeys put a wrap on plastic bags," The Canadian Press, 27 November 2008, http://www.cbc.ca/consumer/story/2008/11/27/loblaw-sobeys-bags.html.
41. Aaron Bernstein, "A Major Swipe at Sweatshops," *BusinessWeek*, 23 May 2005, 98–100; "Stamping Out Sweatshops," *BusinessWeek*, 23 May 2005, 136; Mari Herreras, "Recent Court Cases Might Help Rewrite Company Policies: Employment Law Update," *Wenatchee Business Journal*, 1 January 2006.
42. "Workers in Contract Factories," Nike, 2008, http://nikeresponsibility.com/pdfs/color/3_Nike_CRR_Workers_C.pdf.
43. Karl Schoenberger, "U.S. Companies Must Follow U.S. Anti-Corruption Law Abroad," San Jose Mercury News, 13 March 2005.

Chapter 5

1. "Proprietorship," Canadian Tax and Financial Information, Taxtips.ca, 2008, http://www.taxtips.ca/smallbusiness/incorporate.htm.
2. Ibid.
3. Elswick, "Loaded Statements: Web-Based Total Compensation Statements Keep Employees in the Know," *Employee Benefit News*, 1 May 2005.
4. Canadian Tax and Financial Information, "Proprietorship."
5. Ibid.
6. "Partnership," Canadian Tax and Financial Information, Taxtips.ca, 2008, http://www.taxtips.ca/glossary.htm#P.
7. Jeff Opdyke, "When Business and Friendship Don't Mix," *The Wall Street Journal*, 17 March 2005; Paulette Thomas, "One Sweet Solution to a Sour Partnership," *The Wall Street Journal*, 23 March 2005.
8. Canadian Tax and Financial Information, "Partnership."
9. Ibid.
10. "Corporations," Canadian Tax and Financial Information, Taxtips.ca, 2008, http://www.taxtips.ca/smallbusiness/incorporate.htm.
11. Ibid.
12. "Federal Budget," H&R Block, 2006, http://www.hrblock.ca/resources/fed_budget.asp.

13. "McCain Business Empire has Deep Roots," CBC.ca, 19 March 2004, http://www.cbc.ca/stories/2004/03/19/mccainbiz_040319.
14. "Professional Advantage: New Rules Spell Tax Breaks for Ontario Professionals," Visa, June 2003, http://www.visa.ca/smallbusiness/articles/article.cfm?articleID=189&catID=90; "Incorporation: Is It Right for You?" Newfoundland and Labrador Medical Association, Winter 2003, http://www.nlma.nf.ca/nexus/issues/winter_2003/articles/article_12.html; "Professional Corporation," Business Centre, 2005, http://www.corporationcentre.ca/docen/pinc/home.asp?t=incpr; "Incorporation Rules Expanded for Ontario Doctors and Dentists," BDO Dunwoody LLP, December 2005, http://www.bdo.ca/en/library/publications/taxpub/fastfacts/IncorporationRulesExpandedRevised.cfm.
15. "The Basics of Corporate Structure," Investopedia.com, 2008, http://www.investopedia.com/articles/basics/03/022803.asp.
16. Janet McFarland, "Business Gets Better at the Business of Disclosure," *The Globe and Mail*, 26 November 2007, http://www.theglobeandmail.com/servlet/story/RTGAM.20071125.wrbgmain26/BNStory/boardgames2007/home.
17. Ibid.
18. Ibid.
19. Sean Silcoff, "Old Dutch Buys Humpty Dumpty," *National Post*, 22 March 2006, FP1.
20. Ibid., FP3.
21. Thomas D. Scholtes, "Board Guidance for Going Private," *Directors & Boards*, 22 March 2005.
22. "Company Overview" and "Divisions," Cara Operations Limited, 2001, http://www.cara.com.
23. Matthew Benjamin, "Deal Mania," *U.S. News & World Report*, 18 April 2005.
24. "Interesting Facts," CANAM Franchise Development Group, 2008, http://www.canamfranchise.com/interestingfacts.cfm.
25. Ibid.
26. "Food Restaurants—Boston Pizza International," Canadian Franchise Association, 2006, http://www.cfa.ca/members/food_restaurants.html#boston_pizza_international.
27. Tiesha Higgins, "Franchising Not Just for Fast Food Anymore," *Gazette Business*, 5 January 2005, A31; Ed Duggan, "Playing the Franchising Game Can Be a Risky Business," *South Florida Business Journal*, 13 May 2005.
28. "Kumon Franchise," Occasionfranchise.ca, 2008, http://canada.occasionfranchise.ca/brochure/43/Kumon-franchise.html.
29. "Franchise FAQ," The Keg Steakhouse & Bar, 2008, http://en.kegsteakhouse.com/franchise/faq#1.
30. Julie Bennett, "A Franchiser's Path to International Success Is Often Paved with Pitfalls," *The Wall Street Journal*, 7 April 2005, D7; Anne Fisher, "Hidden Risk," *Fortune*, 26 December 2005.
31. "About Us," Yogen Früz, 2008, http://www.yogenfruz.com/home/about-us; "Our Company," Couche-Tard, 2008, http://www.couche-tard.com/the-network.html; "Beavertails Pastry," *World Franchising*, 2004, http://www.worldfranchising.com/profiles/BeaverTail.htm; "Taco Chain Heads East," *Canadian Business Franchise*, 2006, http://www.cgb.ca/hotnews1.html.
32. "Cooperatives in Canada," Coop Zone, [2008?], http://www.coopzone.coop/en/coopsincda; "About Co-ops in Canada," Government of Canada, 22 August 2008, http://www.agr.gc.ca/rcs-src/coop/index_e.php?s1=info_coop&page=intro; "About Cooperatives," Canadian Co-Operative Association, 2008, http://www.coopscanada.coop/aboutcoop/.

Chapter 6

1. "Key Small Business Statistics," Industry Canada, January 2009, http://www.ic.gc.ca/eic/site/sbrp-rppe.nsf/vwapj/KSBS-PSRPE_Jan2009_eng.pdf/$FILE/KSBS-PSRPE_Jan2009_eng.pdf; "Latest Release from the Labour Force Survey," Statistics Canada, 5 September 2008, http://www.statcan.ca/english/Subjects/Labour/LFS/lfs-en.htm; Tiana Velez, "New Generation of High-Tech Entrepreneurs Gathers Steam," *Arizona Daily Star*, 31 January 2005; "A Definition of Entrepreneurship," Internet Center for Management and Business Administration, Inc., 19992007, http://www.quickmba.com/entre/definition/.
2. "Entrepreneurship vs. Small Business," Internet Center for Management and Business Administration, Inc., 1999–2007, http://www.quickmba.com/entre/definition/; "Entrepreneurship vs. Small Business," Ryerson University, 2008, http://www.ryerson.ca/career/jobsearch/searchjob/entrepreneurship/.
3. Retrieved 16 June 2009 from the following company Web sites: http://www.jimpattison.com, and http://www.jeancoutu.com. Retrieved 27 May 2004 from the following company Web sites:

www.leons.ca/history/default.asp, www2.canadiantire.ca/CTenglish/h_ourstory.html, www.sobeys.ca, http://www.leons.ca/history/default.asp, and http://www.irvingoilco.com/aboutus.htm.

4. "About Us," Travel CUTS, 2008, http://www.travelcuts.com/en/01%20Home/About%20Us.asp.

5. "The Museum," Anne of Green Gables Store, [n.d.], http://www.annesociety.org/anne/index.cfm?id=206.

6. "Lessons from the Leaders," PROFIT, June 2008, 31; Samuel Fromartz, "Newbiz: Entrepreneurs Not Braking for Economic Slowdown," Reuters Business Report, 20 March 2002; Kathy Wagstaff, "Pointers Offered for Small Businesses," Atlanta Journal and Constitution, 30 May 2002, J3; Sarah Kwak, "Students Succeed as Entrepreneurs," University Wire, 3 June 2005; Karen E. Klein, "Rekindling an Entrepreneur's Passion," BusinessWeek Online, 15 December 2005; Pallavi Gogoi, "Startup Secrets of the Successful," BusinessWeek Online, 18 January 2006; Ben Whitney, "Alumni Profile: Extreme Success," queensbusiness.ca, Winter 2006, https://business.queensu.ca/alumni/docs/inqw06_profile_rechichi.pdf.

7. Industry Canada, "Key Small Business Statistics;" "CIBC Report Predicts Canada Will Be Home to One Million Women Entrepreneurs by 2010," Canada NewsWire, 28 June 2005, http://proquest.umi.com/pqdweb.

8. Virginia Galt, "CAREER COACH; Before Blaming the Boss, Expert Advises You Take Stock of Your Situation," The Globe and Mail, 11 March 2006, B11.

9. Thomas M. Cooney, "What Is An Entrepreneurial Team?" International Small Business Journal, 1 June 2005, "Management Advisory Group to Advise Paxson," South Florida Business Journal, 16 January 2006.

10. Helle Neergaard, "Networking Activities in Technology-Based Entrepreneurial Teams," International Small Business Journal, 16 January 2005.

11. Industry Canada "Key Small Business Statistics."

12. Ibid.

13. Dan Strempel, "UConn Mulls Stamford Tech Incubator," Fairfield County (Connecticut) Business Journal, 11 April 2005; Emily Le Coz, "Incubators Provide Tools for Entrepreneurs," Northeast Mississippi Daily Journal, 6 January 2006; Nancy Cambria, "'Incubator' Loan Program Will Foster Small Businesses," St. Louis Post-Dispatch, 19 January 2006.

14. Sammi King, "Internet a Boon to Home-Based Businesses," Arlington Heights (Illinois) Daily Herald, 22 February 2005; Steve Jones, "Home Businesses Can Be Path to Freedom," Myrtle Beach (South Carolina) Sun News, 15 May 2005; Kristen Millares Bolt, "Moms Setting Up Online Businesses," Seattle Post-Intelligencer, 5 February 2005.

15. Deb Gruver, "Small-Business Owners Face Pros, Cons of Home-Based Enterprises," Wichita Eagle, 3 June 2005; Deb Gruver, "Home-Based Businesses Need to Use Caution with Deductions," Wichita Eagle, 18 March 2005; "Parenting, Work-at-Home Experts Join to Author Book Series for Busy Moms," PR Newswire, 31 January 2005; Janel Stephens, "Disciplined Commute from Bed to Home Office," Sarasota Herald Tribune, 17 March 2005.

16. "E-Commerce Sales Now over $60B," Canwest News Service, 25 April 2008, http://www.canada.com/theprovince/news/money/story.html?id=6919a090-7616-4f8e-bd75-f6bb13de52b6&k=3365.

17. Ibid.

18. Simon Avery, "Pioneers of E-Commerce," Cincinnati Post, 6 August 2005.

19. Larry Olmsted, "Nonstop Innovation: How One Company Transforms Its Employees into Entrepreneurs," Inc., July 2005, 34; Alan Deutschman, "Building a Better Skunk Works," Fast Company, March 2005, 68–73; Nicole Marie Richardson, "What It Takes to Be a Successful Intrapreneur," Black Enterprise, 1 December 2005.

20. Phil Bishop, "Strengthening the Innovation Chain," Electronic Business, 1 December 2004; Robert D. Ramsey, "Gaining the Edge over the Competition," Supervision, 1 May 2005.

21. "Business Incubation," Canadian Association of Business Incubation 2008, http://www.cabi.ca/business-incubation.php; "How Many Business Incubators Are There?," National Incubation Association, 22 August 2008, http://www.nbia.org/resource_center/bus_inc_facts/index.php; "Canada Business—About Us," Government of Canada, 8 December 2005, http://www.cbsc.org/servlet/ContentServer?cid=1063391060815
&pagename=CBSC_FE/CBSC_WebPage/CBSC_WebPage_Temp&lang=eng&c=CBSC_WebPage; "Aboriginal Business Service Network," Government of Canada, 5 August 2003, http://www.cbsc.org/servlet/ContentServer?cid=1091626045548&pagename=ABSN_FE%2FCBSC_WebPage%2FCBSC_WebPage_Temp&lang=en&c=CBSC_WebPage; "Business Incubation," Canadian Association of Business Incubation, 2006, http://www.cabi.ca/page_05.htm; "Business Incubation FAQ," National Incubation Association, 31 March 2006, http://www.nbia.org/resource_center/bus_inc_facts/index.php; Jean-Pierre Trudel, "Laval's Biotech City Adds Two New Biotech Development Centres to Its Complex," LifeSciencesWorld, 26 April 2003, http://www.biotecfind.com/pages/articles_eg/laval/laval.htm.

22. Industry Canada, "Key Small Business Statistics,".

23. Ibid.

24. Ibid.

25. Andy Holloway, "Fill Your Shoes: Small-Business Succession," Canadian Business, March 27–April 9, 2006, http://www.canadianbusiness.com/managing/strategy/article.jsp?content=20060327_75741_75741.

26. "Governance for the Family Business," KPMG in Canada, 2008, http://www.kpmg.ca/en/services/enterprise/issuesGrowthGovernance.html.

27. "BBB Tips Give Entrepreneurs the Inside Track on Small Business Start-Up," Business Wire, 24 August 2005, Perri Capell, "Typical Funding Mistakes That You Should Avoid," The Wall Street Journal, 12 April 2005.

28. "Where Does the Money Come From?," Canadian Bankers Association, 2008, http://www.cba.ca/en/viewDocument.asp?fl=6&sl=111&tl=&docid=251&pg=1.

29. "Venture Capitalists Invested $4.63 Billion During the First Three Months of 2005," Purchasing, 19 May 2005; Amanda Fung, "Startups Find Few VC Funds," Crain's New York Business, 1 August 2005; Tricia Bishop, "Fewer Venture Capital-Funded Companies Go Public in 2005," Baltimore Sun, 4 January 2006.

30. Jim Melloan, "Angels with Angles," Inc., July 2005, 93–104; Lee Gomes, "Angel Investors Return and They Are Serious," The Wall Street Journal, 12 April 2005; Kevin Allison, "Angel Investing Takes Flight Again," Financial Times, 3 May 2005, 12; Arlene Weintraub, "Where VCs Fear to Tread," BusinessWeek, 7 March 2005, 86–87.

31. "Canada's Venture Capital Industry in 2008," Thomas Reuters, 2009, http://www.cvca.ca/files/Downloads/Final_English_Q4_2008_VC_Data_Deck.pdf.

32. Rick Spence, "2006 Financing Guide: Get cash now," PROFIT, August 2007, http://www.canadianbusiness.com/entrepreneur/financing/article.jsp?content=20060210_145411_1560.

33. John Canter, "How and Why I Hired My Tax Accountant," The Wall Street Journal, 25 February 2005.

34. Megan Harman, "Angel Investors: Spreading Your Wings," Canadian Business, 17 March 2008, http://www.canadianbusiness.com/managing/strategy/article.jsp?content=20080226_198715_198715.

35. "The Amazing Race: Cervélo Cycles," PROFIT, May 2006, http://www.canadian business.com/entrepreneur/managing/article.jsp?content=20060404_153018_5420.

36. Keith Lowe, "Why You Need an Accountant," Entreprenuer.com, 3 June 2002.

37. "Welcome Note," The Forzani Group Ltd., 2006, http://www.forzanigroup.com/home_forzani_group.aspx.

Chapter 7

1. Jack Welch and Suzy Welch, "How to Be a Good Leader," Newsweek, 4 April 2005, 45–48.

2. Greg Thompson, "Great Expectations, the Secret to Coaching," CMA Magazine, April 2008, 22–23.

3. Gary Hamel, "The Why, What, and How of Management Innovation," Harvard Business Review, February 2006, 72–84.

4. Peter Cappelli and Monika Hamori, "The New Road to the Top," Harvard Business Review, January 2005, 25–32.

5. Marcus Buckingham, "What Great Managers Do," Harvard Business Review, March 2005, 70–79.

6. Elizabeth Fenner, "Happiness," Fortune, 21 February 2005, 36.

7. Kenneth R. Brousseau, Michael J. Driver, Gary Hourihon, and Rikard Larsson. "The Seasoned Executive's Decision-Making Style," Harvard Business Review, February 2006, 111–121.

8. John E. West, "Listening to the Customer," *Quality Digest*, February 2006, 16.
9. Jack Welch, "It's All in the Sauce," *Fortune*, 18 April 2005, 138–144.
10. Sholnn Freeman, "What Drives Them," *Washington Post*, 11 January 2006, D1 and D3.
11. Jonathan Fahey, "Hydrogen Gas," *Forbes*, 25 April 2005, 78–83.
12. Bill Breen, "The Clear Leader," *Fast Company*, March 2005, 65–67.
13. Janel M. Radtke, "How to Write a Mission Statement," *TCCI Magazine Online*, 2005.
14. Giovanni Gavetti and Jan W. Rivkin, "How Strategists Really Think," *Harvard Business Review*, April 2005, 54–63.
15. Neal E. Boudette, "Powerful Nostalgia," *The Wall Street Journal*, 10 January 2006, B1.
16. Michael C. Mankins and Richard Steele, "Stop Making Plans: Start Making Decisions," *Harvard Business Review*, January 2006, 76–84.
17. Robert J. Samuelson, "No Joke: CEOs Do Some Good," *Newsweek*, 18 April 2005, 49.
18. Andrew Nikiforuk, "Avian Flu—Winging It?" *Canadian Business*, 24 April–7 May 2006, 57.
19. "The Next Pandemic?" CBC News Online, 21 March 2006, http://www.cbc.ca/news/background/avianflu/.
20. Public Health Agency of Canada, "The Public Health Agency of Canada's Pandemic Preparedness Activities," 27 March 2006, http://www.phac-aspc.gc.ca/influenza/pha-asp-prep_e.html.
21. Ibid.
22. "The New Contingency Plan—Health-Related Emergencies," 27 May 2003, Toronto: Morneau Sobeco. Retrieved from http://www.morneausobeco.com/PDF/SARSCommuniqué_E.pdf.
23. Roma Luciw, "Is Your Company Ready for a Sisaster?" *The Globe and Mail*, 21 June 2006, http://www.theglobeandmail.com/servlet/story/RTGAM.20060621.wdisaster0621/BNStory/Business.
24. Ibid.
25. Gary Silverman, "How May I Help You?" *Financial Times*, 4/5 February 2006, W1 and W2.
26. Paul Rogers and Marcia Blenko, "Who Has the D?" *Harvard Business Review*, January 2006, 53–61.
27. Chris Penttila, "Musical Chairs," *Entrepreneur*, April 2006, 24.
28. "Making Loblaw Best Again", 27 November 2007, www.loblaw.ca/en/inv_analyst_materials.html
29. Andreas Priestland and Robert Hanig, "Developing First-Level Leaders," *Harvard Business Review*, June 2005, 113–120.
30. Robert Kutz, "Skills of an Effective Administrator," Harvard Business Review, Sept – Oct 1974, 90-101.
31. Anthony Davis, "Sky High," *PROFIT Guide*, March 2004, http://www.profitguide.com/shared/print.jsp?content_20040213_171556_4580.
32. P. Fraser Johnson and Robert D. Klassen, "E-Procurement," *MIT Sloan Management Review*, Winter 2005, 7–10.
33. WestJet Airlines Limited, "2005 Annual Report," http://www.westjet.com/pdffile/WestJet2005AR.pdf.
34. Mahender Singh, "Supply Chain Reality Check," *MIT Sloan Management Review*, Spring 2005, 96.
35. Murray Johannsen, "Nine Characteristics of Successful Entrepreneurs and Business Leaders," http://www.legacee.com/Info/Leadership/LeadershipEntrepreneurial.html.
36. Murray Johannsen, "Nine Spheres of Leadership Influence' http://www.legacee.com/Info/Leadership/Influence.html.
37. "Transformational Leadership," *Changing*minds.org, http://changingminds.org/disciplines/leadership/styles/transformational_leadership.
38. Chris Sorensen, "WestJet Apologizes to Air Canada for Snooping," *Financial Post*, 30 May 2006, http://www.canada.com/nationalpost/financialpost/story.html?id=6ca8461a-fb61-4bcc-be49-002f092c337f&p=2.
39. Ibid.
40. Bertrand Marotte, "Management Guru Assails Excessive CEO Salaries," *The Globe and Mail*, 8 May 2003, B7.
41. Virginia Galt, "Anything but Middling," *The Globe and Mail*, 11 April 2003, C1.
42. H. James Harrington, "Knowledge Management Takes Us from Chance to Choice," *Quality Digest*, April 2003, 14–16.
43. Laura Bogomolny, "Most Innovative Exec/Canadian Tire—Janice Wismer," *Canadian Business*, 2004, http://www.canadianbusiness.com/allstars/best_innovative_exec.html.
44. Joy Riggs, "Empowering Workers by Setting Goals," *Nation's Business*, January 1995, 6.

Chapter 8

1. "Latest Indicators, Population Estimate (January 2009)," Statistics Canada, 26 March 2009, http://www.statcan.gc.ca/start-debut-eng.html; "World POPClock Projection," U.S. Census Bureau, 7 January 2009, http://www.census.gov/ipc/www/popclockworld.html; Matt Rosenberg, "Capitals of Every Independent Country," About.com, 25 March 2009, http://geography.about.com/od/countryinformation/a/capitals.htm.
2. "Current World Population," Nations Online, 2008, http://www.nationsonline.org/oneworld/world_population.htm.
3. "Developed Countries—Population, Births, and Deaths," French National Institute of Demographic Studies, 3 April 2008, http://www.ined.fr/en/pop_figures/developed_countries/population_births_deaths/. This percentage was calculated by adding up the 51 developed countries listed on this site and then dividing by the 195 countries on earth.
4. "Scotiabank Reaches Agreement to Buy E*TRADE Canada," CNW Group, 14 July 2008, http://www.newswire.ca/en/releases/archive/July2008/14/c4216.html.
5. "Canada's Fastest-Growing Companies—LIJA," *Profit*, June 2008, 50–51.
6. "Hargrove calls for help from feds after another round of Chrysler cuts," CBC.ca, 24 July 2008, http://www.cbc.ca/canada/story/2008/07/24/chrysler-caw.html; Nicolas Van Praet, "Polywheels grinds to halt in Oakville," *Financial Post*, 10 July 2008, http://network.nationalpost.com/np/blogs/fpposted/archive/2008/07/10/polywheels-grinds-to-halt-in-oakville.aspx; "2,000 jobs lost as auto-parts plants close," The Canadian Press, 3 July 2008, http://www.cbc.ca/canada/toronto/story/2008/07/03/plant-closure.html.
7. Erin White, "Future CEOs May Need to Have Broad Liberal-Arts Foundation," *The Wall Street Journal*, 12 April 2005, B4.
8. Guy DeJonquieres, "Going Global Is Always a Risky Business," *Financial Times*, 8 March 2005, 15; Christine Hall, "Understanding Culture Is Key to Global Mindset," *Houston Business Journal*, 13 January 2006.
9. Frank Vargo, "U.S. Trade Policy: Free Trade Agreements Level the Playing Field for Everyone," *Rubber & Plastics News*, 2 May 2005; "Free Trade Winds in the Mideast," *The Wall Street Journal*, 11 January 2006.
10. Dave Abler, "Glossary—Absolute Advantage," Penn State University, 2008, http://450.aers.psu.edu/glossary_search.cfm?letter=a.
11. "Absolute Advantage," Wikimedia Foundation, Inc., 22 July 2008, http://en.wikipedia.org/wiki/Absolute_advantage.
12. "Key Small Business Statistics," Industry Canada, July 2008, http://www.ic.gc.ca/epic/site/sbrp-rppe.nsf/vwapj/KSBS_July2008_Eng.pdf/$FILE/KSBS_July2008_Eng.pdf ; "Canada's State of Trade—Trade and Investment Update 2008, Export Establishments by Employee Size," Foreign Affairs and International Trade Canada, 8 May 2008, http://www.international.gc.ca/eet/trade/sot_2008/sot-2008-en.asp.
13. "Anticipating Needs, Delivering Results, EDC in an Evolving Trade Environment," Export Development Canada, May 2008, http://www.edc.ca/english/docs/LegReview_2008_e.pdf.
14. "Canada's State of Trade: Trade and Investment Update—2009," Foreign Affairs and International Trade Canada, 2009, http://www.international.gc.ca/economist-economiste/assets/pdfs/DFAIT_SoT_2009_en.pdf.
15. Ibid.
16. Ibid.
17. Ibid.
18. Ibid.
19. "Canada's State of Trade: Trade and Investment Update—2009," Foreign Affairs and International Trade Canada, 2009, http://www.international.gc.ca/economist-economiste/assets/pdfs/DFAIT_SoT_2009_en.pdf; "Seizing Global Advantage: A Global Commerce Strategy for Securing Canada's Growth & Prosperity," Foreign Affairs and International Trade Canada, 2008, http://www.international.gc.ca/commerce/assets/pdfs/GCS-en.pdf; "A Global Commerce Strategy for Securing Canada's Growth and Prosperity, A Message from the Minister," Foreign Affairs and International Trade Canada, 12 August 2008, http://www.international.gc.ca/commerce/strategy-strategie/minister-ministre.aspx; Jim Middlemiss, "Canada Readying to Ride the Tiger," *Financial Post*, 28 May 2008, http://www.financialpost.com/reports/legal/story.html?id=546037; "International Science and Technology Partnerships Program—

ISTPP," Foreign Affairs and International Trade Canada, 5 June 2007, http://www.infoexport.gc.ca/science/istpp-en.htm.

20. "Tokyo Disney Parks Operator Sees Sales, Profit Fall," *Kyodo World News Service*, 9 May 2005.

21. "Workers in Contract Factories," Nike, 2007, http://www.nike.com/nikebiz/nikeresponsibility/pdfs/color/3_Nike_CRR_Workers_C.pdf.

22. "FouFou Dog," *PROFIT*, 2009, http://list.canadianbusiness.com/rankings/hot50/2008/DisplayProfile.aspx?profile=32; Jerry Langton, "Canine Couture," *Toronto Star*, 17 November 2008, http://www.thestar.com/Business/SmallBusiness/article/538014; "About Us," FouFou Dog, 2009, http://www.foufoudog.com/about.html.

23. "In a joint venture, Lotus and Jaguar are developing a new engine called Omnivore," Auto123.com, 12 August 2008, http://www.auto123.com/en/news/car-news/in-a-joint-venture-lotus-and-jaguar-are-developing-a-new-engine-called-omnivore?artid=100249.

24. Lee Hawkins Jr. and Joann S. Lublin, "Emergency Repairman: GM's Wagoner Aims to Make Auto Company More Global," *The Wall Street Journal*, 6 April 2005, B1; "Shanghai Automotive Industry Corporation Guide to China's Auto Market," *Automotive News*, 9 March 2005; Martin Strathnairn, "SAIC Car Sales to Get Boost from GM," *Birmingham Post*, 9 January 2006.

25. Kenneth Fox, "Seeing the Invisible," *Business & Economics Review*, April–June 2005, 17.

26. Haig Simonian, "A Case of Two Heads Being Better Than One," *Financial Times*, 4 March 2005, 9.

27. Brent Jang, "Air Canada, Continental join forces; Move Counters WestJet-Southwest deal," *The Globe and Mail*, 25 July 2008, B3.

28. Ibid.

29. "GroupM and Consilient Form Alliance to Expand Mobile Email Advertising in Asia Pacific," Consilient Technologies Corporation, 10 April 2008, http://www.consilient.com/media/press/groupm-consilient-alliance.php.

30. Ibid.

31. Foreign Affairs and International Trade Canada, "Canada's State of Trade: Trade and Investment Update—2009."

32. Kim Shiffman, "HOT 50 Overview: Canada's hottest startups," *PROFIT*, October 2007, http://rankings.canadianbusiness.com/hot50/article.asp?pageID=article&year=2007&content=overview&type=overview.

33. "The World of Nestle," Nestlé S.A., [2009?], http://www.nestle.com/Resource.axd?Id=602C42FE-04D6-4669-BEE1-1027492FE5E8; Tom Wright, "Nestlé Focuses on Health to Fatten Its Profit-Bucking Global Trend," *International Herald Tribune*, 9 April 2005.

34. Mark Srite, "Levels of Culture and Individual Behavior: An Integrative Perspective," *Journal of Global Information Management*, 1 April 2005.

35. Eric Bellman and Kris Hudson, "Wal-Mart Trains Sights on India's Retail Market," *The Wall Street Journal*, 18 January 2006, A9.

36. Steve H. Hanke, "The Strong Dollar Charade," *Forbes*, 3 February 2003, 122.

37. Ed Zwirn, "Dollar Doldrums," *CFO*, May 2005, 35–38.

38. Matt Krantz, "Regulators Look Closely at Bartering," *USA Today*, 21 May 2002, 35.

39. Alan O. Sykes, "New Directions in Law and Economics," *American Economist*, 1 April 2002, 10.

40. Peter Fritsch and Timothy Mapes, "In Indonesia, a Tangle of Bribes Creates Trouble for Monsanto," *The Wall Street Journal*, 5 April 2005, A1–A6.

41. "The 2007 Results," Transparency International, 26 September 2007, http://www.transparency.org/news_room/latest_news/press_releases/2007/2007_09_26_cpi_2007_en.

42. Ibid.

43. Alma Olaechea, "Globalization Is Best for All," *University Wire*, 13 February 2002.

44. "Washington to Fight New Tariffs on U.S. Corn," CBC News, 6 December 2005, http://www.cbc.ca/story/business/national/2005/12/16/corn-051216.html.

45. "China Delays WTO Probe on Auto Part Tariffs," CBC.ca, 28 September 2006, http://www.cbc.ca/money/story/2006/09/28/chinawto.html.

46. "WTO Rules Against China Over Auto Parts Dispute," Xinhua News Agency, 19 July 2008, http://news.xinhuanet.com/english/2008-07/19/content_8573630.htm.

47. "About the Export and Import Controls Bureau (EICB) Controlled Goods," Foreign Affairs and International Trade Canada, 3 January 2007, http://www.dfait-maeci.gc.ca/eicb/eicbintro-en.asp.

48. "Important Information Related to Canada's Sanctions Against Burma," Foreign Affairs and International Trade Canada, 7 July 2008, http://www.international.gc.ca/international/Sanctions_Burma-Birmanie.aspx.

49. John Zarocostas, "WTO to Focus on Barriers," *Footwear News*, 10 January 2005; Evan Ramstad, "Tech Companies Push for Tariff Overhauls as Products Converge," *The Wall Street Journal*, 15 December 2005.

50. Chester Dawson, "A China Price for Toyota," *BusinessWeek*, 21 February 2005, 50–51; Clay Chandler, "Full Speed Ahead," *Fortune*, 7 February 2005, 79–84.

51. "Mad Cow in Canada: The Science and the Story," CBC.ca, 13 March 2006, http://www.cbc.ca/news/background/madcow/.

52. "Members and Observers," World Trade Organization, 23 July 2008, http://www.wto.org/english/thewto_e/whatis_e/tif_e/org6_e.htm; Elizabeth Wasserman, "Happy Birthday WTO," *Inc.*, January 2005, 21–23; Julian Morris, "The Future of World Trade," *The Wall Street Journal*, 20 December 2005.

53. "Developing Countries," World Trade Organization, 2008, http://www.wto.org/english/res_e/doload_e/inbr_e.pdf.

54. "The WTO Launches World Trade Report 2008: Trade in a Globalizing World," World Trade Organization, 15 July 2008, http://www.wto.org/english/news_e/pres08_e/pr534_e.htm.

55. "North American Free Trade Agreement," Wikimedia Foundation, Inc., 30 August 2008, http://en.wikipedia.org/wiki/NAFTA.

56. "European Union," Wikimedia Foundation, Inc., 2 June 2009, http://en.wikipedia.org/wiki/European_union.

57. "Europa, Key Facts and Figures about Europe and the Europeans," EUROPA [2008?], http://europa.eu/abc/keyfigures/index_en.htm; Graham Bowley, "Enlarged EU Portrayed as a 'Job Machine,'" *International Herald Tribune*, 21 May 2005; Paul Ames, "EU Mulls Plan to Create Rival to MIT in Bid to Counter Trans-Atlantic Brain Drain," *AP Worldstream*, 13 January 2006.

58. "EU Ready to Negotiate New Trade Deal with Canada," CBC News, 27 April 2009, http://www.cbc.ca/world/story/2009/04/27/eu-trade.html.

59. *The 2005 CIA World Fact Book* (www.cia.gov/cia/publications/factbook); "Exporting an Uber-Brand," *BusinessWeek*, 4 April 2005, 74.

60. Joe Studwell, "China's Boom Has Led to Only Partial Change," *Financial Times*, 4 April 2005, 15.

61. Frederik Balfour, "Fakes," *BusinessWeek*, 7 February 2005, 54–64.

62. Peter Mandelson, "India's New Leadership Role: An Economic Giant," *International Herald Tribune*, 15 January 2005; Foster Klug, "Lawmaker Says Tour of China and India a 'Reality Check on Asia's Growing Economies,'" *AP Worldstream*, 6 January 2006.

63. Mary Dejevsky, "Forget the China Story, Russia Offers a Greater Prize for Western Investors," *Independent*, 22 April 2005.

64. Pete Engardio, "The Future of Outsourcing," *BusinessWeek*, 30 January 2006, 50–58.

65. Anne Fisher, "Offshoring Could Boost Your Career," *Fortune*, 24 January 2005, 36.

Chapter 9

1. "Innovation in Canada," Sackville: Centre for Canadian Studies at Mount Allison University, http://www.mta.ca/faculty/arts/canadian_studies/english/about/innovation/.

2. *Innovation Analysis Bulletin*, Vol. 6, No. 1, March 2004, http://www.statcan.gc.ca/pub/88-003-x/88-003-x2004001-eng.pdf.

3. "Spending on research and development," *The Daily*, 20 December 2007, Statscan.ca/Daily/English/071220/d071220b.htm.

4. Statistics Canada "Science Statistics," December 2007, http://www.statcan.gc.ca/pub/88-001-x/88-001-x2007007-eng.pdf.

5. "Business Research and Development Spending Slumps in 2006, According to Canada's Top 100 Corporate R&D Spenders List," Re$earch Infosource, Inc, press release, 22 October 2007, http://researchinfosource.com/pressroom/20071022/top100_gen.pdf.

6. "Canada's Top 100 Corporate R&D Spenders List 2007 Analysis," Re$earch Infosource, Inc., 2007, Researchinfosource.com/2007analysis.pdf.

7. Canadian Manufacturers & Exporters, "Canada's Manufacturing Industry Drives Our Economy," 2004, http://www.cme-mec.ca/national/template_na.asp?p=4.

8. Kathryn Jones, "The Dell Way," *Business 2.0*, February 2003, 61–66.
9. Spencer E. Ante, "The New Blue," *Business Week*, 17 March 2003, 80–88.
10. Daniel Eisenberg, "There's a New Way to Think @ Big Blue," *Time*, 20 January 2003, 49–53.
11. Pete Engardio, Aaron Bernstein, and Manjeet Kripalani, "Is Your Job Next?" *Business Week*, 3 February 2003, 50–60.
12. David Atkin, "HP Toronto Plant Aimed at Dell," *The Globe and Mail*, 14 November 2003, B1.
13. "Hoover's Profile: Gilden Activewear, Inc.," Answers.com, http://www.Answers.com/topic/gildan-activewear-inc.
14. Richard Wilding, "The Ghost in the Machine," *Financial Times*, 7 April 2006, p. 5 of a section called "Mastering Uncertainty."
15. Gordon Pitts, "Kodiak Comes Home," *The Globe and Mail*, 15 May 2006, B5.
16. Douglas M. Lambert and A. Michael Knemeyer, "We're in This Together," *Harvard Business Review*, December 2004, 114–22.
17. Gary Norris, "Honda Putting New Assembly Plant in U.S.; Ontario Gets $154M Engine Factory," Canadian Business Online, 17 May 2006, http://www.canadianbusiness.com/markets/headline_news/article.jsp?content=b051777A.
18. David Crane, "We've Got to Use Our Brains More than Our Brawn," *Toronto Star*, D2.
19. CBC News Online, "Outsourcing: Contracting Out Becomes Big Business," 7 March 2006, http://www.cbc.ca/news/background/economy/outsourcing.html.
20. CORE Centre for Outsourcing Research and Education, www.core-outsourcing.org
21. Gordon Pitts, "Small Producer Cleans Up Making Soap," *The Globe and Mail*, 28 July 2003, B1.
22. "IT Outsourcing to Canada," IMEX Systems, Inc., www.imexsystems.com/pdf/Outsourcing_USA.pdf.
23. Virginia Galt, "Take Our Business, Take Our People: BMO," *The Globe and Mail*, 19 May 2003, B1.
24. Canadian Vehicle Manufacturers Association, "The Automotive Industry in Canada," 2006, http://www.cvma.ca/eng/industry/industry.asp.
25. Richard Waters, "Manufacturing Glitches Dent Xbox Sales," *Financial Times*, 27 January 2006, 17.
26. Michelle Conlin, "Call Centers in the Rec Room," *BusinessWeek*, 23 January 2006, 76–77.
27. Janet Bealer Rodie, "Brückner, M-Tec Partner to Provide Carpet Solutions," *Textile World*, 1 May 2005.
28. Davis Balestracci, "When Processes Moonlight as Trends," *Quality Digest*, June 2005, 18.
29. "More about NQI" and "Canada Awards for Excellence," Toronto: National Quality Institute, http://www.nqi.ca.
30. John E. (Jack) West, "Continuous Improvement and Your QMS," *Quality Digest*, April 2006, 16.
31. Scott M. Paton, "The Cost of Quality," *Quality Digest*, January 2006, 128.
32. "ISO Standards," International Organization for Standardization, www.iso.org/iso/iso_catalogue.htm.
33. SNC-Lavalin Group Inc., "Quality Policy," http://www.snclavalin.com/en/6_0/6_10.aspx.
34. "Extensive debate improves consensus on future ISO 26000 standard on social responsibility," International Organization for Standardization, 4 June 2009, http://www.iso.org/iso/pressrelease.htm?refid=Ref1229.
35. "Grocery Chain in Drive to Improve," *National Post*, 31 October 2001, JV3.
36. "The Juggling Act Behind the Cirque," *National Post*, 31 October 2001, JV4.
37. Gordon Pitts, "Kodiak Comes Home," *The Globe and Mail*, 15 May 2006, http://www.theglobeandmail.com/servlet/story/LAC.20060515.RKODIAK15/TPStory/?query=kodiak.
38. Robyn Waters, "The Secret of Feel-Good Shopping," *Kiplinger's*, January 2006, 20–22.
39. Wikimedia Foundation Inc., "Economic Order Quantity," 3 May 2006, http://en.wikipedia.org/wiki/Economic_order_quantity.
40. "Royal Canadian Mint," September 2003, Cognos, http://www.cognos.com/products/applications/success.html.
41. Ibid.
42. Centre for Research and Information on Canada, "Background," 11 May 2006, http://www.cric.ca/en_html/guide/border/border.html#faqs.
43. Daren Fonda, "Why the Most Profitable Cars Made in the U.S.A. are Japanese and German," *Time*, June 2003, A9–A13.
44. Horst-Henning Wolf, "Making the Transition to Strategic Purchasing," *MIT Sloan Management Review*, Summer 2005, 17–24.
45. Greg Keenan, "Ford's New Maxim: Flex Manufacturing; New Oakville Plant Should Be Able to Switch Models in Days, not Weeks," *The Globe and Mail*, 10 May 2006, B3.
46. Ibid.
47. Derrell S. James, "Using Lean and Six Sigma in Project Management," *Quality Digest*, August 2005, 49–55; Bill Ritsch, "Breaking the Bottleneck," *Quality Digest*, March 2006, 41.
48. Julia Boorstin, "Adidas Expands Its Footprint," *Fortune*, 30 May 2005, 33.
49. Robyn Waters, "The Secret of Feel-Good Shopping," *Kiplinger's*," January 2006, 20–22.

Chapter 10

1. Financial Consumer Agency of Canada, "About the Financial Services Sector," 22 February 2009, www.fcac-acfc.gc.ca.
2. Financial Consumer Agency of Canada, "About the Financial Services Sector—Facts & Figures," 22 February 2009, www.fcac-acfc.gc.ca/eng/media/facts/default.asp.
3. Canadian Bankers Association, "Competition in the Canadian Financial Services Sector," May 2004, www.cba.ca/en/content/stats/fastfacts/040528_Competitionffact.pdf.
4. Financial Consumer Agency of Canada, "How the Industry Is Regulated," 22 February 2009, www.fcac-acfc.gc.ca/eng/industry/actsregs/default.asp.
5. The Canada Deposit Insurance Corporation, 29 January 2004, www.cdic.ca.
6. Evan I. Schwartz, "How You'll Pay," *Technology Review*, January 2003, 50–56.
7. Bank of Canada, "Counterfeit Detection," www.bankofcanada.ca/en/banknotes/counterfeit/security/index100b.html.
8. Catherine Siskos, "Cash in a Flash," *Kiplinger's*, October 2002, 30–31.
9. "Deflation Warning," *Washington Times*, 14 May 2003, A20.
10. Patrick Barta and Michelle Higgins, "Dollar's Fall Could End Many Bargains," *The Wall Street Journal*, 9 January 2003, D1, D4.
11. Bank of Canada, "Canada's Money Supply," January 2000, www.bankofcanada.ca/en/backgrounders/bg-m2.htm; Bank of Canada, "Target for the Overnight Rate," July 2001, www.bankofcanada.ca/en/backgrounders/bg-p9.htm.
12. Bank of Canada, "Canada's Money Supply."
13. Bank of Canada, "Target for the Overnight Rate."
14. Canadian Bankers Association, "Bank Earnings," April 2003, www.cba.ca/en/ViewDocument.asp?fl_6&sl_111&tl_&docid_420.
15. Canadian Bankers Association, "Income Statement—Net Income," February 2009, www.cba.ca/en/content/stats/DB251-2007-eng updated.pdf.
16. Julie Rawe, "A Mini-Mall in Your ATM," *Time*, 8 April 2002, 61.
17. Michelle Higgins, "ATMs to Go Far Beyond Cash," *The Wall Street Journal*, 6 June 2002, D1, D2.
18. Stephanie Miles, "What's a Check?" *The Wall Street Journal*, 21 October 2002, p. R5.
19. Pallavi Gogoi, "The Hot News in Banking: Bricks and Mortar," *BusinessWeek*, 21 April 2003, 83–84.
20. Insurance Bureau of Canada, "Facts on the General Insurance Industry in Canada," www.ibc.ca/pdffiles/publications/brochures/consumer/FactsBook2005.html.
21. Insurance Bureau of Canada, "Facts of the General Insurance Industry of Canada," www.ibc.ca/en/need_more_info/documents/facts book 2009_eng.pdf.
22. Financial Consumer Agency of Canada, "Financial Consumer Agency of Canada Glossary—Investment Dealer Definition," 26 February 2004, www.fcac-acfc.gc.ca/eng/glossary.asp; Investment Dealers Association of Canada, "Canadian Securities IndustryProfile," www.ida.ca/IndIssues/IndProfile_en.asp; Department of Finance Canada., "The Canadian Securities Industry—The Canadian Financial System—June 2000," 5 September 2003, www.fin.gc.ca/toce/2000/cansec_e.html.
23. Bertrand Marotte, "Regulator Assails Plan for National Stock Watchdog," *The Globe and Mail*, 22 January 2004, B6; Karen Howlett and Heather Scoffield, "Consensus Elusive over Regulator," *The Globe and Mail*, 20 January 2004, B6; "What Is the CSA?" and "Who Are the Canadian Securities Administrators?" June 2001: Canadian Securities Administrators, www.csa-acvm.ca/html_CSA/about_who_are_csa.html and www.csa-acvm.ca/html_CSA/about.html.

24. Financial Consumer Agency of Canada, "Financial Consumer Agency of Canada Glossary—Securities Commission Definition," 26 February 2004, www.fcac-acfc.gc.ca/eng/glossary.asp.

25. "Demen Found Guilty of Securities Violations," *The Gazette*, 30 September 2008, www.canada.com/montrealgazette/news/business/story.html?id=dc8f3467-0591-490f-bf65-ea5b76b732d2.

26. Financial Consumer Agency of Canada, "Financial Consumer Agency of Canada Glossary—Security Definition," 26 February 2004, www.fcac-acfc.gc.ca/eng/glossary.asp.

27. "The Case for Going Private: Corporate Ownership," *The Economist*, 25 January 2003, 67.

28. Ben White and Kathleen Day, "SEC Approves Wall Street Settlement; Conflict of Interest Targeted," *Washington Post*, 29 April 2003, A1.

29. Mara Der Hovanesian, "The Market's Closed—Wake Up," *BusinessWeek*, 3 March 2003, 132.

30. Ben White, "A Crisis of Trust on Wall Street," *Washington Post*, 4 May 2003, F1.

31. Eric Troseth, "Finding a Rally in Bearish Times," *Christian Science Monitor*, 5 May 2003, 14.

32. Jyoti Thottam, "Are Penny Stocks Worth a Look?" *Time*, 12 August 2002, 46.

33. "Hillsdale Hedge Funds Prepared for May 1st S&P/TSE Composite Index Changes," Hillsdale Investment Management, February 2002, www.hillsdaleinv.com/research/pdf/tse_change.pdf.

34. Matt Krantz, "Microsoft Stock Splits into 10 Billion Shares," *USA Today*, 19 February 2003, 1B.

35. The Investment Funds Institute of Canada, "Industry Statistics," October 2008, www.ific.ca/eng/home/index.asp.

36. John Rekenthaler, "When Mutual Funds Die, Companies Bury Their Mistakes, Distorting Returns," *Money*, April 2003, 49–53.

Chapter 11

1. Jane von Bergen, "Calling All Accountants," *Philadelphia Enquirer*, 12 October 2005; David Simanoff, "Accountants Can Count on More Job Offers," *Tampa Tribune*, 26 June 2005; Mike Allen, "Supply and Demand Works in Accountants' Favor: Firms Are Desperately Seeking Skilled CPAs," *San Diego Business Journal*, 16 January 2006.

2. Nanette Byrnes and Louis Lavelle, "The Corporate Tax Game," *BusinessWeek*, 31 March 2003, 78–83.

3. Gary McWilliams, "Dell Puts Cash Flow to Work," *The Wall Street Journal*, 25 April 2005, C3.

4. Michael Hunstad, "Better Forecasting: Know Your Cash Flows," *Financial Executive*, 1 May 2005; Kenneth L. Parkinson, "Cash Flow Forecasting: Do It Better and Save," *Financial Executive*, 1 January 2006.

5. Patrick Kilts, "Effective Cash Flow Management Improves Investment Outlook," *Crain's Cleveland Business*, 19 September 2005; Bruce Perryman, "Grow with the Flow," *Stitches Magazine*, 1 January 2005; Andi Gray, "The Optimum Growth Model," *Fairfield County Business Journal*, 30 January 2006.

6. Tim Reason, "Budgeting in the Real World," *CFO*, July 2005, 43–48.

7. Mara Der Hovanesian, "Cash: Burn, Baby, Burn," *BusinessWeek*, 28 April 2003, 82–83.

8. Jordan I. Shifrin, "All Boards Must Grapple with Budget Issues," *Daily Herald*, 4 June 2005.

9. Charles Mulford, "A Best Practices Approach to Cash Flow Reporting: Implications for Analysis," *Business Credit*, 1 January 2005.

10. Anne Tergesen, "Cash-Flow Hocus-Pocus," *BusinessWeek*, 16 July 2002, 130–32.

11. Paul Katzeff, "Manage Accounts Receivable Upfront Before There's a Problem," *Investors Business Daily*, 27 January 2003, A4.

12. Krissah Williams Washington, "How Stores Play Their Cards: They'll Give Discounts and Awards to Get Interest and Bigger Sales," *Washington Post*, 2 February 2003, H5.

13. Linda Stern, "Credit Card Issuers Offer Some Good Deals," *Reuters Business*, 1 March 2003.

14. Lisa McLaughlin, "New Brew on the Block," *Time*, 20 January 2003, 143.

15. Courtney McGrath, "Bankers You Can Love," *Kiplinger's*, April 2003, 46–48.

16. Susan C. Thompson, "Mixing Personal, Business Funds Is a Formula for Bankruptcy," *St. Louis Post-Dispatch*, 5 August 2005; Carolyn M. Brown, "Borrowing from Dad: Financing

from Relatives and Friends Has Risks and Rewards," *Black Enterprise*, 1 January 2005.

17. Kate Ashford, "Lend to a Friend (Without Regret): Four Things to Do When a Pal Asks for a Loan," *Money*, 1 November 2005.

18. Janice Revell, "How Debt Triggers Can Sink a Stock," *Fortune*, 18 March 2002, 147–51.

19. John M. Berry, "Low Interest Rates Are Allowing Corporations to Boost Profit," *Washington Post*, 19 April 2003, D12.

20. Liza Casabona, "Origins of Factoring Come Full Circle," *WWD*, 19 September 2005; "Texas Oil Drill Bit Manufacturer Taps into a $1 Million Factoring Credit Line," *PR Newswire*, 1 February 2006.

21. Toni Clarke and Jed Stelzer, "Merck Profit Rises on Higher Drug Sales," *Reuters Business*, 21 April 2003.

22. Jean Ende, "Card Issuers Charge After Owners," *Crain's New York Business*, 18 July 2005.

23. Amy Barrett, "Pfizer's Funk," *BusinessWeek*, 28 February 2005; Jennifer Bayot, "Pfizer's Pain Inflamed by Weak Sales," *International Herald Tribune*, 6 April 2005.

24. The Canadian Securities Course 1993 (Toronto: The Canadian Securities Institute, 1992), 63.

25. Justin Fox, "Show Us the Money," *Fortune*, 3 February 2003, 76–78.

26. Walter Updegrave, "Dividend Mania, What the Bush Dividend Plan Would Really Mean for You," *Money*, 1 March 2003, 69–74.

27. "The Preferred Route to Income Preferred Stocks Offer the Most Sumptuous Dividend Payments Around," *Money*, 1 March 2003, 54B.

28. Michael Barbaro, "Primus Agrees to Sell Convertible Preferred Stock," *Washington Post*, 1 January 2003, E5.

Appendix B

1. Nitin Nohria, "Risk, Uncertainty, and Doubt," *Harvard Business Review*, February 2006, 39–40.

2. Andrew Jack, "The Bird Flu Issue Has Landed," *Financial Times*, 10 January 2006, 8.

3. Eric Schoeniger, "How to Plug the $13 Billion Leak," *BusinessWeek*, 20 March 2006, 2–5; M. Eric Johnson, "A Broader Context for Information Security," a special section in *Financial Times* called "Mastering Risk," 16 September 2005, 1–12.

4. Charlie Ross, "Jackson Action," *The Wall Street Journal*, 15 September 2005, A21.

5. Michel Crouhy, Dan Galai, and Robert Mark, *The Essentials of Risk Management*, (New York: McGraw Hill, 2006), 1–11.

6. James Altucher, "Living with Bird Flu, Sharks and Hurricanes," *Financial Times*, 4 April 2006, 10.

7. Deborah Wince-Smith, "Innovate at Your Own Risk," *Harvard Business Review*, May 2005, 25.

8. Keith Goffin and Rick Mitchell, "The Risks of Innovation," a special section in *Financial Times* called "Managing Risk," 30 September 2005, 1–12.

9. Norm Brodsky, "How Much Risk Can You Take?," *Inc.*, December 2005, 73–74.

10. Maggie Urry, "Business Stands By and Sees Profits Go to Blazes," *Financial Times*, 25 April 2006, 4.

11. Tamsyn Burgmann and Joan Bryden, "Health Officials Tie Listeria Outbreaks to Maple Leaf Meats," *The Globe and Mail*, 23 August 2008, www.theglobeandmail.com/servlet/story/RTGAM.20080823.wmapleleaf0823/BNStory/National.

12. Erin White, "Smaller Companies Join the Outsourcing Trend," *The Wall Street Journal*, 8 May 2006, B3. 15. Jack Kemp, "How Congress Stalks the Economic Upturn," *Washington Times*, 4 August 2005, p. A17.

13. Amy Borrus, Mike McNamee, and Howard Gleckman, "Up to His Neck in the Risk Pool," *BusinessWeek*, 6 June 2005, 109–11; Andrea Siedsma, "Insurance Well Spent," *Hispanic Business*, March 2006, 48–50.

14. Jeffrey Kluger, "Global Warming," *Time*, 3 April 2006, 28–42; Thomas G. Donlan, "Take the Hot Air Out of Global Warming," *Barron's*, 5 December 2005, 47.

15. David Ignatius, "Corporate Green," *Washington Post*, 11 May 2005, A17.

16. Holman W. Jenkins, "A Global Warming Worksheet," *The Wall Street Journal*, 1 February 2006, A15.

17. Chip Giller and David Roberts, "Green Gets Going," *Fast Company*, March 2006, 73–78.

Photo Credits

Subject Index